HEGEL'S *LECTURES ON THE HISTORY OF PHILOSOPHY*

HUMANITIES PAPERBACK LIBRARY

Published

Commentary to Kant's "Critique of Pure Reason"
Norman Kemp Smith

The Foundations of Metaphysics in Science
Errol E. Harris

Fundamentals of Philosophy
Errol E. Harris

Hegel's Science of Logic
Translated by A. V. Miller

Karl Jaspers: Basic Philosophical Writings
*Karl Jaspers; edited and translated by Edith Ehrlich,
Leonard H. Ehrlich, and George B. Pepper*

Philosophy and Truth: Selections from
Nietzsche's Notebooks of the Early 1870's
*Friedrich Nietzsche; edited and
translated by Daniel Breazeale*

The Principal Upanisads
*Edited with Introduction, Text, Translation
and Notes by S. Radhakrishnan*

Reason and Revolution
Herbert Marcuse

The Worlds of Existentialism:
A Critical Reader
*Edited, with Introductions and
Conclusions by Maurice Friedman*

Hypothesis and Perception
The Roots of Scientific Method
Errol E. Harris

Hegel's *Lectures on the History of Philosophy*
Introduction by Tom Rockmore
Translated by E. S. Haldane and Frances H. Simson

Hegel's *Lectures on the History of Philosophy*

Abridged Student Edition

With an Introduction by
Tom Rockmore

TRANSLATED BY

E. S. Haldane
and
Frances H. Simson

HUMANITIES PRESS
NEW JERSEY

This abridged edition first published in 1996 by
Humanities Press International, Inc., 165 First Avenue,
Atlantic Highlands, New Jersey 07716

Introduction © 1996 by Tom Rockmore

Library of Congress Cataloging-in-Publication Data

Hegel, Georg Wilhelm Friedrich, 1770–1831.
　[Vorlesungen über die Geschichte der Philosophie.
　English] Hegel's Lectures on the history of philosophy.
　— Abridged student ed. / with an introd. by Tom
Rockmore; translated by E.S. Haldane and Frances
H. Simson.
　　　p.　　cm. — (Humanities paperback library)
　　Includes index.
　　ISBN 0-391-03957-1　　(pbk. : alk. paper)
　　1. Philosophy—History.　I. Rockmore, Tom, 1942–
II. Haldane, Elizabeth Sanderson, 1862–1937.
III. Simson, Frances H.　IV. Title.
B2936.E5H3　1996
109—dc20
　　　　　　　　　　　　　　　　　　　　　96–25490
　　　　　　　　　　　　　　　　　　　　　　CIP

Printed in the United States of America

10 9 8 7 6 5 4 3 2 1

CONTENTS

PART ONE

PART THREE

INTRODUCTION TO THE ABRIDGED
STUDENT EDITION

THE purpose of this one-volume abridgment of Hegel's famous *Lectures on the History of Philosophy* is to increase the availability of the lectures at a time when heightened attention is being directed to Hegel and to the history of philosophy. Hegel's *Lectures* are important for an understanding of his thought, for an understanding of selected thinkers, and for a general understanding of the philosophical tradition.

Interest in the history of philosophy and in Hegel are presently increasing for different reasons. Interest in the history of philosophy is clearly on the rise as a result of the sea change now under way in philosophy in general, including analytic philosophy. Analytic philosophy has historically been either indifferent or even antipathetic to the history of philosophy. The founders of the analytic tradition (Russell, Moore, and Wittgenstein) were uninterested in prior thought. Except for Russell's interest in Leibniz, they were basically unconcerned with anyone earlier than Frege whose main work was done in the last quarter of the nineteenth century. This negative attitude has remained constant in later analytic thought. Quine's reported quip about a distinction between those interested in the history of philosophy and those interested in philosophy pretty well describes the view, widespread among analytic philosophers, that the prior history of philosophy is at least irrelevant to philosophy as it is currently understood.

This conviction is certainly not limited to analytic philosophers. Although continental thinkers are generally better informed about the history of philosophy than are their analytic colleagues—in the case of Cassirer or Gadamer, exceptionally well informed—others are either comparatively uninformed or even actively hostile to it. Husserl, for instance, was comparatively unaware of the philosophical tradition. Although he desired to make a new or true beginning, he had only a very general idea of the prior philosophical discussion. Despite his unusual grasp of the history of philosophy, Heidegger was increasingly hostile to it; he later came to see it as no more than a series of mistakes.

The prevalent view that a philosopher does best not to consider the prior philosophical tradition, since concerns with philosophy and the history of philosophy are simply incompatible, is a frequent theme virtually throughout the entire philosophical tradition. With the prominent exception of Aristotle, who routinely examines prior views in the process of arriving at his own, ancient Greek philosophers were mainly unconcerned to survey earlier ideas. They were not actively unfriendly to prior philosophy; yet they displayed little interest in it for the obvious reason that there does not seem to have been any conviction that philosophy is itself historical. This is hardly surprising since, although such ancient Greek historians as Thucydides wrote on history, there was no more than the most minimal effort to understand the nature of history. This general philosophical disinterest in the philosophical tradition changes in modern philosophy, which is often actively antagonistic to the history of philosophy.

Modern philosophy is dominated by the widespread conviction of the need to begin again, to finally make a true beginning, a conviction that is often understood to imply that, despite the immense efforts of many talented individuals, nothing of value has so far been accomplished. In modern philosophy, two main attitudes toward the history of philosophy are represented by Descartes and Kant. For Descartes, we need to begin again in order finally to make a true beginning in independence of anything that has previously gone before to defeat skepticism. For Kant, we need to begin again by noting the mistakes of our predecessors that suggest the need to select a different approach. Whereas Descartes turns away from earlier views on the grounds that, since they disagree, none is acceptable, Kant turns away from them on the grounds that they are committed to an incorrect strategy. For Descartes, we cannot build on earlier theories, and for Kant, we can do so only in the sense that they collectively indicate a deep-seated mistake to be avoided. Both Descartes and Kant hold that there is nothing positive to be learned from earlier thought. This influential idea is widely found throughout later philosophy, among analytic thinkers, but also among occasional continental thinkers.

With exceptions, among continental philosophers the disregard of earlier thought never ran very deep. Numerous continental thinkers in our time are distinguished by their grasp and appreciation of prior philosophy. The typical analytic tendency to disregard earlier theories is now changing as analytic thinkers devote increasing intention, if not to a historical conception of knowledge, at least to an ever wider selection of figures in the history of philosophy. It is only when the idea emerges that philosophy can learn from and build upon the preceding tradition that the history of philosophy becomes relevant to philosophy. Hence, one reason why we should read Hegel's *Lectures on the History of Philosophy* now is because it has been increasingly realized in recent years that the philosophical tradition is not irrelevant, but precisely relevant, to philosophy.

xiiINTRODUCTION

Another reason is related to the increasing interest in
Hegel. We are presently in the midst of a Hegel renais-
sance, with books on his thought appearing almost faster
than anyone can read them. The explosion of interest
in Hegel is far-reaching, touching both continental and
analytic writers. In the United States, the Hegel discussion began in German settlements during the second
half of the nineteenth century, particularly in Cincinati
and St. Louis; in England, it began with the publication of J. H. Stirling's *The Secret of Hegel* in 1865. Yet
since the rise of analytic philosophy at the beginning of
this century as the result of the revolt against British
Hegelianism, with obvious exceptions such as Findlay
and Taylor, until relatively recently few analytically trained
philosophers were even faintly concerned with Hegel. That
period is now past. Roughly since the middle 1980s,
analytic thinkers are increasingly turning to Hegel in a
burgeoning series of studies of various aspects of his
thought, frequently with an epistemological bent. Recent examples include studies by Solomon, Wood, Pip-
pin, Pinkard, Hardimon, K. Westphal, and Forster. Those
who write from a continental perspective have certainly
not slackened the pace of their production, as witnessed
by new works by H. S. Harris, E. Harris, Olson,
McCumber, Desmond, M. Westphal, and others. At
present, it is fair to say that with Descartes, Kant, and
perhaps one or two others, Hegel is one of the few modern
philosophers who regularly attracts scholarly attention across
the board from both continental and analytic perspectives.

Increasing interest in Hegel provides two further reasons to turn to his *Lectures on the History of Philosophy*. One reason concerns the nature of Hegel's view.
Although generations of Hegel's students, particularly in
English-language circles, have continued to study his
theory apart from the philosophical tradition, this is hardly
an approach to be recommended. Since Hegel is a his-

torical thinker, in fact the outstanding example of a philosopher who thinks on the basis of the prior philosophical debate, his own theory simply cannot be understood apart from his reading of other views. Unlike so many other philosophers, who attempt to begin again, often as if no one had ever attempted to philosophize before, Hegel takes seriously the need to engage prior thought as a condition of working out his own theory. Like Newton, who modestly claimed to have seen farther than others since he stood on the shoulders of giants, Hegel consciously stands on the shoulders of his great philosophical predecessors. He clearly seeks to take up in his own theory all the achievements of the preceding discussion. His position literally emerges out of his effort to come to grips with the philosophy of his time, especially Kant's critical theory. Later he extends his effort to appropriate the positive results of prior thinkers through a dialogue with the entire philosophical tradition. Since his theory literally depends on his reading of prior thinkers and the tradition as a whole, an appreciation of his grasp of the history of philosophy is central for more than the most superficial reading of his own thought.

A second reason to turn to the *Lectures* follows from Hegel's specific contribution to our understanding of the history of philosophy. As interest in the philosophical tradition increases, it becomes ever more important to understand the link between philosophy and the history of philosophy. The main representative of the view that the history of philosophy is an integral part of philosophy is certainly Hegel. To an unrivaled extent, more than such recent figures as Cassirer or Heidegger in our time, or Schelling in the nineteenth century, and more than Aristotle among the ancients, in fact more than anyone else in the philosophical tradition, Hegel combines a deep grasp of the history of philosophy with a philosophical theory of the first rank. The obvious anwer

as to why we should read Hegel's *Lectures* on this topic
is that Hegel was not only a great philosopher, argu-
ably one of the few thinkers on the highest level who
continues to speak to succeeding generations in different ways; he was also a great historian of philosophy,
in some ways even the first great historian of philosophy, on whose work all later historians continue to build.

Hegel's conception of the history of philosophy follows from his view of knowledge as an intrinsically historical enterprise. He famously holds that we do not
know absolutely, but only from the perspective of our
time and place. It follows that philosophy, which he
defines as its own time captured in thought, is linked to
the historical moment in which it appears, for Stoicism,
say, to a time of universal fear and bondage.

In his *Phenomenology of Spirit*, Hegel presents a series of cognitive perspectives, or what, borrowing a term
from his *Encyclopedia of the Philosophical Sciences*, we
can call attitudes of thought to objectivity. The perspectives distinguished are related among themselves like
a series of nesting Chinese boxes, all of which are contained within the final perspective, or absolute knowing
(*das absolute Wissen*). In his *Lectures on the History
of Philosophy*, he maintains that at least since Parmenides
all thinkers are concerned with finding a solution to the
problem of knowledge through a demonstration of the
unity of thought and being.

Socrates presupposed in engaging his interlocutors in
discussion that truth can emerge from a free debate between representatives of different points of view. Hegel
transposes this idea to the philosophical tradition as a
whole. For Hegel, the philosophical tradition resembles
an ongoing Socratic dialogue in which successive thinkers come to grips with earlier theories, upon which they
build, in order to arrive at an acceptable view of knowledge, Hegel's approach to the philosophical tradition as

in effect an ongoing dialogue enables him to see the many theories as resulting from a dialectical interaction between different thinkers.

This approach is obviously distinctive. The difference between the standard approach and Hegel's approach to the philosophical tradition is clear. All historians of philosophy prior to Hegel and too many since his day depict the history of philosophy as a mere compilation of different, unrelated theories. Russell, the author of *A History of Western Philosophy*, was never able to see connections among theories. Copleston's more recent *A History of Philosophy* is scarcely better in that regard. Hegel provides the first philosophical treatment of the philosophical tradition. Since Hegel literally created the philosophical treatments of the philosophical tradition, all such later treatments, including those due to Windelband, Kroner, and Löwith, are indebted to his own approach.

We can end with a few words, but no more than that, about the work you are about to read. Hegel's *Lectures on the History of Philosophy* is not, as the name suggests, a finished book, but rather no more than lecture notes. Hegel lectured on this topic nine times throughout his career, initially in Jena in the winter of 1805/ 1806, twice more in Heidelberg (winter of 1816/1817 and 1817/1818), and then six times in Berlin (summer of 1819, winter of 1820/1821, 1823/1824, 1825/1826, 1827/1828, and 1829/1830). He had already begun the tenth series of lectures on this topic when he died suddenly at the age of sixty-one, at the height of his powers, during a cholera epidemic in 1831. Hegel's *Lectures* ended more than a century and a half ago. But although the nature of the debate has changed, and although we often possess better texts of the ancient writers than were available in Hegel's day, astonishingly, with the exception of a few details, there is almost nothing, certainly no central thesis in his views of his predecessors, that must be abandoned. Now as before, one can look to Hegel's reading of his predecessors for deep insight into the nature of the particular theories. For example, the immense attention devoted to Kant's moral theory has added nothing to Hegel's critique of the intrinsic vacuousness of universal laws that apply to everything and nothing. And Heidegger's discussion of the Aristotelian conceptual of *energeia* as central to Greek thought is fully anticipated by Hegel.

Hegel's *Lectures on the History of Philosophy* can be read with great profit by anyone interested either in the philosophical tradition, in Hegel's views of it, or in his detailed discussion, with which he opens his *Lectures*, of the nature of the history of philosophy and its relation to other intellectual concerns. His *Lectures* are a constant source of insight into particular positions as well as into nature of the philosophical tradition as a whole. Hegel's reading of the prior tradition has important limitations. One is the fact that, although he was formed in the Tübinger Stift, a Protestant seminary in Tübingen, a small town in southwestern Germany, hence he was presumably familiar with the full range of Scholastic writings, he has very little to say about Scholastic thought. Another limitation lies in his self-congratulatory view of German idealism. As befits a great philosopher, Hegel's standards were very high. It is well known that he considered that among his contemporaries only Fichte and Schelling were philosophers worthy of the name. Yet although he acknowledged their significance, he also tended to depict their theories invidiously, less through their intrinsic importance than as leading up to his own theory. This influential view of German idealism as beginning in Kant and peaking in Hegel has for generations tended to distort our understanding of the other great philosophers who belong to this movement, particularly Fichte and Schelling, although recent work has increasingly removed them from the limitations of Hegel's reading of them.

Although not perfect, Hegel's *Lectures on the History of Philosophy*, like the theory of ethics Aristotle advances in the *Nicomachean Ethics*, represents the best thinking we have on the topic. Hegel's *Lectures*, essential for a grasp of his theory, can be read with profit by anyone interested in the philosophical tradition in whole or in part, by anyone seeking a philosophical analysis of a prior philosophical position, or even by anyone who merely wants to see a great philosopher striving to come to grips with the views of his predecessors.

TOM ROCKMORE

TRANSLATOR'S NOTE

It is perhaps unnecessary to say anything respecting the difficulty of making any adequate translation of Hegel's writings. In the case of the History of Philosophy, that difficulty is possibly enhanced by the fact that the greater part of the book is put together from the notes of different courses of lectures delivered on the subject at various times. Hegel, as we learn from Michelet, in his preface to the first edition of this work, lectured in all nine times on the History of Philosophy: first in Jena in 1805-1806, then in Heidelberg in 1816-1817 and 1817-1818, and the other six times in Berlin between the years 1819 and 1830. He had begun the tenth course on the subject in 1831 when death cut his labours short. It was only for the first course of lectures—that delivered in Jena—that Hegel fully wrote out his lectures; this was evidently done with the intention of future publication in book form. At Heidelberg he composed a short abstract of his subject, giving in a few terse words the main points dealt with in each system of Philosophy. In the later courses of lectures Hegel trusted to extempore speaking, but at the same time made considerable use of the above writings, the margins of which he annotated with subsequent additions. Besides these annotations he left behind him a large number of miscellaneous notes, which have proved of the greatest value. The present translation is taken from the second and amended edition of the "Geschichte der Philosophie," published in 1840. This edition is derived from no one set of lectures in particular, but carefully prepared by Michelet—himself one of Hegel's pupils—from all available sources, including the notes of students.   The Jena volume is, however, made the basis, as representing the main elements of the subject afterwards to be more fully amplified; or, in Michelet's words, as the skeleton which was afterwards to be clothed with flesh.

I have endeavoured to make this translation as literal as possible consistently with intelligibility, and have attempted, so far as might be, to give the recognized symbols for the words for which we have in English no satisfactory equivalents.   " Begriff," when used in its technical sense, is translated by " Notion," " Idee " by " Idea," as distinguished from the colloquial "idea"; " Vorstellung " is usually rendered by "popular" or " ordinary conception."

Miss Frances H. Simson has rendered very valuable assistance in going carefully over most of the proofs of the first volume, and she is now engaged with me in the translation of the volumes following.

E. S. H.

INAUGURAL ADDRESS

DELIVERED AT HEIDELBERG ON THE 28TH OCTOBER, 1816

GENTLEMEN,—Since the History of Philosophy is to be the subject of these lectures, and to-day I am making my first appearance in this University, I hope you will allow me to say what satisfaction it gives me to take my place once more in an Academy of Learning at this particular time. For the period seems to have been arrived at when Philosophy may again hope to receive some attention and love—this almost dead science may again raise its voice, and hope that the world which had become deaf to its teaching, may once more lend it an ear. The necessities of the time have accorded to the petty interests of every-day life such overwhelming attention: the deep interests of actuality and the strife respecting these have engrossed all the powers and the forces of the mind—as also the necessary means—to so great an extent, that no place has been left to the higher inward life, the intellectual operations of a purer sort; and the better natures have thus been stunted in their growth, and in great measure sacrificed. Because the spirit of the world was thus occupied, it could not look within and withdraw into itself. But since this stream of actuality is checked, since the German nation has cut its way out of its most material conditions, since its nationality, the basis of all higher life, has been saved, we may hope that, in addition to the State, which has swallowed up all other interests in its own, the Church may now resume her high position—that in addition to the kingdom of the world to which all thoughts and efforts have hitherto been

directed, the Kingdom of God may also be considered. In
other words, along with the business of politics and the
other interests of every-day life, we may trust that Science,
the free rational world of mind, may again flourish.

We shall see in the History of Philosophy that in other
European countries in which the sciences and the cultivation of the understanding have been prosecuted with zeal
and with respect, Philosophy, excepting in name, has
sunk even from memory, and that it is in the German
nation that it has been retained as a peculiar possession.
We have received the higher call of Nature to be the con-
servers of this holy flame, just as the Eumolpidæ in Athens
had the conservation of the Eleusinian mysteries, the inhabitants of the island of Samothrace the preservation and
maintenance of a higher divine service ; and as, earlier still,
the World-spirit reserved to the Jewish nation the highest
consciousness that it should once more rise from thence as a
new spiritual force. We have already got so far, and have
attained to a seriousness so much greater and a consciousness so much deeper, that for us ideas and that which our
reason justifies, can alone have weight ; to speak more
plainly, the Prussian State is a State constituted on principles of intelligence. But the needs of the time and the
interests of the events in the world already mentioned, have
repressed a real and earnest effort after Philosophy and
driven hence any general attention to it. It has thus happened that because vigorous natures turned to the practical,
insipidity and dulness appropriated to themselves the pre-
eminence in Philosophy and flourished there. It may
indeed be said that since Philosophy began to take a place
in Germany, it has never looked so badly as at the present
time—never have emptiness and shallowness overlaid it so
completely, and never have they spoken and acted with such
arrogance, as though all power were in their hands ! To
combat the shallowness, to strive with German earnestness
and honesty, to draw Philosophy out of the solitude into

which it has wandered—to do such work as this we may hope that we are called by the higher spirit of our time. Let us together greet the dawn of a better time in which the spirit, hitherto a prey to externalities, may return within itself, come to itself again, and win space and room for a kingdom of its own, where true minds will rise above the interests of the moment, and obtain the power to receive the true, eternal and divine, the power to consider and to grasp the highest.

We elders, who in the storms of the age have ripened into men, may think you happy whose youth falls in the day in which you may devote the same undisturbed to Science and to Truth. I have dedicated my life to Science, and it is a true joy to me to find myself again in this place where I may, in a higher measure and more extensive circle, work with others in the interests of the higher sciences, and help to direct your way therein. I hope that I may succeed in deserving and obtaining your confidence. But in the first place, I can ask nothing of you but to bring with you, above all, a trust in science and a trust in yourselves. The love of truth, faith in the power of mind, is the first condition in Philosophy. Man, because he is Mind, should and must deem himself worthy of the highest; he cannot think too highly of the greatness and the power of his mind, and, with this belief, nothing will be so difficult and hard that it will not reveal itself to him. The Being of the universe, at first hidden and concealed, has no power which can offer resistance to the search for knowledge; it has to lay itself open before the seeker—to set before his eyes and give for his enjoyment, its riches and its depths.

PREFATORY NOTE

In the History of Philosophy the observation is immediately forced upon us that it certainly presents great interest if its subject is regarded from a favourable point of view, but that it would still possess interest even if its end were regarded as opposite to what it is. Indeed, this interest may seem to increase in the degree in which the ordinary conception of Philosophy, and of the end which its history serves, is reversed; for from the History of Philosophy a proof of the futility of the science is mainly derived.

The demand that a history, whatever the subject may be, should state the facts without prejudice and without any particular object or end to be gained by its means, must be regarded as a fair one. But with a commonplace demand like this, we do not get far; for the history of a subject is necessarily intimately connected with the conception which is formed of it. In accordance with this what is important in it is determined, and the relation of the events to the end regulates the selection of facts to be recorded, the mode of comprehending them, and the point of view under which they are regarded. It may happen from the ideas formed of what a State really is, that a reader of the political history of a country may find therein nothing of what he looks for. Still more may this be the case in the history of Philosophy, and representations of this history may be instanced in which everything, excepting what was supposed to be Philosophy, appears to be found.

In other histories we have a clear conception of their subjects, at least so far as their principal points are concerned ; we know whether they concern a particular land, people or race, or whether their subject is the science of mathematics, physics, &c., or an art, such as painting. The science of Philosophy has, however, this distinguishing feature, and, if you will, this disadvantage as compared with other sciences, that we find the most varied points of view as regards its Notion, and regarding that which it ought to and can accomplish. If this first assumption, the conception of the subject of the history, is not established, the history itself is necessarily made vacillating, and it only obtains consistency when it sets forth a definite conception : but then in view of the various ways of regarding its subject, it easily draws upon itself the reproach of one-sidedness.

That drawback relates, however, only to an external consideration of this narrative ; there is another and greater disadvantage allied to it. If there are different Notions of the science of Philosophy, it is the true Notion alone that puts us in a position to understand the writings of philosophers who have worked in the knowledge of it. For in thought, and particularly in speculative thought, comprehension means something quite different from understanding the grammatical sense of the words alone, and also from understanding them in the region of ordinary conception only. Hence we may possess a knowledge of the assertions, propositions, or of the opinions of philosophers ; we may have occupied ourselves largely with the grounds of and deductions from these opinions, and the main point in all that we have done may be wanting—the comprehension of the propositions. There is hence no lack of voluminous and even learned histories of Philosophy in which the knowledge of the matter itself about which so much ado has been made, is absent. The authors of such histories may be compared to animals which have listened to all the tones in some music, but to whose senses the unison, the harmony of their tones, has not penetrated.

The circumstance mentioned makes it in no science so necessary as in the history of Philosophy to commence with an Introduction, and in it correctly to define, in the first place, the subject of the history about to be related. For it may be said, How should we begin to treat a subject, the name of which is certainly mentioned often enough, but of whose nature we as yet know nothing? In treating the history of Philosophy thus, we could have no other guidance than that of seeking out and taking up whatever has received the name of Philosophy, anywhere or any time. But in fact, when the Notion of Philosophy is established, not arbitrarily but in a scientific way, such treatment becomes the science of Philosophy itself. For in this science the peculiar characteristic is that its Notion forms the beginning in appearance merely, and it is only the whole treatment of the science that is the proof, and indeed we may say the finding of its Notion; and this is really a result of that treatment.

In this Introduction the Notion of the science of Philosophy, of the subject of its history, has thus likewise to be set forth. At the same time, though this Introduction professes to relate to the history of Philosophy only, what has just been said of Philosophy on the whole, also holds good. What can be said in this Introduction is not so much something which may be stated beforehand, as what can be justified or proved in the treatment of the history. These preparatory explanations are for this reason only, not to be placed in the category of arbitrary assumptions. But to begin with stating what in their justification are really results, can only have the interest which may be possessed by a summary, given in advance, of the most general contents of a science. It must serve to set aside many questions and demands which might, from our ordinary prejudices, arise in such a history.

INTRODUCTION

THERE are various aspects under which the History of Philosophy may possess interest. We shall find the central point of this interest in the essential connection existing between what is apparently past and the present stage reached by Philosophy. That this connection is not one of the external considerations which may be taken into account in the history of Philosophy, but really expresses its inner character : that the events of this history, while they perpetuate themselves in their effects like all other events, yet produce their results in a special way—this it is which is here to be more clearly expounded.

What the history of Philosophy shows us is a succession of noble minds, a gallery of heroes of thought, who, by the power of Reason, have penetrated into the being of things, of nature and of spirit, into the Being of God, and have won for us by their labours the highest treasure, the treasure of reasoned knowledge.

The events and actions of this history are therefore such that personality and individual character do not enter to any large degree into its content and matter. In this respect the history of Philosophy contrasts with political history, in which the individual, according to the peculiarity of his disposition, talents, affections, the strength or weakness of his character, and in general, according to that through which he is this individual, is the subject of actions and events. In Philosophy, the less deserts and merits are accorded to the particular individual, the better is the history; and the more it deals with thought as free, with the universal character of man as man, the more this thought, which is devoid of special characteristic, is itself shown to be the producing subject.

The acts of thought appear at first to be a matter of history, and, therefore, things of the past, and outside our real existence. But in reality we are what we are through history : or, more accurately, as in the history of Thought, what has passed away is only one side, so in the present, what we have as a permanent possession is essentially bound up with our place in history. The possession of self-conscious reason, which belongs to us of the present world, did not arise suddenly, nor did it grow only from the soil of the present. This possession must be regarded as previously present, as an inheritance, and as the result of labour—the labour of all past generations of men. Just as the arts of outward life, the accumulated skill and invention, the customs and arrangements of social and political life, are the result of the thought, care, and needs, of the want and the misery, of the ingenuity, the plans and achievements of those who preceded us in history, so, likewise, in science, and specially in Philosophy, do we owe what we are to the tradition which, as Herder has put it,[1] like a holy chain, runs through all that was transient, and has therefore passed away. Thus has been preserved and transmitted to us what antiquity produced.

But this tradition is not only a stewardess who simply guards faithfully that which she has received, and thus delivers it unchanged to posterity, just as the course of nature in the infinite change and activity of its forms ever remains constant to its original laws and makes no step in advance. Such tradition is no motionless statue, but is alive, and swells like a mighty river, which increases in

[1] Zur Philosophie und Geschichte. Pt. V. pp. 184—186. (Edition of 1828, in 12 vols.)

size the further it advances from its source. The
of this tradition is that which the intellectual world has
brought forth, and the universal Mind does not remain
stationary. But it is just the universal Mind with which we
have to do. It may certainly be the case with a single
nation that its culture, art, science—its intellectual activities
as a whole—are at a standstill. This appears, perhaps, to
be the case with the Chinese, for example, who may have
been as far advanced in every respect two thousand years
ago as now. But the world-spirit does not sink into this
rest of indifference; this follows from its very nature, for
its activity is its life. This activity presupposes a material
already present, on which it acts, and which it does not
merely augment by the addition of new matter, but completely fashions and transforms. Thus that which each
generation has produced in science and in intellectual
activity, is an heirloom to which all the past generations
have added their savings, a temple in which all races of
men thankfully and cheerfully deposit that which rendered
aid to them through life, and which they had won from the
depths of Nature and of Mind. To receive this inheritance
is also to enter upon its use. It constitutes the soul of
each successive generation, the intellectual substance of the
time; its principles, prejudices, and possessions; and this
legacy is degraded to a material which becomes metamor-
phosed by Mind. In this manner that which is received is
changed, and the material worked upon is both enriched
and preserved at the same time.

This is the function of our own and of every age: to
grasp the knowledge which is already existing, to make it
our own, and in so doing to develop it still further and to
raise it to a higher level. In thus appropriating it to ourselves we make it into something different from what it was
before. On the presupposition of an already existing
intellectual world which is transformed in our appropria-
tion of it, depends the fact that Philosophy can only arise

in connection with previous Philosophy, from which of necessity it has arisen. The course of history does not show us the Becoming of things foreign to us, but the Becoming of ourselves and of our own knowledge.,

The ideas and questions which may be present to our mind regarding the character and ends of the history of Philosophy, depend on the nature of the relationship here given. In this lies the explanation of the fact that the study of the history of Philosophy is an introduction to Philosophy itself. The guiding principles for the formation of this history are given in this fact, the further discussion of which must thus be the main object of this introduction. We must also, however, keep in mind, as being of fundamental importance, the conception of the aim of Philosophy. And since, as already mentioned, the systematic exposition of this conception cannot here find a place, such discussion as we can now undertake, can only propose to deal with the subject provisionally and not to give a thorough and conclusive account of the nature of the Becoming of Philosophy.

This Becoming is not merely a passive movement, as we suppose movements such as those of the sun and moon to be. It is no mere movement in the unresisting medium of space and time. What we must represent to ourselves is the activity of free thought; we have to present the history of the world of thought as it has arisen and produced itself.

There is an old tradition that it is the faculty of thought which separates men from beasts; and to this tradition we shall adhere. In accordance with this, what man has, as being nobler than a beast, he has through thinking. Everything which is human, however it may appear, is so only because the thought contained in it works and has worked. But thought, although it is thus the essential, substantial, and effectual, has many other elements. We must, however, consider it best when Thought does not pursue anything else, but is occupied only with itself—with what is noblest—when it has sought and found itself. The history which we have before us is the history of Thought finding itself, and it is the case with Thought that it only finds itself in producing itself; indeed, that it only exists and is actual in finding itself. These productions are the philosophic systems; and the series of discoveries on which Thought sets out in order to discover itself, forms a work which has lasted twenty-five hundred years.

If the Thought which is essentially Thought, is in and for itself and eternal, and that which is true is contained in Thought alone, how, then, does this intellectual world come to have a history? In history what appears is transient, has disappeared in the night of the past and is no more. But true, necessary thought—and it is only with such that we have to do—is capable of no change. The question here raised constitutes one of those matters first to be brought under our consideration. But in the second place, there are also many most important things outside of Philosophy, which are yet the work of Thought, and which are left unconsidered. Such are Religion, Political History, forms of Government, and the Arts and Sciences. The question arises as to how these operations differ from the subject of consideration, and how they are related in history? As regards these two points of view, it is desirable to show in what sense the history of Philosophy is here taken, in order to see clearly what we are about. Moreover, in the third place, we must first take a general survey before we descend to particulars, else the whole is not seen for the mere details—the wood is not seen for the trees, nor Philosophy for mere philosophies. We require to have a general idea of the nature and aim of the whole in order to know what to look for. Just as we first desire to obtain a general idea of a country, which we should no longer see in going into detail, so we desire to see the relation which single philosophies bear to the whole; for in reality, the high value of the detail lies in its relation to the whole. This is nowhere more the case than with Philosophy, and also with its history. In the case of a history, indeed, the establishment of the Universal seems to be less needful than in that of one of the sciences proper. For history seems at first to be a succession of chance events, in which each fact stands isolated by itself, which has Time alone as a connecting-link. But even in political history we are not satisfied with this. We see, or at least divine in it, that essential connection in which the individual events have their place and relation to an end or aim, and in this way obtain significance. For the significant in history is such only through its relation to and connection with a Universal. To perceive this Universal is thus to apprehend the significance.

There are, therefore, the following points with which I wish to deal in this introduction.

The first of these will be to investigate the character of the history of Philosophy, its significance, its nature, and its aim, from which will follow inferences as to its treatment. In particular, we shall get an insight into the relation of the history of Philosophy to the science of Philosophy, and this will be the most interesting point of all. That is to say, this history represents, not merely the external, accidental, events contained within it, but it shows how the content, or that which appears to belong to mere history, really belongs to the science of Philosophy. The history of Philosophy is itself scientific, and thus essentially becomes the science of Philosophy.

In the second place, the Notion of Philosophy must be more adequately determined, and from it must be deduced what should be excluded from the history of Philosophy out of the infinite material and the manifold aspects of the intellectual culture of the nations. Religion, certainly, and the thoughts contained in and regarding it, particularly when these are in the form of mythology, are, on account of their matter, and the sciences with their ideas on the state, duties and laws, on account of their form, so near Philosophy that the history of the science of Philosophy threatens to become quite indefinite in extent. It might be supposed that the history of Philosophy should take account of all these ideas. Has not everything been called Philosophy and philosophizing? On the one hand, the close connection has to be further considered in which Philosophy stands with its allied subjects, religion, art, the other sciences, and likewise with political history. On the other hand, when the province of Philosophy has been correctly defined, we reach, with the determination of what Philosophy is and what pertains to it, the starting-point of its history, which must be distinguished from the commencements of religious ideas and mere thoughtful conjectures.

From the idea of the subject which is contained in these first two points of view, it is necessary to pass on to the consideration of the third point, to the general review of this history and to the division of its progress into natural periods—such an arrangement to exhibit it as an organic, progressive whole, as a rational connection through which this history attains the dignity of a science. And I will not occupy further space with reflections on the use of the history of Philosophy, and other methods of treating it. The use is evident. But, in conclusion, I wish to consider the sources of the history of Philosophy, for this is customary.

A

THE NOTION OF THE HISTORY OF PHILOSOPHY.

THE thought which may first occur to us in the history of Philosophy, is that the subject itself contains an inner contradiction. For Philosophy aims at understanding what

is unchangeable, eternal, in and for itself: its end is
Truth.   But history tells us of that which has at one time
existed, at another time has vanished, having been expelled by something else.   Truth is eternal; it does not
fall within the sphere of the transient, and has no history.
But if it has a history, and as this history is only the representation of a succession of past forms of knowledge, the
truth is not to be found in it, for the truth cannot be what
has passed away.

It might be said that all this argument would affect not
only the other sciences, but in like degree the Christian
religion, and it might be found inconsistent that a history
of this religion and of the other sciences should exist; but
it would be superfluous further to examine this argument,
for it is immediately contradicted by the very fact that
there are such histories.   But in order to get a better
understanding of this apparent contradiction, we must
distinguish between the outward history of a religion or a
science and the history of the subject itself.   And then we
must take into account that the history of Philosophy
because of the special nature of its subject-matter, is
different from other histories.   It is at once evident that
the contradiction in question could not refer to the outward
history, but merely to the inward, or that of the content
itself.   There is a history of the spread of Christianity and
of the lives of those who have avowed it, and its existence has formed itself into that of a Church.   This in itself
constitutes an external existence such that being brought
into contact with temporal affairs of the most diverse kind,
its lot is a varied one and it essentially possesses a history.   And of the Christian doctrine it is true that it, too,
has its history, but it necessarily soon reached its full
development and attained to its appointed powers.   And
this old creed has been an acknowledged influence to every
age, and will still be acknowledged unchanged as the
Truth, even though this acknowledgment were become no

more than a pretence, and the words an empty form. But the history of this doctrine in its wider sense includes two elements: first the various additions to and deviations from the truth formerly established, and secondly the combating of these errors, the purification of the principles that remain from such additions, and a consequent return to their first simplicity.

The other sciences, including Philosophy, have also an external history like Religion. Philosophy has a history of its origin, diffusion, maturity, decay, revival; a history of its teachers, promoters, and of its opponents—often, too, of an outward relation to religion and occasionally to the State. This side of its history likewise gives occasion to interesting questions. Amongst other such, it is asked why Philosophy, the doctrine of absolute Truth, seems to have revealed itself on the whole to a small number of individuals, to special nations, and how it has limited itself to particular periods of time. Similarly with respect to Christianity, to the Truth in a much more universal form than the philosophical, a difficulty has been encountered in respect to the question whether there is a contradiction in the fact that this religion should have appeared so late in time, and that it should have remained so long and should still remain limited to special races of men. But these and other similar questions are too much a matter of detail to depend merely on the general conflict referred to, and when we have further touched upon the peculiar character of philosophic knowledge, we may go more specially into the aspects which relate to the external existence and external history of Philosophy.

But as regards the comparison between the history of Religion and that of Philosophy as to inner content, there is not in the latter as there is in Religion a fixed and fundamental truth which, as unchangeable, is apart from history. The content of Christianity, which is Truth, has, however, remained unaltered as such, and has therefore little history or as good as none.[1] Hence in Religion, on account of its very nature as Christianity, the conflict referred to disappears. The errors and additions constitute no difficulty. They are transitory and altogether historical in character.

The other sciences, indeed, have also according to their content a History, a part of which relates to alterations, and the renunciation of tenets which were formerly current. But a great, perhaps the greater, part of the history relates to what has proved permanent, so that what was new, was not an alteration on earlier acquisitions, but an addition to them. These sciences progress through a process of juxta-position. It is true that in Botany, Mineralogy, and so on, much is dependent on what was previously known, but by far the greatest part remains stationary and by means of fresh matter is merely added to without itself being affected by the addition. With a science like Mathematics, history has, in the main, only the pleasing task of recording further additions. Thus to take an example, elementary geometry in so far as it was created by Euclid, may from his time on be regarded as having no further history.

The history of Philosophy, on the other hand, shows neither the motionlessness of a complete, simple content, nor altogether the onward movement of a peaceful addition of new treasures to those already acquired. It seems merely to afford the spectacle of ever-recurring changes in the whole, such as finally are no longer even connected by a common aim.

1. COMMON IDEAS REGARDING THE HISTORY OF PHILOSOPHY.

At this point appear these ordinary superficial ideas regarding the history of Philosophy which have to be referred to and corrected. As regards these very current

---

[1] S. Marheineke: "Lehrbuch des Christlichen Glaubens und Lebens." Berlin, 1823. § 133, 134.

views, which are doubtless known to you, gentlemen, for indeed they are the reflections most likely to occur in one's first crude thoughts on a history of Philosophy, I will shortly explain what requires explanation, and the explanation of the differences in philosophies will lead us further into the matter itself.

a. *The History of Philosophy as an accumulation of Opinions.*

History, at the first glance, includes in its aim the narration of the accidental circumstances of times, of races, and of individuals, treated impartially partly as regards their relation in time, and partly as to their content. The appearance of contingency in time-succession is to be dealt with later on. It is contingency of content which is the idea with which we have first to deal—the idea of contingent actions. But thoughts and not external actions, or griefs, or joys, form the content of Philosophy. Contingent thoughts, however, are nothing but opinions, and philosophical opinions are opinions relating to the more special content of Philosophy, regarding God, Nature and Spirit.

Thus we now meet the view very usually taken of the history of Philosophy which ascribes to it the narration of a number of philosophical opinions as they have arisen and manifested themselves in time. This kind of matter is in courtesy called opinions; those who think themselves more capable of judging rightly, call such a history a display of senseless follies, or at least of errors made by men engrossed in thought and in mere ideas. This view is not only held by those who recognize their ignorance of Philosophy. Those who do this, acknowledge it, because that ignorance is, in common estimation, held to be no obstacle to giving judgment upon what has to do with the subject; for it is thought that anybody can form a judgment on its character and value without any comprehension of it whatever. But the same view is even held by those who write or have written on the history of Philosophy. This history, considered only as the enumeration of various opinions, thus becomes an idle tale, or, if you will, an erudite investigation. For erudition is, in the main, acquaintance with a number of useless things, that is to say, with that which has no intrinsic interest or value further than being known. Yet it is thought that profit is to be derived from learning the various opinions and reflections of other men. It stimulates the powers of thought and also leads to many excellent reflections ; this signifies that now and then it occasions an idea, and its art thus consists in the spinning one opinion out of the other.

If the history of Philosophy merely represented various opinions in array, whether they be of God or of natural and spiritual things existent, it would be a most superfluous and tiresome science, no matter what advantage might be brought forward as derived from such thought-activity and learning. What can be more useless than to learn a string of bald opinions, and what more unimportant ? Literary works, being histories of Philosophy in the sense that they produce and treat the ideas of Philosophy as if they were opinions, need be only superficially glanced at to find how dry and destitute of interest everything about them is.

An opinion is a subjective conception, an uncontrolled thought, an idea which may occur to me in one direction or in another : an opinion is mine,[1] it is in itself a universal thought which is existent in and for itself. But Philosophy possesses no opinions, for there is no such thing as philosophical opinions. When we hear a man speaking of philosophical opinions, even though he be an historian of philosophy itself, we detect at once this want of fundamental education. Philosophy is the objective science of truth, it is science of necessity, conceiving knowledge, and neither opinion nor the spinning out of opinions.

The more precise significance of this idea is that we get

[1] " *Meinung ist mein.*"

to know opinions only, thus laying emphasis upon the word Opinion. Now the direct opposite of opinion is the Truth; it is Truth before which mere opinion pales. Those who in the history of Philosophy seek mere theories, or who suppose that on the whole only such are to be found within it, also turn aside when that word Truth confronts them. Philosophy here encounters opposition from two different sides. On the one hand piety openly declares Reason or Thought to be incapable of apprehending what is true, and to lead only to the abyss of doubt; it declares that independent thought must be renounced, and reason held in bounds by faith in blind authority, if Truth is to be reached. Of the relation existing between Religion and Philosophy and of its history, we shall deal later on. On the other hand, it is known just as well, that so-called reason has maintained its rights, abandoning faith in mere authority, and has endeavoured to make Christianity rational, so that throughout it is only my personal insight and conviction which obliges me to make any admissions. But this affirmation of the right of reason is turned round in an astonishing manner, so that it results in making knowledge of the truth through reason an impossibility. This so-called reason on the one hand has combated religious faith in the name and power of thinking reason, and at the same time it has itself turned against reason and is true reason's adversary. Instinct and feeling are maintained by it against the true reason, thus making the measure of true value the merely subjective—that is a particular conviction such as each can form in and for himself in his subjective capacity. A personal conviction such as this is no more than the particular opinion that has become final for men.

If we begin with what meets us in our very first conceptions, we cannot neglect to make mention of this aspect in the history of Philosophy. In its results it permeates culture generally, being at once the misconception and true sign of our times. It is the principle through which

men mutually understand and know each other; an
hypothesis whose value is established and which is the
ground of all the other sciences. In theology it is not so
much the creed of the church that passes for Christianity, as
that every one to a greater or less degree makes a christianity of his own to tally with his conviction. And in history
we often see theology driven into acquiring the knowledge
of various opinions in order that an interest may thus be
furnished to the science, and one of the first results of the
attention paid them is the honour awarded to all convictions, and the esteem vouchsafed to what has been constituted merely by the individual. The endeavour to know
the Truth is then of course relinquished. It is true that
personal conviction is the ultimate and absolute essential
which reason and its philosophy, from a subjective point of
view, demand in knowledge. But there is a distinction
between conviction when it rests on subjective grounds
such as feelings, speculations and perceptions, or, speaking
generally, on the particular nature of the subject, and when
it rests on thought proceeding from acquaintance with the
Notion and the nature of the thing. In the former case
conviction is opinion.

This opposition between mere opinion and truth now
sharply defined, we already recognize in the culture of the
period of Socrates and Plato—a period of corruption in
Greek life—as the Platonic opposition between opinion
(δόξα) and Science (ἐπιστήμη). It is the same opposition as that which existed in the decadence of Roman
public and political life under Augustus, and subsequently
when Epicureanism and indifference set themselves up
against Philosophy. Under this influence, when Christ said,
"I came into the world that I should bear witness unto the
Truth," Pilate answered, "What is Truth?" That was
said in a superior way, and signifies that this idea of truth
is an expedient which is obsolete: we have got further, we
know that there is no longer any question about knowing

the Truth, seeing that we have gone beyond it. Who
makes this statement has gone beyond it indeed. If this is
made our starting point in the history of Philosophy, its
whole significance will consist in finding out the particular
ideas of others, each one of which is different from the
other : these individual points of view are thus foreign to
me : my thinking reason is not free, nor is it present in
them : for me they are but extraneous, dead historic matter,
or so much empty content, and to satisfy oneself with
empty vanity is mere subjective vanity itself.

To the impartial man, the Truth has always been a heart-
stirring word and one of great import. As to the assertion that the Truth cannot be known, we shall consider it
more closely in the history of Philosophy itself where it
appears. The only thing to be here remarked is that if this
assumption be allowed, as was the case with Tennemann, it
is beyond conception why anyone should still trouble about
Philosophy, since each opinion asserts falsely in its turn
that it has found the truth. This immediately recalls to
me the old belief that Truth consists in knowledge, but that
an individual only knows the Truth in so far as he reflects
and not as he walks and stands : and that the Truth cannot
be known in immediate apprehension and perception, whether
it be external and sensuous, or whether it be intellectual
perception (for every perception as a perception is sensuous)
but only through the labour of thought.

b. *Proof of the futility of Philosophical Knowledge
obtained through the History of Philosophy itself.*

From another point of view another consequence ensues
from the above conception of the history of Philosophy
which may at will be looked at as an evil or a benefit. In
view of such manifold opinions and philosophical systems
so numerous, one is perplexed to know which one ought
to be accepted. In regard to the great matters to which

man is attracted and a knowledge of which Philosophy
would bestow, it is evident that the greatest minds
have erred, because they have been contradicted by
others. "Since this has been so with minds so great,
how then can *ego homuncio* attempt to form a judgment ? " This consequence, which ensues from the
diversity in philosophical systems, is, as may be supposed,
the evil in the matter, while at the same time it is a
subjective good. For this diversity is the usual plea urged
by those who, with an air of knowledge, wish to make a show
of interest in Philosophy, to explain the fact that they, with
this pretence of good-will, and, indeed, with added motive
for working at the science, do in fact utterly neglect it.
But this diversity in philosophical systems is far from being
merely an evasive plea. It has far more weight as a genuine
serious ground of argument against the zeal which Philosophy requires. It justifies its neglect and demonstrates
conclusively the powerlessness of the endeavour to attain
to philosophic knowledge of the truth. When it is
admitted that Philosophy ought to be a real science,
and one Philosophy must certainly be the true, the
question arises as to which Philosophy it is, and when it
can be known. Each one asserts its genuineness, each even
gives different signs and tokens by which the Truth can be
discovered ; sober reflective thought must therefore hesitate
to give its judgment.

This, then, is the wider interest which the history of
Philosophy is said to afford. Cicero (De natura Deorum I.
8 sq.) gives us from this point of view, a most slovenly
history of philosophic thought on God. He puts it in the
mouth of an Epicurean, but he himself knew of nothing
more favourable to say, and it is thus his own view.
The Epicurean says that no certain knowledge has been
arrived at. The proof that the efforts of philosophy are
futile is derived directly from the usual superficial view
taken of its history ; the results attendant on that history

make it appear to be a process in which the most various thoughts arise in numerous philosophies, each of which opposes, contradicts and refutes the other. This fact, which cannot be denied, seems to contain the justification, indeed the necessity for applying to Philosophy the words of Christ, " Let the dead bury their dead ; arise, and follow Me." The whole of the history of Philosophy becomes a battlefield covered with the bones of the dead ; it is a kingdom not merely formed of dead and lifeless individuals, but of refuted and spiritually dead systems, since each has killed and buried the other. Instead of " Follow thou Me," here then it must indeed be said, " Follow thine own self "—that is, hold by thine own convictions, remain steadfast to thine own opinion, why adopt another ?

It certainly happens that a new philosophy makes its appearance, which maintains the others to be valueless; and indeed each one in turn comes forth at first with the pretext that by its means all previous philosophies not only are refuted, but what in them is wanting is supplied, and now at length the right one is discovered. But following upon what has gone before, it would rather seem that other words of Scripture are just as applicable to such a philosophy—the words which the Apostle Peter spoke to Ananias, " Behold the feet of them that shall carry thee out are at the door." Behold the philosophy by which thine own will be refuted and displaced shall not tarry long as it has not tarried before.

c. *Explanatory remarks on the diversity in Philosophies.*

Certainly the fact is sufficiently well established that there are and have been different philosophies. The Truth is, however, one ; and the instinct of reason maintains this irradicable intuition or belief. It is said that only one philosophy can be true, and, because philosophies are different, it is concluded that all others must be erroneous. But, in fact, each one in turn gives every assurance, evidence and proof of being the one and true Philosophy. This is a common mode of reasoning and is what seems in truth to be the view of sober thought. As regards the sober nature of the word at issue—thought—we can tell from everyday experience that if we fast we feel hunger either at once or very soon. But sober thought always has the fortunate power of not resulting in hunger and desire, but of being and remaining as it is, content. Hence the thought expressed in such an utterance reveals the fact that it is dead understanding; for it is only death which fasts and yet rests satisfied. But neither physical life nor intellectual remains content with mere abstention; as desire it presses on through hunger and through thirst towards Truth, towards knowledge itself. It presses on to satisfy this desire and does not allow itself to feast and find sufficiency in a reflection such as this.

As to this reflection, the next thing to be said of it is that however different the philosophies have been, they had a common bond in that they were Philosophy. Thus whoever may have studied or become acquainted with a philosophy, of whatever kind, provided only that it is such, has thereby become acquainted with Philosophy. That delusive mode of reasoning which regards diversity alone, and from doubt of or aversion to the particular form in which a Universal finds its actuality, will not grasp or even allow this universal nature, I have elsewhere [1] likened to an invalid recommended by the doctor to eat fruit, and who has cherries, plums or grapes, before him, but who pedantically refuses to take anything because no part of what is offered him is fruit, some of it being cherries, and the rest plums or grapes.

But it is really important to have a deeper insight into the bearings of this diversity in the systems of Philosophy.

[1] Cf. Hegels Werke, vol. VI. § 13, pp. 21, 22.

Truth and Philosophy known philosophically, make such diversity appear in another light from that of abstract opposition between Truth and Error. The explanation of how this comes about will reveal to us the significance of the whole history of Philosophy. We must make the fact conceivable, that the diversity and number of philosophies not only does not prejudice Philosophy itself, that is to say the possibility of a philosophy, but that such diversity is, and has been, absolutely necessary to the existence of a science of Philosophy and that it is essential to it.

This makes it easy to us to comprehend the aim of Philosophy, which is in thought and in conception to grasp the Truth, and not merely to discover that nothing can be known, or that at least temporal, finite truth, which also is an untruth, can alone be known and not the Truth indeed. Further we find that in the history of Philosophy we have to deal with Philosophy itself. The facts within that history are not adventures and contain no more romance than does the history of the world. They are not a mere collection of chance events, of expeditions of wandering knights, each going about fighting, struggling purposelessly, leaving no results to show for all his efforts. Nor is it so that one thing has been thought out here, another there, at will; in the activity of thinking mind there is real connection, and what there takes place is rational. It is with this belief in the spirit of the world that we must proceed to history, and in particular to the history of Philosophy.

2. Explanatory Remarks upon the Definition of the History of Philosophy.

The above statement, that the Truth is only one, is still abstract and formal. In the deeper sense it is our starting point. But the aim of Philosophy is to know this one Truth as the immediate source from which all else proceeds,

both all the laws of nature and all the manifestations of
life and consciousness of which they are mere reflections,
or to lead these laws and manifestations in ways apparently
contrary, back to that single source, and from that source to
comprehend them, which is to understand their derivation.
Thus what is most essential is to know that the single
truth is not merely a solitary, empty thought, but one
determined within itself. To obtain this knowledge we
must enter into some abstract Notions which, as such,
are quite general and dry, and which are the two principles
of *Development* and of the *Concrete.* We could, indeed,
embrace the whole in the single principle of development;
if this were clear, all else would result and follow of its
own accord. The product of thinking is the thought;
thought is, however, still formal; somewhat more defined
it becomes Notion, and finally Idea is Thought in its
totality, implicitly and explicitly determined. Thus the
Idea, and it alone is Truth. Now it is essentially in the
nature of the Idea to develop, and only through development to arrive at comprehension of itself, or to become
what it is. That the Idea should have to make itself what
it is, seems like a contradiction; it may be said that it is
what it is.

a. *The Notion of Development.*

The idea of development is well known, but it is the
special characteristic of Philosophy to investigate such
matters as were formerly held as known. What is dealt
with or made use of without consideration as an aid to
daily life, is certainly the unknown to man unless he be
informed in Philosophy. The further discussion of this
idea belongs to the science of Logic.

In order to comprehend what development is, what may
be called two different states must be distinguished. The
first is what is known as capacity, power, what I call being-
in-itself (*potentia, δύναμις*); the second principle is that

of being-for-itself, actuality (*actus, ἐνέργεια*). If we say, for example, that man is by nature rational, we would mean that he has reason only inherently or in embryo : in this sense, reason, understanding, imagination, will, are possessed from birth or even from the mother's womb. But while the child only has capacities or the actual possibility of reason, it is just the same as if he had no reason ; reason does not yet exist in him since he cannot yet do anything rational, and has no rational consciousness. Thus what man is at first implicitly becomes explicit, and it is the same with reason. If, then, man has actuality on whatever side, he is actually rational ; and now we come to reason.

What is the real meaning of this word ? That which is in itself must become an object to mankind, must arrive at consciousness, thus becoming for man. What has become an object to him is the same as what he is in himself ; through the becoming objective of this implicit being, man first becomes for himself ; he is made double, is retained and not changed into another. For example, man is thinking, and thus he thinks out thoughts. In this way it is in thought alone that thought is object ; reason produces what is rational : reason is its own object. The fact that thought may also descend to what is destitute of reason is a consideration involving wider issues, which do not concern us here. But even though man, who in himself is rational, does not at first seem to have got further on since he became rational for himself—what is implicit having merely retained itself—the difference is quite enormous : no new content has been produced, and yet this form of being for self makes all the difference. The whole variation in the development of the world in history is founded on this difference. This alone explains how since all mankind is naturally rational, and freedom is the hypothesis on which this reason rests, slavery yet has been, and in part still is, maintained by many peoples, and men have remained contented under it. The only distinction between the Africans and the Asiatics on the one hand, and the Greeks, Romans, and moderns on the other, is that the latter know and it is explicit for them, that they are free, but the others are so without knowing that they are, and thus without existing as being free. This constitutes the enormous difference in their condition. All knowledge, and learning, science, and even commerce have no other object than to draw out what is inward or implicit and thus to become objective.

Because that which is implicit comes into existence, it certainly passes into change, yet it remains one and the same, for the whole process is dominated by it. The plant, for example, does not lose itself in mere indefinite change. From the germ much is produced when at first nothing was to be seen; but the whole of what is brought forth, if not developed, is yet hidden and ideally contained within itself. The principle of this projection into existence is that the germ cannot remain merely implicit, but is impelled towards development, since it presents the contradiction of being only implicit and yet not desiring so to be. But this coming without itself has an end in view; its completion fully reached, and its previously determined end is the fruit or produce of the germ, which causes a return to the first condition. The germ will produce itself alone and manifest what is contained in it, so that it then may return to itself once more thus to renew the unity from which it started. With nature it certainly is true that the subject which commenced and the matter which forms the end are two separate units, as in the case of seed and fruit. The doubling process has apparently the effect of separating into two things that which in content is the same. Thus in animal life the parent and the young are different individuals although their nature is the same.

In Mind it is otherwise: it is consciousness and therefore it is free, uniting in itself the beginning and the end. As with the germ in nature, Mind indeed resolves itself back into unity after constituting itself another. But what is in itself becomes for Mind and thus arrives at being for itself. The fruit and seed newly contained within it on the other hand, do not become for the original germ, but for us alone; in the case of Mind both factors not only are implicitly the same in character, but there is a being for the other and at the same time a being for self. That for which the " other " is, is the same as that " other ; " and thus alone Mind is at home with itself in its " other." The development of Mind lies in the fact that its going forth and separation constitutes its coming to itself.

[handwritten: 1° DESIRE]

This being-at-home-with-self, or coming-to-self of [Mind] may be described as its complete and highest end : it is this alone that it desires and nothing else. Everything that from eternity has happened in heaven and earth, the life of God and all the deeds of time simply are the struggles for Mind to know itself, to make itself objective to itself, to find itself, be for itself, and finally unite itself to itself; it is alienated and divided, but only so as to be able thus to find itself and return to itself. Only in this manner does Mind attain its freedom, for that is free which is not connected with or dependent on another. True self-possession and satisfaction are only to be found in this, and in nothing else but Thought does Mind attain this freedom. In sense-perception, for instance, and in feeling, I find myself confined and am not free ; but I am free when I have a consciousness of this my feeling. Man has particular ends and interests even in will; I am free indeed when this is mine. Such ends, however, always contain " another," or something which constitutes for me " another," such as desire and impulse. It is in Thought alone that all foreign matter disappears from view, and that Mind is absolutely free. All interest which is contained in the Idea and in Philosophy is expressed in it.

[handwritten right margin: FREEDOM ONLY IN THOUGHT]

b. *The Notion of the Concrete.*

As to development, it may be asked, what does develop

and what forms the absolute content? Development is considered in the light of a formal process in action and as destitute of content. But the act has no other end but activity, and through this activity the general character of the content is already fixed. For being-in-self and being-for-self are the moments present in action; but the act is the retention of these diverse elements within itself. The act thus is really one, and it is just this unity of differences which is the concrete. Not only is the act concrete, but also the implicit, which stands to action in the relation of subject which begins, and finally the product is just as concrete as the action or as the subject which begins. Development in process likewise forms the content, the Idea itself; for this we must have the one element and then the other : both combined will form a unity as third, because the one in the other is at home with, and not without, itself. Thus the Idea is in its content concrete within itself, and this in two ways : first it is concrete potentially, and then it is its interest that what is in itself should be there for it.

It is a common prejudice that the science of Philosophy deals only with abstractions and empty generalities, and that sense-perception, our empirical self-consciousness, natural instinct, and the feelings of every-day life, lie, on the contrary, in the region of the concrete and the self-determined. As a matter of fact, Philosophy is in the region of thought, and has therefore to deal with universals; its content is abstract, but only as to form and element. In itself the Idea is really concrete, for it is the union of the different determinations. It is here that reasoned knowledge differs from mere knowledge of the understanding, and it is the business of Philosophy, as opposed to understanding, to show that the Truth or the Idea does not consist in empty generalities, but in a universal; and that is within itself the particular and the determined. If the Truth is abstract it must be untrue.

Healthy human reason goes out towards what is concrete; the reflection of the understanding comes first as abstract and untrue, correct in theory only, and amongst other things unpractical. Philosophy is what is most antagonistic to abstraction, and it leads back to the concrete.

If we unite the Notion of the concrete with that of development we have the motion of the concrete. Since the implicit is already concrete within itself, and we only set forth what is implicitly there, the new form which now looks different and which was formerly shut up in the original unity, is merely distinguished. The concrete must become for itself or explicit; as implicit or potential it is only differentiated within itself, not as yet explicitly set forth, but still in a state of unity. The concrete is thus simple, and yet at the same time differentiated. This, its inward contradiction, which is indeed the impelling force in development, brings distinction into being. But thus, too, its right to be taken back and reinstated extends beyond the difference; for its truth is only to be found in unity. Life, both that which is in Nature and that which is of the Idea, of Mind within itself, is thus manifested. Were the Idea abstract, it would simply be the highest conceivable existence, and that would be all that could be said of it; but such a God is the product of the understanding of modern times. What is true is rather found in motion, in a process, however, in which there is rest; difference, while it lasts, is but a temporary condition, through which comes unity, full and concrete.

We may now proceed to give examples of sensuous things, which will help us further to explain this Notion of the concrete. Although the flower has many qualities, such as smell, taste, form, colour, &c., yet it is one. None of these qualities could be absent in the particular leaf or flower: each individual part of the leaf shares alike all the qualities of the leaf entire. Gold, similarly contains in every particle all its qualities unseparated and entire. It

is frequently allowed with sensuous things that such varied
elements may be joined together, but, in the spiritual, differentiation is supposed to involve opposition. We do not
controvert the fact, or think it contradictory, that the smell
and taste of the flower, although otherwise opposed, are
yet clearly in one subject ; nor do we place the one
against the other. But the understanding and understanding thought find everything of a different kind,
placed in conjunction, to be incompatible. Matter,
for example, is complex and coherent, or space is continuous and uninterrupted. Likewise we may take separate
points in space and break up matter dividing it ever
further into infinity. It then is said that matter consists of atoms and points, and hence is not continuous.
Therefore we have here the two determinations of continuity and of definite points, which understanding regards
as mutually exclusive, combined in one. It is said that
matter must be clearly either continuous or divisible into
points, but in reality it has both these qualities. Or when
we say of the mind of man that it has freedom, the understanding at once brings up the other quality, which in this
case is necessity, saying, that if Mind is free it is not in
subjection to necessity, and, inversely, if its will and
thought are determined through necessity, it is not free—
the one, they say, excludes the other. The distinctions
here are regarded as exclusive, and not as forming something concrete. But that which is true, the Mind, is
concrete, and its attributes are freedom and necessity.
Similarly the higher point of view is that Mind is free in
its necessity, and finds its freedom in it alone, since its
necessity rests on its freedom. But it is more difficult for
us to show the unity here than in the case of natural
objects. Freedom can, however, be also abstract freedom
without necessity, which false freedom is self-will, and
for that reason it is self-opposed, unconsciously limited, an
imaginary freedom which is free in form alone.

The fruit of development, which comes third, is a result of motion, but inasmuch as it is merely the result of one stage in development, as being last in this stage, it is both the starting point and the first in order in another such stage. Goethe somewhere truly says, "That which is formed ever resolves itself back into its elements." Matter —which as developed has form—constitutes once more the material for a new form. Mind again takes as its object and applies its activity to the Notion in which in going within itself, it has comprehended itself, which it is in form and being, and which has just been separated from it anew. The application of thought to this, supplies it with the form and determination of thought. This action thus further forms the previously formed, gives it additional determinations, makes it more determinate in itself, further developed and more profound. As concrete, this activity is a succession of processes in development which must be represented not as a straight line drawn out into vague infinity, but as a circle returning within itself, which, as periphery, has very many circles, and whose whole is a large number of processes in development turning back within themselves.

c. *Philosophy as the apprehension of the development of the Concrete.*

Having thus generally explained the nature of the Concrete, I now add as regards its import, that the Truth thus determined within itself is impelled towards development. It is only the living and spiritual which internally bestirs and develops itself. Thus the Idea as concrete in itself, and self-developing, is an organic system and a totality which contains a multitude of stages and of moments in development. Philosophy has now become for itself the apprehension of this development, and as conceiving Thought, is itself this development in Thought. The more progress made in this development, the more perfect is the Philosophy.

This development goes no further out than into externality, but the going without itself of development also is a going inwards. That is to say, the universal Idea continues to remain at the foundation and still is the all-embracing and unchangeable. While in Philosophy the going out of the Idea in course of its development is not a change, a becoming "another," but really is a going within itself, a self-immersion, the progress forward makes the Idea which was previously general and undetermined, determined within itself. Further development of the Idea or its further determination is the same thing exactly. Depth seems to signify intensiveness, but in this case the most extensive is also the most intensive. The more intensive is the Mind, the more extensive is it, hence the larger is its embrace. Extension as development, is not dispersion or falling asunder, but a uniting bond which is the more powerful and intense as the expanse of that embraced is greater in extent and richer. In such a case what is greater is the strength of opposition and of separation; and the greater power overcomes the greater separation.

These are the abstract propositions regarding the nature of the Idea and of its development, and thus within it Philosophy in its developed state is constituted : it is one Idea in its totality and in all its individual parts, like one life in a living being, one pulse throbs throughout all its members. All the parts represented in it, and their systematization, emanate from the one Idea; all these particulars are but the mirrors and copies of this one life, and have their actuality only in this unity. Their differences and their various qualities are only the expression of the Idea and the form contained within it. Thus the Idea is the central point, which is also the periphery, the source of light, which in all its expansion does not come without itself, but remains present and immanent within itself. Thus it is both the system of necessity and its own necessity, which also constitutes its freedom.

3. Results obtained with respect to the Notion of the History of Philosophy.

Thus we see that Philosophy is system in development, the history of Philosophy is the same; and this is the main point to be noted and the first principle to be dealt with in this treatise on that history. In order to make this evident, the difference in respect to the possible modes of manifestation must first be pointed out. That is to say, the progression of the various stages in the advance of Thought may occur with the consciousness of necessity, in which case each in succession deduces itself, and this form and this determination can alone emerge. Or else it may come about without this consciousness as does a natural and apparently accidental process, so that while inwardly, indeed, the Notion brings about its result consistently, this consistency is not made manifest. This is so in nature; in the various stages of the development of twigs, leaves, blossom and fruit, each proceeds for itself, but the inward Idea is the directing and determining force which governs the progression. This is also so with the child whose bodily powers, and above all whose intellectual activities, make their appearance one after the other, simply and naturally, so that those parents who form such an experience for the first time, marvel whence all that is now showing itself from within, comes from; for the whole of these manifestations merely have the form of a succession in time.

The one kind of progression which represents the deduction of the forms, the necessity thought out and recognized, of the determinations, is the business of Philosophy; and because it is the pure Idea which is in question and not yet its mere particularized form as Nature and as Mind, that representation is, in the main, the business of logical Philosophy. But the other method, which represents the part played by the history of Philosophy, shows the different stages and moments in development in time, in manner of occurrence, in particular places, in particular people or political circumstances, the complications arising thus, and, in short, it shows us the empirical form. This point of view is the only one worthy of this science. From the very nature of the subject it is inherently the true one, and through the study of this history it will be made manifest that it actually shows and proves itself so.

Now in reference to this Idea, I maintain that the sequence in the systems of Philosophy in History is similar to the sequence in the logical deduction of the Notion-determinations in the Idea. I maintain that if the fundamental conceptions of the systems appearing in the history of Philosophy be entirely divested of what regards their outward form, their relation to the particular and the like, the various stages in the determination of the Idea are found in their logical Notion. Conversely in the logical progression taken for itself, there is, so far as its principal elements are concerned, the progression of historical manifestations ; but it is necessary to have these pure Notions in order to know what the historical form contains. It may be thought that Philosophy must have another order as to the stages in the Idea than that in which these Notions have gone forth in time ; but in the main the order is the same. This succession undoubtedly separates itself, on the one hand, into the sequence in time of History, and on the other into succession in the order of ideas. But to treat more fully of this last would divert us too far from our aim.

I would only remark this, that what has been said reveals that the study of the history of Philosophy is the study of Philosophy itself, for, indeed, it can be nothing else. Whoever studies the history of sciences such as Physics and Mathematics, makes himself acquainted with Physics and Mathematics themselves. But in order to obtain a knowledge of its progress as the development of the Idea in the empirical, external form in which Philosophy appears in History, a corresponding knowledge of the Idea is absolutely essential, just as in judging of human affairs one must have a conception of that which is right and fitting. Else, indeed, as in so many histories of Philosophy, there is presented to the vision devoid of idea, only a disarranged collection of opinions. To make you acquainted with this Idea, and consequently to explain the manifestations, is the business of the history of Philosophy, and to do this is my object in undertaking to lecture on the subject. Since the observer must bring with him the Notion of the subject in order to see it in its phenomenal aspect and in order to expose the object faithfully to view, we need not wonder at there being so many dull histories of Philosophy in which the succession of its systems are represented simply as a number of opinions, errors and freaks of thought. They are freaks of thought which, indeed, have been devised with a great pretension of acuteness and of mental exertion, and with everything else which can be said in admiration of what is merely formal. But, considering the absence of philosophic mind in such historians as these, how should they be able to comprehend and represent the content, which is reasoned thought?

It is shown from what has been said regarding the formal nature of the Idea, that only a history of Philosophy thus regarded as a system of development in Idea, is entitled to the name of Science : a collection of facts constitutes no science. Only thus as a succession of phenomena established through reason, and having as content just what is reason and revealing it, does this history show that it is rational : it shows that the events recorded are in reason. How should the whole of what has taken place in reason not itself be rational? That faith must surely be the more reasonable in which chance is not made ruler over human affairs, and it is the business of Philosophy to recognize that however much its own manifestations may be history likewise, it is yet determined through the Idea alone.

Through these general preliminary conceptions the categories are now determined, the more immediate application
of which to the history of Philosophy we have now to consider. This application will bring before us the most
significant aspects in this history.

a. *The development in Time of the various Philosophies.*

The first question which may be asked in reference to this
history, concerns that distinction in regard to the manifestation of the Idea, which has just been noticed. It is the
question as to how it happens that Philosophy appears to
be a development in time and has a history. The answer to
this question encroaches on the metaphysics of Time, and
it would be a digression from our object to give here more
than the elements on which the answer rests.

It has been shown above in reference to the existence of
Mind, that its Being is its activity. Nature, on the contrary,
is, as it is; its changes are thus only repetitions, and its
movements take the form of a circle merely. To express
this better, the activity of Mind is to know itself. I am,
immediately, but this I am only as a living organism ; as
Mind I am only in so far as I know myself. Γνῶθι σεαυτόν,
Know thyself, the inscription over the temple of the oracle
at Delphi, is the absolute command which is expressed by
Mind in its essential character. But consciousness really
implies that for myself, I am object to myself. In forming
this absolute division between what is mine and myself,
Mind constitutes its existence and establishes itself as
external to itself. It postulates itself in the externality
which is just the universal and the distinctive form of
existence in Nature. But one of the forms of externality
is Time, and this form requires to be further examined both
in the Philosophy of Nature and the finite Mind.

This Being in existence and therefore Being in time
is a moment not only of the individual consciousness,

which as such is essentially finite, but also of the development of the philosophical Idea in the element of Thought. For the Idea, thought of as being at rest, is, indeed, not in Time. To think of it as at rest, and to preserve it in the form of immediacy is equivalent to its inward perception. But the Idea as concrete, is, as has been shown, the unity of differences; it is not really rest, and its existence is not really sense-perception, but as differentiation within itself and therefore as development, it comes into existent Being and into externality in the element of Thought, and thus pure Philosophy appears in thought as a progressive existence in time. But this element of Thought is itself abstract and is the activity of a single consciousness. Mind is, however, not only to be considered as individual, finite consciousness, but as that Mind which is universal and concrete within itself; this concrete universality, however, comprehends all the various sides and modes evolved in which it is and becomes object to the Idea. Thus Mind's thinking comprehension of self is at the same time the progression of the total actuality evolved. This progression is not one which   TOTALITY takes its course through the thought of an individual and exhibits itself in a single consciousness, for it shows itself to be universal Mind presenting itself in the history of the world in all the richness of its form. The result of this development is that one form, one stage in the Idea comes to consciousness in one particular race, so that this race and this time expresses only this particular form, within which it constructs its universe and works out its conditions. The higher stage, on the other hand, centuries later reveals itself in another race of people.

Now if we thus grasp the principles of the Concrete and of Development, the nature of the manifold obtains quite another signification, and what is said of the diversity in philosophies as if the manifold were fixed and stationary and composed of what is mutually exclusive, is at once

refuted and relegated to its proper place. Such talk is that
in which those who despise Philosophy think they possess
an invincible weapon against it, and in their truly beggarly
pride in their pitiful representations of it, they are in perfect
ignorance even of what they have and what they have to know
in any meagre ideas attained, such as in that of the manifold
and diverse. Yet this category is one which anybody can
understand ; no difficulty is made in regard to it, for it is
thoroughly known, and those who use it think they can
do so as being entirely comprehensible—as a matter of
course they understand what it is. But those who believe
the principle of diversity to be one absolutely fixed, do not
know its nature, or its dialectic ; the manifold or diverse is
in a state of flux ; it must really be conceived of as in the
process of development, and as but a passing moment.
Philosophy in its concrete Idea is the activity of development in revealing the differences which it contains within
itself ; these differences are thoughts, for we are now
speaking of development in Thought. In the first
place, the differences which rest in the Idea are
manifested as thoughts. Secondly, these distinctions
must come into existence, one here and the other there ;
and in order that they may do this, they must be complete,
that is, they must contain within themselves the Idea in its
totality. The concrete alone as including and supporting
the distinctions, is the actual ; it is thus, and thus alone, that
the differences are in their form entire.

A complete form of thought such as is here presented, is
a Philosophy. But the Idea contains the distinctions in a
peculiar form. It may be said that the form is indifferent,
and that the content, the Idea, is the main consideration ;
and people think themselves quite moderate and reasonable
when they state that the different philosophies all contain
the Idea, though in different forms, understanding by this
that these forms are contingent. But everything hangs on
this : these forms are nothing else than the original distinc-

tions in the Idea itself, which is what it is only in them. They are in this way essential to, and constitute the content of the Idea, which in thus sundering itself, attains to form. The manifold character of the principles which appear, is, however, not accidental, but necessary: the different forms constitute an integral part of the whole form. They are the determinations of the original Idea, which together constitute the whole; but as being outside of one another, their union does not take place in them, but in us, the observers. Each system is determined as one, but it is not a permanent condition that the differences are thus mutually exclusive. The inevitable fate of these determinations must follow, and that is that they shall be drawn together and reduced to elements or moments. The independent attitude taken up by each moment is again laid aside. After expansion, contraction follows—the unity out of which they first emerged. This third may itself be but the beginning of a further development. It may seem as if this progression were to go on into infinitude, but it has an absolute end in view, which we shall know better later on; many turnings are necessary, however, before Mind frees itself in coming to consciousness.

The temple of self-conscious reason is to be considered from this the point of view alone worthy of the history of Philosophy. It is hence rationally built by an inward master worker, and not in Solomon's method, as freemasons build. The great assumption that what has taken place on this side, in the world, has also done so in conformity with reason—which is what first gives the history of Philosophy its true interest—is nothing else than trust in Providence, only in another form. As the best of what is in the world is that which Thought produces, it is unreasonable to believe that reason only is in Nature, and not in Mind. That man who believes that what, like the philosophies, belongs to the region of mind must be merely contingent, is insincere in his belief in divine rule, and what he says of it is but empty talk.

A long time is undoubtedly required by Mind in working out Philosophy, and when one first reflects on it, the length of the time may seem astonishing, like the immensity of the space spoken of in astronomy. But it must be considered in regard to the slow progress of the world-spirit, that there is no need for it to hasten :—" A thousand years are in Thy sight as one day." It has time enough just because it is itself outside of time, because it is eternal. The fleeting events of the day pass so quickly that there is not time enough for all that has to be done. Who is there who does not die before he has achieved his aims? The world-spirit has time enough, but that is not all. It is not time alone which has to be made use of in the acquisition of a conception ; much else is required. The fact that so many races and gene- rations are devoted to these operations of its consciousness by Mind, and that the appearance is so perpetually presented of rising up and passing away, concern it not at all; it is rich enough for such displays, it pursues its work on the largest possible scale, and has nations and individuals enough and to spare. The saying that Nature arrives at its end in the shortest possible way, and that this is right, is a trivial one. The way shown by mind is indirect, and accommodates itself to circumstances. Considerations of finite life, such as time, trouble, and cost, have no place here. We ought, too, to feel no disappointment that particular kinds of knowledge cannot yet be attained, or that this or that is still absent. In the history of the world progression is slow.

b. *The application of the foregoing to the treatment of Philosophy.*

The first result which follows from what has been said, is that the whole of the history of Philosophy is a progression impelled by an inherent necessity, and one which is im- plicitly rational and *à priori* determined through its Idea ; and this the history of Philosophy has to exemplify. Contingency must vanish on the appearance of Philosophy. Its history is just as absolutely determined as the development of Notions, and the impelling force is the inner dialectic of the forms. The finite is not true, nor is it what it is to be—its determinate nature is bound up with its existence. But the inward Idea abolishes these finite forms : a philosophy which has not the absolute form identical with the content, must pass away because its form is not that of truth.

What follows secondly from what we have said, is that every philosophy has been and still is necessary. Thus none have passed away, but all are affirmatively contained as elements in a whole. But we must distinguish between the particular principle of these philosophies as particular, and the realization of this principle throughout the whole compass of the world. The principles are retained, the most recent philosophy being the result of all preceding, and hence no philosophy has ever been refuted. What has been refuted is not the principle of this philosophy, but merely the fact that this principle should be considered final and absolute in character. The atomic philosophy, for example, has arrived at the affirmation that the atom is the absolute existence, that it is the indivisible unit which is also the individual or subject; seeing, then, that the bare unit also is the abstract being-for-self, the Absolute would be grasped as infinitely many units. The atomic theory has been refuted, and we are atomists no longer. Mind is certainly explicitly existent as a unit or atom, but that is to attribute to it a barren character and qualities incapable of expressing anything of its depth. The principle is indeed retained, although it is not the absolute in its entirety. This same contradiction appears in all development. The development of the tree is the negation of the germ, and the blossom that of the leaves, in so far as that they show that these do not form the highest and truest existence of the tree. Last of all, the blossom finds its negation in the fruit. Yet none of them can come into actual existence excepting as preceded by all the earlier stages. Our attitude to a philosophy must thus contain an affirmative side and a negative; when we take both of these into consideration, we do justice to a philosophy for the first time. We get to know the affirmative side later on both in life and in science; thus we find it easier to refute than to justify.

In the third place, we shall limit ourselves to the particular consideration of the principle itself. Each principle has reigned for a certain time, and when the whole system of the world has been explained from this special form, it is called a philosophical system. Its whole theory has certainly to be learned, but as long as the principle is abstract it is not sufficient to embrace the forms belonging to our conception of the world. The Cartesian principles, for instance, are very suitable for application to mechanism, but for nothing further; their representation of other manifestations in the world, such as those of vegetable and animal nature, are insufficent, and hence uninteresting. Therefore we take into consideration the principles of these philosophies only, but in dealing with concrete philosophies we must also regard the chief forms of their development and their applications. The subordinate philosophies are inconsistent; they have had bright glimpses of the truth, which are, however, independent of their principles. This is exemplified in the Timæus of Plato, a philosophy of nature, the working out of which is empirically very barren because its principle does not as yet extend far enough, and it is not to its principle that we owe the deep gleams of thought there contained.

In the fourth place it follows that we must not regard the history of Philosophy as dealing with the past, even though it is history. The scientific products of reason form the content of this history, and these are not past. What is obtained in this field of labour is the True, and, as such, the Eternal; it is not what exists now, and not then; it is true not only to-day or to-morrow, but beyond all time, and in as far as it is in time, it is true always and for every time. The bodily forms of those great minds who are the heroes of this history, the temporal existence and outward lives of the philosophers, are, indeed, no more, but their works and thoughts have not followed suit, for they neither conceived nor dreamt of the rational import of their works. Philosophy is not somnambulism, but is developed consciousness; and what these heroes have done is to bring that which is implicitly rational out of the depths of Mind, where it is found at first as substance only, or as inwardly existent, into the light of day, and to advance it into consciousness and knowledge. This forms a continuous awakening. Such work is not only deposited in the temple of Memory as forms of times gone by, but is just as present and as living now as at the time of its production. The effects produced and work performed are not again destroyed or interrupted by what succeeds, for they are such that we must ourselves be present in them. They have as medium neither canvas, paper, marble, nor representation or memorial to preserve them. These mediums are themselves transient, or else form a basis for what is such. But they do have Thought, Notion, and the eternal Being of Mind, which moths cannot corrupt, nor thieves break through and steal. The conquests made by Thought when constituted into Thought form the very Being of Mind. Such knowledge is thus not learning merely, or a knowledge of what is dead, buried and corrupt: the history of Philosophy has not to do with what is gone, but with the living present.

c. *Further comparison between the History of Philosophy and Philosophy itself.*

We may appropriate to ourselves the whole of the riches apportioned out in time : it must be shown from the succession in philosophies how that succession is the systematization of the science of Philosophy itself. But a distinction is

to be noted here : that which first commences is implicit,
immediate, abstract, general—it is what has not yet advanced; the more concrete and richer comes later, and the
first is poorer in determinations. This may appear contrary to one's first impressions, but philosophic ideas are
often enough directly opposed to ordinary ideas, and
what is generally supposed, is not found to be the case. It
may be thought that what comes first must be the concrete.
The child, for instance, as still in the original totality of
his nature, is thought to be more concrete than the man,
hence we imagine the latter to be more limited, no longer
forming a totality, but living an abstract life. Certainly
the man acts in accordance with definite ends, not bringing
his whole soul and mind into a subject, but splitting his life
into a number of abstract unities. The child and the youth,
on the contrary, act straight from the fulness of the heart.
Feeling and sense-perception come first, thought last, and
thus feeling appears to us to be more concrete than thought,
or the activity of abstraction and of the universal. In
reality, it is just the other way. The sensuous consciousness is certainly the more concrete, and if poorer
in thought, at least richer in content. We must thus
distinguish the naturally concrete from the concrete of
thought, which on its side, again, is wanting in sensuous
matter. The child is also the most abstract and the poorest
in thought: as to what pertains to nature, the man is abstract, but in thought he is more concrete than the child.
Man's ends and objects are undoubtedly abstract in general
affairs, such as in maintaining his family or performing his
business duties, but he contributes to a great objective
organic whole, whose progress he advances and directs. In
the acts of a child, on the other hand, only a childish and, indeed, momentary " I," and in those of the youth the subjective
constitution or the random aim, form the principle of action.
It is in this way that science is more concrete than sense-
perception.

In applying this to the different forms of Philosophy, it follows in the first place, that the earliest philosophies are the poorest and the most abstract. In them the Idea is least determined; they keep merely to generalities not yet realized. This must be known in order that we may not seek behind the old philosophies for more than we are entitled to find; thus we need not require from them determinations proceeding from a deeper consciousness. For instance, it has been asked whether the philosophy of Thales is, properly speaking, Theism or Atheism,[1] whether he asserted a personal God or merely an impersonal, universal existence. The question here regards the attribution of subjectivity to the highest Idea, the conception of the Personality of God. Such subjectivity as we comprehend it, is a much richer, more concentrated, and therefore much later conception, which need not be sought for in distant ages. The Greek gods had, indeed, personality in imagination and idea like the one God of the Jewish religion, but to know what is the mere picture of fancy, and what the insight of pure Thought and Notion, is quite another thing. If we take as basis our own ideas judged by these deeper conceptions, an ancient Philosophy may undoubtedly be spoken of as Atheism. But this expression would at the same time be false, for the thoughts as thoughts in beginning, could not have arrived at the development which we have reached.

From this it follows—since the progress of development is equivalent to further determination, and this means further immersion in and a fuller grasp of the Idea itself—that the latest, most modern and newest philosophy is the most developed, richest and deepest. In that philosophy everything which at first seems to be past and gone must be preserved and retained, and it must itself be a mirror of the whole history. The original philosophy is the most abstract, because it is the original and has not as yet made any move-

[1] Flatt: De Theismo Thaleti Milesio abjudicando. Tub. 1785. 4.

ment forward; the last, which proceeds from this forward and impelling influence, is the most concrete. This, as may at once be remarked, is no mere pride in the philosophy of our time, because it is in the nature of the whole process that the more developed philosophy of a later time is really the result of the previous operations of the thinking mind; and that it, pressed forwards and onwards from the earlier standpoints, has not grown up on its own account or in a state of isolation.

It must also be recollected that we must not hesitate to say, what is naturally implied, that the Idea, as comprehended and shown forth in the latest and newest philosophy, is the most developed, the richest and deepest. I call this to remembrance because the designation, new or newest of all in reference to Philosophy, has become a very common by-word. Those who think they express anything by using such terms might quite easily render thanks respecting any number of philosophies just as fast as their inclination directs, regarding either every shooting-star and even every candle-gleam in the light of a sun, or else calling every popular cry a philosophy, and adducing as proof that at any rate there are so many philosophies that every day one displaces another. Thus they have the category in which they can place any apparently significant philosophy, and through which they may at the same time set it aside; 'this they call a fashion-philosophy.

> " Scoffer, thou call'st this but a fleeting|phase
> When the Spirit of Man once again and anew,
> Strives earnestly on, towards forms that are higher."

A second consequence has regard to the treatment of the older philosophies. Such insight also prevents us from ascribing any blame to the philosophies when we miss determinations in them which were not yet present to their culture, and similarly it prevents our burdening them with deductions and assertions which were neither made nor thought of by them, though they might correctly enough allow themselves to be derived from the thought of such a philosophy. It is necessary to set to work on an historical basis, and to ascribe to Philosophy what is immediately given to us, and that alone. Errors crop up here in most histories of Philosophy, since we may see in them a number of metaphysical propositions ascribed to a philosopher and given out as an historical statement of the views which he has propounded, of which he neither thought nor knew a word, and of which there is not the slightest trace found in history. Thus in Brucker's great History of Philosophy (Pt. I. pp. 465—478 seq.) a list of thirty, forty, or a hundred theorems are quoted from Thales and others, no idea of which can be traced in history as having been present to these philosophers. There are also propositions in support of them and citations taken from discussions of a similar kind with which we may occupy ourselves long enough. Brucker's method is to endow the single theorem of an ancient philosopher with all the consequences and premises which must, according to the idea of the Wolffian Metaphysics, be the premises and conclusions of that theorem, and thus easily to produce a simple, naked fiction as if it were an actual historical fact. Thus, according to Brucker, Thales said, *Ex nihilo fit nihil*, since he said that water was eternal. Thus, too, he was to be counted amongst the philosophers who deny creation out of nothing ; and of this, historically at least, Thales was ignorant. Professor Ritter, too, whose history of Ionic Philosophy is carefully written, and who on the whole is cautious not to introduce foreign matter, has very possibly ascribed to Thales more than is found in history. He says (pp. 12, 13), " Hence we must regard the view of nature which we find in Thales as dynamic in principle. He regarded the world as the all-embracing, living animal which has developed from a germ like every other animal, and this germ, like that of all other animals, is either damp or water. Thus the fundamental idea of Thales is that the world is a living whole which has developed from a germ and carries on its life as does an animal, by means of nourishment suitable to its nature" (cf. p. 16). This is quite a different account from that of Aristotle, and none of it is communicated by the ancients regarding Thales. The sequence of thought is evident, but historically it is not justified. We ought not by such deductions to make an ancient philosophy into something quite different from what it originally was.

We are too apt to mould the ancient philosophers into our own forms of thought, but this is just to constitute the progress of development ; the difference in times, in culture and in philosophies, depends on whether certain reflections, certain thought determinations, and certain stages in the Notion have come to consciousness, whether a consciousness has been developed to a particular point or not. The history of Philosophy has simply to deal with this development and bringing forth of thought. The determinations involved certainly follow from a proposition, but whether they are put forth as yet or not is quite another thing, and the bringing forth of the inner content is the only matter of importance. We must therefore only make use of the words which are actually literal, for to use further thought determinations which do not yet belong to the consciousness of the philosopher in question, is to carry on development. Thus Aristotle states that Thales has defined the principle (ἀρχή) of every thing to be water. But Anaximander first made use of ἀρχή, and Thales thus did not possess this determination of thought at all; he recognized ἀρχή as commencement in time, but not as the fundamental principle. Thales did not once introduce the determination of cause into his philosophy, and first cause is a further determination still. There are whole nations which have not this conception at all; indeed it involves a great step forward in development. And seeing that difference in culture on the whole depends on difference in the thought determinations which are manifested, this must be so still more with respect to philosophies.

Now, as in the logical system of thought each of its forms has its own place in which alone it suffices, and this form becomes, by means of ever-progressing development, reduced to a subordinate element, each philosophy is, in the third place, a particular stage in the development of the whole process and has its definite place where it finds its true value and significance. Its special character is really to be conceived of in accordance with this determination, and it is to be considered with respect to this position in order that full justice may be done to it. On this account nothing more must be demanded or expected from it than what it actually gives, and the satisfaction is not to be sought for in it, which can only be found in a fuller development of knowledge. We must not expect to find the questions of our consciousness and the interest of the present world responded to by the ancients; such questions presuppose a certain development in thought. Therefore every philosophy belongs to its own time and is restricted by its own limitations, just because it is the manifestation of a particular stage in development. The individual is the offspring of his people, of his world, whose constitution and attributes are alone manifested in his form ; he may spread himself out as he will, he cannot escape out of his time any more than out of his skin, for he belongs to the one universal Mind which is his substance and his own existence. How should he escape from this ? It is the same universal Mind that is embraced by thinking Philosophy ; that Philosophy is Mind's thought of itself and therefore its determinate and substantial content. Every philosophy is the philosophy of its own day, a link in the whole chain of spiritual development. and thus it can only find satisfaction for the interests belonging to its own particular time.

On this account an earlier philosophy does not give satisfaction to the mind in which a deeper conception reigns. What Mind seeks for in Philosophy is this conception which already constitutes its inward determination and the root of its existence conceived of as object to thought; Mind demands a knowledge of itself. But in the earlier philosophy the Idea is not yet present in this determinate character. Hence the philosophy of Plato and Aristotle, and indeed all philosophies, ever live and are present in their principles, but Philosophy no longer has the particular form and aspect possessed by that of Plato and of Aristotle. We cannot rest content with them, and they cannot be revived; hence there can be no Platonists, Aristotelians, Stoics, or Epicureans to-day. To re-awaken them would be to try to bring back to an earlier stage the Mind of a deeper culture and self-penetration. But this cannot be the case; it would be an impossibility and as great a folly as were a man to wish to expend his energies in attaining the standpoint of the youth, the youth in endeavouring to be the boy or child again; whereas the man, the youth, and the child, are all one and the same individual. The period of revival in the sciences, the new epoch in learning which took place in the fifteenth and sixteenth centuries, began not only with the revived study of, but also with the re-animation of the old philosophies. Marsilius Ficinus was a Platonist; an Academy of Platonic philosophy was established and installed with professors by Cosmos de Medici, and Ficinus was placed at the head of it. There were pure Aristotelians like Pomponius : Gassendi later on maintained the Epicurean philosophy, for his philosophy dealt with Physics after the manner of the Epicureans ; Lipsius wished to be a Stoic, and so on. The sense of opposition was so great, ancient philosophy and Christianity —from or in which no special philosophy had developed— were so diverse, that no philosophy peculiar to itself could develop in Christianity. What was or could be had as philosophy, either in conformity with or in opposition to Christianity, was a certain ancient philosophy which was thus taken up anew. But mummies when brought amongst living beings cannot there remain. Mind had for long possessed a more substantial life, a more profound Notion of itself, and hence its thought had higher needs than such as could be satisfied by these philosophies. A revival such as this is then to be regarded only as the transitory period in which we learn to know the forms which are implied and which have gone before, and as the renewal of former struggles through the steps necessary in development. Such reconstructions and repetitions in a distant time of principles which have become foreign to Mind, are in history transitory only, and formed in a language which is dead. Such things are translations only and not originals, and Mind does not find satisfaction excepting in knowledge of its own origination.

When modern times are in the same way called upon to revert to the standpoint of an ancient philosophy (as is recommended specially in regard to the philosophy of Plato) in order to make this a means of escaping from the complications and difficulties of succeeding times, this reversion does not come naturally as in the first case. This discreet counsel has the same origin as the request to cultivated members of society to turn back to the customs and ideas of the savages of the North American forests, or as the recommendation to adopt the religion of Melchisedec which Fichte[1] has maintained to be the purest and simplest possible, and therefore the one at which we must eventually arrive. On the one hand, in this retrogression the desire for an origin and for a fixed point of departure is unmistakable, but such must be sought for in thought and Idea alone and not in an authoritatively given form. On the other hand, the return of the developed, enriched Mind to a simplicity such as this—which means to an abstraction, an abstract condition or thought—is to be regarded only as the escape of an incapacity which cannot enjoy the rich material

[1] Grundzüge des gegenwärtigen Zeitalters, pp. 211, 212; cf. Anweisung zum Seligen Leben, pp. 178, 348.

of development which it sees before it, and which demands to be controlled and comprehended in its very depths by thought, but seeks a refuge in fleeing from the difficulty and in mere sterility.

From what has been said it is quite comprehensible how so many of those who, whether induced by some special attraction such as this, or simply by the fame of a Plato or ancient philosophy in general, direct their way thereto in order to draw their own philosophy from these sources, do not find themselves satisfied by the study, and unjustifiably quit such altogether. Satisfaction is found in them to a certain extent only. We must know in ancient philosophy or in the philosophy of any given period, what we are going to look for. Or at least we must know that in such a philosophy there is before us a definite stage in the development of thought, and in it those forms and necessities of Mind which lie within the limits of that stage alone are brought into existence. There slumber in the Mind of modern times ideas more profound which require for their awakening other surroundings and another present than the abstract, dim, grey thought of olden times. In Plato, for instance, questions regarding the nature of freedom, the origin of evil and of sin, providence, &c., do not find their philosophic answer. On such subjects we certainly may in part take the ordinary serious views of the present time, and in part philosophically set their consideration altogether aside, or else consider sin and freedom as something negative only. But neither the one plan nor the other gives freedom to Mind if such subjects have once been explicitly for it, and if the opposition in self-consciousness has given it the power of sinking its interests therein. The case is similar with regard to questions regarding the limits of knowledge, the opposition between subjectivity and objectivity which had not yet come up in Plato's age. The independence of the " I " within itself and its explicit existence was foreign to him; man had not yet gone back within himself, had not yet set himself forth as explicit. The subject was indeed the individual as free, but as yet he knew himself only as in unity with his Being. The Athenian knew himself to be free, as such, just as the Roman citizen would, as *ingenuus*. But the fact that man is in and for himself free, in his essence and as man, free born, was known neither by Plato, Aristotle, Cicero, nor the Roman legislators, even though it is this conception alone which forms the source of law. In Christianity the individual, personal mind for the first time becomes of real, infinite and absolute value; God wills that all men shall be saved. It was in the Christian religion that the doctrine was advanced that all men are equal before God, because Christ has set them free with the freedom of Christianity. These principles make freedom independent of any such things as birth, standing or culture. The progress made through them is enormous, but they still come short of this, that to be free constitutes the very idea of man. The sense of this existent principle has been an active force for centuries and centuries, and an impelling power which has brought about the most tremendous revolutions; but the conception and the knowledge of the natural freedom of man is a knowledge of himself which is not old.

B

THE RELATION OF PHILOSOPHY TO OTHER DEPARTMENTS OF KNOWLEDGE.

The History of Philosophy has to represent this science in that form of time and individualities from which its outward form has resulted. Such a representation has, however, to shut out from itself the external history of the time, and to take into account only the general character of the people and time, and likewise their circumstances as a whole. But as a matter of fact, the history of Philosophy does present this character, and that indeed in the highest possible

c

degree ; its connection with it is of the closest kind, and the particular appearance presented by a philosophy belonging to one special period, is only a particular aspect or element in the character. Because of this inward correspondence we have partly to consider more closely the particular relation borne by a philosophy to its historical surroundings, and partly, but pre-eminently, what is proper to itself, from which alone, after separating everything related however closely, we can fix our standpoint. This connection, which is not merely external but essential, has thus two sides, which we must consider. The first is the distinctly historical side, the second is the connection with other matters—the connection of Philosophy with Religion, for instance, by which we at once obtain a deeper conception of Philosophy itself.

1. THE HISTORICAL SIDE OF THIS CONNECTION.

It is usually said that political affairs and such matters as Religion are to be taken into consideration because they have exercised a great influence on the Philosophy of the time, and similarly it exerts an influence upon them. But when people are content with such a category as " great influence " they place the two in an external relationship, and start from the point of view that both sides are for themselves independent. Here, however, we must think of this relationship in another category, and not according to the influence or effect of one upon the other. The true category is the unity of all these different forms, so that it is one Mind which manifests itself in, and impresses itself upon these different elements.

a. *Outward and historical conditions imposed upon Philosophy.*

It must be remarked in the first place, that a certain stage is requisite in the intellectual culture of a people in order that it may have a Philosophy at all. Aristotle says, " Man first begins to philosophize when the necessities of life are supplied " (Metaphysics, I. 2) ; because since Philosophy is a free and not self-seeking activity, cravings of want must have disappeared, a strength, elevation and inward fortitude of mind must have appeared, passions must be subdued and consciousness so far advanced, before what is universal can be thought of. Philosophy may thus be called a kind of luxury, in so far as luxury signifies those enjoyments and pursuits which do not belong to external necessity as such. Philosophy in this respect seems more capable of being dispensed with than anything else ; but that depends on what is called indispensable. From the point of view of mind, Philosophy may even be said to be that which is most essential.

b. *The commencement in History of an intellectual necessity for Philosophy.*

However much Philosophy, as the thought and conception of the Mind of a particular time, is *à priori*, it is at the same time just as really a result, since the thought produced and, indeed, the life and action are produced to produce themselves. This activity contains the essential element of a negation, because to produce is also to destroy ; Philosophy in producing itself, has the natural as its starting point in order to abrogate it again. Philosophy thus makes its appearance at a time when the Mind of a people has worked its way out of the indifference and stolidity of the first life of nature, as it has also done from the standpoint of the emotional, so that the individual aim has blotted itself out. But as Mind passes on from its natural form, it also proceeds from its exact code of morals and the robustness of life to reflection and conception. The result of this is that it lays hold of and troubles this real, substantial kind of existence, this morality and faith, and thus the period of destruction commences. Further progress is then made through the gathering up of thought within itself. It may be said that Philosophy first commences when a race for the most part has left its concrete life, when separation and change of class have begun, and the people approach toward their fall ; when a gulf has arisen between inward strivings and external reality, and the old forms of Religion, &c., are no longer satisfying; when Mind manifests indifference to its living existence or rests unsatisfied therein, and moral life becomes dissolved. Then it is that Mind takes refuge in the clear space of thought to create for itself a kingdom of thought in opposition to the world of actuality, and Philosophy is the reconciliation following upon the destruction of that real world which thought has begun. When Philosophy with its abstractions paints grey in grey, the freshness and life of youth has gone, the reconciliation is not a reconciliation in the actual, but in the ideal world. Thus the Greek philosophers held themselves far removed from the business of the State and were called by the people idlers, because they withdrew themselves within the world of thought.

This holds good throughout all the history of Philosophy. It was so with Ionic Philosophy in the decline of the Ionic States in Asia Minor. Socrates and Plato had no more pleasure in the life of the State in Athens, which was in the course of its decline ; Plato tried to bring about something better with Dionysius. Thus in Athens, with the ruin of the Athenian people, the period was reached when Philosophy appeared. In Rome, Philosophy first expanded in the decline of the Republic and of Roman life proper, under the despotism of the Roman Emperors : a time of misfortune for the world and of decay in political life, when earlier religious systems tottered and everything was in the process of struggle and disintegration. With the decline of the Roman Empire, which was so great, rich and glorious, and yet inwardly dead, the height and indeed the zenith of ancient Philosophy is associated through the Neo-Platonists at Alexandria. It was also in the fifteenth and sixteenth centuries, when the Teutonic life of the Middle Ages acquired another form, that Philosophy first became taught, though it was later on that it attained to independence. Before that, political life still existed in unity with Religion, or if the State fought against the Church, the Church still kept the foremost place, but now the gulf between Church and State came into existence. Philosophy thus comes in at a certain epoch only in the development of the whole.

c. *Philosophy as the thought of its time.*

But men do not at certain epochs, merely philosophize in general, for there is a definite Philosophy which arises among a people, and the definite character of the standpoint of thought is the same character which permeates all the other historical sides of the spirit of the people, which is most intimately related to them, and which constitutes their foundation. The particular form of a Philosophy is thus contemporaneous with a particular constitution of the people amongst whom it makes its appearance, with their institutions and forms of government, their morality, their social life and the capabilities, customs and enjoyments of the same ; it is so with their attempts and achievements in art and science, with their religions, warfares and external relationships, likewise with the decadence of the States in which this particular principle and form had maintained its supremacy, and with the origination and progress of new States in which a higher principle finds its manifestation and development. Mind in each case has elaborated and expanded in the whole domain of its manifold nature the principle of the particular stage of self-consciousness to which it has attained. Thus the Mind of a people in its richness is an organization, and, like a Cathedral, is divided into numerous vaults, passages, pillars and vestibules, all of which have proceeded out of one whole and are directed to one end. Philosophy is one form of these many aspects. And which is it? It is the fullest blossom, the Notion of Mind in its entire form, the consciousness and spiritual essence of all things, the spirit of the time as spirit present in itself. The multifarious whole is reflected in it as in the single focus, in the Notion which knows itself.

The Philosophy which is essential within Christianity could not be found in Rome, for all the various forms of the whole are only the expression of one and the same determinate character. Hence political history, forms of government, art and religion are not related to Philosophy as its causes, nor, on the other hand, is Philosophy the ground of their existence—one and all have the same common root, the spirit of the time. It is one determinate existence, one determinate character which permeates all sides and manifests itself in politics and in all else as in different elements; it is a condition which hangs together in all its parts, and the various parts of which contain nothing which is really inconsistent, however diverse and accidental they may appear to be, and however much they may seem to contradict one another. This particular stage is the product of the one preceding. But to show how the spirit of a particular time moulds its whole actuality and destiny in accordance with its principle, to show this whole edifice in its conception, is far from us—for that would be the object of the whole philosophic world-history. Those forms alone concern us which express the principle of the Mind in a spiritual element related to Philosophy.

This is the position of Philosophy amongst its varying forms, from which it follows that it is entirely identical with its time. But if Philosophy does not stand above its time in content, it does so in form, because, as the thought and knowledge of that which is the substantial spirit of its time, it makes that spirit its object. In as far as Philosophy is in the spirit of its time, the latter is its determined content in the world, although as knowledge, Philosophy is above it, since it places it in the relation of object. But this is in form alone, for Philosophy really has no other content. This knowledge itself undoubtedly is the actuality of Mind, the self-knowledge of Mind which previously was not present : thus the formal difference is also a real and actual difference. Through knowledge, Mind makes manifest a distinction between knowledge and that which is ; this knowledge is thus what produces a new form of development. The new forms at first are only special modes of knowledge, and it is thus that a new Philosophy is produced : yet since it already is a wider kind of spirit, it is the inward birth-place of the spirit which will later arrive at actual form. We shall deal further with this in the concrete below, and we shall then see that what the Greek Philosophy was, entered, in the Christian world, into actuality.

2. Separation of Philosophy from other allied departments of Knowledge.

The history of the other Sciences, of culture and above all the history of art and of religion are, partly in regard to the elements contained in them, and partly to their particular objects, related to the history of Philosophy. It is through this relationship that the treatment of the history of Philosophy has been so confused. If it is to concern itself with the possession of culture generally and then with scientific culture, and then again with popular myths and the dogmas contained only in them, and yet farther with the religious reflections which are already thoughts of a speculative kind, and which make their appearance in them, no bounds are left to Philosophy at all. This is so, partly on account of the amount of material itself and the labour required in working it up and preparing it, and partly because it is in immediate connection with so much else. But the separation must not be made arbitrarily or as by chance, but must be derived from fundamental determinations. If we merely look at the name of Philosophy, all this matter will pertain to its history.

I shall speak of this material from three points of view, for three related aspects are to be eliminated and separated from Philosophy. The first of these is that which is generally considered to be the domain of science, and in which are sound the beginnings of understanding thought. The second region is that of mythology and religion; the relation of Philosophy to them seems often to be inimical both in the time of the Greeks and of the Christians. The third is that of philosophizing and the metaphysics of the understanding. While we distinguish what is related to Philosophy, we must also take note of the elements in this related matter which belong to the Notion of Philosophy, but which appear to us to be partially separated from it : and thus we may become acquainted with the Notion of Philosophy.

a. *Relation of Philosophy to Scientific Knowledge.*

Knowledge and thought certainly form the element of whatever has to do with particular sciences as they form the element of Philosophy ; but their subjects are mainly finite subjects and appearance. A collection of facts known about this content is by its nature excluded from Philosophy : neither this content nor such a form has anything to do with it. But even if the sciences are systematic and contain universal principles and laws from which they proceed, they are still related to a limited circle of objects. The ultimate principles are assumed as are the objects themselves ; that is, the outward experience or the feelings of the heart, natural or educated sense of right and duty, constitute the source from which they are created. Logic and the determinations and principles of thought in general are in their methods assumed.

The forms of thought or the points of view and principles which hold good in the sciences and constitute the ultimate support of all their matter, are not peculiar to them, but are common to the condition and culture of the time and of the people. This culture consists mainly in the general ideas and aims, in the whole extent of the particular intellectual powers dominating consciousness and life. Our consciousness has these ideas and allows them to be considered ultimate determinations; it makes use of them as guiding and connecting links, but does not know them and does not even make them the objects of its consideration. To give an abstract example, each act of consciousness has and requires the whole abstract thought-determination of Being. " The sun is in the heavens, the bunch of grapes is ripe," and so on into infinitude. Again, in a higher culture, such relations as those of cause and effect are involved, as also those of force and its manifestation. All its knowledge and ideas are permeated and governed by a metaphysic such as this ; it is the net in which all the concrete matter which occupies mankind in action and in impulses, is grasped. But this web and its knots in our ordinary consciousness are sunk into a manifold material, for it contains the objects and interests which we know and which we have before us. These common threads are not drawn up and made explicitly the objects of our reflection.

We Germans seldom now count general scientific knowledge as Philosophy. And yet traces of this are found, as for instance, in the fact that the philosophic Faculty contains all the Sciences which have not as their immediate aim the Church and State. In connection with this, the significance of the name of Philosophy, which is even now an important matter of discussion in England, comes in question. Natural Sciences are in England called Philosophy. A " Philosophic Journal " in England, edited by Thompson, treats of Chemistry, Agriculture, Manuring, Husbandry, Technology, like Hermbstädt's Journal, and gives inventions connected

therewith.   The English call physical instruments, such as
the barometer and thermometer, philosophical instruments.
Theories too, and especially morality and the moral
sciences, which are derived from the feelings of the human
heart or from experience, are called Philosophy, and finally
this is also so with the theories and principles of Political
Economy.   And thus at least in England, is the name of
Philosophy respected.   Some time ago a banquet took place
under the presidency of Lord Liverpool, at which the
minister Canning was also present.   The latter in returning
thanks congratulated England in having philosophic principles of government there brought into operation.   There,
at least, Philosophy is no by-word.

In the first beginnings of culture, however, we are more
often met by this admixture of Philosophy and general
knowledge.   There comes a time to a nation when mind
applies itself to universal objects, when, for example, in seeking to bring natural things under general modes of understanding, it tries to learn their causes.   Then it is said that
a people begins to philosophize, for this content has thought
in common with Philosophy.   At such a time we find
deliverances about all the common events of Nature,
as we also find intellectual maxims, moral sentences,
general principles respecting morality, the will, duty,
and the like, and those who expressed them have been
called wise men or philosophers.   Thus in the beginnings of
Greek Philosophy we find the seven sages and the Ionic
Philosophers.   From them a number of ideas and discoveries are conveyed to us which seem like philosophic propositions.   Thus Thales, amongst others, has explained that
the eclipse of sun and moon is due to the intervention of
the moon or earth.   This is called a theorem.   Pythagoras
found out the principle of the harmony of sounds.   Others
have had ideas about the stars : the heavens were supposed
to be composed of perforated metal, by which we see
throughout the empyrean region, the eternal fire which sur-

rounds the world. Such propositions as products of the understanding, do not belong to the history of Philosophy, although they imply that the merely sensuous gaze has been left behind, as also the representation of those objects by the imagination only. Earth and heaven thus become un-peopled with gods, because the understanding distinguishes things in their outward and natural qualities from Mind.

In a later time the epoch of the revival in the sciences is as noteworthy in this respect. General prin-ciples regarding the state, &c., were given expression to, and in them a philosophic side cannot be mistaken. To this place the philosophic systems of Hobbes and Descartes belong : the writings of the latter contain philosophic prin-ciples, but his Philosophy of Nature is quite empirical. Hugo Grotius composed an international law in which what was historically held by the people as law, the *consensus gentium,* was a main element. Though earlier, medicine was a collection of isolated facts and a theosophic com-bination mixed up with astrology, &c. (it is not so long ago since cures were effected by sacred relics), a mode of regard-ing nature came into vogue according to which men went forth to discover the laws and forces of Nature. The *à priori* reasoning regarding natural things, according to the metaphysics of the Scholastic Philosophy or to Religion, has now been given up. The Philosophy of Newton contains nothing but Natural Science, that is, the know-ledge of the laws, forces, and general constitution of Nature, derived from observation and from experience. However much this may seem to be contrary to the principle of Philosophy, it has in common with it the fact that the bases of both are universal, and still further that *I* have made this experience, that it rests on my consciousness and obtains its significance through me.

This form is in its general aspect antagonistic to the positive, and has come forward as particularly opposed to Religion and to that which is positive in it. If, in the

Middle Ages, the Church had its dogmas as universal truths, man, on the contrary, has now obtained from the testimony of his "own thought," feeling and ideas, a mistrust of these. It is merely to be remarked of this that "my own thought" is in itself a pleonasm, because each individual must think for himself, and no one can do so for another. Similarly this principle has turned against the recognized constitutions and has sought different principles instead, by them to correct the former. Universal principles of the State have now been laid down, while earlier, because religion was positive, the ground of obedience of subjects to princes and of all authority were also so. Kings, as the anointed of the Lord, in the sense that Jewish kings were so, derived their power from God, and had to give account to Him alone, because all authority is given by God. So far theology and jurisprudence were on the whole fixed and positive sciences, wherever this positive character might have been derived. Against this external authority reflection has been brought to bear, and thus, especially in England, the source of public and civil law became no longer mere authority derived from God like the Mosaic Law. For the authority of kings other justification was sought, such as the end implied in the State, the good of the people. This forms quite another source of truth, and it is opposed to that which is revealed, given and positive. This substitution of another ground than that of authority has been called philosophizing.

The knowledge was then a knowledge of what is finite— the world of the content of knowledge. Because this content proceeded through the personal insight of human reason, man has become independent in his actions. This independence of the Mind is the true moment of Philosophy, although the Notion of Philosophy through this formal determination, which limits it to finite objects, has not yet been exhausted. This independent thought is respected, has been called human wisdom or worldly wisdom, for it has had what is earthly as its object, and it took its origin in the world. This was the meaning of Philosophy, and men did rightly to call it worldly wisdom. Frederick von Schlegel revived this by-name for Philosophy, and desired to indicate by it that what concerns higher spheres, such as religion, must be kept apart; and he had many followers. Philosophy, indeed, occupies itself with finite things, but, according to Spinoza, as resting in the divine Idea: it has thus the same end as religion. To the finite sciences which are now separated also from Philosophy, the Churches objected that they led men away from God, since they have as objects only what is finite. This defect in them, conceived of from the point of view of content, leads us to the second department allied to Philosophy,— that is, to Religion.

b. *Relation of Philosophy to Religion.*

As the first department of knowledge was related to Philosophy principally by means of formal and independent knowledge, Religion, though in its content quite different from this first kind or sphere of knowledge, is through it related to Philosophy. Its object is not the earthly and worldly, but the infinite. In the case of art and still more in that of Religion, Philosophy has in common a content composed entirely of universal objects; they constitute the mode in which the highest Idea is existent for the unphilosophical feeling, the perceiving and imagining consciousness. Inasmuch as in the progress of culture in time the manifestation of Religion precedes the appearance of Philosophy, this circumstance must really be taken account of, and the conditions requisite for beginning the History of Philosophy have to depend on this, because it has to be shown in how far what pertains to Religion is to be excluded from it, and that a commencement must not be made with Religion.

In Religion, races of men have undoubtedly expressed their idea of the nature of the world, the substance of nature and of intellect and the relation of man thereto. Absolute Being is here the object of their consciousness; and as such, is for them pre-eminently the "other," a "beyond," nearer or further off, more or less friendly or frightful and alarming. In the act and forms of worship this opposition is removed by man, and he raises himself to the consciousness of unity with his Being, to the feeling of, or dependence on, the Grace of God, in that God has reconciled mankind to Himself. In conception, with the Greeks, for instance, this existence is to man one which is already in and for itself and friendly, and thus worship is but the enjoyment of this unity. This existence is now reason which is existent in and for itself, the universal and concrete substance, the Mind whose first cause is objective to itself in consciousness; it thus is a representation of this last in which not only reason in general, but the universal infinite reason is. We must, therefore, comprehend Religion, as Philosophy, before everything else, which means to know and apprehend it in reason; for it is the work of self-revealing reason and is the highest form of reason. Such ideas as that priests have framed a people's Religion in fraud and self-interest are consequently absurd; to regard Religion as an arbitrary matter or a deception is as foolish as it is perverted. Priests have often profaned Religion—the possibility of which is a consequence of the external relations and temporal existence of Religion. It can thus, in this external connection, be laid hold of here and there, but because it is Religion, it is really that which stands firm against finite ends and their complications and constitutes a region exalted high above them. This region of Mind is really the Holy place of Truth itself, the Holy place in which are dissolved the remaining illusions of the sensuous world, of finite ideas and ends, and of the sphere of opinion and caprice.

Inasmuch as it really is the content of religions, this rational matter might now seem to be capable of being abstracted and expressed as a number of historical theorems. Philosophy stands on the same basis as Religion and has the same object—the universal reason existing in and for itself; Mind desires to make this object its own, as is done with Religion in the act and form of worship. But the form, as it is present in Religion, is different from what is found to be contained in Philosophy, and on this account a history of Philosophy is different from a history of Religion. Worship is only the operation of reflection; Philosophy attempts to bring about the reconciliation by means of thinking knowledge, because Mind desires to take up its Being into itself. Philosophy is related in the form of thinking consciousness to its object; with Religion it is different. But the distinction between the two should not be conceived of so abstractly as to make it seem that thought is only in Philosophy and not in Religion. The latter has likewise ideas and universal thoughts. Because both are so nearly related, it is an old tradition in the history of Philosophy to deduce Philosophy from Persian, Indian, or similar philosophy, a custom which is still partly retained in all histories of Philosophy. For this reason, too, it is a legend universally believed, that Pythagoras, for instance, received his Philosophy from India and Egypt ; the fame of the wisdom of these people, which wisdom is understood also to contain Philosophy, is an old one. The Oriental ideas and religious worship which prevailed throughout the West up to the time of the Roman Empire, likewise bear the name of Oriental Philosophy. The Christian Religion and Philosophy are thought of in the Christian world, as more definitely divided ; in these Eastern days, on the other hand, Religion and Philosophy are still conceived of as one in so far as that the content has remained in the form in which it is Philosophy. Considering the prevalence of these ideas and in order to have

a definite limit to the relations between a history of Philosophy and religious ideas, it is desirable to note some further
considerations as to the form which separates religious ideas
from philosophical theorems.

Religion has not only universal thought as inward content *implicite* contained in its myths, ideas, imaginations
and in its exact and positive histories, so that we require
first of all to dig this content out of such myths in the
form of theorems, but it often has its content *explicite* in the
form of thought. In the Persian and Indian Religions
very· deep, sublime and speculative thoughts are even
expressed. Indeed, in Religion we even meet philosophies
directly expressed, as in the Philosophy of the Fathers.
The scholastic Philosophy really was Theology; there is
found in it a union or, if you will, a mixture of Theology
and Philosophy which may very well puzzle us. The question which confronts us on the one side is, how Philosophy
differs from Theology, as the science of Religion, or from
Religion as consciousness? And then, in how far have we
in the history of Philosophy to take account of what pertains to Religion? For the reply to this last question
three aspects have again to be dealt with; first of all the
mythical and historical aspect of Religion and its relation
to Philosophy; in the second place the theorems and
speculative thoughts directly expressed in Religion; and
in the third place we must speak of Philosophy within
Theology.

a. *Difference between Philosophy and Religion.*

The consideration of the mythical aspect of Religion or
the historical and positive side generally, is interesting,
because from it the difference in respect of form will show
in what this content is antagonistic to Philosophy. Indeed,
taken in its connections, its difference passes into apparent
inconsistency. This diversity is not only found in our con-

templation but forms a very definite element in history. It is required by Philosophy that it should justify its beginning and its manner of knowledge, and Philosophy has thus placed itself in opposition to Religion. On the other hand Philosophy is combated and condemned by Religion and by the Churches. The Greek popular religion indeed, proscribed several philosophers; but the opposition is even more apparent in the Christian Church. The question is thus not only whether regard is to be paid to Religion in the history of Philosophy, for it has been the case that Philosophy has paid attention to Religion, and the latter to the former. Since neither of the two has allowed the other to rest undisturbed, we are not permitted to do so either. Of their relations, therefore, we must speak definitely, openly and honestly—*aborder la question,* as the French say. We must not hesitate, as if such a discussion were too delicate, nor try to help ourselves out by beating about the bush; nor must we seek to find evasions or shifts, so that in the end no one can tell what we mean. We must not seem to wish to leave Religion alone. This is nothing else than to appear to wish to conceal the fact that Philosophy has directed its efforts against Religion. Religion, that is, the theologians, are indeed the cause of this; they ignore Philosophy, but only in order that they may not be contradicted in their arbitrary reasoning.

It may appear as if Religion demanded that man should abstain from thinking of universal matters and Philosophy because they are merely worldly wisdom and represent human operations. Human reason is here opposed to the divine. Men are, indeed, well accustomed to a distinction between divine teaching and laws and human power and inventions, such that under the latter everything is comprehended which in its manifestation proceeds from the consciousness, the intelligence or the will of mankind; which makes all this opposed to the knowledge of God and to things rendered divine by divine revelation. But the

depreciation of what is human expressed by this opposition
is then driven further still, inasmuch as while it implies the
further view that man is certainly called upon to admire
the wisdom of God in Nature, and that the grain, the
mountains, the cedars of Lebanon in all their glory, the
song of the birds in the bough, the superior skill and the
domestic instincts of animals are all magnified as being the
work of God, it also implies that the wisdom, goodness and
justice of God is, indeed, pointed out in human affairs, but not
so much in the disposition or laws of man or in actions performed voluntarily and in the ordinary progress of the world,
as in human destiny, that is, in that which is external and
even arbitrary in relation to knowledge and free-will.   Thus
what is external and accidental is regarded as emphatically
the work of God, and what has its root in will and conscience, as the work of man.   The harmony between outward relations, circumstances and events and the general
aims of man is certainly something of a higher kind, but this
is the case only for the reason that this harmony is considered
with respect to ends which are human and not natural—
such as those present in the life of a sparrow which finds its
food.   But if the summit of everything is found in this,
that God rules over Nature, what then is free-will ?   Does
He not rule over what is spiritual, or rather since He himself is spiritual, in what is spiritual ? and is not the ruler
over or in the spiritual region higher than a ruler over
or in Nature ?   But is that admiration of God as revealed
in natural things as such, in trees and animals as opposed
to what is human, far removed from the religion of the
ancient Egyptians, which derived its knowledge of what is
divine from the ibis, or from cats and dogs ? or does it differ
from the deplorable condition of the ancient and the modern
Indians, who held and still hold cows and apes in reverence, and are scrupulously concerned for the maintenance
and nourishment of these animals, while they allow men
to suffer hunger ; who would commit a crime by removing

the pangs of starvation through their slaughter or even by partaking of their food ?

It seems to be expressed by such a view that human action as regards Nature is ungodly ; that the operations of Nature are divine operations, but what man produces is ungodly. But the productions of human reason might, at least, be esteemed as much as Nature. In so doing, however, we cede less to reason than is permitted to us. If the life and the action of animals be divine, human action must stand much higher, and must be worthy to be called divine in an infinitely higher sense. The pre-eminence of human thought must forthwith be avowed. Christ says on this subject (Matt. vi. 26—30), "Behold the fowls of the air," (in which we may also include the Ibis and the *Kokilas,*) "are ye not much better than they ? Wherefore, if God so clothe the grass of the field, which to-day is, and to-morrow is cast into the oven, shall He not much more clothe you ? " The superiority of man, of the image of God, to animals and plants is indeed implicitly and explicitly established, but in asking wherein the divine element is to be sought and seen —in making use of such expressions—none of the superior, but only the inferior nature, is indicated. Similarly, in regard to the knowledge of God, it is remarkable that Christ places the knowledge of and faith in Him not in any admiration of the creatures of nature nor in marvelling at any so-called dominion over them, nor in signs and wonders, but in the witness of the Spirit. Spirit is infinitely high above Nature, in it the Divine Nature manifests itself more than in Nature.

But the form in which the universal content which is in and for itself, first belongs to Philosophy is the form of Thought, the form of the universal itself. In Religion, however, this content is for immediate and outward perception, and further for idea and sensation through art. The import is for the sensuous nature ; it is the evidence of the Mind which comprehends that content. To make this clearer, the difference must be recollected between that which we are and have, and how we know the same—that is, in what manner we know it and have it as our object. This distinction is an infinitely important matter, and it alone is concerned in the culture of races and of individuals. We are men and have reason; what is human, or above all, what is rational vibrates within us, both in our feelings, mind and heart and in our subjective nature generally. It is in this corresponding vibration and in the corresponding motion effected that a particular content becomes our own and is like our own. The manifold nature of the determinations which it contains is concentrated and wrapt up within this inward nature—an obscure motion of Mind in itself and in universal substantiality. The content is thus directly identical with the simple abstract certainty of ourselves and with self-consciousness. But Mind, because it is Mind, is as truly consciousness. What is confined within itself in its simplicity must be objective to itself and must come to be known. The whole difference lies in the manner and method of this objectivity, and hence in the manner and method of consciousness.

This method and manner extends from the simple expression of the dulness of mere feeling to the most objective form, to that which is in and for itself objective, to Thought. The most simple, most formal objectivity is the expression of a name for that feeling and for the state of mind according with it, as seen in these words, worship, prayer, etc. Such, expressions as " Let us pray " and " Let us worship " are simply the recalling of that feeling. But " Let us think about God " brings with it something more ; it expresses the absolutely embracing content of that substantial feeling, and the object, which differs from mere sensation as subjective self-conscious activity ; or which is content distinguished from this activity as form. This object, however, comprehending in itself the whole substantial content, is itself still undeveloped and entirely undetermined. To develop that content, to comprehend, express and bring to consciousness its relations, is the commencement, creation and manifestation of Religion. The form in which this developed content first possesses objectivity is that of immediate perception, of sensuous idea or of a more defined idea deduced from natural, physical or mental manifestations and conditions.

Art brings about this consciousness, in that it gives permanence and cohesion to the fleeting visible appearance through which objectivity passes in sensation. The shapeless, sacred stone, the mere place, or whatever it is to which the desire for objectivity first attaches itself, receives from art, form, feature, determinate character and content which can be known and which is now present for consciousness. Art has thus become the instructress of the people. This was the case with Homer and Hesiod for instance, who, according to Herodotus (II. 53), "Made the Greeks their Theogony," because they elevated and consolidated ideas and traditions in unison with the spirit of the people, wherever and in whatever confusion they might be found, into definite images and ideas. This is not the art which merely gives expression in its own way to the content, already perfectly expressed, of a Religion which in thought, idea and words has already attained complete development ; that is to say, which puts its matter into stone, canvas, or words as is done by modern art, which, in dealing either with religious or with historical objects, takes as its groundwork ideas and thoughts which are already there. The consciousnss of this Religion is rather the product of thinking imagination, or of thought which comprehends through the organ of imagination alone and finds expression in its forms.

If the infinite Thought, the absolute Mind, has revealed and does reveal itself in true Religion, that in which it reveals itself is the heart, the representing consciousness and the understanding of what is finite. Religion is not merely directed to every sort of culture. "To the poor is the Gospel preached," but it must as being Religion expressly directed towards heart and mind, enter into the sphere of subjectivity and consequently into the region of finite methods of representation. In the perceiving and, with reference to perceptions, reflecting consciousness, man possesses for the speculative relations belonging to the absolute, only finite relations, whether taken in an exact or in a symbolical sense, to serve him to comprehend and express those qualities and relationships of the infinite.

In Religion as the earliest and the immediate revelations of God, the form of representation and of reflecting finite thought cannot be the only form in which He gives existence to Himself in consciousness, but it must also appear in this form, for such alone is comprehensible to religious consciousness. To make this clearer, something must be said as to what is the meaning of comprehension. On the one hand, as has been remarked above, there is in it the substantial basis of content, which, coming to Mind as its absolute Being, affects it in its innermost, finds an answering chord, and thereby obtains from it confirmation. This is the first absolute condition necessary to comprehension; what is not implicitly there cannot come within it or be for it—that is, a content which is infinite and eternal. For the substantial as infinite, is just that which has no limitations in that to which it is related, for else it would be limited and not the true substantial. And Mind is that alone which is not implicit, which is finite and external; for what is finite and external is no longer what is implicit but what is for another, what has entered into a relation. But, on the other hand, because the true and eternal must be for Mind, become known, that is, enter into finite consciousness, the Mind for which it is, is finite and the manner of its consciousness consists in the ideas and forms of finite things and relations. These forms are familiar and well known to consciousness, the ordinary mode of finality, which mode it has appropriated to itself, having constituted it the universal medium of its representation, into which everything that comes to consciousness must be resolved in order that it may have and know itself therein.

The assertion of Religion is that the manifestation of Truth which is revealed to us through it, is one which is given to man from outside, and on this account it is also asserted that man has humbly to assent to it, because human reason cannot attain to it by itself. The assertion of positive Religion is that its truths exist without having their source known, so that the content as given, is one which is above and beyond reason. By means of some prophet or other divine instrument, the truth is made known : just as Ceres and Triptolemus who introduced agriculture and matrimony, for so doing were honoured by the Greeks, men have rendered thanks to Moses and to Mahomed. Through whatever individual the Truth may have been given, the external matter is historical, and this is indifferent to the absolute content and to itself, since the person is not the import of the doctrine. But the Christian Religion has this characteristic that the Person of Christ in His character of the Son of God, Himself partakes of the nature of God. If Christ be for Christians only a teacher like Pythagoras, Socrates or Columbus, there would be here no universal divine content, no revelation or knowledge imparted about the Nature of God, and it is regarding this alone that we desire to obtain knowledge.

Whatever stage it may itself have reached, the Truth must undoubtedly in the first place come to men from without as a present object, sensuously represented, just as Moses saw God in the fiery bush, and as the Greek brought the god into conscious being by means of sculpture or other representations. But there is the further fact, that neither in Religion nor in Philosophy does this

external form remain, nor can it so remain. A form of
the imagination or an historical form, such as Christ, must
for the spirit be spiritual; and thus it ceases to be an
external matter, seeing that the form of externality is dead.
We must know God "in Spirit and in Truth." He is the
absolute and actual Spirit. The relation borne by the
human spirit to this Spirit involve the following considerations.

When man determines to adopt a Religion he asks himself, "What is the ground of my faith?" The Christian
Religion replies—"The Spirit's witness to its content."
Christ reproved the Pharisees for wishing to see miracles;
the Spirit alone comprehends Spirit, the miracle is only a
presentiment of that Spirit; and if the miracle be the suspension of natural laws, Spirit itself is the real miracle
in the operations of nature. Spirit in itself is merely this
comprehension of itself. There is only one Spirit, the
universal divine Spirit. Not that it is merely everywhere; it
is not to be comprehended as what is common to everything,
as an external totality, to be found in many or in all
individuals, which are essentially individuals; but it must
be understood as that which permeates through everything,
as the unity of itself and of a semblance of its "other,"
as of the subjective and particular. As universal, it is object
to itself, and thus determined as a particular, it is this individual: but as universal it reaches over this its "other," so
that its "other" and itself are comprised in one. The
true universality seems, popularly expressed, to be two—
what is common to the universal itself and to the particular.
A division is formed in the understanding of itself, and the
Spirit is the unity of what is understood and the understanding person. The divine Spirit which is comprehended,
is objective; the subjective Spirit comprehends. But Spirit
is not passive, or else the passivity can be momentary
only; there is one spiritual substantial unity. The sub-
ective Spirit is the active, but the objective Spirit is itself

this activity; the active subjective Spirit is that which comprehends the divine, and in its comprehension of it it is itself the divine Spirit. The relation of Spirit to self alone is the absolute determination; the divine Spirit lives in its own communion and presence. This comprehension has been called Faith, but it is not an historical faith; we Lutherans—I am a Lutheran and will remain the same— have only this original faith. This unity is not the Substance of Spinoza, but the apprehending Substance in self-consciousness which makes itself eternal and relates to universality. The talk about the limitations of human thought is futile; to know God is the only end of Religion. The testimony of the Spirit to the content of Religion is itself Religion; it is a testimony that both bears witness and at the same time is that witness. The Spirit proves itself, and does so first in the proof; it is only proved because it proves itself and shows or manifests itself.

It has further to be said, that this testimony, this inward stirring and self-consciousness, reveals itself, while in the enshrouded consciousness of devotion it does not arrive at the proper consciousness of an object, but only at the consciousness of immersion in absolute Being. This permeating and permeated Spirit now enters into conception; God goes forth into the " other " and makes Himself objective. All that pertains to revelation and its reception, and which comes before us in mythology, here appears; everything which is historical and which belongs to what is positive has here its proper place. To speak more definitely, we now have the Christ who came into the world nearly two thousand years ago. But He says, "I am with you even unto the ends of the earth; where two or three are gathered together in My Name, there will I be in the midst." I shall not be seen of you in the flesh, but " The Spirit of Truth will guide you into all Truth." The external is not the true relation; it will disappear.

The two stages have here been given, the first of which

is the stage of devotion, of worship, such as that reached in partaking of the Communion. That is the perception of the divine Spirit in the community in which the present, indwelling, living Christ as self-consciousness has attained to actuality. The second stage is that of developed consciousness, when the content becomes the object; here this present, indwelling Christ retreats two thousand years to a small corner of Palestine, and is an individual historically manifested far away at Nazareth or Jerusalem. It is the same thing in the Greek Religion where the god present in devotion changes into prosaic statues and marble; or in painting, where this externality is likewise arrived at, when the god becomes mere canvas or wood. The Supper is, according to the Lutheran conception, of Faith alone; it is a divine satisfaction, and is not adored as if it were the Host. Thus a sacred image is no more to us than is a stone or thing. The second point of view must indeed be that with which consciousness begins; it must start from the external comprehension of this form: it must passively accept report and take it up into memory. But if it remain where it is, that is the unspiritual point of view: to remain fixed in this second standpoint in this dead far-away historic distance, is to reject the Spirit. The sins of him who lies against the Holy Ghost cannot be forgiven. That lie is the refusal to be a universal, to be holy, that is to make Christ become divided, separated, to make Him only another person as this particular person in Judea; or else to say that He now exists, but only far away in Heaven, or in some other place, and not in present actual form amongst His people. The man who speaks of the *merely* finite, of *merely* human reason, and of the limits to mere reason, lies against the Spirit, for the Spirit as infinite and universal, as self-comprehension, comprehends itself not in a "merely" nor in limits, nor in the finite as such. It has nothing to do with this, for it comprehends itself within itself alone, in its infinitude.

If it be said of Philosophy that it makes reality the subject of its knowledge, the principal point is that the reality should not be one outside of that of which it is the reality. For example, if from the real content of a book, I abstract the binding, paper, ink, language, the many thousand letters that are contained in it, the simple universal content as reality, is not outside of the book. Similarly law is not outside of the individual, but it constitutes the true Being of the individual. The reality of my Mind is thus in my Mind itself and not outside of it; it is my real Being, my own substance, without which I am without existence. This reality is, so to speak, the combustible material which may be kindled and lit up by the universal reality as such as objective; and only so far as this phosphorus is in men, is comprehension, the kindling and lighting up, possible. Feeling, anticipation, knowledge of God, are only thus in men; without such, the divine Mind would not be the in and for itself Universal. Reality is itself a real content and not the destitute of content and undetermined; yet, as the book has other content besides, there is in the individual mind also a great amount of other matter which belongs only to the manifestation of this reality, and the individual surrounded with what is external, must be separated from this existence. Since reality is itself Spirit and not an abstraction, " God is not a God for the dead but for the living," and indeed for living spirits.

> The great Creator was alone
> And experienced desire,
> Therefore He created Spirits,
> Holy mirrors of His holiness.
> The noblest Being He found no equal;
> From out the bowl of all the spiritual world,
> There sparkled up to Him infinitude.

Religion is also the point of view from which this existence is known. But as regards the different forms of knowledge existing in Religion and Philosophy, Philosophy

appears to be opposed to the conception in Religion that
the universal mind first shows itself as external, in the
objective mode of consciousness. Worship, commencing
with the external, then turns against and abrogates it as
has just been said, and thus Philosophy is justified through
the acts and forms of worship, and only does what they
do. Philosophy has to deal with two different objects;
first as in the Religion present in worship, with the substantial content, the spiritual soul, and secondly with bringing this before consciousness as object, but in the form of
thought. Philosophy thinks and conceives of that which
Religion represents as the object of consciousness, whether
it is as the work of the imagination or as existent facts in
history. The form of the knowledge of the object is, in
religious consciousness, such as pertains to the ordinary idea,
and is thus more or less sensuous in nature. In Philosophy
we do not say that God begot a Son, which is a relation derived from natural life. Thought, or the substance of such
a relation, is therefore still recognized in Philosophy. Since
Philosophy thinks its object, it has the advantage of
uniting the two stages of religious consciousness—which in
Religion are different moments—into one unity in philosophic thought.

It is these two forms which are different from one another
and which, as opposed, may therefore seem to be mutually
conflicting; and it is natural and it necessarily seems to be
the case, that on first definitely coming to view they are
so to speak conscious of their diversity, and hence at first
appear as inimical to one another. The first stage in the
order of manifestation is definite existence, or a determinate
Being-for-self as opposed to the other. The later form is
that Thought embraces itself in the concrete, immerses itself
in itself, and Mind, as such, comes in it to consciousness.
In the earlier stage, Mind is abstract, and in this constraint it knows itself to be different, and in opposition to
the other. When it embraces itself in the concrete, it is no

more simply confined in determinate existence, only knowing or possessing itself in that diversity, but it is the
Universal which, inasmuch as it determines itself, contains
its "other" within itself. As concrete intelligence, Mind
thus comprehends the substantial in the form which seemed
to differ from it, of which it had only grasped the outward
manifestation and had turned away from it; it recognizes
itself in its inward content, and so it for the first time
grasps its object, and deals justice to its opposite.

Generally speaking, the course of this antithesis in history
is that Thought first of all comes forth within Religion,
as not free and in separate manifestations. Secondly, it
strengthens itself, feels itself to be resting upon itself, holds
and conducts itself inimically towards the other form, and
does not recognize itself therein. In the third place, it
concludes by acknowledging itself as in this other. Or else
Philosophy has to begin with carrying on its work entirely
on its own account, isolating Thought from all popular
beliefs, and taking for itself quite a different field of
operation, a field for which the world of ordinary ideas lies
quite apart, so that the two exist peacefully side by side,
or, to put it better, so that no reflection on their opposition
is arrived at. Just as little did the thought of reconciling
them occur, since in the popular beliefs the same content
appeared as in any external form other than the notion—
the thought that is, of explaining and justifying popular
belief, in order thus to be able again to express the conceptions of free thought in the form of popular religion.

Thus we see Philosophy first restrained and confined
within the range of the Greek heathen world; then resting upon itself, it goes forth against popular religion
and takes up an unfriendly attitude to it, until it grasps
that religion in its innermost and recognizes itself therein.
Thus the ancient Greek philosophers generally respected
the popular religion, or at least they did not oppose it, or
reflect upon it. Those coming later, including even Xeno-

phanes, handled popular ideas most severely, and thus
many so-called atheists made their appearance. But as the
spheres of popular conception and abstract thought stood
peacefully side by side, we also find Greek philosophers of
even a later period in development, in whose case speculative thought and the act of worship, as also the pious invo-
cation upon and sacrifice to the gods, coexist in good faith,
and not in mere hypocrisy. Socrates was accused of teaching other gods than those belonging to the popular religion ;
his δαιμόνιον was indeed opposed to the principles of Greek
morals and religion, but at the same time he followed quite
honestly the usages of his religion, and we know besides
that his last request was to ask his friends to offer a cock
to Æsculapius—a desire quite inconsistent with his conclusions regarding the existence of God and above all regarding morality. Plato declaimed against the poets and
their gods. It was in a much later time that the Neo-
platonists first recognized in the popular mythology rejected
earlier by the philosophers, the universal content; they
transposed and translated it into what is significant for
thought, and thus used mythology itself as a symbolical
imagery for giving expression to their formulas.

Similarly do we see in the Christian Religion, thought
which is not independent first placing itself in conjunction
with the form belonging to this Religion and acting within
it—that is to say, taking the Religion as its groundwork,
and proceeding from the absolute assumption of the
Christian doctrine. We see later on the opposition between
so-called faith and so-called reason ; when the wings of
thought have become strengthened, the young eaglet flies
away for himself to the sun of Truth; but like a bird of
prey he turns upon Religion and combats it. Latest of all
Philosophy permits full justice to be done to the content of
Religion through the speculative Notion, which is through
Thought itself. For this end the Notion must have grasped
itself in the concrete and penetrated to concrete spirituality.

This must be the standpoint of the Philosophy of the present time ; it has begun within Christianity and can have no other content than the world-spirit. When that spirit comprehends itself in Philosophy, it also comprehends itself in that form which formerly was inimical to Philosophy.

Thus Religion has a content in common with Philosophy the forms alone being different; and the only essential point is that the form of the Notion should be so far perfected as to be able to grasp the content of Religion. The Truth is just that which has been called the mysteries of Religion. These constitute the speculative element in Religion such as were called by the Neo-platonists μνεῖν, μνεῖσθαι (being initiated), or being occupied with speculative Notions. By mysteries is meant, superficially speaking, the secret, what remains such and does not arrive at being known. But in the Eleusinian mysteries there was nothing unknown ; all Athenians were initiated into them, Socrates alone shut himself out. Openly to make them known to strangers was the one thing forbidden, as indeed it was made a crime in the case of certain people. Such matters however, as being holy, were not to be spoken of. Herodotus often expressly says (e.g. ii. 45—47) that he would speak of the Egyptian Divinities and mysteries in as far as it was pious so to do : he knew more, but it would be impious to speak of them. In the Christian Religion dogmas are called mysteries. They are that which man knows about the Nature of God. Neither is there anything mysterious in this; it is known by all those who are partakers in that Religion, and these are thus distinguished from the followers of other Religions. Hence mystery here signifies nothing unknown, since all Christians are in the secret. Mysteries are in their nature speculative, mysterious certainly to the understanding, but not to reason; they are rational, just in the sense of being speculative. The understanding does not comprehend the speculative which simply is the concrete because it holds to the differences in their separation; their contradiction is indeed contained in the mystery, which, however, is likewise the resolution of the same.

Philosophy, on the contrary, is opposed to the so-called Rationalism of the new Theology which for ever keeps reason on its lips, but which is dry understanding only ; no reason is recognizable in it as the moment of independent thought which really is abstract thought and that alone. When the understanding which does not comprehend the truths of Religion, calls itself the illuminatiug reason and plays the lord and master, it goes astray. Rationalism is opposed to Philosophy in content and form, for it has made the content empty as it has made the heavens, and has reduced all that is, to finite relations—in its form it is a reasoning process which is not free and which has no conceiving power. The supernatural in Religion is opposed to rationalism, and if indeed the latter is related in respect of the real content to Philosophy, yet it differs from it in form, for it has become unspiritual and wooden, looking for its justification to mere external authority. The scholastics were not supernaturalists in this sense; they knew the dogmas of the Church in thought and in conception. If Religion in the inflexibility of its abstract authority as opposed to thought, declares of it that "the gates of Hell shall not triumph over it," the gates of reason are stronger than the gates of Hell, not to overcome the Church but to reconcile itself to the Church. Philosophy, as the conceiving thought of this content, has as regards the idea of Religion, the advantage of comprehending both sides—it comprehends Religion and also comprehends both rationalism and supernaturalism and itself likewise. But this is not the case on the other side. Religion from the standpoint of idea, comprehends only what stands on the same platform as itself, and not Philosophy, the Notion, the universal thought determinations. Often no injustice is done to a Philosophy when its opposition to Religion has been made matter of reproach; but often, too, a wrong has been inflicted where this is done from the religious point of view.

The form of Religion is necessary to Mind as it is in and for itself; it is the form of truth as it is for all men, and for every mode of consciousness. This universal mode is first of all for men in the form of sensuous consciousness, and then, secondly, in the intermingling of the form of the universal with sensuous manifestation or reflection—the representing consciousness, the mythical, positive and historical form, is that pertaining to the understanding. What is received in evidence of Mind only becomes object to consciousness when it appears in the form of the understanding, that is to say, consciousness must first be already acquainted with these forms from life and from experience. Now, because thinking consciousness is not the outward universal form for all mankind, the consciousness of the true, the spiritual and the rational, must have the form of Religion, and this is the universal justification of this form.

We have here laid down the distinction between Philosophy and Religion, but taking into account what it is we wish to deal with in the history of Philosophy, there is something still which must be remarked upon, and which partly follows from what has been already said. There is the question still confronting us as to what attitude we must take in reference to this matter in the history of Philosophy.

β. The religious element to be excluded from the content of the History of Philosophy.

aa. Mythology first meets us, and it seems as if it might be drawn within the history of Philosophy. It is indeed a product of the imagination, but not of caprice, although that also has its place here. But the main part of mythology is the work of the imaginative reason, which makes reality its object, but yet has no other means

D

of so doing, than that of sensuous representation, so that the gods make their appearance in human guise. Mythology can now be studied for art, &c. But the thinking mind must seek out the substantial content, the thought and the theory implicitly contained therein, as reason is sought in Nature. This mode of treating mythology was that of the Neo-platonists; in recent times it has for the most part become the work of my friend Creuzer in symbolism. This method of treatment is combated and condemned by others. Man, it is said, must set to work historically alone, and it is not historic when a theory unthought of by the ancients, is read into a myth, or brought out of it. In one light, this is quite correct, for it points to a method adopted by Creuzer, and also by the Alexandrians who acted in a similar way. In conscious thought the ancients had not such theories before them, nor did anyone maintain them, yet to say that such content was not implicitly present, is an absurd contention. As the products of reason, though not of thinking reason, the religions of the people, as also the mythologies, however simple and even foolish they may appear, indubitably contain as genuine works of art, thoughts, universal determinations and truth, for the instinct of reason is at their basis. Bound up with this is the fact that since mythology in its expression takes sensuous forms, much that is contingent and external becomes intermingled, for the representation of the Notion in sensuous forms always possesses a certain incongruity, seeing that what is founded on imagination cannot express the Idea in its real aspect. This sensuous form produced as it is by an historic or natural method, must be determined on many sides, and this external determination must, more or less, be of such a nature as not to express the Idea. It may also be that many errors are contained in that explanation, particularly when a single one is brought within our notice; all the customs, actions, furnishings, vestments, and offerings taken together, may undoubtedly contain something of the Idea in analogy, but the connection is far removed, and many contingent circumstances must find their entrance. But that there is a Reason there, must certainly be recognized, and it is essential so to comprehend and grasp mythology.

But Mythology must remain excluded from our history of Philosophy. The reason of this is found in the fact that in Philosophy we have to do not with theorems generally, or with thoughts which only are *implicite* contained in some particular form or other, but with thoughts which are explicit, and only in so far as they are explicit and in so far as a content such as that belonging to Religion, has come to consciousness in the form of Thought. And this is just what forms the immense distinction which we saw above, between capacity and actuality. The theorems which are *implicite* contained within Religion do not concern us; they must be in the form of thoughts, since Thought alone is the absolute form of the Idea.

In many mythologies, images are certainly used along with their significance, or else the images are closely attended by their interpretation. The ancient Persians worshipped the sun, or fire, as being the highest existence; the first cause in the Persian Religion is Zervane Akerene— unlimited time, eternity. This simple eternal existence possesses according to Diogenes Lærtius (I. 8), "the two principles Ormuzd ('Ωρομάσδης) and Ahriman ('Αρειμάνιος), the rulers over good and evil." Plutarch in writing on Isis and Osiris (T. II. p. 369, ed. Xyl.) says, "It is not one existence which holds and rules the whole, but good is mingled with evil; nature as a rule brings forth nothing pure and simple; it is not one dispenser, who, like a host, gives out and mixes up the drink from two different barrels. But through two opposed and inimical principles of which the one impels towards what is right, and the other in the opposite direction, if not the whole world, at

least this earth is influenced in different ways. Zoroaster
has thus emphatically set up the one principle (Ormuzd)
as being the Light, and the other (Ahriman) as the Darkness.
Between the two ($\mu\acute{\epsilon}\sigma\sigma\varsigma$ $\delta\grave{\epsilon}$ $\mathring{a}\mu\phi o\hat{\imath}\nu$) is Mithra, hence called
by the Persians the Mediator ($\mu\epsilon\sigma\acute{\imath}\tau\eta\varsigma$)." Mithra is then
likewise substance, the universal existence, the sun raised
to a totality. It is not the mediator between Ormuzd and
Ahriman by establishing peace and leaving each to remain
as it was ; it does not partake of good and evil both, like
an unblest middle thing, but it stands on the side of
Ormuzd and strives with him against the evil. Ahriman
is sometimes called the first-born son of the Light, but
Ormuzd only remained within the Light. At the creation
of the visible world, Ormuzd places on the earth in his
incomprehensible kingdom of Light, the firm arches of
the heavens which are above yet surrounded on every side
with the first original Light. Midway to the earth is the
high hill Albordi, which reaches into the source of Light.
Ormuzd's empire of Light extended uninterruptedly over
the firm vault of the heavens and the hill Albordi, and
over the earth too, until the third age was reached. Then
Ahriman, whose kingdom of night was formerly bound
beneath the earth, broke in upon Ormuzd's corporeal world
and ruled in common with him. Now the space between
heaven and earth was divided into light and night. As
Ormuzd had formerly only a spiritual kingdom of light,
Ahriman had only one of night, but now that they were
intermingled he placed the terrestrial light thus created in
opposition to the terrestrial night. From this time on, two
corporeal worlds stand opposed, one pure and good, and
one impure and evil, and this opposition permeates all
nature. On Albordi, Ormuzd created Mithra as mediator
for the earth. The end of the creation of the bodily world
is none other than to reinstate existence, fallen from its
creator, to make it good again, and thus to make the evil
disappear for ever. The bodily world is the battle-ground

between good and evil; but the battle between light and darkness is not in itself an absolute and irreconcilable opposition, but one which can be conquered, and in it Ormuzd, the principle of Light, will be the conqueror.

I would remark of this, that when we consider the elements in these ideas which bear some further connection with Philosophy, the universal of that duality with which the Notion is necessarily set forth can alone be interesting and noteworthy to us; for in it the Notion is just the immediate opposite of itself, the unity of itself with itself in the "other:" a simple existence in which absolute opposition appears as the opposition of existence, and the sublation of that opposition. Because properly the Light principle is the only existence of both, and the principle of Darkness is the null and void,—the principle of Light identifies itself with Mithra, which was before called the highest existence. The opposition has laid aside the appearance of contingency, but the spiritual principle is not separate from the physical, because the good and evil are both determined as Light and Darkness. We thus here see thought breaking forth from actuality, and yet not such a separation as only takes place in Religion, when the supersensuous is itself again represented in a manner sensuous, notionless and dispersed, for the whole of what is dispersed in sensuous form is gathered together in the one single opposition, and activity is thus simply represented. These determinations lie much nearer to Thought; they are not mere images or symbols, but yet these myths do not concern Philosophy. In them Thought does not take the first place, for the myth-form remains predominant. In all religions this oscillation between form and thought is found, and such a combination still lies outside Philosophy.

This is also so in the Sanchuniathonic Cosmogony of the Phœnicians. These fragments, which are found in Eusebius (Præpar. Evang. I. 10), are taken from the translation of the Sanchuniathon from Phœnician into

Greek made by a Grammarian named Philo from Biblus. Philo lived in the time of Vespasian and ascribes great antiquity to the Sanchuniathon. It is there said, " The principles of things are found in Chaos, in which the elements exist undeveloped and confused, and in a Spirit of Air.. The latter permeated the chaos, and with it engendered a slimy matter or mud (ἰλύν) which contained within it the living forces and the germs of animals. By mingling this mud with the component matter of chaos and the resulting fermentation, the elements separated themselves. The fire elements ascended into the heights and formed the stars. Through their influence in the air, clouds were formed and the earth was made fruitful. From the mingling of water and earth, through the mud converted into putrefying matter, animals took their origin as imperfect and senseless. These again begot other animals perfect and endowed with senses. It was the crash of thunder in a thunder-storm that caused the first animals still sleeping in their husks to waken up to life." [1]

The fragments of Berosus of the Chaldeans were collected from Josephus, Syncellus and Eusebius under the title *Berosi Chaldaica*, by Scaliger, as an appendix to his work *De emendatione temporum*, and they are found complete in the Greek Library of Fabricius (T. xiv. pp. 175—211). Berosus lived in the time of Alexander, is said to have been a Priest of Bel and to have drawn upon the archives of the temple at Babylon. He says, " The original god is Bel and the goddess Omoroka (the sea), but beside them there were yet other gods. Bel divided Omoroka in two, in order to create from her parts heaven and earth. Hereupon he cut off his own head and the human race originated from the drops of his divine blood. After the creation of man, Bel banished the darkness, divided heaven and earth, and formed the world into its natural shape. Since certain parts of the

[1] Sanchuniathonis Fragm. ed. Rich. Cumberland, Lond. 1720, 8; German by J. P. Kassel, Magdeburg, 1755, 8, pp. 1—4.

earth seemed to him to be insufficiently populated, he compelled another god to lay hands upon himself, and from his
blood more men and more kinds of animals were created.
At first the men lived a wild and uncultivated life, until a
monster " (called by Berosus, Oannes) " joined them into a
state, taught them arts and sciences, and in a word brought
Humanity into existence. The monster set about this end
with the rising of the sun out of the sea, and with its
setting he again hid himself under the waves."

$\beta\beta$. What belongs to Mythology may in the second place
make a pretence of being a kind of Philosophy. It has
produced philosophers who availed themselves of the
mythical form in order to bring their theories and systems
more prominently before the imagination, for they made
the thoughts the content of the myth. But the myth is
not a mere cloak in the ancient myths; it is not merely
that the thoughts were there and were concealed. This
may happen in our reflecting times ; but the first poetry
does not start from a separation of prose and poetry. If
philosophers used myths, it was usually the case that they
had the thoughts and then sought for images appropriate
to them; Plato has many beautiful myths of this kind.
Others likewise have spoken in myths, as for example,
Jacobi, whose Philosophy took the form of the Christian
Religion, through which he gave utterance to matter of a
highly speculative nature. But this form is not suitable to
Philosophy. Thought which has itself as object, must have
raised itself to its own form, to the form of thought.
Plato is often esteemed on account of his myths; he is
supposed to have evinced by their means greater genius than
other philosophers were capable of. It is contended here
that the myths of Plato are superior to the abstract form of
expression, and Plato's method of representation is certainly
a wonderful one. On closer examination we find that it is
partly the impossibility of expressing himself after the manner
of pure thought that makes Plato put his meaning so, and

also such methods of expression are only used by him in introducing a subject. When he comes to the matter in point, Plato expresses himself otherwise, as we see in the Parmenides, where simple thought determinations are used without imagery. Externally these myths may certainly serve when the heights of speculative thought are left behind, in order to present the matter in an easier form, but the real value of Plato does not rest in his myths. If thought once attains power sufficient to give existence to itself within itself and in its element, the myth becomes a superfluous adornment, by which Philosophy is not advanced. Men often lay hold of nothing but these myths. Hence Aristotle has been misunderstood just because he intersperses similes here and there; the simile can never be entirely in accord with thought, for it always carries with it something more. The difficulty of representing thoughts as thoughts always attaches to the expedient of expression in sensuous form. Thought, too, ought not to be concealed by means of the myth, for the object of the mythical is just to give expression to and to reveal thought. The symbol is undoubtedly insufficient for this expression; thought concealed in symbols is not yet possessed, for thought is self-revealing, and hence the myth does not form a medium adequate for its conveyance. Aristotle (Metaph. III. 4) says, "It is not worth while to treat seriously of those whose philosophy takes a mythical form." Such is not the form in which thought allows itself to be stated, but only is a subordinate mode.

Connected with this, there is a similar method of representing the universal content by means of numbers, lines and geometric figures. These are figurative, but not concretely so, as in the case of myths. Thus it may be said that eternity is a circle, the snake that bites its own tail. This is only an image, but Mind does not require such a symbol. There are people who value such methods of representation, but these forms do not go far. The most abstract determinations can indeed be thus expressed, but any further progress brings about confusion. Just as the freemasons have symbols which are esteemed for their depth of wisdom—depth as a brook is deep when one cannot see the bottom—that which is hidden very easily seems to men deep, or as if depth were concealed beneath. But when it is hidden, it may possibly prove to be the case that there is nothing behind. This is so in freemasonry, in which everything is concealed to those outside and also to many people within, and where nothing remarkable is possessed in learning or in science, and least of all in Philosophy. Thought is, on the contrary, simply its manifestation; clearness is its nature and itself. The act of manifestation is not a condition which may be or may not be equally, so that thought may remain as thought when it is not manifested, but its manifestation is itself, its Being. Numbers, as will be remarked in respect of the Pythagoreans, are unsuitable mediums for expressing thoughts; thus μονάς, δυάς, τριάς are, with Pythagoras, unity, difference, and unity of the unity and of the difference. The two first of the three are certainly united by addition ; this kind of union is, however, the worst form of unity. In Religion the three make their appearance in a deeper sense as the Trinity, and in Philosophy as the Notion, but enumeration forms a bad method of expression. There is the same objection to it as would exist to making the mensuration of space the medium for expressing the absolute. People also quote the Philosophy of the Chinese, of the Foï, in which it is said that thoughts are represented by numbers. Yet the Chinese have explained their symbols and hence have made their meaning evident. Universal simple abstractions have been present to all people who have arrived at any decree of culture.

γγ. We have still to remark in the third place, that Religion, as such, does not merely form its representations after the manner of art ; and also that Poetry likewise con-

tains actual thoughts. In the case of the poets whose art
has speech as medium, we find all through deep universal
thought regarding reality; these are more explicitly
expressed in the Indian Religion, but with the Indians
everything is mixed up. Hence it is said that such races
have also had a Philosophy proper to themselves; but the
universal thoughts of interest in Indian books limit themselves to what is most abstract, to the idea of rising up
and passing away, and thus of making a perpetual round.
The story of the Phœnix is well known as an example of
this; it is one which took its origin in the East. We are
able similarly to find thoughts about life and death and
of the transition of Being into passing away; from life
comes death and from death comes life; even in Being,
in what is positive, the negation is already present.
The negative side must indeed contain within it the
positive, for all change, all the process of life is founded
on this. But such reflections only occasionally come forth;
they are not to be taken as being proper philosophic
utterances. For Philosophy is only present when thought,
as such, is made the absolute ground and root of everything else, and in these modes of representation this is not
so.

Philosophy does not reflect on any particular thing or
object already existing as a first substratum; its content
is just Thought, universal thought which must plainly
come first of all; to put it otherwise, the Absolute must
in Philosophy be in the form of thought. In the Greek
Religion we find the thought—determination "eternal
necessity;" which means an absolute and clearly universal
relation. But such thought has other subjects besides; it
only expresses a relation, the necessity to be the true
and all-embracing Being. Thus neither must we take this
form into our consideration. We might speak in that way
of a philosophy of Euripides, Schiller or Goethe. But all
such reflection respecting, or general modes of represent-

ing what is true, the ends of men, morality and so on, are in part only incidentally set forth, and in part they have not reached the proper form of thought, which implies that what is so expressed must be ultimate, thus constituting the Absolute.

γ. *Particular theories found in Religion.*

In conclusion, the philosophy which we find within Religion does not concern us. We find deep, speculative thoughts regarding the nature of God not only in the Indian Religions, but also in the Fathers and the Schoolmen. In the history of dogmatism there is a real interest in becoming acquainted with these thoughts, but they do not belong to the history of Philosophy. Nevertheless more notice must be taken of the Schoolmen than of the Fathers, for they were certainly great philosophers to whom the culture of Christendom owes much. But their speculations belong in part to other philosophies such as to that of Plato, which must in so far be considered for themselves; partly, too, they emanate from the speculative content of Religion itself which already exists as independent truth in the doctrine of the Church, and belongs primarily to faith. Thus such modes of thought rest on an hypothesis and not on Thought itself; they are not properly speaking themselves Philosophy or thought which rests on itself, but as ideas already firmly rooted, they act on its behalf either in refuting other ideas and conclusions or in philosophically vindicating against them their own religious teaching. Thought in this manner does not represent and know itself as the ultimate and absolute culmination of the content, or as the inwardly self-determining Thought. Hence, too, when the Fathers, seeing that the content of the Christian Religion can only be grasped after the speculative form, did, within the teaching of the Church, produce thoughts of a highly speculative nature, the ultimate justification of these was not found in Thought as such, but in the teaching of the Church. Philosophic teaching here finds itself within a strongly bound system and not as thought which emanates freely from itself. Thus with the scholastics, too, Thought does not construct itself out of itself, but depends upon hypotheses ; and although it ever rests more and more upon itself, it never does so in opposition to the doctrine of the Church. Both must and do agree, since Thought has to prove from itself what the Church has already verified.

c. *Philosophy proper distinguished from Popular Philosophy.*

Of the two departments of knowledge allied to Philosophy we found that the one, that of the special sciences, could not be called a philosophy in that it, as independent seeing and thinking immersed in finite matter, and as the active principle in becoming acquainted with the finite, was not the content, but simply the formal and subjective moment. The second sphere, Religion, is deficient in that it only had the content or the objective moment in common with Philosophy. In it independent thought was an essential moment, since the subject had an imaginary or historical form. Philosophy demands the unity and intermingling of these two points of view ; it unites the Sunday of life when man in humility renounces himself, and the working-day when he stands up independently, is master of himself and considers his own interests. A third point of view seems to unite both elements, and that is popular Philosophy. It deals with universal objects and philosophizes as to God and the world; and thought is likewise occupied in learning about these matters. Yet this Philosophy must also be cast aside. The writings of Cicero may be put under this category ; they contain a kind of philosophy that has its own place and in which excellent things are said. Cicero formed many experiences both in the affairs of life and mind, and from them and after observing what takes place in the world, he deduced the truth. He expresses himself with

culture on the concerns most important to man, and hence
his great popularity. Fanatics and mystics may from another
point of view be reckoned as in this category. They give
expression to a deep sense of devotion, and have had experiences in the higher regions. They are able to express
the highest content, and the result is attractive. We thus
find the brightest gleams of thought in the writings of a
Pascal—as we do in his *Pensées.*

But the drawback that attaches to this Philosophy is
that the ultimate appeal — even in modern times—is
made to the fact that men are constituted such as they
are by nature, and with this Cicero is very free. Here the
moral instinct comes into question, only under the name
of feeling; Religion now rests not on what is objective but
on religious feeling, because the immediate consciousness
of God by men is its ultimate ground. Cicero makes
copious use of the *consensus gentium;* in more modern
times this appeal has been more or less left alone, since the
individual subject has to rest upon himself. Feeling is first
of all laid hold of, then comes reasoning from what is given,
but in these we can appeal to what is immediate only.
Independent thought is certainly here advanced; the content too, is taken from the self; but we must just as
necessarily exclude this mode of thinking from Philosophy.
For the source from which the content is derived is of the
same description as in the other cases. Nature is the
source in finite sciences, and in Religion it is Spirit; but
here the source is in authority; the content is given and
the act of worship removes but momentarily this externality. The source of popular Philosophy is in the heart,
impulses and capacities, our natural Being, my impression
of what is right and of God; the content is in a form which
is of nature only. I certainly have everything in feeling,
but the whole content is also in Mythology, and yet in
neither is it so in veritable form. The laws and doctrines
of Religion are that in which this content always comes

to consciousness in a more definite way, while in feeling there still is intermingled the arbitrary will of that which is subjective.

3. COMMENCEMENT OF PHILOSOPHY AND OF ITS HISTORY.

Now that we have thus defined the Notion of Philosophy to be thè Thought which, as the universal content, is complete Being, it will be shown in the history of Philosophy how the determinations in this content make their appearance little by little. At first we only ask where Philosophy and its History begin.

a. *Freedom of Thought as a first condition.*

The general answer is in accordance with what has been said. Philosophy begins where the universal is comprehended as the all-embracing existence, or where the existent is laid hold of in a universal form, and where thinking about thought first commences. Where, then, has this occurred? Where did it begin? That is a question of history. Thought must be for itself, must come into existence in its freedom, liberate itself from nature and come out of its immersion in mere sense-perception; it must as free, enter within itself and thus arrive at the consciousness of freedom. Philosophy is properly to be commenced where the Absolute is no more in the form of ordinary conception, and free thought not merely thinks the Absolute but grasps its Idea. That is to say where Thought grasps as Thought, the Being (which may be Thought itself), which it recognizes as the essence of things, the absolute totality and the immanent essence of everything, and does so as an external Being. The simple existence which is not sensuous and which the Jews thought of as God (for all Religion is thinking), is thus not a subject to be treated of by Philosophy, but just such a proposition as that "The existence or principle of things is water, fire or thought."

Thought, this universal determination which sets forth

itself, is an abstract determinateness; it is the beginning of Philosophy, but this beginning is at the same time in history, the concrete form taken by a people, the principle of which constitutes what we have stated above. If we say that the consciousness of freedom is connected with the appearance of Philosophy, this principle must be a fundamental one with those with whom Philosophy begins; a people having this consciousness of freedom founds its existence on that principle seeing that the laws and the whole circumstances of the people are based only on the Notion that Mind forms of itself, and in the categories which it has. Connected with this on the practical side, is the fact that actual freedom develops political freedom, and this only begins where the individual knows himself as an independent individual to be universal and real, where his significance is infinite, or where the subject has attained the consciousness of personality and thus desires to be esteemed for himself alone. Free, philosophic thought has this direct connection with practical freedom, that as the former supplies thought about the absolute, universal and real object, the latter, because it thinks itself, gives itself the character of universality. Thinking means the bringing of something into the form of universality; hence Thought first treats of the universal, or determines what is objective and individual in the natural things which are present in sensuous consciousness, as the universal, as an objective Thought. Its second attribute is that in recognizing and knowing this objective and infinite universal, I, at the same time, remain confronting it from the standpoint of objectivity.

On account of this general connection between political freedom and the freedom of Thought, Philosophy only appears in History where and in as far as free institutions are formed. Since Mind requires to separate itself from its natural will and engrossment in matter if it wishes to enter upon Philosophy, it cannot do so in the form with which the world-spirit commences and which takes precedence of that separation. This stage of the unity of Mind with Nature which as immediate is not the true and perfect state, is mainly found in the Oriental conception of existence, therefore Philosophy first begins in the Grecian world.

b. Separation of the East and its Philosophy.

Some explanations have to be given regarding this first form. Since Mind in it, as consciousness and will, is but desire, self-consciousness still stands upon its first stage in which the sphere of its idea and will is finite. As intelligence is thus finite too, its ends are not yet a universal for themselves; but if a people makes for what is moral, if laws and justice are possessed, the character of universality underlies its will. This presupposes a new power in Mind with which it commences to be free, for the universal will as the relation of thought to thought or as the universal, contains a thought which is at home with itself. If a people desire to be free, they will subordinate their desires to universal laws, while formerly that which was desired was only a particular. Now finitude of the will characterizes the orientals, because with them the will has not yet grasped itself as universal, for thought is not yet free for itself. Hence there can but be the relation of lord and slave, and in this despotic sphere fear constitutes the ruling category. Because the will is not yet free from what is finite, it can therein be comprehended and the finite can be shown forth as negative. This sensation of negation, that something cannot last, is just fear as distinguished from freedom which does not consist in being finite but in being for itself, and this cannot be laid hold of. Religion necessarily has this character, since the fear of the Lord is the essential element beyond which we cannot get. " The fear of the Lord is the beginning of wisdom " is indeed a true saying ; man must begin with this in order to know the finite ends in their negative character. But man must also have overcome fear through the relinquishment of finite ends, and the satisfaction which that Religion affords is confined to what is finite, seeing that the chief means of reconciliation are natural forms which are impersonated and held in reverence.

The oriental consciousness raises itself, indeed, above the natural content to what is infinite; but it only knows itself as accidental in reference to the power which makes the individual fear. This subordination may take two forms and must indeed from one extreme pass to the other. The finite, which is for consciousness, may have the form of finitude as finite, or it may become the infinite, which is however an abstraction. The man who lives in fear, and he who rules over men through fear, both stand upon the same platform; the difference between them is only in the greater power of will which can go forth to sacrifice all that is finite for some particular end. The despot brings about what his caprice directs, including certainly what is good, not as law, but as arbitrary will : the passive will, like that of slavery, is converted into the active energy of will, which will, however, is arbitrary still. In Religion we even find self-immersion in the deepest sensuality represented as the service of God, and then there follows in the East a flight to the emptiest abstraction as to what is infinite, as also the exaltation attained through the renunciation of everything, and this is specially so amongst the Indians, who torture themselves and enter into the most profound abstraction. The Indians look straight before them for ten years at a time, are fed by those around, and are destitute of other spiritual content than that of knowing what is abstract, which content therefore is entirely finite. This, then, is not the soil of freedom.

In the East, Mind indeed begins to dawn, but it is still true of it that the subject is not presented as a person, but appears in the objectively substantial, which is represented as partly supersensuous and partly, and even more, material, as negative and perishing. The highest point attainable by the individual, the everlasting bliss, is made an immersion into substance, a vanishing away of consciousness, and thus of all distinction between substance and individuality—hence an annihilation. A spiritually dead relation thus comes into existence, since the highest point there to be reached is insensibility. So far, however, man has not attained that bliss, but finds himself to be a single existent individual, distinguished from the universal substance. He is thus outside the unity, has no significance, and as being what is accidental and without rights, is finite only; he finds himself limited through Nature—in caste for instance. The will is not here the substantial will; it is the arbitrary will given up to what is outwardly and inwardly contingent, for substance alone is the affirmative. With it greatness, nobility, or exaltitude of character, are certainly not excluded, but they are only present as the naturally determined or the arbitrary will, and not in the objective forms of morality and law to which all owe respect, which hold good for all, and in which for that same reason all are recognized. The oriental subject thus has the advantage of independence, since there is nothing fixed; however undetermined is the substance of the Easterns, as undetermined, free and independent may their character be. What for us is justice and morality is also in their state, but in a substantial, natural, patriarchal way, and not in subjective freedom. Conscience does not exist nor does morality. Everything is simply in a state of nature, which allows the noblest to exist as it does the worst.

The conclusion to be derived from this is that no philosophic knowledge can be found here. To Philosophy belongs the knowledge of Substance, the absolute Universal, that whether I think it and develop it or not, confronts me still as for itself objective; and whether this is to me substantial or not, still just in that I think it, it is mine, that in which I possess my distinctive character or am affirmative: thus my thoughts are not mere subjective determinations or opinions, but, as being my thoughts, are also thoughts of what is objective, or they are substantial thoughts. The Eastern form must therefore be excluded from the History of Philosophy, but still, upon the whole, I will take some notice of it. I have touched on this elsewhere,[1] for some time ago we for the first time reached a position to judge of it. Earlier a great parade was made about the Indian wisdom without any real knowledge of what it was; now this is for the first time known, and naturally it is found to be in conformity with the rest.

c. *Beginnings of Philosophy in Greece.*

Philosophy proper commences in the West. It is in the West that this freedom of self-consciousness first comes forth; the natural consciousness, and likewise Mind disappear into themselves. In the brightness of the East the individual disappears; the light first becomes in the West the flash of thought which strikes within itself, and from thence creates its world out of itself. The blessedness of the West is thus so determined that in it the subject as such endures and continues in the substantial; the individual mind grasps its Being as universal, but universality is just this relation to itself. This being at home with self, this personality and infinitude of the " I " constitutes the Being of Mind; it is thus and can be none else. For a people to know themselves as free, and to be only as universal, is for them to be; it is the principle of their whole life as regards morality and all else. To take an example, we only know our real Being in so far as personal freedom is its first condition, and hence we never can be slaves. Were the mere arbitrary will of

---

[1] That is to say in the Lectures preceding these, delivered in the Winter Session 1825—1826.

the prince a law, and should he wish slavery to be introduced, we would have the knowledge that this could not
be.   To sleep, to live, to have a certain office, is not our
real Being, and certainly to be no slave is such, for that
has come to mean the being in nature.   Thus in the West
we are upon the soil of a veritable Philosophy.

Because in desire I am subject to another, and my Being
is in a particularity, I am, as I exist, unlike myself; for I
am " I," the universal complete, but hemmed in by passion.
This last is self-will or formal freedom, which has desire as
content.   Amongst the Greeks we first find the freedom
which is the end of true will, the equitable and right,
in which I am free and universal, and others, too, are free,
are also " I " and like me; where a relationship between
free and free is thus established with its actual laws, determinations of the universal will, and justly constituted states.
Hence it is here that Philosophy began.

In Greece we first see real freedom flourish, but still
in a restricted form, and with a limitation, since slavery
was still existent, and the states were by its means conditioned.   In the following abstractions we may first of all
superficially describe the freedom of the East, of Greece,
and of the Teutonic world.   In the East only one individual
is free, the despot; in Greece the few are free; in the
Teutonic world the saying is true that all are free, that is,
man is free as man.   But since the one in Eastern countries
cannot be free because that would necessitate the others
also being free to him, impulse, self-will, and formal freedom, can there alone be found.   Since in Greece we have to
deal with the particular, the Athenians, and the Spartans,
are free indeed, but not the Messenians or the Helots.
The principle of the "few" has yet to be discovered, and
this implies some modifications of the Greek point of view
which we must consider in connection with the History of
Philosophy.   To take these into consideration means simply
to proceed to the dividing up of Philosophy.

C

Division, Sources, and Method adopted in treating of the History of Philosophy.

1. Division of the History of Philosophy.

Since we set to work systematically this division must present itself as necessary. Speaking generally, we have properly only two epochs to distinguish in the history of Philosophy, as in ancient and modern art—these are the Greek and the Teutonic. The Teutonic Philosophy is the Philosophy within Christendom in so far as it belongs to the Teutonic nations; the Christian-European people, inasmuch as they belong to the world of science, possess collectively Teutonic culture; for Italy, Spain, France, England, and the rest, have through the Teutonic nations, received a new form. The influence of Greece also reaches into the Roman world, and hence we have to speak of Philosophy in the territory of the Roman world; but the Romans produced no proper Philosophy any more than any proper poets. They have only received from and imitated others, although they have often done this with intelligence; even their religion is derived from the Greek, and the special character that it has, makes no approach to Philosophy and Art, but is unphilosophical and inartistic.

A further description of these two outstanding opposites must be given. The Greek world developed thought as far as to the Idea; the Christian Teutonic world, on the contrary, has comprehended Thought as Spirit; Idea and Spirit are thus the distinguishing features. More particularly the facts are as follows. Because God, the still undetermined and immediate Universal, Being, or objective Thought, jealously allowing nothing to exist beside Him, is the substantial groundwork of all Philosophy, which never alters, but ever sinks more deeply within itself, and through the development of determinations manifests itself and brings to consciousness, we may designate the particular

character of the development in the first period of Philosophy by saying that this development is a simple process
of determinations, figurations, abstract qualities, issuing
from the one ground that potentially already contains the
whole.

The second stage in this universal principle is the gathering up of the determinations manifested thus, into ideal,
concrete unity, in the mode of subjectivity. The first
determinations as immediate, were still abstractions, but
now the Absolute, as the endlessly self-determining
Universal, must furthermore be comprehended as active
Thought, and not as the Universal in this determinate
character. Hence it is manifested as the totality of determinations and as concrete individuality. Thus, with the
νοῦς of Anaxagoras, and still more with Socrates, there
commences a subjective totality in which Thought grasps
itself, and thinking activity is the fundamental principle.

The third stage, then, is that this totality, which is at first
abstract, in that it becomes realized through the active,
determining, distinguishing thought, sets itself forth even
in the separated determinations, which, as ideal, belong to
it. Since these determinations are contained unseparated
in the unity, and thus each in it is also the other, these
opposed moments are raised into totalities. The quite
general forms of opposition are the universal and the
particular, or, in another form, Thought as such, external
reality, feeling or perception. The Notion is the identity
of universal and particular; because each of these is thus
set forth as concrete in itself, the universal is in itself
at once the unity of universality and particularity, and
the same holds good of particularity. Unity is thus
posited in both forms, and the abstract moments can
be made complete through this unity alone; thus it has
come to pass that the differences themselves are each raised
up to a system of totality, which respectively confront one
another as the Philosophy of Stoicism and of Epicureanism.

The whole concrete universal is now Mind; and the whole concrete individual, Nature. In Stoicism pure Thought develops into a totality; if we make the other side from Mind —natural being or feeling—into a totality, Epicureanism is the result. Each determination is formed into a totality of thought, and, in accordance with the simple mode which characterizes this sphere, these principles seem to be for themselves and independent, like two antagonistic systems of Philosophy. Implicitly both are identical, but they themselves take up their position as conflicting, and the Idea is also, as it is apprehended, in a one-sided determinateness.

The higher stage is the union of these differences. This may occur in annihilation, in scepticism; but the higher point of view is the affirmative, the Idea in relation to the Notion. If the Notion is, then, the universal—that which determines itself further within itself, but yet remains there in its unity and in the ideality and transparency of its determinations which do not become independent—the further step is, on the other hand, the reality of the Notion in which the differences are themselves brought to totalities. Thus the fourth stage is the union of the Idea, in which all these differences, as totalities, are yet at the same time blended into one concrete unity of Notion. This comprehension first takes place without constraint, since the ideal is itself only apprehended in the element of universality.

The Greek world got as far as this Idea, since they formed an ideal intellectual world; and this was done by the Alexandrian Philosophy, in which the Greek Philosophy perfected itself and reached its end. If we wish to represent this process figuratively, *A*. Thought, is (*a*) speaking generally abstract, as in universal or absolute space, by which empty space is often understood; (β) then the most simple space determinations appear, in which we commence with the point in order that we may arrive at the line and angle; (γ) what comes third is their union into the triangle, that which is indeed concrete, but which is still

retained in this abstract element of surface, and thus is only
the first and still formal totality and limitation which corresponds to the νοῦς. *B.* The next point is, that since we
allow each of the enclosing lines of the triangle to be again
surface, each forms itself into the totality of the triangle
and into the whole figure to which it belongs; that is the
realization of the whole in the sides as we see it in Scepticism or Stoicism. *C.* The last stage of all is, that these
surfaces or sides of the triangle join themselves into a body
or a totality: the body is for the first time the perfect spacial
determination, and that is a reduplication of the triangle.
But in as far as the triangle which forms the basis is outside
of the pyramid, this simile does not hold good.

Grecian Philosophy in the Neo-platonists finds its end in
a perfect kingdom of Thought and of bliss, and in a potentially existent world of the ideal, which is yet unreal
because the whole only exists in the element of universality.
This world still lacks individuality as such, which is an
essential moment in the Notion; actuality demands that in
the identity of both sides of the Idea, the independent
totality shall be also posited as negative. Through this
self-existent negation, which is absolute subjectivity, the
Idea is first raised into Mind. Mind is the subjectivity
of self-knowledge; but it is only Mind inasmuch as it
knows what is object to itself, and that is itself, as a
totality, and is for itself a totality. That is to say, the
two triangles which are above and below in the prism
must not be two in the sense of being doubled, but they
must be one intermingled unity. Or, in the case of body,
the difference arises between the centre and the peripheral
parts. This opposition of real corporeality and centre as the
simple existence, now makes its appearance, and the totality
is the union of the centre and the substantial —not, however,
the simple union, but a union such that the subjective
knows itself as subjective in relation to the objective and
substantial. Hence the Idea is this totality, and the Idea

which knows itself is essentially different from the substantial; the former manifests itself independently, but in such a manner that as such it is considered to be for itself substantial. The subjective Idea is at first only formal, but it is the real possibility of the substantial and of the potentially universal; its end is to realize itself and to identify itself with substance. Through this subjectivity and negative unity, and through this absolute negativity, the ideal becomes no longer our object merely, but object to itself, and this principle has taken effect in the world of Christianity. Thus in the modern point of view the subject is for itself free, man is free as man, and from this comes the idea that because he is Mind he has from his very nature the eternal quality of being substantial. God becomes known as Mind which appears to itself as double, yet removes the difference that it may in it be for and at home with itself. The business of the world, taking it as a whole, is to become reconciled with Mind, recognizing itself therein, and this business is assigned to the Teutonic world.

The first beginning of this undertaking is found in the Religion which is the contemplation of and faith in this principle as in an actual existence before a knowledge of the principle has been arrived at. In the Christian Religion this principle is found more as feeling and idea; in it man as man is destined to everlasting bliss, and is an object of divine grace, pity and interest, which is as much as saying that man has an absolute and infinite value. We find it further in that dogma revealed through Christ to men, of the unity of the divine and human nature, according to which the subjective and the objective Idea—man and God —are one. This, in another form, is found in the old story of the Fall, in which the serpent did not delude man, for God said, "Behold, Adam has become as one of us, to know good and evil." We have to deal with this unity of subjective principle and of substance; it constitutes the process of Mind that this individual one or independent existence of subject should put aside its immediate character and bring itself forth as identical with the substantial. Such an aim is pronounced to be the highest end attainable by man. We see from this that religious ideas and speculation are not so far asunder as was at first believed, and I maintain these ideas in order that we may not be ashamed of them, seeing that we still belong to them, and so that if we do get beyond them, we may not be ashamed of our progenitors of the early Christian times, who held these ideas in such high esteem.

The first principle of that Philosophy which has taken its place in Christendom is thus found in the existence of two totalities. This is a reduplication of substance which now, however, is characterized by the fact that the two totalities are no longer external to one another, but are clearly both required through their relation to one another. If formerly Stoicism and Epicureanism, whose negativity was Scepticism, came forth as independent, and if finally the implicitly existent universality of both was established, these moments are now known as separate totalities, and yet in their opposition they have to be thought of as one. We have here the true speculative Idea, the Notion in its determinations, each of which is brought into a totality and clearly relates to the other. We thus have really two Ideas, the subjective Idea as knowledge, and then the substantial and concrete Idea; and the development and perfection of this principle and its coming to the consciousness of Thought, is the subject treated by modern Philosophy. Thus the determinations are in it more concrete than with the ancients. This opposition in which the two sides culminate, grasped in its widest significance, is the opposition between Thought and Being, individuality and substance, so that in the subject himself his freedom stands once more within the bounds of necessity; it is the opposition between subject and object, and between Nature and Mind, in so far as this last as finite stands in opposition to Nature.

The Greek Philosophy is free from restraint because it does not yet have regard to the opposition between Being and Thought, but proceeds from the unconscious presupposition that Thought is also Being. Certainly certain stages in the Greek Philosophy are laid hold of which seem to stand on the same platform as the Christian philosophies. Thus when we see, for instance, in the Philosophy of the Sophists, the new Academics, and the Sceptics, that they maintain the doctrine that the truth is not capable of being known, they might appear to accord with the later subjective philosophies in asserting that all thought-determinations were only subjective in character, and that hence from these no conclusions could be arrived at as regards what is objective. But there is really a difference. In the case of ancient philosophies, which said that we know only the phenomenal, everything is confined to that; it is as regards practical life that the new Academy and the Sceptics also admitted the possibility of conducting oneself rightly, morally and rationally, when one adopts the phenomenal as one's rule and guide in life. But though it is the phenomenal that lies at the foundation of things, it is not asserted that there is likewise a knowledge of the true and existent, as in the case of the merely subjective idealists of a more modern day. These last still keep in the background a potentiality, a beyond which cannot be known through thought or through conception. This other knowledge is an immediate knowledge—a faith in, a view of, and a yearning after, the beyond such as was evinced by Jacobi. The ancients have no such yearning: on the contrary, they have perfect satisfaction and rest in the certitude that only that which appears is for Knowledge. Thus it is necessary in this respect to keep strictly to the point of view from which we start, else through the similarity of the results, we come to see in that old Philosophy all the determinate character of modern subjectivity. Since in the simplicity of ancient philosophy the phenomenal was itself the only sphere, doubts as to objective thought were not present to it.

The opposition defined, the two sides of which are in modern times really related to one another as totalities, also has the form of an opposition between reason and faith, between individual perception and the objective truth which must be taken without reason of one's own, and even with a complete disregard for such reason. This is faith as understood by the church, or faith in the modern sense, i.e. a rejection of reason in favour of an inward revelation, called a direct certainty or perception, or an implicit and intuitive feeling. The opposition between this knowledge, which has first of all to develop itself, and that knowledge which has already developed itself inwardly, arouses a peculiar interest. In both cases the unity of thought or subjectivity and of Truth or objectivity is manifested, only in the first form it is said that the natural man knows the Truth since he intuitively believes it, while in the second form the unity of knowledge and Truth is shown, but in such a way that the subject raises itself above the immediate form of sensuous consciousness and reaches the Truth first of all through Thought.

The final end is to think the Absolute as Mind, as the Universal, that which, when the infinite bounty of the Notion in its reality freely emits its determinations from itself, wholly impresses itself upon and imparts itself to them, so that they may be indifferently outside of or in conflict with one another, but so that these totalities are one only, not alone implicitly, (which would simply be our reflection) but explicitly identical, the determinations of their difference being thus explicitly merely ideal. Hence if the starting-point of the history of Philosophy can be expressed by saying that God is comprehended as the immediate and not yet developed universality, and that its end—the grasping of the Absolute as Mind through the two and a half thousand years' work of the thus far inert world-spirit—is the end of our time, it makes it easy for us from one determination to go on through the manifestation of its needs, to others. Yet in the course of history this is difficult.

We thus have altogether two philosophies—the Greek and the Teutonic. As regards the latter we must distinguish the time when Philosophy made its formal appearance as Philosophy and the period of formation and of preparation for modern times. We may first begin Teutonic philosophy where it appears in proper form as Philosophy. Between the first period and those more recent, comes, as an intermediate period, that fermentation of a new Philosophy which on the one side keeps within the substantial and real existence and does not arrive at form, while on the other side, it perfects Thought, as the bare form of a presupposed truth, until it again knows itself as the free ground and source of Truth. Hence the history of Philosophy falls into three periods—that of the Greek Philosophy, the Philosophy of the Middle Ages and the modern Philosophy. Of these the first is speaking generally, regulated by Thought, the second falls into the opposition between existence and formal reflection, but the third has the Notion as its ground. This must not be taken to mean that the first contains Thought alone; it also has conceptions and ideas, just as the latter begins from abstract thoughts which yet constitute a duality.

First Period.—This commences at the time of Thales, about 600 B.C., and goes on to the coming to maturity of the Neoplatonic philosophy with Plotinus in the third century; from thence to its further progress and development with Proclus in the fifth century until the time when all philosophy was extinguished. The Neo-platonic philosophy then made its entrance into Christianity later on, and many philosophies within Christianity have this philosophy as their only groundwork. This is a space of time extending to about 1000 years, the end of which coincides with the migration of the nations and the decline of the Roman Empire.

Second Period.—The second period is that of the Middle Ages. The Scholastics are included in it, and Arabians and Jews are also historically to be noticed, but this philosophy mainly falls within the Christian Church. This period is of something over 1000 years' duration.

Third Period.—The Philosophy of modern times made its first independent appearance after the Thirty Years' War, with Bacon, Jacob Böhm and Descartes; it begins with the distinction contained in : *cogito ergo sum.* This period is one of a couple of centuries and the philosophy is consequently still somewhat modern.

2. Sources of the History of Philosophy.

We have to seek for sources of another kind in this than in political history. There historians are the fountainheads, which again have as sources the deeds and sayings of individuals ; and the historians who are not original have over and above performed their work at secondhand. But historians always have the deeds already present in history, that is to say, here brought into the form of ordinary conception ; for the name of history has two meanings : it signifies on the one hand the deeds and events themselves, and on the other, it denotes them in so far as they are formed through conception for conception. In the history of Philosophy there are, on the contrary, not any sources which can be derived from historians, but the deeds themselves lie before us, and these—the philosophic operations themselves—are the true sources. If we wish to study the history of Philosophy in earnest, we must go to such springs as these. Yet these operations form too wide a field to permit of our keeping to it alone in this history.

In the case of many philosophers it is absolutely necessary to confine oneself to the original authors, but in many periods, in which we cannot obtain original sources, seeing that they have not been preserved to us, (as, for instance, in that of the older Greek philosophy) we must certainly confine our attention simply to historians and other writers. There are other periods, too, where it is desirable that others should have read the works of the philosophers and that we should receive abstracts therefrom. Several schoolmen have left behind them works of sixteen, twenty-four and twenty-six folios, and hence we must in their case confine ourselves to the researches of others. Many philosophic works are also rare and hence difficult to obtain. Many philosophers are for the most part important from an historic or literary point of view only, and hence we may limit ourselves to the compilations in which they are dealt with. The most noteworthy works on the history of Philosophy are, however, the following, regarding which I refer for particulars to the summary of Tennemann's History of Philosophy, by A. Wendt, since I do not wish to give any complete list.

1. One of the first Histories of Philosophy, which is only interesting as an attempt, is the "History of Philosophy," by Thomas Stanley (London, 1655, folio ed. III., 1701. 4. translated into Latin by Godofr. Olearius, Lipsiæ, 1711, 4). This history is no longer much used, and only contains the old philosophic schools in the form of sects and as if no new ones had existed. That is to say, it keeps to the old belief commonly held at that time, that there only were ancient philosophies and that the period of philosophy came to an end with Christianity, as if Philosophy were something belonging to heathendom and the truth only could be found in Christianity. In it a distinction was drawn between Truth as it is created from the natural reason in the ancient philosophies, and the revealed truth of the Christian religion, in which there was

consequently no longer any Philosophy. In the time of
the Revival of Learning there certainly were no proper
philosophies, and above all in Stanley's time systems of
Philosophy proper were too young for the older generations
to have the amount of respect for them necessary to allow
of their being esteemed as realities.

2. *Jo. Jac. Bruckeri Historia critica philosophiæ Lipsiæ,*
1742—1744, four parts, or five volumes in four, for the
fourth part has two volumes. The second edition, unaltered,
but with the addition of a supplement, 1766—1767, four
parts in six quartos, the last of which forms the supplement.
This is an immense compilation which is not formed straight
from the original sources, but is mixed with. reflections
after the manner of the times. As we have seen from an
example above (p. 43) the accounts given are in the highest
degree inaccurate. Brucker's manner of procedure is entirely
unhistoric, and yet nowhere ought we to proceed in a more
historic manner than in the history of Philosophy. This
work is thus simply so much useless ballast. An epitome of
the same is *Jo. Jac. Bruckeri Institutiones historiæ philoso-
phicæ, usui academicæ juventutis adornatæ. Lipsiæ,* 1747,
8; second edition, Leipzig, 1756; third edition prepared
by Born, Leipzig, 1790, 8.

3. Dietrich Tiedmann's *Geist der Speculativen Philosophie,* Marburg, 1791—1797, 6 vols., 8. He treats of political
history diffusely, but without any life, and the language is
stiff and affected. The whole work is a melancholy example
of how a learned professor can occupy his whole life with
the study of speculative philosophy, and yet have no idea at
all of speculation. His *argumenta* to the Plato of Brucker
are of the same description. In every history he makes
abstracts from the philosophers so long as they keep to
mere ratiocination, but when the speculative is arrived
at, he becomes irate, declaring it all to be composed of
empty subtleties, and stops short with the words " we know
better." His merit is that he has supplied valuable abstracts

from rare books belonging to the Middle Ages and from cabalistic and mystical works of that time.

4. Joh. Gottlieb Buhle : *Lehrbuch der Geschichte der Philosophie und einer kritischen Literatur derselben.* Göttingen, 1796 to 1804. Eight parts, 8. Ancient philosophy is treated with disproportionate brevity ; the further Buhle went on, the more particular he became. He has many good summaries of rare works, as for instance those of Giordano Bruno, which were in the Göttingen Library.

5. Wilh. Gottl. Tennemann's *Geschichte der Philosophie,* Leipzig, 1798—1819, eleven parts, 8. The eighth part, the Scholastic Philosophy, occupies two volumes. The philosophies are fully described, and the more modern times are better done than the ancient. The philosophies of recent times are easier to describe, since it is only necessary to make an abstract or to interpret straight on, for the thoughts contained in them lie nearer to ours. It is otherwise with the ancient philosophers, because they stand in another stage of the Notion, and on this account they are likewise more difficult to grasp. That is to say, what is old is easily overthrown by something else more familiar to us, and where Tennemann comes across such he is almost useless. In Aristotle, for instance, the misinterpretation is so great, that Tennemann foists upon him what is directly opposite to his beliefs, and thus from the adoption of the opposite to what Tennemann asserts to be Aristotle's opinion, a correct idea of Aristotelian philosophy is arrived at. Tennemann is then candid enough to place the reference to Aristotle underneath the text, so that the original and the interpretation often contradict one another. Tennemann thinks that it is really the case that the historian should have no philosophy, and he glories in that ; yet he really has a system and he is a critical philosopher. He praises philosophers, their work and their genius, and yet the end of the lay is that all of them will be pronounced to be wanting in that they have one defect, which is not to

be Kantian philosophers and not yet to have sought the
source of knowledge. From this the result is that the Truth
could not be known.

Of compendiums, three have to be noticed. 1. Frederick
Aft's *Grundriss einer Geschichte der Philosophie.* (Landshut
1807, 8 ; second edition, 1825) is written from a better point
of view ; the Philosophy is that of Schelling for the most
part, but it is somewhat confused. Aft by some formal
method has distinguished ideal philosophy from real. 2.
Professor Wendt's Göttingen edition of Tennemann (fifth
edition, Leipzig, 1828, 8). It is astonishing to see what
is represented as being Philosophy, without any consideration as to whether it has any meaning or not. Such so-
called new philosophies grow like mushrooms out of the
ground. There is nothing easier than to comprehend in
harmony with a principle ; but it must not be thought that
hence something new and profound has been accomplished.
3. Rirner's *Handbuch der Geschichte der Philosophie,* 3
vols., Sulzbach, 1822—1823, 8 (second amended edition,
1829) is most to be commended, and yet I will not assert
that it answers all the requirements of a History of Philosophy. There are many points which leave much to desire,
but the appendices to each volume in which the principal
original authorities are quoted, are particularly excellent
for their purpose. Selected extracts, more specially from
the ancient philosophers, are needed, and these would not
be lengthy, since there are not very many passages to be
given from the philosophers before Plato.

3. METHOD OF TREATMENT ADOPTED IN THIS HISTORY OF PHILOSOPHY.

As regards external history I shall only touch upon that
which is the concern of universal history, the spirit or the
principle of the times, and hence I will treat of conditions
of life in reference to the outstanding philosophers. Of
philosophies, however, only those are to be made mention

of the principles of which have caused some sensation, and through which science has made an advance; hence I shall put aside many names which would be taken up in a learned treatise, but which are of little value in respect to Philosophy. The history of the dissemination of a doctrine, its fate, those who have merely taught a particular doctrine, I pass over, as the deduction of the whole world from one particular principle.

The demand that in Philosophy an historian should have no system, should put into the philosophy nothing of his own, nor assail it with his ideas, seems a plausible one. The history of Philosophy should show just this impartiality, and it seems in so far that to give only summaries of the philosophers proves a success. He who understands nothing of the matter, and has no system, but merely historic knowledge, will certainly be impartial. But political history has to be carefully distinguished from the history of Philosophy. That is to say, though in the former, one is not indeed at liberty to limit oneself to representing the events chronologically only, one can yet keep to what is entirely objective, as is done in the Homeric epic. Thus Herodotus and Thucydides, as free men, let the objective world do freely and independently as it would; they have added nothing of their own, neither have they taken and judged before their tribunal the actions which they represented. Yet even in political history there is also a particular end kept in view. In Livy the main points are the Roman rule, its enlargement, and the perfecting of the constitution; we see Rome arise, defend itself, and exercise its mastery. It is thus that the self-developing reason in the history of Philosophy makes of itself an end, and this end is not foreign or imported, but is the matter itself, which lies at the basis as universal, and with which the individual forms of themselves correspond. Thus when the history of Philosophy has to tell of deeds in history, we first ask, what a deed in Philosophy is, and whether any particular thing is philosophic or not. In external history everything is in action—certainly there is in it what is important and that which is unimportant—but action is the idea immediately placed before us. This is not the case in Philosophy, and on this account the history of Philosophy cannot be treated throughout without the introduction of the historian's views.

PART ONE

GREEK PHILOSOPHY

INTRODUCTION

THE name of Greece strikes home to the hearts of men of education in Europe, and more particularly is this so with us Germans. Europeans have taken their religion, the life to come, the far-off land, from a point somewhat further off than Greece—they took it from the East, and more especially from Syria. But the here, the present, art and science, that which in giving liberty to our spiritual life, gives it dignity as it likewise bestows upon it ornament, we know to have proceeded from Greece either directly or indirectly—through the circuitous road of Rome. The latter of these two ways was the earlier form in which this culture came to us; it also came from the formerly universal church which derived its origin as such from Rome, and has retained its speech even until now. The sources of authority in addition to the Latin Gospels have been the Fathers. Our law, too, boasts of deriving its most perfect forms from Rome. Teutonic strength of mind has required to pass through the hard discipline of the church and law which came to us from Rome, and to be kept in check; it is in this way that the European character first obtained its pliability and capacity for freedom. Thus it was after European manhood came to be at home with itself and to look upon the present, that the historical and that which is of foreign derivation was given. When man began to be at home with himself, he turned to the Greeks to find enjoyment in it. Let us leave the Latin and the Roman to the church and to jurisprudence. Higher, freer philosophic science, as also the beauty of our untrammelled art, the taste for, and love of the same, we know to have taken their root in Greek life and to have created therefrom their spirit. If we were to have an aspiration, it would be for such a land and such conditions.

But what makes us specially at home with the Greeks is that they made their world their home; the common spirit of homeliness unites us both. In ordinary life we like best the men and families that are homely and contented in themselves, not desiring what is outside and above them, and so it is with the Greeks. They certainly received the substantial beginnings of their religion, culture, their common bonds of fellowship, more or less from Asia, Syria and Egypt; but they have so greatly obliterated the foreign nature of this origin, and it is so much changed, worked upon, turned round, and altogether made so different, that what they, as we, prize, know, and love in it, is essentially their own. For this reason, in the history of Greek life, when we go further back and seem constrained so to go back, we find we may do without this retrogression and follow within the world and manners of the Greeks, the beginnings, the germination and the progress of art and science up to their maturity, even seeing the origin of their decay—and this completely comprehended within their own range. For their spiritual development requires that which is received or foreign, as matter or stimulus only; in such they have known and borne themselves as men that were free. The form which they have given to the foreign principle is this characteristic breath of spirituality, the spirit of freedom and of beauty which can in the one aspect be regarded as form, but which in another and higher sense is simply substance.

They have thus not only themselves created the substantial in their culture and made their existence their own, but they have also held in reverence this their spiritual rebirth, which is their real birth. The foreign origin they have so to speak thanklessly forgotten, putting it in the background—perhaps burying it in the darkness of the mysteries which they have kept secret from themselves. They have not only done this, that is they have not only used and enjoyed all that they have brought forth and formed, but they have become aware of and thankfully and joyfully placed before themselves this at-homeness [Heimathlichkeit] in their whole existence, the ground and origin of themselves, not merely existing in it, possessing and making use of it. For their mind, when transformed in this spiritual new birth, is just the living in their life, and also the becoming conscious of that life as it has become actual. They represent their existence as an object apart from themselves, which manifests itself independently and which in its independence is of value to them ; hence they have made for themselves a history of everything which they have possessed and have been. Not only have they represented the beginning of the world—that is, of gods and men, the earth, the heavens, the wind, mountains and rivers—but also of all aspects of their existence, such as the introduction of fire and the offerings connected with it, the crops, agriculture, the olive, the horse, marriage, property, laws, arts, worship, the sciences, towns, princely races, &c. Of all these it is pleasingly represented through tales how they have arisen in history as their own work.

It is in this veritable homeliness, or, more accurately, in the spirit of homeliness, in this spirit of ideally being-at-home-with-themselves in their physical, corporate, legal, moral and political existence ; it is in the beauty and the freedom of their character in history, making what they are to be also a sort of Mnemosyne with them, that the kernel of thinking liberty rests ; and hence it was requisite that Philosophy should arise amongst them.

Philosophy is being at home with self, just like the homeliness of the Greek; it is man's being at home in his
mind, at home with himself.   If we are at home with the
Greeks, we must be at home more particularly in their
Philosophy; not, however, simply as it is with them, for
Philosophy is at home with itself, and we have to do with
Thought, with what is most specially ours, and with what is
free from all particularity.   The development and unfolding
of thought has taken place with them from its earliest
beginning, and in order to comprehend their Philosophy
we may remain with them without requiring to seek for
further and external influences.

But we must specify more particularly their character
and point of view.   The Greeks have a starting-point in
history as truly as they have arisen from out of themselves :
this starting-point, comprehended in thought, is the
oriental substantiality of the natural unity between the
spiritual and the natural.   To start from the self, to live
in the self, is the other extreme of abstract subjectivity, when it is still empty, or rather has made
itself to be empty; such is pure formalism, the abstract
principle of the modern world.   The Greeks stand between
both these extremes in the happy medium; this therefore is
the medium of beauty, seeing that it is both natural and
spiritual, but yet that the spiritual still remains the governing,
determining subject.   Mind immersed in nature is in substantial unity with it, and in so far as it is consciousness, it
is essentially sensuous perception : as subjective consciousness it is certainly form-giving though it is devoid of measure.   For the Greeks, the substantial unity of nature and
spirit was a fundamental principle, and thus being in the
possession and knowledge of this, yet not being overwhelmed
in it, but having retired into themselves, they have avoided
the extreme of formal subjectivity, and are still in unity
with themselves.   Thus it is a free subject which still possesses that original unity in content, essence and substratum,

and fashions its object into beauty. The stage reached by Greek consciousness is the stage of beauty. For beauty is the ideal; it is the thought which is derived from Mind, but in such a way that the spiritual individuality is not yet explicit as abstract subjectivity that has then in itself to perfect its existence into a world of thought. What is natural and sensuous still pertains to this subjectivity, but yet the natural form has not equal dignity and rank with the other, nor is it predominant as is the case in the East. The principle of the spiritual now stands first in rank, and natural existence has no further value for itself, in its existent forms, being the mere expression of the Mind shining through, and having been reduced to be the vehicle and form of its existence. Mind, however, has not yet got itself as a medium whereby it can represent itself in itself, and from which it can form its world.

Thus free morality could and necessarily did find a place in Greece, for the spiritual substance of freedom was here the principle of morals, laws and constitutions. Because the natural element is, however, still contained in it, the form taken by the morality of the state is still affected by what is natural; the states are small individuals in their natural condition, which could not unite themselves into one whole. Since the universal does not exist in independent freedom, that which is spiritual still is limited. In the Greek world what is potentially and actually eternal is realized and brought to consciousness through Thought; but in such a way that subjectivity confronts it in a determination which is still accidental, because it is still essentially related to what is natural; and in this we find the reason as promised above, for the fact that in Greece the few alone are free.

The measureless quality of substance in the East is brought, by means of the Greek mind, into what is measurable and limited; it is clearness, aim, limitation of forms, the reduction of what is measureless, and of infinite splendour and

riches, to determinateness and individuality. The riches of
the Greek world consist only of an infinite quantity of
beautiful, lovely and pleasing individualities in the serenity
which pervades all existence; those who are greatest
amongst the Greeks are the individualities, the connoisseurs
in art, poetry, song, science, integrity and virtue. If the
serenity of the Greeks, their beautiful gods, statues, and
temples, as well as their serious work, their institutions and
acts, may seem—compared to the splendour and sublimity,
the colossal forms of oriental imagination, the Egyptian
buildings of Eastern kingdoms—to be like child's play,
this is the case yet more with the thought that comes into
existence here. Such thought puts a limit on this wealth
of individualities as on the oriental greatness, and reduces
it into its one simple soul, which, however, is in itself the
first source of the opulence of a higher ideal world, of the
world of Thought.

"From out of thy passions, oh, man," exclaimed an
ancient, "thou hast derived the materials for thy gods,"
just as the Easterns, and especially the Indians, did from the
elements, powers and forms of Nature. One may add, " out
of Thought thou takest the element and material for God."
Thus Thought is the ground from which God comes forth,
but it is not Thought in its commencement that constitutes
the first principle from which all culture must be grasped.
It is quite the other way. In the beginning, thought comes
forth as altogether poor, abstract, and of a content which is
meagre in comparison to that given to his subject by the
oriental; for as immediate, the beginning is just in the form
of nature, and this it shares with what is oriental. Because it
thus reduces the content of the East to determinations which
are altogether poor, these thoughts are scarcely worth observation on our part, since they are not yet proper thoughts,
neither being in the form of, or determined as thought, but
belonging really to Nature. Thus Thought is the Absolute,
though not as Thought. That is, we have always two

things to distinguish, the universal or the Notion, and the reality of this universal, for the question here arises as to whether the reality is itself Thought or Nature. We find in the fact that reality at first has still the immediate form and is only Thought potentially, the reason for commencing with the Greeks and from the natural philosophy of the Ionic school.

As regards the external and historical condition of Greece at this time, Greek philosophy commences in the sixth century before Christ in the time of Cyrus, and in the period of decline in the Ionic republics in Asia Minor. Just because this world of beauty which raised itself into a higher kind of culture went to pieces, Philosophy arose. Crœsus and the Lydians first brought Ionic freedom into jeopardy; later on the Persians were those who destroyed it altogether, so that the greater part of the inhabitants sought other spots and created colonies, more particularly in the West. At the time of the decline in Ionic towns, the other Greece ceased to be under its ancient lines of kings; the Pelopideans and the other, and for the most part foreign, princely races had passed away. Greece had in many ways come into touch with the outside world and the Greek inhabitants likewise sought within themselves for a bond of fellowship. The patriarchal life was past, and in many states it came to be a necessity that they should constitute themselves as free, organized and regulated by law. Many individuals come into prominence who were no more rulers of their fellow-citizens by descent, but who were by means of talent, power of imagination and scientific knowledge, marked out and reverenced, and such individuals came into many different relations with their fellows. Part of them became advisers, but their advice was frequently not followed; part of them were hated and despised by their fellow-citizens, and they drew back from public affairs; others became violent, if not fierce governors of the other citizens, and others again finally became the administrators of liberty.

Amongst these men just characterized, the seven sages
—in modern times excluded from the history of Philosophy—take their place. In as far as they may be
reckoned as milestones in the history of Philosophy, something about their character should, in the commencement of Philosophy, be shortly said. They came into
prominence, partly as taking part in the battles of
the Ionic towns, partly as expatriated, and partly as
individuals of distinction in Greece. The names of the
seven are given differently : usually, however, as Thales,
Solon, Periander, Cleobulus, Chilon, Bias, Pittacus.
Hermippus in Diogenes Laertius (1, 42) specifies seventeen,
and, amongst these, various people pick out seven in various
ways. According to Diogenes Laertius (1, 41) Dicæarchus,
who came still earlier in history, only names four, and these
are placed amongst the seven by all; they are Thales, Bias,
Pittacus and Solon. Besides these, Myson, Anacharsis,
Acusilaus, Epimenides, Pherecydes, &c., are mentioned.
Dicæarchus in Diogenes (1, 40), says of them that they are
neither wise men (σοφούς) nor philosophers, but men of
understanding (συνετούς) and law-givers ; this judgment
has become the universal one and is held to be just. They
come in a period of transition amongst the Greeks—a transition from a patriarchal system of kings into one of law or
force. The fame of the wisdom of these men depends, on
the one hand, on the fact that they grasped the practical
essence of consciousness, or the consciousness of universal
morality as it is in and for itself, giving expression to
it in the form of moral maxims and in part in civil laws,
making these actual in the state ; on the other hand it
depends on their having, in theoretic form, expressed the
same in witty sayings. Some of these sayings could not
merely be regarded as thoughtful or good reflections, but in
so far, as philosophic and speculative ; they have a comprehensive, universal significance ascribed to them, which,
however, does not explain them. These men have not

really made science and Philosophy their aim; it is expressly said of Thales that it was in the latter part of his life that he first took to Philosophy. What had relation to politics appeared most frequently; they were practical men, men of affairs, but not in our sense of the word; with us practical activity devotes itself to a special line of administration or to a particular business, or to economics, &c. They lived in democratic states and thus shared the responsibilities of the general administration and rule. They were not statesmen like the great Greek personalities, like Miltiades, Themistocles, Pericles and Demosthenes, but they were statesmen in a time when safety, preservation and, indeed, the whole well-being, disposition and well nigh the very foundation of civic life were in question; and certainly when this was so with the foundations of legally established institutions.

Thales and Bias thus appear as the representatives of the Ionic towns. Herodotus (I. 169—171) speaks of both, and says of Thales that he advised even before the overthrow of the Ionians (apparently through Crœsus), that they should constitute a supreme council (ἐν βουλευτήριον) in Teos, in the centre of the Ionian people, and thus make a federal state with a capital and principal federal town, so that they might still remain separate nations (δῆμοι) as before. However, they did not follow this advice, and this isolated and weakened them, and the result was their conquest; it has always been a difficult thing for the Greeks to give up their individuality. Later on, when Harpagus, the general of Cyrus who accomplished their overthrow, pressed in upon them, the Ionians took no better the most excellent advice of Bias of Priene, given them at the decisive moment when they were assembled at Panionium, " to go in a common fleet to Sardinia, there to found an Ionic state. By so doing they would escape servitude, be happy, and, inhabiting the largest island, subdue the others. But if they remained in Ionia there was no hope of liberty to be seen for them." Herodotus gives his corroboration to this advice—" If they had followed him they would have been the happiest of Greeks." Such things take place, but through force and not voluntarily.

We find the other sages under similar conditions. Solon was an administrator in Athens, and thereby became famous; few men have attained the honourable position of being a law-giver. Solon shares it with Moses, Lycurgus, Zaleucus, Numa, &c., alone. No individuals can be found amongst Teutonic peoples who possess the distinction of being the law-givers of their people. Nowadays there can be law-givers no longer ; legal institutions and regulations are in modern times always ready to hand, and the little that can still be done by means of the law-giver and by law-making assemblies is simply the further modification of details or making very insignificant additions. What is dealt with is the compilation, wording and perfecting of the particular only ; and yet neither Solon and Lycurgus did more than respectively bring the Ionic mind and the Doric character—being that which had been given them and which was implicitly present—into the form of conscious-ness, and obviate the temporary inconvenience of disorder through effective laws. Solon was thus not a perfect statesman ; this is manifest from the sequel of his history. A constitution which allowed Pisistratus in Solon's own time to raise himself into the Tyranny, showing itself to be so destitute of strength and organization that it could not prevent its own overthrow, (and by what a power !) manifests some inward want. This may seem strange, for a constitution must be able to afford resistance to such an attack. But let us see what Pisistratus did.

What the so-called tyrants really were, is most clearly shown by the relation borne by Solon to Pisistratus. When orderly institutions and laws were necessary to the Greeks, we find law-givers and regents of states appearing, who laid down laws, and ruled accordingly. The law, as universal, seemed and still seems now to the individual to be force, inasmuch as he does not have regard to or comprehend the law : it applies first to all the people, and then only, to the individual; it is essential first of all to use constraint until the individual attains discernment, and law to him becomes his law, and ceases to be something foreign. Most of the law-givers and administrators of states undertook themselves to constrain the people and to be their tyrants. In states where they did not undertake it, it had to be done by other individuals, for it was essential. According to Diogenes Laertius' account (I. 48—50), we find Solon—whom his friends advised to secure the mastery for himself since the people held to him (προςεῖχον), and would have liked to see him become tyrant—repulse them, and try to prevent any such occurrence, when he became suspicious of Pisistratus' intentions. What he did when he remarked upon the attitude of Pisistratus, was to come into the assembly of the people, and tell them the design of Pisistratus, accoutred in armour and shield; this was then unusual, for Thucydides (1, 6) makes it a distinguishing feature between Greeks and Barbarians, that the former, and pre-eminently the Athenians, put aside their arms in time of peace. He said, " Men of Athens, I am wiser than some and braver than others : I am wiser than those who do not see the deceit of Pisistratus, braver than those who certainly see it, but say nothing from fear." As he could not do anything, he left Athens. Pisistratus is said to have then written a most honourable letter to Solon in his absence, which Diogenes (I. 53, 54) has preserved for us, inviting him to return to Athens, and live with him as a free citizen. " Not only am I not the only one of the Greeks to have seized the tyranny, but I have not taken anything which was not my due, for I am of the race of Codrus. I have only taken back to myself what the Athenians swore they would preserve to Codrus and his race, and yet took from them. Moreover I am doing no evil toward gods and

men, but as thou hast given laws to the Athenians, I take
care (ἐπιτροπῶ) that in civil life they shall carry them out
(πολιτεύειν.)" His son Hippias did the same. "And these
relations are carried out better than they would be in a
democracy, for I allow nobody to do evil (ὑβρίζειν), and as
Tyrant, I lay claim to no more (πλεῖόν τι φέρομαι) than
such consideration and respect and specified gifts
(τὰ ῥητὰ γέρα) as would have been offered to the kings
in earlier times. Every Athenian gives the tenth part
of his revenue, not to me, but towards the cost of
the public offering, and besides for the commonwealth,
and for use in case of war. I am not angry that thou
hast disclosed my project. For thou didst it more out
of love to the people than hate against me, and because
thou didst not know how I would conduct my rule. For
if thou hadst known this, thou wouldst have submitted
to it willingly, and wouldst not have taken flight;" and
so he goes on. Solon, in the answer given by Diogenes,
(I. 66, 67) says, that he "has not a personal grudge against
Pisistratus, and he must call him the best of tyrants; but
to turn back does not befit him. For he made equality of
rights essential in the Athenian constitution, and himself
refused the tyranny. By his return he would condone
what was done by Pisistratus." The rule of Pisistratus
accustomed the Athenians to the laws of Solon, and brought
them into usage, so that after this usage came to be
general, supremacy was superfluous; his sons were hence
driven out of Athens, and for the first time the constitution of Solon upheld itself. Solon undoubtedly gave the
laws, but it is another thing to make such regulations
effectual in the manners, habits and life of a people. What
was separate in Solon and Pisistratus, we find united in
Periander in Corinth, and Pittacus in Mitilene.

This may be enough about the outward life of the seven
sages. They are also famed for the wisdom of the sayings
which have been preserved to us; these sayings seem in

great measure, however, to be superficial and hackneyed. The reason for this is found in the fact that, to our reflection, general propositions are quite usual; much in the Proverbs of Solomon seems to us to be superficial and commonplace for the same reason. But it is quite another thing to bring to the ordinary conception for the first time this same universal in the form of universality. Many distichs are ascribed to Solon which we still retain; their object is to express in maxims general obligations towards the gods, the family and the country. Diogenes (I. 58) tells us that Solon said: "Laws are like a spider's web; the small are caught, the great tear it up: speech is the image of action," &c. Such sayings are not philosophy, but general reflections, the expression of moral duties, maxims, necessary determinations. The wisdom of the sages is of this kind; many sayings are insignificant, but many seem to be more insignificant than they are. For instance, Chilon says: "Stand surety, and evil awaits thee" ($\dot{\epsilon}\gamma\gamma\acute{\nu}a$, $\pi\acute{a}\rho a$ δ' $\mathring{a}\tau a$). On the one hand this is quite a common rule of life and prudence, but the sceptics gave to this proposition a much higher universal significance, which is also accredited to Chilon. This sense is, "Ally thyself closely to any particular thing, and unhappiness will fall upon thee." The sceptics adduced this proposition independently, as demonstrating the principle of scepticism, which is that nothing is finite and definite in and for itself, being only a fleeting, vacillating phase which does not last. Cleobulus says, $\mu\acute{\epsilon}\tau\rho o\nu$ $\mathring{a}\rho\iota\sigma\tau o\nu$, another $\mu\eta\delta\grave{\epsilon}\nu$ $\mathring{a}\gamma a\nu$, and this has likewise a universal significance which is that limitation, the $\pi\acute{\epsilon}\rho a\varsigma$ of Plato as opposed to the $\mathring{a}\pi\epsilon\iota\rho o\nu$—the self-determined as opposed to undetermined—is what is best; and thus it is that in Being limit or measure is the highest determination.

One of the most celebrated sayings is that of Solon in his conversation with Crœsus, which Herodotus (I. 30—33) has in his own way given us very fully. The result arrived at is this :—" Nobody is to be esteemed happy before his death." But the noteworthy point in this narrative is that from it we can get a better idea of the standpoint of Greek reflection in the time of Solon. We see that happiness is put forward as the highest aim, that which is most to be desired and which is the end of man ; before Kant, morality, as eudæmonism, was based on the determination of happiness. In Solon's sayings there is an advance over the sensuous enjoyment which is merely pleasant to the feelings. Let us ask what happiness is and what there is within it for reflection, and we find that it certainly carries with it a certain satisfaction to the individual, of whatever sort it be—whether obtained through physical enjoyment or spiritual—the means of obtaining which lie in men's own hands. But the fact is further to be observed that not every sensuous, immediate pleasure can be laid hold of, for happiness contains a reflection on the circumstances as a whole, in which we have the principle to which the principle of isolated enjoyment must give way. Eudæmonism signifies happiness as a condition for the whole of life ; it sets up a totality of enjoyment which is a universal and a rule for individual enjoyment, in that it does not allow it to give way to what is momentary, but restrains desires and sets a universal standard before one's eyes. If we contrast it with Indian philosophy, we find eudæmonism to be antagonistic to it. There the liberation of the soul from what is corporeal, the perfect abstraction, the necessity that the soul shall, in its simplicity, be at home with itself, is the final end of man. With the Greeks the opposite is the case ; the satisfaction there is also satisfaction of the soul, but it is not attained through flight, abstraction, withdrawal within self, but through satisfaction in the present, concrete satisfaction in relation to the surroundings. The stage of reflection that we reach in happiness, stands midway between mere desire and the other extreme, which is right as right and duty as duty. In happiness, the individual enjoyment has disappeared ; the form of universality is there, but the universal does not yet come forth on its own account, and this is the issue of the conversation between Crœsus and Solon. Man as thinking, is not solely engrossed with present enjoyment, but also with the means for obtaining that to come. Crœsus points out to him these means, but Solon still objects to the statement of the question of Crœsus. For in order that any one should be conceived of as happy, we must await his death, for happiness depends upon his condition to the end, and upon the fact that his death should be a pious one and be consistent with his higher destiny. Because the life of Crœsus had not yet expired, Solon could not deem him happy. And the history of Crœsus bears evidence that no momentary state deserves the name of happiness. This edifying history holds in its embrace the whole standpoint of the reflection of that time.

In the consideration of Greek philosophy we have now to distinguish further three important periods :—in the first place the period from Thales to Aristotle ; secondly, Greek philosophy in the Roman world ; thirdly, the Neo-platonic philosophy.

1. We begin with thought, as it is in a quite abstract, natural or sensuous form, and we proceed from this to the Idea as determined. This first period shows the beginning of philosophic thought, and goes on to its development and perfection as a totality of knowledge in itself ; this takes place in Aristotle as representing the unity of what has come before. In Plato there is just such a union of what came earlier, but it is not worked out, for he only represents the Idea generally. The Neo-platonists have been called eclectics, and Plato was said to have brought about the unity ; they were not, however, eclectics, but they had a conscious insight into the necessity for uniting these philosophies.

2. After the concrete Idea was reached, it came forth as if in opposites, perfecting and developing itself. The second period is that in which science breaks itself up into

different systems. A one-sided principle is carried through the whole conception of the world; each side is in itself formed into a totality, and stands in the relation of one extreme to another. The philosophical systems of Stoicism and Epicureanism are such; scepticism forms the negative to their dogmatism, while the other philosophies disappear.

3. The third period is the affirmative, the withdrawal of the opposition into an ideal world or a world of thought, a divine world. This is the Idea developed into totality, which yet lacks subjectivity as the infinite being-for-self.

CHAPTER II

FIRST PERIOD, SECOND DIVISION

B.—SOCRATES.

Consciousness had reached this point in Greece, when in Athens the great form of Socrates, in whom the subjectivity of thought was brought to consciousness in a more definite and more thorough manner, now appeared. But Socrates did not grow like a mushroom out of the earth, for he stands in continuity with his time, and thus is not only a most important figure in the history of Philosophy—perhaps the most interesting in the philosophy of antiquity—but is also a world-famed personage. For a mental turning-point exhibited itself in him in the form of philosophic thought. If we shortly recall the periods already passed over, we find that the ancient Ionic philosophers certainly thought, but without reflecting on the thought or defining its product as thought. The Atomists made objective existence into thoughts, but these were to them only abstractions, pure entities. Anaxagoras, on the other hand, raised thought as

[1] Sext Empir. adv. Math. VII. 83, 84.

such, into a principle which thereby presented itself as the all-powerful Notion, as the negative power over all that is definite and existent. Protagoras finally expresses thought as real existence, but it is in this its movement, which is the all-resolving consciousness, the unrest of the Notion. This unrest is in itself at the same time something restful or secure. But the fixed point of motion as such, is the ' I,' for it has the moments of movement outside of it; as the self-retaining, which only abrogates what is different, the ' I ' is negative unity, but just in that very way individual, and not yet the universal reflected within itself. Now we here find the ambiguity of dialectic and sophistry, which rests in the fact that if the objective disappears, the signification of the fixed subjective is either that of the individual opposed to the objective, and thereby the contingent and lawless will, or that of the objective and universal in itself. Socrates expresses real existence as the universal ' I,' as the consciousness which rests in itself ; but that is the good as such, which is free from existent reality, free from individual sensuous consciousness of feeling and desire, free finally from the theoretically speculative thought about nature, which, if indeed thought, has still the form of Being and in which I am not certain of my existence.

Socrates herein adopted firstly the doctrine of Anaxagoras that thought, the understanding, is the ruling and self-determining universal, though this principle did not, as with the Sophists, attain the form of formal culture or of abstract philosophizing. Thus, if with Socrates, as with Protagoras, the self-conscious thought that abrogates all that is determined, was real existence, with Socrates this was the case in such a way that he at the same time grasped in thought rest and security. This substance existing in and for itself, the self-retaining, has become determined as end, and further as the true and the good.

To this determination of the universal, we have, in the second place, to add that this good, which has by me to be esteemed as substantial end, must be known by me; with this the infinite subjectivity, the freedom of self-consciousness in Socrates breaks out. This freedom which is contained therein, the fact that consciousness is clearly present in all that it thinks, and must necessarily be at home with itself, is in our time constantly and plainly demanded; the substantial, although eternal and in and for itself, must as truly be produced through me; but this my part in it is only the formal activity. Thus Socrates' principle is that man has to find from himself both the end of his actions and the end of the world, and must attain to truth through himself. True thought thinks in such a way that its import is as truly objective as subjective. But objectivity has been the significance of substantial universality, and not of external objectivity; thus truth is now posited as a product mediated through thought, while untrained morality, as Sophocles makes Antigone say (vers. 454—457), is "the eternal law of the Gods " :

" And no one knew from whence it came."

But though in modern times we hear much said of immediate knowledge and belief, it is a misconception to maintain that their content, God, the Good, Just, &c., although the content of feeling and conception, is not, as spiritual content, also posited through thought. The animal has no religion, because it only feels; but what is spiritual rests on the mediation of thought, and pertains to man.

Since Socrates thus introduces the infinitely important element of leading back the truth of the objective to the thought of the subject, just as Protagoras says that the objective first is through relation to us, the battle of Socrates and Plato with the Sophists cannot rest on the ground that these, as belonging to the old faith, maintained against the others the religion and customs of Greece, for the violation of which Anaxagoras was condemned. Quite the contrary. Reflection, and the reference of any judgment to consciousness, is held by Socrates in common with the Sophists. But the opposition into which Socrates and Plato were in their philosophy necessarily brought in regard to the Sophists, as the universal philosophic culture of the times, was as follows :—The objective produced through thought, is at the same time in and for itself, thus being raised above all particularity of interests and desires, and being the power over them. Hence because, on the one hand, to Socrates and Plato the moment of subjective freedom is the directing of consciousness into itself, on the other, this return is also determined as a coming out from particular subjectivity. It is hereby implied that contingency of events is abolished, and man has this outside within him, as the spiritual universal. This is the true, the unity of subjective and objective in modern terminology, while the Kantian ideal is only phenomenal and not objective in itself.

In the third place Socrates accepted the Good at first only in the particular significance of the practical, which nevertheless is only one mode of the substantial Idea ; the universal is not only for me, but also, as end existent in and for itself, the principle of the philosophy of nature, and in this higher sense it was taken by Plato and Aristotle. Of Socrates it is hence said, in the older histories of Philosophy, that his main distinction was having added ethics as a new conception to Philosophy, which formerly only took nature into consideration. Diogenes Laertius, in like manner says (III., 56), that the Ionics founded natural philosophy, Socrates ethics, and Plato added to them dialectic. Now ethics is partly objective, and partly subjective and reflected morality [Sittlichkeit und Moralität],[1] and the

---

[1] The distinction between these two words is a very important one. Schwegler, in explaining Hegel's position in his " History of Philosophy," states that Hegel asserts that Socrates set *Moralität*, the subjective morality of individual conscience, in the place of *Sittlichkeit*, " the spontaneous, natural, half-unconscious (almost.

teaching of Socrates is properly subjectively moral, because in it the subjective side, my perception and meaning, is the prevailing moment, although this determination of self-positing is likewise sublated, and the good and eternal is what is in and for itself. Objective morality is, on the contrary, natural, since it signifies the knowledge and doing of what is in and for itself good. The Athenians before Socrates were objectively, and not subjectively, moral, for they acted rationally in their relations without knowing that they were particularly excellent. Reflective morality adds to natural morality the reflection that this is the good and not that; the Kantian philosophy, which is reflectively moral, again showed the difference.

Because Socrates in this way gave rise to moral philosophy, all succeeding babblers about morality and popular philosophy constituted him their patron and object of adoration, and made him into a cloak which should cover all false philosophy. As he treated it, it was undoubtedly popular ; and what contributed to make it such was that his death gave him the never-failing interest derived from innocent suffering. Cicero (Tusc. Quæst. V. 4), whose manner of thought was, on the one hand, of the present, and who, on the other hand, had the belief that Philosophy should yield itself up, and hence succeeded in attaining to no content in it, boasted of Socrates (what has often enough

---

instinctive) virtue that rests in obedience to established custom (use and wont, natural objective law, that is at bottom, according to Hegel, rational, though not yet subjectively cleared, perhaps, into its rational principles)." As Dr. Stirling says in his Annotations to the same work (p. 394), "There is a period in the history of the State when people live in tradition; that is a period of unreflected *Sittlichkeit*, or natural observance. Then there comes a time when the observances are questioned, and when the right or truth they·involve is reflected into the subject. This is a period of Aufklärung, and for *Sittlichkeit* there is substituted *Moralität*, subjective morality : the subject will approve nought but what he finds inwardly true to himself, to his conscience."—[TRANSLATOR'S NOTE.]

been said since) that his most eminent characteristic was
to have brought Philosophy from heaven to earth, to the
homes and every-day life of men, or, as Diogenes
Laertius expresses it (II. 21), "into the market place."
There we have what has just been said. This would seem
as if the best and truest Philosophy were only a domestic
or fireside philosophy, which conforms to all the ordinary
ideas of men, and in which we see friends and faithful ones
talk together of righteousness, and of what can be known
on the earth, without having penetrated the depths of the
heavens, or rather the depths of consciousness. But this
last is exactly what Socrates, as these men themselves
indicate, first ventured to do. And it was not incumbent on
him to reflect upon all the speculations of past Philosophy,
in order to be able to come down in practical philosophy
to inward thought. This gives a general idea of his
principle.

We must examine more closely this noteworthy
phenomenon, and begin with the history of Socrates' life.
This is, however, closely intertwined with his interest in
Philosophy, and the events of his life are bound up with his
principles. We have first of all to consider the begin-
ning of his life only. Socrates, whose birth occurs in the
fourth year of the 77th Olympiad (469 B.C.), was the son of
Sophroniscus, a sculptor, and of Phænarete, a midwife.
His father brought him up to sculpture, and it is said that
Socrates acquired skill in the art, and long after, statues of
draped Graces, found in the Acropolis, were ascribed to him.
But his art did not satisfy him; a great desire for
Philosophy, and love of scientific research, got possession
of him. He pursued his art merely to get money for a
necessary subsistence, and to be able to apply himself to
the study of the sciences; and it is told of Crito, an
Athenian, that he defrayed the cost of Socrates' instruction
by masters in all the arts. During the exercise of his art,
and specially after he gave it up altogether, he read the

works of ancient philosophers in so far as he could get possession of them. At the same time he attended Anaxagoras' instructions, and, after his expulsion from Athens, at which time Socrates was thirty-seven years old, those of Archelaus, who was regarded as Anaxagoras' successor, besides those of Sophists celebrated in other sciences. Amongst these he heard Prodicus, a celebrated teacher of oratory, whom, according to Xenophon (Memorab. II. c. 1, §§ 21, 34), he mentions with affection, and other teachers of music, poetry, etc. He was esteemed as on all sides a man of culture, who was instructed in everything then requisite thereto.[1]

Another feature in his life was that he fulfilled the duty of protecting his country, which rested on him as an Athenian citizen. Hence he made three campaigns in the Peloponnesian war, which occurred during his life. The Peloponnesian war led to the dissolution of Greek life, inasmuch as it was preparatory to it; and what took place politically was by Socrates carried out in thinking consciousness. In these campaigns he not only acquired the fame of a brave warrior, but, what was best of all, the merit of having saved the lives of other citizens. In the first, he was present at the tedious siege of Potidæa in Thrace. Here Alcibiades had already attached himself to him, and, according to Plato, he recited in the Banquet (p. 219—222, Steph.; p. 461—466, Bekk.), a eulogy on Socrates for being able to endure all toil, hunger and thirst, heat and cold, with mind at rest and health of body. In an engagement in this campaign he saw Alcibiades wounded in the midst of the enemy, lifted him up, forced his way through, and saved both him and his arms. The generals rewarded him with a wreath, which was the prize of the bravest; Socrates did not, however, take it, maintaining that it was given to Alcibiades. In this campaign it is said that once, sunk in

---

[1] Diog. Laert. II. 44 (cf. Menag. ad h. 1); 18—20, 22.

deep meditation, he stood immovable on one spot the whole day and night, until the morning sun awoke him from his trance—a condition in which he is said often to have been. This was a cataleptic state, which may bear some relation to magnetic somnambulism, in which Socrates became quite dead to sensuous consciousness. From this physical setting free of the inward abstract self from the concrete bodily existence of the individual, we have, in the outward manifestation, a proof of how the depths of his mind worked within him. In him we see pre-eminently the inwardness of consciousness that in an anthropological way existed in the first instance in him, and became later on a usual thing. He made his other campaign in Bœotia at Delium, a small fortification which the Athenians possessed not far from the sea, and where they had an unfortunate, though not an important engagement. Here Socrates saved another of his favourites, Xenophon; he saw him in the flight, for Xenophon, having lost his horse, lay wounded on the ground. Socrates took him over his shoulders, carried him off, defending himself at the same time with the greatest tranquillity and presence of mind from the pursuing enemy. Finally he made his last campaign at Amphipolis in Edonis, on the Strymonian Bay.[1]

Besides this, he occupied various civil offices. At the time when the democratic constitution of Athens hitherto existing, was taken away by the Lacedemonians, who now introduced everywhere an aristocratic and indeed tyrannical rule, whereby they in great measure put themselves at the head of affairs, he was chosen for the council, which, as a representative body, took the place of the people. Here he distinguished himself by his immovable firmness in what he held to be right as against the wills of the thirty tyrants, as formerly against the will of the people. For he sat in the tribunal which condemned the ten

---

[1] Diog. Laert. II. 22, 23; Plat. Apol. Socr. p. 28 (p. 113).

generals to death, because, as admirals at the battle of Arginusæ, though they certainly had conquered, yet, being kept back through storm, they had not dragged out the bodies nor buried them on the shore, and because they neglected to erect trophies; *i.e.* really because they did not stand their ground, and thus appeared to have been beaten. Socrates alone did not agree with this decision, declaring himself more emphatically against the people than against the rulers.[1] To-day he fares badly who says anything against the people. " The people have excellent intelligence, understand everything, and have only the most excellent intentions." As to rulers, governments, ministers, it is self-evident that "they understand nothing, and only desire and bring forth what is bad."

Along with these to him more accidental relationships to the State, in which he acted only from the ordinary sense of citizenship, without spontaneously making the affairs of the State his real business, or pressing on to the head of public affairs, the real business of his life was to discuss moral philosophy with any who came in his way. His philosophy, which asserts that real existence is in consciousness as a universal, is still not a properly speculative philosophy, but remained individual; yet the aim of his philosophy was that it should have a universal significance. Hence we have to speak of his own individual being, of his thoroughly noble character, which usually is depicted as a complete catalogue of the virtues adorning the life of a private citizen; and these virtues of Socrates are certainly to be looked at as his own, and as made habitual to him by his own will. It has to be noted that with the ancients these qualities have generally more of the character of virtue, because with the ancients, in ordinary morality, individuality, as the form of the universal, was given free

---

[1] Diog. Laert. II. 24; Xenoph. Memorab. I. c. 1, § 18; Plat. Apol. Socrat. p. 32 (pp. 120—122); Epist. VII. pp. 324,·325 (p. 429).

scope, so that virtues were regarded more as the actions of
the individual will, and thus as personal qualities; while
with us they seem to be less what is meritorious to the
individual, or what comes from himself as this unit. We
are accustomed to think of them much more as what
exists, as duty, because we have a fuller consciousness
of the universal, and consider the pure individual, the
personal inward consciousness, as real existence and duty.
With us virtues are hence actually either elements in our
dispositions and nature, or they have the form of the
universal and of what is necessary; but with Socrates they
have the form, not of ordinary morality or of a natural or
necessary thing, but of an independent determination. It
is well known that his appearance indicated naturally low
and hateful qualities, which, as indeed he says, he himself
subdued.

He lived amongst his fellow-citizens, and stands before us
as one of those great plastic natures consistent through
and through, such as we often see in those times—resembling a perfect classical work of art which has brought itself
to this height of perfection. Such individuals are not
made, but have formed themselves into what they are;
they have become that which they wished to be, and are
true to this. In a real work of art the distinguishing point
is that some idea is brought forth, a character is presented in which every trait is determined by the idea, and,
because this is so, the work of art is, on the one hand,
living, and, on the other, beautiful, for the highest beauty
is just the most perfect carrying out of all sides of the
individuality in accordance with the one inward principle.
Such works of art are also seen in the great men of every
time. The most plastic individual as a statesman is
Pericles, and round him, like stars, Sophocles, Thucydides,
Socrates, &c., worked out their individuality into an
existence of its own—into a character which regulated
their whole being, and which was one principle running

throughout the whole of their existence. Pericles alone lived with the sole end of being a statesman. Plutarch (in Pericle, c. 5, 7) says of him that, from the time that he devoted himself to the business of the State, he laughed no more, and never again went to a feast. Thus, too, Socrates formed himself, through his art and through the power of self-conscious will, into this particular character, and acquired this capacity for the business of his life. Through his principle he attained that far-reaching influence which has lasted to the present day in relation to religion, science, and justice, for since his time the genius of inward conviction has been the basis which must be fundamental. And since this principle proceeded from the plasticity of his character, it is very inappropriate when Tennemann regrets (Vol. II. p. 26) " that though we know what he was, we do not know how he became such."

Socrates was a peaceful, pious example of the moral virtues —of wisdom, discretion, temperance, moderation, justice, courage, inflexibility, firm sense of rectitude in relation to tyrants and people ; he was equally removed from cupidity and despotism. His indifference to money was due to his own determination, for, according to the custom of the times, he could acquire it through the education of youth, like other teachers. On the other side, this acquisition was purely matter of choice, and not, as with us, something which is accepted. so that to take nothing would be to break through a custom, thus to present the appearance of wishing to become conspicuous, and to be more blamed than praised. For this was not yet a State affair; it was under the Roman emperors that there first were schools with payment. This moderation of his life was likewise a power proceeding from conscious knowledge, but this is not a principle found to hand, but the regulation of self in accordance with circumstances ; in company he was, how-ever, a good fellow. His sobriety in respect to wine is best depicted iu Plato's " Symposium," in a very characteristic scene in which we see what Socrates called virtue. Alcibiades there appears, no longer sober, at a feast given by Agathon, on the occasion of a success which his tragedy had obtained on the previous day at the games. Since the company had drunk much on the first day of the feast, the assembled guests, amongst whom was Socrates, this evening took a resolution, in opposition to the Greek custom at meals, to drink little. Alcibiades, finding that he was coming in amongst abstemious men, and that there was no one else in his own frame of mind, made himself king of the feast, and offered the goblet to the others, in order to bring them into the condition reached by himself; but with Socrates he said that he could do nothing, because he remained as he was, however much he drank. Plato then makes the individual who tells what happened at the Banquet, also tell that he, with the others, at last fell asleep on the couch, and as he awoke in the morning, Socrates, cup in hand, still talked with Aristophanes and Agathon about comedy and tragedy, and whether one man could write both comedies and tragedies, and then went at the usual time into the public places, to the Lyceum, as if nothing had happened, and walked about the whole day as usual.[1] This is not a moderation which exists in the least possible enjoyment, no aimless abstemiousness and self-mortification, but a power belonging to consciousness, which keeps its self-possession in bodily excess. We see from this that we have not to think of Socrates throughout after the fashion of the litany of moral virtues.

His behaviour to others was not only just, true, open, without rudeness, and honourable, but we also see in him an example of the most perfect Attic urbanity; i.e. he moves in the freest possible relations, has a readiness for conversation which is always judicious, and, because it has an inward universality, at the same time always has the right

[1] Plat. Convivium, pp. 212, 176, 213, 214, 223 (pp. 447, 376—378, 449, 450, 468, 469).

living relationship to the individual, and bears upon the case on which it operates. The intercourse is that of a most highly cultured man who, in his relation to others, never places anything personal in all his wit, and sets aside all that is unpleasant. Thus Xenophon's, but particularly Plato's Socratic Dialogues belong to the highest type of this fine social culture.

Because the philosophy of Socrates is no withdrawal from existence now and here into the free, pure regions of thought, but is in a piece with his life, it does not proceed to a system ; and the manner of his philosophizing, which appears to imply a withdrawal from actual affairs as it did to Plato, yet in that very way gives itself this inward connection with ordinary life. For his more special business was his philosophic teaching, or rather his philosophic social intercourse (for it was not, properly speaking, teaching) with all ; and this outwardly resembled ordinary Athenian life in which the greater part of the day was passed without any particular business, in loitering about the market-place, or frequenting the public Lyceum, and there partly partaking of bodily exercises, and partly and principally, talking with one another. This kind of intercourse was only possible in the Athenian mode of life, where most of the work which is now done by a free citizen—by a free republican and free imperial citizen alike—was performed by slaves, seeing that it was deemed unworthy of free men. A free citizen could in Athens certainly be a handicraftsman, but he had slaves who did the work, just as a master now has workmen. At the present day such a life of movement would not be suitable to our customs. Now Socrates also lounged about after this manner, and lived in this constant discussion of ethical questions.[1] Thus what he did was what came naturally to him, and what can in general be called moralizing ; but its nature and method

---

[1] Xenoph. Memorab. I. c. 1, § 10.

was not that of preaching, exhortation or teaching; it was not a dry morality. For amongst the Athenians and in Attic urbanity, this had no place, since it is not a reciprocal, free, and rational relationship. But with all men, however different their characters, he entered on one kind of dialogue, with all that Attic urbanity which, without presumption on his part, without instructing others, or wishing to command them, while maintaining their perfect right to freedom, and honouring it, yet causes all that is rude to be suppressed.

1. In this conversation Socrates' philosophy is found, as also what is known as the Socratic method, which must in its nature be dialectic, and of which we must speak before dealing with the content. Socrates' manner is not artificial; the dialogues of the moderns, on the contrary, just because no internal reason justifies their form, are necessarily tedious and heavy. But the principle of his philosophy falls in with the method itself, which thus far cannot be called method, since it is a mode which quite coincides with the moralizing peculiar to Socrates. For the chief content is to know the good as the absolute, and that particularly in relation to actions. Socrates gives this point of view so high a place, that he both puts aside the sciences which involve the contemplation of the universal in nature, mind, &c., himself, and calls upon others to do the same.[1] Thus it can be said that in content his philosophy had an altogether practical aspect, and similarly the Socratic method, which is essential to it, was distinguished by the system of first bringing a person to reflection upon his duty by any occasion that might either happen to be offered spontaneously, or that was brought about by Socrates. By going to the work-places of tailors and shoemakers, and entering into discourse with them, as also with youths and old men, Sophists, statesmen, and citizens of all kinds, he in

---

[1] Xenoph. Memorab. I. c. 1, § 11—16; Aristot. Metaph. I. 6.

the first place took their interests as his topic—whether these were household interests, the education of children, or the interests of knowledge or of truth. Then he led them on from a definite case to think of the universal, and of truths and beauties which had absolute value, since in every case, from the individual's own thoughts, he derived the conviction and consciousness of that which is the definite right. This method has two prominent aspects, the one the development of the universal from the concrete case, and the exhibition of the notion which implicitly exists in every consciousness,[1] and the other is the resolution of the firmly established, and, when taken immediately in consciousness, universal determinations of the sensuous conception or of thought, and the causing of confusion between these and what is concrete.

a. If we proceed from the general account of Socrates' method to a nearer view, in the first place its effect is to inspire men with distrust towards their presuppositions, after faith had become wavering and they were driven to seek that which is, in themselves. Now whether it was that he wished to bring the manner of the Sophists into disrepute, or that he was desirous to awaken the desire for knowledge and independent thought in the youths whom he attracted to himself, he certainly began by adopting the ordinary conceptions which they considered to be true. But in order to bring others to express these, he represents himself as in ignorance of them, and, with a seeming ingenuousness, puts questions to his audience as if they were to instruct him, while he really wished to draw them out. This is the celebrated Socratic irony, which in his case is a particular mode of carrying on intercourse between one person and another, and is thus only a subjective form of dialectic, for real dialectic deals with the reasons for things. What he wished to effect was, that

---

[1] Aristot. Metaph. XIII. 4.

when other people brought forward their principles, he, from each definite proposition, should deduce as its consequence the direct opposite of what the proposition stated, or else allow the opposite to be deduced from their own inner consciousness without maintaining it directly against their statements. Sometimes he also derived the opposite from a concrete case. But as this opposite was a principle held by men as firmly as the other, he then went on to show that they contradicted themselves. Thus Socrates taught those with whom he associated to know that they knew nothing ; indeed, what is more, he himself said that he knew nothing, and therefore taught nothing. It may actually be said that Socrates knew nothing, for he did not reach the systematic construction of a philosophy. He was conscious of this, and it was also not at all his aim to establish a science.

On the one view, this irony seems to be something untrue. But when we deal with objects which have a universal interest, and speak about them to one and to another, it is always the case that one does not understand another's conception of the object. For every individual has certain ultimate words as to which he presupposes a common knowledge. But if we really are to come to an understanding, we find it is these presuppositions which have to be investigated. For instance, if in more recent times belief and reason are discussed as the subjects of present intellectual interest, everyone pretends that he knows quite well what reason, &c., is, and it is considered ill-bred to ask for an explanation of this, seeing that all are supposed to know about it. A very celebrated divine, ten years ago,[1] published ninety theses on reason, which contained very interesting questions, but resulted in nothing, although they were much discussed, because one person's assertions issued from the point of view of faith, and the other's from that of reason, and each remained in this state of oppo-

---

[1] From the Lectures of the winter 1825–1826.—(NOTE BY EDITOR.)

sition, without the one's knowing what the other meant. Thus what would make an understanding possible is just the explanation of what we think is understood, without really being so. If faith and knowledge certainly differ from one another at the first, yet through this declaration of their notional determinations the common element will at once appear; in that way questions like these and the trouble taken with them may, for the first time, become fruitful; otherwise men may chatter this way and that for years, without making any advance. For if I say I know what reason, what belief is, these are only quite abstract ideas; it is necessary, in order to become concrete, that they should be explained, and that it should be understood that what they really are, is unknown. The irony of Socrates has this great quality of showing how to make abstract ideas concrete and effect their development, for on that alone depends the bringing of the Notion into consciousness.

In recent times much has been said about the Socratic irony which, like all dialectic, gives force to what is taken immediately, but only in order to allow the dissolution inherent in it to come to pass; and we may call this the universal irony of the world. Yet men have tried to make this irony of Socrates into something quite different, for they extended it into a universal principle; it is said to be the highest attitude of the mind, and has been represented as the most divine. It was Friedrich von Schlegel who first brought forward this idea, and Ast repeated it, saying, " The most ardent love of all beauty in the Idea, as in life, inspires Socrates' words with inward, unfathomable life." This life is now said to be irony! But this irony issues from the Fichtian philosophy, and is an essential point in the comprehension of the conceptions of most recent times. It is when subjective consciousness maintains its independence of everything, that it says, " It is I who through my educated thoughts can annul all determinations of right, morality, good, &c., because I am clearly master of

them, and I know that if anything seems good to me I can
easily subvert it, because things are only true to me in
so far as they please me now." This irony is thus only a
trifling with everything, and it can transform all things into
show : to this subjectivity nothing is any longer serious,
for any seriousness which it has, immediately becomes dissipated again in jokes, and all noble or divine truth vanishes
away or becomes mere triviality. But the Greek gaiety, as
it breathes in Homer's poems, is ironical, for Eros mocks the
power of Zeus and of Mars; Vulcan, limping along, serves the
gods with wine, and brings upon himself the uncontrollable
laughter of the immortal gods. Juno boxes Diana's ears.
Thus, too, there is irony in the sacrifices of the ancients,
who themselves consumed the best; in the pain that laughs,
in the keenest joy which is moved to tears, in the scornful
laughter of Mephistopheles, and in every transition from one
extreme to another—from what is best to what is worst.
Sunday morning may be passed in deep humility, profoundest contrition and self-abasement, in striking the
breast in penitence, and the evening in eating and drinking to the full, going the round of pleasures, thus
allowing self to re-assert its independence of any such
subjection. Hypocrisy, which is of the same nature,
is the truest irony. Socrates and Plato were falsely stated
to be the originators of this irony, of which it is said that
it is the " inmost and deepest life," although they possessed
the element of subjectivity; in our time it was not permitted
to us to give effect to this irony. Ast's " inmost, deepest
life " is just the subjective and arbitrary will, the inward
divinity which knows itself to be exalted above all. The
divine is said to be the purely negative attitude, the perception of the vanity of everything, in which my vanity
alone remains. Making the consciousness of the nullity of
everything ultimate, might indeed indicate depth of life,
but it only is the depth of emptiness, as may be seen from
the ancient comedies of Aristophanes. From this irony of

our times, the irony of Socrates is far removed; as is also
the case with Plato, it has a significance which is limited.
Socrates' premeditated irony may be called a manner of
speech, a pleasant rallying; there is in it no satirical
laughter or pretence, as though the idea were nothing but
a joke. But his tragic irony is his opposition of subjective
reflection to morality as its exists, not a consciousness of
the fact that he stands above it, but the natural aim of
leading men, through thought, to the true good and to the
universal Idea.

b. Now the second element is what Socrates has
called the art of midwifery—an art which came to him
from his mother.[1] It is the assisting into the world of the
thought which is already contained in the consciousness
of the individual—the showing from the concrete, unreflected consciousness, the universality of the concrete, or
from the universally posited, the opposite which already
is within it. Socrates hence adopts a questioning attitude,
and this kind of questioning and answering has thus been
called the Socratic method; but in this method there is more
than can be given in questions and replies. For the answer
seems occasionally to be quite different from what was intended by the question, while in printed dialogue, answers
are altogether under the author's control; but to say
that in actual life people are found to answer as they are
here made to do, is quite another thing. To Socrates those
who reply may be called pliable youths, because they reply
directly to the questions, which are so formed that they
make the answer very easy, and exclude any originality in
reply. To this plastic manner, which we see in the method
of Socrates, as represented by Plato and Xenophon, it is
objected that we do not answer in the same relation in
which the questioner asks; while, with Socrates, the relation which the questioner adopts is respected in the reply.

[1] Platonis Theætetus, p. 210 (p. 322).

The other way, which is to bring forward another
point of view, is undoubtedly the spirit of an animated
conversation, but such emulation is excluded from this
Socratic method, in which the principal matter is to keep
to the point. The spirit of dogmatism, self-assertion, stopping short when we seem to get into difficulties, and escaping from them by a jest, or by setting them aside—all these
attitudes and methods are here excluded ; they do not constitute good manners, nor do they have a place in Socrates'
dialogues. In these dialogues, it is hence not to be wondered at that those questioned answered so precisely to the
point, while in the best modern dialogues there is always an
arbitrary element.

This difference concerns only what is external and
formal. But the principal point, and the reason why
Socrates set to work with questions in bringing the good
and right into consciousness in universal form, was that he
did not proceed from what is present in our consciousness
in a simple form through setting forth the conception allied
to it in pure necessity, which would be a deduction, a proof
or, speaking generally, a consequence following from the conception. But this concrete, as it is in natural consciousness
without thinking of it, or universality immersed in matter, he
analyzed, so that through the separation of the concrete, he
brought the universal contained therein to consciousness as
universal. We see this method also carried on to a large
extent in Plato's dialogues, where there is, in this regard,
particular skill displayed. It is the same method which
forms in every man his knowledge of the universal ; an
education in self-consciousness, which is the development of
reason. The child, the uncultured man, lives in concrete
individual ideas, but to the man who grows and educates
himself, because he thereby goes back into himself as thinking, reflection becomes reflection on the universal and the
permanent establishment of the same ; and a freedom—formerly that of moving in concrete ideas—is now that of so

doing in abstractions and in thoughts. We see such a development of universal from particular, where a number of examples are given, treated in a very tedious way. For us who are trained in presenting to ourselves what is abstract, who are taught from youth up in universal principles, the Socratic method of so-called deference, with its eloquence, has often something tiresome and tedious about it. The universal of the concrete case is already present to us as universal, because our reflection is already accustomed to the universal, and we do not require, first of all, to take the trouble of making a separation ; and thus, if Socrates were now to bring what is abstract before consciousness, we should not require, in order to establish it as universal, that all these examples should be adduced, so that through repetition the subjective certainty of abstraction might arise.

c. The next result of this method of procedure may be that consciousness is surprised that what it never looked for should be found in consciousness. If we reflect, for example, on the universally known idea of Becoming, we find that what becomes is not and yet it is; it is the identity of Being and non-being, and it may surprise us that in this simple conception so great a distinction should exist.

The result attained was partly the altogether formal and negative one of bringing home to those who conversed with Socrates, the conviction that, however well acquainted with the subject they had thought themselves, they now came to the conclusion, "that what we knew has refuted itself." Socrates thus put questions in the intent that the speaker should be drawn on to make admissions, implying a point of view opposed to that from which he started. That these contradictions arise because they bring their ideas together, is the drift of the greater part of Socrates' dialogues ; their main tendency consequently was to show the bewilderment and confusion which exist in

knowledge. By this means, he tries to awaken shame, and
the perception that what we consider as true is not the
truth, from which the necessity for earnest effort after
knowledge must result. Plato, amongst others, gives
these examples in his Meno (p. 71—80, Steph. ; p. 327—346,
Bekk.). Socrates is made to say, " By the gods, tell me what
is virtue." Meno proceeds to make various distinctions :
" Man's virtue is to be skilful in managing state affairs,
and thereby to help friends and harm foes ; woman's to
rule her household ; other virtues are those of boys, of young
men, of old men," &c. Socrates interrupts him by saying,
that it is not that about which he inquires, but virtue in
general, which comprehends every thing in itself. Meno says
" It is to govern and rule over others." Socrates brings forward the fact that the virtue of boys and slaves does not consist in governing. Meno says that he cannot tell what is
common in all virtue. Socrates replies that it is the same
as figure, which is what is common in roundness, square-
ness, &c. There a digression occurs. Meno says, " Virtue
is the power of securing the good desired." Socrates inter-
poses that it is superfluous to say the good, for from the
time that men know that something is an evil, they do not
desire it; and also the good must be acquired in a right
way. Socrates thus confounds Meno, and he sees that
these ideas are false. The latter says, " I used to hear of
you, before I knew you, that you were yourself in doubt
(ἀπορεῖς), and also brought others into doubt, and now
you cast a spell on me too, so that I am at my wits' end
(ἀπορίας). You seem, if I may venture to jest, to be
like the torpedo fish, for it is said of it that it makes
torpid (ναρκᾶν) those who come near it and touch it.
You have done this to me, for I am become torpid in body
and soul, and I do not know how to answer you, although I
have talked thousands of times about virtue with many
persons, and, as it seemed to me, talked very well. But
now I do not know at all what to say. Hence you do well

not to travel amongst strangers, for you might be put to death as a magician." Socrates again wishes to " inquire." Now Meno says, " How can you inquire about what you say you do not know ? Can you have a desire for what you do not know ? And if you find it out by chance, how can you know that it is what you looked for, since you acknowledge that, you do not know it ? " A number of dialogues end in the same manner, both in Xenophon and Plato, leaving us quite unsatisfied as to the result. It is so in the Lysis, where Plato asks the question of what love and friendship secures to men ; and similarly the Republic commences by inquiring what justice is. Philosophy must, generally speaking, begin with a puzzle in order to bring about reflection ; everything must be doubted, all pre-suppositions given up, to reach the truth as created through the Notion.

2. This, in short, is Socrates' method. The affirmative, what Socrates develops in the consciousness, is nothing but the good in as far as it is brought forth from con-sciousness through knowledge—it is the eternal, in and for itself universal, what is called the Idea, the true, which just in so far as it is end, is the Good. In this regard Socrates is opposed to the Sophists, for the proposition that man is the measure of all things, to them still comprehends particular ends, while to Socrates the universal brought forth through free thought is thereby expressed in objective fashion. Nevertheless, we must not blame the Sophists because, in the aimlessness of their time, they did not discover the principle of the Good ; for every discovery has its time, and that of the Good, which as end in itself is now always made the starting point, had not yet been made by Socrates. It now seems as if we had not yet shown forth much of the Socratic philosophy, for we have merely kept to the prin-ciple ; but the main point with Socrates is that his know-ledge for the first time reached this abstraction. The Good is nevertheless no longer as abstract as the νοῦς of Anaxagoras,

but is the universal which determines itself in itself, realizes itself, and has to be realized as the end of the world and of the individual. It is a principle, concrete within itself, which, however, is not yet manifested in its development, and in this abstract attitude we find what is wanting in the Socratic standpoint, of which nothing that is affirmative can, beyond this, be adduced.

a. As regards the Socratic principle, the first determination is the great determination which is, however, still merely formal, that consciousness creates and has to create out of itself what is the true. This principle of subjective freedom was present to the consciousness of Socrates himself so vividly that he despised the other sciences as being empty learning and useless to mankind ; he has to concern himself with his moral nature only in order to do what is best—a one-sidedness which is very characteristic of Socrates. This religion of the Good is to Socrates, not only the essential point to which men have to direct their thoughts, but it is that exclusively. We see him showing how from every individual this universal, this absolute in consciousness may be found as his reality. Here we see law, the true and good, what was formerly present as an existent, return into consciousness. But it is not a single chance manifestation in this individual Socrates, for we have to comprehend Socrates and his manifestation. In the universal consciousness, in the spirit of the people to which he belongs, we see natural turn into reflective morality, and he stands above as the consciousness of this change. The spirit of the world here begins to change, a change which was later on carried to its completion. From this higher standpoint, Socrates, as well as the Athenian people and Socrates in them, have to be considered. The reflection of consciousness into itself begins here, the knowledge of the consciousness of self as such, that it is real existence—or that God is a Spirit, or again, in a cruder and more sensuous form, that God takes human form. This epoch begins where essence is given up as Being—even though it be, as hitherto, abstract Being, Being as thought. But this epoch in a naturally moral people in the highest state of development, makes its appearance as the destruction threatening them or breaking in upon them unprevented. For its morality, as was usually so with the ancients, consisted in the fact that the Good was present as a universal, without its having had the form of the conviction of the individual in his individual consciousness, but simply that of the immediate absolute. It is the authoritative, present law, without testing investigation, but yet an ultimate ground on which this moral consciousness rests. It is the law of the State ; it has authority as the law of the gods, and thus it is universal destiny which has the form of an existent, and is recognized as such by all. But moral consciousness asks if this is actually law in itself ? This consciousness turned back within itself from everything that has the form of the existent, requires to understand, to know, that the above law is posited in truth, *i.e.* it demands that it should find itself therein as consciousness. In thus returning into themselves the Athenian people are revealed to us : uncertainty as to existent laws as existent has arisen, and a doubt about what was held to be right, the greatest freedom respecting all that is and was respected. This return into itself represents the highest point reached by the mind of Greece, in so far as it becomes no longer the mere existence of these moralities, but the living consciousness of the same, which has a content which is similar, but which, as spirit, moves freely in it. This is a culture which we never find the Lacedæmonians reach. This deepest life of morality is so to speak a free personal consciousness of morality or of God, and a happy enjoyment of them. Consciousness and Being have here exactly the same value and rank ; what is, is consciousness ; neither is powerful above another. The authority of law is no oppressive bond to consciousness, and all reality is likewise no obstacle to it, for it is secure in itself. But this return is just on the point of abandoning the content, and indeed of positing itself as abstract consciousness, without the content, and, as existent, opposed to it. From this equilibrium of consciousness and Being, consciousness takes up its position as independent. This aspect of separation is an independent conception, because consciousness, in the perception of its independence, no longer immediately acknowledges what is put before it, but requires that this should first justify itself to it, *i.e.* it must comprehend itself therein. Thus this return is the isolation of the individual from the universal, care for self at the cost of the State; to us, for instance, it is the question as to whether I shall be in eternal bliss or condemnation, whereas philosophic eternity is present now in time, and is nothing other than the substantial man himself. The State has lost its power, which consisted in the unbroken continuity of the universal spirit, as formed of single individuals, so that the individual consciousness knew no other content and reality than law. Morals have become shaken, because we have the idea present that man creates his maxims for himself. The fact that the individual comes to care for his own morality, means that he becomes reflectively moral; when public morality disappears, reflective morality is seen to have arisen. We now see Socrates bringing forward the opinion, that in these times every one has to look after his own morality, and thus he looked after his through consciousness and reflection regarding himself; for he sought the universal spirit which had disappeared from reality, in his own consciousness. He also helped others to care for their morality, for he awakened in them this consciousness of having in their thoughts the good and true, *i.e.* having the potentiality of action and of knowledge. This is no longer there immediately, but must be provided, just as a ship must make provision of water when it goes to places where none is to be found. The immediate has no further authority but must justify itself to thought. Thus we comprehend the special qualities of Socrates, and his method in Philosophy, from the whole; and we also understand his fate from the same.

This direction of consciousness back into itself takes the form—very markedly in Plato—of asserting that man can learn nothing, virtue included, and that not because the latter has no relation to science. For the good does not come from without, Socrates shows; it cannot be taught, but is implied in the nature of mind. That is to say, man cannot passively receive anything that is given from without like the wax that is moulded to a form, for everything is latent in the mind of man, and he only seems to learn it. Certainly everything begins from without, but this is only the beginning; the truth is that this is only an impulse towards the development of spirit. All that has value to men, the eternal, the self-existent, is contained in man himself, and has to develop from himself. To learn here only means to receive knowledge of what is externally determined. This external comes indeed through experience, but the universal therein belongs to thought, not to the subjective and bad, but to the objective and true. The universal in the opposition of subjective and objective, is that which is as subjective as it is objective; the subjective is only a particular, the objective is similarly only a particular as regards the subjective, but the universal is the unity of both. According to the Socratic principle, nothing has any value to men to which the spirit does not testify. Man in it is free, is at home with himself, and that is the subjectivity of spirit. As it is said in the Bible, "Flesh of my flesh, and bone of my bone," that which is held by me as truth and right is spirit of my spirit. But what spirit derives from itself must come from it as from the spirit which acts in a universal manner, and not from its passions, likings, and arbitrary desires. These, too, certainly come from something inward which is "implanted in us by nature," but which is only in a natural way our own, for it belongs to the particular ; high above it is true thought, the Notion, the rational. Socrates opposed to the contingent and particular inward, that universal, true inward of thought. And Socrates awakened this real conscience, for he not only said that man is the measure of all things, but man as thinking is the measure of all things. With Plato we shall, later on, find it formulated that what man seems to receive he only remembers.

As to the question of what is the Good, Socrates recognized its determination as being not only a determination in particularity to the exclusion of the natural side, as determination is understood in empirical science, but even in relation to the actions of men, he holds the Good to be still undetermined, and the ultimate determinateness, or the determining, is what we may call subjectivity generally That the Good should be determined, primarily signifies that while, at first, in opposition to the Being of reality, it was a general maxim only, that to which the activity of individuality was still wanting, in the second place it was not permitted to be inert, to be mere thought, but had to be present as the determining and actual, and thus as the effectual. It is such only through subjectivity, through the activity of man. That the Good is a determinate thus further means that individuals know what the Good is, and we call this standpoint reflective morality, while natural morality does right unconsciously. Thus to Socrates virtue is perception. For to the proposition of the Platonic Protagoras that all other virtues have a relationship to one another, but that it is not so with valour, since many brave men are to be found who are the most irreligious, unjust, intemperate and uncultured of people (such as a band of robbers), Plato makes Socrates answer that valour, like all virtues, also is a science, that is, it is the knowledge and the right estimation of what is to be feared.[1] By this the distinctive qualities of valour are certainly not unfolded. The naturally moral and upright man is such without his having considered the matter at all; it is his character, and what is good is securely rooted within him. When, on the other hand, consciousness is concerned, the question arises as to whether I directly desire the good or not. Hence this consciousness of morality easily becomes dangerous, and causes the individual to be puffed up by a good opinion of himself, which proceeds from the consciousness of his own power to decide for the good. The 'I' is then the master, he who chooses the Good, and in that there is the conceit of my knowing that I am an excellent man. With Socrates this opposition of the good and the subject as choosing is not reached, for what is dealt with is only the determination of the Good and the connection therewith of subjectivity; this last, as an individual person who can choose, decides upon the inward universal. We have here on the one side the knowledge of the Good, but, on the other, it is implied that the subject is good, since this is his ordinary character; and the fact that the subject is such, was by the ancients called virtue.

We understand from this the following criticism which Aristotle makes (Magna Mor. I. 1) on the quality of virtue as expounded by Socrates. He says : " Socrates spoke better of virtue than did Pythagoras, but not quite justly, for he made virtues into a science ($\dot{\epsilon}\pi\iota\sigma\tau\dot{\eta}\mu\alpha\varsigma$). But this is impossible, since, though all knowledge has some basis ($\lambda\acute{o}\gamma o\varsigma$) this basis only exists in thought. Consequently, he places all the virtues in the thinking ($\lambda o\gamma\iota\sigma\tau\iota\kappa\hat{\wp}$) side of the soul. Hence it comes to pass that he does away with the feeling ($\check{\alpha}\lambda o\gamma o\nu$) part of the soul, that is, the inclination ($\pi\hat{\alpha}\theta o\varsigma$) and the habits ($\mathring{\eta}\theta o\varsigma$)," which, however, also pertain to virtue. " But

---

[1] Plat. Protag. p. 349 (pp. 224, 225); pp. 360, 361 (pp. 245—247).

Plato rightly distinguished the thinking and the feeling sides of the soul." This is a good criticism. We see that what Aristotle misses in the determination of virtue in Socrates, is the side of subjective actuality, which we now call the heart. Certainly virtue is determination in accordance with universal, and not with particular ends, but perception is not the only element in virtue. For in order that the good perceived should be virtue, it must come to pass that the whole man, the heart and mind, should be identical with it, and this aspect of Being or of realization generally, is what Aristotle calls τὸ ἄλογον. If we understand the reality of the good as universal morality, substantiality is wanting to the perception; but matter, when we regard the inclination of the individual subjective will as this reality. This double want may also be considered as a want of content and of activity, in so far as to the universal development is wanting; and in the latter case, determining activity comes before us as negative only in reference to the universal. Socrates thus omits, in characterizing virtue, just what we saw had also disappeared in actuality, that is, first the real spirit of a people, and then reality as the sympathies of the individual. For it is just when consciousness is not yet turned back into itself, that the universal good appears to the individual as the object of his sympathy. To us, on the other hand, because we are accustomed to put on one side the good or virtue as practical reason, the other side, which is opposed to a reflective morality, is an equally abstract sensuousness, inclination, passion, and hence the bad. But in order that the universal should be reality, it must be worked out through consciousness as individual, and the carrying into effect pertains to this individuality. A passion, as for example, love, ambition, is the universal itself, as it is self-realizing, not in perception, but in activity; and if we did not fear being misunderstood, we should say that for the individual the universal is his own interests. Yet this is not the place in which to unravel all the false ideas and contradictions present in our culture.

Aristotle (Eth. Nicom. VI. 13), supplementing the one-sidedness of Socrates, further says of him : ' Socrates in one respect worked on right lines, but not in the other. For to call virtue scientific knowledge is untrue, but to say that it is not without scientific basis is right. Socrates made virtues into perceptions (λόγους), but we say that virtue exists with perception." This is a very true distinction ; the one side in virtue is that the universal of end belongs to thought. But in virtue, as character, the other side, active individuality, real soul, must necessarily come forth; and indeed with Socrates the latter appears in a characteristic form of which we shall speak below (p. 421 et seq.).

b. If we consider the universal first, it has within it a positive and a negative side, which we find both united in Xenophon's " Memorabilia," a work which aims at justifying Socrates. And if we inquire whether he or Plato depicts Socrates to us most faithfully in his personality and doctrine, there is no question that in regard to the personality and method, the externals of his teaching, we may certainly receive from Plato a satisfactory, and perhaps a more complete representation of what Socrates was. But in regard to the content of his teaching and the point reached by him in the development of thought, we have in the main to look to Xenophon.

The fact that the reality of morality had become shaken in the mind of the people, came to consciousness in Socrates ; he stands so high because he gave expression to what was present in the times. In this consciousness he elevated morality into perception, but this action is just the bringing to consciousness of the fact that it is the power of the Notion which sublates the determinate existence and the immediate value of moral laws and the sacredness of their implicitude. When perception likewise posi-

tively acknowledges as law that which was held to be law
(for the positive subsists through having recourse to laws),
this acknowledgment of them always passes through the
negative mode, and no longer has the form of absolute
being-in-itself: it is, however, just as far from being a
Platonic Republic. To the Notion too, because to it the
determinateness of laws in the form in which they have
value to unperceiving consciousness has dissolved, only
the purely implicit universal Good is the true. But since
this is empty and without reality, we demand, if we are
not satisfied with a dull monotonous round, that again a
movement should be made towards the extension of the
determination of the universal. Now because Socrates
remains at the indeterminateness of the good, its determination means for him simply the expression of the particular
good. Then it comes to pass that the universal results
only from the negation of the particular good; and since
this last is just the existing laws of Greek morality, we
have here the doubtlessly right, but dangerous element in
perception, the showing in all that is particular only its deficiencies. The inconsistency of making what is limited into
an absolute, certainly becomes unconsciously corrected in the
moral man; this improvement rests partly on the morality of
the subject and partly on the whole of the social life ; and
unfortunate extremes resulting in conflict are unusual
and unfrequent. But since the dialectic sublates the
particular, the abstract universal also becomes shaken.

a. Now as regards the positive side, Xenophon tells us
in the fourth book of the Memorabilia (c. 2, § 40), how
Socrates, once having made the need for perception
sensible to the youths, then actually instructed them,
and no longer wandered through mere subtleties in his
talk, but taught them the good in the clearest and most
open way. That is, he showed them the good and true in
what is determined, going back into it because he did not
wish to remain in mere abstraction. Xenophon gives

an example of this (Memorab. IV. c. 4, §§ 12—16, 25) in a
dialogue with the Sophist Hippias. Socrates there asserts
that the just man is he who obeys the law, and that these
laws are divine. Xenophon makes Hippias reply by asking
how Socrates could declare it to be an absolute duty to obey
the laws, for the people and the governors themselves often
condemn them by changing them, which is allowing that
they are not absolute. But Socrates answers by demand-
ing if those who conduct war do not again make peace,
which is not, any more than in the other case, to condemn
war, for each was just in its turn. Socrates thus says, in a
word, that the best and happiest State is that in which the
citizens are of one mind and obedient to law. Now this is
the one side in which Socrates looks away from the contradiction and makes laws and justice, as they are accepted
by each individually, to be the affirmative content. But if
we here ask what these laws are, they are, we find, just
those which have a value at some one time, as they happen
to be present in the State and in the idea; at another time
they abrogate themselves as determined, and are not held
to be absolute.

β. We hence see this other negative side in the same
connection when Socrates brings Euthydemus into the
conversation, for he asks him whether he did not strive
after the virtue without which neither the private man nor
the citizen could be useful to himself or to his people or
the State. Euthydemus declares that this undoubtedly is
so. But without justice, replies Socrates, this is not
possible, and he further asks whether Euthydemus had thus
attained to justice in himself. Euthydemus answers affirmatively, for he says that he thinks he is no less just than any
other man. Socrates now replies, "Just as workmen can
show their work, the just will be able to say what their
works are." This he also agrees to, and replies that he
could easily do so. Socrates now proposes if this is so
to write, " on the one hand under Δ the actions of the just,

and on the other, under A, those of the unjust?" With the
approbation of Euthydemus, lies, deceit, robbery, making a
slave of a free man, thus fall on the side of the unjust.
Now Socrates asks, "But if a general subdues the enemy's
State, would this not be justice?" Euthydemus says
"Yes." Socrates replies, "Likewise if he deceives and
robs the enemy and makes slaves?" Euthydemus has to
admit the justice of this. It is thus shown "that the
same qualities come under the determination both of justice
and of injustice." Here it strikes Euthydemus to add the
qualification that he intended that Socrates should understand the action to be only in reference to friends ; as
regards them it is wrong. Socrates accepts this, but proceeds, "If a general at the decisive moment of the battle
saw his own army in fear, and he deceived them by falsely
saying that help was coming in order to lead them on to
victory, could it be deemed right?" Euthydemus acknowledges that it could. Socrates says, "If a father gives a sick
child a medicine which it does not wish to take, in its food,
and makes it well through deceit, is this right?" Euthydemus—"Yes." Socrates—"Or is anyone wrong who takes
arms from his friend secretly or by force, when he sees him
in despair, and in the act of taking his own life?" Euthydemus has to admit that this is not wrong.[1] Thus it is
again shown here, that as regards friends also, the same determinations have to hold good on both sides, as justice as
well as injustice. Here we see that abstention from lying,
deceit, and robbery, that which we naturally hold to be
established, contradicts itself by being put into connection
with something different, and something which holds
equally good. This example further explains how through
thought, which would lay hold of the universal in the form
of the universal only, the particular becomes uncertain.

γ. The positive, which Socrates sets in the place of what

---

[1] Xenoph. Memorab. IV. c. 2, §§ 11—17.

was fixed and has now become vacillating, in order to give a content to the universal, is, on the one hand, and in opposition to this last, obedience to law (p. 416), that is, the mode of thought and idea which is inconsistent; and, on the other hand, since such determinations do not hold good for the Notion, it is perception, in which the immediately posited has now, in the mediating negation, to justify itself as a determination proceeding out of the constitution of the whole. But it is both true that we do not find this perception present in Socrates, for it remains in its content undetermined, and that in reality it is a contingent, which is seen in the fact, that the universal commands, such as "Thou shalt not kill," are connected with a particular content which is conditioned. Now whether the universal maxim in this particular case has value or not, depends first on the circumstances; and it is the perception which discovers the conditions and circumstances whereby exceptions to this law of unconditioned validity arise. However, because through this contingency in the instances, the fixed nature of the universal principle disappears, since it, too, appears as a particular only, the consciousness of Socrates arrives at pure freedom in each particular content. This freedom, which does not leave the content as it is in its dissipated determination to the natural consciousness, but makes it to be penetrated by the universal, is the real mind which, as unity of the universal content and of freedom, is the veritable truth. Thus if we here consider further what is the true in this consciousness, we pass on to the mode in which the realization of the universal appeared to Socrates himself.

Even the uneducated mind does not follow the content of its consciousness as this content appears in it; but, as mind, it corrects that which is wrong in its consciousness, and is thus implicitly, if not explicitly as consciousness, free. That is, though this consciousness expresses the universal law, "Thou shalt not kill," as a duty, that consciousness—

if no cowardly spirit dwells within it—will still bravely attack and slay the enemy in war. Here, if it is asked whether there is a command to kill one's enemies, the reply would be affirmative, as likewise when a hangman puts to death a criminal. But when in private life we become involved with adversaries, this command to kill one's enemies will not occur to us. We may thus call this the mind which thinks at the right time, first of the one, and then of the other; it is spirit, but an unspiritual consciousness. The first step towards reaching a spiritual consciousness is the negative one of acquiring freedom for one's consciousness. For since perception attempts to prove individual laws, it proceeds from a determination to which, as a universal basis, particular duty is submitted; but this basis is itself not absolute, and falls under the same dialectic. For example, were moderation commanded as a duty on the ground that intemperance undermined the health, health is the ultimate which is here considered as absolute; but it is at the same time not absolute, for there are other duties which ordain that health, and even life itself, should be risked and sacrificed. The so-called conflict of duties is nothing but duty, which is expressed as absolute, showing itself as not absolute; in the constant contradiction morals become unsettled. For a consciousness which has become consistent, law, because it has then been brought into contact with its opposite, has been sublated. For the positive truth has not yet become known in its determination. But to know the universal in its determination, *i.e.* the limitation of the universal which comes to us as fixed and not contingent, is only possible in connection with the whole system of actuality. Thus if with Socrates the content has become spiritualized, yet manifold independent grounds have merely taken the place of manifold laws. For the perception is not yet expressed as the real perception of these grounds over which it rules; but the truth of consciousness simply is this very movement of pure perception. The true ground is, however, spirit, and the spirit of the people—a perception of the constitution of a people, and the connection of the individual with this real universal spirit. Laws, morals, the actual social life, thus have in themselves their own corrective against the inconsistent, which consists of the expression of a definite content as absolute. In ordinary life we merely forget this limitation of universal principles, and these still hold their place with us; but the other point of view is thus when the limitation comes before our consciousness.

When we have the perfect consciousness that in actual life fixed duties and actions do not exist, for each concrete case is really a conflict of many duties which separate themselves in the moral understanding, but which mind treats as not absolute, comprehending them in the unity of its judgment, we call this pure, deciding individuality, the knowledge of what is right, or conscience, just as we call the pure universal of consciousness not a particular but an all-comprehensive one, duty. Now both sides here present, the universal law and the deciding spirit which is in its abstraction the active individual, are also necessary to the consciousness of Socrates as the content and the power over this content. That is, because with Socrates the particular law has become vacillating, there now comes in the place of the universal single mind, which, with the Greeks, was unconscious determination through unreflective morality, individual mind as individuality deciding for itself. Thus with Socrates the deciding spirit is transformed into the subjective consciousnesss of man, since the power of deciding originates with himself; and the first question now is, how this subjectivity appears in Socrates himself. Because the person, the individual, now gives the decision, we come back to Socrates as person, as subject, and what follows is a development of his personal relations. But since the moral element is generally placed in the personality of Socrates, we see the contingent nature of the instruction and of the culture which was obtained through Socrates' character; for it was the actual basis on which men fortified themselves in associating with Socrates, by actual communication with him and by their manner of life. Thus it was true that "the intercourse with his friends was, on the whole, beneficial and instructive to them, but in many cases they became unfaithful to Socrates," [1] because not everyone attains to perception, and he who possesses it may remain at the negative. The education of the citizens, life in the people, is quite a fresh force in the individual, and does not mean that he educates himself through arguments; hence, however truly educative the intercourse with Socrates was, this contingency still entered into it. We thus see as an unhappy symptom of disorder, how Socrates' greatest favourites, and those endowed with the most genial natures (such as Alcibiades, that genius of levity, who played with the Athenian people, and Critias, the most active of the Thirty) afterwards experienced the fate of being judged in their own country, one as an enemy and traitor to his fellows, and the other as an oppressor and tyrant of the State. They lived according to the principle of subjective perception, and thus cast a bad light on Socrates, for it is shown in this how the Socratic principle in another form brought about the ruin of Greek life.[2]

c. The characteristic form in which this subjectivity—this implicit and deciding certainty—appears in Socrates, has still to be mentioned. That is, since everyone here has this personal mind which appears to him to be his mind, we see how in connection with this, we have what is known under the name of the Genius (δαιμόνιον) of Socrates; for it implies that now man decides in accordance with his perception and by himself. But in this Genius of Socrates—notorious

---

[1] Xenoph. Memorab. IV. c. 1, § 1 ; c. 2, § 40.
[2] Cf. Xenoph. Memorab. I. c. 2, §§ 12—16, sqq.

as a much discussed *bizarrerie* of his imagination—we are neither to imagine the existence of protective spirit, angel, and such-like, nor even of conscience. For conscience is the idea of universal individuality, of the mind certain of itself, which is at the same time universal truth. But the Genius of Socrates is rather all the other and necessary sides of his universality, that is, the individuality of mind which came to consciousness in him equally with the former. His pure consciousness stands over both sides. The deficiency in the universal, which lies in its indeterminateness, is unsatisfactorily supplied in an individual way, because Socrates' judgment, as coming from himself, was characterized by the form of an unconscious impulse. The Genius of Socrates is not Socrates himself, not his opinions and conviction, but an oracle which, however, is not external, but is subjective, his oracle. It bore the form of a knowledge which was directly associated with a condition of unconsciousness; it was a knowledge which may also appear under other conditions as a magnetic state. It may happen that at death, in illness and catalepsy, men know about circumstances future or present, which, in the understood relations of things, are altogether unknown. These are facts which are usually rudely denied. That in Socrates we should discover what comes to pass through reflection in the form of the unconscious, makes it appear to be an exceptional matter, revealed to the individual only, and not as being what it is in truth. Thereby it certainly receives the stamp of imagination, but there is nothing more of what is visionary or superstitious to be seen in it, for it is a necessary manifestation, though Socrates did not recognize the necessity, this element being only generally before his imagination.

In connection with what follows, we must yet further consider the relationship of the Genius to the earlier existent form of decision, and that into which it led Socrates; regarding both Xenophon expresses himself in his history most distinctly. Because the standpoint of the Greek mind was natural morality, in which man did not yet determine himself, and still less was what we call conscience present, since laws were, in their fundamental principles, regarded as traditional, these last now presented an appearance of being sanctioned by the gods.   We know that the Greeks undoubtedly had laws on which to form their judgments, but on the other hand, both in private and public life, immediate decisions had to be made.   But in them the Greeks, with all their freedom, did not decide from the subjective will. The general or the people did not take upon themselves to decide as to what was best in the State, nor did the individual do so in the family.   For in making these decisions, the Greeks took refuge in oracles, sacrificial animals, soothsayers, or, like the Romans, asked counsel of birds in flight. The general who had to fight a battle was guided in his decision by the entrails of animals, as we often find in Xenophon's Anabasis.   Pausanias tormented himself thus a whole day long before he gave the command to fight.[1]   This element, the fact that the people had not the power of decision but were determined from without, was a real factor in Greek consciousness ; and oracles were everywhere essential where man did not yet know himself inwardly as being sufficiently free and independent to take upon himself to decide as we do.   This subjective freedom, which was not yet present with the Greeks, is what we mean in the present day when we speak of freedom; in the Platonic Republic we shall see more of it.   Our responsibility for what we do is a characteristic of modern times; we wish to decide according to grounds of common sense, and consider this as ultimate.   The Greeks did not possess the knowledge of this infinitude.

In the first book of Xenophon's Memorabilia (chap. 1, §§ 7—9), on the occasion of the defence by Socrates of his δαιμόνιον, Socrates says at the very beginning : "The gods

---

[1] Herodot. IX. 33, seq.

have reserved to themselves what is most important in knowledge. Architecture, agriculture, forging, are human arts,
as also government, the science of law, management of the
household and generalship. In all this man can attain to
skill, but for the other, divination is necessary. He who
cultivates a field does not know who will enjoy the fruit, nor
does he who builds a house know who will inhabit it; the
general does not know whether the army should be brought
into the field; he who rules a State whether it is good for him "
(the individual) " or bad. Nor does he who marries a wife
know whether he will experience happiness or whether grief
and sorrow will not come through this to him; neither can
he who has powerful relations in the State, know whether, on
account of these, he may not be banished from the State.
Because of this uncertainty, men have to take refuge in
divination." Regarding it Xenophon expresses himself
(ibid. §§ 3, 4) to the effect that it manifests itself in
different ways through oracles, sacrifices, flight of birds,
&c., but to Socrates this oracle is his Genius. To hold
the future, or what is foreseen by the somnambulist or at
death to be a higher kind of insight, is a perversion which
easily arises even in our ideas; but looked at more closely,
we find in this the particular interests of individuals merely,
and the knowledge of what is right and moral is something
much higher. If anyone wishes to marry or to build a
house, &c., the result is important to the individual only.
The truly divine and universal is the institution of agriculture, the state, marriage, &c.; compared to this it is a trivial
matter to know whether, when I go to sea, I shall perish or
not. The Genius of Socrates moreover reveals itself in him
through nothing other than the counsel given respecting these particular issues, such as when and whether
his friends ought to travel. To anything true, existing in
and for itself in art and science, he made no reference, for
this pertains to the universal mind, and these dæmonic
revelations are thus much more unimportant than those of

his thinking mind. There is certainly something universal in them, since a wise man can often foresee whether anything is advisable or not. But what is truly divine pertains to all, and though talents and genius are also personal characteristics, they find their first truth in their works which are universal.

Now because with Socrates judgment from within first begins to break free from the external oracle, it was requisite that this return into itself should, in its first commencement, still appear in physiological guise (*supra*, pp. 390, 391). The Genius of Socrates stands midway between the externality of the oracle and the pure inwardness of the mind; it is inward, but it is also presented as a personal genius, separate from human will, and not yet as the wisdom and free will of Socrates himself. The further investigation of this Genius consequently presents to us a form which passes into somnambulism, into this double of consciousness; and in Socrates there clearly appears to be something of the kind, or something which is magnetic, for, as we already mentioned (p. 390), he is said often to have fallen into trances and catalepsy. In modern times we have seen this in the form of a rigid eye, an inward knowledge, perception of this thing and that, of what is gone, of what is best to do, &c.; but magnetism carries science no further than this. The Genius of Socrates is thus to be taken as an actual state, and is remarkable because it is not morbid but was necessarily called up through a special condition of his consciousness. For the turning point in the whole world-famed change of views constituting the principle of Socrates, is that in place of the oracle, the testimony of the mind of the individual has been brought forward and that the subject has taken upon itself to decide.

3. With this Genius of Socrates as one of the chief points of his indictment, we now enter upon the subject of his fate, which ends with his condemnation. We may find this fate out of harmony with his professed business of instructing his

fellow-citizens in what is good, but taken in connection with what Socrates and his people were, we shall recognize the necessity of it. The contemporaries of Socrates, who came forward as his accusers before the Athenian people, laid hold on him as the man who made known that what was held as absolute was not absolute. Socrates, with this new principle, and as one who was an Athenian citizen whose express business was this form of instruction, came, through this his personality, into relationship with the whole Athenian people; and this relationship was not merely with a certain number or with a commanding number, but it was a living relationship with the spirit of the Athenian people. The spirit of this people in itself, its constitution, its whole life, rested, however, on a moral ground, on religion, and could not exist without this absolutely secure basis. Thus because Socrates makes the truth rest on the judgment of inward consciousness, he enters upon a struggle with the Athenian people as to what is right and true. His accusation was therefore just, and we have to consider this accusation as also the end of his career. The attacks which Socrates experienced are well known, and were from two sources; Aristophanes attacked him in the " Clouds," and then he was formally accused before the people.

Aristophanes regarded the Socratic philosophy from the negative side, maintaining that through the cultivation of reflecting consciousness, the idea of law had been shaken, and we cannot question the justice of this conception. Aristophanes' consciousness of the one-sidedness of Socrates may be regarded as a prelude to his death; the Athenian people likewise certainly recognized his negative methods in condemning him. It is known that Aristophanes brought upon the stage along with Socrates, not only such men as Aeschylus, and more specially Euripides, but also the Athenians generally and their generals—the personified Athenian people and the gods themselves—a freedom which

we would not dream of were it not historically authenticated.   We have not here to consider the real nature of the
Comedy of Aristophanes, nor the wanton way in which he
was said to have treated Socrates.   As to the first, it
should not startle us, nor do we require to justify
Aristophanes or to excuse him.   The Comedy of Aristophanes is in itself as real a part of the Athenian
people, and Aristophanes is as essential a figure, as were
the sublime Pericles, the happy Alcibiades, the divine
Sophocles, and the moral Socrates, for he belongs as much
as any other to this circle of luminaries (Vol. I., p. 322). Thus
much can alone be said, that it certainly goes against
our German seriousness to see how Aristophanes brings on
the boards men living in the State, by name, in order to
make a jest of them; and we feel this specially in regard
to so upright a man as Socrates.

By chronological considerations, some have tried hard to
refute the fact that Aristophanes' representations had no
influence on the condemnation of Socrates.   It is seen that,
on the one hand, Socrates was treated quite unjustly; but
then we must recognize the merit of Aristophanes, who in
his "Clouds" was perfectly right.   This poet, who exposed Socrates to scorn in the most laughable and bitter
way, was thus no ordinary joker and shallow wag who
mocked what is highest and best, and sacrificed all to wit
with a view to making the Athenians laugh.   For everything has to him a much deeper basis, and in all his jokes
there lies a depth of seriousness.   He did not wish merely
to mock; and moreover to mock what was worthy of
honour would be perfectly bald and flat.   It is a pitiful
wit which has no substance, and does not rest on contradictions lying in the matter itself.   But Aristophanes was
no bad jester.   It is, generally speaking, not possible to
joke in an external way about what does not contain matter
for joking or irony in itself.   For what really is comic is
to show a man or a thing as they disclose themselves in

their extent; and if the thing is not itself its contradiction, the comic element is superficial and groundless. Hence, when Aristophanes makes merry over the Democracy, there is a deep political earnestness at heart, and from all his works it appears what a noble, excellent, true Athenian citizen he was. We thus have a real patriot before us, who, though it involved the punishment of death, did not fear in one of his works to counsel peace. In him, as one who had a patriotism of the most enlightened kind, we find the blissful self-satisfied enjoyment of a people giving free rein to itself. There is, in what is humorous, a self-security which, though with all seriousness it strives after some particular thing, while the opposite of what it aims at always comes to pass, never has for that reason any doubts nor any reflection about itself, since it remains perfectly certain of itself and of what concerns it. We enjoy in Aristophanes this side of the free Athenian spirit, this perfect enjoyment of itself in loss, this untroubled certainty of itself in all miscarriage of the result in real life, and this is the height of humour.

In the "Clouds" we do not indeed see this natural humour, but a contradiction with definite intention. Aristophanes indeed depicts Socrates humorously too, for he brings forth in his moral works the opposite of that from which he starts, and his scholars derive delight from the far-extending discoveries reached through him, which they think are made by their own good luck, but which afterwards turn hateful to them, and become the very opposite of what they intended. The wonderful perception which the followers of Socrates are here represented as having attained, is just a perception of the nullity of the laws of the determinate good as it is to the natural consciousness. Aristophanes made fun of the fact that Socrates occupied himself with elementary researches as to how far fleas spring, and of his putting wax on their feet in order to discover this. This is not historic, but it is well known that Socrates had in his philosophy the side which Aristophanes showed up with such acrimony. Shortly, the fable of the "Clouds" is this : Strepsiades, an honourable Athenian citizen of the old school, had great trouble with his new-fashioned extravagant son, who, spoiled by mother and uncle, kept horses and led a life out of keeping with his position. The father thus got into trouble with his creditors, and went in distress to Socrates, and became his disciple. There the old man learned that not this or that, but another is the right, or rather he learned the stronger (κρείττων) and weaker reasons (ἥττων λόγος). He learned the dialectic of laws, and how, by reasoning, the payment of debts can be disregarded, and he then required that his son should go to the School of Socrates ; and the latter likewise profited from his wisdom. But we find the result ensuing from the universal which has now through the Socratic dialectic become empty, in the private interest or the wrong spirit of Strepsiades and his son, which spirit is merely the negative consciousness of the content of laws. Equipped with this new wisdom of reasons, and the discovery of reasons, Strepsiades is armed against the chief evil that presses on him, as regards his threatening creditors. These now come one after another to obtain payment. But Strepsiades knows how to put them off with excellent reasons, and to argue them away, for he pacifies them by all sorts of *titulos*, and shows them that he does not need to pay them ; indeed he even mocks them, and is very glad that he learned all this from Socrates. But soon the scene changes, and the whole affair alters. The son comes, behaves in a very unseemly way to his father, and finally beats him. The father cries to the supreme power, as if this were the last indignity, but the son shows him, with equally good reasons, obtained by the method derived by him from Socrates, that he had a perfect right to strike him. Strepsiades ends the comedy with execrations on the Socratic dialectic, with a return to his old ways, and with the burning of Socrates' house. The exaggeration which may be ascribed to Aristophanes, is that he drove this dialectic to its bitter end, but it cannot be said that injustice is done to Socrates by this representation. Indeed we must admire the depth of Aristophanes in having recognized the dialectic side in Socrates as being a negative, and—though after his own way—in having presented it so forcibly. For the power of judging in Socrates' method is always placed in the subject, in conscience, but where this is bad, the story of Strepsiades must repeat itself.

With regard to the formal public accusation of Socrates, we must not, like Tennemann (Vol. II., p. 39 seq.), say of Socrates' treatment, that "it is revolting to humanity that this excellent man had to drink the cup of poison as a sacrifice to cabals—so numerous in democracies. A man like Socrates, who had made right" (right is not being discussed, but we may ask what right? The right of moral freedom) "the sole standard of his action, and did. not stray from the straight path, must necessarily make many enemies" (Why? This is foolish; it is a moral hypocrisy to pretend to be better than others who are then called enemies) "who are accustomed to act from quite different motives. When we think of the corruption, and of the rule of the thirty tyrants, we must simply wonder that he could have worked on to his sixtieth year unmolested. But since the Thirty did not venture to lay hands on him themselves, it is the more to be wondered at that in the reconstituted and just rule and freedom which followed the overthrow of despotism"—in that very way the danger in which their principle was, came to be known —"a man like Socrates could be made a sacrifice to cabals. This phenomenon is probably explained by the fact that the enemies of Socrates had first of all to gain time in order to obtain a following, and that under the rule of the Thirty, they played too insignificant a part," and so on.

Now, as regards the trial of Socrates, we have to distinguish two points, the one the matter of the accusation, the judgment of the court, and the other the relation of Socrates to the sovereign people. In the course of justice there are thus these two parts—the relation of the accused to the matter on account of which he is accused, and his relation to the competency of the people, or the recognition of their majesty. Socrates was found guilty by the judges in respect of the content of his accusation, but was condemned to death because he refused to recognize the competency and majesty of the people as regards the accused.

a. The accusation consisted of two points : " That Socrates did not consider as gods those who were held to be such by the Athenian people, but introduced new ones; and that he also led young men astray." [1] The leading away of youth was his casting doubt on what was held to be immediate truth. The first accusation has in part the same foundation, for he made it evident that what was usually so considered, was not acceptable to the gods ; and in part it is to be taken in connection with his Dæmon, not that he called this his god. But with the Greeks this was the direction which the individuality of judgment took; they took it to be a contingency of the individual, and hence, as contingency of circumstances is an external, they also made the contingency of judgment into something external, *i.e.* they consulted their oracles—conscious that the individual will is itself a contingent. But Socrates, who placed the contingency of judgment in himself, since he had his Dæmon in his own consciousness, thereby abolished the external universal Dæmon from which the Greeks obtained their judgments. This accusation, as also Socrates' defence, we wish now to examine further; Xenophon represents both to us, and Plato has also supplied us with an Apology. Meanwhile we may not rest

[1] Xenoph. Apologia Socrat. § 10 ; Memorab. I. c. 1, § 1 Plat. Apologia Socrat. p. 24 (p. 104).

content with saying that Socrates was an excellent man who suffered innocently, &c. (p. 430), for in this accusation it was the popular mind of Athens that rose against the principle which became fatal to him.

a. As regards the first point of the accusation, that Socrates did not honour the national gods, but introduced new ones, Xenophon[1] makes him answer that he always brought the same sacrifices as others to the public altars, as all his fellow-citizens could see—his accusers likewise. But as to the charge that he introduced new Dæmons, in that he heard the voice of God showing him what he should do, he appealed to them whether by soothsayers the cry and flight of birds, the utterances of men (like the voice of Pythia), the position of the entrails of sacrificial animals, and even thunder and lightning were not accepted as divine revelations. That God knows the future beforehand, and, if He wishes, reveals it in these ways, all believe with him; but God can also reveal the future otherwise. He could show that he did not lie in maintaining that he heard the voice of God, from the testimony of his friends, to whom he often announced what was said; and in its results this was always found to be true. Xenophon (Memorab. I. c. 1, § 11) adds, "No one ever saw or heard Socrates do or say anything godless or impious, for he never tried to find out the nature of the Universe, like most of the others, when they sought to understand how what the Sophists called the world began." That is, from them came the earlier atheists, who, like Anaxagoras, held that the sun was a stone.[2]

The effect which the defence against this part of the accusation made on the judges is expressed thus by Xenophon:[3] " One section of them was displeased because they did not believe what Socrates said, and the other part because they were envious that he was more highly honoured

---

[1] Apologia Socrat. §§ 11—13; Memorab. I. c. 1, §§ 2—6; 19.
[2] Plat. Apol. Socrat. p. 26 (108, 109).
[3] Apologia Socrat. § 14 (cf. Memorab. I. c. 1, § 17).

of the gods than they." This effect is very natural. In our times this also happens in two ways. Either the individual is not believed when he boasts of special manifestations, and particularly of manifestations which have to do with individual action and life ; it is neither believed that such manifestations took place at all, or that they happened to this subject. Or if anyone does have dealings with such divinations, rightly enough his proceedings are put an end to, and he is shut up. By this it is not denied in a general way that God foreknows everything, or that He can make revelations to individuals ; this may be admitted *in abstracto,* but not in actuality, and it is believed in no individual cases. Men do not believe that to him, to this individual, there has been a revelation. For why to him more than to others ? And why just this trifle, some quite personal circumstances—as to whether someone should have a successful journey, or whether he should converse with another person, or whether or not he should in a speech properly defend himself ? And why not others amongst the infinitely many things which may occur to the individual ? Why not much more important things, things concerning the welfare of whole States ? Hence it is not believed of an individual, in spite of the fact that if it is possible, it must be to the individual that it happens. This unbelief, which thus does not deny the general fact and general possibility, but believes it in no particular case, really does not believe in the actuality and truth of the thing. It does not believe it because the absolute consciousness—and it must be such—certainly knows nothing of a positive kind of trivialities such as form the subject of these divinations and also those of Socrates ; in spirit such things immemediately vanish away. The absolute consciousness does not know about the future as such, any more than about the past ; it knows only about the present. But because in its present, in its thought, the opposition of future and past to present becomes apparent, it likewise knows about future

P

and past, but of the past as something which has taken shape. For the past is the preservation of the present as reality, but the future is the opposite of this, the Becoming of the present as possibility, and thus the formless. From out of this formlessness the universal first comes into form in the present; and hence in the future no form can be perceived. Men have the dim feeling that when God acts it is not in a particular way, nor for particular objects. Such things are held to be too paltry to be revealed by God in a particular case. It is acknowledged that God determines the individual, but by this the totality of individuality, or all individualities, is understood; hence it is said that God's way of working is found in universal nature.

Now while with the Greeks judgment had the form of a contingency externally posited through the flight and cries of birds, in our culture we decide by an inward contingency, because I myself desire to be this contingency, and the knowledge of individuality is likewise a consciousness of this contingency. But if the Greeks, for whom the category of the contingency of consciousness was an existent, a knowledge of it as an oracle, had this individuality as a universal knowledge of which everyone could ask counsel, in Socrates—in whom what was here externally established had become inward consciousness, as with us, though not yet fully, being still represented as an actual voice, and conceived of as something which he separated from his individuality—the decision of the single individual had the form of personality as a particular, and it was not a universal individuality. This his judges could not in justice tolerate, whether they believed it or not. With the Greeks such revelations had to have a certain nature and method; there were, so to speak, official oracles (not subjective), such as Pythia, a tree, etc. Hence when this appeared in any particular person like a common citizen, it was considered incredible and wrong; the Dæmon of Socrates was a medium of a different kind to any formerly respected in the Greek Religion. It is so much the more noteworthy, that nevertheless the oracle of the Delphian Apollo, Pythia, declared Socrates to be the wisest Greek.[1] Socrates it was who carried out the command of the God of knowledge, "Know Thyself," and made it the motto of the Greeks, calling it the law of the mind, and not interpreting it as meaning á mere acquaintanceship with the particular nature of man. Thus Socrates is the hero who established in the place of the Delphic oracle, the principle that man must look within himself to know what is Truth. Now seeing that Pythia herself pronounced that utterance, we find in it a complete revolution in the Greek mind, and the fact that in place of the oracle, the personal self-consciousness of every thinking man has come into play. This inward certainty, however, is undoubtedly another new god, and not the god of the Athenians existing hitherto, and thus the accusation of Socrates was quite just.

β. If we now consider the second point of the accusation, that Socrates led youth astray, we find that he first sets against it the fact that the oracle of Delphi declared that none could be nobler, juster or wiser than he.[2] And then he sets against this accusation his whole manner of life, and asks whether by the example that he gave, particularly to those with whom he went about, he ever led any into evil.[3] The general accusation had to be further defined and witnesses came forward. "Melitus said that he knew some whom he advised to obey him rather than their parents."[4] This point of the accusation principally related to Anytus, and since he made it good by sufficient testi-

---

[1] Plato. Apol. Socrat. p. 21 (p. 97).
[2] Xenoph. Apol. Socrat. § 14.
[3] Xenoph. Apol. Socrat. §§ 16—19; Memorab. I. c. 2, §§ 1—8.
[4] Xenoph. Apol. Socrat. § 20; cf. Memorab. I. c. 2, § 49 seq.

mony, the point was undoubtedly proved in accordance
with law. Socrates explained himself further on this point
when he left the court. For Xenophon tells us (Apol.
Socr. §§ 27, 29—31) that Anytus was inimical to Socrates,
because he said to Anytus, a respected citizen, that he
should not bring up his son to the trade of a tanner, but in
manner befitting a free man. Anytus was himself a tanner,
and although his business was mostly conducted by slaves,
it was in itself not ignominious, and Socrates' expression was
hence wrong, although, as we have seen (p. 366), quite in the
spirit of Greek thought. Socrates added that he had made
acquaintance with this son of Anytus and discovered no
evil in him, but he prophesied that he would not remain at
this servile work to which his father kept him. Nevertheless, because he had no rational person near to look after
him, he would come to have evil desires and be brought into
dissolute ways. Xenophon added that Socrates' prophecy had
come to pass literally, and that the young man gave himself
up to drink, and drank day and night, becoming totally
depraved. This can be easily understood, for a man who
feels himself to be fit for something better (whether truly
so or not) and through this discord in his mind is discon-
tented with the circumstances in which he lives, yet capable
of attaining to no other, is led out of this disgust into listless-
ness, and is thus on the way to the evil courses which so
often ruin men. The prediction of Socrates is thus quite
natural. (*Supra*, p. 424.)

To this definite accusation that he led sons into disobedience to their parents, Socrates replied by asking the question whether in selecting men for public offices, such as
that of general, parents, or those experienced in war, were
selected. Similarly in all cases those most skilful in an
art or science are picked out. He demanded whether it
was not matter of astonishment that he should be brought
before a judge because he was preferred to parents by the
sons in their aspirations after the highest human good

which is to be made a noble man.[1] This reply of Socrates
is, on the one hand, quite just, but we see at the same time
that we cannot call it exhaustive, for the real point of the
accusation is not touched. What his judges found unjust was
the intrusion morally of a third into the absolute relation between parents and children. On the whole not much can be
said on this point, for all depends on the mode of intervention, and if it is necessary in certain cases, it need not take
place generally, and least of all when some private individual
takes that liberty. Children must have the feeling of
unity with their parents ; this is the first immediately moral
relationship ; every teacher must respect it, keep it pure,
and cultivate the sense of being thus connected. Hence,
when a third person is called into this relation between
parents and children, what happens through the new element introduced, is that the children are for their own good
prevented from confiding in their parents, and made to think
that their parents are bad people who harm them by their
intercourse and training ; and hence we find this revolting.
The worst thing which can happen to children in regard to
their morality and their mind, is that the bond which must
ever be held in reverence should become loosened or even
severed, thereby causing hatred, disdain, and ill-will. Whoever does this, does injury to morality in its truest form.
This unity, this confidence, is the mother's milk of morality
on which man is nurtured; the early loss of parents is therefore a great misfortune. The son, like the daughter, must
indeed come out of his natural unity with the family and
become independent, but the separation must be one which
is natural or unforced, and not defiant and disdainful. When
a pain like this has found a place in the heart, great strength
of mind is required to overcome it and to heal the wound.
If we now speak of the example given us by Socrates, he
seems, through his intervention, to have made the young

[1] Xenoph. Apol. Socrat. §§ 20, 21 ; Memorab. I. c. 2, §§ 51—55 ;
Plat. Apol. Socrat. pp. 24—26 (pp. 103—107).

man dissatisfied with his position. Anytus' son might, indeed, have found his work generally speaking uncongenial, but it is another thing when such dislike is brought into consciousness and established by the authority of a man such as Socrates. We may very well conjecture that if Socrates had to do with him, he strengthened and developed in him the germ of the feeling of incongruity. Socrates remarked on the subject of his capacities, saying that he was fit for something better, and thus established a feeling of dissatisfaction in the young man, and strengthened his dislike to his father, which thus became the reason of his ruin. Hence this accusation of having destroyed the relationship of parents and children may be regarded as not unfounded, but as perfectly well established. It was also thought very bad in Socrates' case particularly, and made a matter of reproach that he had such followers as Critias and Alcibiades, who brought Athens almost to the brink of ruin (*supra*, p. 421). For when he mixed himself in the education which others gave their children, men were justified in the demand that the result should not belie what he professed to do for the education of youth.

The only question now is, how the people came to take notice of this, and in how far such matters can be objects of legislation and be brought into court. In our law, as regards the first part of the accusation, divination such as Cagliostro's is illegal, and it would be forbidden as it formerly was by the Inquisition. Respecting the second point, such a moral interference is no doubt more recognized with us, where there is a particular office having this duty laid upon it; but this interference must keep itself general, and dare not go so far as to call forth disobedience to parents, which is the first immoral principle. But should such questions come before the court? This first of all brings up the question of what is the right of the State, and here great laxity is now allowed. Nevertheless, when some professor or preacher attacks a particular religion, the

legislature would certainly take notice of it, and it would
have a complete right to do so, although there would be
an outcry when it did it. There is undoubtedly a limit
which in liberty of thought and speech is difficult to define
and rests on tacit agreement ; but there is a point beyond
which we find what is not allowed, such as direct incitement to insurrection. It is indeed said, that "bad principles destroy themselves by themselves and find no
entrance." But that is only true in part, for with the popu-
lace the eloquence of sophistry stirs up their passions. It
is also said, "This is only theoretic, no action follows."
But the State really rests on thought, and its existence
depends on the sentiments of men, for it is a spiritual and
not a physical kingdom. Hence it has in so far maxims
and principles which constitute its support, and if these
are attacked, the Government must intervene. Added to
this, it was the case that in Athens quite a different state
of things was present than with us ; in order to be able to
judge rightly of Socrates' case we must first consider the
Athenian State and its customs. According to Athenian
laws, *i.e.* according to the spirit of the absolute State, both
these things done by Socrates were destructive of this
spirit, while in our constitution the universal of the states
is a stronger universal, which last undoubtedly permits of
individuals having freer play, since they cannot be so dangerous to this universal. Hence it would undoubtedly in
the first place mean the subversion of the Athenian State,
if this public religion on which everything was built and
without which the State could not subsist, went to pieces ;
with us the State may be called an absolute and independent power. The Dæmon is now, in fact, a deity
differing from any known, and because it stood in contradiction to the public religion, it gave to it a subjective arbitrariness. But since established religion was
identified with public life so closely that it constituted
a part of public law, the introduction of a new god who

formed self-consciousness into a principle and occasioned
disobedience, was necessarily a crime. We may dispute
with the Athenians about this, but we must allow that they
are consistent. In the second place, the moral connection
between parents and children is stronger, and much more
the moral foundation of life with the Athenians than with
us, where subjective freedom reigns; for family piety is
the substantial key-note of the Athenian State. Socrates
thus attacked and destroyed Athenian life in two fundamental points; the Athenians felt and became conscious of it. Is it then to be wondered at that Socrates
was found guilty? We might say that it had to be so.
Tennemann (Vol. II., p. 41) says: "Though these charges
contained the most palpable untruths, Socrates was condemned to death because his mind was too lofty for him
to descend to the common unworthy means, by which the
judgment of the court was usually perverted." But all
this is false; he was found guilty of these deeds, but not
for that reason condemned to death.

b. We here come to the second occurrence in his history.
In accordance with Athenian laws, the accused had, after
the Heliasts (resembling the English jury) pronounced him
guilty, the liberty of suggesting (ἀντιτιμᾶσθαι) a penalty
different from the punishment which the accuser proposed;
this implied a mitigation of the punishment without a formal
appeal—an excellent provision in Athenian law, testifying
to its humanity. In this penalty the punishment in itself is
not brought into question, but only the kind of punishment; the judges had decided that Socrates deserved punishment. But when it was left to the accused to determine
what his punishment should be, it might not be arbitrary,
but must be in conformity with the crime, a money or
bodily punishment (ὅ, τι χρὴ παθεῖν ἢ ἀποτῖθαι).[1] But it
was implied in the guilty person's constituting himself his

---

[1] Meier und Schömann: Der Attische Process, pp. 173—177.

own judge, that he submitted himself to the decision of the court and acknowledged himself to be guilty. Now Socrates declined to assign a punishment for himself consisting either of fine or banishment, and he had the choice between these and death, which his accusers proposed. He declined to choose the former punishment because he, according to Xenophon's account (Apol. Socr. § 23), in the formality of the exchange-penalty (τὸ ὑποτιμᾶσθαι), as he said, would acknowledge guilt; but there was no longer any question as to the guilt, but only as to the kind of punishment.

This silence may indeed be considered as moral greatness, but, on the other hand, it contradicts in some measure what Socrates says later on in prison, that he did not wish to flee, but remained there, because it seemed better to the Athenians and better to him to submit to the laws (Vol. I., p. 342). But the first submission would have meant that as the Athenians had found him guilty, he respected this decision, and acknowledged himself as guilty. Consistently he would thus have held it better to impose his punishment, since thereby he would not only have submitted himself to the laws, but also to the judgment. We see in Sophocles (Antig., verses 925, 926), the heavenly Antigone, that noblest of figures that ever appeared on earth, going to her death, her last words merely stating—

> " If this seems good unto the gods,
>   Suffering, we may be made to know our error."

Pericles also submitted himself to the judgment of the people as sovereign ; we saw him (Vol. I., p. 328) going round the citizens entreating for Aspasia and Anaxagoras. In the Roman Republic we likewise find the noblest men begging of the citizens. There is nothing dishonouring to the individual in this, for he must bend before the general power, and the real and noblest power is the people. This acknowledgment the people must have direct from those who raise themselves amongst them. Here, on the contrary, Socrates disclaims the submission to, and humiliation before the power of the people, for he did not wish to ask for the remission of his punishment. We admire in him a moral independence which, conscious of its own right, insists upon it and does not bend either to act otherwise, or to recognize as wrong what it itself regards as right. Socrates hence exposed himself to death, which could not be regarded as the punishment for the fault of which he was found guilty; for the fact that he would not himself determine the punishment, and thus disdained the juridical power of the people, was foremost in leading to his condemnation. In a general way he certainly recognized the sovereignty of the people, but not in this individual case; it has, however, to be recognized, not only in general, but in each separate case. With us the competency of the court is presupposed, and the criminal judged without further ado; to-day the whole matter is also open to the light of day and accepted as an acknowledged fact. But with the Athenians we find the characteristic request that the prisoner should, through the act of imposing on himself a penalty, sanction the judge's sentence of guilt. In England this is certainly not the case, but there still remains a like form of asking the accused by what law he wishes to be judged. He then answers, by the law of the land and by the judges of his country. Here we have the recognition of legal operations.

Socrates thus set his conscience in opposition to the judges' sentence, and acquitted himself before its tribunal. But no people, and least of all a free people like the Athenians, has by this freedom to recognize a tribunal of conscience which knows no consciousness of having fulfilled its duty excepting its own consciousness. To this government and law, the universal spirit of the people, may reply: " If you have the consciousness of having done your duty, we must also have the consciousness that you have so done."

For the first principle of a State is that there is no reason or conscience or righteousness or anything else, higher than what the State recognizes as such. Quakers, Anabaptists, &c., who resist any demands made on them by the State, such as to defend the Fatherland, cannot be tolerated in a true State. This miserable freedom of thinking and believing what men will, is not permitted, nor any such retreat behind personal consciousness of duty. If this consciousness is no mere hypocrisy, in order that what the individual does should be recognized as duty, it must be recognized as such by all. If the people can make mistakes the individual may do so much more easily, and he must be conscious that he can do this much more easily than the people. Now law also has a conscience and has to speak through it; the law-court is the privileged conscience. Now if the miscarriage of justice in a trial is shown by every conscience clamouring for something different, the conscience of the court alone possesses any value as being the universal legalized conscience, which does not require to recognize the particular conscience of the accused. Men are too easily convinced of having fulfilled their duty, but the judge finds out whether duty is in fact fulfilled, even if men have the consciousness of its being so.

We should expect nothing else of Socrates than that he should go to meet his death in the most calm and manly fashion. Plato's account of the wonderful scene his last hours presented, although containing nothing very special, forms an elevating picture, and will be to us a permanent representation of a noble deed. The last dialogue of Plato is popular philosophy, for the immortality of the soul is here first brought forward ; yet it brings no consolation, for, as Homer makes Achilles say in the nether world, he would prefer to be a ploughboy on the earth.

But though the people of Athens asserted through the execution of this judgment the rights of their law as against the attacks of Socrates, and had punished the injury caused to their moral life by Socrates, Socrates was still the hero who possessed for himself the absolute right of the mind, certain of itself and of the inwardly deciding consciousness, and thus expressed the higher principle of mind with consciousness. Now because, as has been said, this new principle by effecting an entrance into the Greek world, has come into collision with the substantial spirit and the existing sentiments of the Athenian people, a reaction had to take place, for the principle of the Greek world could not yet bear the principle of subjective reflection. The Athenian people were thus, not only justified, but also bound to react against it according to their law, for they regarded this principle as a crime. In general history we find that this is the position of the heroes through whom a new world commences, and whose principle stands in contradiction to what has gone before and disintegrates it : they appear to be violently destroying the laws. Hence individually they are vanquished, but it is only the individual, and not the principle, which is negated in punishment, and the spirit of the Athenian people did not in the removal of the individual, recover its old position. The false form of individuality is taken away, and that, indeed, in a violent way, by punishment ; but the principle itself will penetrate later, if in another form, and elevate itself into a form of the world-spirit. This universal mode in which the principle comes forth and permeates the present is the true one ; what was wrong was the fact that the principle came forth only as the peculiar possession of one individual. His own world could not comprehend Socrates, but posterity can, in as far as it stands above both. It may be conceived that the life of Socrates had no need to have such an·end, for Socrates might have lived and died a private philosopher, and his teaching might have been quietly accepted by his disciples, and have spread further still without receiving any notice from State or people ; the accusation thus would seem to have been contingent. But it must be said that it was through the manner of that event that this principle became so highly honoured. The principle is not merely something new and peculiar to itself, but it is an absolutely essential moment in the self-developing consciousness of self which is designed to bring to pass as a totality, a new and higher actuality. The Athenians perceived correctly that this principle not only meant opinion and doctrine, for its true attitude was that of a direct and even hostile and destructive relation to the actuality of the Greek mind; and they proceeded in accordance with this perception. Hence, what follows in Socrates' life is not contingent, but necessarily follows upon his principle. Or the honour of having recognized that relation, and indeed of having felt that they themselves were tinged with this principle, is due to the Athenians.

c. The Athenians likewise repented of their condemnation of Socrates, and punished some of his accusers with death itself, and others with banishment; for according to Athenian laws, the man who made an accusation, and whose accusation was found to be false, usually underwent the same punishment that otherwise the criminal would have borne. This is the last act in this drama. On the one hand the Athenians recognized through their repentance the individual greatness of the man; but on the other (and this we find by looking closer) they also recognized that this principle in Socrates, signifying the introduction of new gods and disrespect to parents, has—while destructive and hostile to it—been introduced even into their own spirit, and that they themselves are in the dilemma of having in Socrates only condemned their own principle. In that they regretted the just judgment of Socrates, it seems to be implied that they wished that it had not occurred. But from the regret it does not follow that in itself it should not have occurred, but only that it should not have happened for their consciousness. Both together constitute the innocence which is guilty and atones for its guilt; it would only be senseless and despicable if there were no guilt. An innocent person who comes off badly is a simpleton; hence it is a very flat and uninteresting matter when tyrants and innocent persons are represented in tragedies, just because this is an empty contingency. A great man would be guilty and overcome the great crisis that ensues; Christ thus gave up his individuality, but what was brought forth by him remained.

The fate of Socrates is hence really tragic, not in the superficial sense of the word and as every misfortune is called tragic. The death of an estimable individual must, in such a sense, be specially tragic, and thus it is said of Socrates, that because he was innocent and condemned to death, his fate was tragic. But such innocent suffering would only be sad and not tragic, for it would not be a rational misfortune. Misfortune is only rational when it is brought about by the will of the subject, who must be absolutely justified and moral in what he does, like the power against which he wars—which must therefore not be a merely natural power, or the power of a tyrannic will. For it is only in such a case that man himself has any part in his misfortune, while natural death is only an absolute right which nature exercises over men. Hence, in what is truly tragic there must be valid moral powers on both the sides which come into collision; this was so with Socrates. His is likewise not merely a personal, individually romantic lot; for we have in it the universally moral and tragic fate, the tragedy of Athens, the tragedy of Greece. Two opposed rights come into collision, and the one destroys the other. Thus both suffer loss and yet both are mutually justified; it is not as though the one alone were right and the other wrong. The one power is the divine right, the natural morality whose laws are identical with the will which dwells therein as in its own essence, freely and nobly; we may call it abstractly objective freedom. The other principle, on the contrary, is the right, as really divine, of consciousness or of subjective freedom ; this is the fruit of the tree of the knowledge of good and evil, *i.e.* of self-creative reason ; and it is the universal principle of Philosophy for all successive times.   It is these two principles which we see coming into opposition in the life and the philosophy of Socrates.

The Athenian people had come into a period of culture, in which this individual consciousness made itself independent of the universal spirit and became for itself.   This was perceived by them in Socrates, but at the same time it was felt that it meant ruin, and thus they punished an element which was their own.   The principle of Socrates is hence not the transgression of one individual, for all were implicated ; the crime was one that the spirit of the people committed against itself.   Through this perception the condemnation of Socrates was retracted ; Socrates appeared to have committed no crime, for the spirit of the people has now generally reached the consciousness which turns back from the universal into itself.   This meant the disintegration of this people, whose mind and spirit consequently soon disappeared from the world, but yet out of its ashes a higher took its rise, for the world-spirit had raised itself into a higher consciousness.   The Athenian State, indeed, endured for long, but the bloom of its character soon faded.   It is characteristic of Socrates that he grasped the principle of the inwardness of knowledge, not practically merely, as did Critias and Alcibiades (*supra*, pp. 421, 438), but in thought, making it valid to thought, and this is the higher method.   Knowledge brought about the Fall, but it also contains the principle of Redemption. Thus what to others was only ruin, to Socrates, because it was the principle of knowledge, was also a principle of healing.   The development of this principle, which constitutes the content of all successive history, is explicitly the reason that the later philosophers withdrew from the affairs of the State, restricted themselves to cultivating an inner world, separated from themselves the universal aim of the moral culture of the people, and took up a position contrary to the spirit of Athens and the Athenians. From this it came to pass that particularity of ends and interests now became powerful in Athens. This has, in common with the Socratic principle, the fact that what seems right and duty, good and useful to the subject in relation to himself as well as to the State, depends on his inward determination and choice, and not on the constitution and the universal. This principle of self-determination for the individual has, however, become the ruin of the Athenian people, because it was not yet identified with the constitution of the people; and thus the higher principle must in every case appear to bring ruin with it where it is not yet identified with the substantial of the people. The Athenian life became weak, and the State outwardly powerless, because its spirit was divided within itself. Hence it was dependent on Lacedæmon, and we finally see the external subordination of these States to the Macedonians.

We are done with Socrates. I have been more detailed here because all the features of the case have been so completely in harmony, and he constitutes a great historic turning point. Socrates died at sixty-nine years of age, in Olympiad 95, 1 (399—400 B.C.), an Olympiad after the end of the Peloponnesian war, twenty-nine years after the death of Pericles, and forty-four years before the birth of Alexander. He saw Athens in its greatness and the beginning of its fall; he experienced the height of its bloom and the beginning of its misfortunes.

CHAPTER III

THE development of philosophic science as science, and, further, the progress from the Socratic point of view to the scientific, begins with Plato and is completed by Aristotle. They of all others deserve to be called teachers of the human race.

A. PLATO.

Plato, who must be numbered among the Socratics, was the most renowned of the friends and disciples of Socrates, and he it was who grasped in all its truth Socrates' great principle that ultimate reality lies in consciousness, since, according to him, the absolute is in thought, and all reality is Thought. He does not understand by this a one-sided thought, nor what is understood by the false idealism which makes thought once more step aside and contemplate itself as conscious thought, and as in opposition to reality; it is the thought which embraces in an absolute unity reality as well as thinking, the Notion and its reality in the movement of science, as the Idea of a scientific whole. While Socrates had comprehended the thought which is existent in and for itself, only as an object for self-conscious will, Plato forsook this narrow point of view, and brought the merely abstract right of self-conscious thought, which Socrates had raised to a principle, into the sphere of science. By so doing he rendered it possible to interpret and apply the principle, though his manner of representation may not be altogether scientific.

Plato is one of those world-famed individuals, his philosophy one of those world-renowned creations, whose influence, as regards the culture and development of the mind, has from its commencement down to the present time been all-important. For what is peculiar in the philosophy of Plato is its application to the intellectual and supersensuous world, and its elevation of consciousness into the realm of spirit. Thus the spiritual element which belongs to thought obtains in this form an importance for consciousness, and is brought into consciousness; just as, on the other hand, consciousness obtains a foothold on the soil of the other. The Christian religion has certainly adopted the lofty principle that man's inner and spiritual nature is his true nature, and takes it as its universal principle, though interpreting it in its own way as man's inclination for holiness; but Plato and his philosophy had the greatest share in obtaining for Christianity its rational organization, and in bringing it into the kingdom of the supernatural, for it was Plato who made the first advance in this direction.

We must begin by mentioning the facts of Plato's life. Plato was an Athenian, born in the third year of the 87th Olympiad, or, according to Dodwell, Ol. 87, 4 (B.C. 429), at the beginning of the Peloponnesian war, in the year in which Pericles died. He was, according to this, thirty-nine or forty years younger than Socrates. His father, Ariston, traced his lineage from Cadrus; his mother, Perictione, was descended from Solon. The paternal uncle of his mother was the celebrated Critias, who was for a time among the associates of Socrates, and who was the most talented and brilliant, but also the most dangerous and obnoxious, of the Thirty Tyrants of Athens (*supra*, Vol. I. p.-

421). Critias is usually represented by the ancients as an atheist, with the Cyrenaic Theodorus and Diagoras of Melos; Sextus Empiricus (adv. Math. IX. 51-54) has preserved to us a fine fragment from one of his poems. Sprung from this noble race, and with no lack of means for his culture, Plato received from the most highly esteemed of the Sophists an education in all the arts which were then thought to befit an Athenian. In his family he was called Aristocles; it was only later that he received from his teacher the name, of Plato. Some say that he was so styled because of the breadth of his forehead; others, because of the richness and breadth of his discourse; others again, because of his well-built form.[1]

In his youth he cultivated poetry, and wrote tragedies— very much like young poets in our day—also dithyrambs and songs. Various specimens of the last are still preserved to us in the Greek anthology, and have as subject his various loves; we have amongst others a well-known epigram on a certain Aster, one of his best friends, which contains a pretty fancy, found also in Shakespeare's Romeo and Juliet:

> " To the stars thou look'st, mine Aster,
>   O would that I were Heaven,
>   With eyes so many thus to gaze on thee." [2]

In his youth he had every intention of devoting himself to politics. He was brought by his father to Socrates when in his twentieth year, and enjoyed intimate friendship with him for eight years. It is related that Socrates dreamt on the preceding night that he had a young swan perched on his knees, whose wings quickly developed, and which then flew up to heaven, singing the sweetest songs. Many such incidents are mentioned by the ancients, and they bear witness to the deep reverence and love with which

---

[1] Diog. Laërt. III. 1-4 (Tennemann, Vol. I. p. 416; II. p. 190).
[2] Diog. Laërt. III. 5, 29.

both contemporaries and those of later times regarded the
calm dignity of Plato, and that loftiness of demeanour
which he combined with extreme simplicity and lovable-
ness, traits of character which won for him the name of
" the divine." Plato did not content himself with the
society and wisdom of Socrates, but studied in addition the
older philosophers, particularly Heraclitus. Aristotle
(Met. I. 6) states that Plato, before he ever came to
Socrates, associated with Cratylus, and had been initiated
into the doctrines of Heraclitus. He also studied the
Eleatics, and very particularly the Pythagoreans, and he
frequented the society of the most noted Sophists. Thus
deeply immersed in Philosophy, he lost his interest in
poetry and politics, and gave them up altogether, that he
might devote himself entirely to scientific pursuits. He
fulfilled, like Socrates, his term of military service as an
Athenian citizen, and is said to have taken part in three
campaigns.[1]

We have already mentioned (Vol. I. p. 448) that, after
Socrates was put to death, Plato, like many other philosophers, fled from Athens, and betook himself to Euclides at
Megara. Leaving Megara before long, he travelled first to
Cyrene in Africa, where he turned his attention specially to
mathematics, under the guidance of the celebrated mathematician Theodorus, whom he introduces as taking part in
several of his dialogues. Plato himself soon attained to high
proficiency in mathematics. To him is attributed the solution of the Delian or Delphic problem, which was proposed
by the oracle, and, like the Pythagorean dogma, has reference to the cube. The problem is, to draw a line the cube
of which will be equal to the sum of two given cubes. This
requires a construction through two curves. The nature of
the tasks then set by the oracles is very curious; on this
particular occasion application had been made to the oracle

---

[1] Plat. Epist. VII., p. 324–326 (p. 428–431); Diog. Laërt. III.,
5, 6, 8.

in a time of pestilence, and it responded by proposing an entirely scientific problem ; the change indicated in the spirit of the oracle is highly significant. From Cyrene Plato went to Italy and Egypt. In Magna Græcia he made the acquaintance of the Pythagoreans of that day, Archytas of Tarentum, the celebrated mathematician, Philolaus and others ; and he also bought the writings of the older Pythagoreans at a high price. In Sicily he made friends with Dion. Returning to Athens, he opened a school of Philosophy in the Academy, a grove or promenade in which stood a gymnasium, and there he discoursed to his disciples.[1] This pleasure-ground had been laid out in honour of the hero Academus, but Plato was the true hero of the Academy who did away with the old significance of the name, and overshadowed the fame of the original hero, whose place he so completely took that the latter comes down to after ages only as connected with Plato.

Plato's busy life in Athens was twice interrupted by a journey to Sicily, to the Court of Dionysius the younger, ruler of Syracuse and Sicily. This connection with Dionysius was the most important, if not the only external relation into which Plato entered ; it had, however, no lasting result. Dion, the nearest relative of Dionysius, and other respected Syracusans, his friends, deluded themselves with vain hopes regarding Dionysius. He had been allowed by his father to grow up almost without education, but his friends had instilled into him some notion of and respect for Philosophy, and had roused in him a desire to make acquaintance with Plato. They hoped that Dionysius would profit greatly by his intimacy with Plato, and that his character, which was still unformed, and to all appearance far from unpromising, would be so influenced by Plato's idea of the constitution of a true state, that this might, through him, come to be realized in Sicily. It was partly

[1] Diog. Laërt. III., 6, 7, 9, 18–21; Plat. Epist. VII., p. 326, 327 (p. 431–433).

his friendship with Dion, and partly and more especially
the high hopes he himself cherished of seeing a true form of
government actually established by Dionysius, that induced
Plato to take the mistaken step of journeying to Sicily.
On the surface it seems an excellent idea that a young
prince should have a wise man at his elbow to instruct and
inspire him; and on this idea a hundred political romances
have been based; the picture has, however, no reality
behind it. Dionysius was much pleased with Plato, it is
true, and conceived such a respect for him that he desired
to be respected by him in turn; but this did not last long.
Dionysius was one of those mediocre natures who may
indeed in a half-hearted way aspire to glory and honour,
but are capable of no depth and earnestness, however much
they may affect it, and who lack all strength of character.
His intentions were good, but the power failed him to
carry them out; it was like our own satirical representations in the theatre, of a person who aspires to be quite a
paragon, and turns out an utter fool. The position of affairs
represented thereby can be nothing but this, seeing that
lack of energy alone allows itself to be guided; but it is also
the same lack of energy which renders impossible of execution even a plan made by itself. The rupture between
Plato and Dionysius took place on personal grounds.
Dionysius fell out with his relative Dion, and Plato became
involved in the quarrel, because he would not give up his
friendship with Dion. Dionysius was incapable of a friendship based on esteem and sympathy in pursuits; it was
partly his personal inclination to Plato, and partly mere
vanity, which had made him seek the philosopher's friendship. Dionysius could not, however, induce Plato to come
under any obligation to him; he desired that Plato should
give himself up to him entirely, but this was a demand that
Plato refused to entertain.[1]

[1] Plat. Epist. VII. p. 327–330 (p. 433–439); III. p. 316, 317
(p. 410, 411).

Plato accordingly took his departure.   After the separation, however, both felt the desire to be again together.
Dionysius recalled Plato, in order to effect a reconciliation
with him; he could not endure that he should have failed
in the attempt to attach Plato permanently to himself, and
he found it specially intolerable that Plato would not give
up Dion.   Plato yielded to the urgent representations, not
only of his family and Dion, but also of Archytas and other
Pythagoreans of Tarentum, to whom Dionysius had applied,
and who were taking an interest in the reconciliation of
Dionysius with Dion and Plato ; indeed, they went so far as
to guarantee safety and liberty of departure to Plato.   But
Dionysius found that he could endure Plato's presence no
better than his absence; he felt himself thereby constrained.   And though, by the influence of Plato and his
other companions, a respect for science had been awakened
in Dionysius, and he had thus become more cultured, he
never penetrated beyond the surface.   His interest in
Philosophy was just as superficial as his repeated attempts
in poetry ; and while he wished to be everything—poet,
philosopher, and statesman—he would not submit to be
under the guidance of others.   Thus no closer tie between
Plato and Dionysius was formed ; they drew together
again, and again parted, so that the third visit to Sicily
ended also in coldness, and the connection was not again
established.   This time the ill-feeling with regard to the
continued relations with Dion ran so high, that when Plato
wished to leave Sicily, on account of the treatment his
friend had met with from Dionysius, the latter deprived
him of the means of conveyance, and at last would have
forcibly prevented his departure from Sicily.   The Pythagoreans of Tarentum came at length to the rescue,[1]

---

[1] This circumstance is assigned by Diogenes Laërtius, in the
passage quoted (III. 21, 22), not to the time of Plato's second journey
to Dionysius the younger, i.e. of his third visit to Sicily, where it is
placed by the writers of Plato's Letters, but to the second journey of

demanded Plato back from Dionysius, got him conveyed away safely, and brought him to Greece. They were aided by the circumstance that Dionysius was afraid of an ill report being spread that he was not on good terms with Plato.[1] Thus Plato's hopes were shattered, and his dream of shaping the constitution in accordance with the demands of his own philosophic ideas, through the agency of Dionysius, proved vain.

At a later date, therefore, he actually refused to be the lawgiver of other States, though they had made application to him for that very purpose; amongst these applicants were the inhabitants of Cyrene and the Arcadians. It was a time when many of the Greek States found their constitutions unsatisfactory, and yet could not devise anything new.[2] Now in the last thirty years[3] many constitutions have been drawn up, and it would be no hard task for anyone having had much experience in this work to frame another. But theorizing is not sufficient for a constitution; it is not individuals who make it; it is something divine and spiritual, which develops in history. So strong is this power of the world-spirit that the thought of an individual is as nothing against it; and when such thoughts do count for something, *i.e.* when they can be realized, they are then none other than the product of this power of the universal spirit. The idea that Plato should become lawgiver was not adapted for the times; Solon and Lycurgus were lawgivers, but in Plato's day such a thing was impracticable. He declined any further compliance with the wishes of these States, because they would not agree to the first condition which he imposed, namely, the abolition

Plato to Sicily, which corresponds with his first visit to Dionysius the younger.—[Editor's note.]

[1] Plat. Epist. VII. p. 337–342 (p. 453–461), p. 344–350 (p. 466–477); III. p. 317, 318 (p. 411–415).

[2] Plat. Epist. VII. p. 326 (p. 431).

[3] From the lectures of 1825.

of all private property,[1] a principle which we shall deal with later, in considering Plato's practical philosophy. Honoured thus throughout the whole land, and especially in Athens, Plato lived until the first year of the 108th Olympiad (B.C. 348); and died on his birthday, at a wedding feast, in the eighty-first year of his age.[2]

We have to speak, in the first place, of the direct mode in which Plato's philosophy has come down to us; it is to be found in those of his writings which we possess; indubitably they are one of the fairest gifts which fate has preserved from the ages that are gone. His philosophy is not, however, properly speaking, presented there in systematic form, and to construct it from such writings is difficult, not so much from anything in itself, as because this philosophy has been differently understood in different periods of time; and, more than all, because it has been much and roughly handled in modern times by those who have either read into it their own crude notions, being unable to conceive the spiritual spiritually, or have regarded as the essential and most significant element in Plato's philosophy that which in reality does not belong to Philosophy at all, but only to the mode of presentation; in truth, however, it is only ignorance of Philosophy that renders it difficult to grasp the philosophy of Plato. The form and matter of these works are alike of interest and importance. In studying them we must nevertheless make sure, in the first place, what of Philosophy we mean to seek and may find within them, and, on the other hand, what Plato's point of view never can afford us, because in his time it was not there to give. Thus it may be that the longing with which we approached Philosophy is left quite unsatisfied; it is, however, better that we should not be altogether satisfied than that such conclusions should be

---

[1] Diog. Laërt. III. 23 (Menag. ad h.l.); Ælian Var. Histor. II. 42; Plutarch. ad principem ineruditum, init. p. 779, ed. Xyl.

[2] Diog. Laërt. III. 2; Bruckeri Hist. Crit. Philos. Vol. I. p. 653.

regarded as final. Plato's point of view is clearly defined and necessary, but it is impossible for us to remain there, or to go back to it; for Reason now makes higher demands. As for regarding it as the highest standpoint, and that which we must take for our own—it belongs to the weaknesses of our time not to be able to bear the greatness, the immensity of the claims made by the human spirit, to feel crushed before them, and to flee from them faint-hearted. We must stand above Plato, *i.e.* we must acquaint ourselves with the needs of thoughtful minds in our own time, or rather we must ourselves experience these needs. Just as the pedagogue's aim is to train up men so as to shield them from the world, or to keep them in a particular sphere—the counting-house, for instance, or bean-planting, if you wish to be idyllic—where they will neither know the world nor be known by it; so in Philosophy a return has been made to religious faith, and therefore to the Platonic philosophy.[1] Both are moments which have their due place and their own importance, but they are not the philosophy of our time. It would be perfectly justifiable to return to Plato in order to learn anew from him the Idea of speculative Philosophy, but it is idle to speak of him with extravagant enthusiasm, as if he represented beauty and excellence in general. Moreover, it is quite superfluous for Philosophy, and belongs to the hypercriticism of our times, to treat Plato from a literary point of view, as Schleiermacher does, critically examining whether one or another of the minor dialogues is genuine or not. Regarding the more important of the dialogues, we may mention that the testimony of the ancients leaves not the slightest doubt.

Then of course the very character of Plato's works, offering us in their manysidedness various modes of treating Philosophy, constitutes the first difficulty standing in the way of a comprehension of his philosophy. If we

[1] Compare Vol. I. p. 47—53.

still had the oral discourses (ἄγραφα δόγματα) of Plato, under
the title " Concerning the Good " (περὶ τἀγαθοῦ), which
his scholars noted down, we should have had his philosophy
before us in simpler, because in more systematic form.[1]
Aristotle seems to have had these discourses before him,
when dealing with the philosophy of Plato, and he quotes
them in his work " On Philosophy," or, " On the Ideas,"
or, " On the Good " (Brandis has written on this topic).
But, as it happens, we have only Plato's Dialogues, and
their form renders it all the more difficult for us to gather
a definite idea of his philosophy. For the dialogue form
contains very heterogeneous elements ; Philosophy proper
in the treatment of absolute Being, and, intermingled with
that, its particular mode of representation. It is just this
which constitutes the manysidedness of Plato's works.

A second difficulty is said to lie in the distinction drawn
between exoteric and esoteric philosophy. Tennemann
(Vol. II. p. 220) says : " Plato exercised the right, which
is conceded to every thinker, of communicating only so
much of his discoveries as he thought good, and of so
doing only to those whom he credited with capacity to
receive it. Aristotle, too, had an esoteric and an exoteric
philosophy, but with this difference, that in his case the
distinction was merely formal, while with Plato it was also
material." How nonsensical! This would appear as if
the philosopher kept possession of his thoughts in the same
way as of his external goods : the philosophic Idea is, however, something utterly different, and instead of being
possessed by, it possesses a man. When philosophers discourse on philosophic subjects, they follow of necessity the
course of their ideas; they cannot keep them in their
pockets ; and when one man speaks to another, if his

---

[1] Brandis : De perditis Aristotelis libris de ideis et de bono, sive
philosophia, p. 1–13. (Compare Michelet : Examen critique de
l'ouvrage d'Aristote intitulé Métaphysique, 1835, p. 28–78.)—[Editor's
note.]

words have any meaning at all, they must contain the idea present to him. It is easy enough to hand over an external possession, but the communication of ideas requires a certain skill; there is always something esoteric in this, something more than the merely exoteric. This difficulty is therefore trifling.

Thirdly, as one of the circumstances that render it difficult to comprehend Plato's own speculative thought, we can scarcely reckon the external consideration that in his Dialogues he does not speak in his own person, but introduces Socrates and many others as the speakers, without always making it plain which of them expresses the writer's own opinion. By reason of this historic circumstance, which seems to bear out the manysidedness of Plato, it has of course been often said, by ancients as well as moderns, that he merely expounded, from a historical point of view, the system and doctrine of Socrates, that he adapted much in the Dialogues from various Sophists, and avowedly advanced many theorems belonging to an earlier date, especially those of the Pythagoreans, Heraclitics, and Eleatics, even adopting, in the last case, the Eleatic mode of treatment. Hence it was said that to these philosophies the whole matter of the treatise belonged, the outward form alone being Plato's. It is therefore necessary to distinguish what is peculiarly his and what is not, or whether the component parts are in harmony. In the Socratic Dialogues that we have from Cicero, the personages can be much more readily made out; but in Cicero there is nothing of real interest offered to us. With Plato there can be no talk of this ambiguity, and the difficulty is only in appearance. In the Dialogues of Plato his philosophy is quite clearly expressed; they are not constructed as are the conversations of some people, which consist of many monologues, in which one person expresses a certain opinion and another person differs from him, and both hold to their own way of thinking. Here, on the contrary, the divergency of opinions which comes out is examined, and a conclusion arrived at as to the truth; or, if the result is negative, the whole process of knowledge is what is seen in Plato. There is, therefore, no need to inquire further as to what belongs to Socrates in the Dialogues, and what belongs to Plato. This further observation we must, however, make, that since Philosophy in its ultimate essence is one and the same, every succeeding philosopher will and must take up into his own, all philosophies that went before, and what falls specially to him is their further development. Philosophy is not a thing apart, like a work of art; though even in a work of art it is the skill which the artist learns from others that he puts into practice. What is original in the artist is his conception as a whole, and the intelligent use of the means already at his command; there may occur to him in working an endless variety of ideas and discoveries of his own. But Philosophy has one thought, one reality, as its foundation; and nothing can be put in the place of the true knowledge of this already attained; it must of necessity make itself evident in later developments. Therefore, as I have already observed (Vol. I. p. 166), Plato's Dialogues are not to be considered as if their aim were to put forward a variety of philosophies, nor as if Plato's were an eclectic philosophy derived from them; it forms rather the knot in which these abstract and one-sided principles have become truly united in a concrete fashion. In giving a general idea of the history of Philosophy, we have already seen (Vol. I. p. 54) that such points of union, in which the true is concrete, must occur in the onward course of philosophical development. The concrete is the unity of diverse determinations and principles; these, in order to be perfected, in order to come definitely before the consciousness, must first of all be presented separately. Thereby they of course acquire an aspect of one-sidedness in comparison with the higher principle which follows: this, nevertheless,

does not annihilate them, nor even leave them where they
were, but takes them up into itself as moments. Thus in
Plato's philosophy we see all manner of philosophic teaching from earlier times absorbed into a deeper principle, and
therein united. It is in this way that Plato's philosophy
shows itself to be a totality of ideas : therefore, as the
result, the principles of others are comprehended in itself.
Frequently Plato does nothing more than explain the
doctrines of earlier philosophers ; and the only particular
feature in his representation of them is that their scope
is extended. His Timæus is, by unanimous testimony,
the amplification of a still extant work of Pythagoras ; [1]
and, in like manner, his amplification of the doctrine of
Parmenides is of such a nature that its principle is freed
from its one-sided character.

These last two difficulties having been disposed of, if we
would likewise solve the first mentioned, we must proceed
to describe the form in which Plato has propounded his
ideas, keeping it, on the other hand, distinct from Philosophy proper, as we find it with him. The form of the
Platonic philosophy is, as is well known, the dialogue. The
beauty of this form is highly attractive : yet we must not
think, as many do, that it is the most perfect form in which
to present Philosophy ; it is peculiar to Plato, and as a work
of art is of course to be much esteemed.

In the first place, scenery and dramatic form belong to
what is external. Plato gives to his Dialogues a setting of
reality, both as regards place and persons, and chooses out
some particular occasion which has brought his characters
together; this in itself is very natural and charming.
Socrates takes the leading part, and among the other actors
there are many stars well known to us, such as Agathon,
Zeno, and Aristophanes. We find ourselves in some parti-
ticular spot; in the Phædrus (p. 229 Steph.; p. 6 Bekk.) it

[1] Scholia in Timæum, p. 423, 424 (ed. Bekk: Commentar crit. in
Plat. Vol. II.).

is at the plane tree beside the clear waters of the Ilyssus, through which Socrates and Phædrus pass; in other dialogues we are conducted to the halls of the gymnasia, to the Academy, or to a banquet. By never allowing himself to appear in person, but putting his thoughts always in the mouth of others, any semblance of preaching or of dogmatizing is avoided by Plato, and the narrator appears just as little as he does in the History of Thucydides or in Homer. Xenophon sometimes brings himself forward, sometimes he entirely loses sight of the aim he had in view, of vindicating by what he tells of them the life of Socrates and his method of instruction. With Plato, on the contrary, all is quite objective and plastic; and he employs great art in removing from himself all responsibility for his assertions, often assigning them even to a third or fourth person.

As regards the tone of the intercourse between the characters in these Dialogues, we find that the noblest urbanity of well-bred men reigns supreme; the Dialogues are a lesson in refinement; we see in them the *savoir faire* of a man acquainted with the world. The term courtesy does not quite express urbanity; it is too wide, and includes the additional notion of testifying respect, of expressing deference and personal obligation; urbanity is true courtesy, and forms its real basis. But urbanity makes a point of granting complete liberty to all with whom we converse, both as regards the character and matter of their opinions, and also the right of giving expression to the same. Thus in our counter-statements and contradictions we make it evident that what we have ourselves to say against the statement made by our opponent is the mere expression of our subjective opinion; for this is a conversation carried on by persons as persons, and not objective reason talking with itself. However energetically we may then express ourselves, we must always acknowledge that our opponent is also a thinking person; just as one must not take to speaking with the air of being an oracle, nor prevent anyone else from opening his mouth in reply. This urbanity is, however, not forbearance, but rather the highest degree of frankness and candour, and it is this very characteristic which gives such gracefulness to Plato's Dialogues.

Finally, this dialogue is not a conversation, in which what is said has, and is meant to have, a merely casual connection, without any exhaustive treatment of the subject. When one talks only for amusement, the casual and arbitrary sequence of ideas is quite to be expected. In the introduction, to be sure, the Dialogues of Plato have sometimes this very character of being mere conversations, and consequently appear to take an accidental form; for Socrates is made to take his start from the particular conceptions of certain individuals, and from the circle of their ideas (Vol. I. p. 397). Later, however, these dialogues become a systematic development of the matter in hand, wherein the subjective character of the conversation disappears, and the whole course of the argument shows a beautifully consistent dialectic process. Socrates talks, turns the conversation, lays down his own views, draws a conclusion, and does all this through the apparent instrumentality of the question; most questions are so framed as to be answered by merely Yes or No. The dialogue seems to be the form best adapted for representing an argument, because it sways hither and thither; the different sides are allotted to different persons, and thus the argument is made more animated. The dialogue has, however, this disadvantage, that it seems to be carried on arbitrarily, so that at the end the feeling always remains that the matter might have turned out differently. But in the Platonic Dialogues this arbitrary character is apparent only; it has been got rid of by limiting the development to the development of the subject in hand, and by leaving very little to be said by the second speaker.

Such personages are, as we already saw in connection with Socrates (Vol. I. p. 402), plastic personages as regards the conversation; no one is put there to state his own views, or, as the French express it, *pour placer son mot.* Just as in the Catechism the answers are prescribed to the questions asked, so is it in these dialogues, for they who answer have to say what the author pleases. The question is so framed that a quite simple answer is alone possible, and, thanks to the artistic beauty and power of the dialogues, such an answer appears at the same time perfectly natural.

In the next place, there is connected with this outward aspect of personality the circumstance that the Platonic philosophy does not proclaim itself to be one particular field, where some one begins a science of his own in a sphere of his own; for it sometimes enters into the ordinary conceptions of culture, like those of Socrates, sometimes into those of the Sophists, at other times into those of earlier philosophers, and in so doing brings before us exemplifications from ordinary knowledge, and also uses the methods of the same. A systematic exposition of Philosophy we cannot in this way find; and of course it is all the less easy for us to take a comprehensive view of the subject, since there are at hand no means of judging whether the treatment has been exhaustive or not. Nevertheless, there is present there one spirit, one definite point of view as regards Philosophy, even though Mind does not make its appearance in the precise form which we demand. The philosophic culture of Plato, like the general culture of his time, was not yet ripe for really scientific work; the Idea was still too fresh and new; it was only in Aristotle that it attained to a systematic scientific form of representation.

Connected with this deficiency in Plato's mode of representation, there is also a deficiency in respect of the concrete determination of the Idea itself, since the various elements of the Platonic philosophy which are represented in these dialogues, namely the merely popular conceptions of Being and the apprehending knowledge of the same, are really mixed up in a loose, popular way, so that the former more especially come to be represented in a myth or parable; such intermingling is inevitable in this beginning of science proper in its true form. Plato's lofty mind, which had a perception or conception of Mind, penetrated through his subject with the speculative Notion, but he only began to penetrate it thus, and he did not yet embrace the whole of its reality in the Notion; or the knowledge which appeared in Plato did not yet fully realize itself in him. Here it therefore happens sometimes that the ordinary conception of reality again separates itself from its Notion, and that the latter comes into opposition with it, without any statement having been made that the Notion alone constitutes reality. Thus we find Plato speaking of God, and again, in the Notion, of the absolute reality of things, but speaking of them as separated, or in a connection in which they both appear separated; and God, as an uncomprehended existence, is made to belong to the ordinary conception. Sometimes, in order to give greater completeness and reality, in place of following out the Notion, mere pictorial conceptions are introduced, myths, spontaneous imaginations of his own, or tales derived from the sensuous conception, which no doubt are determined by thought, but which this has never permeated in truth, but only in such a way that the intellectual is determined by the forms of ordinary conception. For instance, appearances of the body or of nature, which are perceptible by the senses, are brought forward along with thoughts regarding them, which do not nearly so completely exhaust the subject as if it had been thoroughly thought out, and the Notion allowed to pursue an independent course.

Looking at this as it bears on the question of how Plato's philosophy is to be apprehended, we find, owing to these two circumstances, that either too much or too little is found in it. Too much is found by the ancients, the so-called Neoplatonists, who sometimes dealt with Plato's philosophy as they dealt with the Greek mythology. This they allegorized and represented as the expression of ideas —which the myths certainly are—and in the same way they first raised the ideas in Plato's myths to the rank of theorems: for the merit of Philosophy consists alone in the fact that truth is expressed in the form of the Notion. Sometimes, again, they took what with Plato is in the form of the Notion for the expression of Absolute Being— the theory of Being in the Parmenides, for instance, for the knowledge of God—just as if Plato had not himself drawn a distinction between them. But in the pure Notions of Plato the ordinary conception as such is not abrogated; either it is not said that these Notions constitute its reality, or they are to Plato no more than a conception, and not reality. Again, we certainly see that too little is found in Plato by the moderns in particular; for they attach themselves pre-eminently to the side of the ordinary conception, and see in it reality. What in Plato relates to the Notion, or what is purely speculative, is nothing more in their eyes than roaming about in abstract logical notions, or than empty subtleties: on the other hand, they take that for theorem which was enunciated as a popular conception. Thus we find in Tennemann (Vol. II. p. 376) and others an obstinate determination to lead back the Platonic Philosophy to the forms of our former metaphysic, *e.g.* to the proof of the existence of God.

However much, therefore, Plato's mythical presentation of Philosophy is praised, and however attractive it is in his Dialogues, it yet proves a source of misapprehensions; and it is one of these misapprehensions, if Plato's myths are held to be what is most excellent in his philosophy. Many propositions, it is true, are made more easily intelligible by being presented in mythical form; nevertheless, hat is not the true way of presenting them; propositions are thoughts which, in order to be pure, must be brought forward as such. The myth is always a mode of representation which, as belonging to an earlier stage, introduces sensuous images, which are directed to imagination, not to thought; in this, however, the activity of thought is suspended, it cannot yet establish itself by its own power, and so is not yet free. The myth belongs to the pedagogic stage of the human race, since it entices and allures men to occupy themselves with the content; but as it takes away from the purity of thought through sensuous forms, it cannot express the meaning of Thought. When the Notion attains its full development, it has no more need of the myth. Plato often says that it is difficult to express one's thoughts on such and such a subject, and he therefore will employ a myth; no doubt this is easier. Plato also says of simple Notions that they are dependent, transitory moments, which have their ultimate truth in God; and in this first mention of God by Plato, He is made a mere conception. Thus the manner of conception and the genuinely speculative element are confounded.

In order to gather Plato's philosophy from his dialogues, what we have to do is to distinguish what belongs to ordinary conception—especially where Plato has recourse to myths for the presentation of a philosophic idea—from the philosophic idea itself; only then do we know that what belongs only to the ordinary conception, as such, does not belong to thought, is not the essential. But if we do not recognize what is Notion, or what is speculative, there is inevitably the danger of these myths leading us to draw quite a host of maxims and theorems from the dialogues, and to give them out as Plato's philosophic propositions, while they are really nothing of the kind, but belong entirely to the manner of presentation. Thus, for instance, in the Timæus (p. 41 Steph.; p. 43 Bekk) Plato makes use of the form, God created the world, and the dæmons had a certain share in the work; this is spoken quite after the manner of the popular conception. If, however, it is taken as a philosophic dogma on Plato's part that God made the world, that higher beings of a spiritual kind exist, and, in the creation of the world, lent God a helping hand, we may see that this stands word for word in Plato, and yet it does not belong to his philosophy. When in pictorial fashion he says of the soul of man that it has a rational and an irrational part, this is to be taken only in a general sense ; Plato does not thereby make the philosophic assertion that the soul is compounded of two kinds of substance, two kinds of thing. When he represents knowledge or learning as a process of recollection, this may be taken to mean that the soul existed before man's birth. In like manner, when he speaks of the central point of his philosophy, of Ideas, of the Universal, as the permanently self-existent, as the patterns of things sensible, we may easily be led to think of these Ideas, after the manner of the modern categories of the understanding, as substances which exist outside reality, in the Understanding of God ; or on their own account and as independent—like the angels, for example. In short, all that is expressed in the manner of pictorial conception is taken by the moderns in sober earnest for philosophy. Such a representation of Plato's philosophy can be supported by Plato's own words ; but one who knows what Philosophy is, cares little for such expressions, and recognizes what was Plato's true meaning.

In the account of the Platonic philosophy to which I must now proceed, the two cannot certainly be separated, but they must be noted and judged of in a very different manner from that which has prevailed amongst the moderns. We have, on the one hand, to make clear Plato's general conception of what Philosophy and Knowledge really are, and on the other to develop the particular branches of Philosophy of which he treats.

In considering his general conception of Philosophy, the

first point that strikes us is the high estimation in which Plato held Philosophy. The lofty nature of the knowledge of Philosophy deeply impressed him, and he shows a real enthusiasm for the thought which deals with the absolute. Just as the Cyrenaics treat of the relation of the existent to the individual consciousness, and the Cynics assert immediate freedom to be reality, Plato upholds the self-mediating unity of consciousness and reality, or knowledge. He everywhere expresses the most exalted ideas regarding the value of Philosophy, as also the deepest and strongest sense of the inferiority of all else; he speaks of it with the greatest energy and enthusiasm, with all the pride of science, and in a manner such as nowadays we should not venture to adopt. There is in him none of the so-called modest attitude of this science towards other spheres of knowledge, nor of man towards God. Plato has a full consciousness of how near human reason is to God, and indeed of its unity with Him. Men do not mind reading this in Plato, an ancient, because it is no longer a present thing, but were it coming from a modern philosopher, it would be taken much amiss. Philosophy to Plato is man's highest possible possession and true reality; it alone has to be sought of man. Out of many passages on this subject I shall quote in the first instance the following from the Timæus (p. 47 Steph.; p. 54 Bekk.): "Our knowledge of what is most excellent begins with the eyes. The distinction between the visible day and the night, the months and courses of the planets, have begotten a knowledge of time, and awakened a desire to know the nature of the whole. From this we then obtained Philosophy, and no greater gift than this, given by God to man, has ever come or will come."

The manner in which Plato expresses his opinions on this subject in the Republic is very well known, as it is greatly decried, because it so completely contradicts the common ideas of men, and it is all the more surprising in that it concerns the relation of Philosophy to the state, and therefore to actuality. For before this, though a certain value might indeed be attributed to Philosophy, it still remained confined to the thoughts of the individual; here, however, it goes forth into questions of constitution, government, actuality. After Plato made Socrates, in the Republic, expound the nature of a true state, he caused Glaucon to interrupt by expressing his desire that Plato should show how it could be possible for such a state to exist. Socrates parries the question, will not come to the point, seeks evasive pleas, and tries to extricate himself by asserting that in describing what is just, he does not bind himself to show how it might be realized in actuality, though some indication must certainly be given of how an approximate, if not a complete realization of it might be possible. Finally, when pressed, he says : "Then it shall be expressed, even though a flood of laughter and utter disbelief overwhelm me. When philosophers rule the states, or the so-called kings and princes of the present time are truly and completely philosophers, when thus political greatness and Philosophy meet in one, and the many natures who now follow either side to the exclusion of the other, come together, then, and not till then, can there be an end, dear Glaucon, either to the evils of the state or, as I believe, to those of the human race. Then only will this state of which I spoke be possible or see the light of day." "This," adds Socrates, "is what I have so long hesitated to say, because I know that it is so much opposed to ordinary ideas." Plato makes Glaucon answer, "Socrates, you have expressed what, you must recollect, would cause many men, and not bad men either, to pull off their coats and seize the first weapon that comes to hand, and set upon you one and all with might and main; and if you don't know how to appease them with your reasons, you will have to answer for it."[1]

[1] Plat. De Republica, V. p. 471–474 (p. 257–261).

Plato here plainly asserts the necessity for thus uniting Philosophy with government. As to this demand, it may seem a piece of great presumption to say that philosophers should have the government of states accorded to them, for the territory or ground of history is different from that of Philosophy. In history, the Idea, as the absolute power, has certainly to realize itself; in other words, God rules in the world. But history is the Idea working itself out in a natural way, and not with the consciousness of the Idea. The action is certainly in accordance with general reflections on what is right, moral, and pleasing to God; but we must recognize that action represents at the same time the endeavours of the subject as such for particular ends. The realization of the Idea thus takes place through an intermingling of thoughts and Notions with immediate and particular ends. Hence it is only on the one side produced through thoughts, and on the other through circumstances, through human actions in their capacity of means. These means often seem opposed to the Idea, but that does not really matter; all those particular ends are really only means of bringing forth the Idea, because it is the absolute power. Hence the Idea comes to pass in the world, and no difficulty is caused, but it is not requisite that those who rule should have the Idea.

In order, however, to judge of the statement that the regents of the people should be philosophers, we must certainly consider what was understood by Philosophy in the Platonic sense and in the sense of the times. The word Philosophy has had in different periods very different significations. There was a time when a man who did not believe in spectres or in the devil was called a philosopher. When such ideas as these pass away, it does not occur to people to call anyone a philosopher for a reason such as this. The English consider what we call experimental physics to be Philosophy; a philosopher to them is anyone who makes investigations in, and possesses a theoretic know-

ledge of chemistry, mechanics, &c. (Vol. I. p. 57).   In
Plato Philosophy becomes mingled with the knowledge of
the supersensuous, or what to us is religious knowledge.
The Platonic philosophy is thus the knowledge of the absolutely true and right, the knowledge of universal ends
in the state, and the recognition of their validity.   In all
the history of the migration of the nations, when the
Christian religion became the universal religion, the only
point of interest was to conceive the supersensuous
kingdom—which was at first independent, absolutely
universal and true—as actualized, and to determine actuality
in conformity thereto.   This has been from that time forth
the business of culture.   A state, a government and constitution of modern times has hence quite a different basis
from a state of ancient times, and particularly from one
of Plato's day.   The Greeks were then altogether dissatisfied with their democratic constitution, and the conditions resulting from it (*supra*, p. 8), and similarly all
philosophers condemned the democracies of the Greek
states in which such things as the punishment of generals
(*supra*, Vol. I. p. 391) took place.   In such a constitution it
might certainly be thought that what was best for the
state would be the first subject of consideration ; but arbitrariness prevailed, and this was only temporarily restrained
by preponderating individualities, or by masters in states-
manship like Aristides, Themistocles, and others.   This
condition of matters preceded the disintegration of the constitution.   In our states, on the other hand, the end of the
state, what is best for all, is immanent and efficacious in
quite another way than was the case in olden times.   The
condition of the laws and courts of justice, of the constitution and spirit of the people, is so firmly established in
itself that matters of the passing moment alone remain to
be decided ; and it may even be asked what, if anything, is
dependent on the individual.

To us government means that in the actual state

procedure will be in accordance with the nature of the thing, and since a knowledge of the Notion of the thing is requisite to this, actuality is brought into harmony with the Notion, and thereby the Idea is realized in existence. The result of this thus is that when Plato says that philosophers should rule, he signifies the determination of the whole matter through universal principles. This is realized much more in modern states, because universal principles really form the bases—certainly not of all, but of most of them. Some have already reached this stage, others are striving to reach it, but all recognize that such principles must constitute the real substance of administration and rule.

What Plato demands is thus, in point of fact, already present. But what we call Philosophy, movement in pure thoughts, has to do with form, and this is something peculiar to itself; nevertheless, the form is not responsible if the universal, freedom, law, is not made a principle in a state. Marcus Aurelius is an example of what a philosopher upon a throne could effect; we have, however, only private actions to record of him, and the Roman Empire was made no better by him. Frederick II. was, on the other hand, justly called the philosopher king. He occupied himself with the Wolffian metaphysics and French philosophy and verses, and was thus, according to his times, a philosopher. Philosophy appears to have been an affair of his own particular inclination, and quite distinct from the fact that he was king. But he was also a philosophic king in the sense that he made for himself an entirely universal end, the well-being and good of the state, a guiding principle in his actions and in all his regulations in respect to treaties with other states, and to the rights of individuals at home; these last he entirely subordinated to absolutely universal ends. If, however, later on, procedure of this kind became ordinary custom, the succeeding princes are no longer called philosophers, even if the same principle is present to them, and the government, and especially the institutions, are founded on it.

In the Republic, Plato further speaks in a figure of the difference between a condition of philosophic culture and a lack of Philosophy: it is a long comparison which is both striking and brilliant. The idea which he makes use of is as follows:—" Let us think of an underground den like a cave with a long entrance opening to the light. Its inhabitants are chained so that they cannot move their necks, and can see only the back of the cave. Far behind their backs a torch burns above them. In the intervening space there is a raised way and also a low wall; and behind this wall " (towards the light) "there are men who carry and raise above it all manner of statues of men and animals like puppets in a marionette show, sometimes talking to one another meanwhile, and sometimes silent. Those who are chained would see only the shadows which fall on the opposite wall, and they would take them for reality; they would hear, moreover, by means of the echo, what was said by those who moved the figures, and they would think that it was the voice of the shadows. Now if one of the prisoners were released, and compelled to turn his neck so as to see things as they are, he would think that what he saw was an illusive dream, and that the shadows were the reality. And if anyone were to take him out of the prison into the light itself, he would be dazzled by the light and could see nothing; and he would hate the person who brought him to the light, as having taken away what was to him the truth, and prepared only pain and evil in its place." [1] This kind of myth is in harmony with the character of the Platonic philosophy, in that it separates the conception of the sensuous world present in men from the knowledge of the supersensuous.

Since we now speak more fully of this matter, we must in the second place consider the nature of knowledge

---

[1] Plat. De Republica VII. pp. 514–516 (pp. 326–328).

according to Plato, and in so doing commence our account of the Platonic philosophy itself.

a. Plato gave a more precise definition of philosophers as those " who are eager to behold the truth."—Glaucon : " That is quite right. But how do you explain it ? " Socrates : " I tell this not to everyone, but you will agree with me in it." " In what ? " " In this, that as the Beautiful is opposed to the Ugly, they are two things." " Why not ? " " With the Just and the Unjust, the Good and the Evil, and every other Idea (εἶδος) the case is the same, that each of them is by itself a One; on the other hand, on account of its combination with actions and bodies and other Ideas springing up on every side, each appears as a Many." " You are right." " I distinguish now, according to this, between the sight-loving, art-loving, busy class on the one side, and those on the other side, of whom we were just speaking as alone entitled to be called philosophers." " What do you mean by that ? " " I mean by that, such as delight in seeing and hearing, who love beautiful voices, and colours, and forms, and all that is composed thereof, while their mind is still incapable of seeing and loving the Beautiful in its own nature." " Such is the case." " Those, however, who have the power of passing on to the Beautiful itself, and seeing what it is in itself (καθ' αὑτό), are they not rare ? " " They are indeed." " He then who sees that beautiful things are beautiful, but does not apprehend Beauty itself, and cannot follow if another should seek to lead him to the knowledge of the same,—think you that he lives his life awake, or in a dream ? " (That is to say, those who are not philosophers are like men who dream.) " For look, is it not dreaming when one in sleep, or even when awake, takes what merely resembles a certain thing to be not something that resembles it, but the very thing that it is like ? " " I should certainly say of such an one that he was dreaming." " The waking man, on the other hand, is he who holds the

Beautiful itself to be the Existent, and can recognize its very self as well as that which only partakes of it (μετέχοντα), and does not confuse between the two." [1]

In this account of Philosophy, we at once see what the so much talked of Ideas of Plato are. The Idea is nothing else than that which is known to us more familiarly by the name of the Universal, regarded, however, not as the formal Universal, which is only a property of things, but as implicitly and explicitly existent, as reality, as that which alone is true. We translate εἶδος first of all as species or kind; and the Idea is no doubt the species, but rather as it is apprehended by and exists for Thought. Of course when we understand by species nothing but the gathering together by our reflection, and for convenience sake, of the like characteristics of several individuals as indicating their distinguishing features, we have the universal in quite an external form. But the specific character of the animal is its being alive; this being alive is that which makes it what it is, and deprived of this, it ceases to exist. To Plato, accordingly, Philosophy is really the science of this implicitly universal, to which, as contrasted with the particular, he always continues to return. "When Plato spoke of tableness and cupness, Diogenes the Cynic said: 'I see a table and a cup, to be sure, but not tableness and cupness.' 'Right,' answered Plato; 'for you have eyes wherewith to see the table and the cup, but mind, by which one sees tableness and cupness, you have not (νοῦν οὐκ ἔχεις).' " [2] What Socrates began was carried out by Plato, who acknowledged only the Universal, the Idea, the Good, as that which has existence. Through the presentation of his Ideas, Plato opened up the intellectual world, which, however, is not beyond reality, in heaven, in another place, but is the real world. With Leucippus, too, the Ideal is brought closer to reality, and not—metaphysically—thrust

---

[1] Plato De Republica, V. p. 475, 476 (p. 265, 266).
[2] Diog. Laërt. VI. 53; cf. Plato De Rep. VI. p. 508 (p. 319).

away behind Nature. The essence of the doctrine of Ideas is thus the view that the True is not that which exists for the senses, but that only what has its determination in itself, the implicitly and explicitly Universal, truly exists in the world ; the intellectual world is therefore the True, that which is worthy to be known—indeed, the Eternal, the implicitly and explicitly divine. The differences are not essential, but only transitory ; yet the Absolute of Plato, as being the one in itself and identical with itself, is at the same time concrete in itself, in that it is a movement returning into itself, and is eternally at home with itself. But love for Ideas is that which Plato calls enthusiasm.

The misapprehension of Plato's Ideas takes two directions ; one of these has to do with the thinking, which is formal, and holds as true reality the sensuous alone, or what is conceived of through the senses—this is what Plato asserts to be mere shadows. For when Plato speaks of the Universal as the real, his conception of it is met either by the statement that the Universal is present to us only as a property, and is therefore a mere thought in our understanding, or else that Plato takes this same Universal as substance, as an existence in itself, which, however, falls outside of us. When Plato further uses the expression that sensuous things are, like images (εἰκόνες), similar to that which has absolute existence, or that the Idea is their pattern and model (παραδεῖγμα), if these Ideas are not exactly made into things, they are made into a kind of transcendent existences which lie somewhere far from us in an understanding outside this world, and are pictures set up which we merely do not see ; they are like the artist's model, following which he works upon a given material, and thereon impresses the likeness of the original. And owing to their not only being removed from this sensuous present reality, which passes for truth, but also being liberated from the actuality of the individual consciousness, their subject, of which they are originally the representations, passes out of consciousness, and even comes to be represented only as something which is apart from consciousness.

The second misapprehension that prevails with regard to these Ideas takes place when they are not transferred beyond our consciousness, but pass for ideals of our reason, which are no doubt necessary, but which produce nothing that either has reality now or can ever attain to it. As in the former view the Beyond is a conception that lies outside the world, and in which species are hypostatized, so in this view our reason is just such a realm beyond reality. But when species are looked on as if they were the forms of reality in us, there is again a misapprehension, just as if they were looked at as æsthetic in nature. By so doing, they are defined as intellectual perceptions which must present themselves immediately, and belong either to a happy genius or else to a condition of ecstasy or enthusiasm. In such a case they would be mere creations of the imagination, but this is not Plato's nor the true sense. They are not immediately in consciousness, but they are in the apprehending knowledge ; and they are immediate perceptions only in so far as they are apprehending knowledge comprehended in its simplicity and in relation to the result ; in other words, the immediate perception is only the moment of their simplicity. Therefore we do not possess them, they are developed in the mind through the apprehending knowledge ; enthusiasm is the first rude shape they take, but knowledge first brings them to light in rational developed form ; they are in this form none the less real, for they alone are Being.

On this account Plato first of all distinguishes Science, the Knowledge of the True, from opinion. " Such thinking (διάνοιαν) as of one who knows, we may justly call knowledge (γνώμην); but the other, opinion (δόξαν). Knowledge proceeds from that which is ; opinion is opposed to it ; but it is not the case that its content is Nothing—

that would be ignorance—for when an opinion is held, it is held about Something. Opinion is thus intermediate between ignorance and science, its content is a mixture of Being and Nothing. The object of the senses, the object of opinion, the particular, only participates in the Beautiful, the Good, the Just, the Universal ; but it is at the same time also ugly, evil, unjust, and so on. The double is at the same time the half. The particular is not only large or small, light or heavy, and any one of these opposites, but every particular is as much the one as the other. Such a mixture of Being and non-Being is the particular, the object of opinion ; " [1]—a mixture in which the opposites have not resolved themselves into the Universal. The latter would be the speculative Idea of knowledge, while to opinion belongs the manner of our ordinary consciousness.

b. Before we commence the examination of the objective implicitly existent content of knowledge, we must consider more in detail, on the one hand, the subjective existence of knowledge in consciousness as we find it in Plato, and, on the other, how the content is or appears in ordinary conception as soul; and the two together form the relation of knowledge, as the universal, to the individual consciousness.

a. The source through which we become conscious of the divine is the same as that already seen in Socrates (Vol. I. pp. 410, 411). The spirit of man contains reality in itself, and in order to learn what is divine he must develop it out of himself and bring it to consciousness. With the Socratics this discussion respecting the immanent nature of knowledge in the mind of man takes the form of a question as to whether virtue can be taught or not, and with the sophist Protagoras of asking whether feeling is the truth, which is allied with the question of the content of scientific knowledge, and with the distinction between that and opinion. But Plato goes on to say that the process by

[1] Plat. De Republ. V. p. 476–479 (p. 266–273).

which we come to know is not, properly speaking, learning, for that which we appear to learn we really only recollect. Plato often comes back to this subject, but in particular he treats of the point in the Meno, in which he asserts (p. 81, 84 Steph. ; p. 349, 355, 356 Bekk.) that nothing can, properly speaking, be learned, for learning is just a recollection of what we already possess, to which the perplexity in which our minds are placed, merely acts as stimulus. Plato here gives the question a speculative significance, in which the reality of knowledge, and not the empirical view of the acquisition of knowledge, is dealt with. For learning, according to the immediate ordinary conception of it, expresses the taking up of what is foreign into thinking consciousness, a mechanical mode of union and the filling of an empty space with things which are foreign and indifferent to this space itself. An external method of effecting increase such as this, in which the soul appears to be a *tabula rasa,* and which resembles the idea we form of growth going on in the living body through the addition of particles, is dead, and is incompatible with the nature of mind, which is subjectivity, unity, being and remaining at home with itself. But Plato presents the true nature of consciousness in asserting that it is mind in which, as mind, that is already present which becomes object to consciousness, or which it explicitly becomes. This is the Notion of the true universal in its movement ; of the species which is in itself its own Becoming, in that it is already implicitly what it explicitly becomes—a process in which it does not come outside of itself. Mind is this absolute species, whose process is only the continual return into itself ; thus nothing is for it which it is not in itself. According to this, the process of learning is not that something foreign enters in, but that the mind's own essence becomes actualized, or it comes to the knowledge of this last. What has not yet learned is the soul, the consciousness represented as natural being. What causes the mind to turn to science is the semblance, and the confusion caused through it, of the essential nature of mind being something different, or the negative of itself—a mode of manifestation which contradicts its real nature, for it has or is the inward certainty of being all reality. In that it abrogates this semblance of other-being, it comprehends the objective, *i.e.* gives itself immediately in it the consciousness of itself, and thus attains to science. Ideas of individual, temporal, transitory things undoubtedly come from without, but not the universal thoughts which, as the true, have their root in the mind and belong to its nature; by this means all authority is destroyed.

In one sense recollection [Erinnerung] is certainly an unfortunate expression, in the sense, namely, that an idea is reproduced which has already existed at another time. But recollection has another sense, which is given by its etymology, namely that of making oneself inward, going inward, and this is the profound meaning of the word in thought. In this sense it may undoubtedly be said that knowledge of the universal is nothing but a recollection, a going within self, and that we make that which at first shows itself in external form and determined as a manifold, into an inward, a universal, because we go into ourselves and thus bring what is inward in us into consciousness. With Plato, however, as we cannot deny, the word recollection has constantly the first and empirical sense. This comes from the fact that Plato propounds the true Notion that consciousness in itself is the content of knowledge, partly in the form of popular idea and in that of myths. Hence here even, the already mentioned (p. 18) intermingling of idea and Notion commences. In the Meno (p. 82-86 Steph.; p. 350-360 Bekk.) Socrates tries to show, by experiment on a slave who had received no instruction, that learning is a recollection. Socrates merely questions him, leaving him to answer in his own way, without either teaching him or asserting the truth of any fact, and at length brings him to the enunciation of a geometrical

proposition on the relation which the diagonal of a square
bears to its side. The slave obtains the knowledge out of
himself alone, so that it appears as though he only recollected what he already knew but had forgotten. Now if
Plato here calls this coming forth of knowledge from consciousness a recollection, it follows that this knowledge has
been already in this consciousness, *i.e.* that the individual
consciousness has not only the content of knowledge implicitly, in accordance with its essential nature, but has also
possessed it as this individual consciousness and not as
universal. But this moment of individuality belongs only
to the ordinary conception, and recollection is not thought;
for recollection relates to man as a sensuous "this," and
not as a universal. The essential nature of the coming
forth of knowledge is hence here mingled with the individual,
with ordinary conception, and knowledge here appears in
the form of soul, as of the implicitly existent reality, the
one, for the soul is still only a moment of spirit. As Plato
here passes into a conception the content of which has no
longer the pure significance of the universal, but of the
individual, he further depicts it in the form of a myth. He
represents the implicit existence of mind in the form of a
pre-existence in time, as if the truth had already been for
us in another time. But at the same time we must remark
that he does not propound this as a philosophic doctrine, but
in the form of a saying received from priests and priestesses
who comprehend what is divine. Pindar and other holy
men say the same. According to these sayings, the human
soul is immortal; it both ceases to be, or, as men say, it
dies, and it comes again into existence, but in no way
perishes. "Now if the soul is immortal and often reappears" (metempsychosis), "and if it has seen that which
is here as well as in Hades," (in unconsciousness) "and
everything else, learning has no more meaning, for it only
recollects what it has already known." [1] Historians seize

----

[1] Plat. Meno, p. 81 (p. 348, 349).

upon this allusion to what is really an Egyptian idea, and a sensuous conception merely, and say that Plato has laid down that such and such was the case. But Plato made no such statement whatever ; what he here says has nothing to do with Philosophy, and more particularly nothing to do with his philosophy, any more than what afterwards is said regarding God.

β. In other Dialogues this myth. is further and more strikingly developed ; it certainly employs remembrance in its ordinary sense, which is that the mind of man has in past time seen that which comes to his consciousness as the true and absolutely existent. Plato's principal effort is, however, to show through this assertion of recollection, that the mind, the soul, thought, is on its own account free, and this has to the ancients, and particularly to the Platonic idea, a close connection with what we call immortality of the soul.

aa. In the Phædrus (p. 245 Steph. ; p. 38 Bekk.) Plato speaks of this in order to show that the Eros is a divine madness (μανία), and is given to us as the greatest happiness. It is a state of enthusiasm, which here has a powerful, predominating aspiration towards the Idea (*supra,* p. 30) : but it is not an enthusiasm proceeding from the heart and feeling, it is not an ordinary perception, but a consciousness and knowledge of the ideal. Plato says that he must expound the nature of the divine and human soul in order to demonstrate the Eros. " The first point is that the soul is immortal. For what moves itself is immortal and eternal, but what obtains its movement from another is transient. What moves itself is the first principle, for it certainly has its origin and first beginning in itself and derived from no other. And just as little can it cease to move, for that alone can cease which derives its motion from another." Plato thus first develops the simple Notion of the soul as of the self-moving, and, thus far, an element in mind ; but the proper life of the mind in and for itself is the consciousness of the absolute nature and freedom of the " I." When we speak of the immortality of the soul, the idea is most frequently present to us that the soul is like a physical thing which has qualities of all kinds, and while these can certainly be changed, it yet seems that, as being independent of them, it is not subject to change. Now thought is one of these qualities, which are thus independent of the thing; and thought is also here defined as a thing, and as if it could pass away or cease to be. As regards this point, the main feature of the idea is that the soul should be able to subsist as an imperishable thing without having imagination, thought, &c. With Plato the immortality of the soul is, on the other hand, immediately connected with the fact that the soul is itself that which thinks; and hence that thought is not a quality of soul, but its substance. It is as with body, where the weight is not a quality, but its substance; for as the body would no longer exist if the weight were abstracted, the soul would not exist if thought were taken away. Thought is the activity of the universal, not an abstraction, but the reflection into self and the positing of self that takes place in all conceptions. Now because thought is an eternal which remains at home with itself in every change, soul preserves its identity in what is different, just as, for instance, in sensuous perception it deals with what is different, with outside matter, and is yet at home with itself. Immortality has not then the interest to Plato which it has to us from a religious point of view; in that to him it is associated in greater measure with the nature of thought, and with the inward freedom of the same, it is connected with the determination that constitutes the principle of what is specially characteristic of Platonic philosophy, it is connected with the supersensuous groundwork which Plato has established. To Plato the immortality of the soul is hence likewise of great importance.

He proceeds : " To seek to make clear the Idea of the soul would involve investigation laborious for any but a god; but the tongue of man may speak of this more easily through a figure." Here follows an allegory in which there is, however, something extravagant and inconsistent. He says: "The soul resembles the united power of a chariot and charioteer." This image expresses nothing to us. "Now the horses" (the desires) "of the gods and the charioteers are good, and of a good breed. With us men, the charioteer at first takes the reins, but one of the horses only is noble and good and of noble origin; the other is ignoble and of ignoble origin. As might be expected, the driving is very difficult. How mortal differ from immortal creatures, we must endeavour to discover. The soul has the care of the inanimate everywhere, and traverses the whole heavens, passing from one idea to another. When perfect and fully winged, she soars upwards" (has elevated thoughts), "and is the ruler of the universe. But the soul whose wings droop roams about till she has found solid ground; then she takes an earthly form which is really moved by her power, and the whole, the soul and body, put together, is called a living creature, a mortal." [1] The one is thus the soul as thought, existence in and for itself; the other is the union with matter. This transition from thought to body is very difficult, too difficult for the ancients to understand; we shall find more about it in Aristotle. From what has been said, we may find the ground for representing Plato as maintaining the dogma that the soul existed independently prior to this life, and then lapsed into matter, united itself to it, contaminating itself by so doing, and that it is incumbent on it to leave matter again. The fact that the spiritual realizes itself from itself is a point not sufficiently examined by the ancients; they take two abstractions, soul and matter, and the connection is expressed only in the form of a deterioration on the part of soul.

[1] Plat. Phædrus, p. 246 (p. 39, 40).

" But as to the immortal," continues Plato, " if we do
not express it in accordance with an apprehending thought,
but form an ordinary conception of it, owing to our
lack of insight and power to comprehend the nature of
God, we conclude that the immortal life of God is that
which has a body and soul which, however, are united in
one nature (συμπεφυκότα),[1] i.e. not only externally but
intrinsically made one.　Soul and body are both abstractions,
but life is the unity of both ; and because God's nature
is to popular conception the holding of body and soul
unseparated in one, He is the Reason whose form and
content are an undivided unity in themselves.　This is an
important definition of God—a great idea which is indeed
none other than the definition of modern times.　It signifies the identity of subjectivity and objectivity, the inseparability of the ideal and real, that is, of soul and body.
The mortal and finite is, on the contrary, correctly
defined by Plato as that of which the existence is not
absolutely adequate to the Idea, or, more definitely, to
subjectivity.

Plato now further explains what happens in the life of
the divine Being, which drama the soul thus has before
it, and how the wasting of its wings occurs.　" The chariots
of the gods enter in bands, led by Zeus, the mighty leader,
from his winged chariot.　An array of other gods and
goddesses follow him, marshalled in eleven bands.　They
present—each one fulfilling his work—the noblest and
most blessed of scenes.　The colourless and formless and
intangible essence requires thought, the lord of the soul,
as its only spectator, and thus true knowledge takes its
rise.　For there it sees what is (τὸ ὄν), and lives in the
contemplation of reality, because it follows in an ever-
recurring revolution " (of ideas).　" In this revolution "
(of gods), " it beholds justice, temperance, and knowledge,

---

[1] Plat. Phædrus, p. 246 (p. 40).

not in the form of what men call things, for it sees what in truth is absolute (τὸ ὄντως ὄν)." This is thus expressed as though it were something which had happened. " When the soul returns from thus beholding, the charioteer puts up his horses at the stall, gives them ambrosia to eat and nectar to drink. This is the life of the gods. But other souls, through fault of charioteer or horses, fall into confusion, with broken wings depart from these heavenly places, cease to behold the truth, nourish themselves on opinion as their food, and fall to the ground; according as a soul has beheld more or less of truth, it takes a higher or lower place. In this condition it retains a recollection of what it has seen, and if it perceives anything beautiful or right, it is rapt in amazement. The wings once more obtain strength, and the soul, particularly that of a philosopher, recollects its former condition in which, however, it had not seen what was beautiful, just, etc., but beauty and justice themselves." [1] Thus because the life of the gods is for the soul, when in individual beauty it is reminded of the universal, it is implied that in the soul, as thus absolutely existing, there is the Idea of the beautiful, good and just, as absolute and as potentially and actually universal. This constitutes the general principle of the Platonic conception. But when Plato speaks of knowledge as of a recollection, he knows all the time that this is only putting the matter in similes and metaphors; he did not ask, as theologians used gravely to do, whether the soul had existed before its birth, and, if so, in what particular place. It cannot be said of Plato that he had any such belief, and he never speaks of the matter in the sense that theologians did; in the same way he never spoke about a Fall from a perfect state, for example, as if man had to look on the present life as an imprisonment. But what Plato expressed as the truth is

---

[1] Plat. Phædrus, pp. 246–251 (pp. 40–50).

that consciousness in the individual is in reason the divine reality and life ; that man perceives and recognizes it in pure thought, and 'that this knowledge is itself the heavenly abode and movement.

$\beta\beta$. Knowledge in the form of soul, is more clearly dealt with in the Phædo, where Plato has further developed the ideas about the immortality of the soul. What in the Phædrus is kept definitely apart as myth and truth respectively, and which is made to appear as such, appears less evidently so in the Phædo—that celebrated dialogue in which Plato makes Socrates speak of the immortality of the soul. That Plato should have connected this discussion with the account of the death of Socrates has in all time been matter of admiration. Nothing could seem more suitable than to place the conviction of immortality in the mouth of him who is in the act of leaving life, and to make this conviction living to us through the scene, just as, on the other hand, a death-scene like this is made living to us through that conviction. We must at the same time remark that in what is fitting the following conditions are implied. It must first be really appropriate for the dying person to occupy himself with himself instead of with the universal, with this certainty of himself as a " this " instead of with the Truth. We hence here meet with the ordinary point of view but slightly separated from that of the Notion, but, although this is so, this ordinary point of view is far removed from sinking into that coarse conception of the soul which considers it to be a thing, and asks about its continuance or subsistence as if it were a thing. Thus we find Socrates expressing himself to the effect that the body and what relates to the body is a hindrance in striving after wisdom, the sole business of Philosophy, because the sensuous perception shows nothing purely, or as it is in itself, and what is true becomes known through the removal of the spiritual from the corporeal. For justice, beauty and such things are what alone exists in verity ;

they are that to which all change and decay is foreign ; and these are not perceived through the body, but only in the soul.[1]

We see in this separation the essence of the soul not considered in a material category of Being, but as the universal ; we see it still more in what follows, by which Plato proves immortality. A principal point in this argument is that already considered, that the soul has existed before this life, because learning is only a recollection,[2] and this implies that the soul is already implicitly what it becomes. We must not think that the bald conception of innate ideas is hereby indicated—such an expression implies the existence of ideas by nature, as though our thoughts were in part already implanted, and had in part a natural existence which did not first produce itself through the movement of the mind. But Plato mainly founds the idea of immortality on the fact that what is put together is liable to dissolution and decay, while the simple can in no manner be dissolved or destroyed ; what is always like itself and the same, is, however, simple. The beautiful, the good, the like, being simple, are incapable of all change ; that, on the contrary, in which these universals are, men, things, &c., are the changeable. They are perceptible by the senses, while the former is the supersensuous. Hence the soul which is in thought, and which applies itself to this, as to what is related to it, must therefore be held to have itself a simple nature.[3] Here, then, we again see that Plato does not take simplicity as the simplicity of a thing—not as if it were of anything like a chemical ingredient, for example, which can no longer be represented as inherently distinguished ; this would only be empty, abstract identity or universality, the simple as an existent.

[1] Plat. Phædo, pp. 65–67 (pp. 18–23).
[2] Ibid. p. 72 (p. 35), p. 75 (p. 41).
[3] Ibid. pp. 78–80 (pp. 46–51).

But finally the universal really does appear to take the form of an existent, as Plato makes Simmias assert : a harmony which we hear is none else than a universal, a simple which is a unity of the diverse ; but this harmony is associated with a sensuous thing and disappears with it, just as music does with the lyre. On the other hand Plato makes Socrates show that the soul is not a harmony in this sense, for the sensuous harmony first exists after its elements, and is a consequence that follows from them. The harmony of the soul is, however, in and for itself, before every sensuous thing. Sensuous harmony may further have diversities within it, while the harmony of the soul has no quantitative distinction.[1] From this it is clear that Plato receives the reality of the soul entirely in the universal, and does not place its true being in sensuous individuality, and hence the immortality of the soul cannot in his case be understood in the ordinary acceptation, as that of an individual thing. Although later on we come across the myth of the sojourn of the soul after death in another and more brilliant earth,[2] we have seen above (pp. 40, 41) what kind of heaven this would be.

γ. The development and culture of the soul must be taken in connection with what precedes. However the idealism of Plato must not be thought of as being subjective idealism, and as that false idealism which has made its appearance in modern times, and which maintains that we do not learn anything, are not influenced from without, but that all conceptions are derived from out of the subject. It is often said that idealism means that the individual produces from himself all his ideas, even the most immediate. But this is an unhistoric, and quite false conception ; if we take this rude definition of idealism, there have been no idealists amongst the philosophers, and Platonic idealism

---

[1] Plat. Phædo, pp. 85, 86 (pp. 62, 63), pp. 92–94 (pp. 74–80).
[2] Ibid. pp. 110–114 (pp. 111–120).

is certainly far removed from anything of the kind. In the seventh book of his Republic (p. 518 Steph., pp. 333, 334 Bekk.) Plato says in connection with what I have already stated (pp. 27-29), and in particular reference to the manner in which this learning is created, by which the universal which before was secreted in the mind, developes out of it alone : "We must believe of science and learning (παιδείας), that its nature is not as some assert" (by this he means the Sophists), "who speak of culture as though knowledge were not contained within the soul, but could be implanted therein as sight into blind eyes." The idea that knowledge comes entirely from without is in modern times found in empirical philosophies of a quite abstract and rude kind, which maintain that everything that man knows of the divine nature comes as a matter of education and habituation, and that mind is thus a quite indeterminate potentiality merely. Carried to an extreme, this is the doctrine of revelation in which everything is given from without. In the Protestant religion we do not find this rude idea in its abstract form, for the witness of the spirit is an essential part of faith, *i.e.* faith demands that the individual subjective spirit shall on its own account accept and set forth the determination which comes to it in the form of something given from without. Plato speaks against any such idea, for, in relation to the merely popularly expressed myth given above, he says : "Reason teaches that every man possesses the inherent capacities of the soul and the organ with which he learns. That is, just as we might imagine the eye not capable of turning from darkness to light otherwise than with the whole body, so must we be turned with the whole soul from the world of Becoming" (contingent feelings and ideas) "to that of Being, and the soul must gradually learn to endure this sight, and to behold the pure light of Being. But we say that this Being is the good. The art of so doing is found in culture, as being the art of the conversion of the soul—that is, the

manner in which a person can most easily and effectually
be converted ; it does not seek to implant (ἐμποιῆσαι)
sight, but—inasmuch as he already possesses it only it
has not been properly turned upon himself and hence he
does not see the objects that he ought to see—it brings
it into operation. The other virtues of the soul are
more in conformity with the body ; they are not originally
in the soul, but come gradually through exercise and habit.
Thought (τὸ φρονῆσαι) on the contrary, as divine, never
loses its power, and only becomes good or evil through
the manner of this conversion." This is what Plato establishes in regard to the inward and the outward. Such
ideas as that mind determines the good from out of
itself are to us much more familiar than to Plato ; but it
was by Plato that they were first maintained.

c. In that Plato places truth in that alone which is produced through thought, and yet the source of knowledge is
manifold—in feelings, sensations, &c.—we must state the
different kinds of knowledge, as given by Plato. Plato is
entirely opposed to the idea that the truth is given through
sensuous consciousness, which is what is known and that
from which we start; for this is the doctrine of the
Sophists with which we met in dealing with Protagoras,
for instance. As regards feeling, we easily make the mistake of placing everything in feeling, as indeed that Platonic
rage for beauty contained the truth in the guise of feeling ;
but this is not the true form of the truth, because feeling is
the entirely subjective consciousness. Feeling as such is
merely a form with which men make the arbitrary will the
principle of the truth, for what is the true content is not
given through feeling; in it every content has a place.
The highest content must likewise be found in feeling ; to
have a thing in thought and understanding is quite different
from having it in heart and feeling, *i.e.* in our most inward
subjectivity, in this " I "; and we say of the content that
it is for the first time in its proper place when it is in the

heart, because it then is entirely identical with our individuality. The mistake, however, is to say that a content is
true because it is in our feeling. Hence the importance of
Plato's doctrine that the content becomes filled by thought
alone ; for it is the universal which can be grasped by the
activity of thought alone. Plato has defined this universal
content as Idea.

At the close of the sixth book of the Republic (pp. 509-
511 Steph. ; pp. 321-325 Bekk.) Plato distinguishes the
sensuous and the intellectual in our knowledge more exactly, so that in each sphere he again presents two modes
of consciousness. " In the sensuous (ὁρατόν) the one
division is the external manifestation, for in it are shadows,
reflections in water, and also in solid, smooth, and polished
bodies, and the like. The second section, of which this is
only the resemblance, includes animals, plants " (this concrete life), " and everything in art. The intelligible (νοητόν)
is also divided into two parts. In the one sub-division the
soul uses the sensuous figures given before, and is obliged
to work on hypotheses (ἐξ ὑποθέσεων) because it does not
go to the principle but to the result." Reflection, which
is not on its own account sensuous, but undoubtedly
belongs to thought, mingles thought with the first sensuous
consciousness, although its object is not as yet a pure
existence of the understanding. " The other division "
(what is thought in the soul itself) " is that in which the
soul, proceeding from an hypothesis, makes its way (μέθοδον)
to a principle which is above hypotheses, not by means of
images, as in the former cases, but through the ideas
themselves. Those who study geometry, arithmetic, and
kindred sciences, assume the odd and the even, the figures,
three kinds of angles, and the like. And since they start
from these hypotheses, they do not think it necessary to
give any account of them, for everybody is supposed to
know them. You further know that they make use of
figures which are visible, and speak of them, although they

are not thinking of them, but of the ideals which they
represent ; for they think of the " (absolute) " square itself
and of its diagonals, and not of the " (sensuous) " images
that they draw. And so it is with other things." Thus,
according to Plato, this is certainly the place where real
knowledge begins, because we have nothing further to do
with the sensuous as such ; at the same time this is not the
true knowledge which considers the spiritual universal on
its own account, but the arguing and reasoning knowledge
that forms universal laws and particular kinds or species
out of what is sensuous. " These figures which they draw
or make, and which also have shadows and images in
water, they use only as images, and seek to behold their
originals, which can only be seen with the understanding "
($\delta\iota\alpha\nu o\acute{\iota}\alpha$).—" That is true."—" This I have named above
that species of the intelligible, in inquiring into which
the soul is compelled to use hypotheses, not proceeding
to a first principle, because it is not able to get above
those hypotheses, but employing those secondary images
as images which are made absolutely similar to the
originals in every respect "—" I understand that you are
speaking of geometry and the kindred arts "—" Now learn
about the other division of the intelligible in which reason
($\lambda\acute{o}\gamma o\varsigma$) itself is concerned, since by the power of the
dialectic it makes use of hypotheses, not as principles, but
only as hypotheses—that is to say, as steps and points of
departure in order to reach a region above hypotheses, the
first principle of all " (which is in and for itself), " and
clinging to this and to that which depends on this, it
descends again to the result, for it requires no sensuous aid
at all, but only ideas, and thus it reaches the ideas finally
through the ideas themselves." To know this is the
interest and business of Philosophy ; this is investigated
by pure thought in and for itself, which only moves in such
pure thoughts. " I understand you, but not perfectly. You
seem to me to wish to assert that what is contemplated in

Being and Knowledge through the science of dialectic is clearer than what is contemplated by the so-called sciences which have hypotheses as their principle, and where those who contemplate them have to do so with the understanding and not with the senses. Yet because in their contemplation they do not ascend to the absolute principle, but speculate from hypotheses, they appear not to exercise thought (νοῦν) upon these objects, although these objects are cognizable by thought if a principle is added to them (νοητῶν ὄντων μετὰ ἀρχῆς). The methods (ἕξιν) of geometry and its kindred sciences you appear to me to call understanding; and that because it stands midway between reason (νοῦς) and 'sensuous' opinion (δόξα)."—"You have quite grasped my meaning. Corresponding to these four sections, I will suppose four faculties (παθήματα) in the soul—conceiving reason (νόησις) has the highest place (ἐπὶ τῷ ἀνωτάτῳ), understanding the second; the third is called faith (πίστις)" —the true conception for animals and plants in that they are living, homogeneous and identical with ourselves; "and the last the knowledge of images (εἰκασία)," opinion. "Arrange them according to the fact that each "stage has as much clearness (σαφηνείας) as that to which it is related has truth." This is the distinction which forms the basis of Plato's philosophy, and which came to be known from his writings.

Now if we go from knowledge to its content, in which the Idea becomes sundered, and thereby organizes itself more completely into a scientific system, this content, according to Plato, begins to fall into three parts which we distinguish as the logical, natural, and mental philosophy. The logical Philosophy the ancients called dialectic, and its addition to philosophy is by the ancient writers on the subject ascribed to Plato (Vol. I. p. 387). This is not a dialectic such as we met with in the Sophists, which merely brings one's ideas altogether into confusion, for this first branch of Platonic philosophy is the dialectic which moves in pure Notions—the movement of the speculatively logical, with which several dialogues, and particularly that of Parmenides, occupy themselves. The second, according to Plato, is a kind of natural philosophy, the principles of which are more especially propounded in the Timæus. The third is the philosophy of the mind—an ethical philosophy —and its representation is essentially that of a perfect state in the Republic. The Critias should be taken in connection with the Timæus and the Republic, but we need not make further reference to it, for it is only a fragment. Plato makes these three dialogues one connected conversation. In the Critias and the Timæus the subject is so divided that while the Timæus dealt with the speculative origin of man and of nature, the Critias was intended to represent the ideal history of human culture, and to be a philosophical history of the human race, forming the ancient history of the Athenians as preserved by the Egyptians. Of this, however, only the beginning has come down to us.[1] Hence if the Parmenides be taken along with the Republic and the Timæus, the three together constitute the whole Platonic system of philosophy divided into its three parts or sections. We now wish to consider the philosophy of Plato more in detail in accordance with these three different points of view.

1. DIALECTIC.

We have already remarked by way of preparation that the Notion of true dialectic is to show forth the necessary movement of pure Notions, without thereby resolving these into nothing; for the result, simply expressed, is that they are this movement, and the universal is just the unity of these opposite Notions. We certainly do not find in Plato a full consciousness that this is the nature of dialectic, but we find dialectic itself present; that is, we find absolute existence

---

[1] Plat. Timæus, p. 20 *et seq.* (p. 10 *seq.*); Critias, p. 108 *seq.* (p. 149 *seq.*).

thus recognized in pure Notions, and the representation of the movement of these Notions. What makes the study of the Platonic dialectic difficult is the development and the manifestation of the universal out of ordinary conceptions. This beginning, which appears to make knowledge easier, really makes the difficulty greater, since it introduces us into a field in which there is quite a different standard from what we have in reason, and makes this field present to us; when, on the contrary, progression and motion take place in pure Notions alone, the other is not remembered at all. But in that very way the Notions attain greater truth. For otherwise pure logical movement might easily appear to us to exist on its own account, like a private territory, which has another region alongside of it, also having its own particular place. But since both are there brought together, the speculative element begins to appear as it is in truth; that is, as being the only truth, and that, indeed, through the transformation of sensuous opinion into thought. For in our consciousness we first of all find the immediate individual, the sensuous real; or there are also categories of the understanding which are held by us to be ultimate and true. But contrasted with merely external reality, it is rather the ideal that is the most real, and it was Plato who perceived that it was the only real, for he characterized the universal or thought as the true, in opposition to what is sensuous.

Thus the aim of many of Plato's Dialogues, which conclude without any positive affirmation (Vol. I. p. 406; II. p. 13), is to show that the immediately existent, the many things that appear to us, although we may have quite true conceptions of them, are still not in themselves, in an objective sense, the true, because they alter and are determined through their relation to something else and not through themselves; thus we must even in the sensuous individuals consider the universal, or what Plato has called the Idea (p. 29). The sensuous, limited, and finite is, in fact, both itself and the

other, which is also considered as existent ; and thus there
is an unsolved contradiction, for the other has dominion in
the first.   We have been before reminded (Vol. I. p. 404 ;
II. p. 33) that the aim of the Platonic dialectic is to confuse
and to resolve the finite ideas of men, in order to bring about
in their consciousness what science demands, the consideration of that which is.   By being thus directed against the
form of the finite, dialectic has in the first place the effect of
confounding the particular, and this is brought about by
the negation therein present being shown forth, so that, in
fact, it is proved that it is not what it is, but that it passes
into its opposite, into the limitations which are essential to it.
But if this dialectic is laid hold of, the particular passes
away and becomes another than that which it is taken to
be.   Formal philosophy cannot look at dialectic in any other
way than as being the art of confusing ordinary conceptions
or even Notions, and demonstrating their nullity, thus
making their result to be merely negative.   For this reason,
Plato in his Republic (VII. pp. 538, 539, Steph. ; pp. 370,
371, Bekk.) advised the citizens not to allow dialectic to be
studied before the thirtieth year, because by its means anyone might transform the beautiful, as he had received it
from his masters, into that which is hateful.   We find this
dialectic a great deal in Plato, both in the more Socratic
and moralizing dialogues, and in the many dialogues which
relate to the conceptions of the Sophists in regard to
science.

In connection with this, the second part of dialectic
makes its first aim the bringing of the universal in men to
consciousness, which, as we formerly remarked when speaking of Socrates (Vol. I. p. 398), was the main interest of
Socratic culture.   From this time on, we may look at such
an aim as having been discarded, and simply remark that a
number of Plato's Dialogues merely aim at bringing to consciousness a general conception, such as we have without
taking any trouble at all (Vol. I. pp. 403, 404) ; hence this

prolixity on Plato's part often wearies us. This dialectic is, indeed, also a movement of thought, but it is really only necessary in an external way and for reflecting consciousness, in order to allow the universal, what is in and for itself, unalterable and immortal, to come forth. Hence these first two sides of the dialectic, directed as they are towards the dissolution of the particular and thus to the production of the universal, are not yet dialectic in its true form : it is a dialectic which Plato has in common with the Sophists, who understood very well how to disintegrate the particular. A subject which Plato very often treats of with this end in view, is virtue, which he proves to be only one (Vol. I. pp. 405, 411), and thereby he makes the universal good emerge from the particular virtues.

Now because the universal which has emerged from the confusion of the particular, *i.e.* the true, beautiful and good, that which taken by itself is species, was at first undetermined and abstract, it is, in the third place, a principal part of Plato's endeavours further to determine this universal in itself. This determination is the relation which the dialectic movement in thought bears to the universal, for through this movement the Idea comes to these thoughts which contain the opposites of the finite within themselves. For the Idea, as the self-determining, is the unity of these differences, and thus the determinate Idea. The universal is hence determined as that which resolves and has resolved the contradictions in itself, and hence it is the concrete in itself ; thus this sublation of contradiction is the affirmative. Dialectic in this higher sense is the really Platonic ; as speculative it does not conclude with a negative result, for it demonstrates the union of opposites which have annulled themselves. Here begins what is difficult for the understanding to grasp. The form of Plato's methods being not yet, however, developed purely on its own account, this is the reason that his dialectic is still often merely reasoning, and that it proceeds from individual points of view and

frequently remains without result. On the other hand,
Plato's own teaching is directed against this merely reasoning dialectic; yet we see that it gives him trouble properly
to show forth the difference.   The speculative dialectic
which commences with him, is thus the most interesting
but also the most difficult part of his work ; hence acquaintance is not usually made with it when the Platonic writings
are studied.   Tennemann, for example, did not at all comprehend what was most important in the Platonic philosophy,
and only gathered some of it together in the form of dry
ontological determinations—for that was what he could
comprehend.   But it shows the greatest lack of intellect in
a historian of Philosophy only to see in a great philosophic
form whether there is anything yielding profit to himself or
not.

What we have thus to deal with in the dialectic of Plato is
the pure thought of reason, from which he very clearly distinguishes the understanding (διάνοια), (supra, p. 47). We
may have thoughts about many things—if indeed, we do
have thought at all—but this is not what Plato means.
Plato's true speculative greatness, and that through
which he forms an epoch in the history of Philosophy, and
hence in the history of the world, lies in the fuller determination of the Idea ; this extension of knowledge is one which
some centuries later constituted the main element in the
ferment which took place in universal history, and in the
transformation which the human mind passed through. This
fuller determination may, from what has gone before, be
understood thus : Plato first comprehended the Absolute
as the Being of Parmenides, but as the Universal which, as
species, is also end, i.e. which rules, penetrates, and produces the particular and manifold.   Plato, however, had not
yet developed this self-producing activity, and hence often
stumbled into an external teleology.   As the union of the
preceding principles, Plato further led this Being into determinateness and into difference, as the latter is contained in

the triad of Pythagorean number-determinations, and expressed the same in thought. That is, he grasped the Absolute as the unity of Being and non-being—in Becoming, as Heraclitus says—or of the one and the many,[1] &c. He further now took into the objective dialectic of Heraclitus the Eleatic dialectic, which is the external endeavour of the subject to show forth contradiction, so that in place of an external changing of things, their inward transition in themselves, *i.e.* in their Ideas, or, as they are here, in their categories, has come to pass out of and through themselves. Plato finally set forth the belief of Socrates, which the latter put forward in regard to the moral self-reflection of the subject only, as objective, as the Idea, which is both universal thought and the existent. The previous philosophies thus do not disappear because refuted by Plato, being absorbed in him.

In addition to Being and non-being, one and many, the unlimited and limiting are, for instance, likewise pure thoughts such as these, in whose absolute contemplation, from an all-embracing point of view, the Platonic investigation occupies itself. The purely logical and quite abstruse consideration of such objects certainly contrasts strongly with our conception of the beautiful, pleasing, and attractive content of Plato. Such consideration to him signifies all that is best in Philosophy, and it is that which he everywhere calls the true method of Philosophy, and the knowledge of the truth ; in it he places the distinction between philosophers and Sophists. The Sophists on their part look at appearances, and these they obtain in opinion ; this, indeed, implies thought, but not pure thought, or what is in and for itself. This is one reason why many turn from the study of Plato's works unsatisfied. When we commence a Dialogue, we find, in the free Platonic method of composition, beautiful scenes in nature, a superb intro-

[1] Cf. Vol. I. pp. 318, 319, and the remarks there made. [Editor's Note.]

duction (p. 14) that promises to lead us through flowery
fields into Philosophy—and that the highest Philosophy, the
Platonic. We meet with elevated thoughts, which are
responded to more specially by youth, but these soon disappear. If at first we have allowed ourselves to be carried
away by these bright scenes, they must now be all renounced, and as we have come to the real dialectic, and truly
speculative, we must keep to the wearisome path, and allow
ourselves to be pricked by the thorns and thistles of
metaphysics. For behold, we then come to what is best and
highest, to investigations respecting the one and many,
Being and nothing ; this was not what was anticipated, and
men go quietly away, only wondering that Plato should seek
knowledge here. From the most profound dialectic investigation, Plato then again proceeds to representations
and images, to the description of dialogues amongst
intelligent men. Thus in the Phædo, for example, which
Mendelssohn has modernized and transformed into Wolffian
metaphysics, the beginning and end are elevating and
beautiful, and the middle deals with dialectic. Hence in
making one's way through Plato's Dialogues very many
mental qualities are called into play, and in their study we
consequently ought to keep our minds open and free as
regards the very various points of interest. If we read
with interest what is speculative, we are apt to overlook
what is most beautiful; if our interest lies in the elevation
and culture of the mind, we forget the speculative element
and find that it does not appeal to us. With some it is like
the young man in the Bible, who had fulfilled his various
duties, and who asked Christ what good thing he still had to
do to become His follower. But when the Lord commanded
him to sell what he had and give to the poor, the young man
went away sorrowful ; this was not what he had anticipated.
Just in the same way many mean well as regards Philosophy ;
they study Fries, and heaven knows whom else. Their
hearts are full of the true, good and beautiful; they would

know and see what they ought to do, but their breasts swell with goodwill alone.

While Socrates remained at the good and universal, at implicitly concrete thoughts, without having developed them or having revealed them through development, Plato certainly goes on to the Idea as determined. His defect, however, is that this determinateness and that universality are still outside one another. We should certainly obtain the determinate Idea by reducing the dialectic movement to its result, and that forms an important element in knowledge. Yet when Plato speaks of justice, beauty, goodness, truth, their origin is not revealed; they are not shown as being results, but merely as hypotheses accepted in their immediacy. Consciousness certainly has an innate conviction that they form the highest end, but this their determination is not discovered. Since Plato's dogmatic expositions of Ideas are lost (*supra*, p. 11), the dialectic of pure thought is only placed before us by the Dialogues dealing with the subject, and these, just because they deal with pure thought, are amongst the most difficult, viz. : the Sophist, the Philebus, and, more especially, the Parmenides. We here pass over the Dialogues which contain only negative dialectic and Socratic dialogue, because they treat only of concrete ideas and not of dialectic in its higher signification; they leave us unsatisfied, because their ultimate end is only to confuse one's opinions, or awaken a sense of the necessity for knowledge. But those three express the abstract speculative Idea in its pure Notion. The embracing of the opposites in one, and the expression of this unity, is chiefly lacking in the Parmenides, which has hence, like some other Dialogues, only a negative result. But both in the Sophist and the Philebus Plato expresses the unity also.

a. The fully worked-out and genuine dialectic is, however, contained in the Parmenides—that most famous masterpiece of Platonic dialectic. Parmenides and Zeno are there represented as meeting Socrates in Athens; but the most important part of it is the dialectic which is put in the mouths of Parmenides and Zeno. At the very beginning the nature of this dialectic is given in detail as follows: Plato makes Parmenides praise Socrates thus: " I notice that in conversing with Aristoteles," (one of those present; it might quite well have been the philosopher, but that he was born sixteen years after Socrates' death) " you were trying to define in what the nature of the beautiful, just and good, and all such ideas lay. This your endeavour is noble and divine. But train and exercise yourself even more in what the multitude call idle chatter, and look on as useless, as long as you are young, for otherwise the truth will escape you.—In what, Socrates asks, does this exercise consist?— I was much pleased because you said before that we must not be content with contemplating the sensuous and its illusions, but must consider that which thought alone can grasp, and that which alone exists." I have before [1] remarked that men at all times have believed that the truth could be found through reflection only, for in reflection thought is found, and that which we have before us in the guise of ordinary conception and of belief is transformed into thought. Socrates now replies to Parmenides: " I believed that I should in that way best discern the like and unlike, and the other general determinations in things." Parmenides replies, " Certainly. But if you begin from a point of view such as that, you must not only consider what follows from such an hypothesis, but also what follows from the opposite of that hypothesis. For example, in the case of the hypothesis 'the many is,' you have to consider what will be the consequences of the relation of the many to itself and to the one, and likewise what the consequences of the relation of the one to itself and to the many." The marvellous fact that meets us in thought when we take determinations such as these by themselves, is that each one

[1] Hegel's Werke, Vol. VI., Pt. 1, p. 8.

is turned round into the opposite of itself. " But again we must consider, if the many is not, as to what will be the result as regards the one and the many, both to themselves and to one another. The same consideration must be employed in respect of identity and non-identity, rest and motion, origination and passing away, and likewise in regard to Being and non-being. We must ask what is each of these in relation to itself, and what is their relation in event of the one or the other being accepted ? In exercising yourself fully in this, you will learn to know real truth."[1] Plato thus lays great stress on the dialectical point of view, which is not the point of view of the merely external, but is a living point of view whose content is formed of pure thoughts only, whose movement consists in their making themselves the other of themselves, and thus showing that only their unity is what is truly justified.

Plato makes Socrates say, as regards the meaning of the unity of the one and many, " If anyone proved to me that I am one and many, it would not surprise me. For since he shows me that I am a many, and points out in me the right and left side, an upper and lower half, a front and back, I partake of the manifold ; and again I partake of unity because I am one of us seven. The case is the same with stone, wood, &c. But if anyone, after determining the simple ideas of similarity and dissimilarity, multiplicity, and unity, rest and movement, and so on, were to show that these in their abstract form admit of admixture and separation, I should be very much surprised."[2] The dialectic of Plato is, however, not to be regarded as complete in every regard. Though his main endeavour is to show that in every determination the opposite is contained, it can still not be said that this is strictly carried out in all his dialectic movements, for there are often external considerations which exercise an influence in his dialectic. For example, Parmenides says :

[1] Plat. Parmenides, pp. 135, 136 (pp. 21–23).
[2] Ibid. p. 129 (pp. 9, 10).

" Are either of the two parts of the one which is—I mean the One and Being—ever wanting to one another ? Is the One ever set free from *being* a part (τοῦ εἶναι μόριον) and Being set free from the *one* part (τοῦ ἐνὸς μορίου)? Once more, each part thus possesses both the one and Being, and the smallest part still always consists of these two parts." [1] In other words : " The one is ; from this it follows that the one is not synonymous with ' is,' and thus the one and ' is ' are distinguished. There hence is in the proposition ' the one is ' a distinction ; the many is therefore contained in it, and thus even with the one I express the many." This dialectic is certainly correct, but it is not quite pure, because it begins from this union of two determinations.

The result of the whole investigation in the Parmenides is summarized at the close by saying " that whether the one is or is not, it, as also the many (τἆλλα), in relation to themselves and in relation to one another—all of them both are and are not, appear and do not appear." [2] This result may seem strange. We are far from accepting, in our ordinary conception of things, quite abstract determinations such as the one, Being, non-being, appearance, rest, move-ment, &c., as Ideas ; but these universals are taken by Plato as Ideas, and this Dialogue thus really contains the pure Platonic doctrine of Ideas. He shows of the one that when it is as well as when it is not, whether like itself or not like itself, both in movement and rest, origination and decay, it both is and is not ; or the unity as well as all these pure Ideas, both are and are not, the one is one as much as it is many. In the proposition "the one is," it is also implied that "the one is not one but many ;" and, con-versely, "the many is " also indicates that "the many is not many, but one." They show themselves dialectically

---

[1] Plat. Parmenides, p. 142 (pp. 35, 36) ; cf. Arist. Eth. Nicom. ed. Michelet, T. I. Præf. p. VII. sqq.

[2] Plat. Parmenides, p. 166 (p. 84) ; cf. Zeller ; Platonische Studien, p. 165.

and are really the identity with their 'other'; and this is the truth. An example is given in Becoming: in Becoming Being and non-being are in inseparable unity, and yet they are also present there as distinguished; for Becoming only exists because the one passes into the other.

In this respect, perhaps, the result arrived at in the Parmenides may not satisfy us, since it seems to be negative in character, and not, as the negation of the negation, expressive of true affirmation. Nevertheless, the Neo-platonists, and more especially Proclus, regard the result arrived at in the Parmenides as the true theology, as the true revelation of all the mysteries of the divine essence. And it cannot be regarded as anything else, however little this may at first appear, and though Tiedemann (Platon. Argumenta, p. 340) speaks of these assertions as merely the wild extravagances of the Neo-platonists. In fact, however, we understand by God the absolute essence of things, which even in its simple Notion is the unity and movement of these pure realities, the Ideas of the one and many, &c. The divine essence is the Idea in general, as it is either for sensuous consciousness or for thought. In as far as the divine Idea is the absolute self-reflection, dialectic is nothing more than this activity of self-reflection in itself; the Neo-Platonists regarded this connection as metaphysical only, and have recognized in it their theology, the unfolding of the secrets of the divine essence. But here there appears the double interpretation already remarked upon (p. 19), which has now to be more clearly expounded. It is that God and the essential reality of things may be understood in two different ways. For, on the one hand, when it is said that the essential reality of things is the unity of opposites, it would seem as though only the immediate essence of these immediately objective things were indicated, and as if this doctrine of real essence or ontology were distinguished from the knowledge of God, or theology. These simple realities and their relation and movement

seem only to express moments of the objective and not
mind, because there is lacking in them one element—that is
to say, reflection into themselves—which we demand for
the existence of the divine essence. For mind, the truly
absolute essence, is not only the simple and immediate, but
that which reflects itself into itself, for which in its opposition
the unity of itself and of that which is opposed is; but
these moments and their movement do not present it as
such, for they make their appearance as simple abstractions.
On the other hand, they may also be taken to be pure
Notions, which pertain purely to reflection into itself. In this
case Being is wanting to them, or what we likewise demand
for reflection into itself as essential to the divine essence;
and then their movement is esteemed an empty round of
empty abstractions, which belong only to reflection and have
no reality. For the solution of this contradiction we must
know the nature of apprehension and knowledge, in order
to obtain in the Notion everything there present. Thus
shall we have the consciousness that the Notion is in truth
neither the immediate only, although it is the simple, nor
merely that which reflects itself into itself, the thing of
consciousness; for it is of spiritual simplicity, thus really
existent—as it is thought turned back on itself, so it is
also Being in itself, *i.e.* objective Being, and consequently
all reality. Plato did not state this knowledge of the
nature of the Notion so expressly, nor did he say that this
essential Being of things is the same as the divine essence.
But really it is simply not put into words, for the fact is
undoubtedly present, and the only distinction is one of
speech as between the mode of the ordinary conception
and that of the Notion. On the one hand, this reflection
into itself, the spiritual, the Notion, is present in the
speculation of Plato; for the unity of the one and many,
&c., is just this individuality in difference, this being-turned-
back-within-itself in its opposite, this opposite which is
implicit; the essential reality of the world is really this

movement returning into itself of that which is turned back within itself. But, on the other hand, for this very reason, this being reflected into self—like the God of ordinary conception—still remains with Plato something separated ; and in his representation of the Becoming of Nature in the Timæus, God, and the essential reality of things, appear as distinguished.

b. In the Sophist Plato investigated the pure Notions or Ideas of movement and rest, self-identity and other-being, Being and non-being. He here proves, as against Parmenides, that non-being is, and likewise that the simple self-identical partakes of other-being, and unity of multiplicity. He says of the Sophists that they never get beyond non-being, and he also refutes their whole ground-principle, which is non-being, feeling, and the many. Plato has thus so determined the true universal, that he makes it the unity of, for example, the one and many, Being and non-being; but at the same time he has avoided, or it was his endeavour to avoid, the double meaning which lies in our talk of the unity of Being and nothing, &c. For in this expression we emphasize the unity, and then the difference disappears, just as if we merely abstracted from it. Plato tried, however, to preserve the difference likewise. The Sophist is a further development of Being and non-being, both of which are applicable to all things ; for because things are different, the one being the other of the other, the determination of the negative is present. First of all, however, Plato expresses in the Sophist a clearer consciousness of Ideas as abstract universalities, and his conviction that this point of view could not endure, because it was opposed to the unity of the Idea with itself. Plato thus first refutes what is sensuous, and then even the Ideas themselves. The first of these points of view is what is later on called materialism, which makes the corporeal alone to be the substantial, admitting nothing to have reality excepting what can be laid hold of by the hand, such as rocks and oaks. "Let us," says Plato, in the second place, "proceed to the other, to the friends of Ideas." Their belief is that the substantial is incorporeal, intellectual, and they separate from it the region of Becoming, of change, into which the sensuous falls, while the universal is for itself. These represent Ideas as immovable, and neither active nor passive. Plato asserts, as against this, that movement, life, soul, and thought, cannot be denied to true Being ($\pi\alpha\nu\tau\epsilon\lambda\hat{\omega}\varsigma$ $\check{o}\nu\tau\iota$), and that the holy reason ($\check{\alpha}\gamma\iota o\nu$ $\nu o\hat{\nu}\nu$) can be nowhere, and in nothing that is unmoved.[1] Plato thus has a clear consciousness of having got further than Parmenides when he says :—

> " Keep your mind from this way of inquiry,
> For never will you show that non-being is."

Plato says that Being in anyone partakes both of Being and non-being ; but what thus participates is different both from Being and non-being as such.[2]

This dialectic combats two things in particular ; and in the first place it is antagonistic to the common dialectic in the ordinary sense, of which we have already spoken. Examples of this false dialectic to which Plato often comes back, are specially frequent amongst the Sophists ; yet he did not show sufficiently clearly how they are distinguished from the purely dialectical knowledge which is in the Notion. For example, Plato expressed his dissent when Protagoras and others said that no determination is absolutely certain—that bitter is not objective, for what to one person is bitter, to another is sweet. Similarly, large and small, more and less, &c., are relative, because the large will be, in other circumstances, small, and the small will be great. That is to say, the unity of opposites is present to us in everything we know, but the common way of looking at things, in which the rational does not come to con-

---

[1] Plat. Sophist. pp. 246–249 (pp. 190–196).
[2] Ibid. p. 258 (p. 219).

sciousness, always holds the opposites asunder, as though they were simply opposed in a determinate way. As in each thing we demonstrate unity, so do we also show its multiplicity, for it has many parts and qualities. In the Parmenides, Plato, as we saw above (p. 58), objected to this unity of opposites, because it must thereby be said that something is one in quite another respect from that in which it is many. We thus do not here bring these thoughts together, for the conception and the words merely go backwards and forwards from the one to the other ; if this passing to and fro is performed with consciousness, it is the empty dialectic which does not really unite the opposites. Of this Plato says, "If anyone thinks he has made a wonderful discovery in ascertaining that he can drag thoughts this way and that, from one determination to another, he may be told that he has done nothing worthy of praise ; for in so doing there is nothing excellent or difficult." The dialectic that annuls a determination because it reveals in it some defect, and then goes on to establish another, is thus wrong. "The point of difficulty, and what we ought to aim at, is to show that what is the other is the same, and what is the same, is another, and likewise in the same regard and from the same point of view to show that the one has in them come into existence if the other determination is revealed within them. But to show that somehow the same is another, and the other also the same, that the great is also small " (*e.g.* Protagoras's die), "and the like also unlike, and to delight in thus always proving opposites, is no true inquiry (ἔλεγχος), but simply proves that he who uses such arguments is a neophyte," in thought, "who has just begun to investigate truth. To separate all existences from one another is the crude attempt of an uncultured and unphilosophical mind. To cause everything to fall asunder means the perfect annihilation of all thought, for thought is the union of ideas."[1]

[1] Plat. Sophist. p. 259 (pp. 220, 221).

Thus Plato expressly speaks against the dialectic of showing how anything may be refuted from some point of view or another. We see that Plato, in respect of content, expresses nothing excepting what is called indifference in difference, the difference of absolute opposites and their unity. To this speculative knowledge he opposes the ordinary way of thinking, which is positive as well as negative; the former, not bringing the thoughts together, allows first one and then the other to have value in their separation; the latter is, indeed, conscious of a unity, though it is of a superficial, differentiating unity in which the two moments are separate, as standing in different aspects.

The second point against which Plato argues is the dialectic of the Eleatics, and their assertion, which in its nature resembles that of the Sophists, that only Being is, and non-being is not. To the Sophists this means, as Plato puts it: Since the negative is not, but only Being is, there is nothing false; everything existent, everything which is for us, is thus necessarily true, and what is not, we do not know or feel. Plato reproaches the Sophists for thus doing away with the difference between true and false.[1] Having arrived at this stage in the knowledge of the dialectic (and the whole matter is merely a difference of stages) the Sophists could allow what they promise—that everything that the individual, according to his belief, makes his end and interest, is affirmative and right. Hence it cannot be said that such and such an act is wrong, wicked, a crime; for this would be to say that the maxim of the action is wrong. No more can it be said that such and such opinion is deceptive, for in the opinion of the Sophists the proposition implies that what I feel or represent to myself, in as far as it is mine, is an affirmative content, and thus true and right. The proposition in itself

[1] Plat. Sophist. pp. 260, 261 (pp. 222–224).

seems quite abstract and innocent, but we first notice what is involved in such abstractions when we see them in concrete form. According to this innocent proposition there would be no wickedness and no crime. The Platonic dialectic is essentially different from this kind of dialectic.

What is further present to the mind of Plato is that the Idea, the absolute universal, good, true, and beautiful, is to be taken for itself. The myth, which I have already quoted (p. 27 *et seq.*), indeed goes to prove that we must not consider a good action, a noble man—not the subject of which these determinations are predicated. For that which appears in such conceptions or perceptions as predicate, must be taken for itself, and this is the absolute truth. This tallies with the nature of the dialectic which has been described. An action, taken in accordance with the empirical conception, may be called right ; in another aspect, quite opposite determinations may be shown to be in it. But the good and true must be taken on their own account without such individualities, without this empirical and concrete character ; and the good and true thus taken alone, constitute that which is. The soul which, according to the divine drama, is found in matter, rejoices in a beautiful and just object ; but the only actual truth is in absolute virtue, justice, and beauty. It is thus the universal for itself which is further determined in the Platonic dialectic; of this several forms appear, but these forms are themselves still very general and abstract. Plato's highest form is the identity of Being and non-being. The true is that which is, but this Being is not without negation. Plato's object is thus to show that non-being is an essential determination in Being, and that the simple, self-identical, partakes of other-being. This unity of Being and non-being is also found in the Sophists ; but this alone is not the end of the matter. For in further investigation Plato comes to the conclusion that non-being, further determined, is the essence of the ' other ': " Ideas mingle, and Being and the other (θάτερον) go through everything and through one another; the other, because it participates (μετασχόν) in Being, certainly *is* through this indwelling Being, but it is not identical with that of which it partakes, being something different, and being other than Being, it is clearly non-being. But since Being likewise partakes of other-being, it also is different from other Ideas, and is not any one of them ; so that there are thousands of ways in which it is not, and as regards all else, whether looked at individually or collectively, it in many respects is, and in many respects is not." [1] Plato thus maintains that the other, as the negative, non-identical, is likewise in one and the same respect the self-identical; there are not different sides which are in mutual opposition.

These are the principal points in Plato's peculiar dialectic. The fact that the Idea of the divine, eternal, beautiful, is absolute existence, is the beginning of the elevation of consciousness into the spiritual, and into the consciousness that the universal is true. It may be enough for the ordinary idea to be animated and satisfied by the conception of the beautiful and good, but thinking knowledge demands the determination of this eternal and divine. And this determination is really only free determination which certainly does not prevent universality—a limitation (for every determination is limitation) which likewise leaves the universal in its infinitude free and independent. Freedom exists only in a return into itself; the undistinguished is the lifeless; the active, living, concrete universal is hence what inwardly distinguishes itself, but yet remains free in so doing. Now this determinateness consists in the one being identical with itself in the ·other, in the many, in what is distinguished. This constitutes the only truth, and the only interest for knowledge in what is called Platonic philosophy, and if this is not known, the main point of it is not known. While in the example already often quoted

---

[1] Plat. Sophist. pp. 258, 259 (pp. 218–220).

(pp.58, 64), in which Socrates is both one and many, the two thoughts are made to fall asunder, it is left to speculative thought alone to bring the thoughts together, and this union of what is different, of Being and non-being, of one and many, &c., which takes place without a mere transition from one to another, constitutes the inmost reality and true greatness of Platonic philosophy. This determination is the esoteric element in Platonic philosophy, and the other is the exoteric; the distinction is doubtless an unwarranted one, indicating, as it seems to do, that Plato could have two such philosophies—one for the world, for the people, and the other, the inward, reserved for the initiated. But the esoteric is the speculative, which, even though written and printed, is yet, without being any secret, hidden from those who have not sufficient interest in it to exert themselves. To this esoteric portion pertain the two dialogues hitherto considered, along with which the Philebus may in the third place be taken.

c. In the Philebus Plato investigates the nature of pleasure; and the opposition of the infinite and finite, or of the unlimited (ἄπειρον) and limiting (πέρας), is there more especially dealt with. In keeping this before us, it would scarcely occur to us that through the metaphysical knowledge of the nature of the infinite and undetermined, what concerns enjoyment is likewise determined; but these pure thoughts are the substantial through which everything, however concrete or seemingly remote, is decided. When Plato treats of pleasure and wisdom as contrasted, it is the opposition of finite and infinite. By pleasure we certainly represent to ourselves the immediately individual, the sensuous; but pleasure is the indeterminate in respect that it is the merely elementary, like fire and water, and not the self-determining. Only the Idea is the self-determinate, or self-identity. To our reflection the infinite appears to be what is best and highest, limitation being inferior to it;

[1] Cf. also Plat. Phileb. p. 14 (p. 138).

and ancient philosophers so determined it. By Plato, however, it is, on the other hand, shown that the limited is the true, as the self-determining, while the unlimited is still abstract; it certainly can be determined in many different ways, but when thus determined it is only the individual. The infinite is the formless; free form as activity is the finite, which finds in the infinite the material for self-realization. Plato thus characterizes enjoyment dependent on the senses as the unlimited which does not determine itself; reason alone is the active determination. But the infinite is what in itself passes over to the finite; thus the perfect good, according to Plato, is neither to be sought for in happiness or reason, but in a life of both combined. But wisdom, as limit, is the true cause from which what is excellent arises.[1] As that which posits measure and end, it is what absolutely determines the end —the immanent determination with which and in which freedom likewise brings itself into existence.

Plato furthur considers the fact that the true is the identity of opposites, thus. The infinite, as the indeterminate, is capable of a more or less, it may be more intensive or not; thus colder and warmer, drier and moister, quicker and slower, &c., are all such. What is limited is the equal, the double, and every other measure; by this means the opposite ceases to be unlike and becomes uniform and harmonious. Through the unity of these opposites, such as cold and warm, dry and moist, health arises; similarly the harmony of music takes its origin from the limitation of high tones and deep, of quicker and slower movement, and, generally speaking, everything beautiful and perfect arises through the union of opposites. Health, happiness, beauty, &c., would thus appear to be begotten, in as far as the opposites are allied thereto, but they are likewise an intermingling of the same. The ancients make copious use of

---

[1] Plat. Phileb. pp. 11–23 (pp. 131–156); pp. 27, 28 (pp. 166, 167).

intermingling, participation, &c., instead of individuality; but for us these are indefinite and inadequate expressions. But Plato says that the third, which is thus begotten, presupposes the cause or that from which it is formed; this is more excellent than those through whose instrumentality that third arose. Hence Plato has four determinations; first the unlimited, the undetermined; secondly the limited, measure, proportion, to which pertains wisdom; the third is what is mingled from both, what has only arisen; the fourth is cause. This is in itself nothing else than the unity of differences, subjectivity, power and supremacy over opposites, that which is able to sustain the opposites in itself; but it is only the spiritual which has this power and which sustains opposition, the highest contradiction in itself. Weak corporeality passes away as soon as 'another' comes into it. The cause he speaks of is divine reason, which governs the world; the beauty of the world which is present in air, fire, water, and in all that lives, is produced thereby.[1] Thus the absolute is what in one unity is finite and infinite.

When Plato speaks thus of the beautiful and good, these are concrete ideas, or rather there is only one idea. But we are still far from these concrete ideas when we begin with such abstractions as Being, non-being, unity, and multiplicity. If Plato, however, has not succeeded in bringing these abstract thoughts through further development and concretion, to beauty, truth, and morality, there at least lies in the knowledge of those abstract determinations, the criterion by which the concrete is determined, as also its sources. This transition to the concrete is made in the Philebus, since the principle of feeling and of pleasure is there considered. The ancient philosophers knew very well what they had of concrete in those abstract thoughts. In the atomic principle of multiplicity we thus find the source of a construction of the state, for the ultimate thought-determination of such state-principles is the logical. The

[1] Plat. Phileb. pp. 23–30 (pp. 156–172).

ancients in their pure Philosophy had not the same end
in view as we—they had not the end of a metaphysical
sequence placed before them like a problem. We, on the
other hand, have something concrete before us, and desire
to reduce it to settled order. With Plato Philosophy offers
the path which the individual must follow in order to attain
to any knowledge, but, generally speaking, Plato places
absolute and explicit happiness, the blessed life itself, in
the contemplation during life of the divine objects named
above.[1] This contemplative life seems aimless, for the
reason that all its interests have disappeared. But to live
in freedom in the kingdom of thought had become the
absolute end to the ancients, and they knew that freedom
existed only in thought.

2. Philosophy of Nature.

With Plato Philosophy likewise commenced to devote
more attention to the understanding of what is further
determined, and in this way the matter of knowledge began
to fall into divisions. In the Timæus the Idea thus makes
its appearance as expressed in its concrete determinateness,
and the Platonic Philosophy of Nature hence teaches us to
have a better knowledge of the reality of the world; we
cannot, however, enter into details, and if we did, they have
little interest. It is more especially where Plato treats of
physiology that his statements in no way correspond with
what we now know, although we cannot fail to wonder at
the brilliant glimpses of the truth there found, which have
been only too much misconceived by the moderns. Plato
derived a great deal from the Pythagoreans; how much is
theirs, however, cannot be satisfactorily determined. We
remarked before (p. 14) that the Timæus is really the
fuller version of a Pythagorean treatise; other would-be
wise persons have indeed said that the treatise is only an

Plat. Phileb. p. 33 (p. 178).

abstract made by a Pythagorean of the larger work of Plato, but the first theory is the more probable. The Timæus has in all times been esteemed the most difficult and obscure of the Platonic dialogues. This difficulty is due in part to the apparent mingling of conceiving knowledge and ordinary perception already mentioned (p. 20), just as we shall presently find an intermingling of Pythagorean numbers; and it is due still more to the philosophic nature of the matter in hand, of which Plato was as yet unconscious. The second difficulty lies in the arrangement of the whole, for what at once strikes one is that Plato repeatedly breaks off the thread of his argument, often appearing to turn back and begin again from the beginning.[1] This moved critics such as August Wolff and others, who could not understand it philosophically, to take the Timæus to be an accumulation of fragments put together, or else to be several works which had only been loosely strung together into one, or into the Platonic portion of which much that is foreign had been introduced. Wolff accordingly thought it was evident from this that the dialogue, like Homer's poems, had been, in its first form, spoken and not written. But although the connection seems unmethodical, and Plato himself makes what may be called copious excuses for the confusion, we shall find how the whole matter really falls into natural divisions, and we shall also find the deep inward reason which makes necessary the frequent return to what apparently is the beginning.

An exposition of the reality of nature or of the becoming of the world is introduced by Plato in the following way: "God is the Good," this stands also at the head of the Platonic Ideas in the verbally delivered discourses (*supra,* p. 11); "goodness, however, has no jealousy of anything, and being free from jealousy, God desired to make all things like Himself."[2] God here is still without determina-

---

[1] Cf. Plat. Tim. p. 34 (p. 31); p. 48 (pp. 56, 57); p. 69 (p. 96).

[2] Ibid. p. 29 (p. 25).

tion, and a name which has no meaning for thought; nevertheless, where Plato in the Timæus again begins from the beginning, he is found to have a more definite idea of God. That God is devoid of envy undoubtedly is a great, beautiful, true, and childlike thought. With the ancients, on the contrary, we find in Nemesis, Dike, Fate, Jealousy, the one determination of the gods: moved by this they cast down the great and bring it low, and suffer not what is excellent and elevated to exist. The later high-minded philosophers controverted this doctrine. For in the mere idea of the Nemesis no moral determination is as yet implied, because punishment there is only the humiliation of what oversteps limits, but these limits are not yet presented as moral, and punishment is thus not yet a recognition of the moral as distinguished from the immoral. Plato's thought is thus much higher than that of most of our moderns, who, in saying that God is a hidden God who has not revealed Himself to us and of whom we can know nothing, ascribe jealousy to God. For why should He not reveal Himself to us if we earnestly seek the knowledge of Him? A light loses nothing by another's being kindled therefrom, and hence there was in Athens a punishment imposed on those who did not permit this to be done. If the knowledge of God were kept from us in order that we should know only the finite and not attain to the infinite, God would be a jealous God, or God would then become an empty name. Such talk means no more than that we wish to neglect what is higher and divine, and seek after our own petty interests and opinions. This humility is sin—the sin against the Holy Ghost.

Plato continues: " God found the visible " ($\pi\alpha\rho\alpha\lambda\alpha\beta\acute{\omega}\nu$) —a mythical expression proceeding from the necessity of beginning with an immediate, which, however, as it presents itself, cannot in any way be allowed—" not at rest, but moving in an irregular and disorderly manner; and out of disorder he brought order, considering that this was far

better than the other." From this it appears as if Plato
had considered that God was only the δημιουργός, *i.e.* the
disposer of matter, and that this, being eternal and independent, was found by Him as chaos; but in view of
what has been said, this is false. These are not the
philosophic doctrines which Plato seriously held, for he
speaks here only after the manner of the ordinary conception, and such expressions have hence no philosophic
content. It is only the introduction of the subject, bringing
us, as it does, to determinations such as matter. Plato
then comes in course of his progress to further determinations, and in these we first have the Notion; we must
hold to what is speculative in Plato, and not to the first-
mentioned ordinary conception. Likewise, when he says
that God esteemed order to be the best, the mode of
expression is naïve. Now-a-days we should ask that God
should first be proved; and just as little should we allow
the visible to be established without much further ado.
What is proved by Plato from this more naïve method of
expression is, in the first place, the true determination of
the Idea, which only appears later on. It is further said:
" God reflecting that of what is visible, the unintelligent
(ἀνόητον) could not be fairer than the intelligent (νοῦς),
and that intelligence could not exist in anything devoid of
soul, for these reasons put intelligence in the soul, and the
soul in the body, and so united them that the world became
a living and intelligent system, an animal." We have
reality and intelligence, and the soul as the bond connecting
the two extremes, without which intelligence could not
have part in the visible body; we saw the true reality
comprehended by Plato in a similar way in the Phædrus
(*supra*, p. 39). "There is, however, only one such
animal, for were there two or more, these would be only
parts of the one, and only one." [1]

Plato now first proceeds to the determination of the

---

[1] Plat. Timæus, p. 30, 31 (pp. 25-27).

Idea of corporeal existence : " Because the world was to become corporeal, visible and tangible, and since without fire nothing can be seen, and without solidity, without earth, nothing can be touched, God in the beginning made fire and earth." In this childlike way Plato introduces these extremes, solidity and life. " But two things cannot be united without a third, there must be a bond between them, uniting both "—one of Plato's simple methods of expression. " The fairest bond, however, is that which most completely fuses itself and that which is bound by it." That is a profound saying, in which the Notion is contained; the bond is the subjective and individual, the power which dominates the other, which makes itself identical with it. " Proportion (ἀναλογία) is best adapted to effect such a fusion; that is, whenever of three numbers or magnitudes or powers, that which is the mean is to the last term what the first term is to the mean, and again when the mean is to the first term as the last term is to the mean " (a : b=b : c) " then the mean having become the first and last, and the first and last both having become means, all things will necessarily come to be the same; but having come to be the same, everything will be one." [1] This is excellent, we have still preserved this in our Philosophy; it is the distinction which is no distinction. This diremption from which Plato proceeds, is the conclusion which we know from logic; it appears in the form of the ordinary syllogism, in which, however, the whole rationality of the Idea is, at least externally, contained. The distinctions are the extremes, and the mean is the identity which in a supreme degree makes them one; the conclusion is thus speculative, and in the extremes unites itself with itself, because all the terms pass through all the different positions. It is hence a mistake to disparage the conclusion and not to recognize it as the highest and absolute form; in respect of the conclusions arrived at by the understanding, on the contrary, we

[1] Plat. Timæus, pp. 31, 32 (pp. 27, 28).

should be right in rejecting it. This last has no such mean ; each of the differences is there recognized as different in its own independent form, as having a character different from that of the other. This, in the Platonic philosophy, is abrogated, and the speculative element in it constitutes the proper and true form of conclusion, in which the extremes neither remain in independence as regards themselves, nor as regards the mean. In the conclusion of the understanding, on the contrary, the unity which is constituted is only the unity of essentially different contents which remain such ; for here a subject, a determination, is, through the mean, simply bound up with another, or "some conception is joined to some other conception." In a rational conclusion, however, the main point of its speculative content is the identity of the extremes which are joined to one another ; in this it is involved that the subject presented in the mean is a content which does not join itself with another, but only through the other and in the other with itself. In other words, this constitutes the essential nature of God, who, when made subject, is the fact that He begot His Son, the world ; but in this reality which appears as another, He still remains identical with Himself, does away with the separation implied in the Fall, and, in the other, merely unites Himself to Himself and thus becomes Spirit. When the immediate is elevated over the mediate and it is then said that God's actions are immediate, there is, indeed, good ground for the assertion ; but the concrete fact is that God is a conclusion which, by differentiating itself, unites itself to itself, and, through the abrogation of the mediation, reinstates its own immediacy. In the Platonic philosophy we thus have what is best and highest ; the thoughts are, indeed, merely pure thoughts, but they contain everything in themselves ; for all concrete forms depend on thought-determinations alone. The Fathers thus found in Plato the Trinity which they wished to comprehend and prove in thought : with Plato the truth really has the same determination as the Trinity. But these forms have been neglected for two thousand years since Plato's time, for they have not passed into the Christian religion as thoughts; indeed they were considered to be ideas which had entered in through error, until quite recent times, when men began to understand that the Notion is contained in these determinations, and that nature and spirit can thus be comprehended through their means.

Plato continues: "Since what is solid requires two means, because it not only has breadth but also depth, God has placed air and water between fire and earth; and indeed He gave to them the same proportion, so that fire is related to air as air to water, and as air is to water, so is water to earth." [1] Thus we have, properly speaking, four methods of representing space, inasmuch as the point is, through line and surface, closely bound up with the solid body. The sundered mean here discovered, again indicates an important thought of logical profundity; and the number four which here appears, is in nature a fundamental number. For as being the different which is turned towards the two extremes, the mean must be separated in itself. In the conclusion in which God is the One, the second (the mediating), the Son; the third, the Spirit; the mean indeed is simple. But the cause why that which in the rational conclusion is merely three-fold, passes in nature to the four-fold, rests in what is natural, because what in thought is immediately the one, becomes separate in Nature. But in order that in Nature the opposition should exist as opposition, it must itself be a two-fold, and thus, when we count, we have four. This also takes place in the conception of God, for when we apply it to the world, we have nature as mean and the existent spirit as the way of return for nature : when the return is made, this is the absolute Spirit. This living process, this separation and unifying of differences, is the living God.

[1] Plat. Timæus, г. 32 (p. 28).

Plato says further : " Through this unity the visible and tangible world has been made. And it comes to pass by God's having given to it these elements entire and unseparated, that it is perfect, and unaffected by age and disease. For old age and disease only arise from a body's being worked upon by a superabundance of such elements from without. But here this is not so, for the world contains those elements entirely in itself, and nothing can come to it from without. The world is spherical in form," (as it was to Parmenides and the Pythagoreans) " as being most perfect, and as containing all others in itself; it is perfectly smooth, since for it there is nothing outside, and it requires no limbs." Finitude consists in this, that a distinction as regards something else is an externality to some other object. In the Idea we certainly have determination, limitation, difference, other-being, but it is at the same time dissolved, contained, gathered together, in the one. Thus it is a difference through which no finitude arises, seeing that it likewise is sublated. Finitude is thus in the infinite itself, and this is, indeed, a great thought. " God gave the world the most appropriate motion of all the seven, being that which harmonizes best with mind and consciousness, motion in a circle ; the other six He took away from it and liberated it from their variations " [1] (movements backwards and forwards). This is only a popular way of putting it.

We read further : " Since God wished to make the world a God, He gave it soul, and this was placed in the centre and diffused through the whole, which was also surrounded by it externally ; and in this way He brought to pass the self-sufficing existence which required no other, and which needed no other friendship or acquaintance than itself. Through these means God created the world as a blessed God." We may say that here, where the world is a totality through the world-soul, we first have the knowledge of the Idea ;

[1] Plat. Timæus, pp. 32-34 (pp. 28-31).

for the first time this newly-begotten God, as the mean and identity, is the true absolute. That first God which was only goodness, is, on the contrary, a mere hypothesis, and hence neither determined nor self-determining. "Now though we have spoken of the soul last," Plato goes on, "it does not for that reason come last; for this is merely our manner of speech. The soul is the ruler, the king, and the body is its subject." It is only Plato's naïvety which ascribes the reversal of the order of the two to a manner of speech. What here appears as contingent is really necessary—that is, to begin with the immediate and then come to the concrete. We must likewise adopt this method, but with the consciousness that when we begin with determinations such as Being, or God, Space, Time, &c., we speak of them in an immediate manner, and this content, in accordance with its nature, is at first immediate, and consequently undetermined in itself. God, for example, with whom we begin as an immediate, is proved only at the last, and then, indeed, as the true first. Thus we can, as already remarked, (p. 72) show Plato's confusion of mind in such presentations; but it depends entirely on what Plato's standard of truth is.

Plato further shows us the nature of the Idea in one of the most famous and profound of passages, where in the essence of the soul he recognizes again the very same idea that he also expressed as the essence of the corporeal. For he says: "The soul is created in the following way: Of the indivisible and unchangeable and also of the divisible which is corporeal, God made a third kind of intermediate essence, which partook of the nature of the same and of the nature of the other or diverse." (The divisible is to Plato likewise the other as such, or in itself, and not of anything else.) "And God in like manner made the soul a sort of intermediate between the indivisible and the divisible." Here the abstract determinations of the one which is identity, of the many or non-identical, which is opposition and difference, once more appear. If we say: "God, the Absolute, is the identity of the identical and non-identical," a cry is raised of barbarism and scholasticism. Those who speak of it so still hold Plato in high esteem, and yet it was thus that he determined the truth. "And taking these three elements as separate, God mingled them all into one Idea, because he forcibly compressed the incongruous nature of the other into the same."[1] This is undoubtedly the power of the Notion, which posits the many, the separate, as the ideal, and that is also the force applied to the understanding when anything is placed before it.

Plato now describes how the self-identical, as itself a moment, and the other or matter, and the third, the apparently dissoluble union which has not returned into the first unity—which three were originally separated—have now, in simple reflection into self and resumption of that beginning, been degraded into moments. "Mingling the identical and the other with the essence (οὐσία)," the third moment, "and making them all one, God again divided this whole into as many parts was as fitting."[2] Since this substance of the soul is identical with that of the visible world, the one whole is for the first time the now systematized substance, the true matter, the absolute element which is internally divided, an enduring and unseparable unity of the one and many ; and no other essence must be demanded. The manner and mode of the division of this subjectivity contain the famous Platonic numbers, which doubtless originally pertain to the Pythagoreans, and respecting which both ancients and moderns, and even Kepler himself in his *Harmonia mundi*, have taken much pains, but which no one has properly understood. To understand would mean two things, and in the first place, the recognition of their speculative significance, their Notion. But, as already remarked of the Pythagoreans (Vol. I. p. 224), these distinctions of

[1] Plat. Timæus, p. 35 (p. 32).
[2] Ibid.

number give only an indefinite conception of difference, and
that only in the earlier numbers; where the relationships
become more complicated, they are quite incapable of desig -
nating them more closely.   In the second place, because of
their being numbers, they express, as differences of magnitude, differences in what is sensuous only.   The system of
apparent magnitude—and it is in the heavenly system that
magnitude appears most purely and freely, liberated from
what is qualitative—must correspond to them.   But these
living number-spheres are themselves systems composed of
many elements—both of the magnitude of distance and of
velocity and mass.   No one of these elements, taken as a
succession of simple numbers, can be likened to the system
of heavenly spheres, for the series corresponding to this
system can, as to its members, contain nothing else than
the system of all these moments.   Now if the Platonic
numbers were also the elements of each system such as this,
it would not be only this element which would have to be
taken into account, for the relationship of moments which
become distinguished in movement has to be conceived
of as a whole, and is the true object of interest and
reason.   What we have to do is to give briefly the main
points as matter of history; we have the most thorough
treatment of it given us by Böckh " On the Constitution
of the World-Soul in the Timæus of Plato," in the third
volume of the Studies of Daub and Creuzer (p. 26 *et seq.*).

The fundamental series is very simple : " God first took
one part out of the whole; then the second, the double of
the first ; the third is one and a half times as many as the
second, or three times the first; the next is double the
second ; the fifth is three times the third ; the sixth is eight
times the first; the seventh is twenty-seven times greater
than the first."   Hence the series is : $1 ; 2 ; 3 ; 4 = 2^2 ;$
$9 = 3^2 ; 8 = 2^3 ; 27 = 3^3$.   " Then God filled up the
double and triple intervals " (the relations $1 : 2$ and $1 : 3$)
" by again abstracting portions from the whole.   These

parts he placed in the intervals in such a way that in each
interval there were two means, the one exceeding and
exceeded by the extremes in the same ratio, the other
being that kind of mean which by an equal number
exceeds and is exceeded by the extremes." That is, the
first is a constant geometric relationship, and the other is
an arithmetical. The first mean, brought about through
the quadration, is thus in the relation 1 : 2, for example,
the proportion $1 : \sqrt{2} : 2$; the other is in the same relation,
the number $1\frac{1}{2}$. Hereby new relations arise which are
again in a specially given and more difficult method inserted
into that first, but this is done in such a way that everywhere something has been left out, and the last relation of
number to number is 256 : 243, or $2^8 : 3^5$.

Much progress is not, however, made with these number-
relations, for they do not present much to the speculative
Notion. The relationships and laws of nature cannot be
expressed by these barren numbers; they form an empirical
relation which does not constitute the basis of the propor-
tions of nature. Plato now says: "God divided this
entire series lengthways into two parts which he set together
crosswise like an X, and he bent their ends into a circular
form and comprehended them in a uniform motion—forming an inner circle and an outer—and he called the motion
of the outer circle the motion of the same, and that of the
inner the motion of the diverse, giving supremacy to the
former, and leaving it intact. But the inner motion he
again split into seven orbits after the same relations; three
of these he made to move with equal velocity, and four with
unequal velocity to the three and to one another. This is the
system of the soul within which all that is corporeal is formed;
the soul is the centre, it penetrates the whole and envelopes
it from without and moves in itself. Thus it has the divine
beginning of a never-ceasing and rational life in itself."[1]

[1] Plat. Timæus, pp. 35, 36 (pp. 32-34).

This is not quite devoid of confusion, and from it we can
only grasp the general fact that as to Plato with the idea
of the corporeal universe that of the soul enters in as the
all-embracing and simple, to him the essence of the corporeal and of the soul is unity in difference. This double
essence, posited in and for itself in difference, becomes
systematized within the one in many moments, which are,
however, movements; thus this reality and that essence
both pertain to this whole in the antithesis of soul and
body, and this again is one. Mind is what penetrates all,
and to it the corporeal is opposed as truly as that it itself is
mind.

This is a general description of the soul which is posited
in the world and reigns over it ; and in as far as the substantial, which is in matter, is similar to it, their inherent
identity is asserted. The fact that in it the same moments
which constitute its reality are contained, merely signifies
that God, as absolute Substance, does not see anything other
than Himself. Plato hence describes the relation of soul to
objective reality thus : it, if it touches any of the moments,
whether dispersed in parts or indivisible, is stirred in all
its powers to declare the sameness and the difference of
that or some other thing, and how, where, and when, the
individual is related to the other and to the universal.
" Now when the orbit of the sensuous, moving in its due
course, imparts knowledge of itself to its whole soul "
(where the different orbits of the world's course show themselves to correspond with the inwardness of mind) "true
opinions and beliefs arise. But when the soul applies
itself to the rational and the orbit of the self-identical
makes itself known, thought is perfected into knowledge." [1]
This is the essential reality of the world as of the inherently
blessed God; here the Idea of the whole is for the first
time perfected, and, in accordance with this Idea, the world

---

[1] Plat. Timæus, p. 37 (p. 35).

first makes its appearance. What had hitherto appeared
was the reality of the sensuous only and not the world as
sensuous, for though Plato certainly spoke before of fire,
&c. (p. 75), he there gave only the reality of the sensuous;
he would hence have done better to have omitted these
expressions. In them we have the reason for its appearing
as if Plato had here begun to consider from the beginning
that of which he has already treated (*supra*, p. 72). For
since we must begin from the abstract in order to reach
the true and the concrete, which first appears later on (*supra*,
p. 79), this last, when it has been found, has the appearance and form of a new commencement, particularly in
Plato's loose style.

Plato now goes on further, for he calls this divine world
the pattern which is in thought (νοητόν) alone, and always
in self-identity ; but he again places this whole in opposition to itself, so that there is a second, the copy of the first,
the world, which has origination and is visible. This
second is the system of the heavenly movement, the first is
the eternally living. The second, which has origination and
becoming within it, cannot be made perfectly like the first,
the eternal Idea. But it is made a self-moving image of
the eternal that remains in the unity ; and this eternal
image that moves rhythmically, after the manner of numbers,
is what we call time. Plato says of it that we are in the
habit of calling the 'was' and 'will be' parts of time, and
we transfer these indications of change which operate in
time, into absolute essence. But the true time is eternal,
or the present. For the substance can neither become
older nor younger, and time, as the immediate image of
the eternal, has neither the future nor the present in its
parts. Time is ideal, like space, not sensuous, but the
immediate mode in which mind comes forth in objective
form, the sensuous non-sensuous. The real moments of
the principle of absolute movement in what is temporal, are
those in which changes appear. " From the mind and will

of God in the creation of time, there arose the sun, moon, and five other stars which are called the planets, and which serve to distinguish and preserve the relations of time." [1] For in them the numbers of time are realized. Thus the heavenly movement, as the true time, is the image of the eternal which yet remains in unity, *i.e.* it is that in which the eternal retains the determination of the ' same.' For everything is in time, that is, in negative unity which does not allow anything to root itself freely in itself, and thus to move and to be moved according to chance.

But this eternal is also in the determinateness of the other reality, in the Idea of the self-changing and variable principle whose universal is matter. The eternal world has a likeness in the world which belongs to time, but opposed to this there is a second world where change really dwells. The ' same ' and the ' other ' are the most abstract opposites that we hitherto have had. The eternal world as posited in time has thus two forms—the form of similarity and the form of differentiality, of variability. The three moments as they appear in the last sphere, are, in the first place, simple essence which is begotten, which has arisen, or determinate matter ; secondly the place in which it is begotten, and thirdly that in which what is begotten has its pattern. Plato gives them thus : " Essence (ὄν), place, and generation." We thus have the conclusion in which space is the mean between individual generation and the universal. If we now oppose this principle to time in its negativity, the mean is this principle of the ' other ' as the universal principle—" a receiving medium like a mother "— an essence which contains everything, gives to everything an independent subsistence and the power to do as is desired. This principle is destitute of form, yet capable of receiving all forms, the universal principle of all that appears different ; it is the false passive matter that we

---

[1] Plat. Timæus, p. 48 (p. 57); pp. 37, 38 (pp. 36, 37).

understand when we speak of it—the relative substantial, existence generally, but external existence here, and only abstract Being-for-self. Form is in our reflection distinguished from it, and this, Plato tells us, first comes into existence through the mother. In this principle we have what we call the phenomenal, for matter is just this subsistence of individual generation, in which division is posited. But what appears herein is not to be posited as the individual of earthly existence, but is to be apprehended as the universal in such determinateness. Since matter, as the universal, is the principle of all that is individual, Plato in the first place reminds us that we cannot speak of these sensuous things—fire, water, earth, air, &c. (which thus once more come before us here) ; for hereby they are expressed as a fixed determination which remains as such— but what remains is only their universality, or they, as universal, are only the fiery, earthly, &c.[1]

Plato further expounds the determinate reality of these sensuous things, or their simple determinateness. In this world of change form is figure in space ; for as in the world, which is the immediate image of the eternal, time is the absolute principle, here the absolute ideal principle is pure matter as such, *i.e.* the existence of space. Space is the ideal essence of this phenomenal world, the mean which unites positivity and negativity, but its determinations are figures. And, indeed, of the different dimensions of space, it is surface which must be taken as true reality, for it is the absolute mean between the line and point in space, and in its first real limitation it is three ; similarly the triangle is first among the figures, while the circle has no limit as such within it. Here Plato comes to the deduction of configuration, in which the triangle forms the principle ; thus triangles form the essence of sensuous things. Hence he says, in Pythagorean fashion, that the compounding and

[1] Plat. Timæus, pp. 47-53 (pp. 55-66).

uniting together of these triangles, as their Idea pertaining to the mean, constitutes once more, according to the original number-relations, the sensuous elements. This is the principle, but how Plato determines the figures of the elements, and the union of the triangles, I refrain from considering. [1]

From this point Plato passes to a system of Physics and Physiology into which we have no intention of following him. It is to be regarded as a first, child-like endeavour to understand sensuous phenomena in their manifold character, but as yet it is superficial and confused. Sensuous manifestations, such as the parts and limbs of the body, are here taken into consideration, and an account of this is given intermingled with thoughts which resemble our formal explanations, and in which the Notion really vanishes. We have to remember the elevated nature of the Idea, as being the main point of excellence in his explanations, for, as far as the realization of the same is concerned, Plato merely felt and expressed it to be a necessity. Speculative thought is often recognizable, but, for the most part, consideration is directed to quite external modes of explanation, such as that of end. The method of treating Physics is a different one from ours, for while with Plato empirical knowledge is still deficient, in modern Physics, on the other hand, the deficiency is found in the Idea. Plato, although he does not seem to conform to our theory of Physics, ignoring as it does the theory of life, and though he proceeds to talk in a childlike way in external analogies, yet in certain cases gives utterance to very deep perceptions, which would be well worthy of our consideration if the contemplation of nature as living had any place with our physicists. His manner of relating the physiological to the physical would be as interesting. Certain portions of his system contain a general element, such as his repre-

[1] Plat. Timæus, pp. 53-56 (pp. 66-72).

sentation of colours, and from this he goes on to more general considerations. For when Plato begins to talk on this subject, he says of the difficulty of distinguishing and recognizing the individual, that in the contemplation of nature there are "two causes to be distinguished, the one necessary and the other divine. The divine must be sought for in all things with the view of attaining to a blessed life" (this endeavour is an end in and for itself, and in it we find happiness) "in as far as our nature admits, but the necessary causes need be sought only for the sake of divine things, considering that without these necessary causes" (as conditions of knowledge) "we cannot know them." Contemplation in accordance with necessity is the external contemplation of objects, their connection, relation, &c. "Of the divine, God Himself was the creator," the divine belongs to that first eternal world—not as to one beyond, but to one now present. "But the creation and disposition of the mortal He committed to His offspring (γεννήμασι)." This is a simple way of passing from the divine to the finite and earthly. "Now they, imitating the divine, because they had received the immortal principle of a soul, fashioned a mortal body, and placed in this a soul of another nature, which was mortal. This mortal nature was subject to violent and irresistible affections—the first of these was pleasure, the greatest‹ incitement to evil, and then pain which is the deterrent (φυγάς) from doing good; also rashness (θάρρος) and fear, two foolish counsellors; anger, hope, &c. These sensations all belong to the mortal soul. And that the divine might not be polluted more than necessary, the subordinate gods separated this mortal nature from the seat of the divine, and gave it a different habitation in another part of the body, placing the neck so as to be the isthmus and boundary between head and breast." The sensations, affections, &c., dwell in the breast or in the heart (we place that which is immortal in the heart); the

spiritual is in the head. But in order to make the former
as perfect as might be, " they placed," for instance, " as a
supporter to the heart which was burnt with passion, the
lung, soft and bloodless, and which had within it hollows
like the pores of a sponge, in order that, receiving the
breath and drink, it might cool the heart and allow of
refreshment and an alleviation of the heat." [1]

What Plato says of the liver is specially worthy of
notice. " Since the irrational part of the soul which desires
eating and drinking does not listen to reason, God made
the liver so that the soul might be inspired with terror
by the power of thought which originates from reason, and
which descends upon the liver as on a mirror, receiving
upon it figures and giving back images. But if this part
of the soul is once more assuaged, in sleep it participates
in visions. For the authors of our being, remembering
the command of their father to make the human race as
good as they could, thus ordered our inferior parts in order
that they also might obtain a measure of truth, and placed
the oracle in them." Plato thus ascribes divination to the
irrational, corporeal part of man, and although it is often
thought that revelation, &c., is by Plato ascribed to reason,
this is a false idea; he says that there is a reason, but in
irrationality. " Herein we have a conclusive proof that God
has given the art of divination to the irrationality of man,
for no man when in his wits, attains prophetic truth and
inspiration, but when he receives the inspiration either his
intelligence is enthralled by sleep or he is demented by
some distemper or possession." Thus Plato makes divination of a lower grade than conscious knowledge. " And
when he has recovered his senses he has to remember and
explain what he has received, for while he is demented, he
cannot judge of it. The ancient saying is therefore very
true, that only a man who has his wits can act or judge

[1] P'at. Timæus, pp. 67-70 (pp. 93-99).

about himself or his own affairs." [1]   Plato is called the
patron saint of mere possession, but, according to this, the
assertion is entirely false.   These are the principal points
in Plato's Philosophy of Nature.

3. Philosophy of Mind.

We have already dealt generally from the theoretical
side with the speculative nature of mind as yet unrealized,
as well as with the highly important differences with
respect to the kinds of knowledge (pp. 28-48).   It must
also be considered that we find in Plato as yet no developed
consciousness of the organization of the theoretic mind,
though certainly sensation, memory, &c., are distinguished
by him from reason; these moments of the mind are,
however, neither accurately discriminated, nor exhibited in
their connection, so as to show the necessary relations
between them.   The only point of interest for us then in
Plato's philosophy of mind is his view of man's moral
nature; and this real, practical side of consciousness is
Plato's greatest glory, and hence must now be specially
dealt with by us.   Its form certainly does not suggest that
Plato gave himself much trouble to discover a supreme
moral principle, as it is now called, which, for the very
reason that it is supposed to be all-embracing, has in it a
certain lack of content.   Neither did he trouble himself
about a natural right, which is but a trivial abstraction
foisted on to the real practical existence, the right; but it
is of man's moral nature that he treats in the Republic.
Man's moral nature seems to us to have little to do with
the State; to Plato, however, the reality of mind—that is,
of mind as opposed to nature—appeared in its highest
truth as the organization of a state which, as such, is
essentially moral; and he recognized that the moral nature

[1] Plat. Timæus, pp. 70-72 (pp. 99-102).

(free will in its rationality) comes to its right, to its reality, only in an actual nation.

We must further remark that in the Republic Plato introduces the investigation of his subject with the object of showing what justice ($\delta\iota\kappa\alpha\iota\sigma\acute{\upsilon}\nu\eta$) is. After much discussion has taken place, and several definitions of justice have been taken into consideration only to be rejected, Plato at last says in his simple way : " The present investigation is very like the case of a man who is required to read small handwriting at a distance ; if it were observed that the same letters were to be seen at a shorter distance and of a larger size, he would certainly prefer to read first the letters where they were written larger, and then would be able to read more easily the small letters also. The same plan should be followed now with justice. Justice is not only in the individual, but also in the state, and the state is greater than the individual ; justice is therefore imprinted on states in larger characters, and is more easily recognizable." (This is different from what the Stoics say of the wise man.) " It is therefore preferable to consider justice as it is to be found in the state." [1] By making this comparison Plato transforms the question anent justice into an investigation of the state ; it is a very simple and graceful transition, though it seems arbitrary. It was great force of insight that really led the ancients to the truth ; and what Plato brings forward as merely simplifying the difficulty, may, in fact, be said to exist in the nature of the thing. For it is not convenience which leads him to this position, but the fact that justice can be carried out only in so far as man is a member of a state, for in the state alone is justice present in reality and truth. Justice, not as the understanding, but as mind in its striving to realize itself, is the existence of freedom here and now, the actuality of the self-conscious, intelligent existence in and

[1] Plat. De Republica, II., pp. 368, 369 (p. 78.)

at home with itself and possessing activity—just as in property, for instance, I place my freedom in this particular thing. But the principle of the state again is the objective reality of justice, the reality in which the whole mind is present and not only the knowledge of myself as this individual. For as the free and reasonable will determines itself, there are laws of freedom; but these laws are nothing else than state-laws, for the Notion of the state implies the existence of a reasoning will. Thus laws have force in the state, and are there matter of practice and of custom; but because self-will is also there in its immediacy, they are not only matter of custom, but must also be a force operating against arbitrary self-will, and showing itself in the courts of justice and in governments. Thus Plato, in order to discern the features of justice, with the instinct of reason fixes his attention on their manner of representation in the state.

Justice in itself is ordinarily represented by us in the form of a natural right, right in a condition of nature; such a condition of nature is, however, a direct moral impossibility. That which is in itself is, by those who do not attain to the universal, held to be something natural, as the necessary moments of the mind are held to be innate ideas. The natural is rather what should be sublated by the mind, and the justice of the condition of nature can only emerge as the absolute injustice of the mind. In contrast with the state, which is the real spirit, the spirit in its simple and as yet unrealized Notion is the abstract implicitude; this Notion must of course precede the construction of its reality; it is this which is conceived of as a condition of nature. We are accustomed to take our start from the fiction of a condition of nature, which is truly no condition of mind, of reasonable will, but of animals among themselves: wherefore Hobbes has justly remarked that the true state of nature is a war of every man against his neighbour. This implicitude of the mind is at the same time the individual man, for in the ordinary conception the universal separates itself from the particular, as if the particular were absolutely and in and for itself what it certainly is, and the Universal did not make it that which it is in truth—as if this were not its essence, but as if the individual element were the most important. The fiction of a state of nature starts from the individuality of the person, his free will, and his relation to other persons according to this free will. Natural justice has thus been a term applied to that which is justice in the individual and for the individual ; and the condition of society and of the state has been recognized only as a medium for the individual person, who is the chief end and object. Plato, in direct contrast with this, lays as his foundation the substantial, the universal, and he does this in such a way that the individual as such has this very universal as his end, and the subject has his will, activity, life and enjoyment in the state, so that it may be called his second nature, his habits and his customs. This moral substance which constitutes the spirit, life and Being of individuality, and which is its foundation, systematizes itself into a living, organic whole, and at the same time it differentiates itself into its members, whose activity signifies the production of the whole.

This relation of the Notion to its reality certainly did not come into consciousness with Plato, and thus we do not find in him a philosophic method of construction, which shows first the absolute Idea, then the necessity, inherently existent, for its realization, and this realization itself. The judgment that has been delivered respecting Plato's Republic therefore is that Plato has therein given a so-called ideal for the constitution of a state ; this has become proverbial as a *sobriquet*, in the sense that this conception is a chimera, which may be mentally conceived of—and in itself, as Plato describes it, it is doubtless excellent and true—that it is also capable of being carried out, but only on the condition that men should be of an excellence such as may possibly be present among the dwellers in the moon, but that it is not realizable for men like those on the earth. But since men must be taken as they are, this ideal cannot be realized by reason of men's wickedness; and to frame such an ideal is therefore altogether idle.

As to this, the first remark to be made is that in the Christian world in general there passes current an ideal of a perfect man which certainly cannot be carried out in the great body of a nation. We may, perhaps, see it realized in monks or Quakers, or other similar pious folk, but a set of melancholy specimens such as these could never form a nation, any more than lice or parasitic plants could exist for themselves, or otherwise than on an organic body. If such men were to constitute a nation, there would have to be an end of this lamb-like gentleness, this vanity which occupies itself exclusively with its own individual self, which pets and pampers itself, and ever has the image and consciousness of its own excellence before its eyes. For life in the universal and for the universal demands, not that lame and cowardly gentleness, but gentleness combined with a like measure of energy, and which is not occupied with itself and its own sins, but with the universal and what is to be done for it. They before whose eyes that false ideal floats of course find men to be always compassed with weakness and depravity, and never find that ideal realized. For they raise into importance the veriest trifles, which no reasonable man would give heed to; and they think such weaknesses and defects are present even when they overlook them. But we need not esteem this forbearance to be generosity; for it rather implies a perception on their part that from what they call weakness and defect proceeds their own destruction, which comes to pass from their making such defects of importance. The man who has them is immediately through himself absolved from them, in so far as he makes nothing of them. The crime

is a crime only when they are real to him, and his destruction is in holding them to be something real. Such an
ideal must therefore not stand in our way, whatever be the
fairness of its form, and this even when it does not appear
exactly as it does to monks and Quakers, but, for instance,
when it is the principle of renouncing sensuous things, and
abandoning energy of action, which principle must bring
to nought much that would otherwise be held of value. It
is contradictory to try to keep intact all our relationships,
for in those that otherwise hold good there always is a side
where opposition is encountered. Moreover, what I have
already said regarding the relation between philosophy and
the state (p. 23 *et seq.*) shows that the Platonic ideal is not
to be taken in this sense. When an ideal has truth in
itself through the Notion, it is no chimera, just because it
is true, for the truth is no chimera. Such an idea is therefore nothing idle and powerless, but the real. It is
certainly permissible to form wishes, but when pious wishes
are all that a man has in regard to the great and true, he
may be said to be godless. It is just as if we could do
nothing, because everything was so holy and inviolable, or
as if we refused to be anything definite, because all that is
definite has its defects. The true ideal is not what ought
to be real, but what is real, and the only real; if an ideal
is held to be too good to exist, there must be some fault in
the ideal itself, for which reality is too good. The Platonic
Republic would thus be a chimera, not because excellence
such as it depicts is lacking to mankind, but because it,
this excellence, falls short of man's requirements. For
what is real, is rational. The point to know, however, is
what exactly is real; in common life all is real, but there
is a difference between the phenomenal world and reality.
The real has also an external existence, which displays
arbitrariness and contingency, like a tree, a house, a plant,
which in nature come into existence. What is on the surface in the moral sphere, men's action, involves much that

is evil, and might in many ways be better; men will ever be wicked and depraved, but this is not the Idea. If the reality of the substance is recognized, the surface where the passions battle must be penetrated. The temporal and transitory certainly exists, and may cause us trouble enough, but in spite of that it is no true reality, any more than the particularity of the subject, his wishes and inclinations, are so.

In connection with this observation, the distinction is to be called to mind which was drawn when we were speaking above (pp. 84, 88) of Plato's Philosophy of Nature : the eternal world, as God holy in Himself, is reality, not a world above us or beyond, but the present world looked at in its truth, and not as it meets the senses of those who hear, see, &c. When we thus study the content of the Platonic Idea, it will become clear that Plato has, in fact, represented Greek morality according to its substantial mode, for it is the Greek state-life which constitutes the true content of the Platonic Republic. Plato is not the man to dabble in abstract theories and principles; his truth-loving mind has recognized and represented the truth, and this could not be anything else than the truth of the world he lived in, the truth of the one spirit which lived in him as well as in Greece. No man can overleap his time, the spirit of his time is his spirit also ; but the point at issue is, to recognize that spirit by its content.

On the other hand, a constitution that would be perfect in respect to one nation, is to be regarded as not, perhaps, suitable for every nation. Thus, when it is said that a true constitution does not do for men as they now are, we must no doubt keep in mind that the more excellent a nation's constitution is, it renders the nation also so much the more excellent ; but, on the other hand, since the morals commonly practised form the living constitution, the constitution in its abstraction is nothing at all in its independence ; it must relate itself to the common morality, and be filled

with the living spirit of the people. It can, therefore, certainly not be said that a true constitution suits any and
every nation; and it is quite the case that for men as they
are—for instance, as they are Iroquois, Russians, French—
not every constitution is adapted. For the nation has its
place in history. But as the individual man is trained in
the state, that is, as individuality is raised into universality,
and the child grows into a man, so is every nation trained;
or barbarism, the condition in which the nation is a child,
passes over into a rational condition. Men do not remain at
a standstill, they alter, as likewise do their constitutions.
And the question here is, What is the true constitution
which the nation must advance towards; just as it is a
question which is the true science of mathematics or of anything else, but not whether children or boys should possess
this science, as they must rather be first so educated that
they may be capable of understanding it. Thus the true
constitution stands before the nation of history, so that it may
advance towards it. Every nation in course of time makes
such alterations in its existing constitution as will bring
it nearer to the true constitution. The nation's mind itself
shakes off its leading-strings, and the constitution expresses
the consciousness of what it is in itself,—the form of truth,
of self-knowledge. If a nation can no longer accept as
implicitly true what its constitution expresses to it as the
truth, if its consciousness or Notion and its actuality are
not at one, then the nation's mind is torn asunder. Two
things may then occur. First, the nation may either by a
supreme internal effort dash into fragments this law which
still claims authority, or it may more quietly and slowly
effect changes on the yet operative law, which is, however,
ro longer true morality, but which the mind has already
passed beyond. In the second place, a nation's intelligence
and strength may not suffice for this, and it may hold to the
lower law; or it may happen that another nation has
reached its higher constitution, thereby rising in the scale,

and the first gives up its nationality and becomes subject to the other. Therefore it is of essential importance to know what the true-constitution is ; for what is in opposition to it has no stability, no truth, and passes away. It has a temporary existence, but cannot hold its ground; it has been accepted, but cannot secure permanent acceptance ; that it must be cast aside, lies in the very nature of the constitution. This insight can be reached through Philosophy alone. Revolutions take place in a state without the slightest violence when the insight becomes universal; institutions, somehow or other, crumble and disappear, each man agrees to give up his right. A government must, however, recognize that the time for this has come ; should it, on the contrary, knowing not the truth, cling to temporary institutions, taking what—though recognized— is unessential, to be a bulwark guarding it from the essential (and the essential is what is contained in the Idea), that government will fall, along with its institutions, before the force of mind. The breaking up of its government breaks up the nation itself ; a new government arises,—or it may be that the government and the unessential retain the upper hand.

Thus the main thought which forms the groundwork of Plato's Republic is the same which is to be regarded as the principle of the common Greek morality, namely, that established morality has in general the relation of the substantial, and therefore is maintained as divine. This is without question the fundamental determination. The determination which stands in contrast to this substantial relation of the individual to established morality, is the subjective will of the individual, reflective morality. This exists when individuals, instead of being moved to action by respect and reverence for the institutions of the state and of the fatherland, from their own convictions, and after moral deliberation, come of themselves to a decision, and determine their actions accordingly. This principle of subjective freedom ·is a later growth, it is the principle of our modern days of culture : it, however, entered also into the Greek world, but as the principle of the destruction of Greek state-life. It was looked on as a crime, because the spirit, political constitution, and laws of the Greeks were not, and could not be calculated to admit of the rise of this principle within them. Because these two elements were not homogeneous, traditional and conventional morality in Greece was overthrown. Plato recognized and caught up the true spirit of his times, and brought it forward in a more definite way, in that he desired to make this new principle an impossibility in his Republic. It is thus a substantial position on which Plato takes his stand, seeing that the substantial of his time forms his basis, but this standpoint is at the same time relative only, in so far as it is but a Greek standpoint, and the later principle is consciously banished This is the universal of Plato's ideal of the state, and it is from this point of view that we must regard it. Investigations as to whether such a state is possible, and the best possible, which start from quite modern points of view, can only lead us astray. In modern states we have freedom of conscience, according to which every individual may demand the right of following out his own interests ; but this is excluded from the Platonic idea.

a. I will now indicate more fully the main features, in so far as they possess philosophic interest. Though Plato represents what the state is in its truth, yet this state has a limit, which we shall learn to know, namely, that the individual—in formal justice—is not opposed to this universality, as in the dead constitution of the ideal states founded on the theory of legal right. The content is but the whole ; the nature of the individual, no doubt, but as reflecting itself into the universal, not unbending, or as having absolute validity ; so that practically the state and the individual are the same in essence. Because Plato thus takes

his start from that justice which implies that the just man
exists only as a moral member of the state, in dealing with
his subject in greater detail, in order to show how this
reality of the substantial mind is produced, he in the first
place opens up before us the organism of the moral commonwealth, *i.e.* the differences which lie in the Notion of moral
substance. Through the development of these moments
it becomes living and existing, but these moments are not
independent, for they are held in unity. Plato regards
these moments of the moral organism under three aspects,
first, as they exist in the state as classes ; secondly, as
virtues, or moments in morality ; thirdly, as moments of
the individual subject, in the empirical actions of the will.
Plato does not preach the morality of reflection, he shows
how traditional morality has a living movement in itself ;
he demonstrates its functions, its inward organism. For it
is inner systematization, as in organic life, and not solid,
dead unity, like that of metals, which comes to pass by
means of the different functions of the organs which go to
make up this living, self-moving unity.

a. Without classes, without this division into great
masses, the state has no organism ; these great distinctions
are the distinction of the substantial. The opposition
which first comes before us in the state is that of the
universal, in the form of state life and business, and the
individual, as life and work for the individual ; these two
fields of activity are so distinct that one class is assigned
to the one, and another to the other. Plato further cites
three systems of reality in the moral, the functions (*aa*) of
legislation, counsel, in short, of diligence and foresight in
the general behalf, in the interest of the whole as such ;
($\beta\beta$) of defence of the commonwealth against foes from
without ; ($\gamma\gamma$) of care for the individual, the supplying
of wants, agriculture, cattle-rearing, the manufacture of
clothing and utensils, the building of houses, &c. Speaking
generally, this is quite as it should be, and yet it appears

to be rather the satisfaction of external necessities, because such wants are found without being developed out of the Idea of mind itself. Further, these distinct functions are allotted to different systems, being assigned to a certain number of individuals specially set apart for the purpose, and this brings about the separate classes of the state, as Plato is altogether opposed to the superficial conception that one and the same must be everything at one time. He accordingly represents three classes, (*aa*) that of the governors, men of learning and wisdom, (*ββ*) that of the warriors, (*γγ*) that of the producers of necessaries, the husbandmen and handicraftsmen. The first he also speaks of as guardians (φύλακας), who are really philosophically educated statesmen, possessing true knowledge ; they have the warriors to work on their behalf (ἐπικούρους τε καὶ βοηθούς), but in such a way that there is no line of separation between the civil and military classes, both being united,[1] and the most advanced in years are the guardians.[2] Although Plato does not deduce this division of the classes, they follow from the constitution of the Platonic state, and every state is necessarily a system within itself of these systems. Plato then passes on to particular determinations, which are in some measure trifling, and might with advantage have been dispensed with; for instance, among other things, he goes so far as to settle for the highest rank their special titles, and he states what should be the duties of the nurses.[3]

---

[1] Following the outline here given by Plato, Hegel, in an earlier attempt to treat the philosophy of Justice (Werke, Vol. I. pp. 380, 381), included in one these two classes, and later named them the general class (Werke, Vol. VIII. p. 267) ; the " other " class (as Hegel expresses it, in the first of the passages referred to above), which by Plato is not included in this, Hegel divided, however, in both his narratives, into the second class (that of city handicraftsmen), and the third (that of tillers of the soil).—[Editor's note.]

[2] Plat. de Republica, II. pp. 369-376 (pp. 79-93); III. p. 414 (pp. 158, 159).

[3] Plat. De Republica, V. p. 433 (p. 211); p. 460 (p. 236).

β. Then Plato points out that the moments which are here realized in the classes, are moral qualities which are present in individuals, and form their true essence, the simple ethical Notion divided into its universal determinations. For he states as the result of this distinction of the classes that through such an organism all virtues are present in the commonwealth ; he distinguishes four of these,[1] and they have been named cardinal virtues.

aa. Wisdom (σοφία) or knowledge appears as the first virtue ; such a state will be wise and good in counsel, not because of the various kinds of knowledge therein present which have to do with the many particular ordinary occupations falling to the multitude, such as the trade of blacksmith, and the tillage of the soil (in short, what we should call skill in the industrial arts, and in finance). The state is called wise, by reason of the true knowledge which is realized in the presiding and governing class, who advise regarding the whole state, and decide upon the policy that is best, both at home and in relation to foreign states. This faculty of perception is properly the peculiar possession of the smallest class.[2]

ββ. The second virtue is courage (ἀνδρία) which Plato defines as a firm opinion about what may justly and lawfully be considered an object of fear, courage which, in its strength of purpose, remains unshaken either by desires or pleasures. To this virtue corresponds the class of the warriors.[3]

γγ. The third virtue is temperance (σωφροσύνη), the mastery over the desires and passions, which like a harmony pervades the whole ; so that, whether understanding, or strength, or numbers, or wealth, or anything else be regarded, the weaker and the stronger work together for one and the same object, and are in agreement one with

---

[1] Plat. De Republica, IX. pp. 427, 428 (pp. 179–181).
[2] Ibid. IV. pp. 428, 429 (pp. 181, 182).
[3] Ibid. pp. 429, 430 (pp. 182–185).

another. This virtue therefore is not, like wisdom and courage, confined to one part of the state, but like a harmony it is shared by governors and governed alike, and is the virtue of all classes.[1] Notwithstanding that this temperance is the harmony in which all work towards one end, it is yet peculiarly the virtue of the third class, to whom it is allotted to procure the necessaries of life by work, although at the first glance the one does not appear to have much correspondence with the other. But this virtue is present precisely when no moment, no determination or particularity isolates itself; or, more closely viewed in a moral aspect, it is when no want asserts its reality and thus becomes a crime. Now work is just this moment of activity concentrating itself on the particular, which nevertheless goes back into the universal, and is for it. Therefore, if this virtue is universal, it yet has special application to the third class, which at first is the only one to be brought into harmony, as it has not the absolute harmony which the other classes possess in themselves.

δδ. Finally, the fourth virtue is justice, which was what Plato began by considering. This, as right-doing, is to be found in the state when each individual does only one kind of work for the state, that work for which by the original constitution of his nature he is best fitted; so that in this way each man is not a jack-of-all-trades, but all have their special work, young and old, women and children, bond and free, handicraftsmen, rulers and subjects. The first remark we make on this is, that Plato here places justice on a level with the other moments, and it thus appears as one of the four determinations. But he now retracts this statement and makes it justice which first gives to wisdom, courage and temperance the power to exist at all, and when they have once come into existence, the power to continue. This is the reason of his also saying that justice will be met

---

[1] Plat. De Republica, IV. pp. 430-432 (pp. 185-188).

with independently, if only the other virtues spoken of are forthcoming.[1] To express it more definitely, the Notion of justice is the foundation, the Idea of the whole, which falls into organic divisions, so that every part is only, as it were, a moment in the whole, and the whole exists through it. Thus the classes or qualities spoken of are nothing else than the moments of this whole. Justice is only the general and all-pervading quality ; but at the same time it implies the independence of every part, to which the state gives liberty of action.

In the second place, it is clear from what he says, that Plato did not understand by justice the rights of property, the meaning which the term commonly bears in jurisprudence, but rather this, that the mind in its totality makes for itself a law as evidence of the existence of its freedom. In a highly abstract sense my personality, my altogether abstract freedom, is present in property. To explain what comes under this science of law, Plato considers on the whole superfluous (De Republica, IV. p. 425 Steph. ; p. 176 Bekk.). To be sure we find him giving laws concerning property, police regulations, &c., "But," he says, "to impose laws about such matters on men of noble character does not repay the trouble." In truth, how can we expect to find divine laws in what contains contingencies alone ? Even in the Laws he considers ethics chiefly, though he gives a certain amount of attention to the rights of property. But as justice, according to Plato, is really the entire being, which presents itself to the individual in such a way that each man learns to do the work he is born to do as well as it can be done, and does it, it is only as determined individuality that man reaches what is law for him ; only thus does he belong to the universal spirit of the state, coming in it to the universal of himself as a " this." While law is a universal with a definite content, and thus a formal

---

[1] Plat. De Republica, IV. pp. 432, 433 (pp. 188–191).

universal only, the content in this case is the whole determined individuality, not this or that thing which is mine by
the accident of possession ; what I properly hold as my own
is the perfected possession and use of my nature. To each
particular determination justice gives its rights, and thus
leads it back into the whole; in this way it is by the particularity of an individual being of necessity developed and
brought into actuality, that each man is in his place and
fulfils his vocation. Justice, therefore, according to its true
conception, is in our eyes freedom in the subjective sense,
because it is the attainment of actuality by the reason, and
seeing that this right on the part of liberty to attain to
actuality is universal, Plato sets up justice as the determination of the whole, indicating that rational freedom comes
into existence through the organism of the state,—an
existence which is then, as necessary, a mode of nature.

γ. The particular subject, as subject, has in the same way
these qualities in himself; and these moments of the subject
correspond with the three real moments of the state. That
there is thus one rhythm, one type, in the Idea of the state,
forms for Plato's state a great and grand basis. This third
form, in which the above moments are exhibited, Plato
characterizes in the following manner. There manifest
themselves in the subject, first of all sundry wants and
desires (ἐπιθυμίαι), like hunger and thirst, each of which
has something definite as its one and only object. Work
for the satisfaction of desires corresponds to the calling
of the third class. But, secondly there is also at the
same time to be found in the individual consciousness
something else which suspends and hinders the gratification
of these desires, and has the mastery over the temptation
thus to gratify them ; this is reasonableness (λόγος). To
this corresponds the class of rulers, the wisdom of the state.
Besides these two ideas of the soul there is a third, anger
(θυμός), which on one side is allied to the desires, but of
which it is just as true that it resists the desires and takes

the side of reason. "It may happen that a man has done wrong to another, and suffers hunger and cold at the hands of him whom he considers entitled to inflict them upon him; in this case, the nobler he is, the less will his anger be excited. But it may also happen that he suffers a wrong; if this is the case, he boils and chafes, and takes the side of what he believes to be justice, and endures hunger and cold and other hardships, and overcomes them, and will not desist from the right until he conquers or dies, or is calmed down by reason, as a shepherd quiets his dog." Anger corresponds with the class of the brave defenders in the state; as these grasp their weapons in behalf of reason within the state, so does anger take the part of reason, if it has not been perverted by an evil upbringing. Therefore wisdom in the state is the same as in the individual, and this is true of courage also. For the rest, temperance is the harmony of the several moments of what pertains to nature; and justice, as in external matters it consists in each doing his own duty, so, in the inner life, it consists in each moment of the mind obtaining its right, and not interfering in the affairs of the others, but leaving them to do as they will.[1] We have thus the deduction of three moments, where the middle place between universality and particularity is filled by anger in its independence and as directed against the objective : it is the freedom which turns back within itself and acts negatively. Even here, where Plato has no consciousness of his abstract ideas, as he has in the Timæus, this of a truth is inwardly present to him, and everything is moulded thereby. This is given as the plan according to which Plato draws up the great whole. To fill up the outlines is a mere detail, which in itself has no further interest.

b. In the second place Plato indicates the means of maintaining the state. As, speaking generally, the whole

[1] Plat. De Republica, IV. pp. 437–443 (pp. 198–210).

commonwealth rests on common morality as the minds of
individuals grown into nature, this question is asked:
How does Plato arrange that everyone takes as his own
that form of activity for which he is specially marked out,
and that it presents itself as the moral acting and willing
of the individual,—that everyone, in harmony with temperance, submits to filling this his post? The main point is
to train the individuals thereto. Plato would produce this
ethical quality directly in the individuals, and first and
foremost in the guardians, whose education is therefore the
most important part of the whole, and constitutes the very
foundation. For as it is to the guardians themselves that
the care is committed of producing this ethical quality
through maintenance of the laws, in these laws special
attention must be given to the guardians' education; after
that also to the education of the warriors. The condition
of affairs in the industrial class causes the state but little
anxiety, "for though cobblers should prove poor and
worthless, and should be only in appearance what they
ought to. be, that is no great misfortune for the state."[1]
The education of the presidents should, however, be carried
on chiefly by means of philosophic science, which is the
knowledge of the universal and absolute. Plato in this
passes over the particular means of education, religion, art,
science. Further on he speaks again and more in detail
on the question of how far music and gymnastic are to be
permitted as means. But the poets Homer and Hesiod he
banishes from his state, because he thinks their representations of God unworthy.[2] For then began in real earnest an
inquiry into the belief in Jupiter and the stories told by
Homer, inasmuch as such particular representations had
been taken as universal maxims and divine laws. At a
certain stage of education childish tales do no harm; but

[1] Plat. De Republica, IV. p. 421 (pp. 167, 168).
[2] Ibid. II. p. 376—III. p. 412 (pp. 93-155); V. p. 472—VII. fin.
(pp. 258-375).

were they to be made the foundation of the truth of morality, as present law, the case would be different. The extermination of the nations which we read of in the writings of the Israelites, the Old Testament, might for instance be taken as a standard of national rights, or we might try to make a precedent of the numerous base acts committed by David, the man of God, or of the horrors which the priesthood, in the person of Samuel, practised and authorized against Saul. Then it would be high time to place these records on a lower level, as something past, something merely historical. Plato would further have preambles to the laws, wherein citizens would be admonished as to their duties, and convinced that these exist, &c.[1] They also should be shown how to choose that which is most excellent, in short, to choose morality.

But here we have a circle: the public life of the state subsists by means of morality, and, conversely, morality subsists by means of institutions. Morals cannot be independent of institutions, that is, institutions cannot be brought to bear on morals through educational establishments or religion only. For institutions must be looked on as the very first condition of morality, for this is the manner in which institutions are subjective. Plato himself gives us to understand how much contradiction he expects to find. And even now his defect is commonly considered to lie in his being too idealistic, while his real deficiency consists in his not being ideal enough. For if reason is the universal force, it is essentially spiritual; thus to the realm of the spiritual belongs subjective freedom, which had already been held up as a principle in the philosophy of Socrates. Therefore reason ought to be the basis of law, and so it is, on the whole. But, on the other hand, conscience, personal conviction,—in short, all the forms of subjective freedom—are essentially therein contained.

[1] Plat. De Legibus, IV. pp. 722, 723 (pp. 367–369).

This subjectivity at first, it is true, stands in opposition to the laws and reason of the state-organism as to the absolute power which desires to appropriate to itself—through the external necessity of wants, in which, however, there is absolute reason—the individual of the family. Individual conscience proceeds from the subjectivity of free-will, connects itself with the whole, chooses a position for itself, and thus makes itself a moral fact. But this moment, this movement of the individual, this principle of subjective freedom, is sometimes ignored by Plato, and sometimes even intentionally disparaged, because it proved itself to be what had wrought the ruin of Greece ; and he considers only how the state may best be organized, and not subjective individuality. In passing beyond the principle of Greek morality, which in its substantial liberty cannot brook the rise of subjective liberty, the Platonic philosophy at once grasps the above principle, and in so doing proceeds still farther.

c. In the third place, in regard to the exclusion of the principle of subjective freedom, this forms a chief feature in the Republic of Plato, the spirit of which really consists in the fact, that all aspects in which particularity as such has established its position, are dissolved in the universal,— all men simply rank as man in general.

a. It specially harmonizes with this particular quality of excluding the principle of subjectivity, that Plato in the first place does not allow individuals to choose their own class ; this we demand as necessary to freedom. It is not, however, birth which marks off the different ranks, and determines individuals for these ; but everyone is tested by the governors of the state, who are the elders of the first class, and have the education of individuals in their hands. According as anyone has natural ability and talents, these elders make choice and selection, and assign each man to a definite occupation.[1] This seems in direct contradiction

---

[1] Plat. De Republica, III. pp. 412–415 (pp. 155–161.)

to our principle, for although it is considered right that
to a certain class there should belong a special capacity
and skill, it always remains a matter of inclination which
class one is to belong to; and with this inclination, as an
apparently free choice, the class makes itself for itself.
But it is not permitted that another individual should
prescribe as to this, or say, for example : " Because you are
not serviceable for anything better, you are to be a
labourer." Everyone may make the experiment for himself ; he must be allowed to decide regarding his own
affairs as subject in a subjective manner, by his own free
will, as well as in consideration of external circumstances ;
and nothing must therefore be put in his way if he says,
for instance : "I should like to apply myself to study."

β. From this determination it further follows that Plato
(De Republica, III. pp. 416, 417 Steph. ; pp. 162–164 Bekk.)
in like manner altogether abolished in his state the principle of private property. For in it individuality, the
individual consciousness, becomes absolute ; or the person
is looked on as implicit, destitute of all content. In law,
as such, I rank as "this" implicitly and explicitly. All
rank thus, and I rank only because all rank, or I rank
only as universal ; but the content of this universality is
fixed particularity. When in a question of law we have to
do with law, as such, to the judges of the case it matters
not a whit whether this or that man actually possesses the
house, and likewise the contending parties think nothing
of the possession of the thing for which they strive, but of
right for right's sake, (as in morality duty is done for
duty's sake) : thus a firm hold is kept of the abstraction, and from the content of reality abstraction is made.
But Being to Philosophy is no abstraction, but the
unity of the universal and reality, or its content. The
content has therefore weight only in as far as it is
negatively posited in the universal ; thus only as returning
into it, and not absolutely. In so far as I use things,—

not in so far as I have them merely in my possession, or as they have worth for me as existent, as definitely fixed on me,—they stand in living relation to me. With Plato, then, those of the other class (cf. *supra*, p. 101, note) carry on handicrafts, trade, husbandry, and procure what will satisfy the general requirements, without acquiring personal property by means of their work, for they are all one family, wherein each has his appointed occupation; but the product of the work is common, and he receives as much as he requires both of his own and of the general product. Personal property is a possession which belongs to me as a certain person, and in which my person as such comes into existence, into reality; on this ground Plato excludes it. It remains, however, unexplained how in the development of industries, if there is no hope of acquiring private property, there can be any incentive to activity; for on my being a person of energy very much depends my capacity for holding property. That an end would be put to all strifes and dissensions and hatred and avarice by the abolition of private property, as Plato thinks, (De Republica, V. p. 464 Steph.; pp. 243, 244 Bekk.) may very well be imagined in a general way; but that is only a subordinate result in comparison with the higher and reasonable principle of the right of property: and liberty has actual existence only so far as property falls to the share of the person. In this way we see subjective freedom consciously removed by Plato himself from his state.

γ. For the same reason Plato also abolishes marriage, because it is a connection in which persons of opposite sex, as such, remain mutually bound to one another, even beyond the mere natural connection. Plato does not admit into his state family life — the particular arrangement whereby a family forms a whole by itself,—because the family is nothing but an extended personality, a relationship to others of an exclusive character within natural morality,—which certainly is morality, but morality of such a character as belongs to the individual as particularity. According to the conception of subjective freedom, however, the family is just as necessary, yea, sacred to the individual as is property. Plato, on the contrary, causes children to be taken away from their mothers immediately after birth, and has them gathered together in a special establishment, and reared by nurses taken from among the mothers who gave them birth ; he has them brought up in common, so that no mother can possibly recognize her child. There are certainly to be marriage celebrations, and each man is to have his particular wife, but in such a way that the intercourse of man and wife does not pre-suppose a personal inclination, and that it should not be their own pleasure which marks out individuals for one another. The women should bear children from the twentieth to the fortieth year, the men should have wives from the thirtieth to the fifty-fifth year. To prevent incest, all the children born at the time of a man's marriage shall be known as his children.[1] The women, whose natural vocation is family life, are by this arrangement deprived of their sphere. In the Platonic Republic it therefore follows that as the family is broken up, and the women no longer manage the house, they are also no longer private persons, and adopt the manners of the man as the universal individual in the state. And Plato accordingly allows the women to take their part like the men in all manly labours, and even to share in the toils of war. Thus he places them on very nearly the same footing as the men, though all the same he has no great confidence in their bravery, but stations them in the rear only, and not even as reserve, but only as *arrière-garde,* in order that they may at least inspire the foe with terror by their numbers, and, in case of necessity, hasten to give aid.[2]

These are the main features of the Platonic Republic,

---

[1] Plat. De Republica, V. pp. 457–461 (pp. 230–239).
[2] Ibid. pp. 451–457 (pp. 219–230) ; p. 471 (p. 257).

which has as its essential the suppression of the principle
of individuality; and it would appear as though the Idea
demanded this, and as if this were the very point on
which Philosophy is opposed to the ordinary way of looking
at things, which gives importance to the individual, and
thus in the state, as also in actualized mind, looks on the
rights of property, and the protection of persons and their
possessions, as the basis of everything that is. Therein,
however, lies the very limit of the Platonic Idea—to
emerge only as abstract idea. But, in fact, the true Idea
is nothing else than this, that every moment should perfectly realize and embody itself, and make itself independent, while at the same time, in its independence, it is for
mind a thing sublated. In conformity with this Idea,
individuality must fully realize itself, must have its sphere
and domain in the state, and yet be resolved in it. The
element of the state is the family, that is, the family is the
natural unreasoning state; this element must, as such, be
present. Then the Idea of the state constituted by reason
has to realize all the moments of its Notion in such a way
that they become classes, and the moral substance divides
itself into portions, as the bodily substance is separated
into intestines and organs, each of which lives on in a particular way of its own, yet all of which together form only
one life. The state in general, the whole, must finally
pervade all. But in exactly the same way the formal
principle of justice, as abstract universality of personality
with individual Being as its existent content, must pervade the whole; one class, nevertheless, specially belongs
to it. There must, then, also be a class in which property
is held immediately and permanently, the possession of the
body and the possession of a piece of land alike; and in the
next place, a class where acquisition is continually going on,
and possession is not immediate, as in the other, but property is ever fluctuating and changing. These two classes
the nation gives up as a part of itself to the principle of

individuality, and allows rights to reign here, permitting the constant, the universal, the implicit to be sought in this principle, which really is a principle of variability. This principle must have its full and complete reality, it must indeed appear in the shape of property. We have here for the first time the true, actual mind, with each moment receiving its complete independence, and the mind itself attaining to being-another in perfect indifference of Being. Nature cannot effect this production of independent life in her parts, except in the great system.[1] This is, as we shall elsewhere see, the great advance of the modern world beyond the ancient, that in it the objective attains to greater, yea, to absolute independence, but for the very same reason returns with all the greater difficulty into the unity of the Idea.

The want of subjectivity is really the want of the Greek moral idea. The principle which became prominent with Socrates had been present up to this time only in a more subordinate capacity; now it of necessity became an even absolute principle, a necessary moment in the Idea itself. By the exclusion of private property and of family life, by the suspension of freedom in the choice of the class, *i.e.* by the exclusion of all the determinations which relate to the principle of subjective freedom, Plato believes he has barred the doors to all the passions; he knew very well that the ruin of Greek life proceeded from this, that individuals, as such, began to assert their aims, inclinations, and interests, and made them dominate over the common mind. But since this principle is necessary through the Christian religion—in which the soul of the individual is an absolute end, and thus has entered into the world as necessary in the Notion of the mind—it is seen that the Platonic state-constitution cannot fulfil what the higher demands of a moral organism require. Plato has not recognized the

[1] Cf. Hegel: On the Scientific Modes of treating Natural Law (Werke, Vol. I.), pp. 383–386.

knowledge, wishes, and resolutions of the individual, nor his self-reliance, and has not succeeded in combining them with his Idea ; but justice demands its rights for this just as much as it requires the higher resolution of the same, and its harmony with the universal. The opposite to Plato's principle is the principle of the conscious free will of individuals, which in later times was by Rousseau more especially raised to prominence : the theory that the arbitrary choice of the individual, the outward expression of the individual, is necessary. In this the principle is carried to the very opposite extreme, and has emerged in its utter one-sidedness. In opposition to this arbitrariness and culture there must be the implicitly and explicitly universal, that which is in thought, not as wise governor or morality, but as law, and at the same time as my Being and my thought, *i.e.* as subjectivity and individuality. Men must have brought forth from themselves the rational along with their interests and their passions, just as it must enter into reality through the necessities, opportunities, and motives that impel them.

There is still another celebrated side of the Platonic philosophy which may be considered, namely æsthetics, the knowledge of the beautiful. In respect to this, Plato has in like manner seized the one true thought, that the essence of the beautiful is intellectual, the Idea of reason. When he speaks of a spiritual beauty, he is to be understood in the sense that beauty, as beauty, is sensuous beauty, which is not in some other place—no one knows where; but what is beautiful to the senses is really the spiritual. The case is the same here as it is with his Idea. As the essence and truth of phenomena in general is the Idea, the truth of phenomenal beauty must also be this Idea. The relation to the corporeal, as a relation of the desires, or of pleasure and utility, is no relation to it as the beautiful ; it is a relation to it as the sensuous alone, or a relation of particular to particular. But the essence of the beautiful is just the simple Idea of reason present to the sensuous apprehension as a thing ; the content of the thing is nothing else than this.[1] The beautiful is essentially of spiritual nature ; it is thus not merely a sensuous thing, but reality subject to the form of universality, to the truth. This universal does not, however, retain the form of universality, but the universal is the content whose form is the sensuous mode ; and therein lies the determination of the beautiful. In science, the universal has again the form of the universal or of the Notion ; but the beautiful appears as an actual thing—or, when put into words, as a popular conception, in which mode the material exists in mind. The nature, essence, and content of the beautiful is recognized and judged by reason alone, as its content is the same as that of Philosophy. But because reason appears in the beautiful in material guise, the beautiful ranks below knowledge, and Plato has for this very reason placed the true manifestation of reason in knowledge, where it is spiritually manifested.

This may be regarded as the kernel of Plato's philosophy. His standpoint is : first, the contingent form of speech, in which men of noble and unfettered nature converse without other interest than that of the theory which is being worked out ; secondly, led on by the content, they reach the deepest Notions and the finest thoughts, like jewels on which one stumbles, if not exactly in a sandy desert, yet at least upon the arid path ; in the third place, no systematic connection is to be found, though one interest is the source of all ; in the fourth place, the subjectivity of the Notion is lacking throughout ; but in the fifth place, the substantial Idea forms the principle.

Plato's philosophy had two stages through which it of necessity developed and worked its way up to a higher principle. The universal which is in reason had first to fall into two divisions opposed to each other in the most direct

[1] Plat. Hippias Major, p. 292 (p. 433); p. 295 sqq. (p. 439 sqq.) p. 302 (pp. 455, 456).

and unmitigated contradiction, in the independence of the personal consciousness which exists for itself : thus in the New Academy self-consciousness goes back into itself, and becomes a species of scepticism—the negative reason, which turns against all that is universal, and fails to find the unity of self-consciousness and the universal, coming accordingly to a standstill at that point. But, in the second place, the Neo-Platonists constitute the return, this unity of self-consciousness and the absolute essence ; to them God is directly present in reason, reasoned knowledge itself is the Divine Spirit, and the content of this knowledge is the Being of God. Both of these we shall consider later.

B. ARISTOTLE.

Here we leave Plato, and we do so with regret. But seeing that we pass to his disciple, Aristotle, we fear that it behoves us to enter even more into detail, since he was one of the richest and deepest of all the scientific geniuses that have as yet appeared—a man whose like no later age has ever yet produced. Because we still possess so large a number of his works, the extent of the material at hand is proportionately greater; unfortunately, however, I cannot give to Aristotle the amount of attention that he deserves. For we shall have to confine ourselves to a general view of his philosophy, and simply remark on one particular phase of it, viz. in how far Aristotle in his philosophy carried out what in the Platonic principle had been begun, both in reference to the profundity of the ideas there contained, and to their expansion ; no one is more comprehensive and speculative than he, although his methods are not systematic.

As regards the general character of Aristotle's writings, he may be said to have extended his attention to the whole circle of human conceptions, to have penetrated all regions of the actual universal, and to have brought under the subjection of the Notion both their riches and their diversitude.

For most of the philosophic sciences have to render thanks to him both for their characterization and first commencement. But although in this way Science throughout falls into a succession of intellectual determinations of determinate Notions, the Aristotelian philosophy still contains the profoundest speculative Notions. Aristotle proceeds in reference to the whole in the same way as in the individual case. But a general view of his philosophy does not give us the impression of its being in construction a self-systematized whole, of which the order and connection pertain likewise to the Notion; for the parts are empirically selected and placed together in such a way that each part is independently recognized as a determinate conception, without being taken into the connecting movement of the science. We need not try to demonstrate necessity from the standpoint of the philosophy of that time. But although Aristotle's system does not appear to be developed in its parts from the Notion, and its parts are merely ranged side by side, they still form a totality of truly speculative philosophy.

One reason for treating of Aristotle in detail rests in the fact that no philosopher has had so much wrong done him by the thoughtless traditions which have been received respecting his philosophy, and which are still the order of the day, although for centuries he was the instructor of all philosophers. For to him views are ascribed diametrically opposite to his philosophy. And while Plato is much read, the treasures contained in Aristotle have for centuries, and until quite modern times, been as good as unknown, and the falsest prejudices reign respecting him. Almost no one knows his speculative and logical works; in modern times more justice has been done to his writings regarding nature, but not to his philosophic views. For instance, there is a quite generally held opinion that the Aristotelian and Platonic philosophies are directly opposed, the one being idealistic and the other realistic, and that, indeed, in the most trivial sense. For Plato is said to have

made the ideal his principle, so that the inward idea creates
from itself; according to Aristotle, on the contrary, we are
told that the soul is made a *tabula rasa*, receiving all its determinations quite passively from the outer world; and his
philosophy is thus mere empiricism—Locke's philosophy at
its worst. But we shall see how little this really is the
case. In fact Aristotle excels Plato in speculative depth,
for he was acquainted with the deepest kind of speculation
—idealism—and in this upholds the most extreme empirical development. Quite false views respecting Aristotle
even now exist in France. An example of how tradition
blindly echoes opinions respecting him, without having
observed from his works whether they are justified or not,
is the fact that in the old Æsthetics the three unities of the
drama—action, time and place—were held to be *règles
d'Aristote, la saine doctrine.* But Aristotle speaks (Poet.
c. 8 et 5) [1] only of the unity of treatment, or very occasionally of the unity of time; of the third unity, that of
place, he says nothing.

As regards Aristotle's life, he was born at Stagira, a
Thracian town on the Strymonian Gulf, but a Greek colony.
Thus, though a Thracian, he was by birth a Greek. This
Greek colony fell, however, like the rest of the country,
under the rule of Philip of Macedon. The year of Aristotle's
birth is the first of the 99th Olympiad (384 B.C.), and if
Plato was born in the third year of the 87th Olympiad
(430 B.C.), Aristotle must have been forty-six years
younger than he. His father Nicomachus was physician to
the Macedonian king, Amyntas, the father of Philip. After
the death of his parents, whom he lost early, he was brought
up by a certain Proxenus, to whom he was ever grateful;

---

[1] In quoting the chapters of Aristotle both hitherto and in future,
Becker's edition is adopted; where a second number is placed in
brackets after the first, different editions are indicated, *e.g.*, for the
Organon, Buhle's edition, for the Nicomachean Ethics those of Zell
and the editor, &c.—[Editor's note.]

and during all his life he held the memory of this friend in such high esteem, that he honoured it by erecting statues to him. He also requited Proxenus for the education given him, by later on bringing up his son Nicanor, adopting him as his own son and making him his heir. In the seventeenth year of his age Aristotle came to Athens, and remained there twenty years in company with Plato.[1] He thus had the best possible opportunity of becoming thoroughly acquainted with Plato's philosophy, and therefore, if we are told that he did not understand it (Vol. I. p. 167), this is shown, by the evident facts of the case, to be an arbitrary and quite unfounded assumption. As regards the relation of Plato to Aristotle, and particularly as regards the fact that Plato did not select Aristotle as his successor in the Academy, but chose Speusippus, a near relative, instead, a number of idle and contradictory anecdotes have come to us from Diogenes (V. 2). If the continuation of the Platonic school was designed to express the hope that the philosophy of Plato, as comprehended by himself, was to be there satisfactorily maintained, Plato could certainly not designate Aristotle as his successor, and Speusippus was the right man to be selected. However, Plato had nevertheless Aristotle as his successor, for Aristotle understood Philosophy in Plato's sense, though his philosophy was deeper and more worked out, and thus he carried it further. Displeasure at being thus passed over is said to have been the cause of Aristotle's leaving Athens after Plato's death, and living for three years with Hermias, the Tyrant of Atarneus in Mysia, who had been a disciple of Plato along with Aristotle, and who had then struck up a close friendship with the latter. Hermias, an independent prince, was, together with other absolute Greek princes

[1] Diog. Laërt. V. 1, 9, 12, 15; Buhle: Aristotelis vita (ante Arist. Opera, T. I.) pp. 81, 82; Ammonius Saccas: Aristotelis vita (ed. Buhle in Arist. Op. T. I.), pp. 43, 44.

and some Republics, brought under the subjection of a
Persian satrap in Asia Minor. Hermias was even sent as
prisoner to Artaxerxes in Persia, and he at once caused
him to be crucified. In order to avoid a similar fate,
Aristotle fled with his wife Pythias, the daughter of
Hermias, to Mitylene, and lived there for some time. He,
however, erected a statue to Hermias in Delphi, with an
inscription which has been preserved. From it we know
that it was by cunning and treachery that he came under
the power of the Persians. Aristotle also honoured his
name in a beautiful hymn on Virtue, which has likewise
come down to us.[1]

From Mitylene he was (Ol. 109, 2 ; 343 B.C.) summoned
by Philip of Macedon to undertake the education of
Alexander, who was then fifteen years old. Philip had
already invited him to do this in the well-known letter that
he addressed to him just after Alexander's birth : " Know
that a son is born to me, but I thank the gods less
that they have given him to me, than that they have
caused him to be born in your time. For I hope that
your care and your wisdom will make him worthy of me
and of his future kingdom." [2] It certainly would appear
to be a brilliant historic destiny to be the instructor of an
Alexander, and Aristotle at this court enjoyed the favour
and esteem of Philip and of Olympias in the highest degree.
What became of Aristotle's pupil is known to all, and the
greatness of Alexander's mind and deeds, as also his
enduring friendship, are the best witnesses of the success,
as also of the spirit of this up-bringing, if Aristotle required
such testimony. Alexander's education utterly refuted the
common talk about the practical uselessness of speculative
philosophy. Aristotle had in Alexander another and
worthier pupil than Plato found in Dionysius. Plato's great

[1] Diog. Laërt. V. 3, 4 ; 7, 8 ; Buhle : Aristotel. vita, pp. 90–92.
[2] Aristotelis Opera (ed. Pac. Aurel. Allobrog, 1607), T. I., in fine :
Aristotelis Fragmenta. (Cf. Stahr. Aristotelia, Pt. I. pp. 85–91.)

interest was his Republic, the ideal of a state; he enters into relation with a person through whom it might be carried out; the individual was thus to him a medium only, and in so far indifferent to him. With Aristotle, on the other hand, this purpose was not present, he merely had the simple individual before him; and his end was to bring up and to develop the individuality as such. Aristotle is known to be a profound, thorough, and abstract metaphysician, and it is evident that he meant seriously with Alexander. That Aristotle did not follow with Alexander the ordinary superficial method of educating princes, might be confidently expected from the earnestness of one who well knew what was truth and true culture. It is also evident from the circumstance that Alexander, while in the midst of his conquests in the heart of Asia, when he heard that Aristotle had made known his acroamatic doctrines in speculative (metaphysical) writings, wrote him a reproachful letter, in which he said that he should not have made known to the common people what the two had worked out together. To this Aristotle replied that, though published, they were really just as much unpublished as before.[1]

This is not the place to estimate Alexander as an historic personage. What can be ascribed in Alexander's education to Aristotle's philosophic instruction is the fact that what was natural to him, the inherent greatness of his mental disposition, acquired inward freedom also, and became elevated into the perfect, self-conscious independence which we see in his aims and deeds. Alexander attained to that perfect certainty of himself which the infinite boldness of thought alone gives, and to an independence of particular and limited projects, as also to their elevation into the entirely universal end of bringing about in the world a social life and intercourse of a mutual kind, through the founda-

[1] Aulus Gellius: Noctis Atticæ, XX. 5.

tion of states which were free from contingent individuality. Alexander thus carried out the plan which his father had already conceived, which was, at the head of the Greeks, to avenge Europe upon Asia, and to subject Asia to Greece; so that as it was in the beginning of Greek history that the Greeks were united, and that only for the Trojan war, this union likewise brought the Greek world proper to an end. Alexander thereby also avenged the faithlessness and cruelty perpetrated by the Persians on Aristotle's friend Hermias. But Alexander further disseminated Greek culture over Asia, in order to elevate into a Greek world this wild medley of utter barbarism, bent solely on destruction, and torn by internal dissensions, these lands entirely sunk in indolence, negation, and spiritual degeneracy. And if it be said that he was merely a conqueror who was unable to establish an enduring kingdom, because his kingdom at his death once more fell to pieces, we must acknowledge that, from a superficial view of the case, this is true, as his family did not retain their rule; Greek rule was, however, maintained. Thus Alexander did not found an extensive kingdom for his family, but he founded a kingdom of the Greek nation over Asia ; for Greek culture and science have since his time taken root there. The Greek kingdoms of Asia Minor, and particularly of Egypt, were for centuries the home of science; and their influence may have extended as far as to India and to China. We certainly do not know definitely whether the Indians may not have obtained what is best in their sciences in this way, but it is probable that at least the more exact portion of Indian astronomy came to them from Greece. For it was from the Syrian kingdom, stretching into Asia Minor as far as to a Greek kingdom in Bactria, that there was doubtless conveyed to the interior of India and China, by means of Greek colonies migrating thither, the meagre scientific knowledge which has lingered there like a tradition, though it has never flourished. For the Chinese, for example, are not skilful enough to make a calendar of their own, or to think for themselves. Yet they exhibited ancient instruments unsuited to any work done by them, and the immediate conjecture was that these had come from Bactria. The high idea that men had of the sciences of the Indians and of the Chinese hence is false.

According to Ritter (Erdkunde, Vol. II. p. 839, of the first edition), Alexander did not set out merely with a view of conquering, but with the idea that he was the Lord. I do not think that Aristotle placed this notion, which was connected with another Oriental conception, in the mind of Alexander. The other idea is that in the East the name of Alexander still flourishes as Ispander, and as Dul-k-ar-nein, *i.e.* the man with two horns, just as Jupiter Ammon is an ancient Eastern hero. The question would now be whether the Macedonian kings did not, through their descent from the ancient race of Indian heroes, claim to rule this land ; by this the progress of Dionysius from Thrace to India could likewise be explained ; whether the "knowledge of this was not the real and fundamental religious idea inspiring the young hero's soul when, before his journey to Asia, he found on the lower Ister (Danube) Indian priestly states where the immortality of the soul was taught, and when, certainly not without the counsel of Aristotle, who, through Plato and Pythagoras, was initiated into Indian wisdom, he began the march into the East, and first of all visited the Oracle of Ammonium (now Siwah), and then destroyed the Persian kingdom and burnt Persepolis, the old enemy of Indian religion, in order to take revenge upon it for all the violence exercised through Darius on the Buddhists and their co-religionists." This is an ingenious theory, formed from a thorough investigation of the connection which exists between Oriental and European ideas from the higher point of view in history. But, in the first place, this conjecture is contrary to the historical basis on which I take my stand.

Alexander's expedition has quite another historic, military, and political character than this, and had not much to do with his going to India; it was, on the face of it, an ordinary conquest. In the second place, Aristotle's metaphysic and philosophy is far from recognizing any such foolish and extravagant imaginations. The elevation of Alexander in the Oriental mind into an acknowledged hero and god, which followed later, is, in the third place, not matter for surprise; the Dalai-Lama is still thus honoured, and God and man are never so very far asunder. Greece likewise worked its way to the idea of a God becoming man, and that not as a remote and foreign image, but as a present God in a godless world: Demetrius Phalereus and others were thus soon after honoured and worshipped in Athens as God. Was the infinite not also now transplanted into self-consciousness? Fourthly, the Buddhists did not interest Alexander, and in his Indian expedition they do not appear; the destruction of Persepolis is, however, sufficiently justified as a measure of Greek vengeance for the destruction by Xerxes of the temples in Greece, especially in Athens.

While Alexander accomplished this great work—for he was the greatest individual at the head of Greece, he ever kept science and art in mind. Just as in modern times we have once more met with warriors who thought of science and of art in their campaigns, we also find that Alexander made an arrangement whereby whatever was discovered in the way of animals and plants in Asia should be sent to Aristotle, or else drawings and descriptions of the same. This consideration on Alexander's part afforded to Aristotle a most favourable opportunity of collecting treasures for his study of nature. Pliny (Histor. natur. VIII., 17 ed. Bip.) relates that Alexander directed about a thousand men, who lived by hunting, fishing and fowling, the overseers of the zoological gardens, aviaries, and tanks of the Persian kingdom, to supply Aristotle with what was remarkable from every place. In this way Alexander's campaign in Asia had the further effect of enabling Aristotle to found the science of natural history, and to be the author; according to Pliny, of a natural history in fifty parts.

After Alexander commenced his journey to Asia, Aristotle returned to Athens, and made his appearance as a public teacher in the Lyceum, a pleasure-ground which Pericles had made for the exercising of recruits; it consisted of a temple dedicated to Apollo (Λύκειος), and shady walks (περίπατοι), which were enlivened by trees, fountains and colonnades. It was from these walks that his school received the name of Peripatetics, and not from any walking about on the part of Aristotle—because, it is said, he delivered his discourses usually while walking. He lived and taught in Athens for thirteen years. But after the death of Alexander there broke out a tempest which had, as it appeared, been long held back through fear of Alexander; Aristotle was accused of impiety. The facts are differently stated : amongst other things it is said that his hymn to Hermias and the inscription on the statue dedicated to him were laid to his charge. When he saw the storm gathering, he escaped to Chalcis in Eubœa, the present Negropont, in order, as he himself said, that the Athenians should not have an opportunity of once more sinning against Philosophy. There he died, in the next year, in the sixty-third year of his age, Ol. 114, 3 (322 B.C.).[1]

We derive Aristotle's philosophy from his writings ; but when we consider their history and nature, so far as externals are concerned, the difficulty of deriving a knowledge of his philosophy from them seems much increased. I cannot certainly enter into details regarding these last. Diogenes Laërtius (V. 21–27) mentions a very large number

---

[1] Diog. Laërt. V. 5, 6 ; Suidas, s. v. Aristoteles ; Buhle : Aristot. vit. p. 100; Ammon. Saccas : Arist. vit. pp. 47, 48; Menag. ad. Diog. Laërt. V. 2; Stahr. Aristotelia, Pt. I. pp. 108, 109 ; Bruckeri Hist. crit. phil. T. I. pp. 788, 789.

of them, but by their titles we do not always quite know
which of those now in our possession are indicated, since
the titles are entirely different. Diogenes gives the number
of lines as four hundred and forty-five thousand, two
hundred and seventy, and, if we count about ten thousand
lines in a printer's alphabet, this gives us forty-four
alphabets. What we now have might perhaps amount to
about ten alphabets, so that we have only about the fourth
part left to us. The history of the Aristotelian manuscripts
has been stated to be such that it would really seem impossible, or almost hopeless, that any one of his writings
should have been preserved to us in its original condition, and not corrupted. Doubts regarding their genuine
character could not in such circumstances fail to exist;
and we can only wonder at seeing them come down to us
even in the condition in which they are. For, as we have
said, Aristotle made them known but little during his life-
time, and he left his writings to Theophrastus, his successor,
with the rest of his immense library. This, indeed, is the
first considerable library, collected as it was by means of
personal wealth along with Alexander's assistance, and
hence it also reveals to us Aristotle's learning. Later on,
it came partially, or in some cases in duplicate, to Alexandria, and formed the basis of the Ptolemaic library, which,
on the taking of Alexandria by Julius Cæsar, became a
prey to fire. But of the manuscripts of Aristotle himself
it is said that Theophrastus left them by will to a certain
Neleus, from whom they came into the hands of ignorant
men, who either kept them without care or estimation of
their value, or else the heirs of Neleus, in order to save
them from the Kings of Pergamus, who were very anxious
to collect a library, hid them in a cellar, where they lay
forgotten for a hundred and thirty years, and thus got into
bad condition. Finally, the descendants of Theophrastus
found them again after long search, and sold them to
Apellicon of Teos, who restored what had been destroyed

by worms and mould, but who did not possess the learning
or the capacity so to do. Hence others went over them,
filled up the blanks as they thought best, replaced what
was damaged, and thus they were sufficiently altered. But
still it was not enough. Just after Apellicon's death, the
Roman Sulla conquered Athens, and amongst the spoil
carried off to Rome were the works of Aristotle. The
Romans, who had just begun to become acquainted with
Greek science and art, but who did not yet appreciate
Greek philosophy, did not know how to profit from this
spoil. A Greek, named Tyrannion, later on obtained permission to make use of and publish the manuscripts of
Aristotle, and he prepared an edition of them, which, however, also bears the reproach of being inaccurate, for here
they had the fate of being given by the dealers into the
hands of ignorant copyists, who introduced a number of
additional corruptions.[1]

This is the way in which the Aristotelian philosophy has
come to us. Aristotle certainly made known much to his
contemporaries, that is to say, the writings in the Alexandrian library, but even those works do not seem to have
been widely known. In fact, many of them are most corrupt, imperfect, and, as, for example, the Poetics, incomplete. Several of them, such as the Metaphysical treatises,
seem to be patched up from different writings, so that the
higher criticism can give rein to all its ingenuity, and,
according to one clever critic, the matter may with much
show of probability be decided in one particular way, while
another ingenious person has a different explanation to
oppose to this.[2] So much remains certain, that the writings
of Aristotle are corrupt, and often both in their details

---

[1] Strabo, XIII. p. 419 (ed. Casaub. 1587); Plutarch in Sulla, c.
26; Brucker. Hist. crit. phil. T. I. pp. 798–800 (cf. Michelet: Examen
critique de l'ouvrage d'Aristote, intitulé Métaphysique, pp. 5–16.)
[2] Cf. Michelet: Examen critique, &c., pp. 17–23; 28–114; 199–
241.

and in the main, not consistent; and we often find whole paragraphs almost verbally repeated. Since the evil is so old, no real cure can certainly be looked for; however, the matter is not so bad as would appear from this description. There are many and important works which may be considered to be entire and uninjured, and though there are others corrupt here and there, or not well arranged, yet, as far as the essentials are concerned, no such great harm has been done as might appear. What we possess therefore places us in a sufficiently good position to form a definite idea of the Aristotelian philosophy, both as a whole, and in many of its details.

But there is still an historic distinction to be noted. For there is an old tradition that Aristotle's teaching was of a twofold nature, and that his writings were of two different kinds, viz. esoteric or acroamatic and exoteric—a distinction which was also made by the Pythagoreans (Vol. I. p. 202). The esoteric teaching was given within the Lyceum in the morning, the exoteric in the evening; the latter related to practice in the art of rhetoric and in disputation, as also to civic business, but the other to the inward and more profound philosophy, to the contemplation of nature and to dialectic proper.[1] This circumstance is of no importance; we see by ourselves which of his works are really speculative and philosophic, and which are rather empirical in character : but they are not to be regarded as antagonistic in their content, and as if Aristotle intended some for the people and others for his more intimate disciples.

a. We have first to remark that the name Aristotelian philosophy is most ambiguous, because what is called Aristotelian philosophy has at different times taken very different forms. It first of all signifies Aristotelian philosophy proper. As regards the other forms of the Aristote-

---

[1] Gellius: Noct. Atticæ, XX. 5; Stahr: Aristotelia, Pt. I. pp. 110–112.

lian philosophy, however, it had, in the second place, at the
time of Cicero, and specially under the name of Peripatetic
philosophy, more of the form of a popular philosophy, in
which attention was principally directed to natural history
and to morals (Vol. I. p. 479). This period does not appear
to have taken any interest in working out and bringing to
consciousness the deep and properly speaking speculative
side of Aristotelian philosophy, and indeed with Cicero
there is no notion of it present. A third form of this
philosophy is the highly speculative form of the Alex-
andrine philosophy, which is also called the Neo-Pythago-
rean or Neo-Platonic philosophy, but which may just as
well be called Neo-Aristotelian—the form as it is regarded
and worked up by the Alexandrines, as being identical
with the Platonic. An important signification of the expression, in the fourth place, is that which it had in the
middle ages where, through insufficient knowledge, the
scholastic philosophy was designated Aristotelian. The
Scholastics occupied themselves much with it, but the form
that the philosophy of Aristotle took with them cannot be
held by us to be the true form. All their achievements,
and the whole extent of the metaphysics of the understanding and formal logic which we discover in them, do
not belong to Aristotle at all. Scholasticism is derived
only from traditions of the Aristotelian doctrines. And
it was not until the writings of Aristotle became better
known in the West, that a fifth Aristotelian philosophy
was formed, which was in part opposed to the Scholastic—
it arose on the decline of scholasticism and with the revival
of the sciences. For it was only after the Reformation
that men went back to the fountainhead, to Aristotle himself. The sixth signification which Aristotelian philosophy
bears, is found in false modern ideas and conceptions, such
as those that we find in Tennemann, who is gifted with too
little philosophic understanding to be able to grasp the
Aristotelian philosophy (Vol. I. p. 113). Indeed, the

general opinion of Aristotelian philosophy now held is that it made what is called experience the principle of knowledge.

b. However false this point of view on the one hand is, the occasion for it may be found in the Aristotelian manner. Some particular passages to which in this reference great importance has been given, and which have been almost the only passages understood, are made use of to prove this idea. Hence we have now to speak of the character of the Aristotelian manner. Since in Aristotle, as we already said (p. 118), we need not seek a system of philosophy the particular parts of which have been deduced, but since he seems to take an external point of departure and to advance empirically, his manner is often that of ordinary ratiocination. But because in so doing Aristotle has a quality, altogether his own, of being throughout intensely speculative in his manner, it is further signified that in the first place he has comprehended the phenomenal as a thinking observer. He has the world of appearance before himself complete and in entirety, and sets nothing aside, however common it may appear. All sides of knowledge have entered into his mind, all have interest for him, and he has thoroughly dealt with all. In the empirical details of a phenomenon abstraction may easily be lost sight of, and its application may be difficult : our progress may be one-sided, and we may not be able to reach the root of the matter at all. But Aristotle, because he looks at all sides of the universe, takes up all those units as a speculative philosopher, and so works upon them that the profoundest speculative Notion proceeds therefrom. We saw, moreover, thought first proceeding from the sensuous, and, in Sophistry, still exercising itself immediately in the phenomenal. In perception, in ordinary conception, the categories appear : the absolute essence, the speculative view of these elements, is always expressed in expressing perceptions. This pure essence in perception Aristotle takes up. When, in the second place, he begins conversely with the universal or the simple, and passes to its determination, this looks as if he were enumerating the number of significations in which it appears; and, after dealing with them all, he again passes all their forms in review, even the quite ordinary and sensuous. He thus speaks of the many significations that we find, for example, in the words οὐσία, ἀρχή, αἰτία, ὁμοῦ, &c. It is in some measure wearisome to follow him in this mere enumeration, which proceeds without any necessity being present, and in which the significations, of which a list is given, manifest themselves as comprehended only in their essence, or in that which is common to all, and not in their determinations; and thus the comprehension is only external. But, on the one hand, this mode presents a complete series of the moments, and on the other, it arouses personal investigation for the discovery of necessity. In the third place, Aristotle takes up the different thoughts which earlier philosophers have had, contradicts them—often empirically—justifies them, reasoning in all sorts of ways, and then attains to the truly speculative point of view. And finally, in the fourth place, Aristotle passes on thoughtfully to consider the object itself of which he treats, *e.g.* the soul, feeling, recollection, thought, motion, time, place, warmth, cold, &c. Because he takes all the moments that are contained within the conception to be, so to speak, united, he does not omit determinations; he does not hold now to one determination and then to another, but takes them as all in one; while reflection of the understanding, which has identity as the rule by which it goes, can only preserve harmony with this by always, while in one determination, forgetting and withholding the other. But Aristotle has the patience to go through all conceptions and questions, and from the investigation of the individual determinations, we have the fixed, and once more restored determination of every object. Aristotle thus forms the Notion, and is in the highest

degree really philosophic, while he appears to be only
empiric. For Aristotle's empiricism is a totality because
he always leads it back again immediately to speculation ;
he may thus be said to be a perfect empiricist, yet at the
same time a thinking one. If, for example, we take away
from space all its empirical determinations, the result will
be in the highest degree speculative, for the empirical,
comprehended in its synthesis, is the speculative Notion.

In this gathering up of determinations into one Notion,
Aristotle is great and masterly, as he also is in regard to
the simplicity of his method of progression, and in the
giving of his decisions in few words. This is a method of
treating of Philosophy which has great efficacy, and which
in our time has likewise been applied, *e.g.* by the French.
It deserves to come into larger use, for it is a good thing
to lead the determinations of the ordinary conception from
an object to thought, and then to unite them in a unity, in
the Notion. But undoubtedly this method in one respect
appears to be empirical, and that, indeed, in the acceptation of objects as we know them in our consciousness ; for
if no necessity is present, this still more appears merely to
pertain to manner externally regarded. And yet it cannot
be denied that with Aristotle the object was not to bring
everything to a unity, or to reduce determinations to a
unity of opposites, but, on the contrary, to retain each in
its determination and thus to follow it up. That may, on
the one hand, be a superficial method, *e.g.* when everything
is brought to an empty determinateness, such as those of
irritability and sensibility, sthenic and asthenic, but, on
the other, it is likewise necessary to grasp reality in simple
determinateness, though without making the latter in this
superficial way the starting point. Aristotle, on the other
hand, simply forsakes determination in another sphere where
it no longer has this form ; but he shows what it is like here,
or what change has taken place within it, and thus it comes
to pass that he often treats one determination after the

other without showing their connection. However, in his
genuine speculation Aristotle is as profound as Plato, and
at the same time more developed and explicit, for with
him the opposites receive a higher determination. Certainly
we miss in him the beauty of Plato's form, the melodious
speech, or, as we might almost call it, chatting—the con-
versational tone adopted, which is as lively as it is cultured
and human. But where in Plato we find, as we do in his
Timæus, the speculative Idea definitely expressed in the
thesis form, we see in it a lack both of comprehension and
purity ; the pure element escapes it, while Aristotle's form
of expression is marked both by purity and intelligibility.
We learn to know the object in its . determination and
its determinate Notion ; but Aristotle presses further into
the speculative nature of the object, though in such a way
that the latter remains in its concrete determination, and
Aristotle seldom leads it back to abstract thought-determinations. The study of Aristotle is hence inexhaustible, but to
give an account of him is difficult, because his teaching must
be reduced to universal principles. Thus in order to set
forth Aristotelian philosophy, the particular content of
each thing would have to be specified. But if we would
be serious with Philosophy, nothing would be more desirable than to lecture upon Aristotle, for he is of all the
ancients the most deserving of study.

    c. What ought to come next is the determination of the
Aristotelian Idea, and here we have to say, in quite a
general way, that Aristotle commences with Philosophy
generally, and says, in the first place, regarding the value
of Philosophy (in the second chapter of the first book of
the Metaphysics), that the object of Philosophy is what is
most knowable, viz. the first and original causes, that
is, the rational. For through these and from these all
else is known, but principles do not become known through
the facts which form their ground-work ($\upsilon\pi o\kappa\epsilon\acute{\iota}\mu\epsilon\nu a$). In
this we already have the opposite to the ordinary point of

view. Aristotle has further declared the chief subject of
investigation, or the most essential knowledge (ἐπιστήμη
ἀρχικωτάτη) to be the knowledge of end; but this is the
good in each thing and, generally speaking, the best in
the whole of nature. This also holds good with Plato and
Socrates; yet the end is the true, the concrete, as against
the abstract Platonic Idea. Aristotle then says of the value
of Philosophy, " Men have begun to philosophize through
wonder," for in it the knowledge of something higher is
at least anticipated. "Thus since man, to escape from
ignorance, began to philosophize, it is clear that for the
sake of knowledge he followed after knowledge, and not
for any utility which it might possess for him. This is
also made evident by the whole course of its external
history. For it was after men had done with all their
absolute requirements, and with what concerns their com-
fort, that they first began to seek this philosophic knowledge. We hence seek it not for the sake of any outside
utility that it may have. And thus as we say that a free
man is he who exists on his own account and not for
another, Philosophy is the only science that is free, because
it alone exists for itself—it is knowledge on account of
knowledge. Therefore in justice it will not be held to be
a human possession," in the sense that, as we said above,
(p. 11) it is not in the possession of a man. "For in many
ways the nature of man is dependent, so that, according
to Simonides, God alone possesses the prerogative (γέρας),
and yet it is unworthy on man's part not to seek after the
science that is in conformity with his own condition (τὴν
καθ᾽ αὑτὸν ἐπιστήμην). But if the poets were right, and
envy characterized divinity, all who would aim higher
must be unfortunate;" Nemesis punishes whatever raises
itself above the common-place, and makes everything
again equal. "But the divine cannot be jealous," *i.e.*
cannot refuse to impart that which it is, as if this knowledge should not come to man (*supra*, pp. 72, 73) "and—

according to the proverb—the poets utter many falsehoods. Nor ought we to consider that any science is more entitled to honour than the one we now investigate, for that which is most divine, is also most worthy of honour." That is to say, what has and imparts what is best is honoured: the gods are thus to be honoured because they have this knowledge. "God is held to be the cause and principle of everything, and therefore God has this science alone, or for the most part." But for this reason it is not unworthy of man to endeavour to seek the highest good which is in conformity with him, this knowledge pertaining to God. "All other sciences are, however, more requisite than Philosophy, but none more excellent."

It is difficult to give a more detailed account of the Aristotelian philosophy, the universal Idea with the more important elements, for Aristotle is much more difficult to comprehend than Plato. In the latter there are myths, and we can pass over the dialectic and yet say that we have read Plato; but with Aristotle we enter at once upon what is speculative. Aristotle always seems to have philosophized only respecting the individual and particular, and not to have risen from it to the thought of the absolute and universal, to the thought of God; he always goes from the individual to the individual. His task concerns what is, and is just as clearly divided off as a professor has his work divided into a half year's course; and though in this course he examines the whole of the world of conception, he yet appears only to have recognized the truth in the particular, or only a succession of particular truths. This has nothing dazzling about it, for he does not appear to have risen to the Idea (as Plato speaks of the nobility of Idea), nor to have led back to it the individual. But if Aristotle on the one hand did not logically abstract the universal Idea, (for then his so-called logic, which is something very different, would have had as its principle the recognition of one Notion in all) on the other

hand there appears in Aristotle the one Absolute, the idea
of God, as itself a particular, in its place beside the others,
although it is all Truth. It is as if we said, "there are
plants, animals, men, and also God, the most excellent of
all."

From the whole list of conceptions which Aristotle enumerates, we shall now select some for further examination, and
I will first speak of his metaphysics and its determinations.
Then I will deal with the particular sciences which have
been treated by Aristotle, beginning by giving the fundamental conception of nature as it is constituted with
Aristotle; in the third place I will say something of mind,
of the soul and its conditions, and finally the logical books
of Aristotle will follow.

1. THE METAPHYSICS.

Aristotle's speculative Idea is chiefly to be gathered
from his Metaphysics, especially from the last chapters of
the twelfth book (Λ) which deal with the divine Thought.
But this treatise has the peculiar drawback noticed above
(p. 128) of being a compilation, several treatises having
been combined into one. Aristotle and the ancients did
not know this work by the name of the Metaphysics; it was
by them called πρώτη φιλοσοφία.[1] The main portion of this
treatise has a certain appearance of unity given to it by the
connection of the argument,[2] but it cannot be said that the
style is orderly and lucid. This pure philosophy Aristotle
very clearly distinguishes (Metaph. IV. 1) from the other
sciences as "the science of that which is, in so far as it is,
and of what belongs to it implicitly and explicitly." The
main object which Aristotle has in view (Metaph. VII. 1)
is the definition of what this substance (οὐσία) really is.

---

[1] Arist. Metaphys. VI. 1; Physic. II. 2; I. 9. (Cf. Michelet:
Examen critique, etc., pp. 23—27.)

[2] Michelet: Examen critique, pp. 115—198.

In this ontology or, as we call it, logic, he investigates and minutely distinguishes four principles (Metaph. I. 3) : first, determination or quality as such, the wherefore of anything, essence or form ; secondly, the matter ; thirdly, the principle of motion ; and fourthly, the principle of final cause, or of the good. In the later part of the Metaphysics Aristotle returns repeatedly to the determination of the Ideas, but here also a want of connection of thought appears, even though all is subsequently united into an entirely speculative Notion.

To proceed, there are two leading forms, which Aristotle characterizes as that of potentiality (δύναμις) and that of actuality (ἐνέργεια) ; the latter is still more closely characterized as entelechy (ἐντελέχεια) or free activity, which has the end (τὸ τέλος) in itself, and is the realization of this end. These are determinations which occur repeatedly in Aristotle, especially in the ninth book of the Metaphysics, and which we must be familiar with, if we would understand him. The expression δύναμις is with Aristotle the beginning, the implicit, the objective ; also the abstract universal in general, the Idea, the matter, which can take on all forms, without being itself the form-giving principle. But with an empty abstraction such as the thing-in-itself Aristotle has nothing to do. It is first in energy or, more concretely, in subjectivity, that he finds the actualizing form, the self-relating negativity. When, on the other hand, we speak of Being, activity is not yet posited : Being is only implicit, only potentiality, without infinite form. To Aristotle the main fact about Substance is that it is not matter merely (Metaph. VII. 3) ; although in ordinary life this is what is generally taken to be the substantial. All that is contains matter, it is true, all change demands a substratum (ὑποκείμενον) to be affected by it ; but because matter itself is only potentiality, and not actuality—which belongs to form—matter cannot truly exist without the activity of form (Metaph. VIII. 1, 2). With Aristotle δύναμις does not therefore mean force (for force is really an imperfect aspect of form), but rather capacity which is not even undetermined possibility; ἐνέργεια is, on the other hand, pure, spontaneous activity. These definitions were of importance throughout all the middle ages. Thus, according to Aristotle, the essentially absolute substance has potentiality and actuality, form and matter, not separated from one another ; for the true objective has most certainly also activity in itself, just as the true subjective has also potentiality.

From this definition we now see clearly the sort of opposition in which the Idea of Aristotle stands to that of Plato, for although the Idea of Plato is in itself essentially concrete and determined, Aristotle goes further. In so far, namely, as the Idea is determined in itself, the relation of the moments in it can be more closely specified, and this relation of the moments to each other is to be conceived of as nothing other than activity. It is easy for us to have a consciousness of what is deficient in the universal, that is, of that which is implicit only. The universal, in that it is the universal, has as yet no reality, for because implicitude is inert, the activity of realization is not yet posited therein. Reason, laws, etc., are in this way abstract, but the rational, as realizing itself, we recognize to be necessary, and therefore we take such universal laws but little into account. Now the standpoint of Plato is in the universal ; what he does is to express Being rather as the objective, the Good, the end, the universal. To this, however, the principle of living subjectivity, as the moment of reality, seems to be lacking, or it appears at least to be put in the background. This negative principle seems indeed not to be directly expressed in Plato, but it is essentially contained in his definition of the Absolute as the unity of opposites ; for this unity is essentially a negative unity of those opposites, which abrogates their being-another, their opposition, and leads them back into itself. But with Aristotle this negativity, this active efficacy, is expressly characterized as energy ; in that it breaks up itself—this independence—abrogating unity, and positing separation ; for, as Aristotle says (Metaph. VII. 13), "actuality separates." The Platonic Idea, on the other hand, is rather that abrogation of opposites, where one of the opposites is itself unity While, therefore, with Plato the main consideration is the affirmative principle, the Idea as only abstractly identical with itself, in Aristotle there is added and made conspicuous the moment of negativity, not as change, nor yet as nullity, but as difference or determination. The principle of individualization, not in the sense of a casual and merely particular subjectivity, but in that of pure subjectivity, is peculiar to Aristotle. Aristotle thus also makes the Good, as the universal end, the substantial foundation, and maintains this position against Heraclitus and the Eleatics. The Becoming of Heraclitus is a true and real determination, but change yet lacks the determination of identity with itself, the constancy of the universal. The stream is ever changing, yet it is nevertheless ever the same, and is really a universal existence. From this it is at once evident that Aristotle (Metaph. IV. 3—6) is controverting the opinions of Heraclitus and others when he says that Being and non-being are not the same (Vol. I. p. 282), and in connection with this lays down the celebrated maxim of contradiction, that a man is not at the same time a ship. This shows at once that Aristotle does not understand by this pure Being and non-being, this abstraction which is really only the transition of the one into the other; but by that which is, he understands Substance, the Idea, Reason, viewed likewise as an impelling end. As he maintains the universal against the principle of mere change, he puts forward activity in opposition to the numbers of the Pythagoreans, and to the Platonic Ideas. However frequently and fully Aristotle controverts both of these, all his objections turn on the remark already quoted (Vol. I. p. 213) that activity is not to be found in these principles, and that to say that real things participate in Ideas is empty talk, and a poetic metaphor. He says also that Ideas, as abstract universal determinations, are only as far as numbers go equal to things, but are not on that account to be pointed out as their causes. Moreover, he maintains that there are contradictions involved in taking independent species, since in Socrates, for instance, there are several ideas included: man, biped, animal (Metaph. I. 7 and 9). Activity with Aristotle is undoubtedly also change, but change that is within the universal, and that remains self-identical; consequently a determination which is self-determination, and therefore the self-realizing universal end : in mere alteration, on the contrary, there is not yet involved the preservation of identity in change. This is the chief point which Aristotle deals with.

Aristotle distinguishes various moments in substance, in so far as the moments of activity and potentiality do not appear as one, but still in separation. The closer determination of this relation of energy to potentiality, of form to matter, and the movement of this opposition, gives the different modes of substance. Here Aristotle enumerates the substances ; and to him they appear as a series of different kinds of substance, which he merely takes into consideration one by one, without bringing them together into a system. The three following are the chief among these :—

a. The sensuous perceptible substance is that in which the matter is still distinguished from the efficient form. Hence this substance is finite ; for the separation and externality of form and matter are precisely what constitute the nature of the finite. Sensuous substance, says Aristotle (Metaph. XII. 2), involves change, but in such a way that it passes over into the opposite ; the opposites disappear in one another, and the third beyond these opposites, that which endures, the permanent in this change, is matter. Now the leading categories of change which Aristotle names are the four differences, in regard to the What (κατὰ τὸ τί), or in regard to quality (ποιόν), or in regard to quantity (ποσόν), or in regard to place where (ποῦ). The first change is the origination and decay of .simple determinate Being (κατὰ τόδε); the second change is that of the further qualities (κατὰ τὸ ᾿πάθος); the third, increase and diminution; the fourth, motion. Matter is the dead substance on which take place the changes which matter passes through. " The change itself is from potential into actual existence; possible whiteness transforms itself into actual whiteness. Thus things do not arise casually out of nothing, but all arises out of what exists, though it exists only in potentiality, not in actuality." The possible is thus really a general implicit existence, which brings about these determinations, without producing one out of the other. Matter is thus simple potentiality, which, however, is placed in opposition to itself, so that a thing in its actuality only becomes that which its matter was also in potentiality. There are thus three moments posited: matter, as the general substratum of change, neutral in respect of what is different (ἐξ οὗ); the opposed determinations of form, which are negative to each other as that which is to be abrogated and that which is to be posited (τι and εἴς τι); the first mover (ὑφ' οὗ), pure activity (Metaph. VII. 7; IX. 8; XII. 3).[1] But activity is the unity of form and matter; how these two are in the other, Aristotle does not, however, further explain. Thus in sensuous substance there appears the diversity of the moments, though not as yet their return into themselves; but activity is the negative which ideally contains in itself the opposite, therefore that also which is about to be.

[1] Not only the form which is to be abrogated, but also matter is spoken of by Aristotle as τι, because in truth the form which is to be abrogated serves only as material for the form which is to be posited; so that he in the first passage names the three moments ἐκ τινος, τι, ὑπό τινος, and in the last passage names them τι, εἴς τι, ὑπό τινος.—[Editor's Note.]

b. A higher kind of substance, according to Aristotle (Metaph. IX. 2; VII. 7; XII. 3), is that into which activity enters, which already contains that which is about to be. This is understanding, absolutely determined, whose content is the aim which it realizes through its activity, not merely changing as does the sensuous form. For the soul is essentially actuality, a general determination which posits itself; not only formal activity, whose content comes from somewhere else. But while the active posits its content in reality, this content yet remains the same; there is an activity present which is different from matter, although substance and activity are allied. Thus here we still have a matter which understanding demands as its hypothesis. The two extremes are matter as potentiality, and thought as efficiency: the former is the passive universal, and the latter the active universal; in sensuous substance the active is, on the contrary, still quite different from matter. In these two moments themselves change does not take place, for they are the implicit universal in opposed forms.

c. The highest point is, however, that in which potentiality, activity and actuality are united; the absolute substance which Aristotle (Metaph. XII. 6, 7; IX. 8), defines in general as being the absolute (ἀΐδιον), the unmoved, which yet at the same time moves, and whose essence is pure activity, without having matter. For matter as such is passive and affected by change, consequently it is not simply one with the pure activity of this substance. Here as elsewhere we certainly see an instance of merely denying a predicate, without saying what its truth is; but matter is nothing else than that moment of unmoved Being. If in later times it has seemed something new to define absolute Being as pure activity, we see that this arises from ignorance as to the Aristotelian conception. But the Schoolmen rightly looked upon this as the definition of God, since they define God as *actus purus;* and higher idealism than this there is none. We may also express this as follows: God is the Substance

which in its potentiality has reality also unseparated from
it ; therein potentiality is not distinguished from form, since
it produces from itself the determinations of its content.   In
this Aristotle breaks away from Plato, and for this reason
controverts number, the Idea, and the universal, because if
this, as inert, is not defined as identical with activity, there
is no movement. Plato's inert Ideas and numbers thus bring
nothing into reality ; but far different is the case with the
Absolute of Aristotle, which in its quiescence is at the same
time absolute activity.

Aristotle further says on this subject (Metaph. XII. 6) :
"It may be that what has potentiality is not real ; it is of
no avail therefore to make substances eternal, as the
idealists do, if they do not contain a principle which can
effect change.   And even this is insufficient, if it is not
active, because in that case there is no change. Yea, even
if it were active, but its substance only a potentiality, there
would be in it no eternal movement, for it is possible that
what is according to potentiality may not exist. We must
therefore have a principle whose substance must be apprehended as activity." Thus in mind energy is substance
itself. "But here a doubt seems to spring up. For all
that is active seems to be possible, but all that is possible
does not seem to energize, so that potentiality seems to be
antecedent," for it is the universal. "But if this were the
case, no one of the entities would be in existence, for it is
possible that a thing may possess a capacity of existence,
though it has never yet existed. But energy is higher than
potentiality. We must thus not assert, as theologians would
have us do, that in the eternal ages there was first chaos or
night " (matter), " nor must we say with natural philosophers that everything existed simultaneously. For how
could the First be changed, if nothing in reality were cause ?
For matter does not move itself, it is the Master who
moves it. Leucippus and Plato accordingly say that motion
has always existed, but they give no reason for the asser-

tion." Pure activity is, according to Aristotle (Metaph.
IX. 8), before potentiality, not in relation to time, but to
essence. That is to say, time is a subordinate moment, far
removed from the universal; for the absolute first Being
is, as Aristotle says at the end of the sixth chapter of the
twelfth book, "that which in like activity remains always
identical with itself." In the former assumption of a
chaos and so on, an activity is posited which has to do
with something else, not with itself, and has therefore a
pre-supposition; but chaos is only bare possibility.

That which moves in itself, and therefore, as Aristotle
continues (Metaph. XII. 7), " that which has circular motion ;" is to be posited as the true Being, " and this is evident
not merely from thinking reason, but also from the fact
itself." From the definition of absolute Being as imparting
motion, as bringing about realization, there follows that it
exists in objectivity in visible nature. As the self-identical
which is visible, this absolute Being is " the eternal
heavens." The two modes of representing the Absolute
are thus thinking reason and the eternal heavens. The
heavens are moved, but they also cause movement. Since
the spherical is thus both mover and moved, there is a
centre-point which causes movement but remains unmoved,
and which is itself at the same time eternal and a substance
and energy.[1] This great definition given by Aristotle of

---

[1] As this explanation by Hegel of Aristotle's celebrated passage
has so many authorities to support it, the editor cannot here, as
frequently elsewhere in these lectures, remain faithful to the directions of his colleagues, quietly to set right anything that is
incorrect. It is, nevertheless, clear that Aristotle is speaking of
three substances: a sublunar world, which the heavens move; the
heavens as the centre which is both mover and moved; and God,
the unmoved Mover. The passage must therefore, on the authority
of Alexander of Aphrodisias (Schol. in Arist. ed. Brandis, p. 804 *b*),
of Cardinal Bessarion (Aristoteles lat. ed. Bekk. p. 525 *b*) and
others, be thus read: ἔστι τοίνυν τι καὶ ὃ κινεῖ (sc. ὁ οὐρανός)· ἐπεὶ δὲ
τὸ κινούμενον καὶ κινοῦν καὶ μέσον τοίνυν, ἔστι τι ὃ οὐ κινούμενον

absolute Being as the circle of reason which returns into itself, is of the same tenor as modern definitions; the unmoved which causes movement is the Idea which remains self-identical, which, while it moves, remains in relation to itself. He explains this as follows : " Its motion is determined in the following manner. That moves which is desired and thought, whereas itself it is unmoved, and the original of both is the same." That is the end whose content is the desire and thought; such an end is the Beautiful or the Good. " For the thing that is desired is that which appears beautiful " (or pleases) : " whose first " (or end), " on which the will is set, is what is beautiful. But it is rather the case that we desire it because it appears beautiful, than that it appears beautiful because we desire it." For if that were so, it would be simply posited by activity, but it is posited independently, as objective Being, through which our desire is first awakened. " But thought is the true principle in this, for thought is moved only by the object of thought. But the intelligible " (we scarcely believe our eyes) " is essentially the other co-element (συστοιχία)" [2] namely, that which is posited as objective, as absolutely existent thought, " and the substance of this other element is the first; but the first substance is simple pure activity. Such are the Beautiful and the Good, and the first is ever the absolutely best or the best possible. But the Notion shows that the final cause belongs to the unmoved. What is moved may also subsist in a different manner. Motion (φορά) is the

κινεῖ. The translation, if this reading be adopted, would be as follows : Besides the heavens in perpetual motion " there is something which the heavens move. But since that which at the same time is moved and causes movement cannot be other than a centre, there is also a mover that is unmoved." (Cf. Michelet : Examen critique, etc., p. 192; Jahrbücher für wissenschaftliche Kritik, November, 1841, No. 84, pp. 668, 669). [Editor's note.]

[2] συστοιχία is a good word, and might also mean an element which is itself its own element, and determines itself only through itself.

first change; the first motion, again, is circular motion,
but this is due to the above cause." Therefore, according
to Aristotle, the Notion, *principium cognoscendi*, is also
that which causes movement, *principium essendi;* he expresses it as God, and shows the relation of God to the
individual consciousness. "The First Cause is necessary.
But the term necessary has three meanings : first what is
accomplished by violence, because it goes contrary to one's
inclination (παρὰ τὴν ὁρμήν); secondly, that without which
the Good does not subsist; thirdly, that which can exist in
no other way than it does, but involves absolute existence.
On such a principle of the unmoved the heavens depend
and the whole of nature "—the visible that is eternal, and
the visible that changes. This system is ever-enduring.
"But to us," as individuals, "there is granted, for a short
time only, a sojourn therein of surpassing excellence. For
the system continues ever the same, but for us that is impossible. Now this activity is in its very self enjoyment,
and therefore vigilance, exercise of the senses, thinking
in general, are most productive of enjoyment; and for the
same reason hopes and memories bring pleasure. But
thinking, in its pure essence, is a thinking of that which
is absolutely the most excellent;" the thought is for itself
absolute end. The difference and contradiction in activity
and the abrogation of the same, Aristotle expresses thus :
" But thought thinks itself by participation (μετάληψιν) in
that which is thought, but thought becomes thought by
contact and apprehension, so that thought and the object
of thought are the same." Thought, as being the unmoved which causes motion, has an object, which, however,
becomes transformed into activity, because its content is
itself something thought, *i.e.* a product of thought, and
thus altogether identical with the activity of thinking.
The object of thought is first produced in the activity of
thinking, which in this way separates the thought as an
object. Hence, in thinking, that which is moved and that

which moves are the same; and as the substance of what
is thought is thought, what is thought is the absolute
cause which, itself unmoved, is identical with the thought
which is moved by it; the separation and the relation are
one and the same. The chief moment in Aristotle's philosophy is accordingly this, that the energy of thinking and
the object of thought are the same; "for thought is that
which is receptive of objects of perception and the existent.
When in possession of these it is in a condition of activity
(ἐνεργεῖ δὲ ἔχων); and thus all this" operation by which
it thinks itself, " is more divine than the divine possession
which thinking reason supposes itself to have,"—the content of thought. It is not the object of thought that is
the more excellent, but the very energy of thinking; the
activity of apprehension brings that to pass which appears
as something that is being apprehended. "Speculation
(ἡ θεωρία) is thus the most pleasing and the best. If
then God has eternally subsisted in such surpassing excellence as for a limited time pertains to us" (in whom
this eternal Thought, which is God Himself, occurs only as
a particular condition), "He is worthy of admiration; if
He possesses it in a more eminent degree, His nature is
still more admirable. But this is His mode of subsistence.
Life is also inherent in Him, for the activity of thought is
life. But He constitutes this efficient power; essential
energy belongs to God as His most excellent and eternal
life. We therefore say that with God there is life perfect
and everlasting." From this substance Aristotle moreover
excludes magnitude.

We in our way of speaking designate the Absolute, the
True, as the unity of subjectivity and objectivity, which is
therefore neither the one nor the other, and yet just as
much the one as the other; and Aristotle busied himself
with these same speculations, the deepest forms of speculation even of the present day, and he has expressed them
with the greatest definiteness. With Aristotle it is thus no

dry identity of the abstract understanding that is indicated, for he distinguishes subjective and objective precisely and decisively. Not dead identity such as this, but energy, is for him what is most to be reverenced, God. Unity is thus a poor, unphilosophic expression, and true Philosophy is not the system of identity; its principle is a unity which is activity, movement, repulsion, and thus, in being different, is at the same time identical with itself. If Aristotle had made the jejune identity of understanding, or experience, his principle, he would never have risen to a speculative Idea like this, wherein individuality and activity are placed higher than universal potentiality. Thought, as the object of thought, is nothing else than the absolute Idea regarded as in itself, the Father; yet this First and unmoved, as distinguished from activity, is, as absolute, simply activity, and is first through this activity set forth as true. In what he teaches respecting the soul we shall find Aristotle recurring to this speculative thought; but to Aristotle it is again an object, like other objects, a kind of condition which he separates from the other conditions of the soul which he understands empirically, such as sleep, or weariness. He does not say that it alone is truth, that all is summed up in Thought, but he says it is the first, the strongest, the most honourable. We, on the other hand, say that Thought, as that which relates to itself, has existence, or is the truth; that Thought comprehends the whole of Truth, even though we ordinarily represent to ourselves sensation and so on, besides thought, as having reality. Thus, although Aristotle does not express himself in modern philosophic language, he has yet throughout the same fundamental theory; he speaks not of a special kind of reason, but of the universal Reason. The speculative philosophy of Aristotle simply means the direction of thought on all kinds of objects, thus transforming these into thoughts; hence, in being thoughts, they exist in truth. The meaning of this is not, however, that natural objects have thus themselves the power of thinking, but as they are subjectively thought by me, my thought is thus also the Notion of the thing, which therefore constitutes its absolute substance. But in Nature the Notion does not exist explicitly as thought in this freedom, but has flesh and blood, and is oppressed by externalities ; yet this flesh and blood has a soul, and this is its Notion. The ordinary definition of truth, according to which it is "the harmony of the conception with the object," is certainly not borne out by the conception ; for when I represent to myself a house, a beam, and so on, I am by no means this content, but something entirely different, and therefore very far from being in harmony with the object of my conception. It is only in thought that there is present a true harmony between objective and subjective ; that constitutes me. Aristotle therefore finds himself at the highest standpoint ; nothing deeper can we desire to know, although he has always the appearance of making ordinary conceptions his starting-point.

Aristotle (Metaph. XII. 9) now solves many other doubtful questions, for instance, whether thought is compound, and whether science is the object of science itself. " Some further doubts arise as to thought (νοῦς), which seems to be of all things the most divine ; but it is only with difficulty that we can conceive under what conditions (πῶς δ' ἔχων) it is a thing of this sort. When it thinks of nothing, but is in a state like that of a sleeper, what constitutes its superiority ? And when it thinks, but something else is dominant all the time (ἄλλο κύριον), that which is its substance is not thought (νόησις), but a potentiality ; " it would not be in eternal activity. " In this way it would not be the highest substance ; for it is " (active) "thought (τὸ νοεῖν) that gives it its high rank. If now, further, thought or thinking is its substance, what does it think ? Itself or another ? And if another, is it always the same, or something different ? Does it also not make a difference,

whether it thinks of what is beautiful or what is casual?
In the first place, if thought is not thinking, but only the
power to think, continuous thinking would be laborious for
it," for every power wears itself out. "In the next place,
something else would be more excellent than thought,
namely that which is thought (νοούμενον); and thinking
and thought (τὸ νοεῖν καὶ ἡ νόησις) will be present to the
mind in understanding what is most inferior. As this is
to be avoided (in the same way that it is better not to see
some things than to see them), thinking would not constitute the best. Thought is therefore this, to think itself,
because it is the most excellent; and it is the thinking,
which is the thinking of thinking. For understanding and
sensation and opinion and deliberation seem always to
have an object other than themselves, and to be their own
objects only in a secondary sense. Further, if thinking
and being thought of are different, in relation to which of
the two is the Good inherent in thought? For the Notion[1]
of thinking and that of the object of thought are not the
same. Or, in the case of some things, does the science
itself constitute that which is the object of science? In
what is practical the thing is the immaterial substance and
the determination of the end (ἡ οὐσία καὶ τὸ τί ἦν εἶναι),
and in what is theoretical it is the reason and the thinking.
As therefore thought and the object of thought are not
different, these opposites, so far as they involve no connection with matter, are the same thing, and there is only a
thought of the thing thought of." Reason which thinks
itself, is the absolute end or the Good, for it only exists for
its own sake. "There still remains a doubt whether that
which thinks is of composite nature or not; for it might
undergo change in the parts of the whole. But the Good

---

[1] The word τὸ εἶναι, when it governs the dative (τὸ εἶναι νοήσει καὶ
νοουμένῳ) invariably expresses the Notion, while, when it governs
the accusative, it denotes concrete existence. (Trendelenburg:
Comment. in Arist. De anima, III. 4, p. 473.) [Editor's Note.]

is not in this or that part, for it is the best in the universe, as distinguished from it. In this way the Thought which is its own object subsists to all eternity."

As this speculative Idea, which is the best and most free, is also to be seen in nature, and not only in thinking reason, Aristotle (Metaph. XII. 8) in this connection passes on to the visible God, which is the heavens. God, as living God, is the universe; and thus in the universe God, as living God, shows Himself forth. He comes forth as manifesting Himself or as causing motion, and it is in manifestation alone that the difference between the cause of motion and that which is moved comes to pass. "The principle and the first cause of that which is, is itself unmoved, but brings to pass the original and eternal and single motion," that is, the heaven of the fixed stars. "We see that besides the simple revolution of the universe, which is brought about by the first unmoved substance, there are other eternal motions, those of the planets." We must not, however, enter into further details on this subject.

Regarding the organization of the universe in general, Aristotle says (Metaph. XII. 10), "We must investigate in what manner the nature of the whole has within it the Good and the Best; whether as something set apart and absolute, or as an order, or in both ways, as in the case of an army. For the good condition of an army depends upon the order enforced, as much as on the general, and the general is the cause of the army's good condition in all the greater degree from the fact of the order being through him, and not from his being through the order. All things are co-ordinated in a certain way, but not all in the same way: take, for example, animals which swim, and those which fly, and plants; they are not so constituted that one of them is not related to another, but they stand in mutual relations. For all are co-ordinated into one system, just as in a house it is by no means permitted to the free inmates to do freely whatever they like, but all that they do, or the most of it, is done according to orderly arrangement. By slaves and animals, on the contrary, little is done for the general good, but they do much that is casual. For the principle of each is his own nature. In the same way it is necessary that all should attain to a position where distinction is drawn" (the seat of judgment) " but there are some things so constituted that all participate in them for the formation of a whole." Aristotle then goes on to refute some other notions ; showing, for instance, the embarrassments into which they fall who make all things proceed from oppositions, and he corroborates, on the other hand, the unity of the principle by quoting Homer's line (Iliad II. 204) :

"It is not good that many govern ; let one alone bear rule."

2. Philosophy of Nature.

Amongst the special sciences treated by Aristotle, the Physics is contained in a whole series of physical treatises, which form a tolerably complete system of what constitutes the Philosophy of Nature in its whole extent. We shall try to give their general plan. Aristotle's first work is his Treatise, in eight books, on Physics, or on the Principles· ($\phi\nu\sigma\iota\kappa\grave{\eta}$ $\dot{a}\kappa\rho\acute{o}a\sigma\iota\varsigma$ $\dot{\eta}$ $\pi\epsilon\rho\grave{\iota}$ $\dot{a}\rho\chi\hat{\omega}\nu$). In this he deals, as is fitting, with the doctrine of the Notion of nature generally, with movement, and with space and time. The first manifestation of absolute substance is movement, and its moments are space and time ; this conception of its manifestation is the universal, which realizes itself first in the corporeal world, passing into the principle of separation. Aristotle's Physics is what for present physicists would, properly speaking, be the Metaphysics of Nature ; for our physicists only say what they have seen, what delicate and excellent instruments they have made, and not what they have thought. This first work by Aristotle is followed by his treatises concerning the Heavens, which deal with the nature of body and the first real bodies, the earth and heavenly bodies in general, as also with the general abstract relation of bodies to one another through mechanical weight and lightness, or what we should call attraction; and finally, with the determination of abstract real bodies or elements. Then follow the treatises on Production and Destruction, the physical process of change, while formerly the ideal process of movement was considered. Besides the physical elements, moments which are only posited in process, as such, now enter in: for instance, warmth, cold, &c. Those elements are the real existent facts, while these determinations are the moments of becoming or of passing away, which exist only in movement. Then comes the Meteorology; it represents the universal physical process in its most real forms. Here particular determinations appear, such as rain, the saltness of the sea, clouds, dew, hail, snow, hoar-frost, winds, rainbows, boiling, cooking, roasting, colours, &c. On certain matters, such as the colours, Aristotle wrote particular treatises. Nothing is forgotten, and yet the presentation is, on the whole, empiric. The book On the Universe, which forms the conclusion, is said not to be genuine; it is a separate dissertation, addressed to Alexander, which contains in part the doctrine of the universality of things, a doctrine found already in the other treatises; hence this book does not belong to this series.

From this point Aristotle proceeds to organic nature, and here his works not only contain a natural history, but also a physiology and anatomy. To the anatomy pertain his works on the Locomotion of Animals, and on the Parts of Animals. He deals with physiology in the works on the Generation of Animals, on the common Movement of Animals; and then he comes to the distinction between Youth and Age, Sleeping and Waking, and treats of Breathing, Dreaming, the Shortness and Length of Life,

&c., all of which he deals with partly in an empiric, and partly in a more speculative manner. Finally, there comes the History of Animals, not merely as a history of Nature, but also as the history of the animal in its entirety—what we may call a kind of physiologico-anatomical anatomy. There is likewise a botanical work On Plants (περὶ φυτῶν) which is ascribed to him. Thus we here find natural philosophy in the whole extent of its outward content.

As regards this plan, there is no question that this is not the necessary order in which natural philosophy or physics must be treated. It is long since physics adopted in its conception the form and tendency derived from Aristotle, of deducing the parts of the science from the whole; and thus even what is not speculative still retains this connection as far as outward order goes. This is plainly to be preferred to the arrangement in our modern text-books, which is a wholly irrational succession of doctrines accidentally put together, and is undoubtedly more suitable to that method of contemplating nature, which grasps the sensuous manifestation of nature quite irrespective of sense or reason. Physics before this contained some metaphysics, but the experience which was met with in endeavouring unsuccessfully to work it out, determined the physicists, so far as possible, to keep it at a distance, and to devote their attention to what they call experience, for they think that here they come across genuine truth, unspoiled by thought, fresh from the hand of nature; it is in their hands and before their faces. They can certainly not dispense with the Notion, but through a kind of tacit agreement they allow certain conceptions, such as forces, subsistence in parts, &c., to be valid, and make use of these without in the least knowing whether they have truth and how they have truth. But in regard to the content they express no better the truth of things, but only the sensuous manifestation. Aristotle and the ancients understand by physics, on the other hand, the comprehension of nature—the universal; and for this reason Aristotle also calls it the doctrine of principles. For in the manifestation of nature this distinction between the principle and what follows it, manifestation, really commences, and it is abrogated only in genuine speculation. Yet if, on the one hand, what is physical in Aristotle is mainly philosophic and not experimental, he yet proceeded in his Physics in what may be called an empiric way. Thus, as it has been already remarked of the Aristotelian philosophy in general that the different parts fall into a series of independently determined conceptions, so we find that this is the case here also; hence an account can only be given of a part of them. One part is not universal enough to embrace the other part, for each is independent. But that which follows, and which has in great measure reference to what is individual, no longer comes under the dominion of the Notion, but becomes a superficial suggestion of reasons, and an explanation from the proximate causes, such as we find in our physics.

In regard to the general conception of nature, we must say that Aristotle represents it in the highest and truest manner. For in the Idea of nature Aristotle (Phys. II. 8) really relies on two determinations : the conception of end and the conception of necessity. Aristotle at once grasps the whole matter in its principles, and this constitutes the old contradiction and divergence of view existing between necessity (*causæ efficientes*) and end (*causæ finales*), which we have inherited. The first mode of consideration is that in accordance with external necessity, which is the same as chance—the conception that all that pertains to nature is determined from without by means of natural causes. The other mode of consideration is the teleological, but conformity to end is either inward or outward, and in the more recent culture the latter has long retained the supremacy. Thus men vibrate in their opinion between these two points of view, seek external causes, and war against the form of an external teleology which places the end outside of nature. These determinations were known to Aristotle, and he thoroughly investigates them and considers what they are and mean. Aristotle's conception of nature is, however, nobler than that of to-day, for with him the principal point is the determination of end as the inward determinateness of natural things. Thus he comprehended nature as life, *i.e.* as that which has its end within itself, is unity with itself, which does not pass into another, but, through this principle of activity, determines changes in conformity with its own content, and in this way maintains itself therein. In this doctrine Aristotle has before his eyes the inward immanent end, to which he considers necessity an external condition. Thus, on the one hand, Aristotle determines nature as the final cause, which is to be distinguished from what is luck or chance; it is thus opposed by him to what is necessary, which it also contains within itself; and then he considers how necessity is present in natural things. In nature we usually think of necessity first, and understand as the essentially natural that which is not determined through end. For long men thought that they determined nature both philosophically and truly in limiting it to necessity. But the aspect of nature has had a stigma removed from it, because, by means of its conformity to the end in view, it is elevated above the common-place. The two moments which we have considered in substance, the active form and matter, correspond with these two determinations.

We must first consider the conception of adaptation to end as the ideal moment in substance. Aristotle begins (Phys. II. 8) with the fact that the natural is the self-maintaining, all that is difficult is its comprehension. "The first cause of perplexity is, what hinders nature from not operating for the sake of an end, and because it is better so to operate, but" being, for example, "like Jupiter, who rains, not that the corn may grow, but from necessity. The vapour driven upwards cools, and the water resulting from this cooling falls as rain, and it happens that the corn is thereby made to grow. In like manner, if the corn of any one is destroyed, it does not rain for the sake of this destruction, but this is an accidental circumstance." That is to say, there is a necessary connection which, however, is an external relation, and this is the contingency of the cause as well as of the effect. "But if this be so," Aristotle asks, "what hinders us from assuming that what appears as parts" (the parts of an animal, for instance) "may thus subsist in nature, too, as contingent? That, for example, the front teeth are sharp and adapted for dividing, and that the back teeth, on the contrary, are broad and adapted for grinding the food in pieces, may be an accidental circumstance, not necessarily brought about for these particular ends. And the same is true with respect to the other parts of the body which appear to be adapted for some end; therefore those living things in which all was accidentally constituted as if for some end, are now, having once been so existent, preserved, although originally they had arisen by chance, in accordance with external necessity." Aristotle adds that Empedocles especially had these reflections, and represented the first beginnings of things as a world composed of all sorts of monstrosities, such as bulls with human heads; such, however, could not continue to subsist, but disappeared because they were not originally constituted so that they should endure; and this went on until what was in conformity with purpose came together. Without going back to the fabulous monstrosities of the ancients, we likewise know of a number of animal tribes which have died out, just because they could not preserve the race. Thus we also require to use the expression development (an unthinking evolution), in our present-day natural philosophy. The conception that the first productions were, so to speak, attempts, of which those which did not show themselves to be suitable could not endure, is easily arrived at by natural philosophy. But

nature, as *entelecheia* or realization, is what brings forth
itself. Aristotle hence replies : " It is impossible to believe
this. For what is produced in accordance with nature is
always, or at least for the most part, produced " (external
universality as the constant recurrence of what has passed
away), " but this is not so with what happens through
fortune or through chance. That in which there is an end
(τέλος), equally in its character as something which precedes and as something which follows, is made into end ;
as therefore a thing is made, so is its nature, and as is its
nature, so is it made ; it exists therefore for the sake of
this." The meaning of nature is that as something is, it
was in the beginning ; it means this inward universality
and adaptation to end that realizes itself ; and thus cause
and effect are identical, since all individual parts are related
to this unity of end. " He who assumes contingent and
accidental forms, subverts, on the other hand, both nature
itself and that which subsists from nature, for that subsists
from nature which has a principle within itself, by whose
means, and being continually moved, it attains its end." In
this expression of Aristotle's we now find the whole of the
true profound Notion of life, which must be considered as
an end in itself—a self-identity that independently impels
itself on, and in its manifestation remains identical
with its Notion : thus it is the self-effectuating Idea.
Leaves, blossoms, roots thus bring the plant into evidence
and go back into it ; and that which they bring to pass
is already present in the seed from which they took
their origin. The chemical product, on the contrary, does
not appear to have itself similarly present, for from acid
and base a third appears to come forth ; but here, likewise,
the essence of both these sides, their relationship, is already
present, though it is there mere potentiality, as it is in the
product merely a thing. But the self-maintaining activity
of life really brings forth this unity in all relationships.
What has here been said is already contained in that which

was asserted by those who do not represent nature in this way, but say, " that which is constituted as though it were constituted for an end, will endure." For this is the self-productive action of nature. In the modern way of looking at life this conception becomes lost in two different ways ; either through a mechanical philosophy, in which we always find as principle pressure, impulse, chemical relationships and forces, or external relations generally—which certainly seem to be inherent in nature, but not to proceed from the nature of the body, seeing that they are an added, foreign appendage, such as colour in a fluid ; or else theological physics maintain the thoughts of an understanding outside of the world to be the causes. In the Kantian philosophy we for the first time have that conception once more awakened in us, for organic nature at least; life has there been made an end to itself. In Kant this indeed had only the subjective form which constitutes the essence of the Kantian philosophy, in which it seems as though life were only so determined by reason of our subjective reasoning; but still the whole truth is there contained that the organic creation is the self-maintaining. The fact that most recent times have brought back the rational view of the matter into our remembrance, is thus none else than a justification of the Aristotelian Idea.

Aristotle also speaks of the end which is represented by organic nature in itself, in relation to the means, of which he says (Phys. II. 8) : "If the swallow builds her nest, and the spider spreads her web, and trees root themselves in the earth, for the sake of nutriment, there is present in them a self-maintaining cause of this kind, or an end." For this instinctive action exhibits an operation of self-preservation, as a means whereby natural existence becomes shut up and reflected into itself. Aristotle then brings what is here said into relation with general conceptions which he had earlier maintained (p. 138) : " Since nature is two-fold as matter and form, but since the latter is end, and the rest are on account of the end, this is final cause." For the active form has a content, which, as content of potentiality, contains the means which make their appearance as adapted for an end, *i.e.* as moments established through the determinate Notion. However much we may, in the modern way of regarding things, struggle against the idea of an immanent end, from reluctance to accept it, we must, in the case of animals and plants, acknowledge such a conception, always re-establishing itself in another. For example, because the animal lives in water or in air, it is so constructed that it can maintain its existence in air or water ; thus it requires water to explain the gills of fishes ; and, on the other hand, because the animal is so constructed, it lives in water. This activity in transformation thus does not depend in a contingent way on life ; it is aroused through the outward powers, but only in as far as conformity with the soul of the animal permits.

In passing, Aristotle here (Phys. II. 8) makes a comparison between nature and art, which also connects what results with what goes before, in accordance with ends. "Nature may commit an error as well as art ; for as a grammarian sometimes makes a mistake in writing, and a physician in mixing a medicinal draught, nature, too, sometimes does not attain its ends. Its errors are monstrosities and deformities, which, however, are only the errors of that which operates for an end. In the production of animals and plants, an animal is not at first produced, but the seed, and even in it corruption is possible." For the seed is the mean, as being the not as yet established, independent, indifferent, free actuality. In this comparison of nature with art we ordinarily have before us the external adaptation to end, the teleological point of view, the making for definite ends. And Aristotle declaims against this, while he remarks that if nature is activity for a certain end, or if it is the implicitly universal, "it is absurd to deny that action is in conformity with end, because that which moves cannot be seen to have deliberated and considered." The understanding comes forward with the determination of this end, and with its instruments and tools, to operate on matter, and we carry this conception of an external teleology over into nature. " But art also," says Aristotle, " does not deliberate. If the form of a ship were the particular inward principle of the timber, it would act as nature prompted. The action of nature is very similar to the exercise of the art whereby anyone heals himself." Through an inward instinct the animal avoids what is evil, and does what is good for him ; health is thus essentially present to him, not as a conscious end, but as an understanding which accomplishes its ends without conscious thought.

As Aristotle has hitherto combated an external teleology, he directs another equally applicable remark (Phys. II. 9) against merely external necessity, and thus we come to the other side, or to how necessity exists in nature. He says in this regard : " Men fancy that necessity exists in this way in generation, just as if it were thought that a house existed from necessity, because heavy things were naturally carried downwards, and light things upwards, and that, therefore, the stones and foundation, on account of their weight, were under the earth, and the earth, because it was lighter, was further up, and the wood in the highest place because it is the lightest." But Aristotle thus explains the facts of the case. "The house is certainly not made without these materials, but not on account of, or through them (unless the material so demands), but it is made for the sake of concealing and preserving certain things. The same takes place in everything which has an end in itself ; for it is not without that which is necessary to its nature, and yet it is not on account of this, unless the matter so demands, but on account of an end. Hence the necessary is from hypothesis only, and not as end, for necessity is in matter, but end is in reason ($\lambda\acute{o}\gamma\wp$). Thus it is clear that matter and its movement are necessity in natural things ;

both have to be set forth as principle, but end is the higher principle." It undoubtedly requires necessity, but it retains it in its own power, does not allow it to give vent to itself, but controls external necessity. The principle of matter is thus turned into the truly active ground of end, which means the overthrow of necessity, so that that which is natural shall maintain itself in the end. Necessity is the objective manifestation of the action of its moments as separated, just as in chemistry the essential reality of both the extremes—the base and the acid—is the necessity of their relation.

This is the main conception of Aristotelian Physics. Its further development concerns the conceptions of the different objects of nature, a material for speculative philosophy which we have spoken of above (pp. 153—155), and regarding which Aristotle puts before us reflections both difficult and profound. Thus he at first (Phys. III. 1—3) proceeds from this point to movement (κίνησις), and says that it is essential that a philosophy of nature should speak of it, but that it is difficult to grasp; in fact, it is one of the most difficult conceptions. Aristotle thus sets to work to understand movement in general, not merely in space and time, but also in its reality; and in this sense he calls it "the activity of an existent thing which is in capacity, so far as it is in capacity." He explains this thus : " Brass is in capacity a statue ; yet the motion to become a statue is not a motion of the brass so far as it is brass, but a motion of itself, as the capacity to become a statue. Hence this activity is an imperfect one (ἀτελής)," *i.e.* it has not its end within itself, " for mere capacity, whose activity is movement, is imperfect." The absolute substance, the moving immovable, the existent ground of heaven which we saw as end, is, on the contrary, both activity itself and the content and object of activity. But Aristotle distinguishes from this what falls under the form of this opposition, " That moving is also moved which has movement as a capacity, and whose immobility is rest. That in which movement is present has immobility as rest; for activity in rest, as such, is movement." That is to say, rest is capacity for motion. "Hence movement is the activity of that which is movable (κινητοῦ),[1] so far as it is movable; but this happens from the contact of that which is motive (κινητικοῦ), so that at the same time it is posited as passive likewise. But that which moves always introduces a certain form or end (εἶδος), either this particular thing (τόδε), or a quality or a quantity, which is the principle and cause of the motion when it moves; thus man, as he is in energy, makes man from man as he is in capacity. Thus, too, it is evident that movement is in the movable thing: for it is the activity of this, and is derived from that which is motive. The activity of that which is motive is likewise not different, for both are necessarily activity. It is motive because it has the capacity for being so; but it causes motion because it energizes. But it is the energetic of the moveable (ἔστιν ἐνεργητικὸν τοῦ κινητοῦ), so that there is one energy of both; just as the relation between one and two is the same as that between two and one, and there also is the same relation between acclivity and declivity, so the way from Thebes to Athens is the same as from Athens to Thebes. Activity and passivity are not originally (κυρίως) the same, but in what they are inherent, in motion, they are the same. In Being (τῷ εἶναι) they are identical, but activity, in so far as it is activity of this in this" (what is moved), "and the activity of this from this" (what moves), "is different as regards its

---

[1] Aristotle here distinguishes four determinations: what is moved in capacity, or the movable [das Bewegbare] .(κινητόν); what is moved in actuality (κινούμενον); the moving in capacity (κινητικόν), or what Hegel calls the motive [das Bewegliche]; the moving in actuality (κινοῦν). It might have been better to translate κινητόν by motive [Beweglich] and κινητικόν by mobile [Bewegerisch].—[Editor's note.]

conception ($\tau\hat{\omega}$ λόγῳ)." Aristotle subsequently deals with
the infinite (Phys. III. 4—8).

"In like manner it is necessary," says Aristotle (Phys.
IV. 1—5), "that the natural philosopher should consider
the subject of place (τόπος)." Here come various definitions and determinations under which space generally and
particular space or place appear. "Is place a body? It
cannot be a body, for then there would be in one and the
same, two bodies. Again, if it is the place and receptacle
(χώρα) of this body, it is evident that it is so also of the
superficies and the remaining boundaries; but the same
reasoning applies to these, for where the superficies of
water were before, there will now be the superficies of air,"
and thus the places of both superficies would be in one.
"But in truth there is no difference between the point and
the place of the point, so that if place is not different from
the other forms of limitation, neither is it something outside of them. It is not an element, and neither consists of
corporeal nor of incorporeal elements, for it possesses magnitude, but not body. The elements of bodies are, however, themselves bodies, and no magnitude is produced
from intelligible elements. Place is not the material of
things, for nothing consists of it—neither the form, nor
the Notion, nor the end, nor the moving cause; and yet
it is something." Aristotle now determines place as the
first unmoved limit of that which is the comprehending:
it comprehends the body whose place it is, and has nothing
of the thing in itself; yet it co-exists with the thing,
because the limits and the limited co-exist. The uttermost
ends of what comprehends and of what is comprehended
are identical, for both are bounds; but they are not
bounds of the same, for form is the boundary of the thing,
place is that of the embracing body. Place, as the comprehending, remains unchangeably passive while the thing
which is moved is moved away; from which we see that
place must be separable from the thing. Or place, accord-

ing to Aristotle, is the boundary, the negation of a body, the assertion of difference, of discretion; but it likewise does not merely belong to this body, but also to that which comprehends. There is thus no difference at all, but unchangeable continuity. "Place is neither the universal (κοινός) in which all bodies are" (heaven), "nor the particular (ἴδιος), in which they are as the first (πρώτῳ)." Aristotle also speaks of above and below in space, in relation to heaven as that which contains, and earth as what is beneath. "That body, outside of which is a comprehending body, is in space. But the whole heavens are not anywhere, since no body comprehends them. Outside the universe nothing is, and hence everything is in the heavens, for the heavens are the whole. Place, however, is not the heavens, but its external quiescent boundary which touches the body moved. Hence the earth is in water, water in air, air in ether, but ether in the heavens."

From this point Aristotle goes on (Phys. IV. 6, 7) to empty space, in which an old question is involved which physicists even now cannot explain : they could do so if they studied Aristotle, but as far as they are concerned there might have been no thought nor Aristotle in the world. "Vacuum, according to ordinary ideas, is a space in which there is no body, and, fancying that all Being is body, they say that vacuum is that in which there is nothing at all. The conception of a vacuum has its justification for one thing in the fact that a vacuum," the negative to an existent form, "is essential to motion ; for a body could not move in a plenum," and in the place to which it does move there must be nothing. "The other argument in favour of a vacuum is found in the compression of bodies, in which the parts press into the empty spaces." This is the conception of varying density and the alteration of the same, in accordance with which an equal weight might consist of an equal number of parts, but these, as being separated by vacuum, might present a greater volume. Aristotle con-

futes these reasonings most adroitly, and first of all in this
way: "The plenum could be changed, and bodies could
yield to one another even if no interval of vacuum separated
them. Liquids as well as solids are not condensed into a
vacuum; something that they contained is expelled, just as
air is expelled if water is compressed."

Aristotle deals more thoroughly, in the first place (Phys.
IV. 8), with the erroneous conception that the vacuum is
the cause of movement. For, on the one hand, he shows
that the vacuum really abolishes motion, and consequently
in vacuum a universal rest would reign. He calls it perfect
indifference as to the greater or less distance to which a
thing is moved; in vacuum there are no distinctions. It
is pure negation without object or difference; there is no
reason for standing still or going on. But body is in
movement, and that, indeed, as distinguished; it has a
positive relation, and not one merely to nothing. On the
other hand, Aristotle refutes the idea that movement is in
vacuum because compression is possible. But this does not
happen in a vacuum; there would be established in it not
one movement, but a movement towards all sides, a general
annihilation, an absolute yielding, where no cohesion would
remain in the body. "Again, a weight or a body is borne
along more swiftly or more slowly from two causes; either
because there is a difference in that through which it is
borne along, as when it moves through air or water or
earth, or because that which is borne along differs through
excess of weight or lightness." As regards difference of
movement on account of the first difference—that in the
density of the medium—Aristotle says: "The medium
through which the body is borne along is the cause of the
resistance encountered, which is greater if the medium is
moving in a contrary direction (and less if it is at rest);
resistance is increased also if the medium is not easily
divided. The difference in velocity is in inverse ratio to
the specific gravity of the medium, air and water, so that if

the medium has only half the density, the rate of progress will be double as quick. But vacuum has to body no such relation of differences of specific gravity. Body can no more contain a vacuum within its dimensions than a line can contain a point, unless the line were composed of points. The vacuum has no ratio to the plenum." But as to the other case, the difference in weight and lightness, which has to be considered as being in bodies themselves, whereby one moves more quickly than another through the same space : " this distinction exists only in the plenum, for the heavy body, by reason of its power, divides the plenum more quickly." This point of view is quite correct, and it is mainly directed against a number of conceptions that prevail in our physics. The conception of equal movement of the heavy and the light, as that of pure weight, pure matter, is an abstraction, being taken as though they were inherently like, only differing through the accidental resistance of the air.

Aristotle (Phys. IV. 9) now comes to the second point, to the proof of the vacuum because of the difference in specific gravity. " Many believe that the vacuum exists because of the rare and the dense :" the former is said to be a rare body, and the latter a perfect continuity; or they at least differ quantitatively from one another through greater or less density. " For if air should be generated from a quantity of water, a given quantity of water must produce a quantity of air the same in bulk, or there must necessarily be a vacuum ; for it is only on the hypothesis of a vacuum that compression and rarefaction are explicable. Now if, as they say, the less dense were that which has many separate void spaces, it is evident that since a vacuum cannot be separated any more than a space can have intervals, neither can the rare subsist in this manner. But if it is not separable, and yet a vacuum is said to exist in the body, in the first place movement could thus only be upwards ; for the rare is the light, and hence they say that fire is rare," because it always moves upwards. " In the next place the vacuum cannot be the cause of motion as that in which something moves, but must resemble bladders that carry up that which adheres to them. But how is it possible that a vacuum can move, or that there can be a place where there is a vacuum ? For that into which it is carried would be the vacuum of a vacuum. In short, as there can be no movement in vacuum, so also a vacuum cannot move." Aristotle set against these ideas the true state of matters, and states generally the ideal conception of nature : " that the opposites, hot and cold, and the other physical contraries, have one and the same matter, and that from what is in capacity that which is in energy is produced ; that matter is not separable though it is different in essence [1] (τῷ εἶναι), and that it remains one and the same in number (ἀριθμῷ) even if it possesses colour, or is hot and cold. And again, the matter of a small body and a large is the same, because at one time a greater proceeds from a smaller, and at another time a smaller from a greater. If air is generated from water it is expanded, but the matter remains the same and without taking to itself anything else ; for that which it was in capacity it becomes in actuality. In a similar way if air is compressed from a greater into a less volume, the process will be reversed, and air will similarly pass into water, because the matter which is in capacity both air and water, also becomes both." Aristotle likewise asserts that increase and decrease of warmth, and its transition into cold, is no addition or otherwise of warm matter, and also one and the same is both dense and rare. This is very different from the physical conceptions which

---

[1] While above (p. 164) we must take the expression τὸ εἶναι as immediate existence because it is opposed to the Notion, here it has the meaning of Notion, because it stands in opposition to immediate existence (καὶ οὐ χωριστὴ μὲν ἡ ὕλη, τῷ δ᾽ εἶναι ἕτερον, καὶ μία τῷ ἀριθμῷ). Cf. Michelet : Comment. in Arist. Eth. Nicom. V. I., pp. 209—214.—[Editor's note.]

assert more or less matter to correspond with more or less density, thus comprehending the difference in specific weight as the external addition of matter. Aristotle, on the contrary, takes this dynamically, though certainly not in the sense in which dynamics are to-day understood, viz. as an increase of intensity or as a degree, for he accepts intensity in its truth as universal capacity. Undoubtedly the difference must also be taken as a difference in amount, but not as an increase and decrease, or as an alteration in the absolute quantity of the matter. For here intensity means force, but again not as being a thing of thought separated from matter, but as indicating that if anything has become more intensive, it has had its actuality diminished, having, however, according to Aristotle, attained to a greater capacity. If the intensity is again directed outwards, and compared with other things, it undoubtedly becomes degree, and therefore magnitude immediately enters in. It then is indifferent whether greater intension or greater extension is posited ; more air is capable of being warmed to the same degree as less, through the greater intensity of the warmth ; or the same air can thereby become intensively warmer.

As regards the investigation of time, Aristotle remarks (Phys. IV. 10, 11, 13) that if time is externally (exoterically, ἐξωτερικῶς) regarded, we are inevitably led to doubt (διαπορῆσαι) whether it has any being whatever, or whether it has bare existence, as feeble (μόλις καὶ ἀμυδρῶς) as if it were only a potentiality. "For one part of it was and is not : another part will be and is not as yet ; but of these parts infinite and everlasting (ἀεὶ λαμβανόμενος), time is composed. But it now appears that time, if composed of things that are not, may be incapable of existence. And also as regards everything divisible, if it exists, either some or all of its parts must be. Time is certainly divisible ; but some of the parts are past, others are future, and no part is present. For the *now* is no part, since a part has a measure, and the whole must consist of the parts ; but time

does not appear to consist of the Now." That is to say,
because the Now is indivisible, it has no quantitative determination which could be measured. " Besides it is not
easy to decide whether the Now remains, or always becomes
another and another. Again, time is not a movement and
change, for movement and change occur in that which is
moved and changed, or accompany time in its course ;
but time is everywhere alike. Besides change is swifter
and slower, but time is not. But it is not without change
and motion " (which is just the moment of pure negativity
in the same) " for when we perceive no change, it appears
as if no time had elapsed, as in sleep. Time is hence in
motion but not motion itself." Aristotle defines it thus :
" We say that time is, when we perceive the before and
after in movement ; but these are so distinguished that we
apprehend them to be another and another, and conceive
that there is something between, as a middle. Now when
we understand that the extremes of the conclusion are
different from the middle, and the soul says that the Now
has two instants, the one prior and the other posterior,
then we say that this is time. What is determined through
the Now, we call time, and this is the fundamental principle.
But when we are sensible of the Now as one, and not as a
prior and posterior in motion, nor as the identity of an earlier
or later, then there does not appear to us to have been any
time, because neither was there any motion." Tedium is
thus ever the same. " Time is hence the number of motion,
according to priority and posteriority ; it is not motion
itself, unless so far as motion has number. We judge of
the more or less through number, but of a greater or less
motion by time. But we call number that which can be
numbered, as well as that with which we number ; but time
is not the number with which we number, but that which
is numbered, and, like motion, always is changing. The
Now is, which is the unity of number, and it measures time.
The whole of time is the same, for the Now which was is

the same" (universality as the Now destroyed) "but in
Being it is another. Time thus is through the Now both
continuous (συνεχής) and discrete (διῄρηται). It thereby
resembles the point, for that also is the continuity of the
line and its division, its principle and limit; but the Now
is not an enduring point. As continuity of time the Now
connects the past and the future, but it likewise divides
time in capacity," the Now is only divisibility and the
moments only ideal. "And in as far as it is such, it is
always another; but, in as far as it unites, it is ever one
and the same. Similarly, in as far as we divide the line,
other and yet other points always arise for thought; but
in as far as it is one, there is only one point. Thus the
Now is both the division of time in capacity, and the limit
and union of both" *i.e.* of the prior and posterior. The
universally dividing point is only one as actual; but this
actual is not permanently one, but ever and again another, so
that individuality has universality, as its negativity, within
it. "But division and union are the same, and similarly
related; however their Notion (τὸ εἶναι)[1] is different." In
one and the same respect the absolute opposite of what was
posited is immediately set forth as existent; in space, on
the other hand, the moments are not set forth as existent,
but in it first appears this being and its motion and contradiction. Thus the identity of the understanding is not
a principle with Aristotle, for identity and non-identity to
him are one and the same. Because the Now is only now,
past and future are different from it, but they are likewise
necessarily connected in the Now, which is not without
before and after; thus they are in one, and the Now, as
their limit, is both their union and their division.

---

[1] Here τὸ εἶναι has again the signification of Notion, as above
(p. 169), because in the preceding words (ἔστι δὲ ταὐτὸ καὶ κατὰ ταὐτὸ ἡ
διαίρεσις καὶ ἡ ἔνωσις) immediate existence is expressed.—[Editor's
note.]

Aristotle (Phys. V. 1) then goes on to movement as
realized in a thing, to change (μεταβολή) or to the physical
processes—while before we had pure movement. "In movement there is first something which moves, also something
which is moved, and the time in which it is moved ; besides
these, that from which, and that into which it is moved."
(Cf. *supra*, p. 141.) "For all motion is from something and
into something; but there is a difference between that
which is first moved and that into which and from which it
is moved, as, for instance, wood, warmth and cold. The
motion is in the wood and not in the form ; for neither form
nor place, nor quantity moves or is moved, but" (in the
order in which they follow) "there is that which is moved
and that which moves, and that into which it is moved.
That to which movement is made, more than that out of
which movement is made, is named change.   Hence to
pass into non-being is also change, although what passes
away is changed from Being : and generation is a mutation
into Being, even though it is from non-being."   The remark
is to be interpreted as meaning that for the first time in
real becoming motion, *i.e.* in change, the relation *whereto*
enters, while the relation *wherefrom* is that in which change
is still the mere ideal motion.   Besides this first form of difference between motion and change, Aristotle further gives
another, since he divides change into three : "into change
from a subject (ἐξ ὑποκειμένου) into a subject; or from a
subject into a non-subject; or from a non-subject into a
subject."   The fourth, "from a non-subject into a non-
subject," which may also appear in the general division,
"is no mutation, for it contains no opposition."   It may
certainly be merely thought or ideal, but Aristotle indicates
the actual phenomenon.   "The mutation from a non-subject
into a subject is generation (γένεσις) ; that from a subject
into a non-subject is corruption (φθορά); that from a
subject into a subject, is motion as such;" because that
which is transformed remains the same, there is no

becoming-another of the actual, but a merely formal becoming-another. This opposition of the materialized motion as mutation, and of merely formal motion, is noteworthy.

In the sixth book Aristotle comes to the consideration of the dialectic of this motion and change as advanced by Zeno, that is, to the endless divisibility which we have already (Vol. I. pp. 266—277) considered. Aristotle solves it through the universal. He says that they are the contradiction of the universal turned against itself; the unity in which its moments dissolve is not a nothing, so that motion and change are nothing, but a negative universal, where the negative is itself again posited as positive, and that is the essence of divisibility.

Of the further details into which Aristotle enters, I shall only give the following. As against atoms and their motion, he remarks (Phys. VI. 10) that the indivisible has no motion and mutation, which is the direct opposite of the proposition of Zeno that only simple indivisible Being and no motion exists. For as Zeno argues from the indivisibility of atoms against motion, Aristotle argues from motion against atoms. " Everything which moves or changes is in the first division of this time partly here and partly there. The atom, as simple indivisible Being, can, however, not have any part of it in both points in space, because it then would be divisible. The indivisible could thus only move if time consisted of the Now; this is, however, impossible, as we proved before." Because atoms thus neither have change in themselves, nor can this come to them from without through impulse, &c., they are really without truth.

The determination of the pure ideality of change is important. Aristotle says of this (Phys. VII. 8), " That which is changed is alone the sensuous and perceptible (αἰσθητόν) ; and forms and figures, as also capacities, are not changed , they arise and disappear in a thing only, without being themselves changed." In other words: the content of change is unchangeable; change as such belongs to mere form. "Virtues or vices belong, for example, to habits acquired. Virtue is the perfection (τελείωσις) in which something has reached the end of its nature. Vice, however, is the corruption and non-attainment of this. They are not changes, for they only arise and pass away while another alters." Or the difference becomes a difference of Being and non-being, *i.e.* a merely sensuous difference.

From these conceptions Aristotle now comes nearer to the first real or physical motion (Phys. VIII. 6, 8, 9; De Cœlo, I. 4): The first principle of motion is itself unmoved. An endless motion in a straight line is an empty creation of thought; for motion is necessarily an effort after something. The absolute motion is the circular, because it is without opposition. For because movement has to be considered in regard to the starting-place and the end in view, in the straight movement the directions from A to B and from B to A are opposed, but in motion in a circle they are the same. The idea that heavenly bodies would of themselves have moved in a straight line, but that they accidentally came into the sphere of solar attraction, is an empty reflection which is far from occurring to Aristotle.

Aristotle then shows (De Cœlo, II. 1; I. 3) that "the whole heavens neither arose nor can pass away, for they are one and eternal: they neither have beginning nor end in eternal time, for they contain infinite time shut up within them." All the other ideas are sensuous which try to speak of essential reality, and in them there always is that present which they think they have excluded. For when they assert a vacuum before the beginning of generation, this is the quiescent, self-identical, *i.e.* the eternal matter, which is thus already established before origination; they will not allow that before origination nothing exists. But in fact a thing does not exist before its origination, *i.e.* in movement there is something to move, and where reality is, there is motion. They do not, however, bring together that vacuum, the self-identical, the un-originated matter and this nothing. "That which has this absolute circular movement is neither heavy nor light; for the heavy is what moves downwards, and the light what moves upwards." In modern physics the heavenly bodies, on the other hand, are endowed with weight, and seek to rush into the sun, but cannot do so on account of another force. "It is indestructible and ungenerated, without decrease or increase, without any change. It is different from earth, fire, air and water; it is what the ancients called ether, as the highest place, from its continuous course (ἀεὶ θεῖν) in infinite time." This ether thus appears to be eternal matter which does not, however, take such a definite form, but which remains as it is, just as the heavens do in our conception, although here the juxtaposition begins ever to strike us more forcibly.

Aristotle (De Cœlo, III. 6) shows further that the elements do not proceed from one body, but from one another; for in generation they neither proceed from what is incorporeal, nor from what is corporeal. In the first case they would have sprung from the vacuum, for the vacuum is the immediate incorporeal; but in that case the vacuum must have existed independently as that in which determinate corporeality arose. But neither do the elements arise from a corporeal, for else this body itself would be a corporeal element before the elements. Thus it only remains that the elements must spring from one another. Regarding this we must remark that Aristotle understands by origination, actual origination—not the transition from the universal to the individual, but the origination of one determinate corporeal, not from its principle, but from the opposite as such. Aristotle does not consider the universal as it contains the negative within it; else the universal would be the absolute matter whose universality, as negativity, is set forth, or is real.

From this point Aristotle comes (De Cœlo, IV. 1—5) to

a kind of deduction of the elements, which is noteworthy. He shows that there must be four of them, in the following way—because he starts from the fundamental conceptions of weight and of lightness, or what we should call attraction and centrifugal force. The corporeal, he says, in its motion is neither light nor heavy, and, indeed, it is not only relative but also absolute. The relatively light and heavy is what, while equal in volume, descends more slowly or quickly. Absolute lightness goes up to the extremity of the heavens, absolute weight down into the middle. These extremes are fire and earth. Between these there are mediums, other than they, which relate to one another like them; and these are air and water, the one of which has weight, and the other lightness, but only relatively. For water is suspended under everything except earth, and air over everything except fire. " Hence," Aristotle concludes, " there now are these four matters, but they are four in such a way that they have one in common; more particularly, because they arise out of one another, but exist as different." Yet it is not the ether that Aristotle designates as this common matter. We must in this regard remark that however little these first determinations may be exhaustive, Aristotle is still far further on than the moderns, since he had not the conception of elements which prevails at the present time, according to which the element is made to subsist as simple. But any such simple determination of Being is an abstraction and has no reality, because such existence would be capable of no motion and change; the element must itself have reality, and it thus is, as the union of opposites, resolvable. Aristotle hence makes the elements, as we have already seen with those who went before (Vol. I., pp. 181, 182; 290—293; 336), arise out of one another and pass into one another; and this is entirely opposed to our Physics, which understands by elements an indelible, self-identical simplicity only. Hence men are wonderfully discerning in reproaching us for calling water, air, &c., elements ! Nor yet in the expression "neutrality" have the modern physicists been able to grasp a universality conceived of as a unity, such as Aristotle ascribes to the elements; in fact, however, the acid which unites with a base is no longer, as is asserted, present within it as such. But however removed Aristotle may be from understanding simplicity as an abstraction, just as little does he recognize here the arid conception of consisting of parts. Quite the contrary. He strives enough against this, as, for instance, in relation to Anaxagoras (De Cœl. III. 4).

I shall further mention the moments of the real process in relation to motion, in which Aristotle finally passes on (De gen. et corr. II. 2—4) to the "principles of perceptible body"; we here see the elements in process, as formerly in their restful determinateness. Aristotle excludes the relations which concern sight, smell, &c., and brings forward the others as being those which are of sensible weight or lightness. He gives as these fundamental principles— warmth and cold, dryness and moisture ; they are the sensible differences for others, while weight and lightness are different for themselves. Now in order to prepare for the transition of the elements into sensible relations, Aristotle says : "Because there are those four principles, and four things have properly six relations to one another, but the opposite cannot here be connected (the moist cannot be connected with the dry, or the warm with the cold), there are four connections of these principles, warm and dry, warm and moist, cold and moist, cold and dry. And these connections follow those first elements, so that thus fire is warm and dry, air warm and moist (vapour), water cold and moist, earth cold and dry." From this Aristotle now makes the reciprocal transformation of the elements into one another comprehensible thus : Origination and decay proceed from the opposite and into the opposite. All elements have a mutual opposite ; each is as non-being to the Being of the other, and one is thus distinguished from the

other as actuality and capacity.   Now amongst these some
have an equal part in common ; fire and water, for example,
have warmth ; thus if in fire dryness were overcome by
moisture, out of fire air would arise.   On the contrary, as
regards those which have nothing in common with one
another, like earth, which is cold and dry, and air, which is
warm and moist, the transition goes more slowly forward.
The transition of all elements into one another, the whole
process of nature, is thus to Aristotle the constant rotation
of their changes.   This is unsatisfactory, because neither
are the individual elements comprehended nor is the
remainder rounded into a whole.

As a matter of fact, Aristotle now goes on, in meteorology,
to the consideration of the universal process of nature.
But here we have reached his limits. Here, in the natural
process, the simple determination as such—this system of
progressive determination—ceases to hold good, and its
whole interest is lost.   For it is in the real process that these
determinate conceptions always lose their signification again
and become their opposite, and in it also this contingent
succession is forced together and united.   In determining
time and motion, we certainly saw Aristotle himself uniting
opposite determinations; but movement, in its true determination, must take space and time back into itself ; it
must represent itself as being the unity of these its real
moments and in them ; that is, as the realization of this ideal.
But still more must the following moments, moisture,
warmth, &c., themselves come back under the conception
of process.   But the sensuous manifestation here begins to
obtain the upper hand ; for the empirical has the nature of
the isolated form, which is to fall out of relation.   The
empirical manifestation thus outstrips thought, which merely
continues everywhere to stamp it as its own, but which has
no longer power to permeate the manifestation, since it
withdraws out of the sphere of the ideal, while it is still in
the region of time, space and movement.

3. The Philosophy of Mind.

As regards the other side from the Philosophy of Nature, the Philosophy of Mind, we find that Aristotle has constituted in it also a separation into special sciences, in a series of works which I shall name. In the first place, his three books "On the Soul" deal partly with the abstract universal nature of the soul, though mainly in an antagonistic spirit; and even more, and in a fashion both profound and speculative, they deal with the soul's essential nature—not with its Being, but with the determinate manner and potentiality of its energy; for this is to Aristotle the Being and essence of the soul. Thus there are several different treatises, viz.: On Sense-perception and the Sensible, On Memory and Recollection, On Sleeping and Waking, On Dreams, On Divination ($\mu\alpha\nu\tau\iota\kappa\acute{\eta}$) through Dreams, besides a treatise on Physiognomy; there is no empirical point of view or phenomenon, either in the natural or the spiritual world, that Aristotle has considered beneath his notice. With respect to the practical side, he in like manner devotes his attention to man in his capacity of householder, in a work on economics ($o\grave{\iota}\kappa o\nu o\mu\iota\kappa\acute{a}$); then he takes into his consideration the individual human being, in a moral treatise ($\acute{\eta}\theta\iota\kappa\acute{a}$), which is partly an inquiry into the highest good or the absolute end, and partly a dissertation on special virtues. The manner of treatment is almost invariably speculative, and sound understanding is displayed throughout. Finally, in his Politics, he gives a representation of the true constitution of a state and the different kinds of constitution, which he deals with from the empirical point of view; and in his Polities an account is given of the most important states, of which we are, however, told very little.

a. Psychology.

In Aristotle's teaching on this subject we must not expect to find so-called metaphysics of the soul. For metaphysical handling such as this really presupposes the soul as a thing, and asks, for example, what sort of a thing it is, whether it is simple, and so on. Aristotle did not busy his concrete, speculative mind with abstract questions such as these, but, as already remarked, he deals rather with the manner of the soul's activity; and though this appears in a general way as a series of progressive determinations which are not necessarily blended into a whole, each determination is yet apprehended in its own sphere with as much correctness as depth.

Aristotle (De Anima, I. 1) makes in the first place the general remark that it appears as if the soul must, on the one hand, be regarded in its freedom as independent and as separable from the body, since in thinking it is independent ; and, on the other hand, since in the emotions it appears to be united with the body and not separate, it must also be looked on as being inseparable from it ; for the emotions show themselves as materialized Notions (λόγοι ἔνυλοι), as material modes of what is spiritual. With this a twofold method of considering the soul, also known to Aristotle, comes into play, namely the purely rational or logical view, on the one hand, and, on the other hand, the physical or physiological; these we still see practised side by side. According to the one view, anger, for instance, is looked on as an eager desire for retaliation or the like ; according to the other view it is the surging upward of the heart-blood and the warm element in man. The former is the rational, the latter the material view of anger; just as one man may define a house as a shelter against wind, rain, and other destructive agencies, while another defines it as consisting of wood and stone ; that is to say, the former gives the determination and the form, or the purpose of the thing, while the latter specifies the material it is made of, and its necessary conditions.

Aristotle characterizes the nature of the soul more closely (De Anima, II. 1) by referring to the three moments of

existence : " First there is matter (ὕλη), which is in itself
no individual thing ; secondly, the form and the universal
(μορφὴ καὶ εἶδος), which give a thing individuality ; thirdly,
the result produced by both, in which matter is potentiality
and form is energy (ἐντελέχεια) ; " matter thus does not exist
as matter, but only implicitly. "The soul is substance, as
being the form of the physical organic body which is
possessed potentially of life; but its substance is energy
(ἐντελέχεια), the energy of a body such as has been described " (endowed with life). "This energy appears in
twofold form : either as knowledge (ἐπιστήμη) or as active
observation (τὸ θεωρεῖν). But it is evident that here it is
to be regarded as the former of these. For the soul is
present with us both when we sleep and when we wake ;
waking corresponds with active observation, and sleep with
possession and passivity. But knowledge is in origination
prior to all else. The soul is thus the first energy of a
physical but organic body." It is in respect of this that
Aristotle gives to the soul the definition of being the
entelechy (*supra*, pp. 143, 144).

In the same chapter Aristotle comes to the question
of the mutual relation of body and soul: "For this
reason " (because soul is form) "we must no more ask
if soul and body are one than we ask if wax and its
form are one, or, in general, if matter and its forms are
one. For though unity and Being are used in various
senses, Being is essentially energy." Were we, namely,
to pronounce body and soul one in the same way that
a house, which consists of a number of parts, or as a
thing and its properties, or the subject and predicate, and
so on, are called one, where both are regarded as things,
materialism results. An identity such as this is an altogether abstract, and therefore a superficial and empty
determination, and a term which it is a mistake to employ,
for form and material do not rank equally as regards Being ;
identity truly worthy of the name is to be apprehended as

nothing else than energy such as has been described. The only question that now arises is whether activity and the organ it employs are one ; and our idea is to answer in the affirmative. The more definite explanation of this relation is to be found in the following : " The soul is substance, but only according to the Notion (κατὰ τὸν λόγον) ; but that is the substantial form (τὸ τί ἦν εἶναι) [1] for such and such a body. For suppose that an instrument, such as an axe, were a natural body, this form, this axehood, would be its substance, and this its form would be its soul, for if this were to be taken away from it, it would no longer be an axe, the name only would remain. But soul is not the substantial form and Notion of such a body as an axe, but of a body which has within itself the principle of movement and of rest." The axe has not the principle of its form in itself, it does not make itself an axe, nor does its form, its Notion, in itself constitute its substance, as its activity is not through itself. " If, for instance, the eye were in itself a living thing, vision would be its soul, for vision is the reality which expresses the Notion of the eye. But the eye, as such, is only the material instrument of vision, for if vision were lost, the eye would be an eye only in name, like an eye of stone or a painted eye." Thus to the question, What is the substance of the eye? Aristotle answers : Are the nerves, humours, tissues, its substance? On the contrary, sight itself is its substance, these material substances are only an empty name. " As this is the case in the part, so it also holds good of the body as a whole. The potentiality of life is not in any such thing as has lost its soul, but in that which still possesses it. The seed or the fruit is such and such a body potentially. Like hewing and seeing," in the axe and the

---

[1] The editor has considered himself justified in adopting this rendering, which was commonly used by the Scholastics, and revived by Leibnitz. (Cf. Michelet, Examen Critique, &c., pp. 165, 261, 265.)

eye, "waking" in general "is activity; but the corporeal is only potentiality. But as the" living "eye is both vision and the eyeball" (the two being connected as actuality and potentiality), "so also are soul and body the living animal, the two are not to be separated. But it is not yet clear whether the soul is the activity of the body in the same way as the steersman is of the ship." That the active form is the true substance, while matter is so only potentially, is a true speculative Notion.

As settling the question asked in the above-mentioned metaphor, we may quote what Aristotle says later (De Anima, II. 4) : " As the principle of motion and as end (οὗ ἕνεκα), and as substance of living bodies, the soul is the cause. For substance is to all objects the cause of their existence, but life is the existence of the living, and its cause and principle is the soul; and further, its energy is the existing Notion of what has potential existence. The soul is cause also as end," that is, as self-determining universality, " for nature, like thought, acts for the sake of an object, which object is its end, but in living beings this is soul. All the parts of the body are thus the organs of the soul, and hence exist for its sake." In like manner Aristotle shows that the soul is the cause of motion.

Aristotle (De Anima, II. 2, 3) further states that the soul is to be determined in three ways, namely as nutrient or vegetable, as sensitive, and as intelligent, corresponding with plant life, animal life and human life. The nutrient soul, when it is alone, belongs to plants ; when it is at the same time capable of sense-perception, it is the animal soul ; and when at once nutrient, sensitive and intelligent, it is the mind of man. Man has thus three natures united in himself ; a thought which is also expressed in modern Natural Philosophy by saying that a man is also both an animal and a plant, and which is directed against the division and separation of the differences in these forms. That difference has also been revived in recent times in the observation of the organic, and it is highly important to keep these sides separate. The only question (and it is Aristotle who raises it) is how far these, as parts, are separable. As to what concerns more nearly the relation of the three souls, as they may be termed (though they are incorrectly thus distinguished), Aristotle says of them, with perfect truth, that we need look for no one soul in which all these are found, and which in a definite and simple form is conformable with any one of them. This is a profound observation, by means of which truly speculative thought marks itself out from the thought which is merely logical and formal. Similarly among figures only the triangle and the other definite figures, like the square, the parallelogram, &c., are truly anything; for what is common to them, the universal figure, is an empty thing of thought, a mere abstraction. On the other hand, the triangle is the first, the truly universal figure, which appears also in the square, &c., as the figure which can be led back to the simplest determination. Therefore, on the one hand, the triangle stands alongside of the square, pentagon, &c., as a particular figure, but—and this is Aristotle's main contention —it is the truly universal figure. In the same way the soul must not be sought for as an abstraction, for in the animate being the nutritive and the sensitive soul are included in the intelligent, but only as its object or its potentiality; similarly, the nutritive soul, which constitutes the nature of plants, is also present in the sensitive soul, but likewise only as being implicit in it, or as the universal. Or the lower soul inheres only in the higher, as a predicate in a subject: and this mere ideal is not to be ranked very high, as is indeed the case in formal thought; that which is for itself is, on the contrary, the never-ceasing return into itself, to which actuality belongs. We can determine these expressions even more particularly. For if we speak of soul and body, we term the corporeal the objective and the soul the subjective; and the misfortune of nature is just this, that it is objective, that is, it is the Notion only implicitly, and not explicitly. In the natural there is, no doubt, a certain activity, but again this whole sphere is only the objective, the implicit element in one higher. As, moreover, the implicit in its sphere appears as a reality for the development of the Idea, it has two sides; the universal is already itself an actual, as, for example, the vegetative soul. Aristotle's meaning is therefore this: an empty universal is that which does not itself exist, or is not itself species. All that is universal is in fact real, as particular, individual, existing for another. But that universal is real, in that by itself, without further change, it constitutes its first species, and when further developed it belongs, not to this, but to a higher stage. These are the general determinations which are of the greatest importance, and which, if developed, would lead to all true views of the organic, &c., since they give a correct general representation of the principle of realization.

a. The nutritive or vegetative soul is therefore, according to Aristotle (De Anima, II. 4), to be conceived as the first, which is energy, the general Notion of the soul itself, just as it is, without further determination; or, as we should say, plant life is the Notion of the organic. What Aristotle goes on to say of nourishment, for instance, whether the like is nourished by the like, or by the opposite, is of little importance. It may, however, be mentioned that Aristotle (De Anima, II. 12) says of the vegetative soul that it is related only to matter, and that only after a material manner, as when we eat and drink, but that it cannot take up into itself the forms of sensible things: we, too, ourselves in practical matters are related as particular individuals to a material existence here and now, in which our own material existence comes into activity.

β. There is more to interest us in Aristotle's determination of sense-perception (De Anima, II. 5), as to which I shall make some further quotations. Sense-perception

is in general a potentiality (we should say a receptivity),
but this potentiality is also activity; it is therefore not
to be conceived as mere passivity.   Passivity and activity
pertain to one and the same, or passivity has two senses.
" On the one hand a passivity is the destruction of one
state by its opposite ; on the other hand, it is a preservation
of what is merely potential by means of what is actual."
The one case occurs in the acquisition of knowledge, which
is a passivity in so far as a change takes place from one
condition ($\xi\xi\iota\varsigma$) into an opposite condition; but there is
another passivity, in which something only potentially
posited is maintained, therefore knowledge is knowing in
an active sense (*supra*, p. 182).   From this Aristotle concludes : " There is one change which is privative ; and
another which acts on the nature and the permanent
energy ($\xi\xi\iota\varsigma$).   The first change in the subject of perception ($\alpha i\sigma\theta\eta\tau\iota\kappa o\hat{v}$) is caused by that which produces the
perception ; but, once produced, the perception is possessed
as knowledge ($\epsilon\pi\iota\sigma\tau\eta\mu\eta$)."   Because that which produces
the change is different from the result, perception is pas-
sivity ; but it is just as much spontaneity, " and sense-
perception, like knowledge ($\theta\epsilon\omega\rho\epsilon\hat{\iota}\nu$), has to do with this
aspect of activity.   But the difference is, that what causes
the perception is external.   The cause of this is that perceptive activity is directed on the particular, while knowledge has as its object the universal ; but the universal is,
to a certain extent, in the soul itself as its substance.
Everyone can therefore think when he will," and for this
very reason thought is free, " but perception does not
depend on him, having the necessary condition that the
object perceived be present."   The influence from without,
as a passivity, comes therefore first ; but there follows the
activity of making this passive content one's own.   This is
doubtless the correct point from which to view perception,
whatever be the manner of further development preferred,
subjective idealism, or any other way.   For it is a matter

of perfect indifference whether we find ourselves subjectively or objectively determined; in both there is contained the moment of passivity, by which the perception comes to pass. The monad of Leibnitz appears, it is true, to be an idea opposed to this, since every monad, every point of my finger, as atom or individual, is an entire universe, the whole of which develops in itself without reference to other monads. Here seems to be asserted the highest idealistic freedom, but it is of no avail to imagine that all in me develops out of me; for we must always recollect that what is thus developed in me is passive, and not free. With this moment of passivity Aristotle does not fall short of idealism; sensation is always in one aspect passive. That is, however, a false idealism which thinks that the passivity and spontaneity of the mind depend on whether the determination given is from within or from without, as if there were freedom in sense-perception, whereas it is itself a sphere of limitation. It is one thing when the matter—whether it be sensation, light, colour, seeing or hearing—is apprehended from the Idea, for it is then shown that it comes to pass from the self-determination of the Idea. But it is different when, in so far as I exist as an individual subject, the Idea exists in me as this particular individual ; there we have the standpoint of finitude established, and therefore of passivity. Thus there need be no standing on ceremony with sense-perception, nor can a system of idealism be based on the theory that nothing comes to us from without: as Fichte's theory about himself was, that when he put on his coat, he constituted it in part by drawing it on, or even by looking at it. The individual element in sensation is the sphere of the individuality of consciousness; it is present therein in the form of one thing as much as of another, and its individuality consists in this fact, that other things exist for it. Aristotle continues: " Speaking generally, the difference is that potentiality is twofold; as we say a boy may become a general, and a grown man may also become so," for the latter has the effective power. "This is the nature of the faculty of sense-perception (αἰσθητικόν); it is in potentiality what the object of sense (αἰσθητόν) is in actuality. Sense-perception is therefore passive, in so far as it does not resemble its object, but after the impression has been made it becomes similar to its object, and is identified with it." The reaction of sense-perception consists therefore in this active receiving into itself of that which is perceived ; but this is simply activity in passivity, the spontaneity which abrogates the' receptivity in sense-perception. Sense-perception, as made like to itself, has, while appearing to be brought to pass by means of an influence working on it, brought to pass the identity of itself and its object. If then subjective idealism declares that there are no external things, that they are but a determination of our self, this must be admitted in respect to pure sense-perception, since sense-perception is a subjective existence or state in me, which yet, however, is not for that reason freedom.

In speaking of sense-perception, Aristotle (De Anima, II. 12) makes use of his celebrated simile, which has so often occasioned misapprehension, because it has been understood quite incorrectly. His words are : " Sense-perception is the receiving of sensible forms without matter, as wax receives only the impress of the golden signet ring, not the gold itself, but merely its form." For the form is the object as universal ; and theoretically we are in the position, not of the individual and sensuous, but of the universal. The case is different with us in our practical relations, where the influence working upon us pre-supposes in return the contact of the material, for which reason, as Aristotle asserts, plants do not perceive (*supra*, p. 186). On the other hand, in receiving form, the material is lost sight of ; for the receiving of form indicates no positive relation to the matter, which is no longer something offering resistance. If, therefore, sense-perceptions are termed in general sensuous impressions, we, in matter-of-fact fashion, do not get beyond this crude way of putting it; and in making the transition to soul, we take refuge behind popular conceptions, which are partly ill-defined Notions, and partly not Notions at all. Thus it is said that all sense-perceptions are impressed on the soul by external things, just as the matter of the signet ring works on the matter of the wax; and then we hear it alleged that this is Aristotle's philosophy. It is the same with most other philosophers; if they give any sort of illustration that appeals to the senses, everyone can understand it, and everyone takes the content of the comparison in its full extent: as if all that is contained in this sensuous relationship should also hold good of the spiritual. No great importance is therefore to be attached to this conception, as it is only an illustration, professing to show by a side comparison that the passive element in sense-perception is in its passivity for pure form only; this form alone is taken up into the percipient subject, and finds a place in the soul. It does not, however, remain in the same relation to it as that in which the form stands to the wax, nor is it as in chemistry where one element is permeated by another as regards its matter. The chief circumstance, therefore, and that which constitutes the difference between this illustration and the condition of the soul is altogether overlooked. That is to say, the wax does not, indeed, take in the form, for the impression remains on it as external figure and contour, without being a form of its real Being; if it were to become such, it would cease to be wax; therefore, because in the illustration there is lacking this reception of form into the Being, no thought is given to it. The soul, on the contrary, assimilates this form into its own substance, and for the very reason, that the soul is in itself, to a certain extent, the sum of all that is perceived by the senses (*infra,* p. 198): as it was said above (p. 183), if the axe had its form in the determination of substance, this form would be the soul of the axe. The illustration of the wax has reference to nothing but the fact that only the form comes to the soul ; and has nothing to do with the form being external to the wax and remaining so, or with the soul having, like wax, no independent form. The soul is by no means said to be passive wax and to receive its determinations from without ; but Aristotle, as we shall soon see (p. 194), really says that the spirit repels matter from itself, and maintains itself against it, having relation only to form. In sense-perception the soul is certainly passive, but the manner in which it receives is not like that of the wax, being just as truly activity of the soul ; for after the perceptive faculty has received the impression, it abrogates the passivity, and remains thenceforth free from it (supra, p. 187). The soul therefore changes the form of the external body into its own, and is identical with an abstract quality such as this, for the sole reason that it itself is this universal form.

This description of sense-perception Aristotle explains more fully in what follows (De Anima, III. 2), and expatiates upon this unity and its contrasts, in the course of which explanation there appear many clear and far-reaching glimpses into the Nature of consciousness. " The bodily organ of each sense-perception receives the object perceived without matter. Hence, when the object of sense is removed, the perceptions and the images which represent them remain in the organs. In the act of sense-perception the object perceived is no doubt identical with the subject that perceives, but they do not exist [1] as the same; for instance, sound and the hearing are the same when in active

---

[1] Here and once again on this page τὸ εἶναι is the immediate existence of the separate sides of sense-perception, therefore their mere potentiality ; while, on the other hand, the active unity of the perceived and the percipient may be expressed as the true Notion of sense-perception.—[Editor's Note.]

exercise, but that which has hearing does not always hear, and that which has sound is not always sounding. When that which is the potentiality of hearing comes into exercise, and likewise that which is the potentiality of sound, hearing and sound, being in full activity, coincide," they do not remain separate energies. " If then movement and action, as well as passivity, have a place in the object on which activity is exercised (ἐν τῷ ποιουμένῳ), it follows necessarily that the energy of hearing and sound is contained in that which potentially is hearing, for the energy of the active and moving is in the passive. As therefore activity and passivity are manifested in the subject which receives the effect, and not in the object which produces it (ποιοῦντι), the energy both of the object and of the faculty of sense-perception is in the faculty itself. For hearing and sounding there are two words, for seeing only one ; seeing is the activity of the person who sees, but the activity of the colour is without name. Since the energy of that which is perceived and that which perceives is one energy, and the aspect they present is alone different, the so-called sounding and hearing must cease simultaneously." There is a body which sounds and a subject which hears ; they are twofold in the aspect they present, but hearing, taken by itself, is intrinsically an activity of both. In like manner, when I have by sense the perception of redness and hardness, my perception is itself red and hard : that is, I find myself determined in that way, even though reflection says that outside of me there is a red, hard thing, and that it and my finger are two ; but they are also one, my eye is red and the thing. It is upon this difference and this identity that everything depends ; and Aristotle demonstrates this in the most emphatic way, and holds firmly to his point. The later distinction of subjective and objective is the reflection of consciousness ; sense-perception is simply the abrogation of this separation, it is that form of identity which abstracts from subjectivity and objectivity. What is simple, the soul

proper or the I, is in sense-perception unity in difference.
"Further, every sense-perception is in its organ, and distinguishes everything that is perceived, like black and white,
and so on. It is thus not possible for separate perceptions,
white and sweet, to be distinguished as separate indifferent
moments, for both must be present (δῆλα) to one subject.
This one subject must therefore determine one thing to be
different from another. This, as distinguished, can also not be
in a different place or time, for it must be undivided and in
undivided time. But it is impossible that one and the same
thing should be affected by contrary movements, in so far
as it is undivided and in undivided time. If sweetness
affects sense-perception in one way, and bitterness in the
contrary way, and whiteness in yet another way, the power
of judging is numerically not discrete nor divisible, but
according to the Notion (τῷ εἶναι) [1] it is distinguished. That
which is the same and indivisible thus possesses in potentiality opposite qualities; but with its true existence (τῷ
εἶναι) that cannot be the case, for in its activity it is separable, and cannot at the same time be both white and black.
Sense-perception and thinking are like that which some term
a point, which, in so far as it is one, is inseparable, and
in so far as it is two, is separable. So far as it is undivided, the judging faculty is one and acts in a single point
of time, but so far as it is divided " (not one) " it employs the
same sign twice simultaneously. So far as it employs two,
it by limitation distinguishes two, and separates them as
having separate origin ; but so far as it is one, it judges by
one act in one single point of time" (*supra*, p. 172). For as

---

[1] *Cf. supra*, p. 169, and note there given. The two significations of
τὸ εἶναι here come into immediate contact with one another, being
likewise intermingled ; for immediate existence (ἀριθμῷ ἀδιαίρετον καὶ
ἀχώριστον), which is opposed to the Notion (τῷ εἶναι) becomes in what
directly follows mere possibility, to which the true reality (τὸ εἶναι) i‹
opposed (δυνάμει μὲν γὰρ τὸ αὐτὸ καὶ ἀδιαίρετον τἀναντία, τῷ δ᾽εἶναι ι.δ,
ἀλλα τῷ ἐνεργεῖσθαι διαίρετον).—[Editor's Note.]

the point in time, which resembles the point in space, contains future and past, and thus is something different and at the same time one and the same, since it is in one and the same respect separation and union ; sense-perception is also one and at the same time separation, separated and not separated, seeing that the faculty of perception has before it in one unity the distinct sense-perception, which by this means receives for the first time a determinate content. Another example is that of number ; one and two are different, and, at the same time, even in two one is used and posited as one.

γ. From sense-perception Aristotle passes on to thought, and becomes here really speculative. "Thinking," he says (De Anima, III. 4) " is not passive (ἀπαθές), but receptive of the form, and is in potentiality similar to it. Therefore the understanding (νοῦς), because it thinks all things, is free from all admixture (ἀμιγής), in order that it may overcome (κρατῇ), as Anaxagoras says, that is, in order that it may acquire knowledge ; for, coming forth in its energy (παρεμφαινόμενον), it holds back what is alien to it, and fortifies itself against it (ἀντιφράττει). Therefore the nature of the understanding is none other than this potentiality." But potentiality itself is here not matter ; that is to say, the understanding has no matter, for potentiality pertains to its very substance. For thinking is really the not being implicit ; and on account of its purity its reality is not the being-for-another, but its potentiality is itself a being-for-self. A thing is real because it is this determinate thing ; the opposite determination, its potentiality to be, for instance, smoke, ashes, and so on, is not posited in it. In the corporeal, therefore, matter, as potentiality, and external form, as reality, are opposed to one another ; but the soul is, in contrast with this, universal potentiality itself, without matter, because its essence is energy. "Understanding, then, in the soul, as that which possesses consciousness, is nothing in reality before it thinks ;" it is absolute activity, but exists only when it is active. "It is therefore not incorporated with the body. For what should it be like, warm or cold? Or should it be an organ? But it is none of these. That it is, however, different from the faculty of sense-perception is clear. For sense-perception cannot perceive after a violent perception; for instance, it cannot smell nor see after experiencing strong smells or colours. But the understanding, after it has thought something which can only be thought with difficulty, will not have more but less difficulty in thinking of something that is easier. For there is no sense-perception independent of the body, but the understanding is separable from it. When it has then become something individual, like him who is really possessed of a faculty of knowing (and this happens when he can energize through himself), it then is also in a certain degree according to potentiality, but yet not so in the same manner as it was before learning and finding." (*Cf. supra*, pp. 182, 187.)

Thinking makes itself into passive understanding, that is, into what is for it the objective; and thus it here becomes plain to what extent the dictum *nihil est in intellectu quod non fuerit in sensu* expresses Aristotle's meaning. Aristotle, raising difficulties, goes on to ask, "If reason is simple and unaffected by impressions, and has nothing in common with other objects, how can it think, since thinking is certainly a state of receptivity?" That is to say, in thinking there is a reference to an object distinct from itself. "For it is when two objects have something in common that the one appears to produce and the other to receive an impression. There is a further difficulty, whether understanding can itself be the object of thought. In that case understanding would either be inherent in other things—unless it is the object of thought in a different sense from that in which other things are so, but there is only one sense in which things can be objects of thought—or, on the other hand, it would have something compounded with it, making it an object of thought as other things are. Now it has been already said that passivity is so determined that understanding is in potentiality all that thought is exercised on : but at the same time it is in actuality nothing before the exercise of thought." That is to say, thought is implicitly the content of the object of what is thought, and in coming into existence it only coincides with itself; but the self-conscious understanding is not merely implicit, but essentially explicit, since it is within itself all things. That is an idealistic way of expressing it; and yet they say that Aristotle is an empiricist.

The passivity of understanding has therefore here only the sense of potentiality before actuality, and that is the great principle of Aristotle; in regard to this he brings forward at the end of the same chapter another much-decried illustration, which has been just as much misunderstood as the preceding. "Reason is like a book upon whose pages nothing is actually written;" that is, however, paper, but not a book. All Aristotle's thoughts are overlooked, and only external illustrations such as this are comprehended. A book on which nothing is written everyone can understand. And the technical term is the well-known *tabula rasa*, which is to be found wherever Aristotle is spoken of : Aristotle is said to have alleged that the mind is a blank page, on which characters are first traced by external objects, so that thinking thus comes to it from without.[1] But that is the very opposite of what Aristotle says. Instead of the Notion being adhered to, casual comparisons such as these have been caught up here and there by the imagination, as if they expressed the matter itself. But Aristotle did not in the least intend that the analogy should be pushed to its furthest extent : the understanding is of a surety not a thing, and has not

[1] Cf. Tenneman, Vol. III. p. 198.

the passivity of a writing-tablet; it is itself the energy,
which is not, as it would be in the case of a tablet, external
to it. The analogy is therefore confined to this, that the
soul has a content only in so far as actual thought is
exercised. The soul is this book unwritten on, and the
meaning consequently is that the soul is all things
implicitly, but it is not in itself this totality; it is like a
book that contains all things potentially, but in reality
contains nothing before it is written on. Before real
activity nothing truly exists; or "Understanding itself can
enter thought, like the objects of thought in general. For
in that which is without matter" (in mind), "the thinker"
(the subjective) "and the thought" (the objective) "are
the same; theoretical knowledge and that which comes
to be known are the same. In that which is material,
thinking is only in potentiality, so that understanding itself
does not belong to it; for understanding is a potentiality
without matter, but the object of thought exists in it,"
while Nature contains the Idea only implicitly. It is plain
from this that the above illustration has been taken in
quite a false sense, utterly contrary to Aristotle's meaning.

Until now we have spoken of the passive understanding,
which is the nature of the soul, but also in equal degree
its faculty of sense-perception and imagination. Aristotle
now proceeds to distinguish active understanding from this,
as follows (De Anima, III. 5) : "In nature as a whole there
is present in every species of things, on the one hand,
matter, which in potentiality is the whole of this species,
and, on the other hand, cause and energy, operative in all
things, in the same way that art is related to matter. It
therefore necessarily follows that in the soul also these
different elements should be present. The faculty of
understanding is thus, in one view of it, the capacity of
becoming all things; but in another view it is the capacity
of creating all things, as is done by an efficient power ($\xi\xi\iota\varsigma$),
light, for instance, which first causes the colours which exist

in potentiality to exist in reality. This understanding is absolute (χωριστός), uncompounded, and not influenced from without, as it is essentially activity. For the active is always more in honour than the passive, and the principle more in honour than the matter that it forms. Knowledge, when in active exercise, is identical with the thing (πρᾶγμα) known; but what is in potentiality" (that is, external reason, imagination, sense-perception) "is certainly prior in respect of time in one and the same individual, but in the universal (ὅλως) it is not even so in respect of time. Active understanding is not such that it sometimes thinks and sometimes does not. When it is absolute, it is the one and only existence; and this alone is eternal and immortal. We, however, do not remember this process, because this understanding is unaffected from without; but the passive understanding is transitory, and without the former it is incapable of thought."

The seventh and eighth chapters are expositions of the maxims contained in the fourth and fifth; they begin with these maxims, and have the appearance of being from the hand of a commentator. "The soul," says Aristotle (De Anima, III. 8), "is in a certain sense the whole of existence. For existent objects are either perceived by the senses or thought; but knowledge itself is in a manner the object of knowledge, and perception the object of perception." What are known and perceived are either the things themselves or their forms. Knowledge and sense-perception are not the things themselves (the stone is not in the soul), but their form; so that the soul is like the hand. As this is the instrument by which we grasp instruments, so the understanding is the form by which we apprehend forms, and sense-perception the form of the objects of sense." Before this Aristotle had remarked (De Anima, III. 4): "It has been truly said that the soul is the *place of ideas* (τόπος εἰδῶν): not the whole soul, but only the thinking soul, and these ideas do not exist in the soul actually, but only potentially." That is to say, the ideas are at first only quiescent forms, not activities, and so Aristotle is not a realist. But the understanding makes these forms, like those of external nature, its objects, its thoughts, its potentiality. Aristotle therefore says in the seventh chapter : "The understanding thinks the abstract (τὰ ἐν ἀφαιρέσει λεγόμενα), just as it conceives snubnosedness not as snubnosedness that cannot be separated from the flesh, but as hollowness." Then in the eighth chapter Aristotle goes on to say : "But as no object is separated from its perceived dimensions, so in the forms perceived by sense there are also objects of thought, both abstract conceptions and the qualities (ἕξεις) and determinations of the objects of sense. In this way he who perceives nothing by his senses learns nothing and understands nothing; when he discerns anything (θεωρῇ), he must necessarily discern it as a pictorial conception, for such conceptions are like sense-perceptions, only without matter. In what way then are our primary ideas distinguished, so as not to be mistaken for conceptions? Or is it not the case also that other thoughts even are not pictorial conceptions, but only that they are never found unassociated with such conceptions?" Since what follows contains no answer to the questions raised here at the very end, this would seem an additional indication that these portions follow later.[1] Aristotle concludes the seventh chapter with the words : "Speaking generally, the understanding is the faculty

[1] While Aristotle's reply is short, and given in the manner usually adopted by him, that of following up by a second question the first question proposed (ἢ οὐδὲ τἆλλα φαντάσματα, ἀλλ' οὐκ ἄνευ φαντασμάτων;), this answer seems quite sufficient. For Aristotle's words certainly bear the meaning that the original thoughts of the active understanding (the reason), in contradistinction to those of the passive understanding, have quite obliterated in themselves the element of pictorial conception; while in the latter this has not been thoroughly carried out, though even in them pictorial conception is not the essential moment.—[Editor's Note.]

which thinks things in their real activity. Whether, however, it can think the absolute or not, unless it be itself
separated from the sensuous, we shall inquire later (ὕστερον)."
This "later" Buhle considers to have reference to the
"highest philosophy." [1]

This identity of the subjective and objective, which
is present in the active understanding—while finite
things and mental states are respectively one separated
from the other, because there the understanding is
only in potentiality—is the highest point which speculation can reach : and in it Aristotle reverts to his metaphysical principles (p. 147), where he termed self-thinking
reason absolute Thought, divine Understanding, or Mind
in its absolute character. It is only in appearance that
thought is spoken of as on a level with what is other than
thought ; this fashion of bringing what is different into
conjunction certainly appears in Aristotle. But what he
says of thought is explicitly and absolutely speculative,
and is not on the same level with anything else, such as
sense-perception, which has only potentiality for thought.
This fact is moreover involved, that reason is implicitly the
true totality, but in that case thought is in truth the
activity which is independent and absolute existence ; that

---

[1] Against this we have only to remember that in Aristotle's way of
speaking ὕστερον and πρότερον always refer to the work they occur in,
while he marks quotations from his other writings by the words :
ἐν ἄλλοις, ἐν ἑτέροις, ἄλλοτε, or εἰς ἐκεῖνον τὸν καιρὸν ἀποκείσθω (De
Ausc. phys. I. 9). And if it be said, as it may be with truth, that
all the physical and psychological works, including the Metaphysics,
form one great scientific system, so that ὕστερον and πρότερον may
very well be used in relating these works to one another, I have yet
proved that the treatise περὶ ψυχῆς must be placed much later than
the Metaphysics (Michelet : Examen Critique, &c., pp. 209–222).
Might not then the expression ὕστερον refer to the following chapter ?
In truth, the difficulty raised at the end of the seventh chapter seems
completely solved by the words of the eighth chapter quoted above
(pp. 198, 199).—[Editor's Note.]

is, the thought of Thought, which is determined thus abstractly, but which constitutes the nature of absolute mind explicitly. These are the main points which are to be taken note of in Aristotle with regard to his speculative ideas, which it is impossible for us, however, to treat in greater detail.

We have now to pass on to what follows, which is a practical philosophy, and in doing so we must first establish firmly the conception of desire, which is really the turning round of thought into its negative side, wherein it becomes practical. Aristotle (De Anima, III. 7 and 6) says: "The object of knowledge and active knowledge are one and the same; what is in potentiality is in the individual prior in point of time, although not so in itself. For all that comes into being originates from that which operates actively. The object perceived by sense appears as that which causes the faculty of perception in potentiality to become the faculty of perception in actuality, for the latter is not receptive of influence, and does not undergo change. On that account it has a different kind of movement from the ordinary, for movement, as we have seen (p. 163) is the activity of an unaccomplished end (ἐνέργεια ἀτελοῦς); pure activity (ἁπλῶς ἐνέργεια), on the contrary, is that of the accomplished end (τοῦ τετελεσμένου)."—"The simple thoughts of the soul are such that in regard to them there can be no falsity; but that in which there is falsity or truth is a combination of thoughts as constituting one conception; for example, 'the diameter is incommensurate.' Or if by mistake white has been stated to be not white, not-white has been brought into connection with it. All this process may, however, just as well be termed separation. But that which makes everything one is reason, which in the form of its thinking thinks the undivided in undivided time and with the undivided action of the soul."—"Sense-perception resembles simple assertion and thought; but pleasant or unpleasant sense-perception has the relation of affirmation or negation," therefore of the positive and negative determination of thought. "And to perceive the pleasant or unpleasant is to employ the activity" (spontaneity)· "of the middle state of sense-perception upon good or evil, in so far as they are such. But desire and aversion are the same in energy ; it is only in manifestation that they are different. To the reasoning soul pictorial conceptions take the place of sense-perceptions, and when the mind affirms or denies something to be good or bad, it desires or avoids its object. It has the relation both of unity and limit. The understanding," as that which determines opposites, "recognizes the forms underlying pictorial conceptions; and in the same manner as what is desirable in them and what is to be avoided have been determined for it, so it also is determined independently of actual sense-perceptions when it is in mental conceptions. And when, in dealing with conception or thought, as if seeing them, it compares the future with the present and passes judgment accordingly, and determines what is pleasant or unpleasant in this respect; it desires or seeks to avoid it, and in general it finds itself in practical operation. But independently of action true and false are of the same character as good or evil."

b. Practical Philosophy.

From this the conception of will, or the practical element is shown to us, and it has to be reckoned as still belonging to the Philosophy of Mind. Aristotle has treated it in several works which we now possess.

a. Ethics.

We have three great ethical works : the Nicomachean Ethics (Ἠθικὰ Νικομάχεια) in ten books, the Magna Moralia (Ἠθικὰ μεγάλα) in two books, and the Eudemean

Ethics ('Hθικὰ Εὐδήμια) in seven books; the last deals for the most part with particular virtues, while in the first two general investigations on the principles are contained. Just as the best that we even now possess in reference to psychology is what we have obtained from Aristotle, so is it with his reflections on the actual agent in volition, on freedom, and the further determinations of imputation, intention, &c. We must simply give ourselves the trouble to understand these, and to translate them into our own form of speech, conception and thought; and this is certainly difficult. Aristotle follows the same course here as in his Physics, determining one after the other, in the most thorough and accurate fashion, the many moments which appear in desire: the purpose, the decision, voluntary or forced action, the act of ignorance, guilt, moral responsibility, &c. I cannot enter upon this somewhat psychological presentation of the subject.[1] I shall only make the following remarks on the Aristotelian definitions.

Aristotle[2] defines the principle of morality or the highest good, as happiness (εὐδαιμονία), which later on became a much disputed expression. It is good generally, not as abstract idea, but in such a way that the moment of realization is what actually answers to it. Aristotle thus does not content himself with the Platonic idea of the good, because it is only general; with him the question is taken in its determinateness. Aristotle then says that the good is what has its end in itself (τέλειον). If we tried to translate τέλειον by "perfect" here, we should translate it badly; it is that which, as having its end (τὸ τέλος) in itself, is not desired for the sake of anything else, but for its own sake (supra, pp. 162, 201). Aristotle determines happiness in this regard as the absolute end existing in and for itself, and

_____

[1] See Michelet, De doli et culpæ in jure criminali notionibus; System der philosophischen Moral. Book II. Part 1; Afzelius, Aristotelis De imputatione actionum doctrina.—[Editor's Note.]

[2] Ethic, Nicom. I. 2–12 (4–12); X. 6–8; Eth. Eudem. II. 1.

gives the following definition of it: It is "the energy of the life that has its end in itself in accordance with absolute virtue (ζωῆς τελείας ἐνέργεια κατ' ἀρετὴν τελείαν)." He makes rational insight an essential condition; all action arising from sensuous desires, or from lack of freedom generally, indicates lack of insight; it is an irrational action, or an action which does not proceed from thought as such. But the absolute rational activity is alone knowledge, the action which in itself satisfies itself, and this is hence divine happiness; with the other virtues, on the contrary, only human happiness is obtained, just as from a theoretic point of view feeling is finite as compared with divine thought. Aristotle goes on to say much that is good and beautiful about virtue and the good and happiness in general, and states that happiness, as the good attainable by us, is not to be found without virtue, &c.; in all of which there is no profound insight from a speculative point of view.

In regard to the conception of virtue I should like to say something more. From a practical point of view, Aristotle first of all distinguishes in soul a rational and an irrational side; in the latter reason only exists potentially; under it come the feelings, passions and affections. On the rational side understanding, wisdom, discretion, knowledge, have their place; but they still do not constitute virtue, which first subsists in the unity of the rational and the irrational sides. When the inclinations are so related to virtue that they carry out its dictates, this, according to Aristotle, is virtue. When the perception is either bad or altogether lacking, but the heart is good, good-will may be there, but not virtue, because the principle—that is reason—which is essential to virtue, is wanting. Aristotle thus places virtue in knowledge, yet reason is not, as many believe, the principle of virtue purely in itself, for it is rather the rational impulse towards what is good; both desire

---

[1] Magn. Moral. I. 5, 35; Eth. Nic. I. 13; Eth. Eud. II. 1.

and reason are thus necessary moments in virtue. Hence it cannot be said of virtue that it is misemployed, for it itself is the employer. Thus Aristotle, as we have already seen (Vol. I. pp. 412--414), blames Socrates, because he places virtue in perception alone. There must be an irrational impulse towards what is good, but reason comes in addition as that which judges and determines the impulse ; yet when a beginning from virtue has been made, it does not necessarily follow that the passions are in accordance, since often enough they are quite the reverse. Thus in virtue, because it has realization as its aim, and pertains to the individual, reason is not the solitary principle ; for inclination is the force that impels, the particular, which as far as the practical side of the individual subject is concerned, is what makes for realization. But then the subject must, in this separation of his activity, bring likewise his passions under the subjection of the universal, and this unity, in which the rational is pre-eminent, is virtue. This is the correct determination ; on the one hand this definition is opposed to these ideals of the utter subjection of the passions, by which men are guided from their youth up, and, on the other, it is opposed to the point of view that declares desires to be good in themselves. Both these extreme views have been frequent in modern times, just as sometimes we hear that the man who by nature is beauteous and noble, is better than he who acts from duty ; and then it is said that duty must be performed as duty, without taking into account the particular point of view as a moment of the whole.

Aristotle then passes through the particular virtues at great length. Because the virtues, considered as the union of the desiring or realizing with the rational, have an illogical moment within them, Aristotle places[1] their prin-

----

[1] Ethic. Nicomach. II. 5–7 (6, 7) ; Magn. Moral. I. 5–9 ; Eth. Eud. II. 3.

ciple on the side of feeling in a mean, so that virtue is
the mean between two extremes; *e.g.* liberality is the mean
between avarice and prodigality; gentleness between passion
and passive endurance; 'bravery between rashness and
cowardice; friendship between egotism and self-effacement,
&c. For the good, and specially that good which has to do
with the senses, which would suffer if affected to an excessive
degree (*supra*, p. 195), is therefore a mean, just because
the sensuous is an ingredient in it. This does not appear
to be a sufficient definition, and it is merely a quantitative
determination, just because it is not only the Notion that
determines, but the empirical side is also present. Virtue
is not absolutely determined in itself, but likewise has a
material element, the nature of which is capable of a more
or a less. Thus if it has been objected to Aristotle's definition of virtue as a difference in degree, that it is unsatisfactory and vague, we may say that this really is involved
in the nature of the thing. Virtue, and determinate virtue
in its entirety, enters into a sphere where that which is
quantitative has a place; thought here is no more as such at
home with itself, and the quantitative limit undetermined.
The nature of particular virtues is of such a kind, that they
are capable of no more exact determination; they can only
be spoken of in general, and for them there is no further
determination than just this indefinite one.[1] But in our
way of looking at things, duty is something absolutely existent in itself, and not a mean between existent extremes
through which it is determined; but this universal
likewise results in being empty, or rather undetermined,
while that determinate content is a moment of being that
immediately involves us in conflicting duties. It is in practice that man seeks a necessity in man as individual, and
endeavours to express it; but it is either formal, or as in
particular virtues, a definite content, which, in so being,
falls a prey to empiricism.

[1] Cf. Arist. Ethic. Nicom. I. 1 (3).

β. Politics.

We have still to speak of Aristotle's Politics ; he was conscious more or less that the positive substance, the necessary organization and realization of practical spirit, is the state, which is actualized through subjective activity, so that this last finds in it its determination and end. Aristotle hence also looks on political philosophy as the sum total of practical philosophy, the end of the state as general happiness. " All science and all capacity (δύναμις)," he says (Magn. Mor. I. 1), " have an end, and this is the good : the more excellent they are, the more excellent is their end ; but the most excellent capacity is the political, and hence its end is also the good." Of Ethics Aristotle recognizes that it indubitably also applies to the individual, though its perfection is attained in the nation as a whole. " Even if the highest good is the same for an individual and for a whole state, it would yet surely be greater and more glorious to win and maintain it for a state ; to do this for an individual were meritorious, but to do it for a nation and for whole states were more noble and god-like still. Such is the object of practical science, and this pertains in a measure to politics." [1]

Aristotle indeed appreciates so highly the state, that he starts at once (Polit. I. 2) by defining man as " a political animal, having reason. Hence he alone has a knowledge of good and evil, of justice and injustice, and not the beast," for the beast does not think, and yet in modern times men rest the distinction which exists in these determinations on sensation, which beasts have equally with men. There is also the sense of good and evil, &c., and Aristotle knows this aspect as well (*supra,* p. 202) ; but that through which it is not animal sensation merely, is thought. Hence rational perception is also to Aristotle the essential condition of virtue, and thus the harmony between the sensational

[1] Arist. Eth. Nic. I. 1 (2).

point of view and that of reason is an essential moment in his eudæmonism. After Aristotle so determines man, he says: "The common intercourse of these, forms the family and the state; in the understanding, however, that the state, in the order of nature" (*i.e.* in its Notion, in regard to reason and truth, not to time) "is prior to the family" (the natural relation, not the rational) "and to the individual among us." Aristotle does not place the individual and his rights first, but recognizes the state as what in its essence is higher than the individual and the family, for the very reason that it constitutes their substantiality. "For the whole must be prior to its parts. If, for example, you take away the whole body, there is not a foot or hand remaining, excepting in name, and as if anyone should call a hand of stone a hand; for a hand destroyed is like a hand of stone." If the man is dead, all the parts perish. "For everything is defined according to its energy and inherent powers, so that when these no longer remain such as they were, it cannot be said that anything is the same excepting in name. The state is likewise the essence of the individuals; the individual when separate from the whole, is just as little complete in himself as any other organic part separated from the whole." This is directly antagonistic to the modern principle in which the particular will of the individual, as absolute, is made the starting-point; so that all men by giving their votes, decide what is to be the law, and thereby a commonweal is brought into existence. But with Aristotle, as with Plato, the state is the *prius*, the substantial, the chief, for its end is the highest in respect of the practical. "But whoever was incapable of this society, or so complete in himself as not to want it, would be either a beast or a god."

From these few remarks it is clear that Aristotle could not have had any thought of a so-called natural right (if a natural right be wanted), that is, the idea of the abstract man outside of any actual relation to others. For the

rest, his Politics contain points of view even now full of
instruction for us, respecting the inward elements of a
state,[1] and a description of the various constitutions;[2] the
latter, however, has no longer the same interest, on account
of the different principle at the base of ancient and modern
states. No land was so rich as Greece, alike in the number
of its constitutions, and in the frequent changes from one
to another of these in a single state ; but the Greeks were
still unacquainted with the abstract right of our modern
states, that isolates the individual, allows of his acting as
such, and yet, as an invisible spirit, holds all its parts
together. This is done in such a way, however, that in no
one is there properly speaking either the consciousness of,
or the activity for the whole ; but because the individual
is really held to be a person, and all his concern is the
protection of his individuality, he works for the whole
without knowing how. It is a divided activity in which
each has only his part, just as in a factory no one makes a
whole, but only a part, and does not possess skill in other
departments, because only a few are employed in fitting
the different parts together. It is free nations alone that
have the consciousness of and activity for the whole ; in
modern times the individual is only free for himself as
such, and enjoys citizen freedom alone—in the sense of
that of a *bourgeois* and not of a *citoyen*. We do not possess
two separate words to mark this distinction. The freedom
of citizens in this signification is the dispensing with
universality, the principle of isolation ; but it is a necessary
moment unknown to ancient states. It is the perfect
independence of the points, and therefore the greater
independence of the whole, which constitutes the higher
organic life. After the state received this principle into
itself, the higher freedom could come forth. These other

[1] Arist. Polit. III. 1; IV. 14–16.
[2] Ibid. III. 7 (5)–IV. 13.

states are sports and products of nature which depend
upon chance and upon the caprice of the individual, but
now, for the first time, the inward subsistence and indestructible universality, which is real and consolidated in
its parts, is rendered possible.

Aristotle for the rest has not tried like Plato to describe
such a state, but in respect of the constitution he merely points
out that the best must rule. But this always takes place,
let men do as they will, and hence he has not so very much
to do with determining the forms of the constitution. By
way of proving that the best must rule, Aristotle says this :
" The best would suffer injustice if rated on an equality
with the others inferior to them in virtue and political
abilities, for a notable man is like a god amongst men."
Here Alexander is no doubt in Aristotle's mind, as one who
must rule as though he were a god, and over whom no one, and
not even law, could maintain its supremacy. " For him there
is no law, for he himself is law. Such a man could perhaps
be turned out of the state, but not subjected to control
any more than Jupiter. Nothing remains but, what is
natural to all, quietly to submit to such an one, and to let
men like this be absolutely and perpetually ($\dot{a}t\delta\iota o\iota$) kings
in the states."[1] The Greek Democracy had then entirely
fallen into decay, so that Aristotle could no longer ascribe
to it any merit.

4. THE LOGIC.

On the other side of the Philosophy of Mind, we have
still Aristotle's science of abstract thought, a Logic, to consider. For hundreds and thousands of years it was just as
much honoured as it is despised now. Aristotle has been
regarded as the originator of Logic : his logical works are the
source of, and authority for the logical treatises of all times ;
which last were, in great measure, only special develop-

[1] **Arist. Polit. III. 13 (8–9).**

ments or deductions, and must have been dull, insipid, imperfect, and purely formal. And even in quite recent
times, Kant has said that since the age of Aristotle, logic—
like pure geometry since Euclid's day—has been a complete
and perfect science which has kept its place even down to
the present day, without attaining to any further scientific
improvements or alteration. Although logic is here mentioned for the first time, and in the whole of the history of
Philosophy that is to come no other can be mentioned (for
no other has existed, unless we count the negation of
Scepticism), we cannot here speak more precisely of its
content, but merely find room for its general characterization. The forms he gives to us come from Aristotle
both in reference to the Notion and to the judgment and
conclusion. As in natural history, animals, such as the
unicorn, mammoth, beetle, mollusc, &c., are considered, and
their nature described, so Aristotle is, so to speak, the de-
scriber of the nature of these spiritual forms of thought;
but in this inference of the one from the other, Aristotle
has only presented thought as defined in its finite application and aspect, and his logic is thus a natural history of
finite thought. Because it is a knowledge and consciousness of the abstract activity of pure understanding, it is not
a knowledge of this and that concrete fact, being pure form.
This knowledge is in fact marvellous, and even more
marvellous is the manner in which it is constituted: this
logic is hence a work which does the greatest honour to the
deep thought of its discoverer and to the power of his abstraction. For the greatest cohesive power in thought is found
in separating it from what is material and thus securing it;
and the strength shows itself almost more, if thus secured
when it, amalgamated with matter, turns about in manifold
ways and is seen to be capable of numberless alterations
and applications. Aristotle also considers, in fact, not
only the movement of thought, but likewise of thought in
ordinary conception. The Logic of Aristotle is contained

in five books, which are collected together under the name
'Οργανον.

a. The Categories (κατηγορίαι), of which the first work
treats, are the universal determinations, that which is predicated of existent things (κατηγορεῖται) : as well that
which we call conceptions of the understanding, as the
simple realities of things.   This may be called an ontology,
as pertaining to metaphysics ; hence these determinations
also appear in Aristotle's Metaphysics.   Aristotle (Categor. I.) now says : " Things are termed homonyms (ὁμώνυμα)
of which the name alone is common, but which have a different substantial definition (λόγος τῆς οὐσίας) ; thus a horse
and the picture of a horse are both called an animal."

Thus the Notion (λόγος) is opposed to the homonym ;
and since Aristotle deduces herefrom τὰ λεγόμενα, of which
the second chapter treats, it is clear that this last expression indicates more than mere predication, and is here
to be taken as determinate Notions.   "Determinate conceptions are either enunciated after a complex (κατὰ
συμπλοκήν) or after an incomplex manner (ἄνευ συμπλοκῆς) ;
the first as ' a man conquers,' ' the ox runs,' and the other
as ' man,' ' ox,' ' to conquer,' ' to run.' "   In the first
rank of this division Aristotle places τὰ ὄντα, which
are undoubtedly purely subjective relations of such as
exist *per se*, so that the relation is not in them but
external to them.   Now although τὰ λεγόμενα and τὰ ὄντα
are again distinguished from one another, Aristotle yet
again employs both λέγεται and ἐστί of the ὄντα, so that
λέγεται is predicated of a species, in relation to its particular ; ἐστί is, on the contrary, employed of a universal, which
is not Idea but only simple.   For Aristotle says, " There
are predicates (ὄντα) which can be assigned to a certain
subject (καθ᾽ ὑποκειμένου λέγεται), yet are in no subject, as
' man ' is predicated of ' some certain man,' and yet he
is no particular man.   Others are in a subject (ἐν ὑποκειμένῳ
ἐστί) yet are not predicated of any subject (I mean by a

thing being in a subject, that it is in any thing not as a part, but as unable to subsist without that in which it is), as 'a grammatical art' (τὶς γραμματική) is in a subject, 'the soul,' but cannot be predicated of any,' or related as genus to a subject.   Some are predicated of a subject (λέγεται) and are in it; science is in the soul and is predicated of the grammatical art.   Some again are neither in, nor are predicated of any subject, as 'a certain man,' the individual, the one in number; but some of them can be in a subject like 'a certain grammatical art.'"   Instead of subject we should do better to speak of substratum, for it is that to which the Notion necessarily relates, *i.e.* that which is neglected in abstraction, and thus the individual opposed to the Notion. We can see that Aristotle has the difference of the genus or universal and the individual present to his mind.

The first thing which Aristotle has indicated in the foregoing is thus the genus, which is predicated of a man, but which is not in him, at least not as a particular quality ; the brave man, for example, is an actual, but expressed as a universal conception.   In formal logic and its conceptions and definitions there is always present opposition to an actual ; and the logical actual is in itself something thought, bravery thus being, for example, a pure form of abstraction.   This logic of the understanding seeks, however, in its three stages to imitate the categories of the absolute. The conception or definition is a logical actual, and thus in itself merely something thought, *i.e.* possible.   In the judgment this logic calls a conception A the actual subject and connects with it another actual as the conception B ; B is said to be the conception and A to be dependent on it—but B is only the more general conception.   In the syllogism necessity is said to be simulated : even in a judgment there is a synthesis of a conception and something whose existence is assumed ; in the syllogism it should bear the form of necessity, because both the opposites are set forth in a third as through the *medius terminus* of reason, *e.g.* as was the case with the mean of virtue (*supra*, p. 206). The major term expresses logical being and the minor term logical potentiality, for Caius is a mere potentiality for logic; the conclusion unites both. But it is to reason that life first unfolds itself, for it is true reality. What comes second in Aristotle is the universal, which is not the genus, *i.e.* it is not in itself the unity of universal and particular—nor is it absolute individuality and hence infinitude. This is the moment or predicate in a subject certainly, but it is not absolutely in and for itself. This relation is now expressed through οὐ λέγεται; for ὅ λέγεται is that which, as universal in itself, is likewise infinite. The third is the particular which is predicated : just as science in itself is infinite and thus the genus, *e.g.* of the grammatical art; but at the same time as universal, or as not individual, it is the moment of a subject. The fourth indicated by Aristotle is what is called immediate conception—the individual. The reservation that something such as a definite grammatical art is also in a subject, has no place here, for the definite grammatical art is not really in itself individual.

Aristotle, himself,[1] makes the following remarks on this matter : "When one thing is predicated (κατηγορεῖται) of another, as of a subject, whatever things are said (λέγεται) of the predicate," *i.e.* what is related to it as a universal, "may be also said of the subject." This is the ordinary conclusion ; from this we see, since this matter is so speedily despatched, that the real conclusion has with Aristotle a much greater significance. "The different genera not arranged under one another (μὴ ὑπ' ἄλληλα τεταγμένα), such as 'animal' and 'science,' differ in their species (διαφοράς). For instance, animals are divided into beasts, bird, fishes—but science has no such distinction. In subordinate genera, however, there may be the same distinctions ; for the superior genera are predicated of the inferior, so that as many distinctions

---

[1] Categor. c. 3 (c. 2, § 3-5.)

as there are of the predicate, so many will there be of the subject."

After Aristotle had thus far spoken of what is enunciated respecting that which is connected, or the complex, he now comes to "that which is predicated without any connection," or the incomplex; for as we saw (p. 212) this was the division which he laid down in the second chapter. That which is predicated without any connection he treats of more fully as the categories proper, in what follows; yet the work in which these categories are laid down is not to be regarded as complete. Aristotle [1] takes ten of them: " Each conception enunciated signifies either Substance (οὐσίαν), or Quality (ποιόν), or Quantity (ποσόν)," matter, " or Relation (πρός τι), or Where (ποῦ), or When (ποτέ), or Position (κεῖσθαι), or Possession (ἔχειν), or Action (ποιεῖν), or Passion (πάσχειν). None of these is considered by itself an affirmation (κατάφασις) or a negation (ἀπόφασις), i.e. none is either true or false." Aristotle adds to these predicables five post predicaments, but he only ranges them all side by side. [2] The categories of relation are the syntheses of quality and quantity, and consequently they belonged to reason; but in as far as they are posited as mere relation, they belong to the understanding and are forms of finitude. Being, essence, takes the first place in them; next to it is possibility, as accident or what is caused; the two are, however, separated. In substance A is Being, B, potentiality; in the relation of causality A and B are Being, but A is posited in B as being posited in a postulation of A. A of substance is logical Being; it is its essence opposed to its existence, and this existence is in logic mere potentiality. In the category of causality the Being of A in B is a mere Being of reflection; B is for itself another. But in reason A is the

---

[1] Categor. c. 4 (c. 2, § 6–8).

[2] Categor. c. 10–14 (8-11); cf. Kant, Kritik der reinen Vernunft, p. 79 (6th Ed.).

Being of B as well as of A, and A is the whole Being of A as well as of B.

Aristotle[1] goes on to speak of Substance; first Substance, "in its strictest (κυριώτατα), first and chief sense" is to him the individual, the fourth class of the divisions enunciated above (pp. 212-214). "Secondary substances are those in which as species (εἴδεσι) these first are contained, that is to say, both these and the genera of these species. Of the subject both name and definition (λόγος) of all things predicated of a subject (τῶν καθ᾽ ὑποκειμένου λεγομένων)—of secondary substances—are predicated; for example of the particular man, as subject, both the name and the definition of ' man ' (living being) are also predicated. But of things which are in a subject (ἐν ὑποκειμένῳ ὄντος) it is impossible to predicate the definition of the " subordinate "subjects, yet with some we predicate the name: the definition of ' whiteness ' thus is not of the body in which it is, but only the name. All other things however," besides Definition (λόγος) and " in most cases name, are related to primary substances as subjects " (the individual), " or are inherent in them. Thus without the primary substances none of the rest could exist, for they are the basis (ὑποκεῖσθαι) of all else. Of secondary substances, species is more substance than genus; for it is nearer to the primary substance, and genus is predicated of the species and not the other way." For species is here the subject, or what does not always require to be something really determined as individual, but which also signifies that which is generally speaking subordinate. " But the species are not more substance one than another, just as in primary substances one is not more substance than the other. Species and genera are likewise, before the rest " (qualities or accidents) " to be called secondary substances: the definition ' man ' before the fact that he is

[1] Categor. c. 5 (3).

'white' or 'runs.'" Abstraction has thus two kinds of objects ; 'man' and 'learned' are both qualities of a certain individual ; but the former only abstracts from the individuality and leaves the totality, and is thus the elevation of the individual into the rational, where nothing is lost but the opposition of reflection. "What is true of substances is also true of differences ; for as synonyms (συνώνυμα) they have both name and definition in common."

b. The second treatise is on Interpretation (περὶ ἑρμηνείας) ; it is the doctrine of judgments and propositions. Propositions exist where affirmation and negation, falsehood and truth are enunciated ;[1] they do not relate to pure thought when reason itself thinks ; they are not universal but individual.

c. The Analytics come third, and there are two parts of them, the Prior and the Posterior ; they deal most fully with proof (ἀπόδειξις) and the syllogisms of the understanding. "The syllogism is a reason (λόγος) in which if one thing is maintained, another than what was maintained follows of necessity."[2] Aristotle's logic ha, treated the general theory of conclusions in the main very accurately, but they do not by any means constitute the universal form of truth ; in his metaphysics, physics, psychology, &c., Aristotle has not formed conclusions, but thought the Notion in and for itself.

d. The Topics (τοπικά) which treat of 'places' (τόποι) come fourth ; in them the points of view from which anything can be considered are enumerated. Cicero and Giordano Bruno worked this out more fully. Aristotle gives a large number of general points of view which can be taken of an object, a proposition or a problem ; each problem can be directly reduced to these different points of

---

[1] Arist. Categor. c. 4 (2) ; De Interpretat. c. 4-6.
[2] Arist. Analytic. prior. I. 1 ; Topic I. 1.

view, that must everywhere appear. Thus these 'places' are, so to speak, a system of many aspects under which an object can be regarded in investigating it; this constitutes a work which seems specially suitable and requisite for the training of orators and for ordinary conversation, because the knowledge of points of view at once places in our hands the possibility of arriving at the various aspects of a subject, and embracing its whole extent in accordance with these points of view (Vol. I. p. 358). This, according to Aristotle, is the function of Dialectic, which he calls an instrument for finding propositions and conclusions out of probabilities.[1] Such 'places' are either of a general kind, such as difference, similarity, opposition, relation, and comparison,[2] or special in nature, such as 'places' which prove that something is better or more to be desired, since in it we have the longer duration of time, that which the one wise man or several would choose, the genus as against the species, that which is desirable for itself; also because it is present with the more honourable, because it is end, what approximates to end, the more beautiful and praiseworthy, &c.[3] Aristotle (Topic VIII. 2) says that we must make use of the syllogism by preference, with the dialectician, but of induction with the multitude. In the same way Aristotle separates[4] the dialectic and demonstrative syllogisms from the rhetorical and every kind of persuasion, but he counts induction as belonging to what is rhetorical.

e. The fifth treatise, finally, deals with the Sophistical Elenchi (σοφιστικοὶ ἔλεγχοι), or 'On Refutations,' as in the unconscious escape of thought in its categories to the material side of popular conception, it arrives at constant contradiction

---

[1] Arist. Topic I. 13 (11) et 1.
[2] Ibid. I. 16–18 (14–16); II. 7, 8, 10.
[3] Ibid. III. 1; Buhle, Argum. p. 18.
[4] Analyt. prior. II. 23 (25).

with itself. The sophistical elenchi betray the unconscious ordinary idea into these contradictions, and make it conscious of them; in order to entrap and puzzle it ; they were mentioned by us in connection with Zeno, and the Sophists sought them out, but it was the Megarics who were specially strong in them. Aristotle goes through a number of such contradictions by the way of solving them ; in so doing he proceeds quietly and carefully, and spares no pains, though they might have been made more dramatic. We have before (Vol. I. pp. 456–459) found specimens of these in treating of the Megarics, and we have seen how Aristotle solves such contradictions through distinction and determination.

Of these five parts of the Aristotelian Organon, what is produced in our ordinary systems of logic is, as a matter of fact, of the slightest and most trivial description, consisting as it does mainly of what is contained in the introduction of Porphyry. More particularly in the first parts, in the Interpretation and in the Analytics, this Aristotelian logic contains these representations of universal forms of thought, such as are now dealt with in ordinary logic, and really form the basis of what in modern times is known as logic. Aristotle has rendered a never-ending service in having recognized and determined the forms which thought assumes within us. For what interests us is the concrete thought immersed as it is in externalities ; these forms constitute a net of eternal activity sunk within it, and the operation of setting in their places those fine threads which are drawn throughout everything, is a master-piece of empiricism, and this knowledge is absolutely valuable. Even contemplation, or a knowledge of the numerous forms and modes assumed by this activity, is interesting and important enough. For however dry and contentless the enumeration of the different kinds of judgments and conclusions, and their numerous limitations may appear to us to be, and though they may not seem to serve their purpose of discovering the truth, at

least no other science in opposition to this one can be elevated
into its place. For instance, if it is held to be a worthy
endeavour to gain a knowledge of the infinite number of
animals, such as one hundred and sixty-seven kinds of
cuckoo, in which one may have the tuft on his head
differently shaped from another, or to make acquaintance
with some miserable new species of a miserable kind of
moss which is no better than a scab, or with an insect,
vermin, bug, &c., in some learned work on entomology, it is
much more important to be acquainted with the manifold
kinds of movement present in thought, than to know about
such creatures. The best of what is stated respecting the
forms of judgment, conclusion, &c., in ordinary logic, is
taken from the works of Aristotle; as far as details are
concerned, much has been spun out and added to it, but
the truth is to be found with Aristotle.

As regards the real philosophic nature of the Aristotelian
logic, it has received in our text-books a position and
significance as though it gave expression only to the
activity of the understanding as consciousness; hence it
is said to direct us how to think correctly. Thus it
appears as though the movement of thought were something independent, unaffected by the object of thought;
in other words, as if it contained the so-called laws of
thought of our understanding, through which we attain to
perception, but through a medium which was not the
movement of things themselves. The result must certainly
be truth, so that things are constituted as we bring them
forth according to the laws of thought; but the manner of
this knowledge has merely a subjective significance, and
the judgment and conclusion are not a judgment and conclusion of things themselves. Now if, according to this
point of view, thought is considered on its own account, it
does not make its appearance implicitly as knowledge, nor
is it without content in and for itself; for it is a formal
activity which certainly is exercised, but whose content is

one given to it. Thought in this sense becomes something subjective ; these judgments and conclusions are in and for themselves quite true, or rather correct—this no one ever doubted ; but because content is lacking to them, these judgments and conclusions do not suffice for the knowledge of the truth. Thus by logicians they are held to be forms whose content is something entirely different, because they have not even the form of the content ; and the meaning which is given to them—namely that they are forms—is found fault with. The worst thing said of them, however, is that their only error is their being formal ; both the laws of thought as such, and also its determinations, the categories, are either determinations of the judgment only, or merely subjective forms of the understanding, while the thing-in-itself is very different. But in that point of view and in the blame awarded the truth itself is missed, for untruth is the form of opposition between subject and object, and the lack of unity in them ; in this case the question is not put at all as to whether anything is absolutely true or not. These determinations have certainly no empirical content, but thought and its movement is itself the content—and, indeed, as interesting a content as any other that can be given; consequently this science of thought is on its own account a true science. But here again we come across the drawback pertaining to the whole Aristotelian manner, as also to all succeeding logic—and that indeed in the highest degree— that in thought and in the movement of thought as such, the individual moments fall asunder ; there are a number of kinds of judgment and conclusion, each of which is held to be independent, and is supposed to have absolute truth as such. Thus they are simply content, for they then have an indifferent, undistinguished existence, such as we see in the famous laws of contradiction, conclusions, &c. In this isolation they have, however, no truth ; for their totality alone is the truth of thought, because this totality is at once subjective and objective. Thus they are only the material of truth, the formless content ; their deficiency is hence not that they are only forms but rather that form is lacking to them, and that they are in too great a degree content. Thus as many individual qualities of a thing are not anything, such as red, hard, &c., if taken by themselves, but only in their unity constitute a real thing, so it is with the unity of the forms of judgment and conclusion, which individually have as little truth as such a quality, or as a rhythm or melody. The form of a conclusion, as also its content, may be quite correct, and yet the conclusion arrived at may be untrue, because this form as such has no truth of its own; but from this point of view these forms have never been considered, and the scorn of logic rests simply on the false assumption that there is a lack of content. Now this content is none other than the speculative Idea. Conceptions of the understanding or of reason constitute the essence of things, not certainly for that point of view, but in truth ; and thus also for Aristotle the conceptions of the understanding, namely the categories, constitute the essential realities of Being. If they are thus in and for themselves true, they themselves are their own, and thus the highest content. But in ordinary logic this is not the case, and even as these are represented in the Aristotelian works they are only universal thought-determinations, between which the abstract understanding makes distinctions. This, however, is not the logic of speculative thought, *i.e.* of reason as distinguished from understanding ; for there the identity of the understanding which allows nothing to contradict itself is fundamental. However little this logic of the finite may be speculative in nature, yet we must make ourselves acquainted with it, for it is everywhere discovered in finite relationships. There are many sciences, subjects of knowledge, &c., that know and apply no other forms of thought than these forms of finite thought, which constitute in fact the general method of dealing with the finite sciences. Mathematics, for instance, is a constant series of syllogisms; jurisprudence is the bringing of the particular under the general, the uniting together of both these sides. Within these relationships of finite determinations the syllogism has now, indeed, on account of its terms being three in number, been called the totality of these determinations, and hence by Kant (Kritik der reinen Vernunft, p. 261) also the rational conclusion; but this syllogism addressed to the intelligence as it appears in the ordinary logical form, is only the intelligible form of rationality, and, as we saw above (p. 76), is very different from the rational syllogism proper. Aristotle is thus the originator of the logic of the understanding; its forms only concern the relationship of finite to finite, and in them the truth cannot be grasped. But it must be remarked that Aristotle's philosophy is not by any means founded on this relationship of the understanding; thus it must not be thought that it is in accordance with these syllogisms that Aristotle has thought. If Aristotle did so, he would not be the speculative philosopher that we have recognized him to be; none of his propositions could have been laid down, and he could not have made any step forward, if he had kept to the forms of this ordinary logic.

Like the whole of Aristotle's philosophy, his logic really requires recasting, so that all his determinations should be brought into a necessary systematic whole—not a systematic whole which is correctly divided into its parts, and in which no part is forgotten, all being set forth in their proper order, but one in which there is one living organic whole, in which each part is held to be a part, and the whole alone as such is true. Aristotle, in the Politics, for instance (*supra*, pp. 207–208), often gives expression to this truth. For this reason the individual logical form has in itself no truth, not because it is the form of thought, but because it is determinate thought, individual form, and to be esteemed as such. But as system and absolute form ruling this content, thought has its content as a distinction in itself, being speculative philosophy in which subject and object are immediately identical, and the Notion and the universal are the realities of things. Just as duty certainly expresses the absolute, but, as determinate, a determinate absolute which is only a moment and must be able again to abrogate its determination, the logical form which abrogates itself as this determinate in this very way gives up its claim to be in and for itself. But in this case logic is the science of reason, speculative philosophy of the pure Idea of absolute existence, which is not entangled in the opposition of subject and object, but remains an opposition in thought itself. Yet we certainly may allow that much in logic is an indifferent form.

At this point we would leave off as far as the Aristotelian philosophy is concerned, and from this it is difficult to break away. For the further we go into its details, the more interesting it becomes, and the more do we find the connection which exists among the subjects. The fulness with which I have set forth the principal content of the Aristotelian philosophy is justified both by the importance of the matter itself, because it offers to us a content of its own, and also by the circumstances already mentioned (p. 118), that against no philosophy have modern times sinned so much as against this, and none of the ancient philosophers have so much need of being defended as Aristotle.

One of the immediate followers of Aristotle was Theophrastus, born Ol. 102, 2 (371 B.C.); though a man of distinction, he can still only be esteemed a commentator on Aristotle. For Aristotle is so rich a treasure-house of philosophic conceptions, that much material is found in him which is ready for further working upon, which may be put forward more abstractly, and in which individual propositions may be brought into prominence. However Aristotle's

manner of procedure, which is to take an empirical starting
point of ratiocination [Raisonnement], and to comprehend
this in the focus of the speculative Notion, is characteristic
of his mind, without being one which, on its own account,
can be freely elevated into a method and a principle.   Thus
of Theophrastus as of many others (Dicæarchus of Messina,
for instance), amongst whom Strato of Lampsacus, the successor of Theophrastus, is best known, there is not much to
tell.   As regards Dicæarchus, Cicero says (Tusc. Quæst. I.
31, 10) that he controverted the immortality of the soul,
for he asserted that "the soul is no more than an empty
name, and the whole of the capacities and powers with
which we act and feel are equally extended over all living
bodies, and inseparable from the body ; for it is nothing
but the body so constituted as to live and feel through a
certain symmetry and proportion in its body."   Cicero
gives in an historical manner a result as he made it comprehensible to himself, without any speculative conception.
Stobæus (Eclog. phys. p. 796), on the other hand, quotes
from Dicæarchus that he held the soul to be "a harmony of
the four elements."   We have only a little general informa-
tion to give of Strato, that he acquired great fame as
a physicist, and that his conception of nature went upon
mechanical lines, and yet not on those of Leucippus and
Democritus, and later, of Epicurus ; for, according to
Stobæus (Eclog. phys. p. 298), he made warmth and cold
into elements.   Hence, if what is said of him is accurate,
he was most unfaithful to the beliefs of Aristotle, because
he led everything back to mechanism and chance and did
away with the immanent end, without accepting the false
teleology of modern times.   At least, Cicero (De nat. Deor.
I. 13) relates of him that he maintained that "divine
strength lies altogether in nature, which has in itself the
causes of origination, of growth, and of decay, but lacks
all sensation and conformation."   The other Peripatetics
occupied themselves more with working up individual

doctrines of Aristotle, with bringing out his works in a commentated form, which is more or less rhetorical in character, though similar in content. But in practical life the Peripatetic school maintained as the principle of happiness, the unity of reason and inclination. We thus may set aside any further expansion of the Peripatetic philosophy, because it has no longer the same interest, and later on tended to become a popular philosophy (Vol. I. p. 479, Vol. II. p. 130); in this mode it no longer remained an Aristotelian philosophy, although this, too, as what is really speculative, must coincide most closely with actuality. This decay of the Aristotelian philosophy is, indeed, closely connected with the circumstance already mentioned (pp. 126–128), that the Aristotelian writings soon disappeared, and that the Aristotelian philosophy did not retain its place so much through these documents as through the traditions in the school, whereby they soon underwent material changes ; and amplifications of Aristotle's doctrines were brought about, as to which it is not known whether some may not have slipped into what pass for his works.

Since Aristotle's leading thought has penetrated all spheres of consciousness, and this isolation in the determination through the Notion, because it is likewise necessary, contains in every sphere the profoundest of true thoughts, Aristotle, to anticipate here the external history of his philosophy as a whole, for many centuries was the constant mainstay of the cultivation of thought. When in the Christian West science disappeared amongst the Christians, the fame of Aristotle shone forth with equal brilliance amongst the Arabians, from whom, in later times, his philosophy was again passed over to the West. The triumph which was celebrated upon the revival of learning, on account of the Aristotelian philosophy having been expelled from the schools, from the sciences, and specially from theology, as from the philosophy which deals with absolute existence, must be regarded in two different

aspects. In the first place we must remember that it was
not the Aristotelian philosophy which was expelled, so
much as the principle of the science of theology which
supported itself thereon, according to which the first truth
is one which is given and revealed—an hypothesis which is
once for all a fundamental one, and by which reason and
thought have the right and power to move to and fro only
superficially. In this form the thought which was awakened
in the Middle Ages reconstructed its theology more especially, entered into all dialectic movements and determinations, and erected an edifice where the material that was
given was only superficially worked up, disposed and
secured. The triumph over this system was thus a triumph
over that principle, and consequently the triumph of free,
spontaneous thought. But another side of this triumph is
the triumph of the commonplace point of view that broke
free from the Notion and shook off the yoke of thought.
Formerly, and even nowadays, enough has been heard of
Aristotle's scholastic subtleties ; in using this name, men
thought that they had a right to spare themselves from
entering on abstraction, and, in place of the Notion, they
thought that it justified them in seeing, hearing, and thus
making their escape to what is called healthy human understanding. In science, too, in place of subtle thoughts,
subtle sight has commenced ; a beetle or a species of bird
is distinguished with as great minuteness as were formerly
conceptions and thoughts. Such subtleties as whether a
species of bird is red or green in colour, or has a more or
less perfect tail, are found more easy than the differences
in thought ; and in the meantime, until a people has educated itself up to the labour of thought, in order to be able
thus to support the universal, the former is a useful preparation, or rather it is a moment in this course of culture.

But inasmuch as the deficiency in the Aristotelian
philosophy rests in the fact, that after the manifold of phenomena was through it raised into the Notion, though this

last again fell asunder into a succession of determinate
Notions, the unity of the absolute Notion which unites
them was not emphasized, and this is what succeeding
time had to accomplish. What now appears is that the
unity of the Notion which is absolute existence, makes its
appearance as necessity, and it presents itself first as the
unity of self-consciousness and consciousness, as pure
thought. The unity of existence as existence is objective
unity, thought, as that which is thought. But unity as
Notion, the implicitly universal negative unity, time as
absolutely fulfilled time, and in its fulfilment as being unity,
is pure self-consciousness. Hence we see it come to pass,
that pure self-consciousness makes itself reality, but, at the
same time, it first of all does so with subjective significance
as a self-consciousness that has taken up its position as
such, and that separates itself from objective existence,
and hence is first of all subject to a difference which it
does not overcome.

Here we have concluded the first division of Greek
philosophy, and we have now to pass to the second period.
The first period of Greek philosophy extended to Aristotle,
to the attainment of a scientific form in which knowledge
has reached the standing of free thought. Thus in Plato
and Aristotle the result was the Idea ; yet we saw in Plato
the universal made the principle in a somewhat abstract
way as the unmoved Idea ; in Aristotle, on the other hand,
thought in activity became absolutely concrete as the
thought which thinks itself. The next essential, one which
now is immediately before us, must be contained in that
into which Philosophy under Plato and Aristotle had
formed itself. This necessity is none other than the fact
that the universal must now be proclaimed free for itself as
the universality of the principle, so that the particular may
be recognized through this universal ; or the necessity of a
systematic philosophy immediately enters in, what we formerly called one in accordance with the unity of the Notion.

We may speak of the Platonic and Aristotelian systems, but they are not in the form of a system; for that it is requisite that one principle should be maintained and consistently carried through the particular. In the perfect complex of the conception of the universe as it is to Aristotle, where everything is in the highest form of scientific knowledge led back to what is speculative, however empiric may be his manner of setting to work, there certainly is one principle brought forward, and that a speculative one, though it is not brought forward as being one. The nature of the speculative has not been explicitly brought to consciousness as the Notion—as containing in itself the development of the manifold nature of the natural and spiritual universe, consequently it is not set forth as the universal, from which the particular was developed. Aristotle's logic is really the opposite of this. He in great measure passes through a series of the living and the dead, makes them confront his objective, that is, conceiving thought, and grasps them in his understanding; each object is on its own account a conception which is laid open in its determinations, and yet he also brings these reflections together, and thereby is speculative. If even Plato on the whole proceeded in an empiric way, taking up this and that idea, each of which is in turn examined, with Aristotle this loose method of procedure appears still more clearly. In the Aristotelian teaching the Idea of the self-reflecting thought is thus grasped as the highest truth; but its realization, the knowledge of the natural and spiritual universe, constitutes outside of that Idea a long series of particular conceptions, which are external to one another, and in which a unifying principle, led through the particular, is wanting. The highest Idea with Aristotle consequently once more stands only as a particular in its own place and without being the principle of his whole philosophy. Hence the next necessity in Philosophy is that the whole extent of what is known must appear as one organization of the Notion; that in this way the manifold reality may be related to that Idea as the universal, and thereby determined. This is the standpoint which we find in this second period.

A systematic philosophy such as this becomes in the first place dogmatism, in antagonism to which, because of its one-sided character, scepticism immediately arises. In the same way the French call what is dogmatic *systématique*, and *système* that in which all the conceptions must consistently proceed from one determination; hence to them *systématique* is synonymous with one-sided. But the philosophies that ensue are one-sided, because in them it was only the necessity of one principle that was recognized, without their meanwhile developing from themselves, as might well have come to pass in and for itself, the Idea as the real universal, and thus comprehending the world in such a way that the content is only grasped as the determination of the self-reflective thought. Hence this principle stands up formally and abstractly, and the particular is not yet deduced from it, for the universal is only applied to the particular and the rules for this application sought out. In Aristotle the Idea is at least implicitly concrete, as the consciousness of the unity of subjective and objective, and therefore it is not one-sided. Should the Idea be truly concrete, the particular must be developed from it. The other relation would be the mere bringing of the particular under the universal, so that both should be mutually distinguished; in such a case the universal is only a formal principle, and such a philosophy is therefore one-sided. But the true difficulty is that the two endeavours, the development of the particular from the Idea, and the bringing of the particular under the universal, collide with one another. The manifestations of the physical and spiritual world must first, from their respective sides, be prepared for and worked into the Notion, so that the other sciences can form therefrom universal laws and principles. Then for the first time can speculative reason present itself in determinate thoughts, and bring perfectly to consciousness the inwardly existing connection between them. As dogmatic, however, those philosophies, it may be further said, are assertive likewise; because in such a method the principle is only asserted and is not truly proved. For a principle is demanded under which everything is subsumed ; thus it is only presupposed as the first principle. Before this we have had abstract principles such as pure Being, but here the particular, with which begins the distinction from what is different, became posited as the purely negative. That necessity, on the other hand, makes for a universal which must likewise be in the particular, so that this should not be set aside, but should have its determinate character through the universal.

This demand for a universal, even though still unproved principle, is henceforth present to knowledge. What answers to this demand now appears in the world through the inward necessity of mind—not externally, but as being in conformity with the Notion. This necessity has produced the philosophy of the Stoics, Epicureans, New Academy, and Sceptics, which we have now to consider. If we have remained too long in the consideration of this period, we may now make amends for this protraction, for in the next period we may be brief.

PART THREE

MODERN PHILOSOPHY

INTRODUCTION

IF we cast a glance back over the period just traversed,* we find that in it a turning-point had been reached, that the Christian religion had placed its absolute content in the mind and will of man, and that it was thus, as a divine and supersensuous content, separated from the world and shut up within itself in the centre-point of the individual. Over against the religious life an external world stood as a natural world—a world of heart or feeling, of desire, of human nature—which had value only in as far as it was overcome. This mutual independence of the two worlds had much attention bestowed on it throughout the Middle Ages; the opposition was attacked on all quarters and in the end overcome. But since the relation of mankind to the divine life exists upon earth, this conquest at first presented the appearance of bringing with it the destruction of the church and of the eternal through the sensuous desires of man. The eternal truth was likewise grafted upon the dry, formal understanding, so that we might say that the separation of self-consciousness has in itself disappeared, and thereby a possibility has been given of obtaining reconciliation. But because this implicit union of the Beyond and the Here was of so unsatisfactory a nature that the better feelings were aroused and forced to turn against it,

---

*Hegel is referring here to the period of the middle Ages, addressed in the *Lectures*' Part Two: "Philosophy of the Middle Ages," omitted from this abridgment.

the Reformation made its appearance, partly, no doubt, as a separation from the Catholic Church, but partly as a reformation from within.   There is a mistaken idea that the Reformation only effected a separation from the Catholic Church ; Luther just as truly reformed the Catholic Church, the corruption of which one learns from his writings, and from the reports of the emperors and of the empire to the Pope ; if further evidence be required, we need only read the accounts given even by the Catholic bishops, the Fathers of the councils at Constance, Basle, &c., of the condition of the Catholic priesthood and of the Roman Court.   The principle of the inward reconciliation of spirit, which was in itself the very Idea of Christianity, was thus again estranged, and appeared as a condition of external, unreconciled alienation and discord ; this gives us an example of the slow operation of the world-spirit in overcoming this externality. It eats away the inward substance, but the appearance, the outward form, still remains ; at the end, however, it is an empty shell, the new form breaks forth.   In such times this spirit appears as if it—having so far proceeded in its development at a snail's pace, and having even retrograded and become estranged from itself—had suddenly adopted seven-leagued boots.

Since thus the reconciliation of self-consciousness with the present is implicitly accomplished, man has attained to confidence in himself and in his thought, in sensuous nature outside of and within him ; he has discovered an interest and pleasure in making discoveries both in nature and the arts.   In the affairs of this world the understanding developed ; man became conscious of his will and his achievements, took pleasure in the earth and its soil, as also in his occupations, because right and understanding were there present.   With the discovery of gunpowder the individual passion of battle was lost.   The romantic impulse towards a casual kind of bravery passed into other adventures, not of hate or revenge, or the so-called deliverance from what men considered the wrongs of innocence, but more harmless adventures, the exploration of the earth, or the discovery of the passage to the East Indies. America was discovered, its treasures and people—nature, man himself; navigation was the higher romance of commerce. The present world was again present to man as worthy of the interests of mind; thinking mind was again capable of action. Now the Reformation of Luther had inevitably to come—the appeal to the *sensus communis* which does not recognize the authority of the Fathers or of Aristotle, but only the inward personal spirit which quickens and animates, in contradistinction to works. In this way the Church lost her power against it, for her principle was within it and no longer lacking to it. To the finite and present due honour is accorded; from this honour the work of science proceeds. We thus see that the finite, the inward and outward present, becomes a matter of experience, and through the understanding is elevated into universality; men desire to understand laws and forces, *i.e.* to transform the individual of perceptions into the form of universality. Worldly matters demand to be judged of in a worldly way; the judge is thinking understanding. The other side is that the eternal, which is in and for itself true, is also known and comprehended through the pure heart itself; the individual mind appropriates to itself the eternal. This is the Lutheran faith without any other accessories—works, as they were called. Everything had value only as it was grasped by the heart, and not as a mere thing. The content ceases to be an objective thing; God is thus in spirit alone, He is not a beyond but the truest reality of the individual.

Pure thought is likewise one form of inwardness; it also approaches absolute existence and finds itself justified in apprehending the same. The philosophy of modern times proceeds from the principle which ancient philosophy had reached, the standpoint of actual self-consciousness—it has as principle the spirit that is present to itself ; it brings the standpoint of the Middle Ages, the diversity between what is thought and the existent universe, into opposition, and it has to do with the dissolution of this same opposition.   The main interest hence is, not so much the thinking of the objects in their truth, as the thinking and understanding of the objects, the thinking this unity itself, which is really the being conscious of a pre-supposed object. The getting rid of the formal culture of the logical understanding and the monstrosities of which it was composed, was more essential than the extension of it : investigation in such a case becomes dissipated and diffused, and passes into the false infinite. The general points of view which in modern philosophy we reach are hence somewhat as follows :—

1. The concrete form of thought which we have here to consider on its own account, really appears as subjective with the reflection of implicitude, so that this has an antithesis in existence ; and the interest is then altogether found in grasping the reconciliation of this opposition in its highest existence, *i.e.* in the most abstract extremes. This highest severance is the opposition between thought and Being, the comprehending of whose unity from this time forward constitutes the interest of all philosophies. Here thought is more independent, and thus we now abandon its unity with theology ; it separates itself there-from, just as with the Greeks it separated itself from mythology, the popular religion, and did not until the time of the Alexandrians seek out these forms again and fill the mythological conceptions with the form of thought. The bond remains, but for this reason it is clearly implicit : theology throughout is merely what philosophy is, for this last is simply thought respecting it.   It does not help theology to strive against philosophy, or to say that it wishes to know nothing about it, and that philosophic maxims are thus to be set aside. It has always to do with the thought that it brings along with it, and these its subjective

conceptions, its home and private metaphysics, are thus frequently a quite uncultured, uncritical thought—the thought of the street. These general conceptions are, indeed, connected with particular subjective conviction, and this last is said to prove the Christian content to be true in a sense all its own ; but these thoughts which constitute the criterion are merely the reflections and opinions which float about the surface of the time. Thus, when thought comes forth on its own account, we thereby separate ourselves from theology ; we shall, however, consider one other in whom both are still in unity. This individual is Jacob Boehme, for since mind now moves in its own domains, it is found partly in the natural and finite world, and partly in the inward, and this at first is the Christian.

While earlier than this, moreover, the spirit, distracted by outward things, had to make its influence felt in religion and in the secular life, and came to be known in the popular philosophy so-called, it was only in the sixteenth and seventeenth centuries that the genuine Philosophy re-appeared, which seeks to grasp the truth as truth because man in thought is infinitely free to comprehend himself and nature, and along with that seeks to understand the present of rationality, reality, universal law itself. For this is ours, since it is subjectivity. The principle of modern philosophy is hence not a free and natural thought, because it has the opposition of thought and nature before it as a fact of which it is conscious. Spirit and nature, thought and Being, are the two infinite sides of the Idea, which can for the first time truly make its appearance when its sides are grasped for themselves in their abstraction and totality. Plato comprehended it as the bond, as limiting and as infinite, as one and many, simple and diverse, but not as thought and Being ; when we first thinkingly overcome this opposition it signifies comprehending the unity. This is the standpoint of philosophic consciousness generally ; but the way in which this unity

must be thinkingly developed is a double one. Philosophy
hence falls into the two main forms in which the opposition
is resolved, into a realistic and an idealistic system of
philosophy, *i.e.* into one which makes objectivity and
the content of thought to arise from the perceptions,
and one which proceeds to truth from the independence
of thought.

a. Experience constitutes the first of these methods, viz.
Realism. Philosophy now signified, or had as its main
attribute, self-thought and the acceptance of the present as
that in which truth lay, and which was thereby knowable.
All that is speculative is pared and smoothed down in order
to bring it under experience. This present is the existent
external nature, and spiritual activity as the political world
and as subjective activity. The way to truth was to begin
from this hypothesis, but not to remain with it in its
external self-isolating actuality, but to lead it to the
universal.

a. The activities of that first method operate, to begin
with, on physical nature, from the observation of which
men derive universal laws, and on this basis their knowledge is founded; the science of nature, however, only
reaches to the stage of reflection. This kind of experimental physics was once called, and is still called philosophy,
as Newton's *Principia philosophiæ naturalis* (Vol. I. p. 59)
show. This work is one in which the methods of the finite
sciences through observation and deduction are alone
present—those sciences which the French still call the
sciences exactes. To this, the understanding of the individual, piety was opposed, and hence in this respect philosophy was termed worldly wisdom (Vol. I. p. 60). Here the
Idea in its infinitude is not itself the object of knowledge;
but a determinate content is raised into the universal, or this
last in its determinateness for the understanding is derived
from observation, just as is, for instance, done in Keppler's
Laws. In Scholastic philosophy, on the other hand, man's

power of observation was set aside, and disputations respecting nature at that time proceeded from abstruse hypotheses.

β. In the second place, the spiritual was observed as in its realization it constitutes the spiritual world of states, in order thus to investigate from experience the rights of individuals as regards one another, and as regards rulers, and the rights of states against states. Before this popes anointed kings, just as was done in Old Testament times to those appointed by God; it was in the Old Testament that the tithe was commanded; the forbidden degrees of relationship in marriage were also adopted from the Mosaic laws. What was right and permissible for kings was demonstrated from Saul's and David's histories, the rights of priesthood from Samuel—in short, the Old Testament was the source of all the principles of public law, and it is in this way even now that all papal bulls have their deliverances confirmed. It may easily be conceived how much nonsense was in this manner concocted. Now, however, right was sought for in man himself, and in history, and what had been accounted right both in peace and in war was explained. In this way books were composed which even now are constantly quoted in the Parliament of England. Men further observed the desires which could be satisfied in the state and the manner in which satisfaction could be given to them, in order thus from man himself, from man of the past as well as of the present, to learn what is right.

b. The second method, that of Idealism, proceeds from what is inward; according to it everything is in thought, mind itself is all content. Here the Idea itself is made the object; that signifies the thinking it and from it proceeding to the determinate. What Realism draws from experience is now derived from thought *à priori;* or the determinate is also comprehended but not led back to the universal merely, but to the Idea.

The two methods overlap one another, however, because experience on its side desires to derive universal laws from observations, while, on the other side, thought proceeding from abstract universality must still give itself a determinate content; thus *a priori* and *a posteriori* methods are mingled. In France abstract universality was the more predominant; from England experience took its rise, and even now it is there held in the greatest respect; Germany proceeded from the concrete Idea, from the inwardness of mind and spirit.

2. The questions of present philosophy, the opposites, the content which occupies the attention of these modern times, are as follows :—

a. The first form of the opposition which we have already touched upon in the Middle Ages is the Idea of God and His Being, and the task imposed is to deduce the existence of God, as pure spirit, from thought. Both sides must be comprehended through thought as absolute unity; the extremest opposition is apprehended as gathered into one unity. Other subjects which engage our attention are connected with the same general aim, namely, the bringing about of the inward reconciliation in the opposition which exists between knowledge and its object.

b. The second form of opposition is that of Good and Evil —the opposition of the assertion of independent will to the positive and universal; the origin of evil must be known. Evil is plainly the "other," the negation of God as Holiness; because He is, because He is wise, good, and at the same time almighty, evil is contradictory to Him; an endeavour is made to reconcile this contradiction.

c. The third form of opposition is that of the freedom of man and necessity.

a. The individual is clearly not determined in any other way than from himself, he is the absolute beginning of determination; in the 'I,' in the self, a power of decision is clearly to be found. This freedom is in opposition to the theory that God alone is really absolutely determining. Further, when that which happens is in futurity, the determining of it through God is regarded as Providence and the foreknowledge of God. In this, however, a new contradiction is involved, inasmuch as because God's knowledge is not merely subjective, that which God knows likewise *is*.

β. Further still, human freedom is in opposition to necessity as the determinateness of nature; man is dependent on nature, and the external as well as the inward nature of man is his necessity as against his freedom.

γ. Considered objectively, this opposition is that between final causes and efficient causes, *i.e.* between the acts of freedom and the acts of necessity.

δ. This opposition between the freedom of man and natural necessity has finally likewise the further form of community of soul and body, of *commercium animi cum corpore*, as it has been called, wherein the soul appears as the simple, ideal, and free, and the body as the manifold, material and necessary.

These matters occupy the attention of science, and they are of a completely different nature from the interests of ancient philosophy. The difference is this, that here there is a consciousness of an opposition, which is certainly likewise contained in the subjects with which the learning of the ancients was occupied, but which had not come to consciousness. This consciousness of the opposition, this ' Fall,' is the main point of interest in the conception of the Christian religion. The bringing about in thought of the reconciliation which is accepted in belief, now constitutes the whole interest of knowledge. Implicitly it has come to pass ; for knowledge considers itself qualified to bring about in itself this recognition of the reconciliation. The philosophic systems are therefore no more than modes of this absolute unity, and only the concrete unity of those opposites is the truth.

3. As regards the stages which were reached in the pro-

gress of this knowledge we have to mention three of the principal.

a. First of all we find the union of those opposites stated ; and to prove it genuine attempts are made, though not yet determined in purity.

b. The second stage is the metaphysical union ; and here, with Descartes, the philosophy of modern times as abstract thought properly speaking begins.

a. Thinking understanding seeks to bring to pass the union, inasmuch as it investigates with its pure thought-determinations ; this is in the first place the standpoint of metaphysics as such.

β. In the second place, we have to consider negation, the destruction of this metaphysics—the attempt to consider knowledge on its own account, and the determinations which proceed from it.

c. The third stage is that this union itself which is to be brought about, and which is the only subject of interest, comes to consciousness and becomes an object. As principle the union has the form of the relationship of knowledge to the content, and thus this question has been put : ' How is, and how can thought be identical with the objective ? ' With this the inward element which lies at the basis of this metaphysic is raised into explicitude and made an object ; and this includes all modern philosophy in its range.

4. In respect to the external history and the lives of the philosophers, it will strike us that from this time on, these appear to be very different from those of the philosophers of ancient times, whom we regarded as self-sufficing indivi-dualities. It is required that a philosopher should live as he teaches, that he should despise the world and not enter into connection with it ; this the ancients have accomplished, and they are such plastic individualities just because the inward spiritual aim of philosophy has likewise frequently deter-mined their external relations and conditions. The object of their knowledge was to take a thoughtful view of

the universe; they kept the external connection with the world all the further removed from themselves because they did not greatly approve of much therein present ; or, at least, it ever proceeds on its way, according to its own particular laws, on which the individual is dependent. The individual likewise participates in the present interests of external life, in order to satisfy his personal ends, and through them to attain to honour, wealth, respect, and distinction ; the ancient philosophers, however, because they remained in the Idea, did not concern themselves with things that were not the objects of their thought. Hence with the Greeks and Romans the philosophers lived in an independent fashion peculiar to themselves, and in an external mode of life which appeared suitable to and worthy of the science they professed ; they conducted themselves independently as private persons, unfettered by outside trammels, and they may be compared to the monks who renounced all temporal goods.

In the Middle Ages it was chiefly the clergy, doctors of theology, who occupied themselves with philosophy. In the transition period the philosophers showed themselves to be in an inward warfare with themselves and in an external warfare with their surroundings, and their lives were spent in a wild, unsettled fashion.

In modern times things are very different; now we no longer see philosophic individuals who constitute a class by themselves. With the present day all difference has disappeared ; philosophers are not monks, for we find them generally in connection with the world, participating with others in some common work or calling. They live, not independently, but in the relation of citizens, or they occupy public offices and take part in the life of the state. Certainly they may be private persons, but if so, their position as such does not in any way isolate them from their other relationships. They are involved in present conditions, in the world and its work and progress.

Thus their philosophy is only by the way, a sort of luxury and superfluity. This difference is really to be found in the manner in which outward conditions have taken shape after the building up of the inward world of religion. In modern times, namely, on account of the reconciliation of the worldly principle with itself, the external world is at rest, is brought into order— worldly relationships, conditions, modes of life, have become constituted and organized in a manner which is conformable to nature and rational. We see a universal, comprehensible connection, and with that individuality likewise attains another character and nature, for it is no longer the plastic individuality of the ancients. This connection is of such power that every individuality is under its dominion, and yet at the same time can construct for itself an inward world. The external has thus been reconciled with itself in such a way that both inward and outward may be self-sufficing and remain independent of one another; and the individual is in the condition of being able to leave his external side to external order, while in the case of those plastic forms the external could only be determined entirely from within. Now, on the contrary, with the higher degree of strength attained by the inward side of the individual, he may hand the external over to chance; just as he leaves clothing to the contingencies of fashion, not considering it worth while to exert his understanding upon it. The external he leaves to be determined by the order which is present in the particular sphere in which his lot is cast. The circumstances of life are, in the true sense, private affairs, determined by outward conditions, and do not contain anything worthy of our notice. Life becomes scholarly, uniform, commonplace, it connects itself with outwardly given relationships and cannot represent or set itself forth as a form pertaining only to itself. Man must not take up the character of showing himself an independent form, and giving himself a position in the world created by himself. Because the objective power of external relationships is infinitely great, and for that reason the way in which I perforce am placed in them has become a matter of indifference to me, personality and the individual life generally are equally indifferent. A philosopher, it is said, should live as a philosopher, *i.e.*, should be independent of the external relationships of the world, and should give up occupying himself with and troubling himself concerning them. But thus circumscribed in respect of all necessities, more especially of culture, no one can suffice for himself; he must seek to act in connection with others. The modern world is this essential power of connection, and it implies the fact that it is clearly necessary for the individual to enter into these relations of external existence; only a common mode of existence is possible in any calling or condition, and to this Spinoza forms the solitary exception. Thus in earlier times bravery was individual; while modern bravery consists in each not acting after his own fashion, but relying on his connection with others—and this constitutes his whole merit. The calling of philosopher is not, like that of the monks, an organized condition. Members of academies of learning are no doubt organized in part, but even a special calling like theirs sinks into the ordinary commonplace of state or class relationships, because admission thereinto is outwardly determined. The real matter is to remain faithful to one's aims.

SECTION TWO

PERIOD OF THE THINKING UNDERSTANDING

AFTER Neo-Platonism and all that is associated with it is left behind, it is not until Descartes is arrived at that we really enter upon a philosophy which is, properly speaking, independent, which knows that it comes forth from reason as independent, and that self-consciousness is an essential moment in the truth. Philosophy in its own proper soil separates itself entirely from the philosophizing theology, in accordance with its principle, and places it on quite another side. Here, we may say, we are at home, and like the mariner after a long voyage in a tempestuous sea, we may now hail the sight of land; with Descartes the culture of modern times, the thought of modern Philosophy, really begins to appear, after a long and tedious journey on the way which has led so far. It is specially characteristic of the German that the more servile he on the one hand is, the more uncontrolled is he on the other; restraint and want of restraint—originality, is the angel of darkness that buffets us. In this new period the universal principle by means of which everything in the world is regulated, is the thought that proceeds from itself; it is a certain inwardness, which is above all evidenced in respect to Christianity, and which is the Protestant principle in accordance with which thought has come to the consciousness of the world at large as that to which every man has a claim. Thus because the independently existent thought, this culminating point of inwardness, is now set forth and firmly grasped as such, the dead externality of authority is set aside and regarded as out of place. It is only through my own free thought within that thought can however be recognized and ratified by me. This likewise signifies that such free thought is the universal business of the world and of individuals ; it is indeed the duty of every man, since everything is based upon it; thus what claims to rank as established in the world man must scrutinize in his own thoughts. Philosophy is thus become a matter of universal interest, and one respecting which each can judge for himself ; for everyone is a thinker from the beginning.

On account of this new beginning to Philosophy we find in the old histories of Philosophy of the seventeenth century—*e.g.* that of Stanley—the philosophy of the Greeks and Romans only, and Christianity forms the conclusion. The idea was that neither in Christianity, nor subsequently, any philosophy was to be found, because there was no longer a necessity for it, seeing that the philosophic theology of the Middle Ages had not free, spontaneous thought as its principle (Vol. I. pp. 111, 112). But though it is true that this has now become the philosophic principle, we must not expect that it should be at once methodically developed out of thought. The old assumption is made, that man only attains to the truth through reflection ; this plainly is the principle. But the determination and definition of God, the world of the manifold as it appears, is not yet revealed as necessarily proceeding from thought ; for we have only reached the thought of a content which is given through ordinary conception, observation, and experience.

On the one hand we see a metaphysic, and, on the other, the particular sciences : on the one hand abstract thought as such, on the other its content taken from experience ; these two lines in the abstract stand opposed to one another, and yet they do not separate themselves so sharply. We shall indeed come to an opposition, viz. to that between *a priori* thought—that the determinations which are to hold good for thought must be taken from thought itself—and the determination that we must commence, conclude and think from experience. This is the opposition between rationalism and empiricism; but it is really a subordinate one, because even the metaphysical mode in philosophy, which only allows validity to immanent thought, does not take what is methodically developed from the necessity of thought, but in the old way derives its content from inward or outward experience, and through reflection and meditation renders it abstract. The form of philosophy which is first reached through thought is metaphysics, the form of the thinking understanding; this period has, as its outstanding figures, Descartes and Spinoza, likewise Malebranche and Locke, Leibnitz and Wolff. The second form is Scepticism and Criticism with regard to the thinking understanding, to metaphysics as such, and to the universal of empiricism; here we shall go on to speak of representatives of the Scottish, German, and French philosophies; the French materialists again turn back to metaphysics.

CHAPTER I

The Metaphysics of the Understanding

Metaphysics is what reaches after substance, and this implies that one unity, one thought is maintained in opposition to dualism, just as Being was amongst the ancients. In metaphysics itself we have, however, the opposition between substantiality and individuality. What comes first is the spontaneous, but likewise uncritical, metaphysics, and it is represented by Descartes and Spinoza, who assert the unity of Being and thought. The second stage is found in Locke, who treats of the opposition itself inasmuch as he considers the metaphysical Idea of experience, that is the origin of thoughts and their justification, not yet entering on the question of whether they are absolutely true. In the third place we have Leibnitz's monad—the world viewed as a totality.

A. First Division.

We here encounter the innate ideas of Descartes. The philosophy of Spinoza, in the second place, is related to the philosophy of Descartes as its necessary development only; the method is an important part of it. A method which stands alongside of Spinozism and which is also a perfected development of Cartesianism, is, in the third place, that by which Malebranche has represented this philosophy.

1. Descartes.

René Descartes is a bold spirit who re-commenced the

whole subject from the very beginning and constituted afresh the groundwork on which Philosophy is based, and to which, after a thousand years had passed, it once more returned. The extent of the influence which this man exercised upon his times and the culture of Philosophy generally, cannot be sufficiently expressed; it rests mainly in his setting aside all former pre-suppositions and beginning in a free, simple, and likewise popular way, with popular modes of thought and quite simple propositions, in his leading the content to thought and extension or Being, and so to speak setting up this before thought as its opposite. This simple thought appeared in the form of the determinate, clear understanding, and it cannot thus be called speculative thought or speculative reason. There are fixed determinations from which Descartes proceeds, but only of thought; this is the method of his time. What the French called exact science, science of the determinate understanding, made its appearance at this time. Philosophy and exact science were not yet separated, and it was only later on that this separation first took place.

To come to the life of Descartes—he was born in 1596, at La Haye in Touraine, of an ancient and noble race. He received an education of the usual kind in a Jesuit school, and made great progress; his disposition was lively and restless; he extended his insatiable zeal in all directions, pursued his researches into all systems and forms; his studies, in addition to ancient literature, embraced such subjects as philosophy, mathematics, chemistry, physics, and astronomy. But the studies of his youth in the Jesuit school, and those studies which he afterwards prosecuted with the same diligence and strenuous zeal, resulted in giving him a strong disinclination for learning derived from books; he quitted the school where he had been educated, and yet his eagerness for learning was only made the keener through this perplexity and unsatisfied yearning. He went as a young man of eighteen to Paris,

and there lived in the great world. But as he here found
no satisfaction, he soon left society and returned to his
studies. He retired to a suburb of Paris and there
occupied himself principally with mathematics, remaining quite concealed from all his former friends. At
last, after the lapse of two years, he was discovered by
them, drawn forth from his retirement, and again introduced to the great world. He now once more renounced
the study of books and threw himself into the affairs of
actual life. Thereafter he went to Holland and entered
the military service; soon afterwards, in 1619, and in the
first year of the Thirty Years' War, he went as a volunteer
with the Bavarian troops, and took part in several
campaigns under Tilly. Many have found learning unsatisfying; Descartes became a soldier—not because he
found in the sciences too little, but because they were too
much, too high for him. Here in his winter quarters he
studied diligently, and in Ulm, for instance, he made
acquaintance with a citizen who was deeply versed in
mathematics. He was able to carry out his studies even
better in winter quarters at Neuberg on the Danube, where
once more, and now most profoundly, the desire awoke in
him to strike out a new departure in Philosophy and
entirely reconstruct it; he solemnly promised the Mother
of God to make a pilgrimage to Loretto if she would
prosper him in this design, and if he should now at last
come to himself and attain to peace. He was also in the
battle at Prague in which Frederick the Elector-Palatine
lost the Bohemian crown. Yet since the sight of these
wild scenes could not satisfy him, he gave up military
service in 1621. He made several other journeys through
the rest of Germany, and then proceeded to Poland,
Prussia, Switzerland, Italy and France. On account of its
greater freedom he withdrew to Holland, in order there to
pursue his projects; here he lived in peace from 1629 to
1644—a period in which he composed and issued most of

his works, and also defended them against the manifold
attacks from which they suffered, and which more especially proceeded from the clergy.   Queen Christina of
Sweden finally called him to her court at Stockholm, which
was the rendezvous for all the most celebrated men of
learning of the time, and there he died in 1650.[1]

As regards his philosophic works, those which contain
his first principles have in particular something very
popular about their method of presentation, which makes
them highly to be recommended to those commencing the
study of philosophy.   Descartes sets to work in a quite
simple and childlike manner, with a narration of his reflections as they came to him.   Professor Cousin of Paris
has brought out a new edition of Descartes in eleven octavo
volumes ; the greater part consists of letters on natural
phenomena.   Descartes gave a new impetus to mathematics
as well as to philosophy.   Several important methods
were discovered by him, upon which the most brilliant
results in higher mathematics were afterwards built.   His
method is even now an essential in mathematics, for
Descartes is the inventor of analytic geometry, and consequently the first to point out the way in this field of
science to modern mathematics.   He likewise cultivated
physics, optics, and astronomy, and made the most important discoveries in these ; we have not, however, to
deal with such matters.   The application of metaphysics
to ecclesiastical affairs, investigations, etc., has likewise no
special interest for us.

1. In Philosophy Descartes struck out quite original
lines ; with him the new epoch in Philosophy begins,
whereby it was permitted to culture to grasp in the form

---

[1] Brucker. Hist. crit. phil. T. IV. P. II. pp. 203-217; Cartes. De
Methodo, I-II (Amstelod. 1672, 4), pp. 2-7 (Œuvres complètes de
Descartes publiées par Victor Cousin, T. I. pp. 125-133; Notes sur
l'éloge de Descartes par Thomas (Œuvres de Descartes publiées par
Cousin, T. I), p. 83, et suiv. ; Tennemann, Vol. X. pp. 210-216.

of universality the principle of its higher spirit in thought, just as Boehme grasped it in sensuous perceptions and forms. Descartes started by saying that thought must necessarily commence from itself; all the philosophy which came before this, and specially what proceeded from the authority of the Church, was for ever after set aside. But since here thought has properly speaking grasped itself as abstract understanding only, in relation to which the more concrete content still stands over on the other side, the determinate conceptions were not yet deduced from the understanding, but taken up only empirically. In Descartes' philosophy we have thus to distinguish what has, and what has not universal interest for us : the former is the process of his thoughts themselves, and the latter the mode in which these thoughts are presented and deduced. Yet we must not consider the process as a method of consistent proof ; it is indeed a deep and inward progress, but it comes to us in an ingenuous and naïve form. In order to do justice to Descartes' thoughts it is necessary for us to be assured of the necessity for his appearance; the spirit of his philosophy is simply knowledge as the unity of Thought and Being. And yet on the whole there is little to say about his philosophy.

a. Descartes expresses the fact that we must begin from thought as such alone, by saying that we must doubt everything (*De omnibus dubitandum est*); and that is an absolute beginning. He thus makes the abolition of all determinations the first condition of Philosophy. This first proposition has not, however, the same signification as Scepticism, which sets before it no other aim than doubt itself, and requires that we should remain in this indecision of mind, an indecision wherein mind finds its freedom. It rather signifies that we should renounce all prepossessions—that is, all hypotheses which are accepted as true in their immediacy—and commence from thought, so that from it we should in the first place attain to some fixed and settled basis, and make a true beginning. In Scepticism this is not the case, for with the sceptics doubt is the end at which they rest.[1] But the doubting of Descartes, his making no hypotheses, because nothing is fixed or secure, does not occur in the interests of freedom as such, in order that nothing should have value except freedom itself, and nothing exist in the quality of an external objective. To him everything is unstable indeed, in so far as the Ego can abstract from it or can think, for pure thought is abstraction from everything. But in consciousness the end is predominant, and it is to arrive at something fixed and objective—and not the moment of subjectivity, or the fact of being set forth, known and proved by me. Yet this last comes along with the other, for it is from the starting point of my thought that I would attain my object; the impulse of freedom is thus likewise fundamental.

In the propositions in which Descartes gives in his own way the ground of this great and most important principle, there is found a naïve and empirical system of reasoning. This is an example : " Because we were born as children, and formed all manner of judgments respecting sensuous things before we had the perfect use of our reason, we are through many preconceived ideas hindered from the knowledge of the truth. From these we appear not to be able to free ourselves in any other way but by once in our lives striving to doubt that respecting which we have the very slightest suspicion of an uncertainty. Indeed it is really desirable to hold as false everything in respect to which we have any doubt, so that we may find more clearly what is most certain and most knowable. Yet this doubt has to be limited to the contemplation of the truth, for in the conduct. of our life we are compelled to choose the

---

[1] Spinoza : Principia philosophiæ Cartesianæ (Benedicti de Spinoza Opera, ed. Paulus. Jenæ, 1802, T. I.), p. 2.

probable, since there the opportunity for action would often pass away before we could solve our doubts. But here, where we have only to deal with the search for truth, we may very reasonably doubt whether any thing sensuous and perceptible exists—in the first place because we find that the senses often deceive us and it is prudent not to trust in what has even once deceived us, and then because every day in dreaming we think we feel or see before ourselves innumerable things which never were, and to the doubter no signs are given by which he can safely distinguish sleeping from waking. We shall hereby likewise doubt everything else, even mathematical propositions, partly because we have seen that some err even in what we hold most certain, and ascribe value to what to us seems false, and partly because we have heard that a God exists who has created us, and who can do everything, so that He may have created us liable to err. But if we conceive ourselves not to derive our existence from God, but from some other source, perhaps from ourselves, we are all the more liable, in that we are thus imperfect, to err. But we have so far the experience of freedom within us that we can always refrain from what is not perfectly certain and well founded."[1] The demand which rests at the basis of Descartes' reasonings thus is that what is recognized as true should be able to maintain the position of having the thought therein at home with itself. The so-called immediate intuition and inward revelation, which in modern times is so highly regarded, has its place here. But because in the Cartesian form the principle of freedom as such is not brought into view, the grounds which are here advanced are for the most part popular.

b. Descartes sought something in itself certain and true,

----

[1] Cartes. Principia philosophiæ, P. I. § 1–6 (Amstelod. 1672, 4), pp. 1, 2 (Œuvres, T. III. pp. 63–66); cf. Meditationes de prima philosophia, I. (Amstelod. 1685, 4), pp. 5–8 (Œuvres, T. I. pp. 235–245); De Methodo, IV. p. 20 (pp. 156–158).

which should neither be only true like the object of faith without knowledge, nor the sensuous and also sceptical certainty which is without truth. The whole of Philosophy as it had been carried on up to this time was vitiated by the constant pre-supposition of something as true, and in some measure, as in the Neo-Platonic philosophy, by not giving the form of scientific knowledge to its matter, or by not separating its moments. But to Descartes nothing is true which does not possess an inward evidence in consciousness, or which reason does not recognize so clearly and conclusively that any doubt regarding it is absolutely impossible. " Because we thus reject or declare to be false everything regarding which we can have any doubt at all, it is easy for us to suppose that there is no God, no heaven, no body—but we cannot therefore say that we do not exist, who think this. For it is contradictory to say that what thinks does not exist. Hence the knowledge that ' I think, therefore I am,' is what we arrive at first of all, and it is the most certain fact that offers itself to everyone who follows after philosophy in an orderly fashion. This is the best way of becoming acquainted with the nature of spirit and its diversity from body. For if we inquire who we are who can set forth as untrue everything which is different from ourselves, we clearly see that no extension, figure, change of position, nor any such thing which can be ascribed to body, constitutes our nature, but only thought alone; which is thus known earlier and more certainly than any corporeal thing." [1] ' I ' has thus significance here as thought, and not as individuality of self-consciousness. The second proposition of the Cartesian philosophy is hence the immediate certainty of thought. Certainty is only knowledge as such in its pure form as self-relating, and this is thought; thus then the unwieldy understanding makes its way on to the necessity of thought.

[1] Cartes.   Principia philosophiæ, P. I. § 7, 8, p. 2 (pp. 66, 67).

Descartes begins, just as Fichte did later on, with the 'I' as indubitably certain; I know that something is presented in me. By this Philosophy is at one stroke transplanted to quite another field and to quite another standpoint, namely to the sphere of subjectivity. Presuppositions in religion are given up; proof alone is sought for, and not the absolute content which disappears before abstract infinite subjectivity. There is in Descartes likewise a seething desire to speak from strong feeling, from the ordinary sensuous point of view, just as Bruno and so many others, each in his own fashion, express as individualities their particular conceptions of the world. To consider the content in itself is not the first matter; for I can abstract from all my conceptions, but not from the 'I.' We think this and that, and hence it is—is to give the common would-be-wise argument of those incapable of grasping the matter in point; that a determinate content exists is exactly what we are forced to doubt—there is nothing absolutely fixed. Thought is the entirely universal, but not merely because I can abstract, but because 'I' is thus simple, self-identical. Thought consequently comes first; the next determination arrived at, in direct connection with it, is the determination of Being. The 'I think' directly involves my Being; this, says Descartes, is the absolute basis of all Philosophy.[1] The determination of Being is in my 'I'; this connection is itself the first matter. Thought as Being and Being as thought—that is my certainty, 'I'; in the celebrated *Cogito, ergo sum* we thus have Thought and Being inseparably bound together.

On the one hand this proposition is regarded as a syllogism: from thought Being is deduced. Kant more especially has objected to this that Being is not contained in thinking, that it is different from thinking. This is

---

[1] Cartes. De Methodo, IV. pp. 20, 21 (p. 158); Spinoza: Principia philosophiæ Cartes, p. 14.

true, but they are still inseparable, or constitute an identity ;
their difference is not to the prejudice of their unity. Yet
this maxim of pure abstract certainty, the universal totality
in which everything implicitly exists, is not proved ;[1] we
must therefore not try to convert this proposition into a
syllogism. Descartes himself says : "There is no syllogism present at all. For in order that there should be
such, the major premise must have been 'all that thinks
exists ' "—from which the subsumption would have followed
in the minor premise, ' now I am.' By this the immediacy
which rests in the proposition would be removed. "But
that major premise" is not set forth at all, being "really
in the first instance derived from the original 'I think,
therefore, I am.' "[2] For arriving at a conclusion three links
are required—in this case we ought to have a third through
which thought and Being should have been mediated,
and it is not to be found here. The 'Therefore' which
binds the two sides together is not the 'Therefore' of a
syllogism ; the connection between Being and Thought is
only immediately posited. This certainty is thus the
prius ; all other propositions come later. The thinking
subject as the simple immediacy of being-at-home-with-me
is the very same thing as what is called Being ; and it is
quite easy to perceive this identity. As universal, thought
is contained in all that is particular, and thus is pure relation to itself, pure oneness with itself. We must not make
the mistake of representing Being to ourselves as a concrete
content, and hence it is the same immediate identity which
thought likewise is. Immediacy is, however, a one-sided
determination ; thought does not contain it alone, but also
the determination to mediate itself with itself, and thereby

---

[1] Cartes. De Methodo, IV. p. 21 (p. 159); Epistol. T. I. ep. 118
(Amstelod. 1682, 4), p. 379 (Œuvres, T. IX. pp. 442, 443).

[2] Cartes. Responsiones ad sec. objectiones, adjunctæ Meditationibus
de prima philosophia, p. 74 (p. 427); Spinoza : Principia philosophiæ
Cartes., pp. 4, 5.

—by the mediation being at the same time the abrogation of the mediation—it is immediacy. In thought we thus have Being; Being is, however, a poor determination, it is the abstraction from the concrete of thought. This identity of Being and Thought, which constitutes the most interesting idea of modern times, has not been further worked out by Descartes; he has relied on consciousness alone, and for the time being placed it in the forefront. For with Descartes the necessity to develop the differences from the ' I think ' is not yet present; Fichte first applied himself to the deduction of all determinations from this culminating point of absolute certainty.

Other propositions have been set against that of Descartes. Gassendi,[1] for example, asks if we might not just as well say *Ludificor, ergo sum :* I am made a fool of by my consciousness, therefore I exist—or properly speaking, therefore I am made a fool of. Descartes himself recognized that this objection merited consideration, but he here repels it, inasmuch as it is the ' I ' alone and not the other content which has to be maintained. Being alone is identical with pure thought, and not its content, be it what it may. Descartes further says : " By thought I, however, understand all that takes place in us within our consciousness, in as far as we are conscious of it ; thus will, conception, and even feeling are identical with thought. For if I say ' I see,' or ' I walk out,' and ' therefore I am,' and understand by this the seeing and walking which is accomplished by the body, the conclusion is not absolutely certain, because, as often happens in a dream, I may imagine that I can see or walk even if I do not open my eyes nor move from my place, and I might also possibly do so supposing I had no body. But if I understand it of the subjective feeling or the consciousness of

---

[1] Appendix ad Cartes. Meditationes, continens objectiones quint. p. 4 (Œuvres, T. II. pp. 92, 93).

seeing or walking itself, because it is then related to the mind that alone feels or thinks that it sees or walks, this conclusion is perfectly certain." [1] "In a dream" is an empirical mode of reasoning, but there is no other objection to it. In willing, seeing, hearing, &c., thought is likewise contained; it is absurd to suppose that the soul has thinking in one special pocket, and seeing, willing, &c., in others. But if I say 'I see,' 'I walk out,' there is present on the one hand my consciousness 'I,' and consequently thought; on the other hand, however, there is present willing, seeing, hearing, walking, and thus a still further modification of the content. Now because of this modification I cannot say 'I walk, and therefore I am,' for I can undoubtedly abstract from the modification, since it is no longer universal Thought. Thus we must merely look at the pure consciousness contained in the concrete 'I.' Only when I accentuate the fact that I am present there as thinking, is pure Being implied; for only with the universal is Being united.

"In this it is implied," says Descartes, " that thought is more certain to me than body. If from the fact that I touch or see the earth I judge that it exists, I must more certainly judge from this that my thought exists. For it may very well happen that I judge the earth to exist, even if it does not exist, but it cannot be that I judge this, and that my mind which judges this does not exist." [2] That is to say, everything which is for me I may assert to be non-existent; but when I assert myself to be non-existent, I myself *assert*, or it is *my* judgment. For I cannot set aside the fact that I judge, even if I can abstract from that respecting which I judge. In this Philosophy has regained its own ground that thought starts from thought as what is certain in itself, and not from something external, not from some-

---

[1] Cartes. Principia philosophiæ, P. I. § 9, pp. 2, 3 (pp. 67, 68).
[2] Ibid. P. I. § 11, p. 3 (pp. 69, 70).

thing given, not from an authority, but directly from the freedom that is contained in the 'I think.' Of all else I may doubt, of the existence of bodily things, of my body itself; or this certainty does not possess immediacy in itself. For 'I' is just certainty itself, but in all else this certainty is only predicate; my body is certain to *me*, it is not this certainty itself.[1] As against the certainty we feel of having a body, Descartes adduces the empirical phenomenon that we often hear of persons imagining they feel pain in a limb which they have lost long ago.[2] What is actual, he says is a substance, the soul is a thinking substance; it is thus for itself, separate from all external material things and independent. That it is thinking is evident from its nature : it would think and exist even if no material things were present; the soul can hence know itself more easily than its body :[3]

All else that we can hold as true rests on this certainty ; for in order that anything should be held as true, evidence is requisite, but nothing is true which has not this inward evidence in consciousness. "Now the evidence of everything rests upon our perceiving it as clearly and vividly as that certainty itself, and on its so entirely depending from, and harmonizing with this principle, that if we wished to doubt it we should also have to doubt this principle likewise" (our *ego*).[4] This knowledge is indeed on its own account

[1] Cartes. Respons. ad sec. object. : Rationes more geometr. dispos., Postulata, p. 86 (pp. 454, 455); Spinoza : Principia philosophiæ, Cartes., p. 13.

[2] Cartes. Princip. philos., P. IV. § 196, pp. 215, 216 (pp. 507-509); Meditation. VI. p. 38 (pp. 329, 330); Spinoza : Principia philos. Cartes., pp. 2, 3.

[3] Cartes. Respons. ad sec. object.: Rat. more geom. dispos., Axiomata V., VI. p. 86 (p. 453), et Propositio IV. p. 91 (pp. 464, 465); Meditationes, II. pp. 9-14 (pp. 246-262).

[4] Cartes. De Methodo, IV. p. 21 (pp. 158, 159); Spinoza : Principia philosoph. Cartes., p. 14.

perfect evidence, but it is not yet the truth ; or if we take that Being as truth, it is an empty content, and it is with the content that we have to do.

c. What comes third is thus the transition of this certainty into truth, into the determinate ; Descartes again makes this transition in a naïve way, and with it we for the first time begin to consider his metaphysics. What here takes place is that an interest arises in further representations and conceptions of the abstract unity of Being and Thought; there Descartes sets to work in an externally reflective manner. " The consciousness which merely knows itself to be certain now however seeks to extend its knowledge, and finds that it has conceptions of many things—in which conceptions it does not deceive itself, so long as it does not assert or deny that something similar outside corresponds to them." Deception in the conceptions has meaning only in relation to external existence. " Consciousness also discovers universal conceptions, and obtains from them proofs which are evident, *e.g.* the geometric proposition that the three angles of a triangle are together equal to two right angles is a conception which follows incontrovertibly from others. But in reflecting whether such things really exist doubts arise."[1] That there is such a thing as a triangle is indeed in this case by no means certain, since extension is not contained in the immediate certainty of myself. The soul may exist without the bodily element, and this last without it ; they are in reality different ; one is conceivable without the other. The soul thus does not think and know the other as clearly as the certainty of itself.[2]

Now the truth of all knowledge rests on the proof of the existence of God. The soul is an imperfect substance,

[1] Cartes. Principia philosophiæ, P. I. § 13, pp. 3, 4 (pp. 71, 72).
[2] Cartes. Respons. ad sec. object : Rationes more geom. dispos., Def. I. p. 85 (pp. 451, 452), et Proposit. IV. p. 91 (pp. 464, 465) ; Meditationes, III. pp. 15-17 (pp. 263-268).

but it has the Idea of an absolute perfect existence within itself; this perfection is not begotten in itself, just because it is an imperfect substance; this Idea is thus innate. In Descartes the consciousness of this fact is expressed by his saying that as long as the existence of God is not proved and perceived the possibility of our deceiving ourselves remains, because we cannot know whether we do not possess a nature ordered and disposed to err (*supra,* p. 226).[1] The form is rather a mistaken one, and it only generally expresses the opposition in which self-consciousness stands to the consciousness of what is different, of the objective ; and we have to deal with the unity of both—the question being whether what is in thought likewise possesses objectivity. This unity rests in God, or is God Himself. I shall put these assertions in the manner of Descartes: " Amongst these various conceptions possessed by us there likewise is the conception of a supremely intelligent, powerful, and absolutely perfect Being; and this is the most excellent of all conceptions." This all-embracing universal conception has therefore this distinguishing feature, that in its case the uncertainty respecting Being which appears in the other conceptions, finds no place. It has the characteristic that " In it we do not recognize existence as something merely possible and accidental, as we do the conceptions of other things which we perceive clearly, but as a really essential and eternal determination. For instance, as mind perceives that in the conception of a triangle it is implied that the three angles are equal to two right angles, the triangle has them ; and in the same way from the fact that mind perceives existence to be necessarily and eternally implied in the Notion of the most perfect reality, it is forced to conclude that the most

---

[1] Cartes. Principia philos., P. I. § 20, p. 6 (pp. 76, 77); Meditationes, III. pp. 17-25 (pp. 268-292); De Methodo, IV. pp. 21, 22 (pp. 159-162); Spinoza : Principia philos. Cartes., p. 10.

perfect reality exists."[1]　For to perfection there likewise
pertains the determination of existence, since the conception of a non-existent is less perfect. Thus we there
have the unity of thought and Being, and the ontological
proof of the existence of God ; this we met with earlier
(p. 63, *seq.*) in dealing with Anselm.

The proof of the existence of God from the Idea of Him
is in this wise : In this Notion existence is implied ; and
therefore it is true. Descartes proceeds further in the same
direction, in so far as after the manner of empirical axioms
he sets forth : (*a*) "There are different degrees of reality or
entity, for the substance has more reality than the accident
or the mode, and infinite substance has more than finite."
(*β*) "In the Notion of a thing existence is implied, either
the merely potential or the necessary," *i.e.* in the ' I ' there
is Being as the immediate certainty of an other-being, of
the not-I opposed to the I.　(*γ*) " No thing or no perfection
of a thing which really exists *actu* can have the Nothing as
original cause of its existence. For if anything could be
predicated of nothing, thought could equally well be predicated of it, and I would thus say that I am nothing because
I think." Descartes here arrives at a dividing line, at an
unknown relationship ; the Notion of cause is reached, and
this is a thought indeed, but a determinate thought.
Spinoza says in his explanation, "That the conceptions
contain more or less reality, and those moments have just
as much evidence as thought itself, because they not only
say that we think, but how we think." These determinate
modes as differences in the simplicity of thought, had, however, to be demonstrated. Spinoza adds to this step in
advance that " The degrees of reality which we perceive in
ideas are not in the ideas in as far as they are considered
merely as kinds of thought, but in so far as the one represents a substance and the other a mere mode of substance,

---

[1] Cartes.　Principia philos. P. I., § 14, p. 4 (pp. 72, 73.)

or, in a word, in so far as they are considered as conceptions of things." (δ) "The objective reality of Notions" (*i.e.*, the entity of what is represented in so far as it is in the Notion), "demands a first cause in which the same reality is contained not merely objectively" (that is to say in the Notion); "but likewise formally or even *eminenter*—formally, that is perfectly likewise: *eminenter*, more perfectly. For there must at least be as much in the cause as in the effect." (ε) "The existence of God is known immediately" —*a priori*—"from the contemplation of His nature. To say that anything is contained in the nature or in the Notion of a thing is tantamount to saying that it is true: existence is directly contained in the Notion of God. Hence it is quite true to say of Him that existence pertains of necessity to Him. There is implied in the Notion of every particular thing either a possible or a necessary existence— a necessary existence in the Notion of God, *i.e.* of the absolutely perfect Being, for else He would be conceived as imperfect."[1]

Descartes likewise argues after this manner: "Problem: to prove *a posteriori* from the mere Notion within us the existence of God. The objective reality of a Notion demands a cause in which the same reality is not merely contained objectively" (as in the finite), "but formally" (freely, purely for itself, outside of us) "or *eminenter*" (as original). (Axiom δ.) "We now have a Notion of God, but His objective reality is neither formally nor *eminenter* contained within us, and it can thus be only in God Himself."[2] Consequently we see that with Descartes this Idea is an hypothesis. Now we should say we find this highest Idea in us. If we then ask whether this Idea exists, why, this is

[1] Cartes. Resp. ad sec. obj.: Rat. more geom. disp., Ax. III.-VI., X., Prop. I. pp. 88, 89 (pp. 458-461); Spinoza: Princ. phil. Cart., pp. 14-17.

[2] Spinoza: Princip. philos. Cart., p. 20; Cartesii Resp. ad sec. obj.: Rat. more geom. dispos., Propos. II. p. 89 (pp. 461, 462).

the Idea, that existence is asserted with it. To say that it is only a conception is to contradict the meaning of this conception. But here it is unsatisfactory to find that the conception is introduced thus: ' We have this conception,' and to find that it consequently appears like an hypothesis. In such a case it is not proved of this content in itself that it determines itself into this unity of thought and Being. In the form of God no other conception is thus here given than that contained in *Cogito, ergo sum*, wherein Being and thought are inseparably bound up—though now in the form of a conception which I possess within me. The whole content of this conception, the Almighty, All-wise, &c., are predicates which do not make their appearance until later; the content is simply the content of the Idea bound up with existence. Hence we see these determinations following one another in an empirical manner, and not philosophically proved—thus giving us an example of how in *a priori* metaphysics generally hypotheses of conceptions are brought in, and these become objects of thought, just as happens in empiricism with investigations, observations, and experiences.

Descartes then proceeds : " Mind is the more convinced of this when it notices that it discovers within itself the conception of no other thing wherein existence is necessarily implied. From this it will perceive that that idea of highest reality is not imagined by it ; it is not chimerical, but a true and unalterable fact which cannot do otherwise than exist, seeing that existence is necessarily involved in it. Our prejudices hinder us from apprehending this with ease, for we are accustomed to distinguish in all other things the essence " (the Notion) "from the existence." Respecting the assertion that thought is not inseparable from existence, the common way of talking is as follows : ' If what men think really existed, things would be different.' But in saying this men do not take into account that what is spoken of in this way is always a particular content, and that in it the essential nature of the finality of things simply signifies the fact that Notion and Being are separable. But how can one argue from finite things to the infinite? " This Notion," Descartes continues, " is furthermore not made by us." It is now declared to be an eternal truth which is revealed in us. " We do not find in ourselves the perfections which are contained in this conception. Thus we are certain that a first cause in which is all perfection, *i.e.* God as really existent, has given them to us ; for it is certain to us that from nothing, nothing arises " (according to Boehme God derived the material of the world from Himself), " and what is perfect cannot be the effect of anything imperfect. From Him we must thus in true science deduce all created things." [1] With the proof of the existence of God the validity of and evidence for all truth in its origin is immediately established. God as First Cause is Being-for-self, the reality which is not merely entity or existence in thought. An existence such as this first cause (which is not what we know as a thing) rests in the Notion of the not-I, not of each determinate thing— since these as determinate are negations—but only in the Notion of pure existence or the perfect cause. It is the cause of the truth of ideas, for the aspect that it represents is that of their Being.

d. Fourthly, Descartes goes on to assert: " We must believe what is revealed to us by God, though we cannot understand it. It is not to be wondered at, since we are finite, that there is in God's nature as inconceivably infinite, what passes our comprehension." This represents the entrance of a very ordinary conception. Boehme on the other hand says (*supra*, p. 212) : ' The mystery of the Trinity is ever born within us.' Descartes, however, concludes : " Hence we must not trouble ourselves with investigations respecting the infinite ; for seeing that we are finite, it is

---

[1] Cartes. Principia philosophiæ, P. I. §. 15 16, 18, 24, pp. 4, 5, 7 (pp. 73-75, 78, 79).

absurd for us to say anything about it." [1]   This matter we shall not, however, enter upon at present.

"Now the first attribute of God is that He is true and the Giver of all light; it is hence quite contrary to His nature to deceive us.   Hence the light of nature or the power of acquiring knowledge given us by God can affect no object which is not really true in as far as it is affected by it" (the power of acquiring knowledge) " *i.e.* as it is perceived clearly and distinctly."   We ascribe truth to God.   From this Descartes goes on to infer the universal bond which exists between absolute knowledge and the objectivity of what we thus know.   Knowledge has objects, has a content which is known ; we call this connection truth.   The truth of God is just this unity of what is thought by the subject or clearly perceived, and external reality or existence.   "Thereby an end is put to doubt, as if it could be the case that what appears quite evident to us should not be really true.   We can thus no longer have any suspicion of mathematical truths.   Likewise if we give heed to what we distinguish by our senses in waking or in sleeping, clearly and distinctly, it is easy to recognize in each thing what in it is true."   By saying that what is rightly and clearly thought likewise is, Descartes maintains that man comes to know by means of thought what in fact is in things ; the sources of errors lie on the other hand in the finitude of our nature.   "It is certain, because of God's truth, that the faculty of perceiving and that of assenting through the will, if it extends no further than to that which is clearly perceived, cannot lead to error.   Even if this cannot be in any way proved, it is by nature so established in all things, that as often as we clearly perceive anything, we assent to it from ourselves and can in no wise doubt that it is true." [2]

[1] Cartes. Principia philosophiæ, P. I. § 24-26, p. 7 (pp. 79, 80).
[2] Ibid. P. I. § 29, 30, 35, 36, 38, 43, pp. 8-11 (pp. 81-86, 89); Meditationes, IV. pp. 25, 26 (pp. 293-297).

All this is set forth very plausibly, but it is still indeterminate, formal, and shallow; we only have the assertion
made to us that this is so. Descartes' method is the
method of the clear understanding merely. Certainty with
him takes the first place ; from it no content is deduced of
necessity, no content generally, and still less its objectivity
as distinguished from the inward subjectivity of the 'I.'
At one time we have the opposition of subjective knowledge and actuality, and at another their inseparable union.
In the first case the necessity of mediating them enters in,
and the truth of God is asserted to be this mediating power.
It consists in this, that His Notion contains reality immediately in itself. The proof of this unity then rests solely
upon the fact of its being said that we find within us the
idea of complete perfection; thus this conception here
appears simply as one found ready to hand. With this
is compared the mere conception of God which contains
no existence within it, and it is found that without existence it would be imperfect. This unity of God Himself,
of His Idea, with His existence, is undoubtedly the Truth ;
in this we find the ground for holding as true what is for
us just as certain as the truth of ourselves. As Descartes
proceeds further we thus find that in reality everything
has truth for him only in so far as it is really an object of
thought, a universal. This truth of God has been, as we
shall see, expressed even more clearly and in a more con-
cise way by a disciple of Descartes, if one may venture
to call him so—I mean Malebranche (who might really be
dealt with here),[1] in his *Recherche de la vérité.*

The first of the fundamental determinations of the
Cartesian metaphysics is from the certainty of oneself to
arrive at the truth, to recognize Being in the Notion of
thought. But because in the thought " I think," I am an
individual, thought comes before my mind as subjective ;

[1] In the Lectures of 1829–1830 the philosophy of Malebranche is
inserted here. (Editor's note).

Being is hence not demonstrated in the Notion of thought itself, for what advance has been made is merely in the direction of separation generally. In the second place the negative of Being likewise comes before self-consciousness, and this negative, united with the positive I, is so to speak implicitly united in a third, in God. God, who before this was a non-contradictory potentiality, now takes objective form to self-consciousness, He is all reality in so far as it is positive, *i.e.* as it is Being, unity of thought and Being, the highest perfection of existence; it is just in the negative, in the Notion of this, in its being an object of thought, that Being is contained. An objection to this identity is now old—Kant urged it likewise—that from the Notion of the most perfect existence more does not follow than that *in* thought existence here and now and the most perfect essence are conjoined, but not *outside* of thought. But the very Notion of present existence is this negative of self-consciousness, not out of thought,—but the thought of the ' out of thought.'

2. Descartes accepts Being in the entirely positive sense, and has not the conception of its being the negative of self-consciousness : but simple Being, set forth as the negative of self-consciousness, is extension. Descartes thus separates extension from God, remains constant to this separation, unites the universe, matter, with God in such a way as to make Him its creator and first cause : and he has the true perception that conservation is a continuous creation, in so far as creation as activity is asserted to be separated. Descartes does not, however, trace extension in a true method back to thought ; matter, extended substances, stand over against the thinking substances which are simple ; in as far as the universe is created by God, it could not be as perfect as its cause. As a matter of fact the effect is less perfect than the cause, since it is that which is posited, if we are to remain at the conception of cause pertaining to the understanding. Hence according to Descartes extension is the

less perfect. But as imperfect the extended substances cannot exist and subsist through themselves or their Notion ; they thus require every moment the assistance of God for their maintenance, and without this they would in a moment sink back into nothing. Preservation is, however, unceasing re-production.[1]

Descartes now proceeds to further particulars, and expresses himself as follows : " We consider what comes under consciousness either as things or their qualities, or as eternal truths which have no existence outside our thought "—which do not belong to this or that time, to this or that place. He calls these last something inborn within us, something not made by us or merely felt,[2] but the eternal Notion of mind itself and the eternal determinations of its freedom, of itself as itself. From this point the conception that ideas are inborn (*innatæ ideæ*) hence proceeds ; this is the question over which Locke and Leibnitz dispute. The expression " eternal truths " is current even in these modern times, and it signifies the universal determinations and relations which exist entirely on their own account. The word ' inborn ' is however a clumsy and stupid expression, because the conception of physical birth thereby indicated, does not apply to mind. To Descartes inborn ideas are not universal, as they are to Plato and his successors, but that which has evidence, immediate certainty, an immediate multiplicity founded in thought itself—manifold conceptions in the form of a Being, resembling what Cicero calls natural feelings implanted in the heart. We would rather say that such is implied in the nature and essence of our mind and spirit. Mind is active and conducts it-

[1] Cartes. Principia philos. P. I. § 22, 23, pp. 6, 7 (pp. 77, 78) ; Responsiones quartæ, p. 133 (p. 70) ; Spinoza : Princip. philos. Cart. pp. 30, 31, 36, 38 ; Buhle : Geschichte der neuern Philosophie, Vol. III. Sec. I. pp. 17, 18.

[2] Cartes. Principia philos. P. I. § 48, p. 12 (p. 92) ; Meditationes, III. p. 17 (pp. 268, 269).

self in its activity in a determinate manner; but this activity has no other ground than its freedom. Yet if this is the case more is required than merely to say so; it must be deduced as a necessary product of our mind. We have such ideas, for instance, in the logical laws: " From nothing comes nothing," "A thing cannot both be and not be," [1] as also in moral principles. These are facts of consciousness which Descartes however soon passes from again; they are only present in thought as subjective, and he has thus not yet inquired respecting their content.

As regards things, on which Descartes now directs his attention, the other side to these eternal verities, the universal determinations of things are substance, permanence, order, &c. [2] He then gives definitions of these thoughts, just as Aristotle draws up a list of the categories. But although Descartes laid it down formerly as essential that no hypotheses must be made, yet now he takes the conceptions, and passes on to them as something found within our consciousness. He defines substance thus : " By substance I understand none other than a thing (*rem*) which requires no other something for existence ; and there is only one thing, namely God, which can be regarded as such a substance requiring no other thing." This is what Spinoza says ; we may say that it is likewise the true definition, the unity of Notion and reality : " All other " (things) " can only exist by means of a concurrence (*concursus*) of God " ; what we still call substance outside of God thus does not exist for itself, does not have its existence in the Notion itself. That is then called the system of assistance (*systema assistentiæ*) which is, however, transcendental. God is the absolute uniter of Notion and actuality ; other things, finite things which have a limit and stand in dependence,

---

[1] Cartes. Principia philosophiæ, P. I. § 49, p. 13 (p. 93).
[2] Ibid. P. I. § 48, p. 12 (p. 92).

require something else. " Hence if we likewise call other things substances, this expression is not applicable both to them and to God *univoce*, as is said in the schools ; that is to say no definite significance can be given to this word which would equally apply both to God and to the creatures." [1]

" But I do not recognize more than two sorts of things ; the one is that of thinking things, and the other that of things which relate to what is extended." Thought, the Notion, the spiritual, the self-conscious, is what is at home with itself, and its opposite is contained in what is extended, spatial, separated, not at home with itself nor free. This is the real distinction (*distinctio realis*) of substances : " The one substance can be clearly and definitely comprehended without the other. But the corporeal and the thinking and creating substance can be comprehended under this common notion, for the reason that they are things which require God's support alone in order to exist." They are universal ; other finite things require other things as conditions essential to their existence. But extended substance, the kingdom of nature, and spiritual substance, do not require one another. They may be called substances, because each of them constitutes an entire range or sphere, an independent totality. But because, Spinoza concluded, each side, the kingdom of thought as well as nature, is one complete system within itself, they are likewise in themselves, that is absolutely, identical as God, the absolute substance ; for thinking spirit this implicit is thus God, or their differences are ideal.

Descartes proceeds from the Notion of God to what is created, to thought and extension, and from this to the

---

[1] Cartes. Princip. philosophiæ, P. I. § 51, p. 14 (p. 95).

[2] Ibid. P. I. § 48, pp. 12, 13 (p. 92); § 60, p. 16 (p. 101); § 52, p. 14 (p. 95); Ration. more geometr. dispos., Definit. X. p. 86 (p. 454).

particular. " Now substances have several attributes without which they cannot be thought"—that signifies their determinateness—"but each has something peculiar to itself which constitutes its nature and essence "—a simple universal determinateness—"and to which the others all relate. Thus thought constitutes the absolute attribute of mind," thought is its quality; " extension is " the essential determination of corporeality, and this alone is " the true nature of body. What remains are merely secondary qualities, modes, like figure and movement in what is extended, imagination, feeling and will in thinking; they may be taken away or thought away. God is the uncreated, thinking substance." [1]

Descartes here passes to what is individual, and because he follows up extension he arrives at matter, rest, movement. One of Descartes' main points is that matter, extension, corporeality, are quite the same thing for thought; according to him the nature of body is fulfilled in its extension, and this should be accepted as the only essential fact respecting the corporeal world. We say that body offers resistance, has smell, taste, colour, transparency, hardness, &c., since without these we can have no body. All these further determinations respecting what is extended, such as size, rest, movement, and inertia, are, however, merely sensuous, and this Descartes showed, as it had long before this been shown by the Sceptics. Undoubtedly that is the abstract Notion or pure essence, but to body or to pure existence, there likewise of necessity pertains negativity or diversity. By means of the following illustration Descartes showed that with the exception of extension, all corporeal determinations may be annihilated, and that none can be absolutely predicated. We draw conclusions respecting the solidity and hardness of matter from the resistance which a body offers to our disturbance,

---

[1] Cartes. Principia philosophiæ, P. I. § 53, 54, p. 14 (pp. 96, 97).

and by means of which it seeks to hold its place. Now if
we admit that matter as we touch it always gives way to us
like space, we should have no reason for ascribing to it
solidity. Smell, colour, taste, are in the same way sensuous
qualities merely; but what we clearly perceive is alone
true. If a body is ground into small parts, it gives way,
and yet it does not lose its nature; resistance is thus not
essential.[1] This not-being-for-itself is however a quantitatively slighter resistance only; the resistance always
remains. But Descartes desires only to think; now he
does not think resistance, colour, &c., but apprehends them
by the senses only. Hence he says that all this must be led
back to extension as being special modifications of the same.
It is undoubtedly to the credit of Descartes that he only
accepts as true what is thought; but the abrogation of these
sensuous qualities simply represents the negative movement
of thought: the essence of body is conditioned through this
thought, that is, it is not true essence.

Descartes now makes his way from the Notion of extension to the laws of motion, as the universal knowledge of
the corporeal in its implicitude; he shows (a) that there
is no vacuum, for that would be an extension without
bodily substance, *i.e.* a body without body; (β) that there
are no atoms (no indivisible independent existence), for the
same reason, viz., because the essence of body is extension.
(γ) He further shows that a body is set in motion by something outside of it, but of itself it continues in a condition
of rest, and likewise it must, when in a condition of movement, be brought to rest by another outside of it—this is
the property of inertia.[2] These are unmeaning propositions, for an abstraction is involved for instance in asserting
simple rest and movement in their opposition.

[1] Cartes. Princip. philos., P. I. § 66-74, pp. 19-22 (pp. 107-117);
P. II. § 4, p. 25 (pp. 123, 124).
[2] Cartes. Principia philos. P. II. § 16, 20, 37, 38, pp. 29-31,
38, 39 (pp. 133, 134, 137, 138, 152-154).

Extension and motion are the fundamental conceptions in mechanical physics; they represent the truth of the corporeal world. It is thus that ideality comes before the mind of Descartes, and he is far elevated above the reality of the sensuous qualities, although he does not reach so far as to the separation of this ideality. He thus remains at the point of view of mechanism pure and simple. Give me matter (extension) and motion and I will build worlds for you, is what Descartes virtually says.[1] Space and time were hence to him the only determinations of the material universe. In this, then, lies the mechanical fashion of viewing nature, or the natural philosophy of Descartes is seen to be purely mechanical.[2] Hence changes in matter are due merely to motion, so that Descartes traces every relationship to the rest and movement of particles, and all material diversity such as colour, and taste—in short, all bodily qualities and animal phenomena—to mechanism. In living beings processes such as that of digestion are mechanical effects which have as principles, rest and movement. We here see the ground and origin of the mechanical philosophy; but further on we find that this is unsatisfactory, for matter and motion do not suffice to explain life. Yet the great matter in all this is that thought goes forward in its determinations, and that it constitutes from these thought-determinations the truth of nature.

In his consideration of the system of the world and the movement of the heavenly bodies, Descartes has worked out the mechanical view more fully. He thus comes to speak of the earth, the sun, &c., and of his conception of the circling motion of the heavenly bodies in the form of vortices: of metaphysical hypotheses as to how small

[1] Buhle : Geschichte der neuern Philosophie, Vol. III. Sec. 1. p. 19; cf. Cartes. Princip. phil., P. III. § 46, 47, p. 65 (pp. 210-212).
[2] Cf. Cartes. Principia philos., P. II. § 64, p. 49 (pp. 178, 179).

particles pass into, out of, and through pores and act on one another ; and finally to saltpetre and gunpowder.[1]

Universal reflections should have the first claim on our attention; but on the other hand the transition to the determinate is accomplished in a system of Physics which is the result of observations and experiences, and this is done entirely by means of the understanding. Descartes thus mingles many observations with a metaphysic of this nature, and to us the result is hence obscure. In this philosophy the thinking treatment of empiricism is thus predominant, and a similar method has been adopted by philosophers from this time on. To Descartes and others, Philosophy had still the more indefinite significance of arriving at knowledge through thought, reflection, and reasoning. Speculative cognition, the derivation from the Notion, the free independent development of the matter itself, was first introduced by Fichte, and consequently what is now called philosophic knowledge is not yet separated in Descartes from the rest of scientific knowledge. In those times all the knowledge of mankind was called philosophy ; in Descartes' metaphysics we thus saw quite empirical reflection and reasoning from particular grounds, from experiences, facts, phenomena, being brought into play in the naïvest manner, and one has no sense of speculation in the matter. The strictly scientific element here really consisted mainly in the method of proof as it has long been made use of in geometry, and in the ordinary method of the formal logical syllogism. Hence it likewise happens that Philosophy, which ought to form a totality of the sciences, begins with logic and metaphysics ; the second part is composed of ordinary physics and mathematics, mingled no doubt with metaphysical speculations, and the third part, ethics, deals

[1] Cartes. Principia philos., P. III. § 5-42, 46 sqq. pp. 51-63, 65 sqq. (pp. 183-208, p. 210 *et suiv.*) ; P. IV. § 1 sqq., 69, 109-115, P. 137 sqq., 116, 178-180 (p. 330 *et suiv.*, 388, 420-425).

with the nature of man, his duties, the state, the citizen.
And this is the case with Descartes. The first part of
the *Principia philosophiæ* treats *De principiis cognitionis
humanæ*, the second *De principiis rerum materialium*. This
natural philosophy, as a philosophy of extension, is, however, none other than what a quite ordinary physics or
mechanics might at that time be, and it is still quite hypothetical; we, on the other hand, accurately distinguish
empirical physics and natural philosophy, even though the
first likewise pertains to thought.

3. Descartes never reached the third part, the philosophy
of Mind, for, while he made a special study of physics, in
the region of ethics he published one tract only, *De pas-
sionibus*. In this reference Descartes treats of thought
and' human freedom. He proves freedom from the fact of
the soul thinking that the will is unrestrained, and of that
constituting the perfection of mankind. And this is quite
true. In respect to the freedom of the will he comes
across the difficulty of how to reconcile it with the divine
prescience. As free, man might do what is not ordained
of God beforehand—this would conflict with the omnipotence and omniscience of God; and if everything is
ordained of God, human freedom would thereby be done
away with. Yet he does not solve the contradiction contained in these two different aspects without falling into
difficulty. But conformably to the method which he adopts,
and which we pointed out above (pp. 238, 239), he says: "The
human mind is finite, God's power and predetermination are
infinite; we are thus not capable of judging of the relationship in which the freedom of the human soul stands to the
omnipotence and omniscience of God—but in self-consciousness we have the certainty of it given us as a fact. And
we must hold only to what is certain." [1]   When he proceeds

---

[1] Cartes. Principia philosoph., P. I. § 37, 39-41, pp. 10, 11
(pp. 85-88).

further much appears to him still incapable of explanation; but we see obstinacy and caprice likewise exhibited in his stopping short at the assertion as to the best of his knowledge. The method of knowledge as set forth by Descartes, takes the form of a reasoning of the understanding, and is thus without special interest.

These, then, are the principal points in the Cartesian system. Some particular assertions made by Descartes, which have been specially instrumental in giving him fame, have still to be mentioned—particular forms which have been formerly considered in metaphysics, and likewise by Wolff. For example, in the first place we gather that Descartes regarded animals and other organisms as machines moved by another, and not possessing the principle of the spontaneity of thought within them [1]—a mechanical physiology, a cut and dry thought pertaining to the understanding, which is of no further importance. In the sharp opposition between thought and extension, the former is not considered as sensation, so that the latter can isolate itself. The organic must as body reduce itself to extension; any further development of this last thus only proves its dependence on the first determinations.

In the second place, the relation between soul and body now becomes an important question, that is, the return of the object within itself in such a way that thought posits itself in another, in matter. As to this, many systems are offered to us in metaphysics. One of these is the *influxus physicus*, that the relation of spirit is of a corporeal nature, that the object is related to mind as bodies are to one another—a conception like this is very crude. How does Descartes understand the unity of soul and body? The former belongs to thought, the latter to extension; and thus because both are substance, neither

---

[1] Cartes. De Methodo, V. pp. 35, 36 (pp. 185-189).

requires the Notion of the other, and hence soul and body are independent of one another and can exercise no direct influence upon one another. Soul could only influence body in so far as it required the same, and conversely— that is, in so far as they have actual relation to one another. But since each is a totality, neither can bear a real relation to the other. Descartes consistently denied the physical influence of one on the other; that would have signified a mechanical relation between the two. Descartes thus established the intellectual sphere in contradistinction to matter, and on it based the independent subsistence of mind; for in his *cogito* ' I ' is at first only certain of itself, since I can abstract from all. Now we find the necessity of a mediator to bring about a union of the abstract and the external and individual. Descartes settles this by placing between the two what constitutes the metaphysical ground of their mutual changes, God. He is the intermediate bond of union, in as far as He affords assistance to the soul in what it cannot through its own freedom accomplish, so that the changes in body and soul may correspond with one another.[1] If I have desires, an intention, these receive corporeal realization; this association of soul and body is, according to Descartes, effected through God. For above (p. 239) we saw that Descartes says of God that He is the Truth of the conception: as long as I think rightly and consistently, something real corresponds to my thought, and the connecting link is God. God is hereby the perfect identity of the two opposites, since He is, as Idea, the unity of Notion and reality. In the Idea of Spinoza this is worked out and developed in its further moments. Descartes' conclusion is quite correct; in finite things this identity is imperfect. Only the form employed by Descartes is inadequate; for it implies that in the beginning there are two things, thought or soul and

[1] Cartes. De Methodo, V. p. 29 (173, 174).

body, and that then God appears as a third thing, outside both—that He is not the Notion of unity, nor are the two elements themselves Notion. We must not however forget that Descartes says that both those original elements are created substances. But this expression ' created' pertains to the ordinary conception only and is not a determinate thought; it was Spinoza, therefore, who first accomplished this return to thought.

2. SPINOZA.

The philosophy of Descartes underwent a great variety of unspeculative developments, but in Benedict Spinoza a direct successor to this philosopher may be found, and one who carried on the Cartesian principle to its furthest logical conclusions. For him soul and body, thought and Being, cease to have separate independent existence. The dualism of the Cartesian system Spinoza, as a Jew, altogether set aside. For the profound unity of his philosophy as it found expression in Europe, his manifestation of Spirit as the identity of the finite and the infinite in God, instead of God's appearing related to these as a Third—all this is an echo from Eastern lands. The Oriental theory of absolute identity was brought by Spinoza much more directly into line, firstly with the current of European thought, and then with the European and Cartesian philosophy, in which it soon found a place.

First of all we must, however, glance at the circumstances of Spinoza's life. He was by descent a Portuguese Jew, and was born at Amsterdam in the year 1632; the name he received was Baruch, but he altered it to Benedict. In his youth he was instructed by the Rabbis of the synagogue to which he belonged, but he soon fell out with them, their wrath having been kindled by the criticisms which he passed on the fantastic doctrines of the Talmud. He was not, therefore, long in absenting himself from the syna-

gogue, and as the Rabbis were in dread lest his example
should have evil consequences, they offered him a yearly
allowance of a thousand gulden if he would keep away from
the place and hold his tongue.   This offer he declined ; and
the Rabbis thereafter carried their persecution of him to
such a pitch that they were even minded to rid themselves
of him by assassination.   After having made a narrow
escape from the dagger, he formally withdrew from the
Jewish communion, without, however, going over to the
Christian Church.   He now applied himself particularly to
the Latin language, and made a special study of the Cartesian philosophy.   Later on he went to Rhynsburg, near
Leyden, and from the year 1664 he lived in retirement,
first at Voorburg, a village near the Hague, and then at the
Hague itself, highly respected by numerous friends : he
gained a livelihood for himself by grinding optical glasses.
It was no arbitrary choice that led him to occupy himself
with light, for it represents in the material sphere the absolute identity which forms the foundation of the Oriental
view of things.   Although he had rich friends and mighty
protectors, among whom even generals were numbered, he
lived in humble poverty, declining the handsome gifts
offered to him time after time.   Nor would he permit Simon
von Vries to make him his heir ; he only accepted from
him an annual pension of three hundred florins ; in the
same way he gave up to his sisters his share of their father's
estate.   From the Elector Palatine, Carl Ludwig, a man of
most noble character and raised above the prejudices of his
time, he received the offer of a professor's chair at Heidelberg, with the assurance that he would have liberty to teach
and to write, because "the Prince believed he would
not put that liberty to a bad use by interfering with the
religion publicly established."   Spinoza (in his published
letters) very wisely declined this offer, however, because
"he did not know within what limits that philosophic
liberty would have to be confined, in order that he might

not appear to be interfering with the publicly established
religion." He remained in Holland, a country highly interesting in the history of general culture, as it was the
first in Europe to show the example of universal toleration,
and afforded to many a place of refuge where they might
enjoy liberty of thought; for fierce as was the rage of the
theologians there against Bekker, for example (Bruck. Hist.
crit. phil. T. IV. P. 2, pp. 719, 720), and furious as were
the attacks of Voetius on the Cartesian philosophy, these
had not the consequences which they would have had in
another land. Spinoza died on the 21st of February, 1677,
in the forty-fourth year of his age. The cause of his death
was consumption, from which he had long been a sufferer;
this was in harmony with his system of philosophy, according
to which all particularity and individuality pass away in the
one substance. A Protestant divine, Colerus by name, who
published a biography of Spinoza, inveighs strongly against
him, it is true, but gives nevertheless a most minute and
kindly description of his circumstances and surroundings—
telling how he left only about two hundred thalers, what
debts he had, and so on. A bill included in the inventory,
in which the barber requests payment due him by M.
Spinoza of blessed memory, scandalizes the parson very
much, and regarding it he makes the observation : " Had
the barber but known what sort of a creature Spinoza was,
he certainly would not have spoken of his blessed memory."
The German translator of this biography writes under the
portrait of Spinoza: *characterem reprobationis in vultu
gerens,* applying this description to a countenance which
doubtless expresses the melancholy of a profound thinker,
but is otherwise mild and benevolent. The *reprobatio* is
certainly correct; but it is not a reprobation in the passive
sense; it is an active disapprobation on Spinoza's part of
the opinions, errors and thoughtless passions of mankind.[1]

[1] Collectanea de vita B. de Spinoza (addita Operibus ed. Paulus

Spinoza used the terminology of Descartes, and also
published an account of his system. For we find the first
of Spinoza's works entitled "An Exposition according to
the geometrical method of the principles of the Cartesian
philosophy." Some time after this he wrote his *Tractatus
theologico-politicus,* and by it gained considerable reputa-
tion. Great as was the hatred which Spinoza roused amongst
his Rabbis, it was more than equalled by the odium which
he brought upon himself amongst Christian, and especially
amongst Protestant theologians—chiefly through the
medium of this essay. It contains his views on inspiration,
a critical treatment of the books of Moses and the like,
chiefly from the point of view that the laws therein
contained are limited in their application to the Jews.
Later Christian theologians have written critically on this
subject, usually making it their object to show that these
books were compiled at a later time, and that they date in
part from a period subsequent to the Babylonian captivity ;
this has become a crucial point with Protestant theologians, and one by which the modern school distinguishes
itself from the older, greatly pluming itself thereon. All
this, however, is already to be found in the above-mentioned
work of Spinoza. But Spinoza drew the greatest odium
upon himself by his philosophy proper, which we must now
consider as it is given to us in his Ethics. While Descartes
published no writings on this subject, the Ethics of Spinoza
is undoubtedly his greatest work ; it was published after
his death by Ludwig Mayer, a physician, who had been
Spinoza's most intimate friend. It consists of five parts ;
the first deals with God (*De Deo*). General metaphysical
ideas are contained in it, which include the knowledge of
God and nature. The second part deals with the nature
and origin of mind (*De natura et origine mentis*). We see

Jenæ 1802-1803, T. II.), pp. 593-604, 612-628 (Spinoza Epist. LIII-
LIV. in Oper. ed. Paul. T. I. pp. 638-640) 642-665 ; Spinozæ Oper. ed.
Paul. T. II. Præf. p. XVI.

thus that Spinoza does not treat of the subject of natural philosophy, extension and motion at all, for he passes immediately from God to the philosophy of mind, to the ethical point of view; and what refers to knowledge, intelligent mind, is brought forward in the first part, under the head of the principles of human knowledge. The third book of the Ethics deals with the origin and nature of the passions (*De origine et natura affectuum*); the fourth with the powers of the same, or human slavery (*De servitute humana seu de affectuum viribus*); the fifth, lastly, with the power of the understanding, with thought, or with human liberty (*De potentia intellectus seu de libertate humana*).[1] Kirchenrath Professor Paulus published Spinoza's works in Jena; I had a share in the bringing out of this edition, having been entrusted with the collation of French translations.

As regards the philosophy of Spinoza, it is very simple, and on the whole easy to comprehend; the difficulty which it presents is due partly to the limitations of the method in which Spinoza presents his thoughts, and partly to his narrow range of ideas, which causes him in an unsatisfactory way to pass over important points of view and cardinal questions. Spinoza's system is that of Descartes made objective in the form of absolute truth. The simple thought of Spinoza's idealism is this: The true is simply and solely the one substance, whose attributes are thought and extension or nature: and only this absolute unity is reality, it alone is God. It is, as with Descartes, the unity of thought and Being, or that which contains the Notion of its existence in itself. The Cartesian substance, as Idea, has certainly Being included in its Notion; but it is only Being as abstract, not as real Being or as extension (*supra*, p. 241). With Descartes corporeality and the thinking 'I'

---

[1] Collectanea de vita B. de Spinoza, pp. 629-641; Spinozæ Ethic. (Oper. T. II.) pp. 1, 3 et not., 33.

are altogether independent Beings; this independence of the two extremes is done away with in Spinozism by their becoming moments of the one absolute Being. This expression signifies that Being must be grasped as the unity of opposites; the chief consideration is not to let slip the opposition and set it aside, but to reconcile and resolve it. Since then it is thought and Being, and no longer the abstractions of the finite and infinite, or of limit and the unlimited, that form the opposition (*supra*, p. 161), Being is here more definitely regarded as extension; for in its abstraction it would be really only that return into itself, that simple equality with itself, which constitutes thought (*supra*, p. 229). The pure thought of Spinoza is therefore not the simple universal of Plato, for it has likewise come to know the absolute opposition of Notion and Being.

Taken as a whole, this constitutes the Idea of Spinoza, and it is just what τὸ ὄν was to the Eleatics (Vol. I. pp. 244, 252). This Idea of Spinoza's we must allow to be in the main true and well-grounded; absolute substance is the truth, but it is not the whole truth; in order to be this it must also be thought of as in itself active and living, and by that very means it must determine itself as mind. But substance with Spinoza is only the universal and consequently the abstract determination of mind; it may undoubtedly be said that this thought is the foundation of all true views—not, however, as their absolutely fixed and permanent basis, but as the abstract unity which mind is in itself. It is therefore worthy of note that thought must begin by placing itself at the standpoint of Spinozism; to be a follower of Spinoza is the essential commencement of all Philosophy. For as we saw above (Vol. I. p. 144), when man begins to philosophize, the soul must commence by bathing in this ether of the One Substance, in which all that man has held as true has disappeared; this negation of all that is particular, to which every philosopher must have come, is the liberation of the mind and its absolute foundation. The difference between our standpoint and that of the Eleatic philosophy is only this, that through the agency of Christianity concrete individuality is in the modern world present throughout in spirit. But in spite of the infinite demands on the part of the concrete, substance with Spinoza is not yet determined as in itself concrete. As the concrete is thus not present in the content of substance, it is therefore to be found within reflecting thought alone, and it is only from the endless oppositions of this last that the required unity emerges. Of substance as such there is nothing more to be said; all that we can do is to speak of the different ways in which Philosophy has dealt with it, and the opposites which in it are abrogated. The difference depends on the nature of the opposites which are held to be abrogated in substance. Spinoza is far from having proved this unity as convincingly as was done by the ancients; but what constitutes the grandeur of Spinoza's manner of thought is that he is able to renounce all that is determinate and particular, and restrict himself to the One, giving heed to this alone.

1. Spinoza begins (Eth. P. I. pp. 35, 36) with a series of definitions, from which we take the following.

a. Spinoza's first definition is of the Cause of itself. He says: " By that which is *causa sui*, its own cause, I understand that whose essence " (or Notion) " involves existence, or which cannot be conceived except as existent." The unity of existence and universal thought is asserted from the very first, and this unity will ever be the question at issue. " The cause of itself " is a noteworthy expression, for while we picture to ourselves that the effect stands in opposition to the cause, the cause of itself is the cause which, while it operates and separates an " other," at the same time produces only itself, and in the production therefore does away with this distinction. The establishing of itself as an other is loss or degeneration, and at the same time the negation of this loss; this is a purely speculative Notion, indeed a fundamental Notion in all speculation. The cause in which the cause is identical with the effect, is the infinite cause (*infra*, p. 263); if Spinoza had further developed what lies in the *causa sui*, substance with him would not have been rigid and unworkable.

b. The second definition is that of the finite. "That thing is said to be finite in its kind which can be limited by another of the same nature." For it comes then to an end, it is not there ; what is there is something else. This something else must, however, be of a like nature ; for those things which are to limit each other must, in order to be able to limit each other, touch each other, and consequently have a relation to each other, that is to say they must be of one nature, stand on a like basis, and have a common sphere. That is the affirmative side of the limit. "Thus a thought is" only "limited by another thought, a body by another body, but thoughts are not limited by bodies nor" conversely "bodies by thoughts." We saw this (p. 244) with Descartes : thought is an independent totality and so is extension, they have nothing to do with one another ; they do not limit each other, each is included in itself.

c. The third definition is that of substance. "By substance I understand that which exists in itself and is conceived by itself, *i.e.* the conception of which does not require the aid of the conception of any other thing for its formation (*a quo formari debeat*) ;" otherwise it would be finite, accidental. What cannot have a conception formed of it without the aid of something else, is not independent, but is dependent upon that something else.

d. In the fourth place Spinoza defines attributes, which, as the moment coming second to substance, belong to it. "By attribute I understand that which the mind perceives as constituting the essence of substance ;" and to Spinoza this alone is true. This is an important determination ; the attribute is undoubtedly a determinateness, but at the same time it remains a totality. Spinoza, like Descartes, accepts only two attributes, thought and extension. The understanding grasps them as the reality of substance, but the reality is not higher than the substance, for it is only reality in the view of the understanding, which falls outside substance. Each of the two ways of regarding substance—extension and thought—contains no doubt the whole content of substance, but only in one form, which the understanding brings with it; and for this very reason both sides are in themselves identical and infinite. This is the true completion; but where substance passes over into attribute is not stated.

e. The fifth definition has to do with what comes third in relation to substance, the mode. " By mode I understand the affections of substance, or that which is in something else, through the aid of which also it is conceived." Thus substance is conceived through itself; attribute is not conceived through itself, but has a relation to the conceiving understanding, in so far as this last conceives reality; mode, finally, is what is not conceived as reality, but through and in something else.

These last three moments Spinoza ought not merely to have established in this way as conceptions, he ought to have deduced them; they are especially important, and correspond with what we more definitely distinguish as universal, particular and individual. They must not, however, be taken as formal, but in their true concrete sense; the concrete universal is substance, the concrete particular is the concrete species; the Father and Son in the Christian dogma are similarly particular, but each of them contains the whole nature of God, only under a different form. The mode is the individual, the finite as such, which enters into external connection with what is " other." In this Spinoza only descends to a lower stage, the mode is only the foregoing warped and stunted. Spinoza's defect

is therefore this, that he takes the third moment as mode
alone, as a false individuality. True individuality and
subjectivity is not a mere retreat from the universal, not
merely something clearly determinate; for, as clearly
determinate, it is at the same time Being-for-itself,
determined by itself alone. The individual, the subjective,
is even in being so the return to the universal; and in
that it is at home with itself, it is itself the universal.
The return consists simply and solely in the fact of the
particular being in itself the universal; to this return
Spinoza did not attain. Rigid substantiality is the last
point he reached, not infinite form; this he knew not,
and thus determinateness continually vanishes from his
thought.

f. In the sixth place, the definition of the infinite is also
of importance, for in the infinite Spinoza defines more
strictly than anywhere else the Notion of the Notion. The
infinite has a double significance, according as it is taken
as the infinitely many or as the absolutely infinite (*infra*,
p. 263). "The infinite in its kind is not such in respect
of all possible attributes; but the absolutely infinite is
that to whose essence all belongs that expresses an essence
and contains no negation." In the same sense Spinoza
distinguishes in the nine-and-twentieth Letter (Oper. T. I.
pp. 526-532) the infinite of imagination from the infinite
of thought (*intellectus*), the actual (*actu*) infinite. Most
men, when they wish to strive after the sublime, get no
further than the first of these; this is the false infinite,
just as when one says "and so on into infinity," meaning
perhaps the infinity of space from star to star, or else the
infinity of time. An infinite numerical series in mathematics
is exactly the same thing. If a certain fraction is
represented as a decimal fraction, it is incomplete; $\frac{1}{7}$ is, on
the contrary, the true infinite, and therefore not an incomplete expression, although the content here is of course
limited. It is infinity in the incorrect sense that one

usually has in view when infinity is spoken of; and even if
it is looked on as sublime, it yet is nothing present, and
only goes ever out into the negative, without being actual
(*actu*). But for Spinoza the infinite is not the fixing of a
limit and then passing beyond the limit fixed—the sensuous
infinity—but absolute infinity, the positive, which has complete and present in itself an absolute multiplicity which
has no Beyond. Philosophic infinity, that which is
infinite *actu*, Spinoza therefore calls the absolute affirmation
of itself. This is quite correct, only it might have been
better expressed as: "It is the negation of negation."
Spinoza here also employs geometrical figures as illustrations of the Notion of infinity. In his *Opera postuma,*
preceding his Ethics, and also in the letter quoted above,

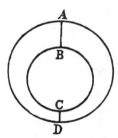

he has two circles, one of which lies
within the other, which have not, however, a common centre.

"The inequalities of the space between A B and C D exceed every
number; and yet the space which lies
between is not so very great." That
is to say, if I wish to determine them
all, I must enter upon an infinite series.
This "beyond" always, however, remains defective, is
always affected with negation; and yet this false infinite
is there to hand, circumscribed, affirmative, actual and
present in that plane as a complete space between the two
circles. Or a finite line consists of an infinite number of
points; and yet the line is present here and determined;
the "beyond" of the infinite number of points, which are
not complete, is in it complete and called back into unity.
The infinite should be represented as actually present, and
this comes to pass in the Notion of the cause of itself,
which is therefore the true infinity. As soon as the cause
has something else opposed to it—the effect—finitude is
present; but here this something else is at the same time

abrogated and it becomes once more the cause itself. The affirmative is thus negation of negation, since, according to the well-known grammatical rule, *duplex negatio affirmat.* In the same way Spinoza's earlier definitions have also the infinite already implied in them, for instance in the case of the just mentioned cause of itself, inasmuch as he defines it as that whose essence involves existence (*supra*, p. 258). Notion and existence are each the Beyond of the other; but cause of itself, as thus including them, is really the carrying back of this "beyond" into unity. Or (*supra*, p. 259) "Substance is that which is in itself and is conceived from itself;" that is the same unity of Notion and existence. The infinite is in the same way in itself and has also its Notion in itself; its Notion is its Being, and its Being its Notion; true infinity is therefore to be found in Spinoza. But he has no consciousness of this; he has not recognized this Notion as absolute Notion, and therefore has not expressed it as a moment of true existence; for with him the Notion falls outside of existence, into the thought of existence.

g. Finally Spinoza says in the seventh place: "God is a Being absolutely infinite, *i.e.* a substance consisting of infinite attributes, each of which expresses an eternal and infinite essence." Does substance, one might here ask, possess an infinite number of attributes? But as with Spinoza there are only two attributes, thought and extension, with which he invests God, "infinite" is not to be taken here in the sense of the indeterminate many, but positively, as a circle is perfect infinity in itself.

The whole of Spinoza's philosophy is contained in these definitions, which, however, taken as a whole are formal; it is really a weak point in Spinoza that he begins thus with definitions. In mathematics this method is permitted, because at the outset we there make assumptions, such as that of the point and line; but in Philosophy the content should be known as the absolutely true. It is all very well to grant the correctness of the name-definition, and acknowledge that the word "substance" corresponds with the conception which the definition indicates, but it is quite another question to determine whether this content is absolutely true. Such a question is not asked in the case of geometrical propositions, but in philosophic investigation it is the very thing to be first considered, and this Spinoza has not done. Instead of only explaining these simple thoughts and representing them as concrete in the definitions which he makes, what he ought to have done was to examine whether this content is true. To all appearance it is only the explanation of the words that is given ; but the content of the words is held to be established. All further content is merely derived from that, and proved thereby ; for on the first content all the rest depends, and if it is established as a basis, the other necessarily follows. "The attribute is that which the understanding thinks of God." But here the question is : How does it come that besides the Deity there now appears the understanding, which applies to absolute substance the two forms of thought and extension ? and whence come these two forms themselves ? Thus everything proceeds inwards, and not outwards ; the determinations are not developed from substance, it does not resolve itself into these attributes.

2. These definitions are followed by axioms and propositions in which Spinoza proves a great variety of points. He descends from the universal of substance through the particular, thought and extension, to the individual. He has thus all three moments of the Notion, or they are essential to him. But the mode, under which head falls individuality, he does not recognize as essential, or as constituting a moment of true existence in that existence ; for it disappears in existence, or it is not raised into the Notion.

a. The main point then is that Spinoza proves from these Notions that there is only One Substance, God. It is a

simple chain of reasoning, a very formal proof. "Fifth
Proposition : There cannot be two or more substances of
the same nature or of the same attribute." This is implied
already in the definitions ; the proof is therefore a useless
and wearisome toil, which only serves to render Spinoza
more difficult to understand. "If there were several"
(substances of the same attribute) "they must be distinguished from one another either by the diversity of their
attributes or by the diversity of their affections" (modes).
"If they are distinguished by their attributes, it would be
directly conceded that there is only one substance having
the same attribute." For the attributes are simply what the
understanding grasps as the essence of the one substance,
which is determined in itself, and not through anything else.
"But if these substances were distinguished by their
affections, since substance is by nature prior to its affections
it would follow that if from substance its affections were
abstracted and it were regarded in itself, *i.e.* in its truth, it
could henceforth not be regarded as distinct from other
substances." "Eighth Proposition : All substance is necessarily infinite. Proof: For otherwise it must be limited by
another substance of the same nature, in which case there
would be two substances of the same attribute, which is
contrary to the fifth proposition." "Every attribute must
be conceived for itself," as determination reflected on itself.
"For attribute is what the mind conceives of substance as
constituting its essence, from which it follows that it must
be conceived through itself," *i.e.* substance is what is
conceived through itself (see the fourth and third definitions). "Therefore we may not argue from the plurality of
attributes to a plurality of substances, for each is conceived
by itself, and they have all been, always and at the same
time, in substance, without the possibility of the one being
produced by the other." "Substance is indivisible. For if
the parts retained the nature of the substance, there would
be several substances of the same nature, which is contrary

to the fifth proposition. If not, infinite substance would cease to exist, which is absurd." [1]

"Fourteenth Proposition: No other substance than God can either exist or be conceived. Proof: God is the absolutely infinite substance, to whom can be denied no attribute which expresses the essence of substance, and He exists necessarily; therefore if there were a substance other than God, it must be explained by means of an attribute of God." Consequently the substance would not have its own being, but that of God, and therefore would not be a substance. Or if it were still to be substance, "then there would necessarily follow the possibility of there being two substances with the same attribute, which according to the fifth proposition is absurd. From this it then follows that the thing extended and the thing that thinks" are not substances, but "are either attributes of God, or affections of His attributes." By these proofs and others like them not much is to be gained. "Fifteenth proposition: What is, is in God, and cannot exist or be conceived without God." "Sixteenth proposition: By the necessity of the divine nature infinite things must follow in infinite modes, *i.e.*, all that can fall under the infinite understanding. God is therefore the absolute First Cause."

Spinoza then ascribes freedom and necessity to God: "God is the absolute free cause, who is determined by nothing outside of Himself, for He exists solely by the necessity of His nature. There is no cause which inwardly or outwardly moves Him to act, except the perfection of His nature. His activity is by the laws of His Being necessary and eternal; what therefore follows from His absolute nature, from His attributes, is eternal, as it follows from the nature of the triangle from eternity and to

---

[1] Spinoz. Ethices, P. I. Prop. V. VIII. X. et Schol., XIII. pp. 37–39, 41, 42, 45.

[2] Spinoz. Ethices, P. I. Prop. XIV. et Coroll. II. Prop. XV. XVI. et Coroll. I. pp. 46, 51.

eternity that its three angles are equal to two right angles."
That is to say, His Being is His absolute power; *actus* and
potentia, Thought and Being, are in Him one. God has not
therefore any other thoughts which He could not have
actualized. "God is the immanent cause of all things, not the
transient (*transiens*)," *i.e.*, external cause. "His essence and
His existence are the same, namely, the truth. A thing
which is determined to perform some action, is, since God is
cause, necessarily determined thereto by God; and a thing
which is thus determined cannot render itself undetermined.
In nature nothing is contingent. Will is not a free cause,
but only a necessary cause, only a mode; it is therefore
determined by another. God acts in accordance with no
final causes (*sub ratione boni*). Those who assert that He
does so, appear to establish something apart from God,
which does not depend on God, and which God in His
working keeps in view, as though it were an end. If this
view is taken, God is not a free cause, but is subject to fate.
It is equally inadmissible to subject all things to the
arbitrary pleasure of God, *i.e.*, to His indifferent will." [1] He
is determined solely by His own nature; the activity of
God is thus His power, and that is necessity. He is then
absolute power in contrast to wisdom, which sets up definite aims, and consequently limitations; particular aims,
thoughts of what is about to come to pass, and the
like are therefore put out of the question. But beyond
this universal, no advance is made; for it must be noticed
as specially singular, that Spinoza in the fiftieth Letter
(Oper. T. I. p. 634) says that every determination is a negation. Moreover, if God is the cause of the world, it is implied that He is finite; for the world is here put beside
God as something different from Him.

b. The greatest difficulty in Spinoza is, in the distinc-

---

[1] Spinoz. Ethices, P. I. Prop. XVII., Coroll. I., II., et Schol., Prop.
XVIII., Prop. XX., et Coroll. I. Prop. XXI., XXVI., XXVII.,
XXIX., XXXII., XXXIII. Schol. II. pp. 51-57, 59, 61, 63, 67, 68.

tions to which he comes, to grasp the relation of this determinate to God, at the same time preserving the determination. "God is a thinking Being, because all individual thoughts are modes which express God's nature in a certain and determinate manner; there pertains therefore to God an attribute the conception of which all individual thoughts involve, and by means of this they also are conceived. God is an extended Being for the same reason." This means that the same substance, under the attribute of thought, is the intelligible world, and under the attribute of extension, is nature; nature and thought thus both express the same Essence of God. Or, as Spinoza says, "The order and system of natural things is the same as the order of the thoughts. Thus, for instance, the circle which exists in nature, and the idea of the existing circle, which is also in God, are one and the same thing" (they are one and the same content), "which is" merely "expressed by means of different attributes. If we therefore regard nature either under the attribute of extension or of thought, or under any other attribute whatever, we shall find one and the same connection of causes, *i.e.*, the same sequence of things. The formal Being of the idea of the circle can be conceived only by means of the mode of thought, as its proximate cause, and this mode again by means of another, and so on infinitely; so that we must explain the order of the whole of nature, or the connection of causes, by the attribute of thought alone, and if things are considered by the attribute of extension, they must be considered only by the attribute of extension, —and the same holds good of other causes."[1] It is one and the same system, which at one time appears as nature, and at another time in the form of thought.

But Spinoza does not demonstrate how these two are

[1] Spinoz. Ethices, P. II. Prop. I., II., VII. et Schol. pp. 78, 79, 82, 83.

evolved from the one substance, nor does he prove why there can only be two of them.   Neither are extension and thought anything to him in themselves, or in truth, but only externally ; for their difference is a mere matter of the understanding, which is ranked by Spinoza only among affections (Eth. P. I. Prop. XXXI. Demonst. p. 62), and as such has no truth.   This has in recent times been served up again by Schelling in the following form : In themselves, the intelligent world and the corporeal world are the same, only under different forms; so that the intelligent universe is in itself the whole absolute divine totality, and the corporeal universe is equally this same totality. The differences are not in themselves ; but the different aspects from which the Absolute is regarded are matters external to it.   We take a higher tone in saying that nature and mind are rational; but reason is for us no empty word, for it means the totality which develops itself within itself.   Again, it is the standpoint of reflection to regard aspects only, and nothing in itself.   This defect appears in Spinoza and Schelling in the fact that they see no necessity why the Notion, as the implicit negative of its unity, should make a separation of itself into different parts; so that out of the simple universal the real, the opposed, itself becomes known.   Absolute substance, attribute and mode, Spinoza allows to follow one another as definitions, he adopts them ready-made, without the attributes being developed from the substance, or the modes from the attributes.   And more especially in regard to the attributes, there is no necessity evident, why these are thought and extension in particular.

c. When Spinoza passes on to individual things, especially to self-consciousness, to the freedom of the ' I,' he expresses himself in such a way as rather to lead back all limitations to substance than to maintain a firm grasp of the individual.   Thus we already found the attributes not to be independent, but only the forms in which the understanding grasps substance in its differences ; what comes third, the modes, is that under which for Spinoza all difference of things alone falls. Of the modes he says (Ethic. P. I. Prop. XXXII. Demonst. et Coroll. II. p. 63) : In every attribute there are two modes ; in extension, these are rest and motion, in thought they are understanding and will (*intellectus et voluntas*). They are mere modifications which only exist for us apart from God; therefore whatever refers to this difference and is specially brought about by it, is not absolute, but finite. These affections Spinoza sums up (Ethices, P. I. Prop. XXIX. Schol. pp. 61, 62) under the head of *natura naturata*: "*Natura naturans* is God regarded as free cause, in so far as He is in Himself and is conceived by Himself : or such attributes of substance as express the eternal and infinite essence. By *natura naturata*, I understand all that follows from the necessity of the divine nature, or from any of the attributes of God, all modes of the divine attributes, in so far as they are regarded as things which are in God, and which without God can neither exist ner be conceived." From God proceeds nothing, for all things merely return to the point whence they came, if from themselves the commencement is made.

These then are Spinoza's general forms, this is his principal idea. Some further determinations have still to be mentioned. He gives definitions of the terms modes, understanding, will, and of the affections, such as joy and sadness.[1] We further find consciousness taken into consideration. Its development is extremely simple, or rather it is not developed at all; Spinoza begins directly with mind. "The essence of man consists of certain modifications of the attributes of God"; these modifications are only something related to our understanding. "If we, therefore, say that the human mind perceives this or that,

[1] Spinoz. Ethic. P. I. Prop. XXX.-XXXII. pp. 62, 63; P. III. Defin. III. p. 132 ; Prop. XI. Schol., p. 141.

it means nothing else than that God has this or that idea, not in so far as He is infinite, but in so far as He is expressed by the idea of the human mind. And if we say that God has this or that idea, not in so far as He constitutes the idea of the human mind, but in so far as He has, along with the human mind, the idea of another thing, then we say that the human mind perceives the thing partially or inadequately." Truth is for Spinoza, on the other hand, the adequate.[1] The idea that all particular content is only a modification of God is ridiculed by Bayle,[2] who argues from it that God modified as Turks and Austrians, is waging war with Himself; but Bayle has not a trace of the speculative element in him, although he is acute enough as a dialectician, and has contributed to the intelligent discussion of definite subjects.

The relation of thought and extension in the human consciousness is dealt with by Spinoza as follows: " What has a place in the object " (or rather in the objective) " of the idea which constitutes the human mind must be perceived by the human mind; or there must necessarily be in the mind an idea of this object. The object of the idea which constitutes the human mind is body, or a certain mode of extension. If, then, the object of the idea which constitutes the human mind, is the body, there can happen nothing in the body which is not perceived by the mind. Otherwise the ideas of the affections of the body would not be in God, in so far as He constitutes our mind, but the idea of another thing : that is to say, the ideas of the affections of our body would not be likewise in our mind." What is perplexing to understand in Spinoza's system is, on the one hand, the absolute identity of thought and Being, and, on the other hand, their absolute

---

[1] Spinoz. Ethices, P. II. Prop. XI. Demonst. et Coroll. pp. 86, 87; Defin. IV. pp. 77, 78.

[2] Dictionnaire historique et critique (édition de 1740, T. IV.), Article Spinosa, p. 261, Note N. No. IV.

indifference to one another, because each of them is a manifestation of the whole essence of God. The unity of the body and consciousness is, according to Spinoza, this, that the individual is a mode of the absolute substance, which, as consciousness, is the representation of the manner in which the body is affected by external things; all that is in consciousness is also in extension, and conversely. " Mind knows itself only in so far as it perceives the ideas of the affections of body," it has only the idea of the affections of its body; this idea is synthetic combination, as we shall immediately see. " The ideas, whether of the attributes of God or of individual things, do not recognize as their efficient cause their objects themselves, or the things perceived, but God Himself, in so far as He is that which thinks." [1] Buhle (Geschichte der neuern Philos. Vol. III. Section II. p. 524) sums up these propositions of Spinoza thus : " Thought is inseparably bound up with extension ; therefore all that takes place in extension must also take place in consciousness." Spinoza, however, also accepts both in their separation from one another. The idea of body, he writes (Epistol. LXVI. p. 673), includes only these two in itself, and does not express any other attributes. The body which it represents is regarded under the attribute of extension; but the idea itself is a mode of thought. Here we see a dividing asunder ; mere identity, the undistinguishable nature of all things in the Absolute, is insufficient even for Spinoza.

The *individuum*, individuality itself, is thus defined by Spinoza (Ethic. P. II. Prop. XIII. Defin. p. 92) : " When several bodies of the same or of different magnitudes are so pressed together that they rest on one another, or when, moving with like or different degrees of rapidity, they communicate their movement to one another in a certain

---

[1] Spinoz. Ethices, P. II. Prop. XII., XIII. et Schol. Prop. XIV., XXIII., V. pp. 87-89, 95, 102, 80, 81.

measure, we say that such bodies are united to one another, and that all together they form one body or individuum, which by this union distinguishes itself from all the other bodies." Here we are at the extreme limit of Spinoza's system, and it is here that his weak point appears. Individuation, the one, is a mere synthesis; it is quite a different thing from the Ichts or self-hood of Boehme (*supra*, pp. 205-207), since Spinoza has only universality, thought, and not self-consciousness. If, before considering this in reference to the whole, we take it from the other side, namely from the understanding, the distinction really falls under that head ; it is not deduced, it is found. Thus, as we have already seen (p. 270) " the understanding in act (*intellectus actu*), as also will, desire, love, must be referred to *natura naturata*, not to *natura naturans*. For by the understanding, as recognized for itself, we do not mean absolute thought, but only a certain mode of thought—a mode which is distinct from other modes like desire, love, etc., and on that account must be conceived by means of absolute thought, *i.e.* by means of an attribute of God which expresses an eternal and infinite essentiality of thought ; without which the understanding, as also the rest of the modes of thought, could neither be nor be conceived to be." (Spinoza, Ethices, P. I. Propos. XXXI. pp. 62, 63). Spinoza is unacquainted with an infinity of form, which would be something quite different from that of rigid, unyielding substance. What is requisite is to recognize God as the essence of essences, as universal substance, identity, and yet to preserve distinctions.

Spinoza goes on to say : " What constitutes the real (*actuale*) existence of the human mind is nothing else than the idea of a particular " (individual) " thing, that actually exists," not of an infinite thing. " The essence of man involves no necessary existence, *i.e.* according to the order of nature a man may just as well be as not be." For the human consciousness, as it does not belong to essence as an attribute, is a mode—a mode of the attribute of thought. But neither is the body, according to Spinoza, the cause of consciousness, nor is consciousness the cause of the body, but the finite cause is here only the relation of like to like ; body is determined by body, conception by conception. " The body can neither determine the mind to thought, nor can the mind determine the body to motion, or rest, or anything else. For all modes of thought have God as Cause, in so far as He is a thinking thing, and not in so far as He is revealed by means of another attribute. What therefore determines the mind to thought, is a mode of thought and not of extension ; similarly motion and rest of the body must be derived from another body." [1]   I might quote many other such particular propositions from Spinoza, but they are very formal, and a continual repetition of one and the same thing.

Buhle (Gesch. d. neuern Phil. Vol. III. Section 2, pp. 525-528), attributes limited conceptions to Spinoza : " The soul experiences in the body all the ' other ' of which it becomes aware as outside of the body, and it becomes aware of this ' other ' only by means of the conceptions of the qualities which the body perceives therein. If, therefore, the body can perceive no qualities of a thing, the soul also can come to no knowledge of it. On the other hand, the soul is equally unable to arrive at the perception of the body which belongs to it ; the soul knows not that the body is there, and knows itself even in no other way than by means of the qualities which the body perceives in things which are outside of it, and by means of the conceptions of the same. For the body is an individual thing, determined in a certain manner, which can only gradually, in association with and amidst other individual things, attain to existence, and can preserve itself in existence only as thus connected, combined and associated with others," *i.e.* in

[1] Spinoz. Ethices, P. II. Prop. XI. (Axiom I. p. 78) et Demonstr. Prop. X. pp. 85-87 ; Prop. VI. p. 81 ; P. III. Prop. II. pp. 133, 134.

infinite progress ; the body can by no means be conceived
from itself. " The soul's consciousness expresses a certain
determinate form of a Notion, as the Notion itself expresses
a determinate form of an individual thing. But the individual thing, its Notion, and the Notion of this Notion are
altogether and entirely one and the same thing, only regarded under different attributes. As the soul is nothing
else than the immediate Notion of the body and is one
and the same thing with this, the excellence of the soul can
never be anything else than the excellence of the body.
The capacities of the understanding are nothing but the
capacities of the body, if they are looked at from the
corporeal point of view, and the decisions of the will are
likewise determinations of the body. Individual things are
derived from God in an eternal and infinite manner " (*i.e.*
once and for all), " and not in a transitory, finite and
evanescent manner : they are derived from one another
merely inasmuch as they mutually produce and destroy
each other, but in their eternal existence they endure unchangeable. All individual things mutually presuppose
each other ; one cannot be thought without the other ; that
is to say they constitute together an inseparable whole ;
they exist side by side in one utterly indivisible, infinite
Thing, and in no other way whatever.

3. We have now to speak of Spinoza's system of morals,
and that is a subject of importance. Its great principle is
no other than this, that the finite spirit is moral in so far
as it has the true Idea, *i.e.* in so far as it directs its knowledge and will on God, for truth is merely the knowledge
of God. It may be said that there is no morality loftier
than this, since its only requisite is to have a clear idea of
God. The first thing Spinoza speaks of in this regard is
the affections : " Everything strives after self-preservation.
This striving is the actual essence of the thing, and involves
only indefinite time ; when referred exclusively to mind, it
is termed will ; when referred to both mind and body to-

gether, it is called desire. Determination of the will
(*volitio*) and Idea are one and the same thing. The sense
of liberty rests on this, that men do not know the determining causes of their actions. The affection is a confused
idea; the more clearly and distinctly, therefore, we know
the affection, the more it is under our control."[1] The influence of the affections, as confused and limited (inadequate) ideas, upon human action, constitutes therefore,
according to Spinoza, human slavery; of the passionate
affections the principal are joy and sorrow; we are in
suffering and slavery in so far as we relate ourselves as a
part.[2]

"Our happiness and liberty consist in an enduring and
eternal love to God; this intellectual love follows from the
nature of mind, in so far as it is regarded as eternal truth
through the nature of God. The more a man recognizes
God's existence and loves Him, the less does he suffer from
evil affections and the less is his fear of death."[3] Spinoza
requires in addition the true kind of knowledge. There
are, according to him, three kinds of knowledge; in the
first, which he calls opinion and imagination, he includes
the knowledge which we obtain from an individual object
through the senses—a knowledge fragmentary and ill-
arranged—also knowledge drawn from signs, pictorial conceptions and memory. The second kind of knowledge is
for Spinoza that which we derive from general conceptions
and adequate ideas of the properties of things. The third
is intuitive knowledge (*scientia intuitiva*) which rises from

[1] Spinoz. Ethices, P. III. Prop. VI.-VIII. Prop. IX. Schol. pp.
139, 140; P. II. Prop. XLIX. Coroll. p. 123; P. III. Prop. II.
Schol. p. 136; P. V. Prop. III. Demonst. et Coroll. pp. 272, 273.

[2] Spinoz. Ethices, P. III. Prop. I. p. 132; Prop. III. p. 138; P.
IV. Præf. p. 199; P. III. Prop. XI. Schol. pp. 141, 142; P. IV.
Prop. II. p. 205; P. III. Prop. III. et Schol. p. 138.

[3] Spinoz. Ethices, P. V. Prop. XXXVI. Schol. Prop. XXXVII.
Demonstr., Prop. XXXVIII. et Schol. pp. 293-295.

the adequate idea of the formal essence of certain attributes of God to the adequate knowledge of the essence of things." [1] Regarding this last he then says : " The nature of reason is not to contemplate things as contingent, but as necessary ... to think of all things under a certain form of eternity (*sub quadam specie œternitatis*) ;" *i.e.* in absolutely adequate Notions, *i.e.* in God. " For the necessity of things is the necessity of the eternal nature of God Himself. Every idea of an individual thing necessarily includes the eternal and infinite essence of God in itself. For individual things are modes of an attribute of God ; therefore they must include in themselves His eternal essence. Our mind, in so far as it knows itself and the body under the form of eternity, has to that extent necessarily the knowledge of God, and knows that it is itself in God and is conceived through God. All Ideas, in so far as they are referable to God, are true." [2] Man must trace back all things to God, for God is the One in All; the eternal essence of God is the one thing that *is*, the eternal truth is the only thing for man to aim at in his actions. With Spinoza this is not a knowledge arrived at through philosophy, but only knowledge of a truth. " The mind can succeed in tracing back all affections of the body or images of things to God. In proportion as the mind regards all things as necessary, it has a greater power over its affections," which are arbitrary and contingent. This is the return of the mind to God, and this is human freedom; as mode, on the other hand, the spirit has no freedom, but is determined from without. " From the third kind of knowledge there arises the repose of the mind; the supreme good of the mind is to know God, and this is its highest virtue. This knowledge necessarily produces the intel-

[1] Spinoz. Ethices, P. II. Prop. XL. Schol. II. pp. 113, 114.
[2] Spinoz. Ethices, P. II. Prop. XLIV. et Coroll. II. pp. 117, 118 ; Prop. XLV. p. 119; P. V. Prop. XXX. p. 289: P. II. Prop. XXXII. p. 107.

lectual love of God; for it produces a joyfulness accompanied by the Idea of God as cause—*i.e.* the intellectual love of God. God Himself loves Himself with an infinite intellectual love." [1] For God can have only Himself as aim and cause; and the end of the subjective mind is to be directed on Him. This is therefore the purest, but also a universal morality.

In the thirty-sixth Letter (pp. 581-582) Spinoza speaks of Evil. The allegation is made that God, as the originator of all things and everything, is also the originator of evil, is consequently Himself evil; in this identity all things are one, good and evil are in themselves the same thing, in God's substance this difference has disappeared. Spinoza says in answer to this: "I assert the fact that God absolutely and truly" (as cause of Himself) "is the cause of everything that has an essential content" (*i e.* affirmative reality) "be it what it may. Now if you can prove to me that evil, error, crime, etc., are something that expresses an essence, I will freely admit to you that God is the originator of crime and evil and error. But I have elsewhere abundantly demonstrated that the form of evil cannot subsist in anything that expresses an essence, and therefore it cannot be said that God is the cause of evil." Evil is merely negation, privation, limitation, finality, mode—nothing in itself truly real. "Nero's murder of his mother, in so far as it had positive content, was no crime. For Orestes did the same external deed, and had in doing it the same end in view—to kill his mother; and yet he is not blamed," and so on. The affirmative is the will, the intention, the act of Nero. "Wherein then consists Nero's criminality? In nothing else but that he proved himself ungrateful, merciless, and disobedient. But it is certain that all this expresses no essence, and therefore God was

[1] Spinoz. Ethices, P. V. Prop. XIV. p. 280; Prop. VI. p. 275; Prop. XXVII. pp. 287, 288; Prop. XXXII. Coroll.; Prop. XXXV. pp. 291, 292.

not the cause of it, though He was the cause of Nero's action and intention." These last are something positive, but yet they do not constitute the crime as such; it is only the negative element, such as mercilessness, etc. that makes the action a crime. "We know that whatever exists, regarded in itself and without taking anything else into consideration, contains a perfection which extends as widely as the essence of the thing itself extends, for the essence is in no way different therefrom."—" Because then," we find in the thirty-second letter (pp. 541, 543), " God does not regard things abstractly, or form general definitions," (of what the thing ought to be) " and no more reality is required of things than the Divine understanding and power has given and actually meted out to them; therefore it clearly follows that such privation exists only and solely in respect to our understanding, but not in respect to God;" for God is absolutely real. It is all very well to say this, but it does not meet the case. For in this way God and the respect to our understanding are different. Where is their unity? How is this to be conceived? Spinoza continues in the thirty-sixth letter: " Although the works of the righteous (*i.e.* of those who have a clear idea of God, to which they direct all their actions and even their thoughts), and " also the works " of the wicked (*i.e.* of those who have no idea of God, but only ideas of earthly things,"—individual, personal interests and opinions,— " by which their actions and thoughts are directed), and all whatsoever exists, necessarily proceed from God's eternal laws and counsels, and perpetually depend on God, they are yet not distinguished from one another in degree, but in essence; for although a mouse as well as an angel depends on God, and sorrow as well as joy, yet a mouse cannot be a kind of angel, and sorrow cannot be a kind of joy,"—they are different in essence.

There is therefore no ground for the objection that Spinoza's philosophy gives the death-blow to morality; we even gain from it the great result that all that is sensuous is mere limitation, and that there is only one true substance, and that human liberty consists in keeping in view this one substance, and in regulating all our conduct in accordance with the mind and will of the Eternal One. But in this philosophy it may with justice be objected that God is conceived only as Substance, and not as Spirit, as concrete. The independence of the human soul is therein also denied, while in the Christian religion every individual appears as determined to salvation. Here, on the contrary, the individual spirit is only a mode, an accident, but not anything substantial. This brings us to a general criticism of the philosophy of Spinoza, in the course of which we shall consider it from three different points of view.

In the first place Spinozism is asserted to be Atheism—by Jacobi, for instance (Werke, Vol. IV. Section I. p. 216)—because in it no distinction is drawn between God and the world; it makes nature the real God, or lowers God to the level of nature, so that God disappears and only nature is established. But it is not so much God and nature that Spinoza sets up in mutual opposition, as thought and extension; and God is unity, not One made up of two, but absolute Substance, in which has really disappeared the limitation of the subjectivity of thought and nature. Those who speak against Spinoza do so as if it were on God's account that they were interested; but what these opponents are really concerned about is not God, but the finite—themselves. The relationship between God and the finite, to which we belong, may be represented in three different ways : firstly, only the finite exists, and in this way we alone exist, but God does not exist—this is atheism; the finite is here taken absolutely, and is accordingly the substantial. Or, in the second place, God alone exists; the finite has no reality, it is only phenomena, appearance. To say, in the third place, that God exists and we also exist is a false synthetic union, an amicable compromise. It is the popular view of the matter

that the one side has as much substantiality as the other;
God is honoured and supreme, but finite things also have
Being to exactly the same extent. Reason cannot remain
satisfied with this "also," with indifference like this. The
philosophic requisite is therefore to apprehend the unity of
these differences in such a way that difference is not let slip,
but proceeds eternally from substance, without being petrified into dualism. Spinoza is raised above this dualism;
religion is so also, if we turn its popular conceptions into
thoughts. The atheism of the first attitude—when men
set up as ultimate the arbitrariness of the will, their own
vanity, the finite things of nature, and the world dwells for
ever in the mind—is not the standpoint of Spinoza, for
whom God is the one and only substance, the world on the
contrary being merely an affection or mode of this substance.
In the respect that Spinoza does not distinguish God from
the world, the finite, it is therefore correct to term his
theory atheism, for his words are these : Nature, the human
mind, the individual, are God revealed under particular forms.
It has been already remarked (pp. 257, 258, 280) that undoubtedly Substance with Spinoza does not perfectly fulfil
the conception of God, since it is as Spirit that He is to be
conceived. But if Spinoza is called an atheist for the sole
reason that he does not distinguish God from the world, it
is a misuse of the term. Spinozism might really just as well
or even better have been termed Acosmism, since according
to its teaching it is not to the world, finite existence, the
universe, that reality and permanency are to be ascribed,
but rather to God alone as the substantial. Spinoza maintains that there is no such thing as what is known as the
world; it is merely a form of God, and in and for itself it is
nothing. The world has no true reality, and all this that we
know as the world has been cast into the abyss of the one
identity. There is therefore no such thing as finite reality, it
has no truth whatever; according to Spinoza what is, is God,
and God alone. Therefore the allegations of those who accuse

Spinoza of atheism are the direct opposite of the truth; with him there is too much God. They say : If God is the identity of mind and nature, then nature or the individual man is God. This is quite correct, but they forget that nature and the individual disappear in this same identity : and they cannot forgive Spinoza for thus annihilating them. Those who defame him in such a way as this are therefore not aiming at maintaining God, but at maintaining the finite and the worldly; they do not fancy their own extinction and that of the world. Spinoza's system is absolute pantheism and monotheism elevated into thought. Spinozism is therefore very far removed from being atheism in the ordinary sense ; but in the sense that God is not conceived as spirit, it is atheism. However, in the same way many theologians are also atheists who speak of God only as the Almighty Supreme Being, etc., who refuse to acknowledge God, and who admit the validity and truth of the finite. They are many degrees worse than Spinoza.

The second point to be considered is the method adopted by Spinoza for setting forth his philosophy ; it is the demonstrative method of geometry as employed by Euclid, in which we find definitions, explanations, axioms, and theorems. Even Descartes made it his starting-point that philosophic propositions must be mathematically handled and proved, that they must have the very same evidence as mathematics. The mathematical method is considered superior to all others, on account of the nature of its evidence ; and it is natural that independent knowledge in its re-awakening lighted first upon this form, of which it saw so brilliant an example. The mathematical method is, however, ill-adapted for speculative content, and finds its proper place only in the finite sciences of the understanding. In modern times Jacobi has asserted (Werke, Vol. IV. Section I. pp. 217-223) that all demonstration, all scientific knowledge leads back to Spinozism, which alone is a logical method of thought ; and because

it must lead thither, it is really of no service whatever, but
immediate knowledge is what we must depend on. It may
be conceded to Jacobi that the method of demonstration
leads to Spinozism, if we understand thereby merely the
method of knowledge belonging to the understanding.
But the fact is that Spinoza is made a testing-point
in modern philosophy, so that it may really be said:
You are either a Spinozist or not a philosopher at all.
This being so, the mathematical and demonstrative
method of Spinoza would seem to be only a defect in the
external form; but it is the fundamental defect of the
whole position. In this method the nature of philosophic
knowledge and the object thereof, are entirely misconceived, for mathematical knowledge and method are merely
formal in character and consequently altogether unsuited
for philosophy. Mathematical knowledge exhibits its proof
on the existent object as such, not on the object as conceived; the Notion is lacking throughout; the content of
Philosophy, however, is simply the Notion and that which
is comprehended by the Notion. Therefore this Notion as
the knowledge of the essence is simply one assumed, which
falls within the philosophic subject; and this is what
represents itself to be the method peculiar to Spinoza's
philosophy. Of this demonstrative manner we have
already seen these examples: (*a*) The definitions from
which Spinoza takes his start—as in geometry a commencement is made with the line, triangle, &c.—concern
universal determinations, such as cause of itself, the finite,
substance, attribute, mode, and so on, which are solely and
simply accepted and assumed, not deduced, nor proved to
be necessary; for Spinoza is not aware of how he arrives at
these individual determinations. (*β*) He further speaks of
axioms, for instance (Ethic. P. I. Ax. I. p. 36): "What
is, is either in itself or in another." The determinations
"in itself" and "in another" are not shown forth in
their necessity: neither is this disjunction proved, it is

merely assumed. (γ) The propositions have, as such, a subject and predicate which are not similar. When the predicate is proved of the subject and necessarily combined with it, the discrepancy remains that the one as universal is related to the other as particular : therefore even although the relation is proved, there is present at the same time a secondary relation. Mathematical science, in its true propositions respecting a whole, escapes from the difficulty by proving also the converse of the propositions, in this way obtaining for them a special definiteness by proving each proposition in both ways. True propositions may, therefore, be looked on as definitions, and the conversion is the proof of the proposition in the form in which it is expressed. But this means of escaping the difficulty Philosophy cannot well employ, since the subject of which something is proved is itself only the Notion or the universal, and the proposition form is therefore quite superfluous and out of place. What has the form of the subject is in the form of an existent thing, as contrasted with the universal, the content of the proposition. The existent thing is taken as signifying existent in the ordinary sense ; it is the word which we use in every-day life, and of which we have a conception that has nothing of the Notion in it. The converse of a proposition would simply read like this : The Notion is that which is thus popularly conceived. This proof from the usage of language—that we also understand this to be the meaning in every-day life, or in other words that the name is correct—has no philosophic significance. But if the proposition is not one like this, but an ordinary proposition, and if the predicate is not the Notion, but some general term or other, a predicate of the subject, such propositions are really not philosophic : we might instance the statement that substance is one and not several, but only that in which substance and unity are the same. Or, in other words, this unity of the two moments is the very thing which the proof has to demonstrate, it is the Notion or the essence. In this case it looks as if the proposition were the matter of chief importance, the truth. But if in these really only so-called propositions, subject and predicate are in truth not alike, because one is individual and the other universal, their relation is essential, *i.e.* the reason for which they are one. The proof has here a false position indeed, as if that subject were implicit or in itself, whereas subject and predicate are, fundamentally even, moments in separation; in the judgment "God is One," the subject itself is universal, since it re- solves itself into unity. On the other side it is im- plied in this false position that the proof is brought in from outside merely, as in mathematics from a preced- ing proposition, and that the proposition is not therefore conceived through itself; thus we see the ordinary method of proof take its middle term, the principle, from anywhere it can, in the same way as in classi- fication it takes its principle of classification. The pro- position is then, as it were, a secondary affair; but we must ask if this proposition is true. The result as pro- position ought to be truth, but is only knowledge. The movement of knowledge, as proof, falls therefore, in the third place, outside of the proposition, which ought to be the truth. The essential moments of the system are really already completely contained in the pre-suppositions of the definitions, from which all further proofs have merely to be deduced. But whence have we these categories which here appear as definitions? We find them doubtless in ourselves, in scientific culture. The existence of the under- standing, the will, extension, is therefore not developed from infinite substance, but it is directly expressed in these determinations, and that quite naturally; for of a truth there exists the One into which everything enters, in order to be absorbed therein, but out of which nothing comes. For as Spinoza has set up the great proposition, all determination implies negation (*supra*, p. 267), and as of everything, even of thought in contrast to extension, it may be shown that it is determined and finite, what is essential in it rests upon negation. Therefore God alone is the positive, the affirmative, and consequently the one substance; all other things, on the contrary, are only modifications of this substance, and are nothing in and for themselves. Simple determination or negation belongs only to form, but is quite another thing from absolute determinateness or negativity, which is absolute form; in this way of looking at it negation is the negation of negation, and therefore true affirmation. This negative self-conscious moment, the movement of knowledge, which pursues its way in the thought which is present before us, is however certainly lacking to the content of Spinoza's philosophy, or at least it is only externally associated with it, since it falls within self-consciousness. That is to say, thoughts form the content, but they are not self-conscious thoughts or Notions: the content signifies thought, as pure abstract self-consciousness, but an unreasoning knowledge, into which the individual does not enter: the content has not the signification of 'I.' Therefore the case is as in mathematics; a proof is certainly given, conviction must follow, but yet the matter fails to be understood. There is a rigid necessity in the proof, to which the moment of self-consciousness is lacking; the 'I' disappears, gives itself altogether up, merely withers away. Spinoza's procedure is therefore quite correct; yet the individual proposition is false, seeing that it expresses only one side of the negation. The understanding has determinations which do not contradict one another; contradiction the understanding cannot suffer. The negation of negation is, however, contradiction, for in that it negates negation as simple determination, it is on the one hand affirmation, but on the other hand also really negation; and this contradiction, which is a matter pertaining to reason, is lacking in the case of Spinoza. There is lacking the infinite form, spirituality and liberty. I have already mentioned before this (pp. 93, 94 ; 129—137) that Lullus and Bruno attempted to draw up a system of form, which should embrace and comprehend the one substance which organizes itself into the universe; this attempt Spinoza did not make.

Because negation was thus conceived by Spinoza in one-sided fashion merely, there is, in the third place, in his system, an utter blotting out of the principle of subjectivity, individuality, personality, the moment of self-consciousness in Being. Thought has only the signification of the universal, not of self-consciousness. It is this lack which has, on the one side, brought the conception of the liberty of the subject into such vehement antagonism to the system of Spinoza, because it set aside the independence of the human consciousness, the so-called liberty which is merely the empty abstraction of independence, and in so doing set aside God, as distinguished from nature and the human consciousness—that is as implicit or in Himself, in the Absolute ; for man has the consciousness of freedom, of the spiritual, which is the negative of the corporeal, and man has also the conscious-ness that his true Being lies in what is opposed to the corporeal. This has been firmly maintained by religion, theology, and the sound common sense of the common consciousness, and this form of opposition to Spinoza appears first of all in the assertion that freedom is real, and that evil exists. But because for Spinoza, on the other hand, there exists only absolute universal substance as the non-particularized, the truly real—all that is particular and individual, my subjectivity and spirituality, has, on the other hand, as a limited modification whose Notion depends on another, no absolute existence. Thus the soul, the Spirit, in so far as it is an individual Being, is for Spinoza a mere negation, like everything in general that is determined. As all differences and determinations of things and of consciousness simply go back into the One substance, one may say that in the system of Spinoza all things are merely cast down into this abyss of annihilation. But from this abyss nothing comes out; and the particular of which Spinoza speaks is only assumed and presupposed from the ordinary conception, without being justified. Were it to be justified, Spinoza would have to deduce it from his Substance; but that does not open itself out, and therefore comes to no vitality, spirituality or activity. His philosophy has only a rigid and unyielding substance, and not yet spirit; in it we are not at home with ourselves. But the reason that God is not spirit is that He is not the Three in One. Substance remains rigid and petrified, without Boehme's sources or springs; for the individual determinations in the form of determinations of the understanding are not Boehme's originating spirits, which energize and expand in one another (*supra*, pp. 202, 203). What we find regarding this particular then is that it is only a modification of absolute substance, which, however, is not declared to be such; for the moment of negativity is what is lacking to this rigid motionlessness, whose single form of activity is this, to divest all things of their determination and particularity and cast them back into the one absolute substance, wherein they are simply swallowed up, and all life in itself is utterly destroyed. This is what we find philosophically inadequate with Spinoza; distinctions are externally present, it is true, but they remain external, since even the negative is not known in itself. Thought is the absolutely abstract, and for that very reason the absolutely negative; it is so in truth, but with Spinoza it is not asserted to be the absolutely negative. But if in opposition to Spinozism we hold fast to the assertion that Spirit, as distinguishing itself from the corporeal, is substantial, actual, true, and in the same way that freedom is not something merely privative, then this actuality in formal thought is doubtless correct, yet it rests only upon feeling ; but the further step is that the Idea essentially includes within itself motion and vitality, and that it consequently has in itself the principle of spiritual freedom.   On the one hand, therefore, the defect of Spinozism is conceived as consisting in its want of correspondence with actuality ; but on the other side it is to be apprehended in a higher sense, I mean in the sense that substance with Spinoza is only the Idea taken altogether abstractly, not in its vitality.

If, in conclusion, we sum up this criticism that we have offered, we would say that on the one hand with Spinoza negation or privation is distinct from substance ; for he merely assumes individual determinations, and does not deduce them from substance.   On the other hand the negation is present only as Nothing, for in the absolute there is no mode ; the negative is not there, but only its dissolution, its return : we do not find its movement, its Becoming and Being.   The negative is conceived altogether as a vanishing moment—not in itself, but only as individual self-consciousness ; it is not like the *Separator* we met with in Boehme's system (*supra,* p. 206).   Self-consciousness is born from this ocean, dripping with the water thereof, *i.e.* never coming to absolute self-hood ; the heart, the independence is transfixed—the vital fire is wanting.   This lack has to be supplied, the moment of self-consciousness has to be added.   It has the following two special aspects, which we now perceive emerging and gaining acceptance ; in the first place the objective aspect, that absolute essence obtains in self-consciousness the mode of an object of consciousness for which the " other " exists, or the existent as such, and that what Spinoza understood by the " modes " is elevated to objective reality as an absolute moment of the absolute; in the second place we have the aspect of self-consciousness, individuality, independence.   As was formerly the case with respect to Bacon and Boehme, the former aspect is here taken up by the Englishman, John Locke, the latter by the German Leibnitz ; in the first case it did not appear as a moment, nor did it in the second appear as absolute Notion. Now while Spinoza only takes notice of these ordinary concep- tions, and the highest point of view he reaches in regard to them is that they sink and disappear in the one Sub- stance, Locke on the contrary examines the genesis of these conceptions, while Leibnitz opposes to Spinoza the infinite multiplicity of individuals, although all these monads have one monad as the basis of their Being. Both Locke and Leibnitz therefore came forward as opponents of the above- mentioned one-sidedness of Spinoza.

B. Second Division.

It was Locke who became the instrument of setting forth this entire manner of thinking in a systematic way, for he worked out Bacon's position more fully. And if Bacon made sensuous Being to be the truth, Locke demonstrated the uni- versal, Thought, to be present in sensuous Being, or showed that we obtained the universal, the true, from experience. From Locke a wide culture proceeds, influencing English philosophers more especially ; the forms adopted by this school were various, but the principle was the same ; it became a general method of regarding things in a popular way, and calls itself Philosophy, although the object of Philosophy is not to be met with here.

1. Locke.

When experience means that the Notion has objective actuality for consciousness, it is indeed a necessary element in the totality ; but as this reflection appears in Locke, signifying as it does that we obtain truth by abstraction from experience and sensuous perception, it is utterly false, since, instead of being a moment, it is made the essence of the truth. It is no doubt true that against the hypothesis of the inward immediacy of the Idea, and against the method of setting it forth in definitions and axioms, as also against absolute substance, the demand that ideas should be represented as results, and the claims of individuality and self-consciousness, assert their rights to recognition. In the philosophy of Locke and Leibnitz, however, these necessities make themselves known in an imperfect manner only ; the one fact which is common to both philosophers is that they, in opposition to Spinoza and Malebranche, take for their principle the particular, finite determinateness and the individual. According to Spinoza and Malebranche substance or the universal is the true, the sole existent, the eternal, that which is in and for itself, without origin, and of which particular things are only modifications which are conceived through substance. But hereby Spinoza has done an injury to this negative ; he hence arrived at no immanent determination, for all that is determined and individual is merely annihilated in his system. Now, on the contrary, the general inclination of consciousness is to maintain the difference, partly in order to, mark itself out as implicitly free in opposition to its object—Being, nature, and God, and partly in order to recognize the unity in this opposition, and from the opposition itself to make the unity emerge. But those who were the instruments of this tendency comprehended themselves but little, they had still no clear consciousness of their task, nor of the manner in which their claims could be satisfied. With Locke, this principle makes its first entrance into Philosophy in a manner so completely at variance with the inflexible undifferentiated identity of the substance of Spinoza, that the sensuous and limited, the immediate present and existent, is the main and fundamental matter. Locke does not get beyond the ordinary point of view of consciousness, viz. that objects outside of us are the real and the true. The finite is thus not grasped by Locke as absolute negativity, *i.e.* in its infinitude; this we shall not find until we come to deal in the third place with Leibnitz. It is in a higher sense that Leibnitz asserts individuality, the differentiated, to be self-existent and indeed objectless, to be true Being. That is to say, it is not according to him finite, but is yet distinguished; thus, each monad is itself the totality. Leibnitz and Locke hence likewise stand in a position of mutual independence and antagonism.

John Locke was born in 1632, at Wrington, in England. He studied for himself the Cartesian philosophy at Oxford, setting aside the scholastic philosophy which was still in vogue. He devoted himself to the study of medicine, which, however, on account of his delicate health, he never really practised. In 1664 he went with an English ambassador for a year to Berlin. After his return to England, he became acquainted with the intellectual Earl of Shaftesbury of that time, who availed himself of his medical advice, and in whose house he lived without requiring to give himself up to practice. When Lord Shaftesbury became Lord Chancellor of England, Locke received an office from him, which, however, he soon lost by a change of ministry. Owing to his dread of falling a prey to consumption, he betook himself in 1675 to Montpellier for the benefit of his health. When his patron came into power again he once more recovered the place he had lost, only to be again deposed on a fresh overthrow of this minister, and he was now compelled to flee from England. "The act by means of which Locke was driven from Oxford" (what post he held there we are not told) "was not an enactment of the University, but of James II., by whose express command, and by the peremptory authority of a written warrant, the expulsion was carried out. From the correspondence that took place, it is evident that the college submitted itself against its will to a measure which it could not resist without compromising the peace and quiet of its members." Locke went to Holland, which was at that time the land wherein all who were obliged to effect their escape from any oppression, whether political or religious, found protection, and in which the most famous and liberal-minded men were to be met with. The Court party persecuted him even here, and by royal warrant he was ordered to be taken prisoner and sent to England ; consequently he had to remain hidden with his friends. When William of Orange ascended the English throne, after the Revolution of 1688, Locke returned with him to England. He was there made Commissioner of Trade and Plantations, gave to the world his famous treatise on the Human Understanding, and finally, having withdrawn from public office on account of the delicacy of his health, he spent his remaining years in the country houses of English nobles ; he died on the 28th day of October, 1704, in the seventy-third year of his life.[1]

The philosophy of Locke is much esteemed ; it is still, for the most part, the philosophy of the English and the French, and likewise in a certain sense of the Germans. To put it in a few words, it asserts on the one hand that truth and knowledge rest upon experience and observation ; and on the other the analysis of and abstraction from general determinations is prescribed as the method of knowledge ; it is, so to speak, a metaphysical empiricism, and this is the ordinary method adopted in the sciences. In respect of method, Locke thus employs an exactly opposite system to that of Spinoza. In the methods of Spinoza and Descartes an account of the origin of ideas may be dispensed with ; they are accepted at once as definitions, such as those of substance, the infinite, mode, extension, etc., all of which constitute a quite incoherent list. But we require to show where these thoughts come in, on what they are founded, and how they are verified. Thus Locke has

---

[1] Buhle: Geschichte der neuern Philosophie, Vol. IV. Sec. 1, pp. 238-241 ; Quarterly Review, April, 1817, pp. 70, 71 ; The Works of John Locke (London, 1812), Vol. I.: The Life of the Author, pp. xix.-xxxix.

striven to satisfy a true necessity. For he has the merit of having deserted the system of mere definitions, which were before this made the starting point, and of having attempted to make deduction of general conceptions, inasmuch as he was, for example, at the pains to show how substantiality arises subjectively from objects. That is a further step than any reached by Spinoza, who begins at once with definitions and axioms which are unverified. Now they are derived, and no longer oracularly laid down, even if the method and manner whereby this authentication is established is not the right one. That is to say, here the matter in question is merely subjective, and somewhat psychological, since Locke merely describes the methods of mind as it appears to us to be. For in his philosophy we have more especially to deal with the derivation of the general conceptions, or ideas, as he called them, that are present in our knowledge, and with their origin as they proceed from what is outwardly and inwardly perceptible. Malebranche no doubt likewise asks how we arrive at conceptions, and thus he apparently has before him the same subject of investigation as has Locke. But firstly, this psychological element in Malebranche is merely the later development, and then to him the universal or God is plainly first, while Locke commences at once with individual perceptions, and only from them does he proceed to Notions, to God. The universal to Locke is, therefore, merely a later result, the work of our minds ; it is simply something pertaining to thought, as subjective. Every man undoubtedly knows that when his consciousness develops empirically, he commences from feelings, from quite concrete conditions, and that it is only later on that general conceptions come in, which are connected with the concrete of sensation by being contained therein. Space, for example, comes to consciousness later than the spacial, the species later than the individual ; and it is only through the activity of my consciousness that the universal is separated from the

particular of conception, feeling, etc.   Feeling undoubtedly
comes lowest, it is the animal mode of spirit; but in its
capacity as thinking, spirit endeavours to transform feeling
into its own form.   Thus the course adopted by Locke is
quite a correct one, but all dialectic considerations are
utterly and entirely set aside, since the universal is merely
analyzed from the empirical concrete.   And in this matter
Kant reproaches Locke with reason, the individual is not
the source of universal conceptions, but the understanding.

As to Locke's further reflections, they are very simple.
Locke considers how the understanding is only consciousness, and in being so is something in consciousness, and
he only recognizes the implicit in as far as it is in the
same.

a. Locke's philosophy is more especially directed against
Descartes, who, like Plato, had spoken of innate ideas.
Locke likewise makes special examination of the "inborn
impressions (*notiones communes in foro interiori descriptæ*)"
which Lord Herbert assumes in his work *De veritate.*   In
the first book of his work Locke combats the so-called
innate ideas, theoretic as well as practical, *i.e.* the universal,
absolutely existent ideas which at the same time are represented as pertaining to mind in a natural way.   Locke said
that we arrive first at *that* which we call idea.   By this he
understands not the essential determinations of man, but
conceptions which we have and which are present and exist
in consciousness as such: in the same way we all have arms
and legs as parts of our bodies, and the desire to eat
exists in everyone.   In Locke we thus have the conception
of the soul as of a contentless *tabula rasa* which is by-and-
by filled with what we call experience.[1]   The expression
" innate principles " was at that time common, and these

[1] Locke: An Essay concerning human Understanding (The Works
of John Locke, Vol. I.), Book I. chap. ii. § 1; chap. iii. § 15,
§ 22.

innate principles have sometimes been foolishly spoken of. But their true signification is that they are implicit, that they are essential moments in the nature of thought, qualities of a germ, which do not yet exist : only in relation to this last there is an element of truth in Locke's conclusions. As diverse conceptions essentially determined they are only legitimatized by its being shown that they are implied in the essential nature of thought ; but as propositions which hold good as axioms, and conceptions which are immediately accepted as laid down in definitions, they undoubtedly possess the form of that which is present and inborn. As they are regarded they are bound to have value in and for themselves ; but this is a mere assertion. From the other point of view the question of whence they come is a futile one. Mind is undoubtedly determined in itself, for it is the explicitly existent Notion ; its development signifies the coming to consciousness. But the determinations which it brings forth from itself cannot be called innate, for this development must be occasioned by an external, and only on that does the activity of mind react, in order that it may for the first time become conscious of its reality.

The grounds on which Locke refutes innate ideas are empirical. "There is nothing more commonly taken for granted than that there are certain principles, both speculative and practical, universally agreed upon by all mankind : which therefore, they argue, must needs be constant impressions which the souls of men receive in their first Beings.'' But this universal consent is not to be found. We may instance the proposition, " Whatsoever is, is ; and It is impossible for the same thing to be and not to be ; which of all others I think have the most allowed title to innate." But this proposition does not hold good for the Notion ; there is nothing either in heaven or earth which does not contain Being and non-Being. Many men, "All children and idiots," says Locke, "have not the least apprehension of these propositions." " No proposition can be said to be in the mind which it never yet knew, which it was never yet conscious of. . . . 'Tis usually answered, That all men know and assent to them " (the propositions) " when they come to the use of reason. . . . If it be meant that the use of reason assists us in the knowledge of these maxims, it would prove them not to be innate." Reason is said to be the deriving from principles already known unknown truths. How then should the application of reason be required to discover supposed innate principles ? This is a weak objection, for it assumes that by innate ideas we understand those which man possesses in consciousness as immediately present. But development in consciousness is something altogether different from any inherent determination of reason, and therefore the expression innate idea is undoubtedly quite wrong. Innate principles must be found " clearest and most perspicuous nearest the fountain, in children and illiterate people, who have received least impression from foreign opinion." Locke gives further reasons of a similar nature, more especially employing those which are of a practical kind—the diversity in moral judgments, the case of those who are utterly wicked and depraved, devoid of sense of right or conscience.[1]

b. In the second book Locke goes on to the next stage, to the origin of ideas, and seeks to demonstrate this process from experience—this is the main object of his efforts. The reason that the positive point of view which he opposes to any derivation from within, is so false, is that he derives his conceptions only from outside and thus maintains Being-for-another, while he quite neglects the implicit. He says: " Every man being conscious to himself, that he thinks ; and that which his mind is applied about, while thinking, being the ideas that are there ; 'tis past doubt, that men have in their minds several ideas, such as those expressed in the words, whiteness, hardness, sweetness, thinking,

---

[1] Locke: An Essay concerning human Understanding (Vol. I.) Book I. chap. ii. § 2-9; § 27; chap. iii. § 1-15.

motion, man, elephant, army, drunkenness, and others."
Idea here signifies both the ordinary conception and thought;
we understand something quite different by the word idea.
" It is in the first place then to be inquired, how he comes
by them " (these ideas) ? Innate ideas have already been
refuted. " Let us then suppose the mind to be, as we
say, white paper, void of all characters, without any ideas ;
how comes it to be furnished ? . . . To this I answer in a
word, from Experience : in that all our knowledge is
founded. " [1]

As to the question in point we must in the first place say
that it is true that man commences with experience if he
desires to arrive at thought. Everything is experienced, not
merely what is sensuous, but also what excites and stimulates my mind. Consciousness thus undoubtedly obtains all
conceptions and Notions from experience and in experience ;
the only question is what we understand by experience.
In a usual way when this is spoken of the idea of nothing
particular is conveyed ; we speak of it as of something
quite well known. But experience is nothing more than
the form of objectivity ; to say that it is something which
is in consciousness means that it has objective form for
consciousness or that consciousness experiences it, it sees it
as an objective. Experience thus signifies immediate knowledge, perception, *i.e.* I myself must have and be something, and the consciousness of what I have and am is
experience. Now there is no question as to this, that
whatever we know, of whatever kind it may be, must be
experienced, that rests in the conception of the thing. It
is absurd to say that one knows anything which is not in
experience. I undoubtedly know men, for instance, from
experience, without requiring to have seen them all, for I
have, as man, activity and will, a consciousness respecting
what I am and what others are. The rational exists, *i.e.* it

[1] Locke: An Essay concerning human Understanding (Vol. I.)
Bk. II. chap. i. § 1, 2.

is as an existent for consciousness, or this last experiences it; it must be seen and heard, it must be there or have been there as a phenomenon in the world. This connection of universal with objective is however in the second place not the only form, that of the implicit is likewise absolute and essential—that is, the apprehension of what is experienced or the abrogation of this apparent other-being and the knowledge of the necessity of the thing through itself. It is now quite a matter of indifference whether anything is accepted as something experienced, as a succession of empirical ideas, if one may so say, or conceptions; or whether the succession is a succession of thoughts, i.e. implicitly existent.

Locke treats of the various kinds of these ideas imperfectly and empirically merely.

a. According to Locke simple ideas arise partly from outward, and partly from inward experience. For experiences, he says, are in the first place sensations; the other side is reflection, the inward determinations of consciousness.[1] From sensation, from the organs of sight for instance, the conceptions of colour, light, etc., arise; there further arises from outward experience the idea of impenetrability, of figure, rest, motion and such like. From reflections come the ideas of faith, doubt, judgment, reasoning, thinking, willing, etc.; from both combined, pleasure, pain, etc. This is a very commonplace account of the matter.

β. After Locke has pre-supposed experience, he goes on to say that it is the understanding which now discovers and desires the universal—the complex ideas. The Bishop of Worcester made the objection that "If the idea of substance be grounded upon plain and evident reason, then we must allow an idea of substance which comes not in by sensation or reflection." Locke replies: "General ideas

[1] Locke: An Essay concerning human Understanding (Vol. I.), Bk. II. chap. i. § 2-5.

come not into the mind by sensation or reflection, but are
the creatures or inventions of the understanding. The
mind makes them from ideas which it has got by sensation
and reflection." The work of the mind now consists in
bringing forth from several simple so-called ideas a number
of new ones, by means of its working upon this material
through comparing, distinguishing and contrasting it,
and finally through separation or abstraction, whereby the
universal conceptions, such as space, time, existence, unity
and diversity, capacity, cause and effect, freedom, necessity,
take their rise. "The mind in respect of its simple ideas
is wholly passive, and receives them all from the existence
and operation of things, such as sensation or reflection
offers them, without being able to make any one idea."
But "the mind often exercises an active power in making
these several combinations. For it being once furnished
with simple ideas it can put them together in several
combinations." According to Locke therefore thought
itself is not the essence of the soul, but one of its powers
and manifestations. He maintains thought to be existent
in consciousness as conscious thought, and thus brings it
forward as a fact in his experience, that we do not always
think. Experience demonstrates dreamless sleep when the
sleep is profound. Locke quotes the example of a man
who remembered no dream until he had reached his
twenty-fifth year. It is as in the Xenien,— [1]

Oft schon war ich, und hab' wirklich an gar nichts gedacht.

That is to say, my object is not a thought. But
sensuous perception and recollection are thought, and
thought is truth.[2] Locke, however, places the reality
of the understanding only in the formal activity of
constituting new determinations from the simple con-

[1] v. Schiller's Xenien.
[2] Locke: An Essay concerning human Understanding (Vol. I,),
Bk. II., chap. ii. § 2, not.; chap. xii. § 1 ; chap. xxii. § 2 ; chap. i.
§ 10-14.

ceptions received by means of perception, through their comparison and the combination of several into one ; it is the apprehension of the abstract sensations which are contained in the objects. Locke likewise distinguishes (Bk. II. chap. xi. § 15-17) beween pure and mixed modes. Pure modes are simple determinations such as power, number, infinitude ; in such expressions as causality we reach, on the other hand, a mixed mode.

Locke now explains in detail the manner in which the mind, from the simple ideas of experience, reaches more complex ideas ; but this derivation of general determinations from concrete perception is most unmeaning, trivial, tiresome and diffuse ; it is entirely formal, an empty tautology. For instance we form the general conception of space from the perception of the distance of bodies by means of sight and feeling.[1] Or in other words, we perceive a definite space, abstract from it, and then we have the conception of space generally ; the perception of distances gives us conceptions of space. This however is no deduction, but only a setting aside of other determinations ; since distance itself is really space, mind thus determines space from space. Similarly we reach the notion of time through the unbroken succession of conceptions during our waking moments,[2] *i.e.* from determinate time we perceive time in general. Conceptions follow one another in a continual succession ; if we set aside the particular element that is present we thereby receive the conception of time. Substance (which Locke does not accept in so lofty a sense as Spinoza), a complex idea, hence arises from the fact that we often perceive simple ideas such as blue, heavy, etc., in association with one another. This association we represent to ourselves as something which so to

---

[1] Locke : An Essay concerning human Understanding (Vol. I.), Bk. II. chap. xiii. § 2 ; chap. iv. § 2.

[2] Ibidem (Vol. I.), Bk. II. chap. xiv. § 3.

speak supports these simple ideas, or in which they exist.[1]
Locke likewise deduces the general conception of power.[2]
The determinations of freedom and necessity, cause and
effect, are then derived in a similar way. " In the notice
that our senses take of the constant vicissitude of things,
we cannot but observe, that several particulars, both
qualities and substance, begin to exist; and that they
receive this their existence from the due application and
operation of some other being. From this observation we
get our ideas of cause and effect," for instance when wax
is melted by the fire.[3] Locke goes on to say : " Every one,
I think, finds in himself a power to begin or forbear,
continue or put an end to several actions in himself. From
the consideration of the extent of this power of the mind
over the actions of the man, which every one finds in
himself, arise the ideas of liberty and necessity."[4]

We may say that nothing can be more superficial than
this derivation of ideas. The matter itself, the essence, is
not touched upon at all. A determination is brought into
notice which is contained in a concrete relationship; hence
the understanding on the one hand abstracts and on the
other establishes conclusions. The basis of this philosophy
is merely to be found in the transference of the determinate
to the form of universality, but it was just this fundamental
essence that we had to explain. As to this Locke confesses
of space, for example, that he does not know what it really is.[5]
This so-called analysis by Locke of complex conceptions,
and his so-called explanation of the same, has, on account
of its uncommon clearness and lucidity of expression, found
universal acceptance. For what can be clearer than to

---

[1] Locke : An Essay concerning human Understanding (Vol. II.),
Bk. II. chap. xxiii. § 1, 2.
[2] Ibidem (Vol. I.), Bk. II. chap. xxi. § 1.
[3] Ibidem (Vol. II.), Bk. II. chap. xxvi. § 1.
[4] Ibidem (Vol. I.), Bk. II. chap. xxi. § 7.
[5] Ibidem (Vol. I.), Bk. II. chap. xiii. § 17, 18.

say that we have the notion of time because we perceive time, if we do not actually see it, and that we conceive of space because we see it ? The French have accepted this most readily and they have carried it further still; their *Idéologie* contains nothing more nor less.

γ. When Locke starts by saying that everything is experience and we abstract for ourselves from this experience general conceptions regarding objects and their qualities, he makes a distinction in respect of external qualities which was before this made by Aristotle (De anima, II. 6), and which we likewise met with in Descartes (*supra,* pp. 245, 246). That is to say, Locke distinguishes between primary and secondary qualities ; the first pertain to the objects themselves in truth, the others are not real qualities, but are founded on the nature of the organs of sensation. Primary qualities are mechanical, like extension, solidity, figure, movement, rest ; these are qualities of the corporeal, just as thought is the quality of the spiritual. But the determinations of our individual feelings such as colours, sounds, smells, taste, etc., are not primary." [1] In Descartes' case this distinction has however another form, for the second class of these determinations is defined by him in such a way as that they do not constitute the essence of body, while Locke says that they exist for sensation, or fall within existence as it is for consciousness. Locke, however, no doubt reckons figure, etc., as still pertaining to reality, but by so doing nothing is ascertained as to the nature of body. In Locke a difference here appears between the implicit and being ' for-another,' in which he declares the moment of ' for-another ' to be unreal—and yet he sees all truth in the relation of ' for-another ' only.

c. Since the universal as such, the idea of species, is, according to Locke, merely a product of our mind, which is not itself objective, but relates merely to objects which are

---

[1] Locke : An Essay concerning human Understanding (Vol. I.), Bk. II. chap. viii. § 9-26.

germane to it, and from which the particular of qualities,
conditions, time, place, etc., are separated, Locke distinguishes essences into real essences and nominal essences;
the former of these express the true essence of things, while
species on the other hand are mere nominal essences which
no doubt express something which is present in the objects,
but which do not exhaust these objects. They serve to
distinguish species for our knowledge, but the real essence
of nature we do not know.[1] Locke gives good reasons for
species being nothing in themselves—for their not being in
nature, or absolutely determined—instancing in exemplification the production of monstrosities (Bk. III. chap. iii.
§ 17): were species absolute no monster would be born.
But he overlooks the fact that since it pertains to species
to exist, it thereby likewise enters into relationship with
other determinations; thus that is the sphere in which
individual things operate upon one another, and may hence
be detrimental to the existence of the species. Locke thus
argues just as one would who wished to prove that the good
does not exist in itself, because there are likewise evil men,
that the circle does not exist absolutely in nature, because
the circumference of a tree, for example, represents a very
irregular circle, or because I draw a circle badly. Nature
just signifies the lack of power to be perfectly adequate to
the Notion; it is only in spirit that the Notion has its true
existence. To say that species are nothing in themselves,
that the universal is not the essential reality of nature, that
its implicit existence is not the object of thought, is tantamount to saying that we do not know real existence: it is
the same litany which has since been so constantly repeated
that we are tired of listening to it:

Das Innere der Natur kennt kein erschaffener Geist,

and which goes on until we have perceived that Being-

[1] Locke: An Essay concerning human Understanding (Vol. II.),
Bk. III. chap. iii. § 6; § 13, 15.

for-another, perception, is not implicit; a point of view which has not made its way to the positive position that the implicit is the universal. Locke is far back in the nature of knowledge, further back than Plato, because of his insistence on Being-for-another.

It is further noteworthy that from the sound understanding Locke argues (Vol. III. Bk. IV. chap. vii. § 8-11) against universal propositions or axioms such as that A = A, *i.e.* if anything is A it cannot be B. He says they are superfluous, of very little use or of no use at all, for nobody yet has built up a science on a proposition which asserts a contradiction. From such the true may be proved as easily as the false; they are tautological. What Locke has further achieved in respect of education, toleration, natural rights or universal state-right, does not concern us here, but has to do with general culture.

This is the philosophy of Locke, in which there is no trace of speculation. The great end of Philosophy, which is to know the truth, is in it sought to be attained in an empiric way; it thus indeed serves to draw attention to general determinations. But such a philosophy not only represents the standpoint of ordinary consciousness, to which all the determinations of its thought appear as if given, humble as it is in the oblivion of its activity, but in this method of derivation and psychological origination that which alone concerns Philosophy, the question of whether these thoughts and relationships have truth in and for themselves, is not present at all, inasmuch as the only object aimed at is to describe the manner in which thought accepts what is given to it. It may be held with Wolff that it is arbitrary to begin with concrete conceptions, as when our conception of identity is made to take its origin from such things as blue flowers and the blue heavens. One can better begin directly from universal conceptions and say that we find in our consciousness the conceptions of time, cause and effect; these are the later facts of consciousness. This method forms the basis of the Wolffian system of reasoning, only here we must still distinguish amongst the different conceptions those that are to be regarded as most essential ; in Locke's philosophy, this distinction cannot really be said to come under consideration. From this time, according to Locke, or in this particular aspect of Philosophy, there is a complete and entire change in the point of view adopted ; the whole interest is limited to the form in which the objective, or individual sensations, pass into the form of conceptions. In the case of Spinoza and Malebranche, we undoubtedly likewise saw that it was made a matter of importance to recognize this relation of thought to what is sensuously perceived, and thus to know it as falling into relation, as passing into the relative ; the main question hence was : How are the two related ? But the question was answered to the effect that it is only this relation for itself that constitutes the point of interest, and this relation itself as absolute substance is thus identity, the true, God, it is not the related parts. The interest does not lie in the related parts ; the related parts as one-sided are not the existent, pre-supposed and permanently established, they are accidental merely. But here the related sides, the things and the subject, have their proper value, and they are pre-supposed as having this value. Locke's reasoning is quite shallow ; it keeps entirely to the phenomenal, to that which is, and not to that which is true.

There is another question however : Are these general determinations absolutely true ? And whence come they not alone into my consciousness, into my mind and understanding, but into the things themselves ? Space, cause, effect, etc., are categories. How do these categories come into the particular ? How does universal space arrive at determining itself ? This point of view, the question whether these determinations of the infinite, of substance, etc., are in and for themselves true, is quite lost sight of.

Plato investigated the infinite and the finite, Being and the determinate, etc., and pronounced that neither of these opposites is of itself true; they are so only as together constituting an identity, wherever the truth of this content may come from. But here the truth as it is in and for itself is entirely set aside and the nature of the content itself is made the main point. It does not matter whether the understanding or experience is its source, for the question is whether this content is in itself true. With Locke, the truth merely signifies the harmony of our conceptions with things; here relation is alone in question, whether the content is an objective thing or a content of the ordinary conception. But it is quite another matter to investigate the content itself, and to ask, " Is this which is within us true ? We must not dispute about the sources, for the Whence, the only important point to Locke, does not exhaust the whole question. The interest of the content in and for itself wholly disappears. when that position is taken up, and thereby the whole of what is aimed at by Philosophy is given up. On the other hand, when thought is from the beginning concrete, when thought and the universal are synonymous with what is set before us, the question of the relation of the two which have been separated by thought is destitute of interest and incomprehensible. How does thought overcome the difficulties which itself has begotten ? Here with Locke none at all have been begotten and awakened. Before the need for reconciliation can be satisfied, the pain of disunion must be excited.

The philosophy of Locke is certainly very comprehensible, but for that very reason it is likewise a popular philosophy to which the whole of the English philosophy as it exists at this day is allied; it is the thinking method of regarding things which is called philosophy carried to its perfection, the form which was introduced into the science which then took its rise in Europe. This is an important moment in culture; the sciences in general and specially the empiric sciences have to ascribe their origin to this movement. To the English, Philosophy has ever signified the deduction of experiences from observations ; this has in a one-sided way been applied to physical and economic subjects. General principles of political economy such as free-trade in the present day, and all matters which rest on thinking experience, the knowledge of whatever reveals itself in this sphere as necessary and useful, signifies philosophy to the English (Vol. I. pp. 57, 58). The scholastic method of starting from principles and definitions has been rejected. The universal, laws, forces, universal matter, etc., have in natural science been derived from perceptions ; thus to the English, Newton is held to be the philosopher κατ' ἐξοχήν. The other side is that in practical philosophy regarding society or the state, thought applies itself to concrete objects such as the will of the prince, subjects and their ends and personal welfare. Inasmuch as we have an object such as that before us, the indwelling and essential universal is made evident ; it must, however, be made clear which conception is the one to which the others must yield. It is in this way that rational politics took their rise in England, because the institutions and government peculiar to the English led them specially and in the first place to reflection upon their inward political and economic relationships. Hobbes must be mentioned as an exemplification of this fact. This manner of reasoning starts from the present mind, from what is our own, whether it be within or without us, since the feelings which we have, the experiences which fall directly within us, are the principles. This philosophy of reasoning thought is that which has now become universal, and through which the whole revolution in the position taken up by mind has come to pass.

C

Third Division

The third development of the philosophy of the understanding is that represented by Leibnitz and Wolff. If Wolff's metaphysics is divested of its rigid form, we have as a result the later popular philosophy.

1. LEIBNITZ.

As in other respects Leibnitz represents the extreme antithesis to Newton, so in respect of philosophy he presents a striking contrast to Locke and his empiricism, and also to Spinoza. He upholds thought as against the perception of the English school, and in lieu of sensuous Being he maintains Being for thought to be the essence of truth, just as Boehme at an earlier time upheld implicit Being. While Spinoza asserted the universality, the oneness of substance merely, and while with Locke we saw infinite determinations made the basis, Leibnitz, by means of his fundamental principle of individuality, brings out the essentiality of the opposite aspect of Spinoza's philosophy, existence for self, the monad, but the monad regarded as the absolute Notion, though perhaps not yet as the "I." The opposed principles, which were forced asunder, find their completion in each other, since Leibnitz's principle of individuation completed Spinoza's system as far as outward aspect goes.

Gottfried Wilhelm, Baron von Leibnitz, was born in 1646 at Leipzig, where his father was professor of Philosophy. The subject that he studied in view of a profession was jurisprudence, but first, in accordance with the fashion of the day, he made a study of Philosophy, and to it he devoted particular attention. To begin with, he picked

up in Leipzig a large and miscellaneous stock of knowledge, then he studied Philosophy and mathematics at
Jena under the mathematician and theosophist Weigel,
and took his degree of Master of Philosophy in Leipzig.
There also, on the occasion of his graduation as Doctor of
Philosophy, he defended certain philosophical theses, some
of which discourses are still contained in his works (ed.
Dutens, T. II. P. I. p. 400). His first dissertation, and
that for which he obtained the degree of doctor of
philosophy, was : *De principio individui,*—a principle
which remained the abstract principle of his whole
philosophy, as opposed to that of Spinoza. After he had
acquired a thorough knowledge of the subject, he wished
to graduate also as Doctor of Laws. But though he
died an imperial councillor, it was his ill fortune to receive
from the Faculty at Leipzig a refusal to confer the
doctorate upon him, his youth being the alleged reason.
Such a thing could scarcely happen nowadays. It may be
that it was done because of his over-great philosophical
attainments, seeing that lawyers are wont to hold the same
in horror. He now quitted Leipzig, and betook himself to
Altdorf, where he graduated with distinction. Shortly
afterwards he became acquainted in Nürnberg with a
company of alchemists, with whose ongoings he became
associated. Here he made extracts from alchemistic
writings, and studied the mysteries of this occult science.
His activity in the pursuit of learning extended also to
historical, diplomatic, mathematical and philosophical
subjects. He subsequently entered the service of the
Elector of Mayence, becoming a member of council, and
in 1672 he was appointed tutor to a son of Von Boineburg,
Chancellor of State to the Elector. With this young man
he travelled to Paris, where he lived for four years. He at
this time made the acquaintance of the great mathematician Huygens, and was by him for the first time

properly introduced into the domain of mathematics. When the education of his pupil was completed, and the Baron Von Boineburg died, Leibnitz went on his own account to London, where he became acquainted with Newton and other scholars, at whose head was Oldenburg, who was also on friendly terms with Spinoza. After the death of the Elector of Mayence, the salary of Leibnitz ceased to be paid ; he therefore left England and returned to France. The Duke of Brunswick-Lüneburg then took him into his service, and gave him the appointment of councillor and librarian at Hanover, with permission to spend as much time as he liked in foreign countries. He therefore remained for some time longer in France, England, and Holland. In the year 1677 he settled down in Hanover, where he became busily engaged in affairs of state, and was specially occupied with historical matters. In the Harz Mountains he had works constructed for carrying off the floods which did damage to the mines there. Notwithstanding these manifold occupations he invented the differential calculus in 1677, on occasion of which there arose a dispute between him and Newton, which was carried on by the latter and the Royal Society of London in a most ungenerous manner. For it was asserted by the English, who gave themselves the credit of everything, and were very unfair to others, that the discovery was really made by Newton. But Newton's *Principia* only appeared later, and in the first edition indeed Leibnitz was mentioned with commendation in a note which was afterwards omitted. From his headquarters in Hanover, Leibnitz, commissioned by his prince, made several journeys through Germany, and also went to Italy in order to collect historical evidence relative to the House of Este, and for the purpose of proving more clearly the relationship between this princely family and that of Brunswick-Lüneburg. At other times he was likewise much occupied with historical questions. Owing to his acquaintance with the consort of Frederick I. of Prussia, Sophia Charlotte, a Hanoverian princess, he was enabled to bring about the foundation of an Academy of Science in Berlin, in which city he lived for a considerable time. In Vienna he also became acquainted with Prince Eugène, which occasioned his being appointed finally an Imperial Councillor. He published several very important historical works as the result of this journey. His death took place at Hanover in 1716, when he was seventy years of age.[1]

It was not only on Philosophy, but also on the most varied branches of science that Leibnitz expended toil and trouble and energy; it was to mathematics, however, that he specially devoted his attention, and he is the inventor of the methods of the integral and differential calculus. His great services in regard to mathematics and physics we here leave out of consideration, and pay attention to his philosophy alone. None of his books can be exactly looked on as giving a complete systematic account of his philosophy. To the more important among them belongs his work on the human understanding (*Nouveaux essais sur l'entendement humain*) in reply to Locke; but this is a mere refutation. His philosophy is therefore scattered through various little treatises which were written in very various connections, in letters, and replies to objections which caused him to bring out one aspect of the question more strongly than another; we consequently find no elaborated systematic whole, superintended or perfected by him. The work which has some appearance of being such, his *Théodicée*, better known to the public than anything else he wrote, is a popular treatise which he drew

---

[1] La vie de Mr. Leibnitz par Mr. le Chevalier de Jaucourt (Essais de Théodicée, par Leibnitz, Amsterdam, 1747, T. I.), pp. 1-28, 45, 59-62, 66-74, 77-80, 87-92, 110-116, 148-151; Brucker. Hist. crit. phil., T. IV. P. II. pp. 335-368; Leibnitzii Opera omnia (ed. Dutens), T. II., P. I. pp. 45, 46.

up for Queen Sophia Charlotte in reply to Bayle, and in which he took pains not to present the matter in very speculative form. A Würtemberg theologian, Pfaff by name, and others who were correspondents of Leibnitz and were themselves only too well versed in philosophy, brought it as a charge against Leibnitz—a charge which he never denied—that his philosophy was written in popular form.[1] They laughed very much afterwards at Wolff, who had taken them to be quite in earnest; his opinion was that if Leibnitz were not perfectly serious in this sense with his *Théodicée*, yet he had unconsciously written his best therein. Leibnitz's *Théodicée* is not what we can altogether appreciate; it is a justification of God in regard to the evil in the world. His really philosophic thoughts are most connectedly expressed in a treatise on the principles of Grace (*Principes de la Nature et de la Grace*),[2] and especially in the pamphlet addressed to Prince Eugène of Savoy.[3] Buhle (Geschichte der neuern Philosophie, vol. iv. section 1, p. 131) says : "His philosophy is not so much the product of free, independent, original speculation, as the result of well-tested earlier" and later "systems, an eclecticism whose defects he tried to remedy in his own way. It is a desultory treatment of Philosophy in letters."

Leibnitz followed the same general plan in his philosophy as the physicists adopt when they advance a hypothesis to explain existing data. He has it that general conceptions of the Idea are to be found, from which the particular may be derived; here, on account of existing data, the general conception, for example the determination of force or matter furnished by reflection, must have its determinations disposed in such a way that it fits in

---

[1] Vie de Mr. Leibnitz, pp. 134-143; Brucker. Hist. crit. philos. T. IV. P. II. pp. 385, 389 ; Tennemann, vol. xi. pp. 181, 182.

[2] Leibnitzii Opera, T. II. P. I. pp. 32-39.

[3] Ibidem, Principia philosophiæ, pp. 20-31.

with the data. Thus the philosophy of Leibnitz seems to be not so much a philosophic system as an hypothesis regarding the existence of the world, namely how it is to be determined in accordance with the metaphysical determinations and the data and assumptions of the ordinary conception, which are accepted as valid [1]—thoughts which are moreover propounded without the sequence pertaining to the Notion and mainly in narrative style, and which taken by themselves show no necessity in their connection. Leibnitz's philosophy therefore appears like a string of arbitrary assertions, which follow one on another like a metaphysical romance; it is only when we see what he wished thereby to avoid that we learn to appreciate its value. He really makes use of external reasons mainly in order to establish relations: "Because the validity of such relations cannot be allowed, nothing remains but to establish the matter in this way." If we are not acquainted with these reasons, this procedure strikes us as arbitrary.

a. Leibnitz's philosophy is an idealism of the intellectuality of the universe; and although from one point of view he stands opposed to Locke, as from another point of view he is in opposition to the Substance of Spinoza, he yet binds them both together again. For, to go into the matter more particularly, on the one hand he expresses in the many monads the absolute nature of things distinguished and of individuality; on the other hand, in contrast to this and apart from it, he expresses the ideality of Spinoza and the non-absolute nature of all difference, as the idealism of the popular conception. Leibnitz's philosophy is a metaphysics, and in sharp contrast to the simple universal Substance of Spinoza, where all that is determined is merely transitory, it makes fundamental the absolute multiplicity of individual substances, which after the example of the ancients he named monads—an expres-

---

[1] cf. Leibnitz: Essais de Théodicée, T. I. P. I. § 10, p. 86.

sion already used by the Pythagoreans. These monads he then proceeds to determine as follows.

Firstly: "Substance is a thing that is capable of activity; it is compound or simple, the compound cannot exist without the simple. The monads are simple substances." The proof that they constitute the truth in all things is very simple; it is a superficial reflection. For instance, one of Leibnitz's maxims is: "Because there are compound things, the principles of the same must be simple; for the compound consists of the simple."[1] This proof is poor enough; it is an example of the favourite way of starting from something definite, say the compound, and then drawing conclusions therefrom as to the simple. It is quite right in a way, but really it is tautology. Of course, if the compound exists, so does the simple; for the compound means something in itself manifold whose connection or unity is external. From the very trivial category of the compound it is easy to deduce the simple. It is a conclusion drawn from a certain premiss, but the question is whether the premiss is true. These monads are not, however, something abstract and simple in itself, like the empty Epicurean atoms, which, as they were in themselves lacking in determination, drew all their determination from their aggregation alone. The monads are, on the contrary, substantial forms, a good expression, borrowed from the Scholastics (*supra*, p. 71), or the metaphysical points of the Alexandrian School (Vol. II. p. 439); they are the entelechies of Aristotle taken as pure activity, which are forms in themselves (Vol. II. pp. 138, 182, 183). " These monads are not material or extended, nor do they originate or decay in the natural fashion, for they can begin only by a creative act of God, and they can end only by annihila-

---

[1] Leibnitz: Principes de la nature et la grace, § 1, p. 32 (Recueil de diverses pièces par Des-Maiseaux, T. II. p. 485); Principia philosophiæ, § 1, 2, p. 20.

tion." [1] Thereby they are distinguished from the atoms, which are regarded simply as principles. The expression creation we are familiar with from religion, but it is a meaningless word derived from the ordinary conception; in order to be a thought and to have philosophic significance, it must be much more closely defined.

Secondly: "On account of their simplicity the monads are not susceptible of alteration by another monad in their inner essence; there is no causal connection between them." Each of them is something indifferent and independent as regards the rest, otherwise it would not be an entelechy. Each of them is so much for itself that all its determinations and modifications go on in itself alone, and no determination from without takes place. Leibnitz says: "There are three ways in which substances are connected: (1) Causality, influence; (2) The relation of assistance; (3) The relation of harmony. The relation of influence is a relation pertaining to a commonplace or popular philosophy. But as it is impossible to understand how material particles or immaterial qualities can pass from one substance into another, such a conception as this must be abandoned." If we accept the reality of the many, there can be no transition at all; each is an ultimate and absolutely independent entity. "The system of assistance," according to Descartes, "is something quite superfluous, a *Deus ex machina,* because continual miracles in the things of nature are assumed." If we, like Descartes, assume independent substances, no causal nexus is conceivable; for this presupposes an influence, a bearing of the one upon the other, and in this way the other is not a substance. "Therefore there remains only harmony, a unity which is in itself or implicit. The monad is therefore simply shut up in itself,

[1] Leibnitzii De ipsa natura sive de vi insita actionibusque creaturarum (Oper. T. II. P. II.), § 11, p. 55, Principia philosophiæ, § 3-6, 18, pp. 20-22; Principes de la nature et de la grace, § 2, p. 32.

and cannot be determined by another; this other cannot be set into it. It can neither get outside itself, nor can others get inside it."[1] That is also Spinoza's way of regarding matters : each attribute entirely represents the essence of God for itself, extension and thought have no influence on each other.

In the third place, "however, these monads must at the same time have certain qualities or determinations in themselves, inner actions, through which they are distinguished from others. There cannot be two things alike, for otherwise they would not be two, they would not be different, but one and the same."[2] Here then Leibnitz's axiom of the undistinguishable comes into words. What is not in itself distinguished is not distinguished. This may be taken in a trivial sense, as that there are not two individuals which are alike. To such sensuous things the maxim has no application, it is *prima facie* indifferent whether there are things which are alike or not; there may also be always a difference of space. This is the superficial sense, which does not concern us. The more intimate sense is, however, that each thing is in itself something determined, distinguishing itself from others implicitly or in itself. Whether two things are like or unlike is only a comparison which we make, which falls within our ken. But what we have further to consider is

---

[1] Leibnitzii Principia philosophiæ, § 7, p. 21; Troisième éclaircissement du système de la communication des substances (Oper. T. II. P. I.), p. 73 (Recueil, T. II. p. 402).

[2] Leibnitzii Principia philosophiæ, § 8, 9, p. 21; Oper. T. II. P. I. pp. 128, 129, § 4, 5 : Il n'y a point deux individus indiscernables. Un gentilhomme d'esprit de mes amis, en parlant avec moi en présence de Mad. l'Electrice dans le jardin de Herrenhausen, crut qu'il trouverait bien deux feuilles entièrement semblables. Mad. l'Electrice l'en défia, et il courut longtemps en vain pour en chercher. Deux gouttes d'eau ou de lait regardées par le microscope se trouveront discernables. C'est un argument contre les Atomes (Recueil, T. I. p. 50).—Cf. Hegel's Werke, Vol. IV. p. 45.

the determined difference in themselves. The difference must be a difference in themselves, not for our comparison, for the subject must have the difference as its own peculiar characteristic or determination, *i.e.* the determination must be immanent in the individual. Not only do we distinguish the animal by its claws, but it distinguishes itself essentially thereby, it defends itself, it preserves itself. If two things are different only in being two, then each of them is one; but the fact of their being two does not constitute a distinction between them; the determined difference in itself is the principal point.

Fourthly: "The determinateness and the variation thereby established is, however, an inward implicit principle; it is a multiplicity of modifications, of relations to surrounding existences, but a multiplicity which remains locked up in simplicity. Determinateness and variation such as this, which remains and goes on in the existence itself, is a perception;" and therefore Leibnitz says all monads perceive or represent (for we may translate *perceptio* by representation [Vorstellung]). In other words, they are in themselves universal, for universality is just simplicity in multiplicity, and therefore a simplicity which is at the same time change and motion of multiplicity. This is a very important determination; in substance itself there is negativity, determinateness, without its simplicity and its implicitude being given up. Further, in it there is this idealism, that the simple is something in itself distinguished, and in spite of its variation, that it yet remains one, and continues in its simplicity. An instance of this is found in "I," my spirit. I have many conceptions, a wealth of thought is in me, and yet I remain one, notwithstanding this variety of state. This identity may be found in the fact that what is different is at the same time abrogated, and is determined as one; the monads are therefore distinguished by modifications in themselves, but not by external determinations. These determinations contained in the monads exist in them in ideal fashion; this ideality in the monad is in itself a whole, so that these differences are only representations and ideas. This absolute difference is what is termed the Notion; what falls asunder in the mere representation is held together. This is what possesses interest in Leibnitz's philosophy. Such ideality in the same way pertains to the material, which is also a multiplicity of monads; therefore the system of Leibnitz is an intellectual system, in accordance with which all that is material has powers of representation and perception. As thus representing, the monad, says Leibnitz, possesses activity; for activity is to be different, and yet to be one, and this is the only true difference. The monad not only represents, it also changes; but in doing so, it yet remains in itself absolutely what it is. This variation is based on activity. "The activity of the inner principle, by means of which it passes from one perception to another, is desire (*appetitus*)." Variation in representation is desire, and that constitutes the spontaneity of the monad; all is now complete in itself, and the category of influence falls away. Indeed, this intellectuality of all things is a great thought on the part of Leibnitz: "All multiplicity is included in unity;"[1] determination is not a difference in respect of something else, but reflected into itself, and maintaining itself. This is one aspect of things, but the matter is not therein complete; it is equally the case that it is different in respect of other things.

Fifthly: These representations and ideas are not necessarily conscious representations and ideas, any more than all monads as forming representations are conscious. It is true that consciousness is itself perception, but a higher grade of the same; perceptions of consciousness Leibnitz calls apperceptions. The difference between the merely representing and the self-conscious monads Leibnitz makes one of degrees of clearness. The expression representation

[1] Leibnitzii Principia philosophiæ, § 10-16, pp. 21, 22; Principes de la nature et de la grace, § 2, p. 32.

has, however, certainly something awkward about it, since
we are accustomed to associate it only with consciousness,
and with consciousness as such ; but Leibnitz admits also
of unconscious representation. When he then adduces
examples of unconscious representations, he appeals to the
condition of a swoon or of sleep, in which we are mere
monads : and that representations without consciousness
are present in such states he shows from the fact of our
having perceptions immediately after awakening out of
sleep, which shows that others must have been there, for
one perception arises only out of others.[1] That is a trivial
and empirical demonstration.

Sixthly : These monads constitute the principle of all
that exists. Matter is nothing else than their passive capability. This passive capability it is which constitutes the
obscurity of the representations, or a confusion which never
arrives at distinction, or desire, or activity.[2] That is a
correct definition of the conception ; it is Being, matter, in
accordance with the moment of simplicity. This is implicitly
activity; " mere implicitness without actualization " would
therefore be a better expression. The transition from obscurity to distinctness Leibnitz exemplifies by the state of
swooning.

Seventhly : Bodies as bodies are aggregates of monads :
they are mere heaps which cannot be termed substances,
any more than a flock of sheep can bear this name.[3] The
continuity of the same is an arrangement or extension, but

---

[1] Leibnitzii Principia philosophiæ, § 19-23, pp. 22, 23 ; Principes
de la nature et de la grace, § 4, pp. 33, 34; Nouveaux essais sur
l'entendement humain (Œuvres philosophiques de Leibnitz par
Raspe), Bk. II. chap. ix. § 4, p. 90.

[2] Leibnitzii De anima brutorum (Op. T. II. P. I.), § 2-4, pp. 230,
231.

[3] Leibnitzii Oper. T. II. P. I. pp. 214, 215, § 3; De ipsa natura
sive de vi insita, § 11, p. 55; Système nouveau de la nature et de la
communication des substances (Op. T. II. P. I.), pp. 50, 53.

space is nothing in itself ;[1] it is only in another, or a unity which our understanding gives to that aggregate.[2]

b. Leibnitz goes on to determine and distinguish more clearly as the principal moments, inorganic, organic, and conscious monads, and he does it in the following way.

a. Such bodies as have no inner unity, whose elements are connected merely by space, or externally, are inorganic; they have not an entelechy or one monad which rules over the rest.[3] The continuity of space as a merely external relation has not the Notion in itself of the likeness of these monads in themselves. Continuity is in fact to be regarded in them as an arrangement, a similarity in themselves. Leibnitz therefore defines their movements as like one another, as a harmony in themselves;[4] but again, this is as much as saying that their similarity is not in themselves. In fact continuity forms the essential determination of the inorganic; but it must at the same time not be taken as something external or as likeness, but as penetrating or penetrated unity, which has dissolved individuality in itself like a fluid. But to this point Leibnitz does not attain, because for him monads are the absolute principle, and individuality does not annul itself.

β. A higher degree of Being is found in bodies with life and soul, in which one monad has dominion over the rest. The body which is bound up with the monad, of which the one monad is the entelechy or soul, is with this soul named a living creature, an animal. One such entelechy

---

[1] Leibnitzii Oper. T. II. P. I. pp. 79, 121, 234-237, 280, 295; Nouveaux essais sur l'entendement humain, Bk. II. chap. xiii. § 15, 17, pp. 106, 107.

[2] Leibnitz : Nouveaux essais sur l'entendement humain, Bk. II. chap. xii. § 7, pp. 102, 103; chap. xxi. § 72, p. 170; chap. xxiv. § 1, p. 185.

[3] Leibnitzii Oper. T. II. P. I. p. 39 ; Nouveaux essais sur l'entendement humain, Bk. III. chap. vi. § 24, p. 278 ; § 39, p. 290.

[4] Leibnitzii Oper. T. II. P. II. p. 60 ; Nouveaux essais sur l'entendement humain, Bk. II. chap. xxiii. § 23, p. 181.

rules over the rest, yet not really, but formally: the limbs of this animal, however, are again themselves such living things, each of which has in its turn its ruling entelechy within it.[1] But ruling is here an inappropriate expression. To rule in this case is not to rule over others, for all are independent; it is therefore only a formal expression. If Leibnitz had not helped himself out with the word rule, and developed the idea further, this dominant monad would have abrogated the others, and put them in a negative position; the implicitness of the other monads, or the principle of the absolute Being of these points or individuals would have disappeared. Yet we shall later on come across this relation of the individuals to one another.

γ. The conscious monad distinguishes itself from the naked (material) monads by the distinctness of the representation. But this is of course only an indefinite word, a formal distinction; it indicates that consciousness is the very thing that constitutes the distinction of the undistinguished, and that distinction constitutes the determination of consciousness. Leibnitz more particularly defined the distinction of man as that " he is capable of the knowledge of necessary and eternal truths,"—or that he conceives the universal on the one hand, and on the other what is connected with it; the nature and essence of self-consciousness lies in the universality of the Notions. "These eternal truths rest on two maxims; the one is that of contradiction, the other is that of sufficient reason." The former of these is unity expressed in useless fashion as a maxim, the distinction of the undistinguishable, $A = A$; it is the definition of thinking, but not a maxim which could contain a truth as content, or it does not express the Notion of distinction as such. The other important principle was, on the other hand: What is not distinguished in thought is not distinguished (p. 333). " The maxim of

---

[1] Leibnitzii Principia philosophiæ, § 65-71, p. 28; Principes de la nature et de la grace, § 3, 4, pp. 32, 33.

the reason is that everything has its reason," [1]—the particular has the universal as its essential reality. Necessary
truth must have its reason in itself in such a manner that
it is found by analysis, *i.e.* through that very maxim of
identity. For analysis is the very favourite plan of
resolving into simple ideas and principles : a resolution
which annihilates their relation, and which therefore in
fact forms a transition into the opposite, though it does
not have the consciousness of the same, and on that account
also excludes the Notion ; for every opposite it lays hold
of only in its identity. Sufficient reason seems to be a
pleonasm ; but Leibnitz understood by this aims, final
causes (*causæ finales*), the difference between which and the
causal nexus or the efficient cause he here brings under
discussion.[2]

c. The universal itself, absolute essence, which with
Leibnitz is something quite different from the monads,
separates itself also into two sides, namely universal Being
and Being as the unity of opposites.

a. That universal is God, as the cause of the world, to
the consciousness of whom the above principle of sufficient
reason certainly forms the transition. The existence of
God is only an inference from eternal truths ; for these
must as the laws of nature have a universal sufficient
reason which determines itself as none other than God.
Eternal truth is therefore the consciousness of the
universal and absolute in and for itself ; and this universal and absolute is God, who, as one with Himself,
the monad of monads, is the absolute *Monas.* Here we
again have the wearisome proof of His existence : He is
the fountain of eternal truths and Notions, and without
Him no potentiality would have actuality ; He has the

[1] Leibnitzii Principia philosophiæ, § 29-31, p. 24 ; Principes de la
nature et de la grace, § 5, p. 34 ; Essais de Théodicée, T. I. P. I.
§ 44, p. 115.

[2] Leibnitz : Principes de la nature et de la grace, § 7, p. 35.

prerogative of existing immediately in His potentiality.[1]
God is here also the unity of potentiality and actuality, but
in an uncomprehending manner; what is necessary, but not
comprehended, is transferred to Him. Thus God is at first
comprehended chiefly as universal, but already in the
aspect of the relation of opposites.

β. As regards this second aspect, the absolute relation of
opposites, it occurs in the first place in the form of
absolute opposites of thought, the good and the evil. "God
is the Author of the world," says Leibnitz; that refers
directly to evil. It is round this relation that philosophy
specially revolves, but to the unity of which it did not
then attain; the evil in the world was not comprehended,
because no advance was made beyond the fixed opposition.
The result of Leibnitz's Théodicée is an optimism supported
on the lame and wearisome thought that God, since a world
had to be brought into existence, chose out of infinitely
many possible worlds the best possible—the most perfect,
so far as it could be perfect, considering the finite element
which it was to contain.[2] This may very well be said in a
general way, but this perfection is no determined thought, but
a loose popular expression, a sort of babble respecting an
imaginary or fanciful potentiality; Voltaire made merry over
it. Nor is the nature of the finite therein defined. Because
the world, it is said, has to be the epitome of finite Beings,
evil could not be separated from it, since evil is negation,
finitude.[3] Reality and negation remain standing in opposition to one another exactly in the same way as before.
That is the principal conception in the Théodicée. But

---

[1] Leibnitz: Principes de la nature et de la grace, § 8, p. 35;
Principia philosophiæ, § 43-46, p. 25.

[2] Leibnitz: Essais de Théodicée, T. I. P. I. § 6-8, pp. 83-85;
Principes de la nature et de la grace, § 10, p. 36.

[3] Leibnitz: Essais de Théodicée, T. I. P. I. § 20, pp. 96, 97; § 32,
33, pp. 106, 107; T. II. P. II. § 153, pp. 57, 58; § 378, pp. 256,
257.

something very like this can be said in every-day life.   If
I have some goods brought to me in the market at some
town, and say that they are certainly not perfect, but the
best that are to be got, this is quite a good reason why I
should content myself with them.   But comprehension is a
very different thing from this.   Leibnitz says nothing
further than that the world is good, but there is also evil
in it; the matter remains just the same as it was before.
" Because it had to be finite " is then a mere arbitrary
choice on the part of God.   The next question would be :
Why and how is there finitude in the Absolute and His
decrees ?   And only then should there be deduced from the
determination of finitude the evil which no doubt exists
therein.

It is true that Leibnitz has a reply to the above question :
" God does not will what is evil ; evil comes only indirectly
into the results " (blind), " because oftentimes the greater
good cculd not be achieved if evils were not present.
Therefore they are means to a good end. '   But why does
not God employ other means ?   They are always external,
not in and for themselves.   " A moral evil may not be
regarded as a means, nor must we, as the apostle says, do
evil that good may come ; yet it has often the relation of a
conditio sine qua non of the good.   Evil is in God only the
object of a permissive will (*voluntatis permissivæ*); " but
everything that is wrong would be such.   " God has therefore among the objects of His will the best possible as the
ultimate object, but the good as a matter of choice (*qualem-
cunque*), also as subordinate ; and things indifferent and
evils often as means.   Evil is, however, an object of His
will only as the condition of something otherwise necessary (*rei alioqui debitæ*), which without it could not exist ;
in which sense Christ said it must needs be that offences
come." [1]

----

[1] Leibnitzii Causa Dei asserta per justitiam ejus (Essais de Théodicée, T. II.), § 34-39, pp. 385, 386.

In a general sense we are satisfied with the answer: "In accordance with the wisdom of God we must accept it as a fact that the laws of nature are the best possible," but this answer does not suffice for a definite question. What one wishes to know is the goodness of this or that particular law; and to that no answer is given. If, for example, it is said that "The law of falling bodies, in which the relation of time and space is the square, is the best possible," one might employ, as far as mathematics are concerned, any other power whatever. When Leibnitz answers: "God made it so," this is no answer at all. We wish to know the definite reason of this law; such general determinations sound pious, but are not satisfying.

γ. He goes on to say that the sufficient reason has reference to the representation of the monads. The principles of things are monads, of which each is for itself, without having influence on the others. If now the Monad of monads, God, is the absolute substance, and individual monads are created through His will, their substantiality comes to an end. There is therefore a contradiction present, which remains unsolved in itself—that is between the one substantial monad and the many monads for which independence is claimed, because their essence consists in their standing in no relation to one another. Yet at the same time, in order to show the harmony that exists in the world, Leibnitz understands the relation of monads to monads more generally as the unity of contrasted existences, namely of soul and body. This unity he represents as a relation without difference, and notionless, *i.e.* as a pre-established harmony.[1] Leibnitz uses here the illustration of two clocks, which are set to the same hour, and keep the same time;[2] in the same way the

---

[1] Leibnitz: Principes de la nature et de la grace, § 3, p. 33; Premier éclaircissement du système de la communication des substances, p. 70.

[2] Leibnitz: Second et troisième éclaircissemens du système de la communication des substances, pp. 71-73.

movement of the kingdom of thought goes on, determined
in accordance with ends, and the movement onward of
the corporeal kingdom which corresponds with it, proceeds
according to a general causal connection.[1] The case is the
same as with Spinoza, that these two sides of the universe
have no connection with each other, the one does not
influence the other, but both are entirely indifferent to
one another; it is really the differentiating relation of the
Notion that is lacking. In abstract thought that is without Notion, that determination now receives the form of
simplicity, of implicitude, of indifference with regard to
what is other, of a self-reflection that has no movement :
in this way red in the abstract is in a position of indifference as regards blue, &c. Here, as before, Leibnitz
forsakes his principle of individuation : it has only the
sense of being exclusively one, and of not reaching to
and including what is other; or it is only a unity of the
popular conception, not the Notion of unity. The soul
has thus a series of conceptions and ideas which are
developed from within it, and this series is from the very
first placed within the soul at its creation, *i.e.* the soul is in
all immediacy this implicit determination ; determination is,
however, not implicit, but the reflected unfolding of this
determination in the ordinary conception is its outward
existence. Parallel with this series of differentiated conceptions, there now runs a series of motions of the body,
or of what is external to the soul.[2] Both are essential
moments of reality ; they are mutually indifferent, but
they have also an essential relation of difference.

Since now every monad, as shut up within itself, has no
influence upon the body and its movements, and yet the infinite multitude of their atoms correspond with one another,
Leibnitz places this harmony in God ; a better definition

---

[1] Leibnitzii Principia philosophiæ, § 82, p. 30; Principes de la
nature et de la grace, § 11, p. 36.

[2] Leibnitz: Système nouveau de la nature et de la communication des substances, pp. 54, 55.

of the relation and the activity of the Monad of monads is therefore that it is what pre-establishes harmony in the changes of the monads.[1] God is the sufficient reason, the cause of this correspondence; He has so arranged the multitude of atoms that the original changes which are developed within one monad correspond with the changes of the others. The pre-established harmony is to be thought of somewhat in this style; when a dog gets a beating, the pain develops itself in him, in like fashion the beating develops itself in itself, and so does the person who administers the beating; their determinations all correspond with one another, and that not by means of their objective connection, since each is independent.[2] The principle of the harmony among the monads does not consequently belong to them, but it is in God, who for that very reason is the Monad of monads, their absolute unity. We saw from the beginning how Leibnitz arrived at this conception. Each monad is really possessed of the power of representation, and is as such a representation of the universe, therefore implicitly the totality of the whole world. But at the same time this representation is not in consciousness; the naked monad is implicitly the universe, and difference is the development of this totality in it.[3] What develops itself therein is at the same time in harmony with all other developments; all is one harmony. "In the universe all things are closely knit together, they are in one piece, like an ocean : the slightest movement transmits its influence far and wide all around."[4] From a single grain of sand, Leibnitz holds, the whole universe might be comprehended in its entire development—if we

---

[1] Leibnitzii Principia philosophiæ, § 90, p. 31 ; Principes de la nature et de la grace, § 12, 13, pp. 36, 37 ; § 15, pp. 37, 38.

[2] Leibnitzii Oper. T. II. P. I. pp. 75, 76.

[3] Leibnitzii Principia philosoph., § 58-62, p. 27; Oper. T. II. P. I. pp. 46, 47.

[4] Leibnitz : Essais de Théodicée, T. I. P. I. § 9, pp. 85, 86.

only knew the sand grain thoroughly. There is not really much in all this, though it sounds very fine ; for the rest of the universe is considerably more than a grain of sand, well though we knew it, and considerably different therefrom. To say that its essence is the universe is mere empty talk : for the fact is that the universe as essence is not the universe. To the sand grain much must be added which is not present ; and since thought adds more than all the grains of sand that exist, the universe and its development may in this way certainly be comprehended. Thus according to Leibnitz every monad has or is the representation of the entire universe, which is the same as saying that it is really representation in general ; but at the same time it is a determinate representation, by means of which it comes to be this particular monad, therefore it is representation according to its particular situation and circumstances.[1]

The representations of the monad in itself, which constitute its universe, develop themselves from themselves, as the spiritual element in it, according to the laws of their own activity and desire, just as the movements of their outer world do according to laws of bodies ; hence liberty is nothing other than this spontaneity of immanent development, but as in consciousness. The magnetic needle, on the contrary, has only spontaneity without consciousness, and consequently without freedom. For, says Leibnitz, the nature of the magnetic needle is to turn to the north; if it had consciousness it would imagine that this was its self-determination ; it would thus have the will to move round in accordance with its nature.[2] But it is clear that in the course of conscious representations there is involved no necessary connection, but contingency and want of sequence

[1] Leibnitz : Principes de la nature et de la grace, § 12, 13, pp. 36, 37 ; Oper. T. II. P. I. p. 337.
[2] Leibnitz : Essais de Théodicée, T. II. P. III. § 291, pp. 184, 185 ; T. I. P. I. § 50, p. 119.

are to be found, the reason of this according to Leibnitz (Oper. T. II. P. I. p. 75) being "because the nature of a created substance implies that it changes incessantly according to a certain order, which order guides it spontaneously (*spontanément*) in all the circumstances which befall it; so that one who sees all things recognizes in the present condition of substance the past also and the future. The law of order, which determines the individuality of the particular substance, has an exact reference to what takes place in every other substance and in the whole universe." The meaning of this is that the monad is not a thing apart, or that there are two views of it, the one making it out as spontaneously generating its representations, so far as form is concerned, and the other making it out to be a moment of the whole of necessity; Spinoza would call this regarding it from both sides. An organic whole, a human being, is thus for instance the assertion of his aim from out of himself: at the same time the being directed on something else is involved in his Notion. He represents this and that to himself, he wills this and that; his activity employs itself and brings about changes. His inward determination thus becomes corporeal determination, and then change going beyond himself; he appears as cause, influencing other monads. But this Being-for-another is only an appearance. For the other, *i.e.* the actual, in so far as the monad determines it or makes it negative, is the passive element which the monad has in itself: all moments are indeed contained therein, and for that very reason it has no need of other monads, but only of the laws of the monads in itself. But if the Being-for-another is mere appearance, the same may be said of Being-for-self; for this has significance only in reference to Being-for-another.

The important point in Leibnitz's philosophy is this intellectuality of representation which Leibnitz, however, did not succeed in carrying out; and for the same reason this intellectuality is at the same time infinite multiplicity, which has remained absolutely independent, because this intellectuality has not been able to obtain mastery over the One. The separation in the Notion, which proceeds as far as release from itself, or appearance in distinct independence, Leibnitz did not succeed in bringing together into unity. The harmony of these two moments, the course of mental representations and the course of things external, appearing mutually as cause and effect, is not brought by Leibnitz into relation in and for themselves ; he therefore lets them fall asunder, although each is passive as regards the other. He moreover considers both of them in one unity, to be sure, but their activity is at the same time not for themselves. Every forward advance becomes therefore incomprehensible when taken by itself, because the course of the representation as through aims in itself, requires this moment of Other-Being or of passivity ; and again the connection of cause and effect requires the universal : each however lacks this its other moment. The unity which according to Leibnitz is to be brought about by the pre-established harmony, namely that the determination of the will of man and the outward change harmonize, is therefore brought about by means of another, if not indeed from without, for this other is God. Before God the monads are not to be independent, but ideal and absorbed in Him.

At this point the demand would come in that in God Himself there should be comprehended the required unity of that which before fell asunder ; and God has the special privilege of having laid on Him the burden of what cannot be comprehended. The word of God is thus the makeshift which leads to a unity which itself is only hypothetical ; for the process of the many out of this unity is not demonstrated. God plays therefore [in the later philosophy a far greater part than in the early, because now the comprehension of the absolute opposition of thought and Being is the chief demand. With Leibnitz the extent to which thoughts advance is the extent of the universe; where comprehension ceases, the universe ceases, and God begins : so that later it was even maintained that to be comprehended was derogatory to God, because He was thus degraded into finitude. In that procedure a beginning is made from the determinate, this and that are stated to be necessary ; but since in the next place the unity of these moments is not comprehended, it is transferred to God. God is therefore, as it were, the waste channel into which all contradictions flow : Leibnitz's Théodicée is just a popular summing up such as this. There are, nevertheless, all manner of evasions to be searched out—in the opposition of God's justice and mercy, that the one tempers the other ; how the fore-knowledge of God and human freedom are compatible—all manner of syntheses which never come to the root of the matter nor show both sides to be moments.

These are the main moments of Leibnitz's philosophy. It is a metaphysic which starts from a narrow determination of the understanding, namely, from absolute multiplicity, so that connection can only be grasped as continuity. Thereby absolute unity is certainly set aside, but all the same it is presupposed; and the association of individuals with one another is to be explained only in this way, that it is God who determines the harmony in the changes of individuals. This is an artificial system, which is founded on a category of the understanding, that of the absoluteness of abstract individuality. What is of importance in Leibnitz lies in the maxims, in the principle of individuality and the maxim of indistinguishability.

CHAPTER II

TRANSITION PERIOD

THE decadence which we find in thought until the philosophy of Kant is reached, is manifested in what was at this time advocated in opposition to the metaphysic of the understanding, and which may be called a general popular philosophy, a reflecting empiricism, which to a greater or less extent becomes itself a metaphysic; just as, on the other hand, that metaphysic, in as far as it extended to particular sciences, becomes empiricism. As against these metaphysical contradictions, as against the artificialities of the metaphysical synthesis, as against the assistance of God, the pre-established harmony, the best possible world, &c., as against this merely artificial understanding, we now find that fixed principles, immanent in mind, have been asserted or maintained respecting what is felt, intuitively perceived and honoured in the cultured human breast. And in distinction to the assertion that we only find the solution in the Beyond, in God, these concrete principles of a fixed and permanent content form a reconciliation here and now, they adopt a position of independence, and assume an intellectual standing-ground which they find in what has generally been termed the healthy human understanding. Such determinations may indeed be found to be perfectly good and valid if the feelings, intuitions, heart and understanding of man be morally and intellectually fashioned; for in that case better and more noble feelings and desires may rule in men and a more universal content may be expressed in these principles. But when men make what we call sound reason—that which is by nature implanted in man's breast—into the content and the principle, the healthy human understanding discovers itself to be identical with a feeling and knowledge belonging to nature. The Indians who worship a cow, and who expose or slay new-born children, and commit all sorts of barbarous deeds, the Egyptians who pray to a bird, the apis, &c., and the Turks as well, all possess a healthy human understanding similar in nature. But the healthy human understanding and the natural feeling of rude and barbarous Turks, when taken as a standard, result in shocking principles. When we speak of healthy human understanding, however, of natural feelings, we always have before our eyes a cultured mind; and those who make the healthy human reason, the natural knowledge, the immediate feelings and inspirations found in themselves, into a rule and standard, do not know that when religion, morality, and rectitude are discovered to be present in the human breast, this is due to culture and education, which are the first to make such principles into natural feelings. Here natural feelings and the healthy human understanding are thus made the principle; and much may be recognized as coming under these heads. This then is the form taken by Philosophy in the eighteenth century. Taken as a whole, three points of view have to be considered; in the first place, Hume must be regarded on his own account, then the Scottish, and, thirdly, the French philosophy. Hume is a sceptic; the Scottish philosophy opposes the scepticism of Hume, the French philosophy has in the "enlightenment" of Germany (by which expression is indicated that form of German philosophy which is not Wolffian metaphysics) an appendage of a feebler form. Since from the metaphysical God we can make no further progress in the concrete, Locke grounds his content on experience. But that empiricism leads thought to no fixed standpoint, Hume demonstrates by denying every universal ; the Scottish philosophers, on the contrary, undoubtedly maintain universal propositions and truths, but not through thought. Hence in empiricism itself the fixed standpoint has now to be adopted ; thus the French find the universal in the actuality which they call *réalité*. They do not, however, find its content in and from thought, but as living substance, as nature and matter. All this is a further working out of reflecting empiricism, and some more details respecting it must still be given.

A.　Idealism and Scepticism.

Thought generally is simple, universal self-identity, but in the form of negative movement, whereby the determinate abrogates itself. This movement of Being-for-self is now an essential moment of thought, while hitherto it was outside it ; and thus grasping itself as movement in itself, thought is self-consciousness—at first indeed formal, as individual self-consciousness. Such a form it has in scepticism, but this distinction marks it off from the older scepticism, that now the certainty of reality is made the starting point. With the ancients, on the contrary, scepticism is the return into individual consciousness in such a way that to it this consciousness is not the truth, in other words that scepticism does not give expression to the results arrived at, and attains no positive significance. But since in the modern world this absolute substantiality, this unity of implicitude and self-consciousness is fundamental—that is, this faith in reality generally —scepticism has here the form of idealism, *i.e.* of expressing self-consciousness or certainty of self as all reality and truth. The crudest form of this idealism is when self-consciousness, as individual or formal, does not proceed further than to say : All objects are our conceptions. We find this subjective idealism in Berkeley,[1] and another form of the same in Hume.

1. BERKELEY.

This idealism, in which all external reality disappears, has before it the standpoint of Locke, and it proceeds directly from him. For we saw that to Locke the source of truth is experience, or Being as perceived. Now since this sensuous Being, as Being, has in it the quality of being for consciousness, we saw that it necessarily came to pass that in Locke's case some qualities, at least, were so determined that they were not in themselves, but only for another; and that colour, figure, &c., had their ground only in the subject, in his particular organization. This Being-for-another, however, was not by him accepted as the Notion, but as falling within self-consciousness—i.e. self-consciousness not looked on as universal,—not within mind, but within what is opposed to the implicit.

George Berkeley was born in 1684 at Kilcrin, near Thomastown, in the county of Kilkenny, Ireland : in 1754 he died as an English Bishop.[2] He wrote the "Theory of Vision," 1709 ; "A Treatise concerning the principles of human knowledge," 1710 ; "Three Dialogues between Hylas and Philonous," 1713. In 1784 his collected works were published in London in two quarto volumes.

Berkeley advocated an idealism which came very near to that of Malebranche. As against the metaphysic of the

[1] In the lectures of 1825-1826 and 1829-1830 Berkeley was passed over by Hegel ; in both courses Hume follows directly after the Scottish and French philosophers, and thus comes immediately before Kant ; in the course of 1825-1826 the French philosophy precedes the Scottish also.

[2] Nachrichten von dem Leben und den Schriften des Bischofs Berkeley (in Berkeley's philosoph. Werk. Pt. I. Leipzig, 1781), pp. 1, 45 ; Buhle : Geschichte der neuern Philosophie, Vol. V. Sect. 1, pp. 86-90.

understanding, we have the point of view that all existence and its determinations arise from feeling, and are constituted by self-consciousness. Berkeley's first and fundamental thought is consequently this: "The Being of whatever is called by us a thing consists alone in its being perceived," *i.e.* our determinations are the objects of our knowledge. "All objects of human knowledge are ideas" (so called by Berkeley as by Locke), "which arise either from the impressions of the outward senses, or from perceptions of the inward states and activities of the mind, or finally, they are such as are constituted by means of memory and imagination through their separation ´and rearrangement. A union of different sensuous feelings appears to us to be a particular thing, *e.g.* the feeling of colour, taste, smell, figure, &c. ; for by colours, smells, sounds, something of which we have a sensation is always understood." [1] This is the matter and the object of knowledge; the knower is the percipient "I," which reveals itself in relation to those feelings in various activities, such as imagination, remembrance, and will.

Berkeley thus indeed acknowledges the distinction between Being-for-self and Other-Being, which in his case, however, itself falls within the "I." Of the matter on which activity is directed, it is no doubt in regard to one portion allowed that it does not exist outside of mind—that is to say, so far as our thoughts, inward feelings and states, or the operations of our imaginary powers are concerned. But in like manner the manifold sensuous conceptions and feelings can only exist in a mind. Locke certainly distinguished extension and movement, for example, as fundamental qualities, *i.e.* as qualities which pertain to the objects in themselves. But Berkeley very pertinently points out inconsistency here from the point of view that

---

[1] Buhle: Geschichte der neuern Philosophie, Vol. V. pp. 90, 91 ; The Works of George Berkeley, Prof. Fraser's edition (Dialogues between Hylas and Philonous), Vol. I. p. 264, seq. et passim.

great and small, quick and slow, hold good as something relative; thus were extension and movement to be inherent or implicit, they could not be either large or small, quick or slow; that is, they could not be, for these determinations rest in the conception¹ of such qualities. In Berkeley the relation of things to consciousness is alone dealt with, and beyond this relationship they do not in his view come. From this it follows that it is only self-consciousness that possesses them; for a perception which is not in a conceiving mind is nothing : it is a direct contradiction. There can be no substance, he says, which neither conceives nor perceives, and which is yet the substratum of perceptions and conceptions. If it is represented that there is something outside of consciousness which is similar to the conceptions, this is likewise contradictory ; a conception can alone be similar to a conception, the idea to the idea alone.²

Thus, while Locke's ultimate point is abstract substance, Being generally with the real determination of a substratum of accidents, Berkeley declares this substance to be the most incomprehensible assumption of all; but the incomprehensibility does not make this Being into an absolute nullity, nor does it make it in itself incomprehensible.³ For Berkeley brings forward against the present existence of external objects only the inconceivability of the relation of a Being to mind. This inconceivability, however, is destroyed in the Notion, for the Notion is the negative of things; and this moved Berkeley and Leibnitz to shut up the two sides in themselves. There nevertheless remains a relationship of what is "other" to us; these feelings do not develop from us as Leibnitz represents, but

¹ Buhle, Geschichte der neuern Philosophie, Vol. V. Sect. 1, pp. 92, 93; The Works of George Berkeley, Vol. I. p. 279 seq.

² Buhle, ibidem, pp. 91, 92 ; Berkeley, ibidem, pp. 288 seq., 300 seq. et passim.

³ Buhle, ibidem, pp. 93, 94; Berkeley, ibidem, pp. 289, 308. seq.

are determined through somewhat else. When Leibnitz speaks of development within the monads, it is nothing but empty talk; for the monads as they follow in succession have no inward connection. Each individual is thus determined through another, and not through us; and it does not matter what this external is, since it remains a contingent. Now in relation to the two sides of Leibnitz which are indifferent to one another, Berkeley says that such an "other" is quite superfluous. Berkeley calls the other the objects; but these, he says, cannot be what we call matter, for spirit and matter cannot come together.[1] But the necessity of conceptions directly contradicts this Being-within-self of the conceiver; for the Being-within-self is the freedom of the conceiver; the latter does not, however, produce the conceptions with freedom; they have for him the form and determinateness of an independent "other." Berkeley likewise does not accept idealism in the subjective sense, but only in respect that there are spirits which impart themselves (in the other case the subject forms his own conceptions), and consequently that it is God alone who brings to pass such conceptions; thus the imaginations or conceptions which are produced by us with our individual activity remain separate from these others,[2] *i.e.* from the implicit.

This conception gives an instance of the difficulties which appear in regard to these questions, and which Berkeley wished to escape from in a quite original way. The inconsistency in this system God has again to make good; He has to bear it all away; to Him the solution of the contradiction is left. In this idealism, in short, the common sensuous view of the universe and the separation of actuality, as also the system of thought, of judgments

[1] Buhle: Geschichte der neuern Philosophie, Vol. V. Sect. 1, pp. 94, 95; The Works of George Berkeley, Vol. I. pp. 308, 335.

[2] Buhle, ibidem, pp. 96-99; Berkeley, ibidem, p. 325, seq. et passim.

devoid of Notion, remain exactly as before; plainly nothing in the content is altered but the abstract form that
all things are perceptions only.[1] Such idealism deals with
the opposition between consciousness and its object merely,
and leaves the extension of the conceptions and the an-
tagonisms of the empirical and manifold content quite un-
touched; and if we ask what then is the truth of these
perceptions and conceptions, as we asked formerly of
things, no answer is forthcoming. It is pretty much a
matter of indifference whether we believe in things or in
perceptions, if self-consciousness remains possessed entirely
by finalities; it receives the content in the ordinary way,
and that content is of the ordinary kind. In its individuality it stumbles about amid the conceptions of an
entirely empirical existence, without knowing and understanding anything else about the content: that is to say
in this formal idealism reason has no content of its own.

As to what Berkeley further states in respect of the
empirical content, where the object of his investigation
becomes entirely psychological, it relates in the main to
finding out the difference between the sensations of sight
and feeling, and to discovering which kind of sensations
belong to the one and which to the other. This kind of
investigation keeps entirely to the phenomenal, and only
therein distinguishes the various sorts of phenomena; or
comprehension only reaches as far as to distinctions. The
only point of interest is that these investigations have in
their course chiefly lighted on space, and a dispute is
carried on as to whether we obtain the conception of
distance and so on, in short all the conceptions relating
to space, through sight or feeling. Space is just this
sensuous universal, the universal in individuality itself,
which in the empirical consideration of empirical multiplicity invites and leads us on to thought (for it itself is
thought), and by it this very sensuous perception and

[1] Cf. Berkeley, ibidem, passim.

reasoning respecting perception is in its action confused. And since here perception finds an objective thought, it really would be led on to thought or to the possession of a thought, but at the same time it cannot arrive at thought in its completion, since thought or the Notion are not in question, and it clearly cannot come to the consciousness of true reality. Nothing is thought in the form of thought, but only as an external, as something foreign to thought.

2. HUME.

We must add to what has preceded an account of the Scepticism of Hume, which has been given a more important place in history than it deserves from its intrinsic nature ; its historic importance is due to the fact that Kant really derives the starting point of his philosophy from Hume.

David Hume was born in 1711 at Edinburgh and died there in 1776. He held a librarian's post in that town for some time, then he became secretary to the Embassy in Paris ; for quite a long period, indeed, he moved in diplomatic circles. In Paris he came to know Jean Jacques Rousseau and invited him to England, but Rousseau's terribly distrustful and suspicious nature very soon estranged the two.[1] Hume is more celebrated as a writer of history than through his philosophic works. He wrote : " A Treatise of human nature," 3 vols., 1739, translated into German by Jacob, Halle, 1790, 8vo ; likewise " Essays and Treatises on several subjects," 2 vols. (Vol. I. containing " Essays moral, political and literary," printed for the first time in Edinburgh, 1742 ; Vol. II. containing an "Inquiry concerning human understanding," a further development of the Treatise, and first printed separately in London, 1748, 8vo). In his " Essays," which contributed most to

[1] Buhle : Geschichte der neuern Philosophie, Vol. V. Sect. 1, pp. 193-200.

his fame as far as the philosophic side is concerned, he
treated philosophic subjects as an educated, thoughtful
man of the world would do—not in a systematic connection,
nor showing the wide range which his thoughts should
properly have been able to attain ; in fact in some of his
treatises he merely dealt with particular points of view.

We must shortly deal with the main aspects of Hume's
philosophy. He starts directly from the philosophic standpoint of Locke and Bacon, which derives our conceptions
from experience, and his scepticism has the idealism of
Berkeley as its object. The sequence of thought is this :
Berkeley allows all ideas to hold good as they are ; in Hume
the antithesis of the sensuous and universal has cleared
and more sharply defined itself, sense being pronounced by
him to be devoid of universality. Berkeley does not make
any distinction as to whether in his sensations there is a
necessary connection or not. Formerly experience was a
mixture of the two elements. Hume tells us that all
perceptions of the mind may be divided into two classes
or species, that of impressions, *i.e.* sensuous perceptions,
and thoughts or ideas ; the latter are similar in content
to the former, but less forcible and lively. All objects of
reason are consequently either relations of thoughts such
as mathematical axioms, or facts of experience.[1] Since
Hume makes these into the content he naturally rejects
innate ideas.[2]

Now when Hume goes on to consider more closely what is
subsumed under experience, he finds categories of the
understanding present there, and more especially the
determination of the universal and of universal necessity ;

[1] Tennemann's Grundriss der Geschichte der Philosophie von
Wendt (Leipzig, 1829), § 370, 'pp. 439, 440 ; Hume : Essays and
Treatises on several subjects, Vol. III. containing an Inquiry con-
cerning human understanding (London, 1770), Sect. 2, pp. 21, 22 ;
Sect. 4, P. I. p. 42 ; Tennemann, Vol. XI. pp. 433, 434.

[2] Hume : Essays and Treatises on several subjects, Vol. III. Not.
A, pp. 283, 284.

he took under his consideration more particularly the category of cause and effect, and in it set forth the rational element, inasmuch as in this causal relationship necessity is especially contained. Here Hume really completed the system of Locke, since he consistently drew attention to the fact that if this point of view be adhered to, experience is indeed the principle of whatever one knows, or perception itself contains everything that happens, but nevertheless the determination of universality and necessity are not contained in, nor were they given us by experience. Hume has thus destroyed the objectivity or absolute nature of thought-determinations. "Our conviction of the truth of a fact rests on feeling, memory, and the reasonings founded on the causal connection, *i.e.* on the relation of cause and effect. The knowledge of this relation is not attained by reasonings *a priori,* but arises entirely from experience; and we draw inferences, since we expect similar results to follow from similar causes, by reason of the principle of the custom or habit of conjoining different manifestations, *i.e.* by reason of the principle of the association of ideas. Hence there is no knowledge and no metaphysics beyond experience." [1]

The simple thought we have here is exactly what Locke says, that we must receive the conception of cause and effect, and thus of a necessary connection, from experience; but experience, as sensuous perception, contains no necessity, has no causal connection. For in what we term such, that which we properly speaking perceive is merely the fact that something first of all happens and that then something else follows. Immediate perception relates only to a content of conditions or things which are

---

[1] Tennemann's Grundriss der Geschichte der Philosophie von Wendt, § 370, p. 440; Hume: Essays and Treatises on several subjects, Vol. III. Sect. 4, Pt. I. pp. 43-45; Sect. 5, pp. 66, 67; Buhle: Geschichte der neuern Philosophie, Vol. V. Sect. 1, pp. 204, 205; Tennemann, Vol. XI. pp. 435, 436.

present alongside of and in succession to one another, but not to what we call cause and effect; in time-succession there is thus no relation of cause and effect, and consequently no necessity either.[1] When we say the pressure of the water is the cause of the destruction of this house, that is no pure experience. We have merely seen the water pressing or moving along in this direction, and subsequently the house falling down; and so with other examples. Necessity is thus not justified by experience, but we carry it into experience; it is accidentally arrived at by us and is subjective merely. This kind of universality which we connect with necessity, Hume calls custom. Because we have often seen results to follow we are accustomed to regard the connection as a necessary one; the necessity to him is thus a quite contingent association of ideas, which is custom.

It is the same thing in respect of the universal. What we perceive are individual phenomena and sensations in which we see that this is now one thing and now another. It may likewise be that we perceive the same determination frequently repeated and in manifold ways. But this is still far removed from universality; universality is a determination which is not given to us through experience. It may be said that this is quite a correct remark on Hume's part, if by experience we understand outward experience. Experience is sensible that something exists, but nevertheless the universal is not as yet present in it. Indeed, sensuous existence as such is something which is set forth as indifferent, not differentiated from anything else; but sensuous existence is likewise universal in itself, or the indifference of its determinateness is not its only determinateness. But since Hume regards necessity, the unity of opposites, as resting quite subjectively on custom, we cannot get any deeper in thought. Custom is indeed

[1] Hume: Essays and Treatises on several subjects, Vol. III. Sect. vii. Pt. 1, pp. 102, 103; Pt. 2, pp. 108, 109; Sect. viii. pp. 118, 119.

so far a necessity in consciousness, and to this extent we really see the principle of this idealism in it; but in the second place this necessity is represented as something quite devoid of thought or Notion.

This custom obtains both in our perception which relates to sensuous nature, and in relation to law and morality. The ideas of justice and morality rest upon an instinct, on a subjective, but very often deceptive moral feeling.[1] From a sceptical point of view the opposite may likewise be demonstrated. From this side Hume considers justice, morality, religious determinations, and disputes their absolute validity. That is to say when it is assumed that our knowledge arises from experience, and that we must consider only what we obtain thereby to be the truth, we find indeed in our feeling, the sentiment *e.g.* that the murderer, the thief, &c., must be punished; and because this is likewise felt by others it is universally allowed. But Hume, like the sceptics of former days, appeals to the various opinions of various nations: amongst different nations and in different times various standards of right have been held.[2] There are those who in this case do not have the feeling of wrong-doing in respect of stealing, *e.g.* the Lacedæmonians or the so-called innocent inhabitants of the South Sea Islands. What is by one nation called immoral, shameful and irreligious, is by another not considered so at all. Thus because such matters rest upon experience, one subject has such and such an experience, finds, for instance, in his religious feelings this determination which inclines him to God, while another subject has different experiences altogether. We are in the

---

[1] Hume: Essays and Treatises on several subjects, Vol. IV. containing an Inquiry concerning the principles of morals, Sect. 1, p. 4; Appendix I. p. 170.

[2] Buhle: Geschichte der neuern Philosophie, Vol. V. Sect. 1, pp. 230, 231; cf. Hume, ibidem, Vol. III. Sect. 12, P. II. p. 221; Vol. IV.; An Inquiry, &c., Sect. 4, pp. 62-65; A dialogue, pp. 235, 236, &c., &c.

habit of allowing one thing to be just and moral, others have another mode of regarding it. Hence if the truth depends upon experience, the element of universality, of objectivity, &c., comes from elsewhere, or is not justified by experience. Hume thus declared this sort of universality, as he declared necessity, to be rather subjectively than objectively existent ; for custom is just a subjective universality of this kind. This is an important and acute observation in relation to experience looked at as the source of knowledge ; and it is from this point that the Kantian reflection now begins.

Hume (Essays and Treatises on several subjects, Vol. III. Sect. 8, 11) then extended his scepticism to the conceptions and doctrines of freedom and necessity, and to the proofs of the existence of God ; and in fact scepticism here possesses a wide field. To such a system of reasoning from thoughts and possibilities another method of reasoning may again be opposed, and this reasoning is no better than the other. What is said to be metaphysically established regarding immortality, God, nature, &c., lacks a real ground for resting upon, such as is professed to be given ; for the inferences on which men ground their proofs are subjectively formed conceptions. But where a universality is found, it does not rest in the matter in itself, but is simply a subjective necessity which is really mere custom. Hence the result which Hume arrives at is necessarily astonishment regarding the condition of human knowledge, a general state of mistrust, and a sceptical indecision—which indeed does not amount to much. The condition of human knowledge regarding which Hume so much wonders, he further describes as containing an antagonism between reason and instinct; this instinct, it is said, which embraces many sorts of powers, inclinations, &c., deceives us in many different ways, and reason demonstrates this. But on the other side it is empty, without content or principles of its own ;

and if a content is in question at all, it must keep to those
inclinations.   In itself reason thus has no criterion whereby
the antagonism between individual desires, and between
itself and the desires, may be settled.[1]   Thus everything
appears in the form of an irrational existence devoid of
thought · the implicitly true and right is not in thought,
but in the form of an instinct, a desire.

SECTION THREE

Recent German Philosophy

In the philosophy of Kant, Fichte, and Schelling, the revolution to which in Germany mind has in these latter days advanced, was formally thought out and expressed; the sequence of these philosophies shows the course which thought has taken. In this great epoch of the world's history, whose inmost essence is laid hold of in the philosophy of history, two nations only have played a part, the German and the French, and this in spite of their absolute opposition, or rather because they are so opposite. The other nations have taken no real inward part in the same, although politically they have indeed so done, both through their governments and their people. In Germany this principle has burst forth as thought, spirit, Notion; in France, in the form of actuality. In Germany, what there is of actuality comes to us as a force of external circumstances, and as a reaction against the same. The task of modern German philosophy is, however, summed up in taking as its object the unity of thought and Being, which is the fundamental idea of philosophy generally, and comprehending it, that is, in laying hold of the inmost significance of necessity, the Notion (*supra*, p. 360). The philosophy of Kant sets forth, in the first place, the formal aspect of the task, but it has the abstract absoluteness of reason in self-consciousness as its sole result, and, in one

o

respect, it carried with it a certain character of shallowness
and want of vigour, in which an attitude of criticism and
negativity is retained, and which, as far as any positive
element is concerned, adheres to the facts of consciousness
and to mere conjecture, while it renounces thought and
returns to feeling.   On the other hand, however, there
sprang from this the philosophy of Fichte, which speculatively grasps the essence of self-consciousness as concrete
egoism, but which does not reach beyond this subjective
form pertaining to the absolute.   From it again comes the
philosophy of Schelling, which subsequently rejects Fichte's
teaching and sets forth the Idea of the Absolute, the truth
in and for itself.

B. Kant.

The philosophy of Kant, which we have now more par-
cularly to consider, made its appearance at the same time
as the above.   While Descartes asserted certainty to be the
unity of thought and Being, we now have the consciousness of thought in its subjectivity, *i.e.* in the first place,

as determinateness in contrast with objectivity, and then as finitude and progression in finite determinations. Abstract thought as personal conviction is that which is maintained as certain; its contents are experience, but the methods adopted by experience are once more formal thought and argument. Kant turns back to the standpoint of Socrates; we see in him the freedom of the subject as we saw it with the Stoics, but the task in respect of content is now placed on a higher level. An endless aiming at the concrete is required for thought, a filling up in accordance with the rule which completion prescribes, which signifies that the content is itself the Idea as the unity of the Notion and reality. With Jacobi thought, demonstration, does not in the first place reach beyond the finite and conditioned, and in the second place, even when God is likewise the metaphysical object, the demonstration is really the making Him conditioned and finite; in the third place the unconditioned, what is then immediately certain, only exists in faith, a subjectively fixed point of view but an unknowable one, that is to say an undetermined, indeterminable, and consequently an unfruitful one. The standpoint of the philosophy of Kant, on the contrary, is in the first place to be found in the fact that thought, has through its reasoning got so far as to grasp itself not as contingent but rather as in itself the absolute ultimate. In the finite, in connection with the finite, an absolute standpoint is raised which acts as a connecting bond; it binds together the finite and leads up to the infinite. Thought grasped itself as all in all, as absolute in judgment; for it nothing external is authoritative, since all authority can receive validity only through thought. This thought, determining itself within itself and concrete, is, however, in the second place, grasped as subjective, and this aspect of subjectivity is the form which from Jacobi's point of view is predominant; the fact that thought is concrete Jacobi has on the other hand for the most part set aside. Both standpoints remain philosophies of subjectivity; since thought is subjective, the capacity of knowing the absolute is denied to it. To Kant God cannot on the one hand be found in experience; He can neither be found in outward experience—as Lalande discovered when he swept the whole heavens and found no God—nor can He be discovered within; though no doubt mystics and enthusiasts can experience many things in themselves, and amongst these God, *i.e.* the Infinite. On the other hand Kant argues to prove the existence of God, who is to him an hypothesis necessary for the explanation of things, a postulate of practical reason. But in this connection another French astronomer made the following reply to the Emperor Napoleon: "*Je n'ai pas eu besoin de cette hypothèse.*" According to this the truth underlying the Kantian philosophy is the recognition of freedom. Even Rousseau represented the absolute to be found in freedom; Kant has the same principle, but taken rather from the theoretic side. The French regard it from the side of will, which is represented in their proverb: '*Il a la tête près du bonnet.*" France possesses the sense of actuality, of promptitude; because in that country conception passes more immediately into action, men have there applied themselves more practically to the affairs of actuality. But however much freedom may be in itself concrete, it was as undeveloped and in its abstraction that it was there applied to actuality; and to make abstractions hold good in actuality means to destroy actuality. The fanaticism which characterized the freedom which was put into the hands of the people was frightful. In Germany the same principle asserted the rights of consciousness on its own account, but it has been worked out in a merely theoretic way. We have commotions of every kind within us and around us, but through them all the German head quietly keeps its nightcap on and silently carries on its operations beneath it.

Immanuel Kant was born at Königsberg in 1724, and there studied theology to begin with; in the year 1755 he entered upon his work as an academic teacher; in 1770 he became professor of logic, and in 1804 he died at Königberg on the 12th of February, having almost attained his eightieth year (Tennemann's Grundriss der Geschichte der Philosophie by Wendt, § 380, pp. 465, 466), without ever having left his native town.

While to Wolff thought as thought was merely positive self-identity and grasped itself as such, we saw the negative self-moving thought, the absolute Notion, appear in all its power in France; and in the *Aufklärung* it likewise made its way to Germany in such a manner that all existence, all action, was called upon to serve a useful purpose, *i.e.* the implicit was done away with and everything had to be for another; and that for which everything had to be is man, self-consciousness, taken, however, as signifying all men generally. The consciousness of this action in abstract form is the Kantian philosophy. It is thus the self-thinking absolute Notion that passes into itself which we see making its appearance in Germany through this philosophy, in such a way that all reality falls within self-consciousness; it is the idealism which vindicates all moments of the implicit to self-consciousness, but which at first itself remains subject to a contradiction, inasmuch as it still separates this implicit from itself. In other words the Kantian philosophy no doubt leads reality back to self-consciousness, but it can supply no reality to this essence of self-consciousness, or to this pure self-consciousness, nor can it demonstrate Being in the same. It apprehends simple thought as having difference in itself, but does not yet apprehend that all reality rests on this difference; it does not know how to obtain mastery over the individuality of self-consciousness, and although it describes reason very well, it does this in an unthinking empiric way which again robs it of the truth it has. Theoretically the Kantian philosophy is the "Illumination" or *Aufklärung* reduced to method; it states that nothing true can be known, but only the phenomenal; it leads knowledge into consciousness and self-consciousness, but from this standpoint maintains it to be a subjective and finite knowledge. Thus although it deals with the infinite Idea, expressing its formal categories and arriving at its concrete claims, it yet again denies this to be the truth, making it a simple subjective, because it has once for all accepted finite knowledge as the fixed and ultimate standpoint. This philosophy made an end of the metaphysic of the understanding as an objective dogmatism, but in fact it merely transformed it into a subjective dogmatism, *i.e.* into a consciousness in which these same finite determinations of the understanding persist, and the question of what is true in and for itself has been abandoned. Its study is made difficult by its diffuseness and prolixity, and by the peculiar terminology found in it. Nevertheless this diffuseness has one advantage, that inasmuch as the same thing is often repeated, the main points are kept before us, and these cannot easily be lost from view.

We shall endeavour to trace the lines which Kant pursued. The philosophy of Kant has in the first place a direct relation to that of Hume as stated above (p. 370). That is to say, the significance of the Kantian philosophy, generally expressed, is from the very beginning to allow that determinations such as those of universality and necessity are not to be met with in perception, and this Hume has already shown in relation to Locke. But while Hume attacks the universality and necessity of the categories generally, and Jacobi their finitude, Kant merely argues against their objectivity in so far as they are present in external things themselves, while maintaining them to be objective in the sense of holding good as universal and necessary, as they do, for instance, in mathematics and natural science.[1] The fact that we crave for universality

---

[1] Kant : Kritik der reinen Vernunft (sixth edition, Leipzig, 1818), pp. 4, 11, 13, 93.

and necessity as that which first constitutes the objective, Kant thus undoubtedly allows. But if universality and necessity do not exist in external things, the question arises " Where are they to be found ? " To this Kant, as against Hume, maintains that they must be *a priori, i.e.* that they must rest on reason itself, and on thought as self-conscious reason; their source is the subject, " I " in my self-consciousness.[1] This, simply expressed, is the main point in the Kantian philosophy.

In the second place the philosophy of Kant is likewise called a critical philosophy because its aim, says Kant, is first of all to supply a criticism of our faculties of knowledge; for before obtaining knowledge we must inquire into the faculties of knowledge. To the healthy human understanding that is plausible, and to it this has been a great discovery. Knowledge is thereby represented as an instrument, as a method and means whereby we endeavour to possess ourselves of the truth. Thus before men can make their way to the truth itself they must know the nature and function of their instrument. They must see whether it is capable of supplying what is demanded of it—of seizing upon the object; they must know what the alterations it makes in the object are, in order that these alterations may not be mixed up with the determinations of the object itself.[2] This would appear as though men could set forth upon the search for truth with spears and staves. And a further claim is made when it is said that we must know the faculty of knowledge before we can know. For to investigate the faculties of knowledge means to know them ; but how we are to know without knowing, how we are to apprehend the truth before the truth, it is impossible to say. It is the old story of the σχολαστικός who would not go into the water till he could swim. Thus

---

[1] Kant : Kritik der reinen Vernunft, pp. 3-5.
[2] Ibidem, Preface, pp. xviii., xix.

since the investigation of the faculties of knowledge is
itself knowing, it cannot in Kant attain to what it aims at
because it is that already—it cannot come to itself because
it is already with itself; the same thing happens as
happened with the Jews, the Spirit passes through the
midst of them and they know it not. At the same time
the step taken by Kant is a great and important one—
that is, the fact that he has made knowledge the subject of
his consideration.

On the one hand this critique of knowledge applies to
the empirical knowledge of Locke, which asserts itself to
be grounded on experience, and, on the other hand, it also
deals with what claims to be on the whole a more metaphysical kind of philosophy—the Wolffian and German—
which had also taken up the line of proceeding on the more
empiric method which has been depicted.   But this last
has at the same time kept itself separate from the merely
empiric method, inasmuch as its main efforts have been
directed towards making such categories of thought as
those of potentiality, actuality, God, &c., have as their
foundation categories of the understanding, and then
reasoning from them.   The Kantian philosophy is in the
first instance directed against both.   Kant takes away the
objective significance of the determinations of the Wolffian
metaphysics, and shows how they must be ascribed to
subjective thought alone.   At the same time Jacobi likewise declared himself against this metaphysic, but since
he started more especially from the standpoint of the
French and Germans, his point of view was different:
he asserts that our finite thought can set forth finite
determinations alone, and thus can only consider God and
Spirit in accordance with finite relationships.   On the practical side there reigned at that time the so-called happiness
theory, since man's inherent Notion and the way to realize
this Notion was apprehended in morality as a satisfaction
of his desires.   As against this Kant has very rightly

shown that it involves a heteronomy and not an autonomy of reason—a determination through nature and consequently an absence of freedom. But because the rational principle of Kant was formal, and his successors could not make any further progress with reason, and yet morality had to receive a content, Fries and others must still be called Hedonists though they avoid giving themselves the name.

In the third place, as regards the relation of the categories to the material which is given through experience, there is according to Kant already inherent in the subjective determinations of thought, *e.g.* in those of cause and effect, the capacity of themselves to bind together the differences which are present in that material. Kant considers thought as in great measure a synthetic activity, and hence he represents the main question of Philosophy to be this, "How are synthetic judgments *a priori* possible?"[1] Judgment signifies the combination of thought-determinations as subject and predicate. Synthetic judgments *a priori* are nothing else than a connection of opposites through themselves, or the absolute Notion, *i.e.* the relations of different determinations such as those of cause and effect, given not through experience but through thought. Space and time likewise form the connecting element; they are thus *a priori, i.e.* in self-consciousness. Since Kant shows that thought has synthetic judgments *a priori* which are not derived from perception, he shows that thought is so to speak concrete in itself. The idea which is present here is a great one, but, on the other hand, quite an ordinary signification is given it, for it is worked out from points of view which are inherently rude and empirical, and a scientific form is the last thing that can be claimed for it. In the presentation of it there is a lack of philosophical abstraction, and it is expressed in the most commonplace way; to say nothing more of the

---

[1] Kant : Kritik der reinen Vernunft, pp. 8, 9, 75, 77, 15.

barbarous terminology, Kant remains restricted and confined by his psychological point of view and empirical methods.

To mention one example only of his barbarous expressions, Kant calls his philosophy (Kritik der reinen Vernunft, p. 19) a Transcendental philosophy, *i.e.* a system of principles of pure reason which demonstrate the universal and necessary elements in the self-conscious understanding, without occupying themselves with objects or inquiring what universality and necessity are; this last would be transcendent. Transcendent and transcendental have accordingly to be clearly distinguished. Transcendent mathematics signifies the mathematics in which the determination of infinitude is made use of in a preeminent degree : in this sphere of mathematics we say, for instance, that the circle consists of an infinitude of straight lines ; the periphery is represented as straight, and since the curve is represented as straight this passes beyond the geometric category and is consequently transcendent. Kant, on the contrary, defines the transcendental philosophy as not a philosophy which by means of categories passes beyond its own sphere, but one which points out in subjective thought, in consciousness, the sources of what may become transcendent. Thought would thus be transcendent if the categories of universality, of cause and effect, were predicated of the object, for in this way men would from the subjective element ' transcend ' into another sphere. We are not justified in so doing as regards the result nor even to begin with, since we merely contemplate thought within thought itself. Thus we do not desire to consider the categories in their objective sense, but in so far as thought is the source of such synthetic relationships ; the necessary and universal thus here receive the significance of resting in our faculties of knowledge. But from this faculty of knowledge Kant still separates the implicit, the thing-in-itself, so that the universality and necessity are all the time a subjective conditionment of knowledge merely, and reason with its universality and necessity does not attain to a knowledge of the truth.[1] For it requires perception and experience, a material empirically given in order, as subjectivity, to attain to knowledge. As Kant says, these form its "constituent parts"; one part it has in itself, but the other is empirically given.[2] When reason desires to be independent, to exist in itself and to derive truth from itself, it becomes transcendent; it transcends experience because it lacks the other constituent, and then creates mere hallucinations of the brain. It is hence not constitutive in knowledge but only regulative; it is the unity and rule for the sensuous manifold. But this unity on its own account is the unconditioned, which, transcending experience, merely arrives at contradictions. In the practical sphere alone is reason constitutive. The critique of reason is consequently not the knowing of objects, but of knowledge and its principles, its range and limitations, so that it does not become transcendent.[3] This is an extremely general account of what we shall now consider in its separate details.

In dealing with this matter Kant adopts the plan of first considering theoretic reason, the knowledge which relates to outward objects. In the second place he investigates the will as self-actualization; and, in the third place, the faculty of judgment, the special consideration of the unity of the universal and individual; how far he gets in this matter we shall likewise see. But the critique of the faculty of knowledge is the matter of main importance.

1. In the first place, as to the theoretic philosophy, Kant in the Critique of Pure Reason sets to work in a psychological manner, *i.e.* historically, inasmuch as he describes

---

[1] Kant: Kritik der reinen Vernunft, pp. 255, 256.

[2] Ibidem, p. 107.

[3] Ibidem, pp. 497, 498; Kritik der prakt. Vernunft (fourth edition, Riga, 1797), p. 254; Kritik der Urtheilskraft (third edition, Berlin, 1799), Preface, p. v.

the main stages in theoretic consciousness. The first faculty is sensuousness generally, the second understanding, the third reason. All this he simply narrates ; he accepts it quite empirically, without developing it from the Notion or proceeding by necessity.

a. The *a priori* fact of sensuous existence, the forms of sensuous existence, constitute the beginning of this transcendentalism. Kant calls the judgment of the same the transcendental æsthetic. Nowadays æsthetic signifies the knowledge of the beautiful. But here the doctrine of intuition or perception is taken from the point of view of its universality, *i.e.* from what in it pertains to the subject as such. Perception, says Kant, is the knowledge of an object given to us through the senses ; sensuousness, however, is the capacity of being affected by conceptions as external. Now, according to Kant, in perception there are to be found all manner of contents, and in dealing with this he first of all distinguishes feeling as external, such as redness, colour, hardness, &c., and then as internal, such as justice, wrath, love, fear, pleasurable and religious feelings, &c. He says content such as this forms the one constituent and pertains to feeling ; all this is subjective and merely subjective. In this sensuous element there is, however, a universal sensuous element likewise contained, which as such does not belong to feeling in so far as it is immediately determined ; in such a content this 'other' consists in the categories of space and time, which of themselves are void and empty. The filling in is performed by the content, by colour, softness, hardness, &c., as regards space ; while as regards time, the same content, so soon as it is something transient, or again some other content, and in particular inward feelings are what causes the determination. Space and time are consequently pure, *i.e.* abstract perceptions in which we place outside of us the content of individual sensations, either in time as succeeding one another, or in space as separate from one another. Here we thus meet with the division between subjectivity and objectivity, for if we isolate the 'alongside of' and 'after' we have space and time. It is the act of *a priori* sensuousness to project the content; the forms of intuition or perception constitute this pure perception.[1] Now everything indeed is termed perception, even thought and consciousness; God, who certainly pertains to thought alone, is said to be comprehended by perception or intuition, the so-called immediate consciousness.

Kant further remarks in this regard, (1) "Space is no empirical Notion which has been derived from outward experiences." But the Notion is never really anything empiric : it is in barbarous forms like this that Kant, however, always expresses himself: "For in order that I may relate my sensations to something outside of me, I must presuppose space." Of time Kant speaks in similar terms : "In order that something outside of me may be represented in separate space or time, the conception of space and time must come first, or it cannot be derived from experience, for experience first becomes possible through this antecedent conception." That is to say, time and space which may appear as objective, since their particular filling in certainly belongs to subjective feeling, are not empirical; for consciousness has time and space first of all in itself." (2) "Space is a necessary conception which lies at the basis of all external perceptions. Space and time are conceptions *a priori*, because we cannot represent things without space and time. Time is a necessary basis for all phenomena." As *a priori*, space and time are universal and necessary, that is to say we find this to be the case; but it does not follow that they must be previously present as conceptions. They are fundamental indeed, but they are likewise an external universal. Kant however places the matter somewhat in this fashion : there

[1] Kant: Kritik der reinen Vernunft, pp. 25-27.

are things-in-themselves outside, but devoid of time and space; consciousness now comes, and it has time and space beforehand present in it as the possibility of experience, just as in order to eat it has mouth and teeth, &c, as conditions necessary for eating. The things which are eaten have not the mouth and teeth, and as eating is brought to bear on things, so space and time are also brought to bear on them; just as things are placed in the mouth and between the teeth, so is it with space and time. (3) " Space and time are not general Notions of the relations of things, but pure intuitive perceptions. For we can only represent to ourselves one space; there are not different component parts of space." The same is the case with time. The abstract conception tree, for example, is in its actuality a number of individual and separate trees, but spaces are not such particulars, nor are they parts; for one immediate continuity remains, and hence a simple unity. Ordinary perception has always something individual before it; space or time are always however one only, and therefore *a priori*. It might however be replied to Kant: The nature of space and time undoubtedly involves their being an abstract universal; but there is in like manner only one blue. (4) " Each Notion or conception certainly comprises an infinite number of conceptions under itself, but not within itself; nevertheless this last is the case in space and time, and they are therefore intuitive perceptions and not Notions or conceptions." [1] Space and time, then, are certainly not thought-determinations, if no thoughts are there present, but a Notion, so soon as we have a Notion of them.

From the transcendental point of view it is likewise maintained that this conception of space and time contains synthetic propositions *a priori*, connected with the consciousness of its necessity. Examples of these synthetic propositions are sought in statements such as that of space

[1] Kant: Kritik der reinen Vernunft, pp. 29, 30; 34-36.

having three dimensions, or in the definition of a straight line, that it is the shortest distance between two points, and likewise in the statement that $5 + 7 = 12$.[1] All these propositions are however very analytic. Kant nevertheless in the first place holds that such propositions do not take their rise from experience, or, as we might better express it, are not an individual contingent perception; this is very true, the perception is universal and necessary. In the second place he states that we acquire them from pure sensuous perception, and not through the understanding or Notion. But Kant does not grasp the two together, and yet this comprehension of them is involved in such propositions being immediately certain even in ordinary perception. When Kant then expresses himself (Kritik der reinen Vernunft, p. 49) to the effect that we have many sensations which constitute "the real matter," with which we externally and inwardly "occupy our minds," and that the mind has in itself in space and time "formal conditions of the mode in which we place them" (those manifold feelings) "in our mind," the question of how mind arrives at having just these special forms now forces itself upon us. But what the nature of time and space is, it does not occur to the Kantian philosophy to inquire. To it what space and time are in themselves does not signify 'What is their Notion,' but 'Are they external things or something in the mind?'

b. The second faculty, the understanding, is something very different from sensuousness; the latter is Receptivity, while Kant calls thought in general Spontaneity —an expression which belongs to the philosophy of Leibnitz. The understanding is active thought, I myself; it "is the faculty of thinking the object of sensuous perception." Yet it has thoughts merely without real content: "Thoughts without content are void and empty,

---

[1] Kant: Kritik der reinen Vernunft, pp. 30, 31, 41; 12, 13, 150.

sensuous perceptions without Notions are blind." The
understanding thus obtains from the sensuous its matter,
both empirical and *a priori*, time and space; and it thinks
this matter, but its thoughts are very different from this
matter. Or it is a faculty of a particular kind, and it is
only when both occur, when the sensuous faculty has
supplied material and the understanding has united to this
its thoughts, that knowledge results.[1] The thoughts of the
understanding as such are thus limited thoughts, thoughts
of the finite only.

Now logic, as transcendental logic, likewise sets forth
the conceptions which the understanding has *a priori* in
itself and "whereby it thinks objects completely *a priori*."
Thoughts have a form which signifies their being the
synthetic function which brings the manifold into a unity.
I am this unity, the transcendental apperception, the pure
apperception of self-consciousness. I=I; *I* must 'accompany' all our conceptions.[2] This is a barbarous exposition
of the matter. As self-consciousness I am the completely
void, general I, completely indeterminate and abstract;
apperception is determination generally, the activity
whereby I transplant an empirical content into my simple
consciousness, while perception rather signifies feeling or
conceiving. In order that a content may enter this One,
it must be infected by its simplicity; it is thus that the
content first becomes my content. The comprehending
medium is 'I'; whatever I have to do with must allow
itself to be forced into these forms of unity. This is a
great fact, an important item of knowledge; what thought
produces is unity; thus it produces itself, for it is the
One. Yet the fact that I am the one and, as thinking,
the simplifier, is not by Kant satisfactorily set forth.
The unity may likewise be called relation; for in so far as

[1] Kant: Kritik der reinen Vernunft, pp. 54, 55.
[2] Ibidem, pp. 59, 97-104.

a manifold is pre-supposed, and as this on the one side remains a manifold while on the other side it is set forth as one, so far may it be said to be related.

Now as ' I ' is the universal transcendental unity of self-consciousness which binds together the empirical matter of conception generally, there are various modes in this relationship, and here we have the transcendental nature of the categories or universal thought-determinations. But Kant (Kritik der reinen Vernunft, pp. 70, 77) approaches these modes of simplicity by accepting them as they are classified in ordinary logic. For he says that in common logic particular kinds of judgment are brought forward ; and since judgment is a special kind of relationship of the manifold, the various functions of thought which ' I ' has in it are shown therein. But the following kinds of judgment have been noticed, viz. Universal, Particular and Singular ; Affirmative, Negative, Infinite ; Categorical, Hypothetical, Disjunctive ; Assertoric, Proble-matic and Apodictic judgments. These particular modes of relationship now brought forward are the pure forms of the understanding. There are thus, according to Kant (Kritik der reinen Vernunft, pp. 75, 76, 78-82), twelve fundamental categories, which fall into four classes ; and it is noteworthy, and deserves to be recognized, that each species of judgment again constitutes a triad. (1) The first kind of categories are those of Quantity, viz. Unity, Plurality and Totality. Plurality is negation of the one, the assertion of difference ; and the third, the bringing of the other two into one, plurality circumscribed, the in-determinate plurality comprehended as one, is the Totality. (2) In the second series are the categories of Quality : Reality, Negation, Limitation. Limitation is as real or positive as negation. (3) The third series comprises the categories of relation, of connection ; and first of all, indeed, the relation of Substantiality, Substance and Acci-dent : then the relation of Causality, the relation of Cause and Effect, and finally Reciprocity. (4) The categories of Modality, of the relation of the objective to our thought, come fourth, viz. Possibility, Existence (actuality) and Necessity. Possibility should come second; in abstract thought, however, the empty conception comes first. It betrays a great instinct for the Notion when Kant says that the first category is positive, the second the negative of the first, the third the synthesis of the two. The triplicity, this ancient form of the Pythagoreans, Neo-Platonists and of the Christian religion, although it here reappears as a quite external *schema* only, conceals within itself the absolute form, the Notion. But since Kant says that a conception can determine itself in me as accidental, as cause, effect, unity, plurality, &c., we thereby have the whole of the metaphysics of the understanding. Kant does not follow up further the derivation of these categories, and he finds them imperfect, but he says that the others are derived from them. Kant thus accepts the categories in an empiric way, without thinking of developing of necessity these differences from unity. Just as little did Kant attempt to deduce time and space, for he accepted them likewise from experience—a quite unphilosophic and unjustifiable procedure.

Thinking understanding is thus indeed the source of the individual categories, but because on their own account they are void and empty, they only have significance through their union with the given, manifold material of perception, feeling, &c. Such connection of sensuous material with categories now constitutes the facts of experience, *i.e.* the matter of sensation after it is brought under the categories; and this is knowledge generally.[1] The matter of perception which pertains to the feelings or sensuous perception is not left in the determination of individuality and immediacy, but I am active in relation to it, inasmuch as I bring it into connection through the

[1] Kant: Kritik der reinen Vernunft, pp. 105-110.

categories and elevate it into universal species, natural laws, &c. The question of whether a completed sensuousness or the Notion is the higher may accordingly be easily decided. For the laws of the heavens are not immediately perceived, but merely the change in position on the part of the stars. It is only when this object of immediate perception is laid hold of and brought under universal thought-determinations that experience arises therefrom, which has a claim to validity for all time. The category which brings the unity of thought into the content of feeling is thus the objective element in experience, which receives thereby universality and necessity, while that which is perceived is rather the subjective and contingent. Our finding both these elements in experience demonstrates indeed that a correct analysis has been made. Kant (Kritik der reinen Vernunft, pp. 119, 120) however connects with this the statement that experience grasps phenomena only, and that by means of the knowledge which we obtain through experience we do not know things as they are in themselves, but only as they are in the form of laws of perception and sensuousness. For the first component part of experience, sensation, is doubtless subjective, since it is connected with our organs. The matter of perception is only what it is in my sensation. I know of this sensation only and not of the thing. But, in the second place, the objective, which ought to constitute the opposite to this subjective side, is itself subjective likewise: it does not indeed pertain to my feeling, but it remains shut up in the region of my self-consciousness; the categories are only determinations of our thinking understanding. Neither the one nor the other is consequently anything in itself, nor are both together, knowledge, anything in itself, for it only knows phenomena—a strange contradiction.

The transition of the category to the empiric is made in the following way: " Pure conceptions of the understanding are quite of a different nature from empiric, indeed from

any sensuous perceptions ; " we have thus " to show how
pure conceptions of the understanding can be applied to
phenomena." This is dealt with by the transcendental
faculty of judgment. For Kant says that in the mind, in
self-consciousness, there are pure conceptions of the understanding and pure sensuous perceptions; now it is the
schematism of the pure understanding, the transcendental
faculty of the imagination, which determines the pure
sensuous perception in conformity with the category and
thus constitutes the transition to experience.[1] The connection of these two is again one of the most attractive
sides of the Kantian philosophy, whereby pure sensuousness and pure understanding, which were formerly expressed as absolute opposites, are now united. There is
thus here present a perceptive understanding or an understanding perception; but Kant does not see this, he does not
bring these thoughts together : he does not grasp the fact
that he has here brought both sides of knowledge into one,
and has thereby expressed their implicitude. Knowledge
itself is in fact the unity and truth of both moments; but
with Kant the thinking understanding and sensuousness
are both something particular, and they are only united in
an external, superficial way, just as a piece of wood and a
leg might be bound together by a cord. Thus, for example, the conception of substance in the *schema* becomes
permanent in time,[2] *i.e.* the pure conception of the understanding, the pure category, is brought into unity with
the form of pure sensuous perception.

In as far as we have to deal with our own determinations
only and as we do not reach the implicit, the true objective,
the Kantian philosophy called itself Idealism. But in this
connection Kant (Kritik der reinen Vernunft, pp. 200, 201)
brings forward a refutation of empirical or material idealism,

---

[1] Kant: Kritik der reinen Vernunft, pp. 129-132.
[2] Ibidem, p. 134.

thus : "I am conscious of my existence as determined in time. But all time-determination presupposes something permanent in perception. This permanence cannot be " a sensuous perception "in me." For all the determining grounds of my existence which are met with in me are conceptions, and as such themselves require a constant element different from them, and in relation to which the change taking place in them—consequently " my existence in time," in which they change, " may be determined." Or I am conscious of my existence as of an empirical consciousness which is only capable of being determined in relation to something which is outside of me; *i.e.* I am conscious of something external to me. Conversely it may be said : I am conscious of external things as determined in time and as changing; these hence presuppose something constant which is not in them but outside of them. And this is ' I,' the transcendental ground of their universality and necessity, of their implicitude, the unity of self-consciousness. On another occasion Kant regards it thus (Kritik der reinen Vernunft, p. 101): These moments confuse themselves, because the constant element is itself a category. Idealism, when we regard it as signifying that nothing exists outside of my individual self-consciousness as individual, as also the refutation of this, the assertion that things exist outside of my self-consciousness as individual, are the one as bad as the other. The former is the idealism of Berkeley, in which self-consciousness as individual is alone in question, or the world of self-consciousness appears as a number of limited, sensuous, individual conceptions, which are as completely devoid of truth as though they were called things. The truth or untruth does not rest in their being things or conceptions, but in their limitation and contingency, whether as conceptions or things. The refutation of this idealism is nothing more than calling attention to the fact that this empirical consciousness does not exist in itself—just as those empiric things do not exist

in themselves.   But the knowing subject does not with
Kant really arrive at reason, for it remains still the individual self-consciousness as such, which is opposed to the
universal.   As a matter of fact there is described in what
we have seen only the empirical finite self-consciousness
which requires a material from outside, or which is limited.
We do not ask whether these facts of knowledge are in and
for themselves true or untrue;   the whole of knowledge
remains within subjectivity, and on the other side there is
the thing-in-itself as an external.   This subjectivity is however concrete in itself ;   even the determinate categories of
the thinking understanding are concrete, and much more
is experience so—the synthesis of the sensation and the
category.[1]

c. The third faculty Kant finds in reason, to which he
advances from the understanding after the same psychological method ; that is to say, he hunts through the soul's
sack to see what faculties are still to be found there ; and
thus by merest chance he lights on Reason.   It would
make no difference if there had been no Reason there, just
as with physicists it is a matter of perfect indifference
whether, for instance, there is such a thing as magnetism
or not.   "All our knowledge begins from the senses,
thence proceeds to the understanding, and finishes up with
reason ; nothing higher than this is to be found in us, for
it signifies the working up of the material of perception,
and the reducing of it to the highest unity of thought."
Reason is therefore, according to Kant, the power of
obtaining knowledge from principles, that is, the power of
knowing the particular in the universal by means of
Notions ; the understanding, on the contrary, reaches its
particular by means of perception.   But the categories are

[1] In the lectures of 1825–1826 the philosophy of Fichte on its
theoretic side is interpolated here, while its practical side is only
shortly mentioned after an account is given of the Critique of Practical
Reason.

themselves particular. The principle of reason, according
to Kant, is really the universal, inasmuch as it finds the
unconditioned involved in the conditioned knowledge of the
understanding. Understanding is hence for him thought
in finite relations; reason, on the contrary, is thought
which makes the unconditioned its object. Since Kant's
time it has become customary in the language of philosophy to distinguish understanding and reason, while
by earlier philosophers this distinction was not drawn.
The·product of reason is, according to Kant, the Idea—
a Platonic expression—and he understands by it the unconditioned, the infinite.[1] It is a great step forward to
say that reason brings forth Ideas; with Kant, however,
the Idea is merely the abstract universal, the indeterminate.

This, the unconditioned, must now be grasped as·concrete,
and therein lies the main difficulty. For to know the unconditioned means to determine it and to deduce its
determinations. Much has been written and said on the
subject of knowledge, without a definition of it ever having
been offered. But it is the business of Philosophy to see
that what is taken for granted as known is really known.
Now on this point Kant says that reason has certainly the
desire to know the infinite, but has not the power. And
the reason which Kant gives for this (Kritik der reinen
Vernunft, pp. 277, 278), is on the one hand that no psycho-
logically sensuous intuition or perception corresponds with
the infinite, that it is not given in outward or inward experience; to the Idea "no congruent or corresponding
object can be discovered in the sensuous world." It
depends, however, on how the·world is looked at; but experience and observation of the world mean nothing else
for Kant than a candlestick standing here, and a snuff-box

---

[1] Kant: Kritik der reinen Vernunft, pp. 257-259, 264, 267, 268,
273.

standing there. It is certainly correct to say that the infinite is not given in the world of sensuous perception ; and supposing that what we know is experience, a synthesis of what is thought and what is felt, the infinite can certainly not be known in the sense that we have a sensuous perception of it. But no one wishes to demand a sensuous proof in verification of the infinite ; spirit is for spirit alone. The second reason for considering that the infinite cannot be known, lies in this, that Reason has no part in it except as supplying the forms of thought which we call categories ; and these doubtless afford what Kant calls objective determinations, but in such a way that in themselves they are still only subjective. If therefore for the determination of the infinite we employ these categories which are applicable only to phenomena, we entangle ourselves in false arguments (paralogisms) and in contradictions (antinomies) ; and it is an important point in the Kantian philosophy that the infinite, so far as it is defined by means of categories, loses itself in contradictions. Although reason, says Kant, becomes transcendent by the exhibition of these contradictions, it still retains its claim to trace perception, experience, and knowledge pertaining to the understanding, back to the infinite. This union of the infinite, the unconditioned, with the finite and conditioned as existing in the knowledge given by the understanding, or even in perception, would signify that the acme of concreteness had been reached.

Of this Unconditioned there are several kinds, objects having special features of their own and proceeding from reason, transcendental Ideas; they are thus themselves particular in their nature. The manner in which Kant arrives at these Ideas is again derived from experience, from formal logic, according to which there are various forms of the syllogism. Because, says Kant, there are three forms of the syllogism, categorical, hypothetical, and disjunctive, the Unconditioned is also threefold in its nature : " Firstly, an Unconditioned of the categorical synthesis in a subject."

Synthesis is the concrete; but the expression is ambiguous, since it indicates an external association of independent elements. "In the second place, an Unconditioned of the hypothetical synthesis of the members of a series will have to be looked for; and in the third place, an Unconditioned of the disjunctive synthesis of the parts in a system." We make the first connection, expressed as object of Reason or transcendental Idea, when we conceive "the thinking subject;" the second "is the sum total of all phenomena, the world;" and the third is "the thing which contains the supreme condition of the possibility of all that can be thought, the Being of all Beings," *i.e.* God. When brought to an ultimate point, the question which meets us is whether Reason can bring these objects to reality, or whether they remain confined to subjective thought. Now, according to Kant, Reason is not capable of procuring reality for its Ideas—otherwise it would be transcendent, its limits would be overstepped; it produces only paralogisms, antinomies, and an ideal without reality.[1]

a. "A paralogism is a syllogism false in its form." Since Reason credits with reality that mode of the Unconditioned which constitutes the categorical synthesis in a subject, and therefore the thinking subject, it is termed substance. Now is the thinking ego a substance, a soul, a soul-thing? Further questions are whether it is permanent, immaterial, incorruptible, personal and immortal, and such as to have a real community with the body. The falsity of the syllogism consists in this, that the idea of the unity of the transcendental subject essential to Reason is expressed as a thing; for it is only in this way that the permanency of the same becomes substance. Otherwise I find myself permanent in my thought, of course, but only within perceiving consciousness, not outside of that. The ego is

---

[1] Kant: Kritik der reinen Vernunft, pp. 261, 262, 274, 275, 284, 288, 289.

therefore the empty, transcendental subject of our thoughts, that moreover becomes known only through its thoughts ; but of what it is in itself we cannot gather the least idea. (A horrible distinction ! For thought is nothing more or less than the " in-itself " or implicit.) We cannot assert of it any present Being, because thought is an empty form, we have a conception of what thinking Beings are through no outward experience, but only by means of self-consciousness,—*i.e.* because we cannot take the " I " in our hands, nor see it, nor smell it. We therefore know very well that the ego is a subject, but if we pass beyond self-consciousness, and say that it is substance, we go farther than we are entitled to do. I cannot therefore assign any reality to the subject.[1]

We here see Kant fall into contradiction, what with the barbarity of the conceptions which he refutes, and the barbarity of his own conceptions which remain behind when the others are refuted. In the first place, he is perfectly correct when he maintains that the ego is not a soul-thing, a dead permanency which has a sensuous present existence ; indeed, were it to be an ordinary thing, it would be necessary that it should be capable of being experienced. But, in the second place, Kant does not assert the contrary of this, namely that the ego, as this universal or as self-thinking, has in itself the true reality which he requires as an objective mode. For he does not get clear of the conception of reality in which reality consists in the possession of a sensuous present existence ; accordingly, because the ego is given in no outward experience, it is not real. For self-consciousness, the ego as such, is not, according to Kant, reality ; it is only *our* thought, or in other words he regards self consciousness as being itself simply and entirely sensuous. The form which Kant accordingly bestows on Being, thing, substance,

[1] Kant: Kritik der reinen Vernunft, pp. 289-299.

would seem to indicate that these categories of the understanding were too high for the subject, too high to be
capable of being predicated of it. But really such determinations are too poor and too mean, for what possesses
life is not a thing, nor can the soul, the spirit, the ego, be
called a thing. Being is the least or lowest quality that
one can assign to spirit, its abstract, immediate identity
with itself; Being thus no doubt pertains to spirit, but it
must be considered as a determination scarcely worth
applying to it.

β. In the second place we have the antinomy, *i.e.* the
contradiction in Reason's Idea of the Unconditioned, an
Idea applied to the world in order to represent it as a
complete summing-up of conditions. That is to say, in the
given phenomena Reason demands the absolute completeness of the conditions of their possibility, so far as these
constitute a series, so that the unconditioned is contained
in the world, *i.e.* the totality of the series. If now this
completeness is expressed as existing, an antinomy is alone
presented, and Reason is presented only as dialectic : *i.e.*
in this object there is on every side a perfect contradiction
found.[1] For phenomena are a finite content, and the world
is a conjunction of the limited ; if this content is now
thought by Reason, and therefore subsumed under the
unconditioned and the unlimited, we have two determinations, finite and infinite, which contradict each other.
Reason demands a perfectly complete synthesis, an absolute
beginning ; but in phenomena we have, on the contrary, a
succession of causes and effects, which never come to an
end. Kant here points out four contradictions (Kritik der
reinen Vernunft, p. 320), which, however, is not enough ;
for in each Notion there are antinomies, since it is not
simple but concrete, and therefore contains different
determinations, which are direct opposites.

[1] Kant : Kritik der reinen Vernunft, pp. 312–314.

aa. These antinomies in the first place involve our making the one determination, limitation, just as valid as non-limitation. "Thesis: The world has a beginning and an end in time, and it is limited in regard to space. Antithesis: It has no beginning and no end in time, and also no limits in space." The one, says Kant, can be proved just as easily as the other; and indeed he does prove each indirectly, though his are not "advocate's proofs." [1] The world, as the universe, is the whole; it is thus a universal idea, and therefore unlimited. The completion of the synthesis in progression as regards time and space is, however, a first beginning of time and space. If therefore the categories of limited and unlimited are applied to the world in order to attain to a knowledge of it, we fall into contradictions, because the categories are not applicable to things-in-themselves.

ββ. The second antinomy is that atoms, from which substance is composed, must necessarily be admitted to exist, therefore simplicity can be proved; but just as easy is it to prove incompleteness, the endless process of division. The thesis is accordingly stated thus: "Every compound substance consists of simple parts," and the antithesis is as follows: "There exists nothing simple." [2] The one is here the limit, a material self-existence, the point which is likewise the enclosing surface; the other is divisibility *ad infinitum.*

γγ. The third antinomy is the opposition between freedom and necessity. The first is the self-determining, the point of view pertaining to infinity: causality according to the laws of freedom is the only causality. The other is: Determinism alone is to be found: everything is determined by means of an external ground or reason. [3]

---

[1] Kant: Kritik der reinen Vernunft, pp. 317, 318, 328, 329, 332.
[2] Ibidem, pp. 318, 336, 337.   [3] Ibidem, pp. 319, 346, 347.

δδ. The fourth antinomy rests on what follows: On the one hand totality completes itself in freedom as a first beginning of action, or in an absolutely necessary Being, as the cause of the world, so that the process is interrupted: but there is opposed to that freedom the necessity of a process according to conditions of causes and effects, and to the necessity of a Being is opposed the consideration that everything is contingent. The absolute necessity of the conditioned world is therefore on the one hand maintained thus: "To the world belongs an absolutely necessary Being." The opposite to this is, "There exists no absolutely necessary Being, either as part of the world or outside of the world." [1]

One of these opposites is just as necessary as the other, and it is superfluous to carry this further here. The necessity of these contradictions is the interesting fact which Kant (Kritik der reinen Vernunft, p. 324) has brought to consciousness; in ordinary metaphysics, however, it is imagined that one of these contradictions must hold good, and the other be disproved. The most important point involved in this assertion of Kant's is, however, unintentional on his part. For he indeed solves these antinomies (Kritik der reinen Vernunft, pp. 385, 386), but only in the particular sense of transcendental idealism, which does not doubt or deny the existence of external things (*supra*, p. 442), but "allows that things are perceived in space and time" (which is the case, whether it allows it or not): for transcendental idealism, however, "space and time in themselves are not things at all," and therefore "do not exist apart from our mind;" *i.e.* all these determinations of a beginning in time, and so on, do not really belong to things, to the implicitude of the phenomenal world, which has independent existence outside of our subjective thought. If such determinations

[1] Kant: Kritik der reinen Vernunft, pp. 319, 354, 355.

belonged to the world, to God, to free agents, there would be an objective contradiction; but this contradiction is not found as absolute, it pertains only to us. Or, in other words, this transcendental idealism lets the contradiction remain, only it is not Being in itself that is thus contradictory, for the contradiction has its source in our thought alone. Thus the same antinomy remains in our mind; and as it was formerly God who had to take upon Himself all contradictions, so now it is self-consciousness. But the Kantian philosophy does not go on to grapple with the fact that it is not things that are contradictory, but self-consciousness itself. Experience teaches that the ego does not melt away by reason of these contradictions, but continues to exist; we need not therefore trouble ourselves about its contradictions, for it can bear them. Nevertheless Kant shows here too much tenderness for things : it would be a pity, he thinks, if they contradicted themselves. But that mind, which is far higher, should be a contradiction—that is not a pity at all. The contradiction is therefore by no means solved by Kant; and since mind takes it upon itself, and contradiction is self-destructive, mind is in itself all derangement and disorder. The true solution would be found in the statement that the categories have no truth in themselves, and the Unconditioned of Reason just as little, but that it lies in the unity of both as concrete, and in that alone.

γ. Kant now goes on to the Idea of God; this third idea is the Being of Beings, which the other ideas presupposed. Kant says (Kritik der reinen Vernunft, pp. 441–452), that according to the definition of Wolff, God is the most real of all Beings; the object then comes to be to prove that God is not only Thought, but that He is, that He has reality, Being. This Kant calls the Ideal of Reason, to distinguish it from the Idea, which is only the sum of all possibility. The Ideal is thus the Idea as existent; just as in art we give the name of ideal to the Idea realized in a sensuous manner. Here Kant takes into consideration the proof of the existence of God, as he asks whether reality can be assigned to this Ideal.

The ontological proof proceeds from the absolute Notion, in order from it to argue up to Being. With Anselm, Descartes, and Spinoza the transition to Being is thus made; and all of them assume in so doing the unity of Being and thought. But Kant says (Kritik der reinen Vernunft, pp. 458–466): To this Ideal of Reason just as little reality can be assigned: there is no transition from the Notion to Being. "Being is not a real predicate," like any other, "a Notion of something which might be added to the Notion of a thing. A hundred real dollars do not contain in the very least more than a hundred possible dollars," they are the same content, *i.e.* the same Notion; they are also a hundred exactly. The one is the Notion, or rather the conception, the other is the object; Being is no new determination of the Notion, otherwise my Notion of a hundred real dollars would contain something different from a hundred real dollars. But "the object, as real, is not contained in my Notion alone; or to my Notion the real hundred dollars are synthetically added." Being cannot therefore be derived from the Notion, because it is not contained therein, but must be added to it. "We must go out of the Notion in order to arrive at existence. With regard to objects of pure thought, there are no means of coming to know of their existence, because it had to be known *a priori;* but our consciousness of all existence belongs entirely to experience." That is to say, Kant does not attain to the comprehension of that very synthesis of Notion and Being, or in other words, he does not comprehend existence, *i.e.* he does not attain to the establishment of it as Notion; existence remains for him something absolutely different from a Notion. The content is no doubt the same for him in what exists and in the Notion: but since Being

is not involved in the Notion, the attempt to derive the one
from the other is unavailing.

Of course the determination of Being is not found as
positive and ready-made in the Notion; the Notion is
something different from reality and objectivity. If we
therefore abide by the Notion, we abide by Being as something different from the Notion, and adhere to the separation of the two; we then have conception, and not Being
at all. That a hundred possible dollars are something
different from a hundred actual ones is a reflection of a
very popular nature, so much so that no proposition has
been so well received as the assertion that no transition can
be made from the Notion to Being; for though I imagine to
myself a hundred dollars, I do not possess them for all that.
But in a like popular fashion it might be said that one must
leave off imagining, for that is mere conception : *i.e.* what
is merely imaginary is untrue, the hundred imaginary dollars
are and remain imaginary. Therefore to believe in them is
a proof of an unsound understanding, and is of no manner
of use; and he is a foolish fellow who indulges in such
fancies and wishes. One possesses a hundred dollars, when
they are real only; if a man has therefore so great a desire
to possess a hundred dollars, he must put his hand to work
in order to obtain them : *i.e.* he must not come to a standstill at the imagination of them, but pass out beyond it.
This subjective side is not the ultimate or the absolute; the
true is that which is not merely subjective. If I possess
a hundred dollars, I have them actually, and at the same
time I form a conception of them to myself. But according to Kant's representation we come to a deadlock at the
difference; dualism is ultimate, and each side has independent validity as an absolute. Against this false idea of
what is to be absolute and ultimate, the healthy human understanding is directed; every ordinary consciousness rises
above it, every action aims at setting aside a subjective
conception and making it into something objective. There

is no man so foolish as that philosophy; when a man feels hungry, he does not call up the imagination of food, but sets about satisfying his hunger. All activity is a conception which does not yet exist, but whose subjectivity is abrogated. Moreover the imaginary hundred dollars become real, and the real ones imaginary : this is a frequent experience, this is their fate; it depends on circumstances entirely outward whether a hundred dollars become my property or not. Of course the mere conception is of no good, if I obstinately hold by it : for I can imagine what I will, but that does not make it exist. The only important point is what I conceive to myself, and then whether I think or comprehend the subjective and Being; by means of this each passes into the other. Thought, the Notion, of necessity implies that the Notion does not remain subjective; this subjective is on the contrary abrogated and reveals itself as objective. Now that unity is expressly affirmed by Descartes solely in reference to the Notion of God, for it is just that which is God; he speaks of no hundred dollars, as these are not an existence which has a Notion in itself. That opposition does away with itself absolutely and entirely, *i.e.* the finite passes away; it holds good only in the philosophy of finitude. If, therefore, there is not a Notion of existence formed, we have in it a notionless, sensuous object of perception; and what is notionless is certainly not a Notion,—therefore sensation, handling, are not Notions. Such existence has of course no Absolute, no real essence : or such existence has no truth, it is only a vanishing moment. This useless thrashing of the empty grainless straw of the common logic is termed philosophizing : it is like Issachar the strong ass, which could not be made to move from the spot where it was (Gen. xlix. 14). People of this kind ·say: We are good for nothing, and because we are good for nothing, we are good for nothing, and wish to be good for nothing. But it is a very false idea of Christian humility and modesty to desire through one's abjectness to attain to excellence; this confession of one's own nothingness is really inward pride and great self-conceit. But for the honour of true humility we must not remain in our misery, but raise ourselves above it by laying hold of the Divine.

The fact to which Kant clings most strongly (Kritik der reinen Vernunft, p. 467) is this, that Being cannot be extracted from the Notion. The result of this is the proposition that to have the thought of the Infinite is certainly Reason; but that from the Idea of Reason is separated determination in general, and especially the determination which is known as Being. The Ideas of Reason cannot be proved from experience, or obtain from it their verification : if they are defined by means of categories, contradictions arise. If the Idea in general is to be defined as existent only, it is nothing more or less than the Notion; and the Being of the existent is still distinguished from it. This result, however, so highly important with reference to knowledge of the understanding, Kant does not, with reference to Reason, carry further than to say that Reason has on its own account nothing but formal unity for the methodical systematization of the knowledge of the understanding. Abstract thinking is adhered to; it is said that the understanding can only bring about order in things; but order is nothing in and for itself, it is only subjective. There therefore remains nothing for Reason except the form of its pure identity with itself, and this extends no further than to the arranging of the manifold laws and relations of the understanding, the classes, kinds and species which the understanding discovers.[1] I, as Reason or conception, and the things external to me, are both absolutely different from one another; and that, according to Kant, is the ultimate standpoint. The animal does not stop at this standpoint, but practically brings about unity. This is the

---

[1] Kritik der reinen Vernunft, pp. 497, 498.

critique of theoretical Reason which Kant gives, and in which he states the *a priori* and determinate character of Reason in itself, without bringing it to the determinateness of individuality.[1]

Mention should still be made of the positive philosophy or metaphysics, which Kant sets *a priori* above objective existence, the content of the object of experience, nature; we have here his natural philosophy, which is a demonstration of the universal conceptions of Nature. But this is on the one-hand very scanty and restricted in content, containing as it does sundry general qualities and conceptions of matter and motion, and with regard to the scientific side or the *a priori,* as Kant calls it, it is likewise altogether unsatisfactory. For Kant assumes all such conceptions as that matter has motion and also a power of attraction and repulsion,[2] instead of demonstrating their necessity. The "Principles of Natural Philosophy" have nevertheless been of great service, inasmuch as at the commencement of a philosophy of nature, attention was called to the fact that physical science employs thought-determinations without further investigation; and these determinations constitute the real foundations of its objects. Density, for instance, is looked on by physical science as a variable quantity, as a mere *quantum* in space : instead of this Kant asserted it to be a certain degree of occupation of space, *i.e.* energy, intensity of action. He demands accordingly (Metaphysische Anfangsgründe der Naturwissenschaft, pp. 65-68) a construction of matter from powers and activities, not from atoms ; and Schelling still holds to this without getting further. Kant's work is an attempt to think, *i.e.* to demonstrate the determinations of thought, whose product consists of such conceptions as matter ; he has

---

[1] Here there is inserted in the lectures of 1825-1826 an examination of what the philosophy of Jacobi has to say on this point.

[2] Kant: Metaphysische Anfangsgründe der Naturwissenschaft (third edition, Leipzig, 1800), pp. 1, 27.

attempted to determine the fundamental Notions and principles of this science, and has given the first impulse to a so-called dynamic theory of Nature.

" Religion within pure Reason " is also a demonstration of dogmas as aspects of Reason, just as in Nature. Thus in the positive dogmas of religion, which the Aufklärung (the clearing-up)—or the Ausklärung (the clearing-out)—made short work of, Kant called to remembrance Ideas of Reason, asking what rational and, first of all, what moral meaning lies in that which men call dogmas of religion, *e.g.* original sin.[1] He is much more reasonable than the *Ausklärung*, which thinks it beneath its dignity to speak of such matters. These are the principal points in respect to the theoretical part of Kant's philosophy.

2. The second subject of review in Kant's philosophy is the practical sphere, the nature and principle of the will; this subject is dealt with in the Critique of Practical Reason, in which Kant accepted Rousseau's conclusion that the will is absolutely free. Kant's idea of theoretic Reason is that when Reason relates itself to an object, this object must be given to it; but when the object is given by Reason to itself, it has no truth; and Reason in knowlege of this kind does not arrive at independence. As practical, on the contrary, Reason is independent in itself; as a moral Being man is free, raised above all natural law and above all phenomena. As the theoretic Reason had in itself categories, *a priori* distinctions, so practical Reason has in turn the moral law in general, the further determinations of which are constituted by the notions of duty and right, lawful and unlawful; and here Reason disdains all the given material which was necessary to it on the theoretic side. The will determines itself within itself; all that is right and moral rests on freedom; in this man has his absolute

---

[1] Kant: Die Religion innerhalb der Grenzen der blossen Vernunft (second edition, Königsberg, 1794), pp. 20-48.

self-consciousness.[1] On this side self-consciousness finds essential reality in itself, as theoretical Reason found it in an "other"; and in the first place, indeed, the ego in its individuality is immediate reality, universality, objectivity; in the second place subjectivity strives after reality, but not after sensuous reality such as we had before, for here Reason holds itself to be the real. Here we have the Notion which is sensible of its own deficiency; this theoretic Reason could not be, as in it the Notion had to remain the Notion. Thus we have the standpoint of absoluteness revealed, since there is an infinite disclosed within the human breast. The satisfying part in Kant's philosophy is that the truth is at least set within the heart; and hence I acknowledge that, and that alone, which is in conformity with my determined nature.

a. Kant divides will into lower and higher faculties of desire; this expression is not inapt. The lower faculties of desire are impulses, inclinations, etc.; the higher faculty is the will as such, which has not external, individual aims, but universal. To the question what the principle of will that should determine man in his actions is, all sorts of answers have been given; for instance, self-love, benevolence, happiness, etc. Such material principles of action, Kant now says, are all reducible to impulses, to happiness; but the rational in itself is purely formal, and consists in the maxim that what is to hold good as law, must be capable of being thought of as a law of universal application, without destroying itself. All morality of action now rests upon the conviction that the act is done with consciousness of the law, for the sake of the law and out of respect for the law and for itself, without any regard to what makes for happiness. As a moral Being man has the moral law in himself, the principle of which is freedom and

---

[1] Kant: Kritik der prakt. Vernunft (fourth edition, Riga, 1797), pp. 3-11, 29-32.

autonomy of the will; for the will is absolute spontaneity. Determinations which are taken from the inclinations are heterogeneous principles as regards the will; or the will is heteronomy if it takes such determinations as its end and aim ; for in that case it takes its determinations from something else than itself. But the essence of the will is to determine itself from itself; for practical Reason gives itself laws. But the empirical will is heteronomous, for it is determined by desires ; and they belong to our nature, not to the realm of freedom. [1]

It is a highly important point in the Kantian philosophy that what self-consciousness esteems reality, law, and implicit Being, is brought back within itself. While a man is striving after this aim and that, according as he judges the world or history in one way or the other, what is he to take as his ultimate aim ? For the will, however, there is no other aim than that derived from itself, the aim of its freedom. It is a great advance when the principle is established that freedom is the last hinge on which man turns, a highest possible pinnacle, which allows nothing further to be imposed upon it ; thus man bows to no authority, and acknowledges no obligations, where his freedom is not respected. Great popularity has from one point of view been won for Kantian philosophy by the teaching that man finds in himself an absolutely firm, unwavering centre-point; but with this last principle it has come to a standstill. While the highest pinnacle of the theoretic Reason is abstract identity, because it can furnish only a canon, a rule for abstract classifications,[2] practical Reason, as law-giving, is immediately regarded as concrete; the law which it gives to itself is the moral law. But even if it is stated that it is concrete in itself, there is the further consideration that

---

[1] Kant: Kritik d. prakt. Vernunft, pp. 40, 41, 56, 126-135, 58, 38, 77.

[2] Kant : Kritik der reinen Vernunft, pp. 62, 500.

this freedom is at first only the negative of everything else ; no bond, nothing external, lays me under an obligation. It is to this extent indeterminate ; it is the identity of the will with itself, its at-homeness with itself. But what is the content of this law ? Here we at once come back to the lack of content. For the sole form of this principle is nothing more or less than agreement with itself, universality ; the formal principle of legislation in this internal solitude comes to no determination, or this is abstraction only. The universal, the non-contradiction of self, is without content, something which comes to be reality in the practical sphere just as little as in the theoretical. The universal moral law Kant therefore expresses thus (and the setting up of such a universal form was at all times the demand of the abstract understanding) : "Act from maxims" (the law is also to be my particular law), "which are capable of becoming universal laws." [1]

Thus for the determination of duty (for the question which meets us is, what is duty for the free will) Kant has contributed nothing but the form of identity, which is the law of abstract Understanding. To defend one's fatherland, to promote the happiness of another, is a duty, not because of the content, but because it is duty ; as with the Stoics, what was thought was true for the very reason that, and in so far as it was thought (Vol. II., pp. 254, 260, 263). The content as such is indeed not what holds good universally in the moral law, because it contradicts itself. For benevolence, for instance, enjoins : "Give your possessions to the poor," but if all give away what they have, beneficence is done away with (Vol. I., pp. 417, 418). Even with abstract identity, however, we do not get a step further, for every content which is put into this form is by being so put freed from self-contradiction. But nothing would be lost if it were not put into this form at all. With regard to property, for

---

[1] Kant : Kritik d. prakt. Vernunft, pp. 54, 58 (35).

instance, the law of my actions is this : Property ought to
be respected, for the opposite of this cannot be universal
law.   That is correct, but it is quite a formal determination :
If property is, then it is.   Property is here presupposed,
but this determination may also in the same way be omitted,
and then there is no contradiction involved in theft : If there
is no such thing as property, then it is not respected.   This
is the defect in the principle of Kant and Fichte, that it is
really formal ; chill duty is the final undigested lump left
within the stomach, the revelation given to Reason.

The first postulate in practical Reason is thus free, independent will which determines itself, but this concrete is
still abstract.   The second and third are forms which remind
us that the will is concrete in a higher sense.

b. The second point is the connection of the Notion of the
will with the particular will of the individual ; the concrete
is here the fact that my particular will and the universal will
are identical, or that I am a moral human being.   The
unity, that man should be moral, is postulated ; but beyond
the "should" and this talk of morality, no advance is made.
It is not said what is moral ; and no thought is given to a
system of the self-realizing spirit.   For really, as theoretic
Reason stands opposed to the objective of the senses, so
practical Reason stands opposed to the practical sensuousness, to impulses and inclinations.   Perfected morality
must remain a Beyond ; for morality presupposes the
difference of the particular and universal will.   It is a
struggle, the determination of the sensuous by the universal ;
the struggle can only take place when the sensuous will is
not yet in conformity with the universal.   The result is,
therefore, that the aim of the moral will is to be attained in
infinite progress only ; on this Kant founds (Kritik der
prakt. Vernunft, pp. 219-223) the postulate of the immortality of the soul, as the endless progress of the subject in
his morality, because morality itself is incomplete, and must
advance into infinitude.   The particular will is certainly

something other than the universal will; but it is not ultimate or really permanent.

c. The third point is the highest concrete, the Notion of the freedom of all men, or the natural world has to be in harmony with the Notion of freedom. That is the postulate of the existence òf God, whom Reason, however, does not recognize. Will has the whole world, the whole of the sensuous, in opposition to it, and yet Reason insists on the unity of Nature or the moral law, as the Idea of the Good, which is the ultimate end of the world. Since, however, it is formal, and therefore has no content on its own account, it stands opposed to the impulses and inclinations of a subjective and an external independent Nature. Kant reconciles the contradiction of the two (Kritik der prakt. Vernunft, pp. 198-200) in the thought of the highest Good, in which Nature is conformed to rational will, and happiness to virtue;—a harmony which does not enter into the question at all, although practical reality consists therein. For happiness is only one's own sensuous consciousness, or the actuality of a particular individual, not universal reality in itself. The unification spoken of itself therefore remains only a Beyond, a thought, which is not actually in existence, but only ought to be. Kant (Kritik der prakt. Vernunft, pp. 205-209) thus agrees entirely with the talk which alleges that in this world it often fares ill with the good, and well with the wicked, and so on ; and he postulates further the existence of God as the Being, the causality, through whom this harmony comes to pass, on behalf both of the sanctity of the moral law, and of the rational end to be attained in Nature, but only in infinite progress ; which postulate, like that of the immortality of the soul, allows the contradiction to remain as it is all the time, and expresses only in the abstract that the reconciliation ought to come about. The postulate itself is always there, because the Good is a Beyond with respect to Nature; the law of necessity and the law of

liberty are different from one another, and placed in this
dualism. Nature would remain Nature no longer, if it
were to become conformed to the Notion of the Good; and
thus there remains an utter opposition between the two
sides, because they cannot unite. It is likewise necessary
to establish the unity of the two ; but this is never actual,
for their separation is exactly what is pre-supposed. Kant
employs popular language thus : evil ought to be overcome, but yet must not have been overcome. God is to
him, therefore, only a faith, an opinion, which is only
subjectively, and not absolutely true.[1] This result is also
of a very popular character.

These postulates express nothing but the synthesis,
devoid of thought, of the different moments which contradict each other on every hand ; they are therefore a
" nest "[2] of contradictions. For instance, the immortality
of the soul is postulated on account of imperfect morality,
i.e. because it is infected with sensuousness. But the
sensuous is implied in moral self-consciousness ; the
end, perfection, is what really destroys morality as such.
Similarly the other aim, the harmony of the sensuous and
the rational, to an equal extent abrogates morality; for
that consists in this very opposition of Reason to the
sensuous. The actuality of the God who produces harmony
is of such a character that it does not enter into consciousness at all ; it is accepted by consciousness for the sake of
harmony, just as children make some kind of scarecrow,
and then agree with each other to pretend to be afraid of
it. The ground on which God is accepted—that by the
conception of a holy law-giver the moral law may acquire
additional reverence—contradicts the fact that morality
really consists in reverence for the law simply for its own
sake.[3] In Practical Reason self-consciousness esteems itself

---

[1] Kant: Kritik d. prakt. Vernunft, pp. 223-227.

[2] Cf. Kant's Kritik d. reinen Vernunft, p. 471.

[3] Kant: Kritik der prakt. Vernunft, p. 146.

to be implicit Being, as contrasted with theoretic Reason, which assigns implicitude to objective existence, but the one, we see, attains just as little as the other to unity and actuality in itself. It is hard for man to believe that Reason actually exists ; but there is nothing real except Reason ; it is the absolute power. The vanity of man aspires to have an ideal before him, in order to be able to find fault with everything alike. We possess all wisdom, it is within us, but is not forthcoming. That is the ultimate standpoint ; it is a high standpoint, no doubt, but in it the truth is never reached. The absolute Good remains "what ought to be," or without objectivity ; and there it has to remain.

3. There is still left for us to consider the third side in Kant's philosophy, the Critique of the Faculty of Judgment, in which the demand for the concrete comes in, the demand that the Idea of unity spoken of before should be established not as a Beyond, but as present ; and this side is of special importance. Kant says that the understanding no doubt regulates in the theoretic sphere and produces categories ; but these remain mere general determinations, beyond which lies the particular (the other element which belongs to every item of knowledge). The two are distinguished from one another for the understanding ; for its distinctions remain in universality. In the practical sphere Reason is certainly the implicit, but its free independence, its law-giving freedom in higher form, is opposed to Nature in its freedom or to Nature's own laws. "In the theoretic sphere Reason can draw conclusions from given laws through syllogisms, only by means of the understanding, and these conclusions never get beyond Nature ; it is only in the practical sphere that Reason itself gives laws. Understanding and " (practical) " Reason have two different regulative systems on one and the same ground of experience, without the one being detrimental to the other. For if the Notion of Nature has but little influence on the giving of laws by the Notion of Freedom,

just as little does the latter interfere with the legislation
of Nature.   The possibility of the existence side by side of
the two regulative systems and of the powers belonging to
them was proved in the Critique of pure Reason."   (! ?)
" Now if a unity is not constituted by these two different
spheres, which certainly do not put a limit on each other in
their regulative action, but do so incessantly in their operations in the sensuous world " (*i.e.* where they encounter
each other), " the reason is this, that the Notion of Nature
represents   its   objects   in   perception,   not   as   things
in themselves, but as mere phenomena, while the Notion
of Freedom, on the other hand, represents in its object a
thing in itself, no doubt, but not in perception.   Consequently neither of them can attain to a theoretic knowledge
of its object (and even of the thinking subject) as a thing-in-
itself, which last would be the supersensuous, an unlimited
and inaccessible realm for our whole faculty of knowledge.   Now truly there is fixed a gulf over which the eye
cannot reach, between the realm of the .Notion of Nature,
as the sensuous, and the realm of the Notion of Freedom,
as the supersensuous, so that it is not possible to pass from
the one to the other, since it is just as if there were two
different worlds, the first of which could have no influence
on the second.   Nevertheless the latter is conceived as
having an influence on the former, or, in other words,
freedom is conceived as having for its mission the realization in the sensuous world of the end indicated by the
laws of freedom.   Consequently Nature must be so conceived that, while in form it realizes its own laws, there
may yet be a possibility of ends being realized in it
according to the laws of freedom.   Therefore there must
surely be some ground for the unity of the supersensuous
which lies at the foundation of Nature with that which
the Notion of Freedom practically contains, the Notion of
which ground of unity, although it attains neither theoretically :nor practically to a knowledge of the same, and

consequently has no peculiar province, yet makes possible the transition from the mode of thought in accordance with the principles of the one, to the mode of thought in accordance with the principles of the other. Between Understanding and Reason there now comes the Faculty of Judgment, as between the powers of knowledge and desire there come pleasure and its opposite; in this faculty must therefore lie the transition from the province of the Notions of Nature to the province of the Notion of Freedom." [1]

Adaptation to ends has its place here, *i.e.* a particular reality, which is determined only through the universal, the end. The understanding is the ground of this unity of the manifold ; the sensuous is therefore here determined by means of the supersensuous. This idea of a universal which implicitly contains the particular is according to Kant the precise object of the faculty of judgment, which he divides as follows :—" If the universal (the rule, principle, law) is given, the faculty of judgment which subsumes the particular under that universal, is determinative,"—the immediate faculty of judgment. But here there is also a particular which is not determined by species. " If, however, only the particular is given, for which the faculty of judgment has to find the universal, it is reflective." The reflective judgment has as its principle the unity of particularity and the abstract universal of the understanding, the idea of a legal necessity which is at the same time free, or of a freedom which is directly one with its content. " This principle can be no other but the fact that since universal laws of Nature have their foundation in our understanding, which prescribes them to nature, although only according to their general conception, the particular, empirical laws, in so far as they are undetermined by universal laws, must

---

[1] Kant: Kritik der Urtheilskraft (third edition, Berlin, 1799), Einleitung, pp. xvii.-xx. xxiv., xxv.

be viewed as containing that unity which they would contain if they had been given by some intelligence—other, it may be, than our own—with express reference to our cognitive faculties, in order to render possible a system of experience according to particular natural laws. It is not as if such an intelligence must be assumed (for it is only the reflective faculty of judgment to which this idea serves as principle) : this faculty gives a law only to itself, not to Nature in addition. Now the conception of an object (if it at the same time contains the ground of the reality of this object), the end, and the harmony of a thing with that quality of things which is only possible in conformity with ends, are termed the adaptation to purpose of the form ; therefore the principle of the faculty of judgment in respect to the form of the things of Nature under empirical laws in general is the adaptability to purpose of Nature in its multiplicity. That is to say, Nature is represented by this Notion as if an intelligence contained the ground of the unity in multiplicity of Nature's empirical laws." [1]

Aristotle already regarded Nature as in itself showing this adaptation to end, and as having in itself νοῦς, intelligence, the Universal, so that in undivided unity one element is moment of another (*v.* Vol. II. pp. 156-162). Purpose is the Notion, and immanent ; not external form and abstraction as distinguished from a fundamental material, but penetrating, so that all that is particular is determined by this universal itself. According to Kant this is Understanding : no doubt the laws of the Understanding, which it implicitly has in knowledge, leave the objective still undetermined ; but because this manifold itself must have a connection in itself, which is yet contingent for human intelligence, "the faculty of judgment must assume as a principle for its own use that what is contingent for us contains a unity, which for us indeed is not knowable, but yet thinkable, in

---

[1] Kant : Kritik der Urtheilskraft, Introduction, pp. xxv.-xxviii.

the connection of the manifold with an implicitly possible experience." [1] This principle hereby at once falls back again into the subjectivity of a thought, and is only a maxim of our reflection, by which nothing is to be expressed regarding the objective nature of the object,[2] because Being-in-itself is once for all fixed outside of self-consciousness, and the Understanding is conceived only in the form of the self-conscious, not in its becoming another.

Now this principle of the reflective faculty of judgment is in itself a twofold adaptation to end, the formal and the material; the faculty of judgment is thus either æsthetic or teleological: of these the former has to do with subjective, the latter with objective, logical adaptation to end. There are thus two objects of the faculty of judgment— the beautiful in works of art and the natural products of organic life—which make known to us the unity of the Notion of Nature and the Notion of Freedom.[3] The consideration of these works involves the fact, that we see a unity of the Understanding and the particular. But as this consideration is only a subjective manner of representing such products, and does not contain the truth of the same, such things are regarded only according to this unity, and they are not in themselves of this nature ; what they are in themselves lies beyond.

a. The Beautiful of the æsthetic faculty of judgment consists in the following : " Pleasure and displeasure are something subjective, which can in no way become a part of knowledge. The object has adaptation to end only to the extent that its conception is directly bound up with the feeling of pleasure ; and this is an æsthetic conception. The taking up of forms into the imaginative faculty can never occur

---

[1] Kant: Kritik der Urtheilskraft, Einleitung, pp. xxvi.-xxxiii.
[2] Ibidem, p. xxxiv.
[3] Ibidem, pp. xlviii.-lii.

without the reflecting faculty of judgment at least comparing them, even unintentionally, by means of its power of
relating perceptions to Notions. Now if in this comparison
the imaginative faculty (as a faculty of perceptions *a
priori?*) " is, by means of a conception given "—something
beautiful,—" unintentionally placed in agreement with the
Understanding, as the faculty of Notions, and thereby a
feeling of pleasure is awakened, the object must then be
looked on as in conformity with end for the reflecting
faculty of judgment. Such a judgment regarding the
adaptability to end of the object, a judgment which is
grounded on no previous Notion of the object, and furnishes
no Notion of it, is an æsthetic judgment. An object whose
form (not the material of its conception as sensation) is
judged to be a cause of the pleasure which springs from the
conception of such an object, is beautiful,"—the first
reasonable thing said about beauty. The sensuous is one
moment of the Beautiful, but it must also express the
spiritual, a Notion. " The Beautiful is what is conceived
without " subjective " interest," but similarly also " without
Notions " (*i.e.* determinations of reflection, laws) " as object
of a universal pleasure. It is related to no inclination,
therefore the subject feels itself quite free therein. It is
not beautiful *for me.* The end is the object of a Notion, so
far as the latter is looked on as the cause of the former "
(the object) ; " and the causality of a Notion in respect to
its object is adaptation to end." To the ideal belongs
" the Idea of reason, which makes the aims of humanity,
as far as they cannot be sensuously conceived, the
principle of judgment of a form through which these
aims reveal themselves as their effect in the phenomenon.
The ideal we may expect to find revealed only in human
form."

The sublime is the effort to give sensuous expression to
an Idea in which the inconceivability of the Idea, and the
impossibility of finding an adequate expression of it by

means of the sensuous, are clearly evidenced.[1] Here in the æsthetic faculty of judgment we see the immediate unity of the universal and the particular; for the Beautiful is this very unity, without Notion and immediate. Because Kant, however, places it in the subject, it is limited, and as æsthetic it also ranks lower, inasmuch as it is not the unity as Notion.

b. The other manner of bringing harmony to pass is the teleological way of regarding Nature, which is found in the objective and material adaptation to end. Here the immediate unity of the Notion and reality is looked upon as objective in the organic products of Nature—this being the purpose of Nature, containing in its universality the particular, in its particularity the species. But such a mode of consideration must be practised not externally, but in conformity with internal teleology. In external adaptation to end one thing has its end in another : " Snow protects the sown crops in cold lands from frost, and facilitates the intercourse of men by permitting of sleighing."[2] Internal adaptation to end signifies, on the contrary, that a thing is in itself end and means, its end is not therefore beyond itself. In the contemplation of the living creature we do not remain at the point of having something sensuous before us, which according to the categories of the Understanding is only brought into relation to something other than itself; for we regard it as cause of itself, as producing itself. This is the self-preservation of the living creature ; as an individual it is no doubt perishable, but in living it produces itself, although for that purpose certain conditions are requisite. The end or purpose of Nature is therefore to be sought for in matter, to the extent that matter is an inwardly organized product of

[1] Kant: Kritik der Urtheilskraft, pp. xliii.–xlv., 16–19, 32, 56, 59, 77.

[2] Ibidem, pp. 279–283.

nature, "in which all is end, and all in turn is means;" [1] because all the members of the organism are at the same time means and end, it is an end in itself. That is the Aristotelian Notion—the infinite that returns into itself, the Idea.

Kant at this point calls to mind the following: "We should find no difference between natural mechanism and the technique of Nature, *i.e.* the connection of ends in the same, were our Understanding not of such a kind that it must pass from the universal to the particular, and the faculty of judgment can therefore pronounce no determining sentences, without having a universal law under which it may subsume the particular. Now the particular as such contains a contingent element in regard to the universal, but nevertheless Reason also demands unity in the connection of particular laws of Nature, and consequently a regulative character, which character when found in the contingent is termed adaptation to end: and the derivation of particular laws from universal is, in regard to the element of contingency which those particular laws contain, *a priori* impossible through the determination of the Notion of the object; the Notion of the adaptation to end of Nature in its products becomes thus a Notion necessary for the human faculty of judgment, but not affecting the determination of the objects themselves, and therefore a subjective principle." [2] An organic Being is therefore, according to Kant (Kritik der Urtheilskraft, p. 354) one in which natural mechanism and end are identical. We regard it as if there dwelt in the sensuous a Notion which brings the particular into conformity with itself. In the organic products of Nature we perceive this immediate unity of the Notion and reality; for in a living creature there is perceived in one unity the soul, or

[1] Kant : Kritik der Urtheilskraft, pp. 286-288, 292-296.
[2] Ibidem, pp. 343, 344.

the universal, and existence or particularity, which is not the case with inorganic Nature. Thus there enters into the Kantian philosophy the conception of the concrete, as that the universal Notion determines the particular. But Kant took these Ideas again in a subjective sense only, as guiding thoughts for the faculty of judgment, by which no Being-in-itself can be expressed; and thus, although he expresses the unity of the Notion and reality, he yet lays fresh emphasis on the side of the Notion. He will not therefore throw off his limitations in the moment in which he assumes them as limitations. This is the perpetual contradiction in Kant's philosophy : Kant exhibited the extremes of opposition in their one-sidedness, and expressed also the reconciliation of the contradiction ; Reason postulates unity, and this we have also in the faculty of judgment. Kant, however, says (Kritik der Urtheilskraft, pp. 355–363) : This is only a mode of our reflecting faculty of judgment, life itself is not so; we are merely accustomed so to regard it. In art it is thus certainly the sensuous mode which gives us the conception of the Idea; reality and ideality are here directly in one. But at this point also Kant says that we must remain at what is one-sided, at the very moment when he is passing out beyond it. The wealth of thought therefore still unfolds itself with Kant in subjective form alone ; all fulness, all content, concentrates in conceiving, thinking, postulating. The objective, according to Kant, is only what is in itself ; and we know not what Things-in-themselves are. But Being-in-itself is only the *caput mortuum*, the dead abstraction of the " other," the empty, undetermined Beyond.

The reason why that true Idea should not be the truth is therefore that the empty abstractions of an understanding which keeps itself in the abstract universal, and of a sensuous material of individuality standing in opposition to the same, are presupposed as the truth. Kant no

doubt expressly advances to the conception of an intuitive
or perceiving understanding, which, while it gives universal laws, at the same time determines the particular;
and the determination thus given is deep; it is the true
concrete, reality determined by the indwelling Notion, or,
as Spinoza says, the adequate Idea. For "to knowledge
there also belongs intuitive perception, and the possession
of a perfect spontaneity of intuition would be a faculty
of knowledge" specifically "distinct from the sensuous,
and quite independent thereof, and therefore it would be
understanding in the most universal sense. Consequently
it is possible to think of an intuitive understanding which
does not pass from the universal to the particular, and thus
proceed through conceptions to the individual—an understanding in which we do not meet with the contingency
of the harmony of Nature in her products, according to
particular laws, with the understanding, a contingency
which makes it so hard for our understanding to bring"
together "into the unity of knowledge the manifold of
Nature." But that this "*intellectus archetypus*" is the
true Idea of the understanding, is a thought which does
not strike Kant. Strange to say, he certainly has this
idea of the intuitive; and he does not know why it should
have no truth—except because our understanding is
otherwise constituted, namely such "that it proceeds
from the analytic universal to the particular."[1] But absolute Reason and Understanding in itself, as we have
already seen (pp. 432, 461), are, in Kant's view, of such a
nature that they have no reality in themselves: the Understanding requires material to work upon, theoretic Reason
spins cobwebs of the brain, practical Reason has to allow
its reality to come to an end with its postulates. In spite
of their directly and definitely expressed non-absoluteness,
they are yet looked on as true knowledge; and intuitive

---

[1] Kant: Kritik der Urtheilskraft, pp. 317, 348 (351).

Understanding, which holds Notion and sensuous perception in one unity, is looked on as a mere thought which we make for ourselves.

c. The highest form in which the conception of the concrete comes into Kant's philosophy is this, that the end is grasped in its entire universality; and thus it is the Good. This Good is an Idea; it is my thought; but there exists the absolute demand that it should be realized also in the world, that the necessity of Nature should correspond with the laws of freedom, not as the necessity of an external Nature, but through what is right and moral in human life, through life in the State,—or in other words that the world in general should be good. This identity of the Good and reality is the demand of practical Reason; but subjective Reason cannot realize this. In every good action a man no doubt accomplishes something good, but this is only limited; universal Good, as the final object of the world, can be attained to only through a third. And this power over the world, which has as its final object the Good in the world, is God.[1] Thus the Critique of the Faculty of Judgment also ends with the postulate of God. Now, although the particular laws of Nature, as independent individual relations, have no relation to the Good, Reason consists in having and desiring unity as the essential or substantial in itself. The opposition of these two, the Good and the world, is contrary to that identity; Reason must therefore demand that this contradiction should be abrogated, that there should be a power which is good on its own account, and is a Power over Nature. This is the position which God assumes in Kant's philosophy: no proof is possible, he says, of God's existence, but the demand is there. The deficiency here is the impossibility of proving God's existence, and it consists in this, that if we admit Kant's dualism, it cannot be shown how the Good

[1] Kant: Kritik der Urtheilskraft, pp. 423, 424.

as abstract Idea in itself is the abrogating of its Idea as abstract ; and how the world in itself is the abrogating of itself in its externality, and in its diversity from the Good —this being done in order that both may reveal themselves to be their truth, which in respect to them appears as the Third, but is at the same time determined as the First. Thus, therefore, according to Kant (Kritik der Urtheilskraft, pp. 460, 461), God can only be believed in. We associate the faith of Jacobi with this ; for in this point Kant agrees with Jacobi.[1]

If now, in accordance with this standpoint of Kant and Jacobi, God is believed in, and we admit this standpoint for an instant, there is certainly a return to the Absolute. But the question remains : What is God ? To define Him as supersensuous is not much, nor is it more to say He is universal, abstract, absolute. What then is His determination ? Were we here, however, to pass over to determinations of the Absolute, the evil result would follow, as far as this standpoint is concerned, that we should pass over to knowledge; for this signifies knowledge of an object which is in itself concrete, *i.e.* determined. But here the furthest point reached is the general statement that God exists with the determination of being infinite, universal, indeterminate. God cannot be known in this way; for in order to be known He must as concrete possess at least two determinations. In this way mediation would be established, for a knowledge of the concrete is at once a mediate knowledge. But this standpoint lacks mediation, and thus remains at the immediate. Paul, in speaking to the Athenians, appeals to the altar which they had dedicated to the Unknown God, and declares to them what God is ; but the standpoint indicated here takes us back to the Unknown God. All the life of Nature, as

---

[1] What falls under this heading in Jacobi's philosophy is inserted here in the lectures of 1825-1826.

of Spirit, is mediation in itself; and to this mediation the philosophy of Schelling now passed on.

If we sum up the Kantian philosophy, we find on all hands the Idea of Thought, which is in itself the absolute Notion, and has in itself difference, reality. In the theoretic and practical Reason it has only abstract difference, but in the Faculty of Judgment, as the unity of the two, Kant goes so far as to establish the difference as actual, establishing not only particularity, but also individuality. But, to be sure, this Philistine conception proceeds from our human faculty of knowledge, which is valid for him in its empirical form, notwithstanding his statement that it does not know the truth, and his further description of the true idea of the same as being merely a thought which we possess. Therefore actuality counts as something sensuous, empirical, for the comprehension of which Kant takes the categories of the Understanding, giving them the same validity as they have in everyday life. This is a complete philosophy of the Understanding, which renounces Reason : the reason why it became so popular was the negative one, that men were once for all free from the old metaphysic. According to Kant something sensuous is produced, having thought-determinations, which, however, is not the thing, for if a man, for instance, feels something hard, Kant says : "I feel hardness, but I do not feel Something." Kant's philosophy thus ends with a dualism, with the relation which is a plainly essential "ought," with the unreconciled contradiction. It is otherwise with Jacobi's faith; he finds the conception of God as immediate existence, and all mediation is untrue for him. With Kant, therefore, the result is: "We know only phenomena;" with Jacobi, on the other hand, it is: "We know only the finite and conditioned." Over these two results there has been unmingled joy among men, because the sloth of Reason (Heaven be praised!) considered itself liberated from every call to reflect, and now, being saved the trouble of penetrating to its own inward meaning and exploring the depths of Nature and Spirit, it could very well leave itself alone. The further result attending this is the autocracy of the subjective Reason, which, seeing that it is abstract and without knowledge, has only subjective certainty and not objective truth. The second cause of rejoicing was the concession to freedom of a perfect right, which I can neither understand nor justify, and need not do so; my subjective liberty of conviction and certainty holds good all round. The third cause of joy was added by Jacobi, who said that it amounted even to a crime to seek to know the truth, because the infinite was thereby only rendered finite. Truth is in a bad way, when all metaphysic is done away with, and the only philosophy acknowledged is not a philosophy at all!

But besides the general idea of synthetic judgments *a priori,* a universal which has difference in itself, Kant's instinct carried this out in accordance with the scheme of triplicity, unspiritual though that was, in the whole system into which for him the entire universe was divided. This he not only practised in the three critiques, but he also followed it out in most of the sub-divisions under the categories, the ideas of Reason, &c. Kant has therefore set forth as a universal scheme the rhythm of knowledge, of scientific movement; and has exhibited on all sides thesis, antithesis and synthesis, modes of the mind by means of which it is mind, as thus consciously distinguishing itself. The first is existence, but in the form of Other-Being for consciousness; for what is only existence is object. The second is Being-for-self, genuine actuality; here the reverse relation enters in, for self-consciousness, as the negative of Being-in-itself, is itself reality. The third is the unity of the two; the absolute, self-conscious actuality is the sum of true actuality, into which are re-absorbed both the objective and the independently existent subjective.

Kant has thus made an historical statement of the moments of the whole, and has correctly determined and distinguished them : it is a good introduction to Philosophy. The defect of Kant's philosophy consists in the falling asunder of the moments of the absolute form ; or, regarded from the other side, our understanding, our knowledge, forms an antithesis to Being-in-itself : there is lacking the negative, the abrogation of the " ought," which is not laid hold of. But thought and thinking had become once for all an absolute requisite that could no longer be set aside. It was consequently in the first place demanded by consistency that particular thoughts should appear as if produced of necessity from the original unity of the ego, and in that way justified. But, in the second place, thought had spread itself over the world, had attached itself to everything, investigated everything, introduced its forms into everything, and systematized everything, so that on every hand thought-determinations had to be followed, instead of any mere feeling or routine or practical common-sense, or what is evidenced in the extraordinary lack of understanding on the part of so-called practical men. And therefore in theology, in governments and their legislation, in the object aimed at by the state, in trades and in mechanics, it is said that men ought to act according to universal determinations, *i.e.* rationally : and men even talk of a rational brewery, a rational brick-kiln, etc. This is the requisite of concrete thought ; while in the Kantian result, which is that of phenomenon, an empty thought was alone present. It is verily also the essence of revealed religion to know what God is. There was, therefore, to be found a yearning desire for content, for truth, since man could not possibly return to the condition of a brute, nor yet sink to the form of sensation, so that this yearning was for him the only thing that held good with regard to the higher life. The first requirement— consistency—Fichte sought to satisfy ; the other—content —Schelling strove to fulfil.

C. Fichte.

Fichte created a great sensation in his time; his philosophy is the Kantian philosophy in its completion, and, as we must specially notice, it is set forth in a more logical way. He does not pass beyond the fundamentals of Kant's philosophy, and at first regarded his own philosophy as no more than a systematic working out of the other.[1] In addition to these systems of philosophies, and that of Schelling, there are none. Any that pretend to be such merely pick out something from these, and over this they fight and wrangle among themselves. *Ils se sont battus. les flancs, pour être de grands hommes.* For in those times there were in Germany many systems of philosophy, such as those of Reinhold, Krug, Bouterweck, Fries, Schulze, &c.; but in them there is only an extremely limited point of view, combined with boastfulness—a strange medley of stray thoughts and conceptions or facts which I find within me. But their thoughts are all derived from Fichte, Kant, or Schelling— that is in so far as there are thoughts there present at all. Or else some slight modification is added, and this for the most part merely consists in making the great principles barren, what points in them were living are destroyed, or else subordinate forms are changed, whereby another principle is said to be set forth, though when we look closer we find that these principles are but the principles of one of those philosophies that have gone before. This may serve as a justification for my not speaking further of all these philosophies; any exposition of them would be no more than a demonstration that everything in them is taken from Kant, Fichte, or Schelling, and that the modification in form is only the semblance of a change, while really it indicates a deterioration in the principles of those philosophies.

---

[1] Fichte : Grundlage der gesammten Wissenschaftslehre (Leipzig, 1794), Preface, p. xii.

Johann Gottlieb Fichte was born on the 19th of May, 1762, at Rammenau, near Bischoffswerda, in Upper Lusatia. He studied at Jena, and for some time was a private tutor in Switzerland. He wrote a treatise on Religion, termed a "Critique of all Revelation," where the Kantian phraseology is employed throughout—so much so that it was thought to be the work of Kant. After this he was in 1793 summoned to Jena by Goethe as Professor of Philosophy, which appointment he, however, resigned in the year 1799, on account of an unpleasantness which had arisen through his essay "On the ground of our Belief in a Divine Government of the World." For Fichte published a journal in Jena, and a paper in it which was by someone else was regarded as atheistical. Fichte might have kept silence, but he published the above-mentioned essay as an introduction to the article. The authorities wished an investigation to be made into the matter. Then Fichte wrote a letter which contained threats, and respecting it Goethe said that a Government ought not to allow itself to be threatened. Fichte now taught privately for some time in Berlin; in 1805 he became professor at Erlangen, and in 1809 at Berlin, at which place he died on the 27th January, 1814.[1] We cannot here deal more particularly with the details of his life.

In what is termed the philosophy of Fichte a distinction must be made between his properly-speaking speculative philosophy, in which the argument is most consistently worked out, and which is less well known, and his popular philosophy, to which belong the lectures delivered in Berlin before a mixed audience, and, for example, the work termed a "Guidance to a Blessed Life." These last have much in them that is affecting and edifying—many who call them-

---

[1] Fichte's Leben und Briefwechsel, edited by his son, Pt. I. pp. 3, 6, 24 seq.; 38 seq.; 142, 189; 337, 338, 348. 349. 353, 354, 358–364; Pt. II. pp. 140–142; Pt. I. pp. 370–372, 442–448, 455; 518, 540; 578.

selves the disciples of Fichte know this side alone—and they are expressed in language most impressive to a cultured, religious temperament. In the history of Philosophy, however, such cannot be taken into consideration, although through their matter they may have the highest possible value; the content has to be speculatively developed, and that is done in Fichte's earlier philosophic works alone.[1]

1. The First Principles of Fichte's Philosophy.

As we mentioned above (p. 478), the shortcoming in the Kantian philosophy was its unthinking inconsistency, through which speculative unity was lacking to the whole system; and this shortcoming was removed by Fichte. It is the absolute form which Fichte laid hold of, or in other words, the absolute form is just the absolute Being-for-self, absolute negativity, not individuality, but the Notion of individuality, and thereby the Notion of actuality; Fichte's philosophy is thus the development of form in itself. He maintained the ego to be the absolute principle, so that from it, the direct and immediate certainty of self, all the matter in the universe must be represented as produced; hence, according to Fichte, reason is in itself a synthesis of Notion and actuality. But this principle he once more in an equally one-sided manner set aside; it is from the very beginning subjective, conditioned by an opposite, and its realization is a continual rushing onward in finitude, a looking back at what has gone before. The form in which it is presented has also the disadvantage, and indeed, the real

---

[1] Fichte's posthumous works, which were not published until after Hegel's death, nevertheless show that the writer in his lectures at the Berlin University likewise worked out scientifically this newly developed point of view in his philosophy; Fichte made a beginning in this regard brocheven in the ure which appeared in 1810: " Die Wissenschaftslehre in ihrem allgemeinen Umrisse" (v. Michelet: Geschichte der letzten Systeme der Philosophie, Pt. I. pp. 441, 442). [Editor's note.]

drawback of bringing the empiric ego ever before one's eyes, which is absurd, and quite distracting to one's point of view.

The claims of Philosophy have advanced so far that in the first place self-consciousness refuses any longer to regard absolute essence as immediate substance which does not in itself possess difference, reality, and actuality. Against this substance self-consciousness ever struggled, for it does not find its explicit Being there, and consequently feels the lack of freedom. But besides this it demanded that this essence, objectively presented, should be personal, living, self-conscious, actual, and not shut up in abstract metaphysical thoughts alone. On the other hand consciousness, for which the other is, demanded the moment of external actuality, Being as such, into which thought must pass, truth in objective existence; and this is what we more especially noticed in connection with the English. This Notion, which is immediately actuality, and this actuality which is immediately its Notion, and that indeed in such a way that there neither is a third thought above this unity, nor is it an immediate unity which does not possess difference, separation, within it, is the ego; it is the self-distinction of opposites within itself. That whereby it distinguishes itself from the simplicity of thought, and distinguishes this other, is likewise immediately for it; it is identical with, or not distinguished from it.[1] Hence it is pure thought, or the ego is the true synthetic judgment *a priori*, as Kant called it. This principle is apprehended actuality, for the taking back of the other-Being into self-consciousness is just apprehension. The Notion of the Notion is from this point of view found in the fact that in what is apprehended self-consciousness has the certainty of itself; what is not apprehended is some-

---

[1] Fichte: Grundlage der gesammten Wissenschaftslehre, pp. 10-12.

thing foreign to it. This absolute Notion or this absolutely existent infinitude it is which has to be developed in knowledge, and its distinction as the whole distinction of the universe has to be represented from itself, and this has in its distinction to remain reflected within itself in equal absoluteness. Nothing other than the ego anywhere exists, and the ego is there because it is there; what is there is only in the ego and for the ego.[1]

Now Fichte merely set forth this Notion; he did not bring it to a scientific realization from itself. For to him this Notion maintains and asserts itself as this Notion; it has absoluteness for him in so far as it is merely the unrealized Notion, and thus indeed comes once more into opposition with reality. The Fichtian philosophy has the great advantage of having set forth the fact that Philosophy must be a science derived from one supreme principle, from which all determinations are necessarily derived. The important point is this unity of principle and the attempt to develop from it in a scientifically consistent way the whole content of consciousness, or, as has been said, to construct the whole world.[2] Beyond this no progress was made.[3] But the great necessity in Philosophy is to possess one living Idea; the world is a flower which is eternally produced from one grain of seed. Thus Fichte does not, like Kant, throw his work into narrative form because he begins with the ego; but he has proceeded further, inasmuch as he sought to bring about a construction of determinations of knowledge from the ego. The whole extent of knowledge in all the world must be developed, and further this knowledge must be the consequence of the development of determinations; but because Fichte says that what is not

---

[1] Fichte: Grundlage der gesammten Wissenschaftslehre, pp. 13, 14.

[2] Fichte: Ueber den Begriff der Wissenschaftslehre (Weimar, 1794), p. 12.

[3] Fichte: Grundlage der ges. Wissenschaftsl., Preface, pp. x., xi.

for us does not concern us, he has not grasped this principle of the ego as Idea, but solely in the consciousness of the activity which we exercise in knowing, and consequently it is still laid hold of in the form of subjectivity.

Thus as Kant treats of cognition [Erkennen], so Fichte sets forth real knowledge [Wissen]. Fichte states that the task of Philosophy is to find a theory of knowledge; universal knowledge is both the object and the starting-point of Philosophy. Consciousness knows, that is its nature; the end of philosophic learning is the knowledge of this knowledge. Hence Fichte called his philosophy the Theory of Knowledge (Begriff der Wissenschaftslehre, p. 18), the science of knowledge. That is to say ordinary consciousness as the active ego finds this and that, occupies itself, not with itself, but with other objects and interests, but the necessity that I bring forth determinations, and which determinations—cause and effect, for example,—lies beyond my consciousness: I bring them forth instinctively and cannot get behind my consciousness. But when I philosophize, I make my ordinary consciousness itself my object, because I make a pure category my consciousness: I know what my ego is doing, and thus I get behind my ordinary consciousness. Fichte thus defines Philosophy as the artificial consciousness, as the consciousness of consciousness.[1]

a. Where Fichte in his system has attained the highest degree of determinateness, he begins, as we saw Kant did before (pp. 437, 438), from the transcendental unity of self-consciousness; in it I—as this—am one, this unity is to Fichte the same and the original. Ego is there a fact, says Fichte, but not yet a proposition. As proposition, as principle, the ego must not remain barren, nor be accepted as one, for to a proposition pertains a synthesis. Now Fichte proceeds in his system from the fact that Philosophy

[1] Fichte: Grundlage der gesammten Wissenschaftslehre, pp. 184, 185.

must begin with an absolutely unconditioned, certain principle, with something indubitably certain in ordinary
knowledge. "It cannot be proved or defined, because it
must be absolutely the first principle."[1] According to
Wendt's account (Tennemann's Grundriss, § 393, pp. 494,
495) Fichte gives an exposition of the necessity of such a
principle as follows : " Scientific knowledge is a system of
cognition obtained through a supreme principle which
expresses the content and form of knowledge. The theory
of knowledge is the science of knowledge which sets forth
the possibility and validity of all knowledge, and proves
the possibility of principles in reference to form and
content, the principles themselves, and thereby the
connection existing in all human knowledge. It must have
a principle which can neither be proved from it nor from
another science ; for it is supreme. If there is a theory of
knowledge there also is a system ; if there is a system there
is also a theory of knowledge and an absolute first
principle—and so on through an inevitable circle." [2]

The simple principle of this knowledge is certainty of
myself, which is the relation of me to myself; what is in
me, that I know. The supreme principle, as immediate and
not derived, must be certain on its own account ; that is,
a determination of the ego only, for it is only from the ego
that I cannot abstract.[3] Fichte thus begins, like Descartes,
with ' I think, therefore I am,' and he expressly brings this
proposition to mind. The Being of the ego is not a dead,
but a concrete Being ; but the highest Being is thought.
Ego, as an explicitly self-existent activity of thought, is
thus knowledge, even if it is only abstract knowledge, as
in the beginning at least it cannot help being. At the

[1] Fichte: Grundlage der gesammten Wissenschaftslehre, p. 3.
[2] Cf. Fichte : Ueber den Begriff der Wissenschaftslehre, pp. 13-
17, 19-39, 50-52.
[3] Fichte: Grundlage der gesammten Wissenschaftslehre, pp. 4, 5.

same time Fichte begins from this absolute certainty with quite other necessities and demands ; for from this ego not only Being but also the larger system of thought has to be derived (*supra,* p. 230). According to Fichte, the ego is the source of the categories and ideas, but all conceptions and thoughts are a manifold reduced to a synthesis through Thought. Thus while with Descartes in connection with the ego other thoughts appear which we simply find already in us, such as God, nature, &c., Fichte sought for a philosophy entirely of a piece, in which nothing empiric was to be admitted from without. With this reflection a false point of view was at once introduced, namely that contained in the old conception of knowledge, of commencing with principles in this form and proceeding from them ; so that the reality which is derived from such a principle is brought into opposition with it, and hence in truth is something different, *i.e.* it is not derived : or that principle for this same reason expresses only the absolute certainty of itself and not the truth. The ego is certain, it cannot be doubted ; but Philosophy desires to reach the truth. The certainty is subjective, and because it is made to remain the basis, all else remains subjective also without there being any possibility of this form being removed. Fichte now analyzes the ego, reducing it to three principles from which the whole of knowledge has to be evolved.

a. The first proposition must be simple, in it predicate and subject must be alike ; for were they unlike, their connection—since in accordance with their diversity the determinations are not directly one—would have to be first of all proved by means of a third. The first principle must thus be identical. Fichte now proceeds further to distinguish in this first principle the form and content ; but in order that this same may be immediately true through itself, form and content must be again the same, and the principle conditioned by neither. It signifies $A = A$, the abstract undetermined identity ; that is the proposition of contradiction, wherein A is an indifferent content. Fichte says, "Thought is by no means essence, but only a particular determination of Being; there are outside of it many other determinations of our Being. I merely remark this, that when 'I am' is overstepped, Spinozism is necessarily reached. Its unity is something which ought to be produced through us, but which cannot be so ; it is not anything that is." The first proposition is then that I am identical with myself, Ego = Ego ;¹ that undoubtedly is the definition of the ego. The subject and the predicate are the content ; and this content of the two sides is likewise their relation, *i.e.* form. Relation requires two sides; the relating and the related are here, however, the same ; for on account of the simplicity of the ego, there is nothing but a relation of the ego to the ego. I have knowledge of myself ; but in so far as I am consciousness, I know of an object which is different from me, and which is then likewise *mine.* But the ego is in such a way identical with its difference that what is different is immediately the same, and what is identical is likewise different ; we have a difference without a difference. Self-consciousness is not dead identity, or non-Being, but the object which is identical with me. This is immediately certain ; all else must be as certain to me, inasmuch as it must be my relation to myself. The content must be transformed into the ego, so that in it I have *my* determination alone. This principle is at first abstract and deficient, because in it no difference, or a formal difference only is expressed ; whereas the principle should possess a content : a subject and a predicate are indeed distinguished in it, but only for us who reflect upon it, *i.e.* in itself there is no difference, and consequently no true content. In the second place, this principle is indeed the imme-

---

¹ Grundlage der gesammten Wissenschaftslehre, pp. 23, 5, 15, 17, 8.

diate certainty of self-consciousness, but self-consciousness is likewise consciousness, and in it there is likewise the certainty that other things exist to which it stands in an attitude of opposition. In the third place, that principle has not the truth in it, for the very reason that the certainty of itself possessed by the ego has no objectivity; it has not the form of the differentiated content within it —or it stands in opposition to the consciousness of an "other"

β. Now in order that determination should come to pass, *i.e.* a content and difference, it is essential for Fichte that a second principle should be established, which in regard to form is unconditioned, but the content of which is conditioned, because it does not belong to the ego. This second principle, set forth under the first, is, "I assert a non-ego in opposition to the ego," and in this something other than absolute self-consciousness is set forth.[1] To this pertains the form therein present, relation; but the content is the non-ego, another content from the ego. We might say that through this content the proposition is independent, since the negative therein is an absolute, as truly as the reverse—that it is independent through the form of opposition which cannot be derived from the original. Here, then, we have no more to do with derivation, although this derivation of opposition from the first proposition was all the same demanded. Inasmuch as I posit another in opposition to the ego, I posit myself as not posited; this non-ego is the object generally, *i.e.* that which is opposed to me. This other is the negative of the ego; thus when Fichte called it the non-ego he was expressing himself in a very happy, suitable, and consistent manner. There has been a good deal of ridicule cast on the ego and non-ego; the expression is new, and therefore to us Germans it seems strange at first.

[1] Fichte; Grundlage der ges. Wissenschaftslehre, pp. 17, 19-22.

But the French say *Moi* and *Non-moi,* without finding
anything laughable in it.   In this principle the positing
belongs, however, to the ego ; but because the non-
ego is independent of the ego, we have two sides,
and self-consciousness relates itself to another.   This
second proposition thus signifies that I posit myself
as limited, as non-ego; but non-ego is something quite
new to be added.   On the one side we thus have before
us a field which is merely appropriated from the ego ;
and in this way we have before us the non-ego as our
object.

γ. To these is added yet a third proposition, in which I
now make this division into ego and non-ego : it is the
synthetic principle, the proposition of ground, which in
content is unconditioned, just as in the second was the
case in regard to form.   This third proposition is the determination of the first two through one another, in such a
way that the ego limits the non-ego.   "In and through the
ego both the ego and the non-ego are posited as capable of
being mutually limited by means of one another, *i.e.* in
such a way that the reality of the one abrogates the reality
of the other."   In limitation both are negated, but "only
in part "; only thus are synthesis and deduction possible.
I posit the non-ego, which is for me, in myself, in my
identity with myself ; thus I take it from its non-identity,
its not-being-I, that is to say I limit it.   This limitation
of the non-ego Fichte expresses thus : "I place in opposition to the ego," and indeed "to the divisible ego, a
divisible non-ego."   The non-ego I destroy as a complete
sphere, which it was according to the second principle, and
posit it as divisible ; I likewise posit the ego as divisible
in so far as the non-ego is present in it.   The whole sphere
which I have before me is supposed indeed to be the ego,
but in it I have not one but two.   The proposition of
ground is thus the relation of reality and negation, *i.e.* it is
limitation ; it contains the ego limited by the non-ego, and

the non-ego limited by the ego.[1] Of this synthesis there is nothing, properly speaking, contained in the two earlier propositions. Even this first presentation of the three principles does away with the immanence of real knowledge. Thus the presentation is here also subject to an opposite from the first, as it is with Kant, even if these are two acts of the ego merely, and we remain entirely in the ego.

Now that limitation may take place for me in two different ways : at one time the one is passive, at another time the other is so. In this limitation the ego may posit the non-ego as limiting and itself as limited, in such a way that the ego posits itself as requiring to have an object ; I know myself indeed as ego, but determined by the non-ego ; non-ego is here active and ego passive. Or, on the other hand, the ego, as abrogating other-being, is that which limits, and non-ego is the limited. I know myself then as clearly determining the non-ego, as the absolute cause of the non-ego as such, for I can think. The first is the proposition of the theoretic reason, of intelligence : the second the proposition of practical reason, of will.[2] The will is this, that I am conscious of myself as limiting the object ; thus I make myself exercise activity upon the object and maintain myself. The theoretic proposition is that the object is before me and it determines me. The ego is, since I perceive, a content, and I have this content in me, which is thus outside of me. This is on the whole the same thing as we meet with in the experience of Kant : it comes to the same thing whether it is by matter or the non-ego that the ego is here determined.

b. In the theoretic consciousness the ego, although the assertive generally, finds itself limited by the non-ego.

[1] Fichte : Grundlage der gesammten Wissenschaftslehre, pp. 34, 31, 23, 27-30 (52), 14, 18.
[2] Ibidem, pp. 52-56, 74.

But it is identical with itself; hence its infinite activity ever sets itself to abrogate the non-ego and to bring forth itself. Now the different methods whereby the ego sets forth itself are the different methods of its activity; these we have to understand in their necessity. But since philosophic knowledge is the consideration of consciousness itself (*supra*, p. 483), I can only know knowledge, the act of the ego. Fichte thus appeals to consciousness, postulates ego and non-ego in their abstraction, and since philosophic knowledge is the consciousness of consciousness, it is not sufficient that I should find its determinations in consciousness, for I produce them with consciousness. Common consciousness, indeed, likewise brings forth all the determinations of the ordinary conception and of thought, but without—on the theoretic side at least—having any knowledge of it; for it is the fact of being limited alone that is present to it. Thus, when I see a large square object, such as a wall, my ordinary consciousness accepts these determinations as they are given to it; the object *is*. In so doing I do not think of seeing, but of the object; seeing, however, is my activity, the determinations of my faculty of sensation are thus posited through me.[1] The ego as theoretic is, indeed, aware in philosophic consciousness that it is the ego which posits; but here it posits that the non-ego posits somewhat in me. The ego thus posits itself as that which is limited by the non-ego. I make this limitation mine; thus is it for me in me, this passivity of the ego is itself the activity of the ego. As a matter of fact, all reality which appears in the object for the ego is a determination of the ego,[2] just as the categories and other determinations were in Kant's case. Thus it is here more especially that we should expect Fichte to demonstrate the return of other-Being into absolute consciousness. How-

---

[1] Fichte's Anweisung zum seligen Leben, pp. 80-82.
[2] Fichte: Grundlage der gesammten Wissenschaftslehre, p. 57.

ever, because after all the other-Being was regarded as unconditioned, as implicit, this return does not come to pass. The ego determines the 'other,' indeed, but this unity is an altogether finite unity; non-ego has thus immediately escaped from determination once more and gone forth from this unity. What we find is merely an alternation between self-consciousness and the consciousness of another, and the constant progression of this alternation, which never reaches any end.[1]

The development of theoretic reason is the following-out of the manifold relationships between the ego and non-ego; the forms of this limitation which Fichte now goes through are the determinations of the object. These particular thought-determinations he calls categories, and he seeks to demonstrate them in their necessity; from the time of Aristotle onwards no one had thought of so doing. The first of these forms is the determination of reciprocity, which we already met with in the third proposition : " By the determination of the reality or negation of the ego, the negation or reality of the non-ego is equally determined ; " the two in one is reciprocal action. In the second place, " Causality is the same degree of activity in the one as of passivity in the other." In so far as something is considered as the reality of the non-ego, the ego is considered as passive, and, on the other hand, in so far as ' I ' am real, the object is passive ; this relation, that the passivity of the object is my activity or reality, and the opposite, is the conception of Causality. " As many parts of negation as the ego posits in itself, so many parts of reality it posits in the non-ego ; it therefore posits itself as self-determining in so far as it is determined, and as suffering determination in so far as it determines itself. In so far," in the third place, " as the ego is regarded as embracing the whole absolutely determined realm of all reality, it is substance ;

[1] Fichte : Grundlage der gesammten Wissenschaftslehre, pp. 78, 79.

on the other hand when it is posited in a not absolutely determined sphere of this realm, in so far there is an accidence in the ego." [1]   That is the first rational attempt that has ever been made to deduce the categories; this progress from one determination to another is, however, only an analysis from the standpoint of consciousness, and is not in and for itself.

The ego is so far the ideal ground of all conceptions of the object; all determination of this object is a determination of the ego.   But in order that it may be object, it must be placed in opposition to the ego, *i.e.* the determinations set forth through the ego are another, the non-ego; this placing of the object in opposition is the real ground of conceptions.   The ego is, however, likewise the real ground of the object; for it is likewise a determination of the ego that the non-ego as object is set in opposition to the ego. Both, the real ground and the ideal ground of the conception, are thus one and the same. [2]   Regarding the ego as ideal principle and the non-ego as real principle, Krug has likewise talked a great deal of nonsense.   Regarded from the one point of view, the ego is active and the non-ego purely passive; while from the other side the ego is passive and the object active and operative.   But since the ego in the non-philosophic consciousness does not have the consciousness of its activity in the conception of the object, it represents to itself its own activity as foreign, *i.e.* as belonging to the non-ego.

We here see the opposition adopting various forms : ego, non-ego; positing, setting in opposition ; two sorts of activity of the ego, &c.   The fact that I represent is undoubtedly my activity, but the matter of main importance is the content of the positing and its necessary connection through itself.   If one occupies oneself only with this con-

---

[1] Fichte : Grundlage der gesammten Wissenschaftslehre, pp. 60, 67, 59, 76.

[2] Ibidem, pp. 121, 122.

tent, that form of subjectivity which is dominant with Fichte, and which remains in his opposition, disappears. As the ego is affirmative and determining, there now is in this determination a negative likewise present; I find myself determined and at the same time the ego is like itself, infinite, *i.e.* identical with itself. This is a contradiction which Fichte indeed endeavours to reconcile, but in spite of it all he leaves the false basis of dualism undisturbed. The ultimate, beyond which Fichte does not get, is only an ' ought,' which does not solve the contradiction; for while the ego should be absolutely at home with itself, *i.e.* free, it should at the same time be associated with another. To Fichte the demand for the solution of this contradiction thus adopts the attitude of being a demanded solution only, of signifying that I ever have to destroy the barriers, that I ever have to reach beyond the limitation into utter infinitude, and that I ever find a new limit; a continual alternation takes place between negation and affirmation, an identity with self which again falls into negation, and from this negation is ever again restored. To speak of the bounds of human reason is, however, an unmeaning form of words. That the reason of the subject is limited is comprehensible from the nature of the case, but when we speak of Thought, infinitude is none other than one's own relation to self, and not to one's limit; and the place in which man is infinite is Thought. Infinitude may then be likewise very abstract, and in this way it is also once more finite; but true infinitude remains in itself.

Fichte further deduces the ordinary conception thus: the fact that the ego in going forth at once finds its activity checked by a limitation, and returns once more into itself, brings about two opposite tendencies in me, between which I waver, and which I try to unite in the faculty of imagination. In order that a fixed determination may exist between the two, I have to make the limit a permanent one, and we have that in the understanding. All further

determinations of the object are, as categories of the understanding, modes of synthesis; but each synthesis is a new
contradiction. New mediations are thus once more necessary, and these are new determinations. Thus Fichte
says: I can always continue to determine the non-ego, to
make it my conception, *i.e.* to take from it its negation
as regards me. I have to deal with my activity alone; but
there is always an externality therein present which still
remains, and which is not explained by my activity. This
Beyond which alone remains to the undetermined ego
Fichte calls the infinite check upon the ego, with which it
ever has to deal, and beyond which it cannot get; thus
the activity which proceeds into infinitude finds itself
checked and driven back by this repulsive force, and then
it reacts upon itself. "The ego in its self-determination
has been considered both as determining and determined;
if we reflect on the fact that the absolutely determined
determining power must be an absolutely indeterminate,
and further, that ego and non-ego are absolutely opposed
to one another, in the one case ego is the indeterminate
and in the other case non-ego."[1]

Inasmuch as the ego here makes the object its conception and negates it, this philosophy is Idealism, in which
philosophy all the determinations of the object are ideal.
Everything determinate which the ego possesses it has
through its own positing; I even make a coat or a boot
because I put them on. There remains only the empty
repulsive force, and that is the Kantian Thing-in-itself,
beyond which even Fichte cannot get, even though the
theoretic reason continues its determination into infinitude.
"The ego as intelligence" ever "remains dependent on
an undetermined non-ego; it is only through this that it is
intelligence."[2] The theoretic side is thus dependent. In

[1] Fichte: Grundlage der gesammten Wissenschaftslehre, pp.
194-197, 204, 221, 222.
[2] Ibidem, p. 228.

it we have not therefore to deal with the truth in and for itself, but with a contingent, because ego is limited, not absolute, as its Notion demands: intelligence is not here considered as spirit which is free. This is Fichte's standpoint as regards the theoretic side.

c. Practical reason comes next; the point of view from which it starts is that "The ego posits itself as determining the non-ego." Now the contradiction has thus to be solved of ego being at home with itself, since it determines its Beyond. The ego is thus infinite activity, and, as ego= ego, the absolute ego, it is undoubtedly abstract. But in order to have a determination, a non-ego must exist; ego is thus activity, causality, the positing of the non-ego. But as with Kant sensuousness and reason remain opposed, the same contradiction is present here, only in a more abstract form, and not in the rude empiricism of Kant. Fichte here turns and twists in all sorts of ways, or he gives the opposition many different forms; the crudest form is that ego is posited as causality, for in it another is necessitated on which it exercises its activity. "The absolute ego has accordingly to be" now "the cause of the non-ego, *i.e.* only of that in the non-ego which remains when we abstract from all demonstrable forms of representation or conception—of that to which is ascribed the check given to the infinitely operative activity of the ego; for the fact that the intelligent ego is, in accordance with the necessary laws of the conception, the cause of the particular determinations of that which is conceived as such, is demonstrated in the theoretic science of knowledge."[1] The limits of intelligence must be broken through, the ego must alone be active; the other side, the infinite repulsion, must be removed, in order that the ego may be liberated.

[1] Fichte: Grundlage der gesammten Wissenschaftslehre, pp. 225, 229, 232.

"According to our hypothesis the ego must now posit a non-ego absolutely, and without any ground, *i.e.* absolutely and without any ground it must limit or in part not posit itself." This, indeed, it already does as intelligent. "It must therefore have the ground of not positing itself" only "in itself." The ego is, however, just the ego, it posits itself, "it must" therefore "have the principle of positing itself within it, and also the principle of not positing itself. Hence the ego in its essence would be contradictory and self-repellent; there would be in it a twofold or contradictory principle, which assumption contradicts itself, for in that case there would be no principle within it. The ego would" consequently "not exist, for it would abrogate itself. All contradictions are reconciled through the further determination of contradictory propositions. The ego must be posited in one sense as infinite, and in another as finite. Were it to be posited as infinite and finite in one and the same sense, the contradiction would be insoluble; the ego would not be one but two. In so far as the ego posits itself as infinite, its activity is directed upon itself and on nothing else but itself. In so far as the ego posits limits, and itself in these limits, its activity is not exercised directly on itself, but on a non-ego which has to be placed in opposition," upon another and again upon another, and so on into infinitude; that is the object, and the activity of the ego "is objective activity."[1] In this way Fichte in the practical sphere also remains at opposition, only this opposition now has the form of two tendencies in the ego, both of which are said to be one and the same activity of the ego. I am called upon to proceed to determine the other in relation to which I am negative, the non-ego, in accordance with my freedom; it has indeed all determinations through the activity of

---

[1] Fichte : Grundlage der gesammten Wissenschaftslehre, pp. 233, 238, 239.

the ego, but beyond my determination the same non-ego. ever continues to appear. The ego clearly posits an object, a point of limitation, but where the limitation is, is undetermined. I may transfer the sphere of my determination, and extend it to an infinite degree, but there always remains a pure Beyond, and the non-ego has no positive self-existent determination.

The last point in respect of the practical sphere is hence this, that the activity of the ego is a yearning or striving [1] —like the Kantian "ought"; Fichte treats this with great prolixity. The Fichtian philosophy consequently has the same standpoint as the Kantian; the ultimate is always subjectivity, as existent in and for itself. Yearning, according to Fichte, is divine; in yearning I have not forgotten myself, I have not forgotten that I possess a superiority in myself; and therefore it is a condition of happiness and satisfaction. This infinite yearning and desire has then been regarded as what is highest and most excellent in the Beautiful, and in religious feelings likewise; and with it is connected the irony of which we have spoken before (Vol. I. pp. 400, 401). In this return the ego is merely an effort, on its side it is fixed, and it cannot realize its endeavours. Striving is thus an imperfect or implicitly limited action. The ultimate result is consequently a "circle" which cannot be broken through, so that "the finite spirit must necessarily posit an absolute outside itself (a thing-in-itself), and yet on the other hand it must recognize that this same is only there for it (a necessary noumenon)." [2] To put it otherwise, we see the ego absolutely determined in opposition only, we see it only as consciousness and self-consciousness which does not get beyond this, and which does not reach so far as to Spirit. The ego is the absolute Notion in so far as it does

---

[1] Fichte: Grundlage der gesammten Wissenschaftslehre, pp. 302, 246, 247.

[2] Ibidem, p. 273.

not yet reach the unity of thought, or in this simplicity does not reach difference, and in motion does not have rest; that is to say, in so far as positing, or the pure activity of the ego, and setting in opposition, are not by it comprehended as the same. Or the ego does not comprehend the infinite repulsion, the non-ego; self-consciousness determines the non-ego, but does not know how to make this Beyond its own.

The deficiency in the Fichtian philosophy is thus firstly that the ego retains the significance of the individual, actual self-consciousness, as opposed to that which is universal or absolute, or to the spirit in which it is itself a moment merely; for the individual self-consciousness simply signifies standing apart as far as another is concerned. Hence, if the ego was ever called absolute existence, the most terrible offence was given, because really the ego only came before us as signifying the individual subject as opposed to the universal.

In the second place, Fichte does not attain to the idea of Reason as the perfected, real unity of subject and object, or of ego and non-ego; it is only, as with Kant, represented as the thought of a union in a belief or faith, and with this Fichte likewise concludes (Grundlage der gesammten Wissenschaftslehre, p. 301). This he worked out in his popular writings. For because the ego is fixed in its opposition to the non-ego, and *is* only as being opposed, it becomes lost in that unity. The attainment of this aim is hence sent further and further back into the false, sensuous infinitude: it is a progression implying just the same contradiction as that found in Kant, and having no present actuality in itself; for the ego has all actuality in its opposition only. The Fichtian philosophy recognizes the finite spirit alone, and not the infinite; it does not recognize spirit as universal thought, as the Kantian philosophy does not recognize the not-true; or it is formal. The knowledge of absolute unity is apprehended as faith in a moral disposition of the world, an absolute hypothesis in accordance with which we have the belief that every moral action that we perform will have a good result.[1] As in Kant's case, this Idea belongs to universal thought. " In a word, when anything is apprehended it ceases to be God ; and every conception of God that is set up is necessarily that of a false God. Religion is a practical faith in the moral government of the world; faith in a supersensuous world belongs, according to our philosophy, to the immediate verities." [2] Fichte thus concludes with the highest Idea, with the union of freedom and nature, but a union of such a nature that, immediately regarded, it is not known ; the opposition alone falls within consciousness. This union of faith he likewise finds in the Love of God. As believed and experienced, this form pertains to Religion, and not to Philosophy, and our only possible interest is to know this in Philosophy. But with Fichte it is still associated with a most unsatisfying externality of which the basis is the non-Idea, for the one determination is essential only because the other is so, and so on into infinitude. " The theory of knowledge is realistic—it shows that the consciousness of finite beings can only be explained by presupposing an independent and wholly opposite power, on which, in accordance with their empirical existence, they themselves are dependent. But it asserts nothing more than this opposed power, which by finite beings can merely be *felt* and not known. All possible determinations of this power or of this non-ego which can come forth into infinity in our consciousness, it pledges itself to deduce from the determining faculties of the ego, and it must actually be able to deduce these, so certainly as it is a theory of knowledge. This knowledge, however, is not transcendent but

[1] Fichte : Ueber den Grund unseres Glaubens an eine göttliche Weltregierung (Fichte's Leben, Part II.), p. 111.

[2] Fichte: Verantwortungsschreiben gegen die Anklage des Atheismus, pp. 51, 53.

transcendental. It undoubtedly explains all consciousness
from something independent of all consciousness, but it
does not forget that this independent somewhat is again a
product of its own power of thought, and consequently
something dependent on the ego, in so far as it has to be
there for the ego.   Every thing is, in its ideality, dependent upon the ego ; but in its reality even the ego is dependent.   The fact that the finite spirit must posit for itself
somewhat outside of itself, which last exists only for it,
is that circle which it may infinitely extend but never
break through."   The further logical determination of the
object is that which in subject and object is identical, the
true connection is that in which the objective is the possession of the ego ; as thought, the ego in itself determines
the object.   But Fichte's theory of knowledge regards the
struggle of the ego with the object as that of the continuous process of determining the object through the
ego as subject of consciousness, without the identity of the
restfully self-developing Notion.

Thirdly, because the ego is thus fixed in its one-
sidedness, there proceeds from it, as representing one
extreme, the whole of the progress that is made in the content of knowledge ; and the deduction of the philosophy of
Fichte, cognition in its content and form, is a progression
from certain determinations to others which do not turn
back into unity, or through a succession of finitenesses
which do not have the Absolute in them at all.   The absolute
point of view, like an absolute content, is wanting.   Thus
the contemplation of nature, for instance, is a contemplation
of it as of pure finitenesses from the point of view of
another, as though the organic body were regarded thus :
" Consciousness requires a sphere entirely its own for its
activity.   This sphere is posited through an original,

----

[1] Fichte: Grundlage der gesammten Wissenschaftslehre, pp. 272-
274.

necessary activity of the ego, in which it does not know itself as free. It is a sensuous perception, a drawing of lines; the sphere of activity thereby becomes something extended in space. As quiescent, continuous, and yet unceasingly changing, this sphere is matter, which, as body, has a number of parts which in relation to one another are called limbs. The person can ascribe to himself no body without positing it as being under the influence of another person. But it is likewise essential that I should be able to check this same influence, and external matter is also posited as resisting my influences on it, *i.e.* as a tough, compact matter."[1] These tough matters must further be separated from one another—the different persons cannot hold together like one mass of dough. For "my body is my body and not that of another; it must further operate and be active without my working through it. It is only through the operation of another that I can myself be active and represent myself as a rational being who can be respected by him. But the other being should treat me immediately as a rational being, I should be for him a rational being even before my activity begins. Or my form must produce an effect through its mere existence in space, without my activity, *i.e.* it must be visible. The reciprocal operation of rational beings must take place without activity; thus a subtle matter must be assumed in order that it may be modified by means of the merely quiescent form. In this way are deduced first Light and then Air."[2] This constitutes a very external manner of passing from one step to another, resembling the method of the ordinary teleology, which makes out, for instance, that plants and animals are given for the nourishment of mankind. This is how it is put: Man must eat, and thus there

---

[1] Fichte: Grundlage des Naturrechts (Jena und Leipzig, 1796), Part I. pp. 55-71.
[2] Ibidem, pp. 78-82.

must be something edible—consequently plants and animals are at once deduced ; plants must have their root in something, and consequently the earth is forthwith deduced. What is altogether lacking is any consideration of the object as what it is in itself ; it is plainly considered only in relation to another. In this way the animal organism appears as a tough, tenacious matter which is " articulated " and can be modified ; light is a subtle matter which is the medium of communication of mere existence, &c.—just as in the other case plants and animals are merely edible. As regards a philosophic consideration of the content there is nothing at all to be found.

Fichte likewise wrote both a Science of Morals and of Natural Rights, but he treats them as sciences pertaining to the understanding only, and his method of procedure is destitute of ideas and carried on by means of a limited understanding. The Fichtian deduction of the conceptions of justice and morality thus remains within the limitations and rigidity of self-consciousness, as against which Fichte's popular presentations of religion and morality present inconsistencies. The treatise on Natural Rights is a special failure, *e.g.* where he, as we have just seen (p. 502), deduces even nature just as far as he requires it. The organization of the state which is described in Fichte's Science of Rights is furthermore as unspiritual as was the deduction of natural objects just mentioned, and as were many of the French constitutions which have appeared in modern times—a formal, external uniting and connecting, in which the individuals as such are held to be absolute, or in which Right is the highest principle. Kant began to ground Right upon Freedom, and Fichte likewise makes freedom the principle in the Rights of Nature ; but, as was the case with Rousseau, it is freedom in the form of the isolated individual. This is a great commencement, but in order to arrive at the particular, they have to accept certain hypotheses. The universal is not the spirit, the substance of the whole, but an external, negative power of the finite understanding directed against individuals. The state is not apprehended in its essence, but only as representing a condition of justice and law, *i.e.* as an external relation of finite to finite. There are various individuals; the whole constitution of the state is thus in the main characterized by the fact that the freedom of individuals must be limited by means of the freedom of the whole.[1] The individuals always maintain a cold attitude of negativity as regards one another, the confinement becomes closer and the bonds more stringent as time goes on, instead of the state being regarded as representing the realization of freedom.

This philosophy contains nothing speculative, but it demands the presence of the speculative element. As the philosophy of Kant seeks in unity its Idea of the Supreme Good, wherein the opposites have to be united, so the Fichtian philosophy demands union in the ego and in the implicitude of faith; in this self-consciousness in all its actions makes its starting-point conviction, so that in themselves its actions may bring forth the highest end and realize the good. In the Fichtian philosophy nothing can be seen beyond the moment of self-consciousness, of self-conscious Being-within-self, as in the philosophy of England we find expressed—in just as one-sided a way—the moment of Being-for-another, or of consciousness, and that not as a moment simply, but as the principle of the truth; in neither of the two is there the unity of both—or spirit.

Fichte's philosophy constitutes a significant epoch in Philosophy regarded in its outward form. It is from him and from his methods that abstract thought proceeds, deduction and construction. Hence with the Fichtian philosophy a revolution took place in Germany. The public had penetrated as far as the philosophy of Kant, and until

---

[1] Fichte: Grundlage des Naturrechts, Part II. p. 21.

the Kantian philosophy was reached the interest awakened by Philosophy was general; it was accessible, and men were curious to know about it, it pertained to the ordinary knowledge of a man of culture (*supra*, p. 218). Formerly men of business, statesmen, occupied themselves with Philosophy; now, however, with the intricate idealism of the philosophy of Kant, their wings droop helpless to the ground. Hence it is with Kant that we first begin to find a line of separation which parts us from the common modes of consciousness; but the result, that the Absolute cannot be known, has become one generally acknowledged. With Fichte the common consciousness has still further separated itself from Philosophy, and it has utterly departed from the speculative element therein present. For Fichte's ego is not merely the ego of the empiric consciousness, since general determinations of thought such as do not fall within the ordinary consciousness have likewise to be known and brought to consciousness; in this way since Fichte's time few men have occupied themselves with speculation. Fichte, it is true, in his later works especially, wrote with a view to meeting the popular ear as we may see in the " Attempt to force the reader into comprehension," but this end was not accomplished. The public was through the philosophy of Kant and Jacobi strengthened in its opinion—one which it accepted *utiliter*—that the knowledge of God is immediate, and that we know it from the beginning and without requiring to study, and hence that Philosophy is quite superfluous.

2. Fichte's System in a Re-constituted Form.

The times called for life, for spirit. Now since mind has thus retreated within self-consciousness, but within self-consciousness as a barren ego, which merely gives itself a content or a realization through finitenesses and individualities which in and for themselves are nothing, the next stage is found in knowing this realization of self-consciousness in itself, in knowing the content in itself as a content which, penetrated throughout by spirit, is self-conscious and spiritual, or a spirit full of content. In his later popular works Fichte thus set forth faith, love, hope, religion, treating them without philosophic interest, and as for a general public: it was a philosophy calculated to suit enlightened Jews and Jewesses, councillors and Kotzebues. He places the matter in a popular form: "It is not the finite ego that is, but the divine Idea is the foundation of all Philosophy; everything that man does of himself is null and void. All existence is living and active in itself, and there is no other life than Being, and no other Being than God; God is thus absolute Being and Life. The divine essence likewise comes forth, revealing and manifesting itself—the world."[1] This immediate unity of the self-conscious ego and its content, or spirit, which merely has an intuition of its self-conscious life and knows it as the truth immediately, manifested itself subsequently in poetic and prophetic tendencies, in vehement aspirations, in excrescences which grew out of the Fichtian philosophy.

3. The more Important of the Followers of Fichte.

On the one hand, in respect of the content which the ego reaches in the philosophy of Fichte, the complete absence of spirituality, the woodenness, and, to put it plainly, the utter foolishness therein evidenced, strike us too forcibly to allow us to remain at his standpoint; our philosophic perception likewise tells us of the one-sidedness and deficiencies of the principle, as also of the evident necessity that the content should prove to be what

---

[1] Rixner: Handbuch d. Gesch. d. Phil. Vol. III., § 192, p. 416; Fichte: Ueber das Wesen des Gelehrten (Berlin, 1806), pp. 4, 5, 15, 25-27.

it is. But on the other hand self-consciousness was therein posited as reality or essence—not as a foreign, alien self-consciousness, but as ego—a signification which all possess, and which finds an answer in the actuality of all. The Fichtian standpoint of subjectivity has thus retained its character of being unphilosophically worked out, and arrived at its completion in forms pertaining to sensation which in part remained within the Fichtian principle, while they were in part the effort—futile though it was— to get beyond the subjectivity of the ego.

a. FRIEDRICH VON SCHLEGEL.

In Fichte's case the limitation is continually re-appearing ; but because the ego feels constrained to break through this barrier, it reacts against it, and gives itself a resting-place within itself; this last ought to be concrete, but it is a negative resting-place alone. This first form, Irony, has Friedrich von Schlegel as its leading exponent. The subject here knows itself to be within itself the Absolute, and all else to it is vain ; all the conclusions which it draws for itself respecting the right and good, it likewise knows how to destroy again. It can make a pretence of knowing all things, but it only demonstrates vanity, hypocrisy, and effrontery. Irony knows itself to be the master of every possible content; it is serious about nothing, but plays with all forms. The other side is this, that subjectivity has cast itself into religious subjectivity. The utter despair in respect of thought, of truth, and absolute objectivity, as also the incapacity to give oneself any settled basis or spontaneity of action, induced the noble soul to abandon itself to feeling and to seek in Religion something fixed and steadfast; this steadfast basis, this inward satisfaction, is to be found in religious sentiments and feelings. This instinct impelling us towards something fixed has forced many into positive forms of religion, into Catholicism, superstition and miracle working, in order that they may find something on which they can rest, because to inward subjectivity everything fluctuates and wavers. With the whole force of its mind subjectivity tries to apply itself to what is positively given, to bend its head beneath the positive, to cast itself, so to speak, into the arms of externality, and it finds an inward power impelling it so to do.

b. SCHLEIERMACHER.

On the other hand the ego finds in the subjectivity and individuality of the personal view of things the height of all its vanity—its Religion. All the various individualities have God within themselves. Dialectic is the last thing to arise and to maintain its place. As this is expressed for philosophic self-consciousness, the foreign intellectual world has lost all significance and truth for ordinary culture; it is composed of three elements, a deity pertaining to a time gone by, and individualized in space and existence, a world which is outside the actuality of self-consciousness, and a world which had yet to appear, and in which self-consciousness would first attain to its reality. The spirit of culture has deserted it, and no longer recognizes anything that is foreign to self-consciousness. In accordance with this principle, the spiritual living essence has then transformed itself into self-consciousness, and it thinks to know the unity of spirit immediately from itself, and in this immediacy to be possessed of knowledge in a poetic, or at least a prophetic manner. As regards the poetic manner, it has a knowledge of the life and person of the Absolute immediately, by an intuition, and not in the Notion, and it thinks it would lose the whole as whole, as a self-penetrating unity, were it not to express the same in poetic form; and what it thus expresses poetically is the intuition of the personal life of self-consciousness.

But the truth is absolute motion, and since it is a motion of
forms and figures [Gestalten], and the universe is a kingdom
of spirits, the Notion is the essence of this movement, and
likewise of each individual form ; it is its ideal form [Form]
and not the real one, or that of figure [Gestalt]. In the
latter case necessity is lost sight of; individual action,
life and heart, remain within themselves, and undeveloped ;
and this poetry vacillates betwixt the universality of the
Notion and the determinateness and indifference of the figure;
it is neither flesh nor fish, neither poetry nor philosophy.
The prophetic utterance of truths which claim to be philosophical, thus belongs to faith, to self-consciousness, which
indeed perceives the absolute spirit in itself, but does not
comprehend itself as self-consciousness, since it places
absolute reality above Knowledge, beyond self-conscious
reason, as was done by Eschenmayer and Jacobi. This
uncomprehending, prophetic manner of speech affirms this
or that respecting absolute existence as from an oracle, and
requires that each man should find the same immediately
in his own heart. The knowledge of absolute reality
becomes a matter pertaining to the heart; there are a
number of would-be inspired speakers, each of whom holds
a monologue and really does not understand the others,
excepting by a pressure of the hands and betrayal of dumb
feeling. What they say is mainly composed of trivialities, if
these are taken in the sense in which they are uttered ; it is
the feeling, the gesture, the fulness of the heart, which first
gives them their significance ; to nothing of more importance
is direct expression given. They outbid one another in
conceits of fancy, in ardent poetry. But before the Truth
vanity turns pale, spitefully sneering it sneaks back into
itself. Ask not after a criterion of the truth, but after the
Notion of the truth in and for itself ; on that fix your gaze.
The glory of Philosophy is departed, for it presupposes a
common ground of thoughts and principles—which is what
science demands—or at least of opinions. But now par-

ticular subjectivity was everything, each individual was proud and disdainful as regards all others. The conception of independent thought—as though there could be a thought which was not such (Vol. I. p. 60)—is very much the same; men have, it is said, to bring forth a particularity of their own, or else they have not thought for themselves. But the bad picture is that in which the artist shows himself; originality is the production of what is in its entirety universal. The folly of independent thought is that it results in each bringing forth something more preposterous than another.

c. Novalis.

Subjectivity signifies the lack of a firm and steady basis, but likewise the desire for such, and thus it evermore remains a yearning. These yearnings of a lofty soul are set forth in the writings of Novalis. This subjectivity does not reach substantiality, it dies away within itself, and the standpoint it adopts is one of inward workings and fine distinctions; it signifies an inward life and deals with the minutiæ of the truth. The extravagances of subjectivity constantly pass into madness; if they remain in thought they are whirled round and round in the vortex of reflecting understanding, which is ever negative in reference to itself.

d. Fries, Bouterweck, Krug.

Yet a last form of subjectivity is the subjectivity of arbitrary will and ignorance. It maintained this, that the highest mode of cognition is an immediate knowledge as a fact of consciousness; and that is so far right. The Fichtian abstraction and its hard understanding has a repellent effect on thought; slothful reason allowed itself to be told the result of the philosophy of Kant and Jacobi, and renounced all consistent thought, all construction. This arbitrariness gave itself entire liberty—the liberty of the *Tabagie*—but in doing so it regarded itself from a poetic or prophetic point of view, as we have just seen (pp. 508, 509). Then it was both more sober and more prosaic, and thus brought the old logic and metaphysic once more into evidence, though with this modification that they are made facts of consciousness. Thus Fries turns back to the faith of Jacobi in the form of immediate judgments derived from reason, and dark conceptions incapable of utterance.[1] He wished to improve the critique of pure reason by apprehending the categories as facts of consciousness; anything one chooses can in such a case be introduced. Bouterweck speaks of "The virtue, the living nature of power ; the fact that subject and object are regarded as one, that is as absolute virtue. With this absolute virtue we have all Being and action, namely the eternal, absolute and pure unity ; in one word we have grasped the world within us and we have grasped ourselves in the world, and that indeed not through conceptions and conclusions, but directly through the power which itself constitutes our existence and our rational nature. To know the All, or indeed to know God in any way, is, however, impossible for any mortal."[2] Krug wrote a "Groundwork of Philosophy," setting forth a "Transcendental Synthesis—that is a transcendental realism and a transcendental idealism inseparably bound together." It is an "original, transcendental synthesis of the real and the ideal, the thinking subject and the corresponding outer world ;" this transcen-

---

[1] Rixner: Handbuch d. Gesch. d. Phil. Vol. III. § 158, pp. 350, 351 ; Fries : Neue Kritik d. Vernunft (First edition, Heidelberg, 1807), Vol. I. pp. 75, 281, 284, 343 ; 206.

[2] Rixner: Handbuch d. Gesch. d. Phil. Vol. III. § 156, pp. 347, 348 ; cf. Bouterweck's Apodiktik (1799), Part II. pp. 206-212.

dental synthesis must "be recognized and asserted without any attempt being made at explaining it." [1]

D. SCHELLING.

It was Schelling, finally, who made the most important, or, from a philosophic point of view, the only important advance upon the philosophy of Fichte ; his philosophy rose higher than that of Fichte, though undoubtedly it stood in close connection with it ; indeed, he himself professes to be a Fichtian. Now the philosophy of Schelling from the first admitted the possibility of a knowledge of God, although it likewise started from the philosophy of Kant, which denies such knowledge. At the same time Schelling makes Jacobi's principle of the unity of thought and Being fundamental, although he begins to determine it more closely. [2] To him concrete unity is this, that the finite is no more true than the infinite, the subjective idea no more than objectivity, and that combinations in which both untruths are brought together in their independence in relation to one another, are likewise combinations of untruths merely. Concrete unity can only be comprehended as process and as the living movement in a proposition. This inseparability is in God alone ; the finite, on the other hand, is that which has this separability within it. In so far as it is a truth it is likewise this unity, but in a limited sphere, and for that reason in the separability of both moments.

Frederick Wilhelm Joseph Schelling, born on the 27th January, 1775, at Schorndorf,[3] in Würtemberg, studied in

[1] Krug : Entwurf eines neuen Organon der Philosophie (Meissen, 1801), pp. 75, 76; Rixner : Handbuch d. Geschichte d. Philosophie, Vol. III. § 157, p. 349.

[2] Schelling's philosophische Schriften (Landshut, 1809, Vol. I. Vom Ich als Princip der Philosophie, pp. 1-114), pp. 3, 4 (first edition, Tübingen, 1795, pp. 4-7).

[3] His birthplace is usually stated to have been Leonberg, a short distance from Schorndorf.—[Translators' note.]

Leipzig and Jena, where he came to be on terms of great intimacy with Fichte. In the year 1807 he became secretary of the Academy of Science in Munich. We cannot with propriety deal fully with his life, for he is still living.[1]

Schelling worked out his philosophy in view of the public. The series of his philosophic writings also represents the history of his philosophic development and the gradual process by which he raised himself above the Fichtian principle and the Kantian content with which he began. It does not thus contain a sequence of separately worked out divisions of Philosophy, but only successive stages in his own development. If we ask for a final work in which we shall find his philosophy represented with complete definiteness none such can be named. Schelling's first writings are still quite Fichtian, and it is only by slow degrees that he worked himself free of Fichte's form. The form of the ego has the ambiguity of being capable of signifying either the absolute Ego or God, or ego in my particularity;[2] this supplied the first stimulus to Schelling. His first and quite short work of four sheets which he wrote in 1795 at Tübingen, while still at the university, was called, "On the Possibility of any Form of Philosophy"; it contains propositions respecting the Fichtian philosophy only. The next work, "On the Ego as principle of Philosophy, or on the Unconditioned in Human Knowledge" (Tübingen, 1795), is likewise quite Fichtian; in this case, however, it is from a wider and more universal point of view, since the ego is therein grasped as an original identity.[3] We find, however, a summary of the Fichtian principle and the Kantian mode of presentation: "It is only by something being originally set in opposition to the ego, and by the ego being itself

---

[1] Lectures of 1816-1817. [Translators' note.]

[2] Schelling's philosophische Schriften: Vom Ich als Princip der Philosophie, p. 99 seq. (p. 178 seq.).

[3] Ibidem, pp. 23, 24 (pp. 38-42).

posited as the manifold (in time), that it is possible for the ego to get beyond the unity which belongs to it of merely being posited, and that, for example, it posits the same content on more than one occasion."[1] Schelling then passed on to natural philosophy, adopted Kantian forms and reflective determinations, such as those of repulsion and attraction, from Kant's "Metaphysics of Nature," and likewise dealt with quite empirical phenomena in expressions taken from Kant. All his first works on this subject come under this category, viz. : "Ideas towards a Philosophy of Nature," 1797 ; "On the World-Soul," 1798, the second edition of which possesses appendices which are entirely inconsistent with what goes before. In the writings of Herder and Kielmeyer[2] we find sensibility, irritability, and reproduction dealt with, as also their laws, such as that the greater the sensibility the less the irritability, &c.—just as the powers or potencies were dealt with by Eschenmayer. It was only later on in relation to these that Schelling first apprehended nature in the categories of thought, and made general attempts of a more definite character in the direction of greater scientific development. It was only through what had been accomplished by these men that he was enabled to come into public notice so young. The spiritual and intellectual side, morality and the state, he represented on the other hand purely in accordance with Kantian principles : thus in his "Transcendental Idealism," although it was written from a Fichtian point of view, he goes no further than Kant did in his "Philosophy of Rights" and his work "On Eternal Peace." Schelling, indeed, later on published a separate treatise on Freedom, deeply speculative in character ; this, however, remains isolated and independent, and deals with this one point alone ; in Philosophy, however, nothing isolated can be worked out or developed.

[1] Ibidem, p. 83 (p. 150).
[2] Schelling's System des transcendentalen Idealismus, p. 257, not. Zeitschrift für speculative Physik, Vol. II. No. 2, p. 92.

In the various presentations of his views Schelling on each occasion began again from the beginning, because, as we may see, what went before did not satisfy him; he has ever pressed on to seek a new form, and thus he has tried various forms and terminologies in succession without ever setting forth one complete and consistent whole. His principal works in this connection are the " First Sketch of a System of Natural Philosophy," 1799; the " System of Transcendental Idealism," 1800, one of his most carefully thoughtout works; "Bruno, a Dialogue on the Divine and Natural Principle of Things," 1802; "Journal of Speculative Physics," 1801; "New Journal of Speculative Physics," 1802 *et seq.* In the second number of the second volume of his " Journal of Speculative Physics," Schelling made the commencement of a detailed treatment of the whole of his philosophy. Here he likewise starts to a certain measure, though unconsciously, from the Fichtian form of construction; but the idea is already present that nature equally with knowledge is a system of reason.

It is not feasible here to go into details respecting what is called the philosophy of Schelling, even if time permitted. For it is not yet a scientific whole organized in all its branches, since it rather consists in certain general elements which do not fluctuate with the rest of his opinions. Schelling's philosophy must still be regarded as in process of evolution, and it has not yet ripened into fruit; [1] we can hence give a general idea of it only.

When Schelling made his first appearance the demands put forward by Philosophy were as follows. With Descartes thought and extension were in some incomprehensible way united in God, with Spinoza it was as motionless substance; and beyond this point of view neither of them ever passed. Later on we saw the form develop, partly in the sciences and partly in the Kantian philosophy. Finally, in the Fichtian

---

[1] Lectures of 1805-1806.

philosophy, the form was subjectivity on its own account, from which all determinations were held to develop. What is thus demanded is that this subjectivity of infinite form which we saw dying into irony or arbitrariness (pp. 507–510) should be delivered from its one-sidedness in order to be united with objectivity and substantiality. To put it otherwise, the substance of Spinoza should not be apprehended as the unmoved, but as the intelligent, as a form which possesses activity within itself of necessity, so that it is the forming power of nature, but at the same time knowledge and comprehension. This then is the object of Philosophy; it is not the formal union of Spinoza that is demanded, nor the subjective totality of Fichte, but totality with the infinite form. We see this developing in the philosophy of Schelling.

1. In one of his earlier writings, the "System of Transcendental Idealism," which we shall consider first of all, Schelling represented transcendental philosophy and natural philosophy as the two sides of scientific knowledge. Respecting the nature of the two, he expressly declared himself in this work, where he once more adopts a Fichtian starting-point: "All knowledge rests on the harmony of an objective with a subjective." In the common sense of the words this would be allowed; absolute unity, where the Notion and the reality are undistinguished in the perfected Idea, is the Absolute alone, or God; all else contains an element of discord between the objective and subjective. "We may give the name of nature to the entire objective content of our knowledge; the entire subjective content, on the other hand, is called the ego or intelligence." They are in themselves identical and presupposed as identical. The relation of nature to intelligence is given by Schelling thus: "Now if all knowledge has two poles which mutually presuppose and demand one another, there must be two fundamental sciences, and it must be impossible to start from the one pole without being driven to the

other." Thus nature is impelled to spirit, and spirit to nature; either may be given the first place, and both must come to pass. "If the objective is made the chief," we have the natural sciences as result, and " the necessary tendency," the end, " of all natural science thus is to pass from nature to intelligence. This is the meaning of the effort to connect natural phenomena with theory. The highest perfection of natural science would be the perfect spiritualization of all natural laws into laws of intuitive perception and thought. The phenomenal (the material element) must entirely disappear, and laws (the formal element) alone remain. Hence it comes to pass that the more that which is in conformity with law breaks forth in nature itself, the more the outward covering disappears; the phenomena themselves become more spiritual, and finally cease altogether. The perfect theory of nature would be that by which the whole of nature should be resolved into an intelligence. The dead and unconscious products of nature are only abortive attempts on the part of nature to reflect itself, but the so-called dead nature is really an immature," torpid, fossilized "intelligence"; it is implicit only, and thus remains in externality; " hence in its phenomena," even though "still unconsciously, the character of intelligence shines through. Its highest end, which is to become object to itself, is first attained by nature" (instead of nature we should call it the Idea of nature), " through its highest and ultimate reflection, which is none other than man, or, more generally, it is that which we call reason, through which nature for the first time returns completely within itself, and whereby it becomes evident that nature is originally identical with what is known in us as intelligence or the conscious. Through this tendency to make nature intelligent natural science becomes the philosophy of nature." The intelligent character of nature is thus spoken of as a postulate of science. The other point of view is "to give the sub

jective the foremost place." Thus here "the problem is
how to add an objective element agreeing with it. To start
from the subjective as from the first and absolute, and to
make the objective arise from it," signifies a new departure; its consideration forms the content of true Transcendental Philosophy, or, as Schelling himself now named this
science, "the other science fundamental to Philosophy."
The organ of transcendental philosophy is the subjective,
the production of inward action. Production and reflection
upon this production, the unconscious and conscious in
one, is the æsthetic act of the imagination.[1] Thus these
two separate processes are as a whole very clearly expressed : the process which leads from nature to the subject,
and that leading from the ego to the object. But the true
process could only be traced out by means of logic, for
it contains pure thoughts ; but the logical point of view
was what Schelling never arrived at in his presentation of
things.

a. In respect of the ego, as principle of the transcendental philosophy, Schelling sets to work in the same
way as did Fichte, inasmuch as he begins from the fact of
knowledge " in which the content is conditioned through
the form, and the form through the content "; this is formal
$A=A$. But does A exist ? The ego is "the point where
subject and object are one in their unmediated condition ";
the ego is just $Ego = Ego$, subject-object; and that
is the act of self-consciousness wherein I am for myself
object to myself. In self-consciousness there is not to be
found a distinction between me and anything else ; what
are distinguished are directly identical, and there is so far
nothing at all in opposition to this self-consciousness.
How the case stands with regard to external objects is the
question which must be decided later, in the further course
of development. It is only the Notion of the ego which is

---

[1] Schelling : System des transcendentalen Idealismus, pp. 1-7, 17-21.

to be laid hold of: "The Notion of the ego, that is the act
whereby thought in general becomes object to itself, and
the ego itself (the object) are absolutely one ; independently
of this act the ego is nothing." It is the act whereby
thought makes itself objective, and wherein the ego is
brought into harmony with the objective, with thought ;
and from this standpoint it had to be demonstrated how
the ego makes its way to objectivity. "The ego, as pure
act, as pure action, is not objective in knowledge itself, for
the reason that it is the principle of all knowledge. If it
is to be object of knowledge, this must come to pass
through a very different kind of knowledge than the
ordinary." The immediate consciousness of this identity
is intuition, but inwardly it becomes "intellectual intuition "·; it " is a knowledge which is the production of its
object : sensuous intuition or perception is perception of
such a nature that the perception itself appears to be different from what is perceived. Now intellectual intuition is
the organ of all transcendental thought," the act of pure
self-consciousness generally. " The ego is nothing else
than a process of production which ever makes itself its
own object. Science can start from nothing objective,"
but from " the non-objective which itself becomes object "
as an " original duplicity. Idealism is the mechanism of
the origination of the objective world from the inward
principle of spiritual activity." [1]

On the one hand Schelling's system is related to the
philosophy of Fichte, and, on the other hand, he, like
Jacobi, makes his principle immediate knowledge—the intelligent intuitive perception which all who wish to philosophize must have. But what comes next is that its
content is no longer the indeterminate, the essence of
essence, but likewise the Absolute, God, the absolutely
self-existent, though expressed as concrete, *i.e.* as mediating

---

[1] Schelling : System des transcendentalen Idealismus, pp. 24-46,
49-52, 55-58, 63-65.

itself within itself, as the absolute unity or indifference of subjective and objective. Intellectual intuition is the Fichtian imagination oscillating between two different points. We have already spoken above (p. 417) of the *form* of intellectual intuition ; it is the most convenient manner of asserting knowledge respecting—anything one likes. But the immediate knowledge of God as spiritual is only in the consciousness of Christian nations, and not for others. This immediate knowledge appears to be still more contingent as the intellectual intuition of the concrete, or the identity of subjectivity and objectivity. This intuition is intellectual indeed, because it is a rational intuition, and as knowledge it is likewise absolutely one with the object of knowledge. But this intuition, although itself knowledge, is not as yet known ; it is the unmediated, the postulated. As it is in this way an immediate we must possess it, and what may be possessed may likewise not be possessed. Thus since the immediate pre-supposition in Philosophy is that individuals have the immediate intuition of this identity of subjective and objective, this gave the philosophy of Schelling the appearance of indicating that the presence of this intuition in individuals demanded a special talent, genius, or condition of mind of their own, or as though it were generally speaking an accidental faculty which pertained to the specially favoured few. For the immediate, the intuitively perceived, is in the form of an existent, and is not thus an essential; and whoever does not understand the intellectual intuition must come to the conclusion that he does not possess it. Or else, in order to understand it, men must give themselves the trouble of possessing it; but no one can tell whether he has it or not—not even from understanding it, for we may merely think we understand it. Philosophy, however, is in its own nature capable of being universal; for its ground-work is thought, and it is through thought that man is man. Schelling's principle is thus indeed clearly a

universal ; but if a definite intuition, a definite consciousness is demanded, such as the consciousness or intuition of
the identity of subjective and objective, this determinate
particular thought is not as yet to be found in it.

It was, however, in this form of knowledge of the
absolute as concrete, and, further, in the form of unity of
subjective and objective, that Philosophy as represented by
Schelling more especially marked itself off .from the
ordinary conceiving consciousness and its mode of reflection.   Even less than Fichte did Schelling attain to popularity (*supra,* pp. 504, 505), for the concrete in its nature
is directly speculative.   The concrete content, God, life, or
whatever particular form it has, is indeed the content and
object of natural consciousness ; but the difficulty lies in
bringing what is contained in the concrete into concrete
thought in accordance with its different determinations,
and in laying hold of the unity.   It pertains to the standpoint of the understanding to divide and to distinguish,
and to maintain the finite thought-determinations in their
opposition ; but Philosophy demands that these different
thoughts should be brought together.   Thought begins by
holding apart infinite and finite, cause and effect, positive
and negative ; since this is the region of reflecting consciousness, the old metaphysical consciousness was able to
take part in so doing : but the speculative point of view is
to have this opposition before itself and to reconcile it.
With Schelling the speculative form has thus again come
to the front, and philosophy has again obtained a special
character of its own ; the principle of Philosophy, rational
thought in itself, has obtained the form of thought.   In
the philosophy of Schelling the content, the truth, has
once more become the matter of chief importance, whereas
in the Kantian philosophy the point of interest was more
especially stated to be the necessity for investigating subjective knowledge.   This is the standpoint of Schelling's
philosophy in its general aspects.

b. Since in further analysis the distinction between subject and object comes into view and is accepted, there follows the relationship of the ego to its other; with Fichte that forms the second proposition, in which the self-limitation of the ego is posited. The ego posits itself in opposition to itself, since it posits itself as conditioned by the non-ego; that is the infinite repulsion, for this conditionment is the ego itself. Schelling, on the one hand, says: "The ego is unlimited as the ego only in so far as it is limited," as it relates to the non-ego. Only thus does consciousness exist, self-consciousness is a barren determination; through its intuition of self the ego becomes finite to itself. "This contradiction only allows itself to be dissolved by the ego becoming in this finitude infinite to itself, *i.e.* by its having an intuitive perception of itself as an infinite Becoming." The relation of the ego to itself and to the infinite check or force of repulsion is a constant one. On the other hand it is said: "The ego is limited only in so far as it is unlimited;" this limitation is thus necessary in order to be able to get beyond it. The contradiction which we find here remains even if the ego always limits the non-ego. "Both activities—that which makes for infinitude, the limitable, real, objective activity, and the limiting and ideal, mutually pre-suppose one another. Idealism reflects merely on the one, realism on the other, transcendental idealism on both." [1] All this is a tangled mass of abstractions.

c. "Neither through the limiting activity nor through the limited does the ego arrive at self-consciousness. There consequently is a third activity, compounded from the other two, through which the ego of self-consciousness arises; this third is that which oscillates between the two —the struggle between opposing tendencies." There is essential relation only, relative identity; the difference

[1] Schelling: System des transcendentalen Idealismus, pp. 69, 70, 72-79.

therein present thus ever remains. "This struggle cannot be reconciled by one such action, but only by an infinite succession of such," *i.e.* the reconciliation of the opposition between the two tendencies of the ego, the inward and the outward, is, in the infinite course of progression, only an apparent one. In order that it may be complete, the whole inward and outward nature must be presented in all its details: but Philosophy can only set forth the epochs which are most important. "If all the intermediate links in sensation could be set forth, that would necessarily lead us to a deduction of all the qualities in nature, which last is impossible." Now this third activity, which contains the union directly in itself, is a thought in which particularity is already contained. It is the intuitive understanding of Kant, the intelligent intuition or intuitively perceiving intelligence; Schelling, indeed, definitely names this absolute unity of contradictions intellectual intuition. The ego here is not one-sided in regard to what is different; it is identity of the unconscious and the conscious, but not an identity of such a nature that its ground rests on the ego itself.[1]

This ego must be the absolute principle : "All philosophy starts from a principle which as absolute identity is non-objective." For if it is objective, separation is at once posited and it is confronted by another; but the principle is the reconciliation of the opposition, and therefore in and for itself it is non-objective. "Now how should a principle such as this be called forth to consciousness and understood, as is required if it is the condition attached to the comprehension of all philosophy? That it can no more be comprehended through Notions [Begriffe] than set forth, requires no proof." Notion to Schelling signifies a category of the ordinary understanding; Notion is, however, the concrete thought which in itself is infinite. "There thus remains

[1] Schelling : System des transcendentalen Idealismus, pp. 85, 86, 89, 98, 442-444.

nothing more than that it should be set forth in an immediate intuition. If there were such an intuition which had as object the absolutely identical, that which in itself is neither subjective nor objective, and if for such, which," however, " can be an intellectual intuition only, one could appeal to immediate experience," the question would be : " How can this intuition be again made objective, *i.e.* how can it be asserted without doubt that it does not rest on a subjective deception, if there is not a universal objectivity in that intuition, which is recognized by all ? " This intellectual principle in itself should thus be given in an experience so that men may be able to appeal to it. " The objectivity of intellectual intuition is art. The work of art alone reflects to me what is otherwise reflected through nothing—that absolute identical which has already separated itself in the ego itself." The objectivity of identity and the knowledge of the same is art ; in one and the same intuition the ego is here conscious of itself and unconscious.[1] This intellectual intuition which has become objective is objective sensuous intuition—but the Notion, the comprehended necessity, is a very different objectivity.

Thus a principle is presupposed both for the content of philosophy and for subjective philosophizing: on the one hand it is demanded that the attitude adopted should be one of intellectual intuition, and, on the other hand, this principle has to be authenticated, and this takes place in the work of art. This is the highest form of the objectivization of reason, because in it sensuous conception is united with intellectuality, sensuous existence is merely the expression of spirituality. The highest objectivity which the subject attains, the highest identity of subjective and objective, is that which Schelling terms the power of imagination. Art is thus comprehended as what is inmost and highest, that which produces the intellectual and real

[1] Schelling: System des transcendentalen Idealismus, pp. 471, 472, 475.

in one, and philosophizing is conceived as this genius of art. But art and power of imagination are not supreme. For the Idea, spirit, cannot be truly given expression to in the manner in which art expresses its Idea. This last is always a method pertaining to intuitive perception ; and on account of this sensuous form of existence the work of art cannot correspond to the spirit. Thus because the point last arrived at is designated as the faculty of imagination, as art, even in the subject this is a subordinate point of view, and thus in itself this point is not the absolute identity of subjectivity and objectivity. In subjective thought, rational, speculative thought is thus indeed demanded, but if this appears false to you nothing further can be said than that you do not possess intellectual intuition. The proving of anything, the making it comprehensible, is thus abandoned ; a correct apprehension of it is directly demanded, and the Idea is thus assertorically pre-established as principle. The Absolute is the absolute identity of subjective and objective, the absolute indifference of real and ideal, of form and essence, of universal and particular ; in this identity of the two there is neither the one nor the other. But the unity is not abstract, empty, and dry ; that would signify logical identity, classification according to something common to both, in which the difference remains all the while outside. The identity is concrete : it is subjectivity as well as objectivity ; the two are present therein as abrogated and ideal. This identity may easily be shown in the ordinary conception : the conception, we may for example say, is subjective ; it has, too, the determinate content of exclusion in reference to other conceptions ; nevertheless, the conception is simple—it is one act, one unity.

What is lacking in Schelling's philosophy is thus the fact that the point of indifference of subjectivity and objectivity, or the Notion of reason, is absolutely pre-supposed, without any attempt being made at showing that this is the truth.

Schelling often uses Spinoza's form of procedure, and
sets up axioms. In philosophy, when we desire to establish
a position, we demand proof. But if we begin with intellectual intuition, that constitutes an oracle to which we have
to give way, since the existence of intellectual intuition was
made our postulate. The true proof that this identity of subjective and objective is the truth, could only be brought
about by means of each of the two being investigated in
its logical, *i.e.* essential determinations; and in regard to
them, it must then be shown that the subjective signifies
the transformation of itself into the objective, and that the
objective signifies its not remaining such, but making
itself subjective. Similarly in the finite, it would have to
be shown that it contained a contradiction in itself, and
made itself infinite ; in this way we should have the unity
of finite and infinite. In so doing, this unity of opposites is
not asserted beforehand, but in the opposites themselves it
is shown that their truth is their unity, but that each taken
by itself is one-sided—that their difference veers round,
casting itself headlong into this unity—while the understanding all the time thinks that in these differences it
possesses something fixed and secure. The result of thinking
contemplation would in this former case be that each moment
would secretly make itself into its opposite, the identity of
both being alone the truth. The understanding certainly
calls this transformation sophistry, humbug, juggling, and
what-not. As a result, this identity would, according to
Jacobi, be one which was no doubt conditioned and of set
purpose produced. But we must remark that a one-sided
point of view is involved in apprehending the result of
development merely as a result ; it is a process which is
likewise mediation within itself, of such a nature that this
mediation is again abrogated and asserted as immediate.
Schelling, indeed, had this conception in a general way,
but he did not follow it out in a definite logical method, for
with him it remained an immediate truth, which can only

be verified by means of intellectual intuition. That is the great difficulty in the philosophy of Schelling. And then it was misunderstood and all interest taken from it. It is easy enough to show that subjective and objective are different. Were they not different, nothing could be made of them any more than of $A = A$; but they are in opposition *as one.* In all that is finite, an identity is present, and this alone is actual; but besides the fact that the finite is this identity, it is also true that it is the absence of harmony between subjectivity and objectivity, Notion and reality; and it is in this that finitude consists. To this principle of Schelling's, form, or necessity, is thus lacking, it is only asserted. Schelling appears to have this in common with Plato and the Neo-Platonists, that knowledge is to be found in the inward intuition of eternal Ideas wherein knowledge is unmediated in the Absolute. But when Plato speaks of this intuition of the soul, which has freed itself from all knowledge that is finite, empirical, or reflected, and the Neo-Platonists tell of the ecstasy of thought in which knowledge is the immediate knowledge of the Absolute, this definite distinction must be noticed, viz., that with Plato's knowledge of the universal, or with his intellectuality, wherein all opposition as a reality is abrogated, dialectic is associated, or the recognized necessity for the abrogation of these opposites ; Plato does not begin with this, for with him the movement in which they abrogate themselves is present. The Absolute is itself to be looked at as this movement of self-abrogation ; this is the only actual knowledge and knowledge of the Absolute. With Schelling this idea has, however, no dialectic present in it whereby those opposites may determine themselves to pass over into their unity, and in so doing to be comprehended.

2. Schelling begins with the idea of the Absolute as identity of the subjective and objective, and accordingly there evinced itself in the presentations of his system which followed, the further necessity of proving this idea ;

this he attempted to do in the two Journals of Speculative Physics. But if that method be once adopted, the procedure is not immanent development from the speculative Idea, but it follows the mode of external reflection. Schelling's proofs are adduced in such an exceedingly formal manner that they really invariably presuppose the very thing that was to be proved. The axiom assumes the main point in question, and all the rest follows as a matter of course. Here is an instance : " The innermost essence of the Absolute can only be thought of as identity absolute, altogether pure and undisturbed. For the Absolute is only absolute, and what is thought in it is necessarily and invariably the same, or in other words, is necessarily and invariably absolute. If the idea of the Absolute were a general Notion " (or conception), " this would not prevent a difference being met with in it, notwithstanding this unity of the absolute. For things the most different are yet in the Notion always one and identical, just as a rectangle, a polygon and a circle are all figures. The possibility of the difference of all things in association with perfect unity in the Notion lies in the manner in which the particular in them is combined with the universal. In the Absolute this altogether disappears, because it pertains to the very idea of the Absolute that the particular in it is also the universal, and the universal the particular ; and further that by means of this unity form and existence are also one in it. Consequently, in regard to the Absolute, from the fact of its being the Absolute, there likewise follows the absolute exclusion from its existence of all difference, and that at once." [1]

In the former of the two above-named works, the " Journal of Speculative Physics," Schelling began by again bringing forward the Substance of Spinoza, simple, absolute Existence, inasmuch as he makes his starting-point

---

[1] Schelling: **Neue Zeitschrift für speculative** Physik, Vol. I. Part I. pp. 52, 53.

the absolute identity of the subjective and objective. Here, like Spinoza, he employed the method of geometry, laying down axioms and proving by means of propositions, then going on to deduce other propositions from these, and so on. But this method has no real application to philosophy. Schelling at this point laid down certain forms of difference, to which he gave the name of potencies, adopting the term from Eschenmayer, who made use of it (p. 514) ;[1] they are ready-made differences, which Schelling avails himself of. But philosophy must not take any forms from other sciences, as here from mathematics. With Schelling, the leading form is that which was brought into remembrance again by Kant, the form of triplicity as first, second, and third potency.

Schelling, like Fichte, begins with $I = I$, or with the absolute intuition, expressed as proposition or definition of the Absolute, that " Reason is the absolute indifference of subject and object " : so that it is neither the one nor the other, for both have in it their true determination ; and their opposition, like all others, is utterly done away with. The true reality of subject and object is placed in this alone, that the subject is not posited in the determination of subject against object, as in the philosophy of Fichte ; it is not determined as in itself existent, but as subject-object, as the identity of the two ; in the same way the object is not posited according to its ideal determination as object, but in as far as it is itself absolute, or the identity of the subjective and objective. But the expression "indifference" is ambiguous, for it means indifference in regard to both the one and the other ; and thus it appears as if the content of indifference, the only thing which makes it concrete, were indifferent. Schelling's next requirement is

---

[1] Kritisches Journal der Philosophie, published by Schelling and Hegel, Vol. I. Part I. p. 67; Schelling : Zeitschrift für speculative Physik, Vol. II. No. II. Preface, p. xiii.

that the subject must not be hampered with reflection ; that would be bringing it under the determination of the understanding, which, equally with sensuous perception, implies the separateness of sensuous things. As to the form of its existence, absolute indifference is with Schelling posited as $A = A$; and this form is for him the knowledge of absolute identity, which, however, is inseparable from the Being or existence of the same.[1]

Thus, therefore, opposition, as form and reality or existence, no doubt appears in this Absolute, but it is determined as a merely relative or unessential opposition : " Between subject and object no other than quantitative difference is possible. For no qualitative difference as regards the two is thinkable," because absolute identity "is posited as subject and object only as regards the form of its Being, not as regards its existence. There is consequently only a quantitative difference left," *i.e.* only that of magnitude: and yet difference must really be understood as qualitative, and must thus be shown to be a difference which abrogates itself. This quantitative difference, says Schelling, is the form *actu :* " The quantitative difference of subjective and objective is the basis of all finitude. Each determined potency marks a determined quantitative difference of the subjective and objective. Each individual Being is the result of a quantitative difference of subjectivity and objectivity. The individual expresses absolute identity under a determined form of Being : " so that each side is itself a relative totality, $A = B$, and at the same time the one factor preponderates in the one, and the other factor in the other, but both remain absolute identity.[2] This is insufficient, for there are other determinations ; difference

---

[1] Schelling : Zeitschrift für speculative Physik, Vol. II. No. II. § 1, pp. 1, 2 ; § 4, p. 4 ; § 16-18, pp. 10-12.

[2] Ibidem, § 22-24, pp. 13-15 ; § 37, 38, pp. 22, 23 ; § 40-42, pp. 25, 26.

is undoubtedly qualitative, although this is not the absolute determination. Quantitative difference is no true difference, but an entirely external relation; and likewise the preponderance of subjective and objective is not a determination of thought, but a merely sensuous determination.

The Absolute itself, in so far as the positing of difference is taken into account, is defined by Schelling as the quantitative indifference of subjective and objective: in respect to absolute identity no quantitative difference is thinkable. " Quantitative difference is only possible outside of absolute identity, and outside of absolute totality. There is nothing in itself outside of totality, excepting by virtue of an arbitrary separation of the individual from the whole. Absolute identity exists only under the form of the quantitative indifference of subjective and objective." Quantitative difference, which appears outside of absolute identity and totality, is therefore, according to Schelling, in itself absolute identity, and consequently thinkable only under the form of the quantitative indifference of the subjective and objective. "This opposition does not therefore occur in itself, or from the standpoint of speculation. From this standpoint A exists just as much as B does; for A like B is the whole absolute identity, which only exists under the two forms, but under both of them alike. Absolute identity is the universe itself. The form of its Being can be thought of under the image of a line," as shown by the following scheme :

$$\frac{\overset{+}{A}=B \qquad A=\overset{+}{B}}{A=A}$$

" in which the same identity is posited in each direction, but with A or B preponderating in opposite directions." [1]

[1] Schelling: Zeitschrift für speculative Physik, Vol. II. No. II. § 25, 26, 28, 30-32, pp. 15-19; § 44, 46, pp. 27-29.

If we go into details, the main points from an elementary point of view are the following.

The first potency is that the first quantitative difference of the Absolute, or " the first relative totality is matter. Proof : A = B is not anything real either as relative identity or as relative duplicity. As identity A = B, in the individual as in the whole, can be expressed only by the line," —the first dimension. " But in that line A is posited throughout as existent," *i.e.* it is at the same time related to B. " Therefore this line presupposes A = B as relative totality throughout; relative totality is therefore the first presupposition, and if relative identity exists, it exists only through relative totality,"—this is duplicity, the second dimension. " In the same way relative duplicity presupposes relative identity. Relative identity and duplicity are contained in relative totality, not indeed *actu*, but yet *potentia*. Therefore the two opposites must mutually extinguish each other in a third " dimension. " Absolute identity as the immediate basis of the reality of A and B in matter, is the force of gravitation. If A preponderates we have the force of attraction, if B preponderates we have that of expansion. The quantitative positing of the forces of attraction and expansion passes into the infinite ; their equilibrium exists in the whole, not in the individual." [1] From matter as the first indifference in immediacy Schelling now passes on to further determinations.

The second potency (A²) is light, this identity itself posited as existent ; in so far as A = B, A² is also posited. The same identity, " posited under the form of relative identity," *i.e.* of the polarity which we find appearing " in A and B, is the force of cohesion. Cohesion is the impression made on matter by the self-hood " of light " or by

[1] Schelling : Zeitschrift für speculative Physik, Vol. II. No. II. § 50, Note 1, § 51, pp. 34-36 ; § 54, p. 40 ; § 56, Appendix 2, § 57 and note, pp. 42-44.

personality, whereby matter first emerges as particular out of the universal identity, and raises itself into the realm of form." Planets, metals and other bodies form a series which under the form of dynamic cohesion expresses particular relations of cohesion, in which on the one hand contraction preponderates, and on the other hand expansion. These potencies appear with Schelling as north and south, east and west polarity : their developments further appear as north-west, south-east, &c. He counts as the last potency Mercury, Venus, the Earth, &c. He continues : " Cohesion outside of the point of indifference I term passive. Towards the negative side " (or pole) " fall some of the metals which stand next to iron, after them the so-called precious metals," then the " diamond, and lastly carbon, the greatest passive cohesion. Towards the positive side, again, some metals fall, in which the cohesive nature of iron gradually diminishes," i.e. approaches disintegration, and lastly " disappears in nitrogen." Active cohesion is magnetism, and the material universe is an infinite magnet. The magnetic process is difference in indifference, and indifference in difference, and therefore absolute identity as such. The indifference point of the magnet is the " neither nor " and the " as well as "; the poles are potentially the same essence, only posited under two factors which are opposed. Both poles depend " only upon whether + or − preponderates "; they are not pure abstractions. " In the total magnet the empirical magnet is the indifference point. The empirical magnet is iron. All bodies are mere metamorphoses of iron—they are potentially contained in iron. Every two different bodies which touch each other set up mutually in each other relative diminution and increase of cohesion. This mutual alteration of cohesion by means of the contact of two different bodies is electricity ; the cohesion-diminishing factor $+E$ is the potency of hydrogen, $−E$ is the potency of oxygen.

" The totality of the dynamic process is represented only by the chemical process." [1]

" By the positing of the dynamic totality the addition of light is directly posited as a product. The expression, the total product, therefore signifies light combined with the force of gravitation ; by the positing of the relative totality of the whole potency, the force of gravity is directly reduced to the mere form of the Being of absolute identity." This is the third potency (A^3), the organism.[2] Schelling launched out into too many individual details, if he desired to indicate the construction of the whole universe. On the one hand, however, he did not complete this representation, and on the other hand, he has confined himself mainly to implicit existence, and has mixed therewith the formalism of external construction according to a presupposed scheme. In this representation he advanced only as far as the organism, and did not reach the presentation of the other side of knowledge, *i.e.* the philosophy of spirit. Schelling began time after time, in accordance with the idea implied in this construction, to work out the natural universe, and especially the organism. He banishes all such meaningless terms as perfection, wisdom, outward adaptability ; or, in other words, the Kantian formula, that a thing appears so and so to our faculty of knowledge, is transformed by him into this other formula, that such and such is the constitution of Nature. Following up Kant's meagre attempt at demonstrating spirit in nature, he devoted special attention to inaugurating anew this mode of regarding nature, so as to recognize in objective

---

[1] Schelling : Zeitschrift für spec. Phys., Vol. II. No. II. § 62-64, pp. 47, 48 ; § 92, 93, pp. 59, 60 ; § 67-69, pp. 49, 50 ; § 95, pp. 64-68 ; (Neue Zeitschrift für speculative Physik, Vol. I. Part II. pp. 92, 93, 98, 117-119 ; Erster Entwurf eines Systems der Natur-philosophie, p. 297) ; § 76-78, p. 53 ; § 83 and Appendix, p. 54 ; § 103, Note, p. 76 ; § 112. p. 84.

[2] Ibidem, § 136, 137, pp. 109, 110 ; § 141, Appendix I. p. 112.

existence the same schematism, the same rhythm, as is present in the ideal. Hence nature represents itself therein not as something alien to spirit, but as being in its general aspect a projection of spirit into an objective mode.

We have further to remark that Schelling by this theory became the originator of modern Natural Philosophy, since he was the first to exhibit Nature as the sensuous perception or the expression of the Notion and its determinations. Natural Philosophy is no new science; we met with it continually—in the works of Aristotle, for instance, and elsewhere. English Philosophy is also a mere apprehension in thought of the physical; forces, laws of Nature, are its fundamental determinations. The opposition of physics and Natural Philosophy is therefore not the opposition of the unthinking and the thinking view of Nature; Natural Philosophy means, if we take it in its whole extent, nothing else than the thoughtful contemplation of Nature; but this is the work of ordinary physics also, since its determinations of forces, laws, &c., are thoughts. The only difference is that in physics thoughts are formal thoughts of the understanding, whose material and content cannot, as regards their details, be determined by thought itself, but must be taken from experience. But concrete thought contains its determination and its content in itself, and merely the external mode of appearance pertains to the senses. If, then, Philosophy passes beyond the form of the understanding, and has apprehended the speculative Notion, it must alter the determinations of thought, the categories of the understanding regarding Nature. Kant was the first to set about this; and Schelling has sought to grasp the Notion of Nature, instead of contenting himself with the ordinary metaphysics of the same. Nature is to him nothing but the external mode of existence as regards the system of thought-forms, just as mind is the existence of the same system in the form of consciousness. That for which we have to thank

Schelling, therefore, is not that he brought thought to bear on the comprehension of Nature, but that he altered the categories according to which thought applied itself to Nature; he introduced forms of Reason, and applied them—as he did the form of the syllogism in magnetism, for instance—in place of the ordinary categories of the understanding. He has not only shown these forms in Nature, but has also sought to evolve Nature out of a principle of this kind.

In the "Further Exposition of the System of Philosophy" which the "New Journal for Speculative Physics" furnishes, Schelling chose other forms; for, by reason of incompletely developed form and lack of dialectic, he had recourse to various forms one after another, because he found none of them sufficient. Instead of the equilibrium of subjectivity and objectivity, he now speaks of the identity of existence and form, of universal and particular, of finite and infinite, of positive and negative, and he defines absolute indifference sometimes in one and sometimes in another form of opposition, just according to chance. All such oppositions may be employed; but they are only abstract, and refer to different stages in the development of the logical principle itself. Form and essence are distinguished by Schelling in this way, that form, regarded on its own account, is the particular, or the emerging of difference, subjectivity. But real existence is absolute form or absolute knowledge immediately in itself, a self-conscious existence in the sense of thinking knowledge, just as with Spinoza it had the form of something objective or in thought. Speculative Philosophy is to be found in this assertion, not that it asserts an independent philosophy, for it is purely organization; knowledge is based on the Absolute. Thus Schelling has again given to transcendental Idealism the significance of absolute Idealism. This unity of existence and form is thus, according to Schelling, the Absolute; or if we regard reality as the universal, and form as the particular, the

Absolute is the absolute unity of universal and particular, or of Being and knowledge. The different aspects, subject and object, or universal and particular, are only ideal oppositions ; they are in the Absolute entirely and altogether one. This unity as form is intellectual intuition, which posits Thinking and Being as absolutely alike, and as it formally expresses the Absolute, it becomes at the same time the expression of its essence. He who has not the power of imagination, whereby he may represent this unity to himself, is deficient in the organ of Philosophy. But in this consists the true absoluteness of all and each, that the one is not recognized as universal, and the other as particular, but the universal in this its determination is recognized as unity of the universal and particular, and in like manner the particular is recognized as the unity of both. Construction merely consists in leading back everything determined and particular into the Absolute, or regarding it as it is in absolute unity ; its determinateness is only its ideal moment, but its truth is really its Being in the Absolute. These three moments or potencies—that of the passing of existence (the infinite) into form (the finite), and of form into existence (which are both relative unities), and the third, the absolute unity, thus recur anew in each individual. Hence Nature, the real or actual aspect, as the passing of existence into form or of the universal into the particular, itself again possesses these three unities in itself, and in the same way the ideal aspect does so ; therefore each potency is on its own account once more absolute. This is the general idea of the scientific construction of the universe—to repeat in each individual alike the triplicity which is the scheme of the whole, thereby to show the identity of all things, and in doing so to regard them in their absolute essence, so that they all express the same unity.[1]

---

[1] Schelling : Neue Zeitschrift für speculative Physik, Vol. I. Part I. pp. 1-77 ; Part II. pp. 1-38.

The more detailed explanation is extremely formal: "Existence passes into form—this taken by itself being the particular (the finite)—by means of the infinite being added to it; unity is received into multiplicity, indifference into difference." The other assertion is: "Form passes into existence by the finite being received into the infinite, difference into indifference." But passing into and receiving into are merely sensuous expressions. "Otherwise expressed, the particular becomes absolute form by the universal becoming one with it, and the universal becomes absolute existence by the particular becoming one with it. But these two unities, as in the Absolute, are not outside of one another, but in one another, and therefore the Absolute is absolute indifference of form and existence," as unity of this double passing-into-one. "By means of these two unities two different potencies are determined, but in themselves they are both the exactly equal roots of the Absolute." [1] That is a mere assertion, the continual return after each differentiation, which is perpetually again removed out of the Absolute.

"Of the first absolute transformation there are copies in phenomenal Nature; therefore Nature, regarded in itself, is nothing else than that first transformation as it exists in the absolute (unseparated from the other). For by means of the infinite passing into the finite, existence passes into form; since then form obtains reality only by means of existence, existence, when it has passed into form without form having (according to the assumption) similarly passed into existence, can be represented only as potentiality or ground of reality, but not as indifference of possibility and actuality. But that which may be described thus, namely as existence, in so far as that is mere ground of reality, and therefore has really passed into form, although form has not in turn passed into it, is what presents itself as Nature.—

[1] Schelling: Ibidem, Vol. I. Part II. p. 39.

Existence makes its appearance in form, but in return form also makes its appearance in existence; this is the other unity," that of mind. "This unity is established by the finite being received into the infinite. At this point form, as the particular, strikes into existence, and itself becomes absolute. Form which passes into existence places itself as absolute activity and positive cause of reality in opposition to the existence which passes into form, and which appears only as ground. The passing of absolute form into existence is what we think of as God, and the images or copies of this transformation are in the ideal world, which is therefore in its implicitude the other unity." [1] Each of these two transformations, then, is the whole totality, not, however, posited and not appearing as totality, but with the one or the other factor preponderating; each of the two spheres has, therefore, in itself again these differences, and thus in each of them the three potencies are to be found.

The ground or basis, Nature as basis merely, is matter, gravity, as the first potency; this passing of form into existence is in the actual world universal mechanism, necessity. But the second potency is "the light which shineth in darkness, form which has passed into existence. The absolute unification of the two unities in actuality, so that matter is altogether form, and form is altogether matter, is organism, the highest expression of Nature as it is in God, and of God as He is in Nature, in the finite." On the ideal side "Knowledge is the essence of the Absolute brought into the daylight of form; action is a transformation of form, as the particular, into the essence of the Absolute. As in the real world form that is identified with essence appears as light, so in the ideal world God Himself appears in particular manifestation as the living form which has emerged in the passing of form into essence, so that in every respect the ideal and real world

---

[1] Schelling: Ibidem, Vol. I. Part II. pp. 39-41.

are again related as likeness and symbol. The absolute unification of the two unities in the ideal, so that material is wholly form and form wholly material, is the work of art; and that secret hidden in the Absolute which is the root of all reality comes here into view, in the reflected world itself, in the highest potency and highest union of God and Nature as the power of imagination." On account of that permeation art and poetry therefore hold the highest rank in Schelling's estimation. But art is the Absolute in sensuous form alone. Where and what could the work of art be, which should correspond to the Idea of the spirit ? " The universe is formed in the Absolute as the most perfect organic existence and the most perfect work of art : for Reason, which recognizes the Absolute in it, it possesses absolute truth ; for the imagination, which represents the Absolute in it, it possesses absolute Beauty. Each of these expresses the very same unity," regarded " from different sides ; and both arrive at the absolute indifference point in the recognition of which lies both the beginning and the aim of real knowledge." [1] This highest Idea, these differences, are grasped as a whole in a very formal manner only.

3. The relation of Nature to Spirit, and to God, the Absolute, has been stated by Schelling elsewhere, *i.e.* in his later expositions, as follows : he defines the existence of God as Nature—in so far as God constitutes Himself its ground or basis, as infinite perception—and Nature is thus the negative moment in God, since intelligence and thought exist only by means of the opposition of one Being. For in one of his writings, directed on some particular occasion against Jacobi, Schelling explains himself further with regard to the nature of God and His relation to Nature. He says : " God, or more properly the existence which is God, is ground : He is ground of Himself as a moral Being.

[1] Schelling, Ibidem, Vol. I. Part II. pp. 41-50.

But" then " it is ground that He makes Himself "—not
cause. Something must precede intelligence, and that
something is Being—" since thought is the exact opposite
of Being. That which is the beginning of an intelligence
cannot be in its turn intelligent, since there would otherwise be no distinction ; but it cannot be absolutely unintelligent, for the very reason that it is the potentiality of an
intelligence. It will accordingly be something between
these, *i.e.* it will operate with wisdom, but as it were with
an innate, instinctive, blind, and yet unconscious wisdom ;
just as we often hear those who are under a spell uttering
words full of understanding, but not uttering them with
comprehension of their meaning, but as it were owing to
an inspiration." God, therefore, as this ground of Himself,
is Nature—Nature as it is in God ; this is the view taken
of Nature in Natural Philosophy.[1] But the work of the
Absolute is to abrogate this ground, and to constitute itself
Intelligence. On this account Schelling's philosophy has
later been termed a Philosophy of Nature, and that in
the sense of a universal philosophy, while at first Natural
Philosophy was held to be only a part of the whole.

It is not incumbent on us here to give a more detailed
account of Schelling's philosophy, or to show points in
the expositions hitherto given by him which are far from
satisfactory. The system is the latest form of Philosophy
which we had to consider, and it is a form both interesting
and true. In the first place special emphasis, in dealing
with Schelling, must be laid on the idea that he has
grasped the true as the concrete, as the unity of subjective
and objective. The main point in Schelling's philosophy
thus is that its interest centres round that deep, specula-

---

[1] Schelling : Denkmal der Schrift von den göttlichen Dingen, pp.
94, 85, 86 (Philosophische Untersuchungen über das Wesen der
menschlichen Freiheit in den Philosophischen Schriften, Vol. I.
Landshut, 1809, p. 429), 89-93.

tive content, which, as content, is the content with which Philosophy in the entire course of its history has had to do. The Thought which is free and independent, not abstract, but in itself concrete, comprehends itself in itself as an intellectually actual world ; and this is the truth of Nature, Nature in itself. The second great merit possessed by Schelling is to have pointed out in Nature the forms of Spirit ; thus electricity, magnetism, &c., are for him only external modes of the Idea. His defect is that this Idea in general, its distinction into the ideal and the natural world, and also the totality of these determinations, are not shown forth and developed as necessitated in themselves by the Notion. As Schelling has not risen to this point of view, he has misconceived the nature of thought; the work of art thus becomes for him the supreme and only mode in which the Idea exists for spirit. But the supreme mode of the Idea is really its own element; thought, the Idea apprehended, is therefore higher than the work of art. The Idea is the truth, and all that is true is the Idea ; the systematizing of the Idea into the world must be proved to be a necessary unveiling and revelation. With Schelling, on the other hand, form is really an external scheme, and his method is the artificial application of this scheme to external objects. This externally applied scheme takes the place of dialectic progress ; and this is the special reason why the philosophy of Nature has brought itself into discredit, that it has proceeded on an altogether external plan, has made its foundation a ready-made scheme, and fitted into it Nature as we perceive it. These forms were potencies with Schelling, but instead of mathematical forms or a type of thought like this, by some other men sensuous forms have been taken as basis, just as were sulphur and mercury by Jacob Boehme. For instance, magnetism, electricity, and chemistry have been defined to be the three potencies in Nature, and thus in the organism reproduction has been termed chemistry ;

irritability, electricity; and sensibility, magnetism.[1] In this way there has crept into Natural Philosophy the great formalism of representing everything as a series, which is a superficial determination without necessity, since instead of Notions we find formulas. Brilliant powers of imagination are displayed, such as were exhibited by Görres. This mistake of applying forms which are taken from one sphere of Nature to another sphere of the same has been carried a long way; Oken, for example, calls wood-fibres the nerves and brain of the plant, and is almost crazy on the subject. Philosophy would in this way become a play of mere analogical reflections ; and it is not with these but with thoughts that we have to do. Nerves are not thoughts, any more than such expressions as pole of contraction, of expansion, masculine, feminine, &c. The formal plan of applying an external scheme to the sphere of Nature which one wishes to observe, is the external work of Natural Philosophy, and this scheme is itself derived from the imagination. That is a most false mode of proceeding; Schelling took advantage of it to some extent, others have made a complete misuse of it. All this is done to escape thought ; nevertheless, thought is the ultimate simple determination which has to be dealt with.

It is therefore of the greatest importance to distinguish Schelling's philosophy, on the one hand, from that imitation of it which throws itself into an unspiritual farrago of words regarding the Absolute; and, on the other hand, from the philosophy of those imitators, who, owing to a failure to understand intellectual intuition, give up comprehension, and with it the leading moment of knowledge, and speak from so-called intuition, *i.e.* they take a glance at the thing in question, and having fastened on it some superficial analogy or definition, they fancy they have expressed its

---

[1] Cf. Schelling's Erster Entwurf der Natur-philosophie, p. 297.

whole nature, while in point of fact they put an end to all capacity for attaining to scientific knowledge. This whole tendency places itself, in the first place, in opposition to reflective thought, or to progress in fixed, steadfast, immovable Notions. But instead of remaining in the Notion and recognizing it as the unresting ego, they have lighted on the opposite extreme of passive intuition, of immediate Being, of fixed implicitude ; and they think that they can make up for the lack of fixity by superficial observation, and can render this observation intellectual by determining it once more by some fixed Notion or other ; or they bring their minds to bear on the object of consideration by saying, for instance, that the ostrich is the fish among birds, because he has a long neck—fish becomes a general term, but not a Notion. This whole mode of reasoning, which has forced its way into natural history and natural science, as well as into medicine, is a miserable formalism, an irrational medley of the crudest empiricism with the most superficial ideal determinations that formalism ever descended to. The philosophy of Locke is not so crude as it is, for it is not a whit better in either its content or its form, and it is combined with foolish self-conceit into the bargain. Philosophy on this account sank into general and well-deserved contempt, such as is for the most part extended to those who assert that they have a monopoly of philosophy. Instead of earnestness of apprehension and circumspection of thought, we find in them a juggling with idle fancies, which pass for deep conceptions, lofty surmises, and even for poetry : and they think they are right in the centre of things when they are only on the surface. Five-and-twenty years ago[1] the case was the same with poetic art ; a taste for ingenious conceits took possession of it, and the effusions of its poetic inspiration came forth blindly from itself, shot out as

---

[1] From the lectures of 1805-1806.

from a pistol. The results were either crazy ravings, or, if they were not ravings, they were prose so dull that it was unworthy of the name of prose. It is just the same in the later philosophies. What is not utterly senseless drivel about the indifference-point and polarity, about oxygen, the holy, the infinite, &c., is made up of thoughts so trivial that we might well doubt our having correctly apprehended their meaning, in the first place because they are given forth with such arrogant effrontery, and in the second place because we cannot help trusting that what was said was not so trivial as it seems. As in the Philosophy of Nature men forgot the Notion and proceeded in a dead unspiritual course, so here they lose sight of spirit entirely. They have strayed from the right road; for by their principle, Notion and perception are one unity, but in point of fact this unity, this spirit, itself emerges in immediacy, and is therefore in intuitive perception, and not in the Notion.

E. Final Result.

The present standpoint of philosophy is that the Idea is known in its necessity; the sides of its diremption, Nature and Spirit, are each of them recognized as representing the totality of the Idea, and not only as being in themselves identical, but as producing this one identity from themselves; and in this way the identity is recognized as necessary. Nature, and the world or history of spirit, are the two realities; what exists as actual Nature is an image of divine Reason; the forms of self-conscious Reason are also the forms of Nature. The ultimate aim and business of philosophy is to reconcile thought or the Notion with reality. It is easy from subordinate standpoints to find satisfaction in modes of intuitive perception and of feeling. But the deeper the spirit goes within itself, the more vehement is the opposition, the more abundant is the wealth without; the depth is to be measured by the greatness of the craving with which spirit seeks to find itself in what lies outside of itself. We saw the thought which apprehends itself appearing; it strove to make itself concrete within itself. Its first activity is formal; Aristotle was the first to say that νοῦς is the thought of thought. The result is the thought which is at home with itself, and at the same time embraces the universe therein, and transforms it into an intelligent world. In apprehension the spiritual and the natural universe are interpenetrated as one harmonious universe, which withdraws into itself, and in its various aspects develops the Absolute into a totality, in order, by the very process of so doing, to become conscious of itself in its unity, in Thought. Philosophy is thus the true theodicy, as contrasted with art and religion and the feelings which these call up—a reconciliation of spirit, namely of the spirit which has apprehended itself in its freedom and in the riches of its reality.

To this point the World-spirit has come, and each stage has its own form in the true system of Philosophy; nothing is lost, all principles are preserved, since Philosophy in its final aspect is the totality of forms. This concrete idea is the result of the strivings of spirit during almost twenty-five centuries of earnest work to become objective to itself, to know itself:

Tantæ molis erat, se ipsam cognoscere mentem.

All this time was required to produce the philosophy of our day; so tardily and slowly did the World-spirit work to reach this goal. What we pass in rapid review when we recall it, stretched itself out in reality to this great length of time. For in this lengthened period, the Notion of Spirit, invested with its entire concrete development, its external subsistence, its wealth, is striving to bring spirit to perfection, to make progress itself and to develop from spirit. It goes ever on and on, because spirit is progress alone. Spirit often seems to have forgotten and lost itself, but

inwardly opposed to itself, it is inwardly working ever forward (as when Hamlet says of the ghost of his father, " Well
said, old mole ! canst work i' the ground so fast ? " [1]), until
grown strong in itself it bursts asunder the crust of
earth which divided it from the sun, its Notion, so that the
earth crumbles away.   At such a time, when the encircling
crust, like a soulless decaying tenement, crumbles away,
and spirit displays itself arrayed in new youth, the seven
league boots are at length adopted.   This work of the
spirit to know itself, this activity to find itself, is the life of
the spirit and the spirit itself.   Its result is the Notion
which it takes up of itself ; the history of Philosophy is a
revelation of what has been the aim of spirit throughout
its history ; it is therefore the world's history in its innermost signification.   This work of the human spirit in the
recesses of thought is parallel with all the stages of reality ;
and therefore no philosophy oversteps its own time.   The
importance which the determinations of thought possessed
is another matter, which does not belong to the history
of Philosophy.   These Notions are the simplest revelation
of the World spirit : in their more concrete form they are
history.

We must, therefore, in the first place not esteem lightly
what spirit has won, namely its gains up to the present
day.   Ancient Philosophy is to be reverenced as necessary,
and as a link in this sacred chain, but all the same nothing
more than a link.   The present is the highest stage reached.
In the second place, all the various philosophies are no
mere fashionable theories of the time, or anything of a
similar nature ; they are neither chance products nor the
blaze of a fire of straw, nor casual eruptions here and there,
but a spiritual, reasonable, forward advance ; they are of
necessity one Philosophy in its development, the revelation
of God, as He knows Himself to be.   Where several

----

[1] Hamlet, Act I. Scene V.

philosophies appear at the same time, they are different sides which make up one totality forming their basis; and on account of their one-sidedness we see the refutation of the one by the other. In the third place we do not find here feeble little efforts to establish or to criticize this or that particular point; instead of that, each philosophy sets up a new principle of its own, and this must be recognized.

If we glance at the main epochs in the whole history of Philosophy, and grasp the necessary succession of stages in the leading moments, each of which expresses a determinate Idea, we find that after the Oriental whirl of subjectivity, which attains to no intelligibility and therefore to no subsistence, the light of thought dawned among the Greeks.

1. The philosophy of the ancients had the absolute Idea as its thought; and the realization or reality of the same consisted in comprehending the existing present world, and regarding it as it is in its absolute nature. This philosophy did not make its starting-point the Idea itself, but proceeded from the objective as from something given, and transformed the same into the Idea; the Being of Parmenides.

2. Abstract thought, νοῦς, became known to itself as universal essence or existence, not as subjective thought; the Universal of Plato.

3. In Aristotle the Notion emerges, free and unconstrained, as comprehending thought, permeating and spiritualizing all the forms which the universe contains.

4. The Notion as subject, its independence, its inwardness, abstract separation, is represented by the Stoics, Epicureans and Sceptics: here we have not the free, concrete form, but universality abstract and in itself formal.

5. The thought of totality, the intelligible world, is the concrete Idea as we have seen it with the Neo-Platonists.

This principle is ideality generally speaking, which is present in all reality, but not the Idea which knows itself : this is not reached until the principle of subjectivity, individuality, found a place in it, and God as spirit became actual to Himself in self-consciousness.

6. But it has been the work of modern times to grasp this Idea as spirit, as the Idea that knows itself. In order to proceed from the conscious Idea to the self-conscious, we must have the infinite opposition, namely the fact that the Idea has come to the consciousness of being absolutely sundered in twain. As spirit had the thought of objective existence, Philosophy thus perfected the intellectuality of the world, and produced this spiritual world as an object existing beyond present reality, like Nature,—the first creation of spirit. The work of the spirit now consisted in bringing this Beyond back to reality, and guiding it into self-consciousness. This is accomplished by self-consciousness thinking itself, and recognizing absolute existence to be the self-consciousness that thinks itself. With Descartes pure thought directed itself on that separation which we spoke of above. Self-consciousness, in the first place, thinks of itself as consciousness ; therein is contained all objective reality, and the positive, intuitive reference of its reality to the other side. With Spinoza Thought and Being are opposed and yet identical; he has the intuitive perception of substance, but the knowledge of substance in his case is external. We have here the principle of reconciliation taking its rise from thought as such, in order to abrogate the subjectivity of thought : this is the case in Leibnitz's monad, which possesses the power of representation.

7. In the second place, self-consciousness thinks of itself as being self-consciousness ; in being self-conscious it is independent, but still in this independence it has a negative relation to what is outside self-consciousness. This is infinite subjectivity, which appears at one time as the critique of thought in the case of Kant, and at another

time, in the case of Fichte, as the tendency or impulse towards the concrete. Absolute, pure, infinite form is expressed as self-consciousness, the Ego.

8. This is a light that breaks forth on spiritual substance, and shows absolute content and absolute form to be identical; —substance is in itself identical with knowledge. Self-consciousness thus, in the third place, recognizes its positive relation as its negative, and its negative as its positive,— or, in other words, recognizes these opposite activities as the same, *i.e.* it recognizes pure Thought or Being as self-identity, and this again as separation. This is intellectual perception; but it is requisite in order that it should be in truth intellectual, that it should not be that merely immediate perception of the eternal and the divine which we hear of, but should be absolute knowledge. This intuitive perception which does not recognize itself is taken as starting-point as if it were absolutely presupposed; it has in itself intuitive perception only as immediate knowledge, and not as self-knowledge: or it knows nothing, and what it perceives it does not really know,—for, taken at its best, it consists of beautiful thoughts, but not knowledge.

But intellectual intuition is knowledge, since, in the first place, in spite of the separation of each of the opposed sides from the other, all external reality is known as internal. If it is known according to its essence, as it is, it shows itself as not existing of itself, but as essentially consisting in the movement of transition. This Heraclitean or Sceptical principle, that nothing is at rest, must be demonstrated of each individual thing; and thus in this consciousness—that the essence of each thing lies in determination, in what is the opposite of itself—there appears the apprehended unity with its opposite. Similarly this unity is, in the second place, to be recognized even in its essence; its essence as this identity is, in the same way, to pass over into its opposite, or to realize itself, to become for itself something different; and thus the opposition in it is brought about by itself. Again, it may be said of the opposition, in the third place, that it is not in the Absolute; this Absolute is existence, the eternal, &c. This is, however, itself an abstraction in which the Absolute is apprehended in a one-sided manner only, and the opposition is apprehended only as ideal (*supra*, p. 536); but in fact it is form, as the essential moment of the movement of the Absolute. This Absolute is not at rest, and that opposition is not the unresting Notion; for the Idea, unresting though it is, is yet at rest and satisfied in itself. Pure thought has advanced to the opposition of the subjective and objective; the true reconciliation of the opposition is the perception that this opposition, when pushed to its absolute extreme, resolves itself; as Schelling says, the opposites are in themselves identical—and not only in themselves, but eternal life consists in the very process of continually producing the opposition and continually reconciling it. To know opposition in unity, and unity in opposition—this is absolute knowledge; and science is the knowledge of this unity in its whole development by means of itself.

This is then the demand of all time and of Philosophy. A new epoch has arisen in the world. It would appear as if the World-spirit had at last succeeded in stripping off from itself all alien objective existence, and apprehending itself at last as absolute Spirit, in developing from itself what for it is objective, and keeping it within its own power, yet remaining at rest all the while. The strife of the finite self-consciousness with the absolute self-consciousness, which last seemed to the other to lie outside of itself, now comes to an end. Finite self-consciousness has ceased to be finite; and in this way absolute self-consciousness has, on the other hand, attained to the reality which it lacked before. This is the whole history of the world in general up to the present time, and the history of Philosophy in particular, the sole work of which is to depict this strife. Now, indeed, it seems to have reached its goal, when this absolute self-consciousness, which it had the work of representing, has ceased to be alien, and when spirit accordingly is realized as spirit. For it becomes such only as the result of its knowing itself to be absolute spirit, and this it knows in real scientific knowledge. Spirit produces itself as Nature, as the State; nature is its unconscious work, in the course of which it appears to itself something different, and not spirit; but in the State, in the deeds and life of History, as also of Art, it brings itself to pass with consciousness; it knows very various modes of its reality, yet they are only modes. In scientific knowledge alone it knows itself as absolute spirit; and this knowledge, or spirit, is its only true existence. This then is the standpoint of the present day, and the series of spiritual forms is with it for the present concluded.

At this point I bring this history of Philosophy to a close. It has been my desire that you should learn from it that the history of Philosophy is not a blind collection of fanciful ideas, nor a fortuitous progression. I have rather sought to show the necessary development of the successive philosophies from one another, so that the one of necessity presupposes another preceding it. The general result of the history of Philosophy is this: in the first place, that throughout all time there has been only one Philosophy, the contemporary differences of which constitute the necessary aspects of the one principle; in the second place, that the succession of philosophic systems is not due to chance, but represents the necessary succession of stages in the development of this science; in the third place, that the final philosophy of a period is the result of this development, and is truth in the highest form which the self-consciousness of spirit affords of itself. The latest philosophy contains therefore those which went before; it embraces in itself all the different stages thereof;

it is the product and result of those that preceded it. We can now, for example, be Platonists no longer. Moreover we must raise ourselves once for all above the pettinesses of individual opinions, thoughts, objections, and difficulties ; and also above our own vanity, as if our individual thoughts were of any particular value. For to apprehend the inward substantial spirit is the standpoint of the individual ; as parts of the whole, individuals are like blind men, who are driven forward by the indwelling spirit of the whole. Our standpoint now is accordingly the know-ledge of this Idea as spirit, as absolute Spirit, which in this way opposes to itself another spirit, the finite, the principle of which is to know absolute spirit, in order that absolute spirit may become existent for it. I have tried to develop and bring before your thoughts this series of successive spiritual forms pertaining to Philosophy in its progress, and to indicate the connection between them. This series is the true kingdom of spirits, the only kingdom of spirits that there is—it is a series which is not a multiplicity, nor does it even remain a series, if we understand thereby that one of its members merely follows on another ; but in the very process of coming to the knowledge of itself it is transformed into the moments of the one Spirit, or the one self-present Spirit. This long proces-sion of spirits is formed by the individual pulses which beat in its life; they are the organism of our substance, an absolutely necessary progression, which expresses nothing less than the nature of spirit itself, and which lives in us all. We have to give ear to its urgency—when the mole that is within forces its way on—and we have to make it a reality. It is my desire that this history of Philosophy should contain for you a summons to grasp the spirit of the time, which is present in us by nature, and—each in his own place—consciously to bring it from its natural condition, *i.e.* from its lifeless seclusion, into the light of day.

I have to express my thanks to you for the attention

with which you have listened to me while I have been making this attempt; it is in great measure due to you that my efforts have met with so great a measure of success. And it has been a source of pleasure to myself to have been associated with you in this spiritual community; I ought not to speak of it as if it were a thing of the past, for I hope that a spiritual bond has been knit between us which will prove permanent. I bid you a most hearty farewell.

(The closing lecture of the series was given on the 22nd March, 1817; on the 14th March, 1818; on the 12th August, 1819; on the 23rd March, 1821; on the 30th March, 1824; on the 28th March, 1828; and on the 26th March, 1830.)

INDEX

Absolute, the: absolute idea,
699; absolute Notion, 633–34,
649–50; absolute Spirit, 702;
in Aristotle, 341, 342, 345;
as the Being of Parmenides
for Plato, 250; in Eastern
philosophy, 122; in Fichte,
652; as mind, 108, 109; as
not at rest, 702; in
philosophy, 90, 91, 94; in
Plato, 198; Schelling on,
670, 676, 678–79, 680,
681–83, 687–89, 691;
Schelling's absolute idealism,
687; in Schlegel, 658; as self-
determining universal, 102;
as unity of Being and
non-being, 251

Academy: Ficinus's Platonic,
46; New, 107, 314; Plato's,
202, 317

Activity, spontaneous
(*energeia*), 336, 339, 340,
341–42

Actuality, 335, 338, 339, 340

Acusilaus, 124

Aesthetics: Aristotle's *Poetics*,
316, 325; Kant on, 619–21;
Plato on, 312–13. *See also*
Art; Beauty

Ahriman, 83, 84

Alcibiades, 139, 144, 170, 187,
196

Alexander the Great, 318–23

Alexandrian philosophy: and
Aristotle, 327; the Idea
achieved by, 103; on
mythology, 82, 432. *See also*
Neo-Platonism

Anacharsis, 124

Anaxagoras: condemned for
impiety, 135; *nous* in, 102,
155; Pericles and, 190; as
precursor of Socrates,
133–34; Socrates and, 134,
139

Anaximander, 44

Ancient philosophy. *See* Greek
philosophy; Roman
philosophy

Anselm of Canterbury, 603

Anytus, 184–85

Apology (Plato), 180

A priori synthetic judgments,
581, 627, 633

Arabians, 110, 423

Arche (principle), 44, 155–56

Archelaus, 139

Archytas of Tarentum, 202,
204

Aristophanes, 150, 175–78, 211

Aristotle, 314–428; accused of
impiety, 323; as Alexander's
teacher, 318–19, 321, 322–23;
on the beautiful, 343; on
Being, 335, 337, 342–43; on

philosophy: of Descartes,
507; of Schelling, 680; of
Spinoza, 480, 488–89,
507–14
German philosophy (Teutonic
philosophy), 573–696;
Bouterweck, 630, 661–63;
comprehending thought as
spirit, 101; French
philosophy contrasted with,
573; Mendelssohn, 252; as
principal form of philosophy,
101, 109; Schleiermacher,
207, 659–61; Schulze, 630.
See also Boehme, Jacob;
Fichte, Johann Gottlieb;
Fries, Jacob Friedrich; Jacobi,
Friedrich Heinrich; Kant,
Immanuel; Krug, Wilhelm
Traugott; Leibnitz, Gottfried
Wilhelm; Novalis, 661;
Schelling, Friedrich Wilhelm
Joseph; Schlegel, Friedrich
von; Wolff, Christian
God: Aristotle on, 333, 334,
345, 349; Bel, 86; in
Berkeley's system, 564;
comprehending
contradictions in Leibnitzian
system, 556–57; Descartes on
omnipotence and
omniscience of, 474;
Descartes's proof of existence
of, 458–63, 603, 605; Eastern
gods, 122; and evil, 503, 549,
550–51; Greek conception
of, 41, 74; as holding body
and soul together, 236;
Hume on proofs of existence
of, 571; Kant on proofs of
existence of, 602–7; Kant's
postulation of existence of,
576, 613–15, 625–27;
knowledge of as end of

religion, 73; Leibnitz's proof
of existence of, 548–49; as
monad of monads, 548, 551,
553; as *natura naturata* and
natura naturans in Spinoza,
495; and nature, 66–67;
Neo-Platonism on, 314; as
not a deceiver for Descartes,
463–66; as only substance for
Spinoza, 489–92; pantheism,
507; philosophy as revelation
of, 698; Platonic proportion
and the Christian, 273, 274;
Plato on, 215, 219, 259,
269–71, 275–77; in Plato's
Timœus, 270–71; Schelling
on, 690–92; as source of
truth for Spinoza, 496, 502;
Spinoza on intellectual love
of, 502–3; Spinoza's
definition of, 488; as uniting
soul and body for Descartes,
476; as the unmoved mover,
340; Wolff's definition of,
602. *See also* Atheism
Goethe, Johann Wolfgang von,
27, 90
Good: knowledge of in
Aristotle's definition of man,
404; Leibnitz on evil and,
549, 550; opposition of evil
and, 436
Good, the: Aristotle on, 337,
343, 344, 348–49, 400; Kant
on, 613–14, 625; Plato on,
241, 263, 269; Socrates on,
136, 155–56, 160–61
Greek philosophy, 117–428;
Archelaus, 139; beauty as
ideal in, 121; beginnings of,
99–100, 123; Being and
thought in, 107;
characteristics of
philosophers of, 439;